The Texas Almanac's

Political History of Texas

By Mike Kingston, Sam Attlesey
&
Mary G. Crawford

EAKIN PRESS * Austin, Texas

FIRST EDITION

Manufactured in the United States of America
By Eakin Press ★ A Division of Sunbelt Media
P.O. Drawer 90159 / Austin, TX 78709-0159

1 2 3 4 5 6 7 8 9

ISBN 0-89015-855-X

Library of Congress Cataloging-in-Publication Data

Kingston, Mike.
   The Texas almanac's political history of Texas / by Mike Kingston, Sam
Attlesey & Mary G. Crawford.
     p.   cm.
   Includes bibliographical references and index.
   ISBN 0-89015-855-X
   1. Texas — Politics and government. I. Attlesey, Sam.
II. Crawford, Mary G. III. Title.
F386.K59 1992
320.4764--dc20   92-5287
                                                 CIP

The Texas Almanac's

Political History of Texas

Table of Contents

Acknowledgments

Writers incur many debts while gathering material for a book like this that includes election returns more than a century old. Texas has not been the best of states in preserving election information, and that makes the task especially difficult.

In the course of chasing down information for this book, we were aided by many people without whose cooperation, courtesy and genuine interest we would not have been able to complete the task.

In the Texas State Library and Archives, Chris La Plante and staff, including Michael R. Green, Jean Carefoot, Donaly Brice, Eddie Williams and Sergio Velasco were most helpful and patient.

George Christian of Austin and Bobby Aikin of Commerce aided Sam Attlesey in his pursuit of information.

Roger Olien's excellent book, *From Token to Triumph*, was an invaluable source for information on Texas Republicans in the early to middle years of the century for Mike Kingston. And Dale Baum at Texas A&M University was helpful in sorting out many questions that arose concerning voting procedures and election fraud.

And the personnel at Common Cause of Texas, the Texas Secretary of State's office, the Texas House Research Organization, and the Texas Legislative Library, the Democratic Party of Texas and the Republican Party of Texas were most accommodating and, as important, patient with our inquiries.

Without the help of these and others, this book would not have been possible. Our thanks to them all. And as always, the errors are those of the authors alone.

MIKE KINGSTON.
SAM ATTLESEY.
MARY G. CRAWFORD.
February 1992

Politics Texas-Style

Politics in Texas can be viewed from many perspectives. The election season can be deadly serious or silly. Candidates can be statesmen or clowns. One thing for certain, the debates will be high volume and even outrageous by many standards.

In many ways, however, the state's politics are important beyond its borders. Consider this: Two of the past six presidents of the United States have been products of the Texas political system. Three speakers of the U.S. House of Representatives this century — John Nance Garner, Sam Rayburn and Jim Wright — have come from Texas. And Texans have chaired most of the important committees in the U.S. House over the past 100 years.

President George Bush could not win a statewide election in Texas, losing twice before winning a congressional office in Houston. Even when he got the Republican presidential nomination, the naturalized Texan had to defeat a ticket featuring another favorite son, Democratic Sen. Lloyd Bentsen.

Since 1845, candidates for governor of Texas have pursued a gamut of strategies from the hell-bent campaign of Pat Neff, who made more than 850 campaign appearances in 1920 to reach Texans in 150 counties, including 37 that had never seen a gubernatorial candidate, to Francis R. Lubbock who didn't campaign at all in 1861 and won the narrowest victory ever in the campaign of that Civil War year. Candidates have projected images from the suave, debonair John Connally in the 1960s to the master showman Pappy Lee O'Daniel and his western band of the Depression years. Alcohol played a role in the state's politics in the early 20th century until Prohibition proved a disastrous failure. Most Texas governors have been moderate drinkers, but Pat Neff boasted that he never touched alcohol or tobacco, while Ann Richards is an acknowledged recovering alcoholic.

Texans have suffered — or chuckled at — wardrobe peculiarities in their leaders from George T. Woods' refusal to wear socks to William

H. R. Runnels, left, holds the distinction of being the only person to defeat Sam Houston in an election after Houston moved to Texas. Runnels beat Houston for the governorship in 1857, but two years later, Houston came back and took the office. Francis R. Lubbock, right, served as lieutenant governor under Runnels. As a gubernatorial candidate in 1861, Lubbock did not campaign, but won the election by 124 votes. Pictures from the Texas State Library.

P. Clements' zest for dazzlingly bizarre sport coats.

  The state spearheaded the populist revolt of the late 19th century, let women vote before most of the rest of the nation and sent a U.S. Senator to Washington via election even before the national constitution was amended to require election to the upper house. On the other hand, Texas embraced white supremacy well past the middle of the century and took no positive action to assure African-Americans or other minorities the right to vote without a court pointing a judicial gun at its head. The white primary was a Texas innovation, and the state perfected the system for denying minority voters a voice in government until almost mid-century. The poll tax remained a criterion for voting into the 1960s. Texans have kept elected representatives around for almost 40 years, as in the case of Sam Rayburn, and they have dismissed others, like George Wood, the state's second governor and first to be voted out of office after the first term, forthwith.

  Through all this, Texans have gone to the polls to express their wills in a variety of ways ranging from giving their voice vote for a candidate to an election judge with no security to feeding their ballot into a portable computer. And sometimes they have taken pencil in hand to cast 100,000 write-in votes for a candidate like Pappy Lee O'Daniel in a performance that amazed some pundits who did not think that many literate Texans would vote for the showman.

Some of the nation's most notorious political bosses like the Parrs (George and Archer), Jim Wells and Renfo Creager in South Texas have operated within the state's borders.

Aliens have been allowed — indeed, even encouraged — to vote in the state's elections. On other occasions, the state abandoned its professed frontier egalitarianism to pare back the electorate to some so-called decent people, all in the name of reform and good government.

Texans elected Annie Webb Blanton to the office of state superintendent of public instruction before women could vote in the general election and denied office to minority candidates who polled the most votes on election day. Statesmanship has marked some elections, while others have been decided or overturned with the exercise of brute force and violence.

Rural areas of the state have exercised influence on elections beyond their numbers, and urban areas have led the way for the development of the Republican Party as a legitimate alternative to the Democratic versions of conservatism and liberalism that marked the last half of the 20th century.

What's Conservative?

The magic word in Texas politics is "conservative," and it covers a multitude of sins. The division is not new. Oran Roberts, a judge, governor and statesman of the 19th century, explained in a history of Texas government in the 1890s that two parties had always existed, though their names changed. "One of them was in favor of a liberal construction of the (U.S.) Constitution in the administration of government, and the other was in favor of a strict construction which would prevent the exercise of any doubtful powers, and the assumption of powers not delegated, in order to meet emergencies in theadministration of government," Roberts wrote. Those were the platforms from which many debates over state and national policy were fought in Texas. As politics developed in the 20th century, the issues often boiled down to spending and white supremacy, which was wholeheartedly embraced by the Democratic Party. Race in the 1930s, 1940s and 1950s became a paramount, if unspoken, issue.

Texas benefited from Franklin D. Roosevelt's New Deal and Fair Deal spending programs of the Depression years, and it was not until the pain of the period began to recede that some of the state's politicians began to rebel against the policies. Some observers suggest that the opposition began to build only after it became apparent that blacks and other minorities were going to benefit from the programs along with whites. As Roosevelt extended his presidency beyond the traditional two

Ann Richards waves a victory banner of sorts in celebration of her upset victory over Republican Clayton Williams in 1990. She was given little chance to win early in the campaign when Williams had a double-digit lead in the polls. Gov. Richards is the second woman to hold the state's highest office. Associated Press Photo.

terms, opposition grew. His vice president, John Nance Garner of Texas, quit in disgust. Opposition mushroomed in the 1940s leading to a break-away "Texas Regulars" movement, a third-party states' rights effort and finally with Texas moving away from liberal Democrats and to Republican Dwight D. Eisenhower's presidential effort.

Attention to government spending lost some of its popularity. Three of the most popular "conservative" governors in this period steered the course of state government into some expensive waters. State spending increased 50 percent in the four years "conservative" Coke Stevenson served as governor from 1943 to 1947, and it almost doubled in Allan Shivers' seven years in office from 1949 to 1957. John Connally, another conservative under whose administration state spending almost doubled again, put it into perspective when asked if he was a liberal or conservative in the 1960s: "On what?" was his response. Usually, in today's parlance, however, the term "conservative" means that the candidate agrees with the voter and "liberal" means that he or she does not.

Despite the definitions of conservatism, Texans occasionally have been on the cutting edge of change in the nation. John Reagan sponsored the legislation that created the Interstate Commerce Commission in the 19th century.

During his presidency, Lyndon B. Johnson, perhaps the state's greatest politician, was responsible for the most sweeping civil rights legislation in the history of the nation. Johnson's Great Society was an extension of New Deal policies designed to eliminate poverty. As a young congressman, he supported FDR and the New Deal in his campaign for Congress and with his votes after elections. When he advanced to the U.S. Senate, Johnson, ironically, held the seat once filled by the so-called "last Democrat," Joseph W. Bailey, one of Texas' great demagogues.

Election Oddities

Texas has allowed candidates to run against themselves, as did Democrat-Republicans Gov. Allan Shivers and U.S. Sen. Price Daniel in 1952, and put on the ballot the names of U.S. Sens. Lyndon B. Johnson and Lloyd Bentsen in pursuit of two offices, senator and vice president of the United States in 1960 and in 1988.

Elections are not limited to the usual election years, either. Special elections are called to fill offices vacated through death or advancement of the officeholder. When that happens, a free-for-all often develops. When long-time Sen. Morris Sheppard died in 1941, twenty-nine candidates entered into a mad scramble that W. Lee O'Daniel won by a razor-thin margin over a young congressman, Lyndon B. Johnson. At the time, a candidate needed only to gain a plurality of the vote to win. That law was changed after 1957 when liberal Ralph Yarborough defeated a field of 22 candidates for the U.S. Senate seat held by Price Daniel, who had left Washington to successfully run for governor.

Crowded as the special election fields were in 1941 and 1957, the election held in 1961 to replace Sen. Johnson, who had been elected vice president, attracted an amazing 71 candidates. In the inevitable runoff, Republican John Tower defeated Democrat William Blakley to open a new political era in Texas.

In recent years, party-switching has been a popular pastime in the state's political scheme. Usually disgruntled Democrats see the grass greener on the Republican side of the fence. But often as not, the plenitude is a mirage.

Swapping Parties

On the threshold of the Republican insurgence, Democrat Jack Cox swapped parties after running a close race with Price Daniel for governor in 1960. But after one good run at John Connally in 1962, Cox faded from the scene. That was the fate that also awaited Kent Hance in the 1980s. A good Democratic primary race with Mark White prompted Hance to seek his fortune in the Republican Party. But he never got the party's nomination. When White's popularity dropped in 1986, Hance would have been a shoo-in for the Democratic nomination, but he was in the process of losing the Republican primary to William P. Clements. The former governor unexpectedly re-entered politics to avenge his 1982 loss to White. While Republican leadership encourages party-swapping, Republican primary voters often grade newcomers against a

Ralph W. Yarborough, left, surprised Texas political leadership with a victory in the 1957 special election to fill one of the state's two U.S. senatorial seats. He later defeated Waggoner Carr and Barefoot Sanders in heated Democratic primaries to hold the office until 1970 when he was beaten by Lloyd Bentsen. Jack Cox, right, ran a good race against Price Daniel in 1960 in the Democratic primary and then swapped parties. In 1962 running as a Republican, he lost a close race for governor to then-Democrat John Connally. Dallas Morning News Photos.

time-in-party standard. Candidates on the local level usually fare better than those higher on the ballot. Several Democratic district judges in Dallas County successfully swapped parties in the early 1980s when it became apparent that the Republican majority in the county would clear the courthouse of Democrats, regardless of job performance.

U.S. Sen. Phil Gramm has proved to be the most successful party-switcher after losing a Democratic primary bid for the U.S. senatorial nomination to incumbent Lloyd Bentsen in 1976. Initially elected to Congress as a Democrat, Gramm in 1982 resigned his House seat and sought re-election as a Republican in a special election. When U.S. Sen. John Tower chose not to run in 1984, Gramm easily won the party nomination and defeated liberal Democrat Lloyd Doggett for the seat in the general election.

Women have played a major role in Texas politics for most of the 20th century, beginning with a determined campaign for the right to vote. Miriam A. Ferguson became the state's first woman governor when she entered the man's world in 1924, carrying the banner of her husband, Jim, who had been impeached, convicted and barred from seeking the state's top office again.

Women Show Punch

Beginning in the early 1950s, women became the muscle of the Republican Party. They manned telephone banks, made surveys, conducted get-out-the-vote campaigns and all the other thankless tasks that are the backbone of a successful political campaign. Republican women's clubs were organized by the dozens and were the focal points of the success the party experienced. Republican gubernatorial candidate Clayton Williams, who in 1990 blew a double-digit lead in the polls to lose to Texas' second woman governor, Ann Richards, made strategic blunders that probably cost him the election. He was insensitive to women's issues, joking about rape, and he ignored basic campaign organization in the urban areas where women traditionally have provided the enthusiasm and determination to attract voters.

On the other hand, Republican Kay Bailey Hutchison of Dallas defeated an all-woman field in the primary and in the general election to take the office of state treasurer in 1990. A former state legislator from Houston, Mrs. Hutchinson is considered one of the party's bright newcomers, as is Rick Perry of Haskell, who defeated incumbent Democrat Jim High-tower for agriculture commissioner, also in 1990.

Although the Greenback and Populist parties were strong and attractive in the late 19th century, Texans have steered away from third-party candidates in the 20th century. Former Alabama governor George Wallace made the most successful third-party presidential bid in 1968, carrying 21 counties (mostly in East Texas) and probably cost Republican Richard M. Nixon the state's electoral votes. Nixon won nationally anyway. In the gubernatorial races, Ramsey Muniz, running as the La Raza Unida Party candidate, got more than 214,000 votes for the best showing as a third-party candidate in the governor's race this century.

Since President Jimmy Carter's loss to conservative Republican Ronald Reagan in 1980, national Democrats have written off Texas' electoral votes, feeling that the conservative tradition of the state was too strong for moderate to liberal Democrats to carry. But the fact remains that no Democrat has won the presidency in the 20th century without winning in Texas.

Regionalism plays an important role in the state's politics. Texas can be broken into eight geographical regions that have distinct political personalities. Perhaps the greatest division in the state, however, is the so-called I-35 split. The interstate highway in many ways is the state's main street, running through most of the population centers like Dallas, Austin, San Antonio and Laredo, and neatly dividing the population, economic resources and political clout into haves and have-nots. More than 80 percent of the population and economic activity in the state takes place along or east of I-35. More than eighty percent of the

Geographical Regions of Texas

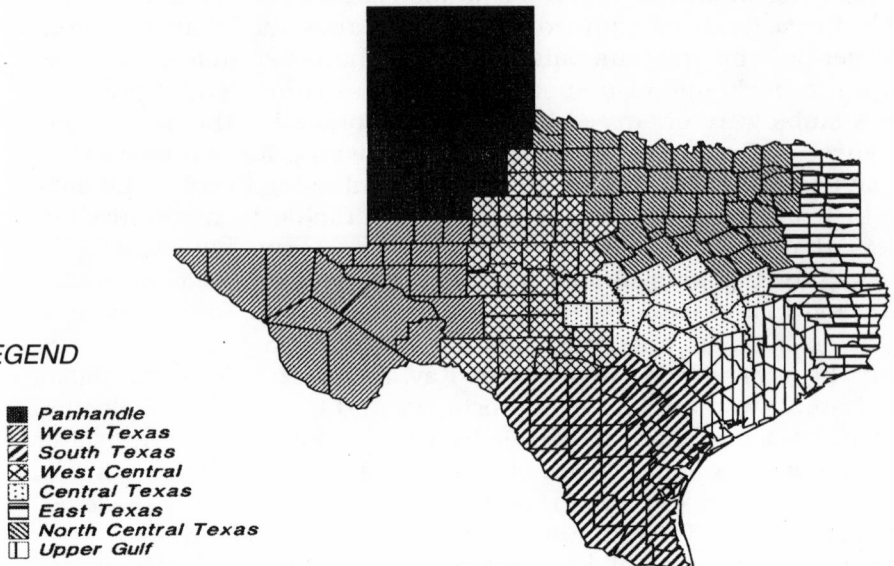

LEGEND

- ▨ Panhandle
- ▨ West Texas
- ▨ South Texas
- ⊠ West Central
- ▨ Central Texas
- ▤ East Texas
- ▧ North Central Texas
- ▢ Upper Gulf

votes in most statewide elections come from the same area. Only oil production is greater west of the line. The situation causes West Texans to despair of having a voice or influence in the affairs of the state, although these western regions get their share of representation on the boards and commissions of the state.

Texas' sprawling size places a financial hardship on candidates for statewide offices. With 26 major media markets in the state, big campaign funds are an absolute necessity to pay for electronic and newspaper advertising. The days of the shoe-leather campaigns of Pat Neff are just not realistic today. Spending in the governor's race has grown from $15 million in 1978 to $50 million in 1990. Raising such huge sums of money makes it difficult for a candidate to retain independence and not acquire political obligations to special interest groups.

With the growth of the Republican Party, expensive campaigns are needed in either primary. William P. Clements and Clayton Williams each "bought" victories in the Republican primaries of 1978 and 1990.

Clements carried momentum that propelled him to victory in the general election. Williams embarked on his general election campaign with an unfortunate series of gaffes that ultimately were his undoing in his loss to Ann Richards.

Texans have been vitally involved in politics as in 1896 when more than 80 percent of the electorate went to polls, and they have been totally bored by the spectacle, as in 1950 when only seven percent of the qualified voters chose to participate in selection of a governor.

The Motor Sputters

Politics can be the motor of society when it is practiced for the benefit of the greatest number of citizens. Conversely, it is a nasty business when special interests control the mechanisms of government for the benefit of a limited number and to the detriment of the majority. Texas has examples of both extremes in its history.

No matter which goal is pursued the most actively, politics can be fun, interesting and educational. In the following chapters, we will try to illuminate briefly many of the themes, issues and tendencies that have driven the engine of government in Texas.

This article was written by Mike Kingston, editor of the Texas Almanac.

Special Elections Are 'Special'

Special elections in Texas have, indeed, been special.

They have made Texas a two-party state. They have been called to replace a U.S. Senator who was simultaneously running for vice president of the United States. They have served as a national laboratory for a political party realignment experiment. They have been called to fill the vacancy left by a U.S. House Speaker forced to resign in disgrace. And they have elected the only black member of Congress from the state.

Special elections in Texas are called by the governor to fill the vacancies left by the death or resignation of incumbents.

In the early part of the century, special elections were noted for the crowds they attracted — on the ballot, not at the polls. In 1941, 29 candidates crowded the field in a race to replace long-time U.S. Senator Morris Sheppard, and Gov. W. Lee O'Daniel walked away with the office. Only a plurality was needed to win a special election. Ralph Yarborough led a field of 23 candidates in 1957 to gain a U.S. Senate seat, and the election resulted in a change in the law. Yarborough, a liberal, was anathema to Texas' political leadership. To prevent further accidental elections, the state law was changed to require a runoff if no candidate received a majority vote in the special election. Yarborough sailed to two general election victories before losing to Lloyd Bentsen in the 1970 Democratic primary.

No special election was more controversial, colorful or contested than the 1961 U.S. Senate race to replace Lyndon B. Johnson, who resigned his Senate seat to become vice president in John F. Kennedy's administration. With the improbable help of liberal Democrats, a conservative Republican college professor from Wichita Falls became the first GOP senator from the South since Reconstruction. John Goodwin Tower was elected in the 1961 special election that drew 71 candidates who were willing to pay a $50 filing fee for some statewide exposure and

Democrat Jim Chapman, left, won a special election for a congressional seat in East Texas in 1985 in a race billed as a preview of a political realignment in Texas. William A. Blakley, right, was not so fortunate. Twice appointed to the U.S. Senate to fill unexpired terms, he lost a special election to Ralph Yarborough in 1957, and in 1961, John Tower defeated him for Lyndon B. Johnson's seat. Blakley is the only person to have served in both the Thomas J. Rusk and Sam Houston successions in the state's U.S. Senate seats. Dallas Morning News Photos.

for a chance to serve in the U.S. Senate.

The race attracted some of the most famous names in Texas politics, including future U.S. House Speaker Jim Wright, Attorney General Will Wilson, State Sen. Henry B. Gonzalez and longtime liberal leader Maury Maverick, Jr. The other major Democratic candidate was conservative William Blakley of Dallas, who was named to serve as interim senator by Gov. Price Daniel. That gave him the incumbent advantage in the special election, but that would not be enough to give him a victory.

Texas Republicans rallied around the diminutive Tower, who repeatedly told his courthouse rally crowds that "my name is Tower but I don't." By the time the special election was held on April 4, 1961, Tower was no longer an unknown son of a Methodist minister. He had established himself as a credible candidate with statewide name identification because he had been the GOP standard bearer in the 1960 race against Johnson.

Taking advantage of a peculiar state law that Johnson had persuaded legislators to adopt in 1959, the powerful Senate majority leader ran for re-election and for vice president at the same time. Drawing support in the GOP strongholds of Dallas and Houston, Tower ran a respectable race against Johnson, garnering 31 percent of the vote.

Many Texans voted against Johnson because they were turned off that he was seeking two offices at the same time. In his political memoirs called *Consequences*, Tower wrote about how he capitalized on that by telling his campaign audiences to "Double your pleasure, double your fun — scratch Lyndon twice."

Tower conceded in his book that much of the support he garnered in the 1960 race was an "anti-Johnson vote." And he confessed that in the contest he was "out to hitch a ride" on the coattails of GOP presidential nominee Richard Nixon. After he lost the 1960 race and Johnson became vice president-elect, Tower never stopped campaigning for the special election that would be held less than six months later. With Republicans backing Tower and conservative Democrats behind Blakley, liberal Democrats could not agree on one of the other major candidates. When votes were counted on Election Day, the two candidates with the most votes were the two most conservative candidates. That would prove to be a key factor in the runoff.

Tower led the pack with 327,308 votes (32 percent). Blakley won a runoff spot, finishing second with 18 percent. Finishing third was Wright with 16 percent followed by Wilson with 12 percent, Maverick with 10 percent and Gonzalez with 9 percent. The other 65 candidates split the rest of the 1,058,124 votes cast on April 4. Looking at the combined vote of the Democratic candidates, Tower and his campaign consultants realized there was only one way to win the runoff: divide and conquer. As Tower recalled in his memoirs, "Our strategy involved holding my conservative base while continuing to paint Blakley, who was just as conservative as I was, as an ally of the Kennedys. This forced Blakley to run against his own president, and that in turn alienated moderate and liberal Democrats."

For liberal Democrats, the choice between two conservatives was so distasteful that many openly talked about "going fishing" — not voting — on Election Day. In his book *Two-Party Texas*, political consultant John Knaggs paints this picture of the liberals' dilemma. "On balmy spring afternoons shortly after the first election, liberals gathered to ponder their situation under the tall trees of Scholz Beer Garten, their quaint old unofficial headquarters in Austin, virtually in the shadows of the state capitol," Knaggs wrote."Over pitchers of cold draft beer, they discussed a steaming dilemma with three major facets:

"(1) Bite the bullet and vote for Tower to promote the two-party system.

"(2) Refuse to vote for either.

"(3) Wait for signals that Blakley might moderate."

On election day, many liberals went fishing, while others voted for Tower for one of two reasons. Some believed Tower would be easier to beat in the next regular election than Blakley. Others believed that a Tower victory would help create a two-party state in which the Democratic Party would be purged of conservatives who would switch to the Republican Party.

On May 27, 1961, Tower ushered in a new day in Texas politics. With the help of some liberal Democrats, the conservative Republican defeated the conservative Democrat by a 10,343 margin out of 886,091 votes cast. Tower received 448,217 votes compared to Blakley's 437,874. The first Republican to win a statewide office in Texas since Reconstruction, Tower would go on to serve in the Senate until he decided not to seek re-election in 1984. His victory forever changed politics in the Lone Star State.

When Tower was killed in an airplane crash in April 1991, he was remembered as either the "founding father of two-party Texas" or as "the father of the Republican Party in Texas."

One of those memorializing Tower was his successor in the Senate, former Texas A&M University economics professor Phil Gramm. Gramm had won the Senate seat vacated by Tower in 1984. But before that campaign, Gramm had been involved in one of the most unusual special elections ever held in Texas. The 1983 special election for the 6th Congressional District was caused by the Gramm's own resignation. In what observers called a dramatic and risky move, Gramm switched from the Democratic to the Republican Party on Jan. 5, 1983, resigned his congressional seat and then announced as a GOP candidate in the special election.

Gramm could have simply switched parties and kept his Central Texas congressional seat. But he said he wanted to give the voters of the district a chance to accept or reject him as a Republican. Democrats, including State Rep. Dan Kubiak, who would challenge Gramm in the Feb. 12 special election, disagreed. "This was all done to satisfy the biggest political ego this side of the Potomac River," Kubiak said at the time.

Gramm's party switch in January 1983 came after a nasty spat with Democratic congressional leaders, including U.S. House Speaker Tip O'Neill and Majority Leader Jim Wright of Fort Worth.

Gramm, who was first elected from the district in 1978, received national attention when he became one of the leaders of the Boll Weevil Democratic congressmen who supported many of the economic policies of Republican President Ronald Reagan. Gramm, while serving as a member of the powerful Budget Committee, became a co-sponsor of a Reagan-backed federal budget reduction resolution. The Democrats then booted Gramm off the committee. That gave him the final excuse he needed to defect to the Republican party, and it set the stage for the special election.

Outgoing GOP Gov. Bill Clements called the election as soon as possible after Gramm's resignation in an effort to prevent challengers from building name identification or war chests. But that did not stop

Craig Washington, left, and Phil Gramm have been two big winners in special elections in the 1980s. Gramm succeeded himself after resigning his congressional seat when he decided to swap parties. The move gave him exposure that he used in a subsequent race to fill the U.S. Senate seat vacated by John Tower. Washington, a long-time state senator, sought the U.S. House seat vacated by the death of Rep. Mickey Leland of Houston in an airplane crash in Africa. Dallas News Photos.

nine Democrats and one Libertarian from running against Gramm in the sprawling district that snaked from southwest Dallas County to the Houston suburbs of Montgomery County. Most of the Democratic Party leadership rallied around Kubiak, the former state representative from Rockdale. The candidacy of nationally-known humorist John Henry Faulk added some color to the race that revolved more around name-calling and political party allegiance than it did issues.

Some observers said the election was a test for "Reaganomics," but others said it was a referendum on Gramm. To some residents of the district, Gramm was a profile in courage or a prince of principles. To others he was a congressional spy or an ambitious political opportunist. Gramm, who had amassed a campaign kitty of $750,000 and a near 100 percent name identification, weathered the attacks. And on Election Day, Gramm finished first with 55 percent, or 46,334 votes out of 84,062 cast. Kubiak, who could raise only about $125,000, finished second with 39 percent, or 33,162 votes. Faulk ran a distant third with less than 4 percent of the vote. The other eight contenders split the rest of the vote.

Gramm became the first Republican congressman from the district, but on election night he proclaimed: "This was not a victory of party, but a triumph of philosophy."

Two years later, Gramm would play a key role in a special election that would serve as a national experiment in political party re-alignment. The laboratory for the experiment would be the 1st Congressional District in Yellow-Dog Democrat Northeast Texas.

In 1985, Gramm, serving as a freshman U.S. Senator, not only helped cause the special election but was influential in hand-picking the lone GOP candidate. A vacancy was created when Gramm selected Boll Weevil Democratic U.S. Rep. Sam Hall of Marshall as his nominee to a vacant federal judgeship. Hall had served as the 1st District's congressman since 1976, having succeeded populist Democrat Wright Patman, who represented the area for almost half a century. No Republican had represented the area since Reconstruction, but Gramm and other GOP leaders felt the time was ripe for their party to begin making inroads in the area.

In the wake of the Ronald Reagan landslide of 1984, political analysts viewed the off-year election as a test of whether political party realignment — a shifting of allegiance from the Democratic to the Republican Party — had become a reality in Texas and the nation.

Party pride was on the line when Democratic Gov. Mark White called the election for June 29, 1985. Eight candidates entered the race, including six Democrats and one independent. Democratic contenders included two state legislators, former State Treasurer Warren G. Harding and a former Hopkins County district attorney named Jim Chapman. The lone Republican was former Texas A&M quarterback star Edd Hargett, a farmer and rancher from Lindale. Gramm played a key role in selecting the political novice and he repeatedly campaigned in the district on Hargett's behalf.

As the race grew in national significance, the Reagan White House became visibly involved. Vice President George Bush and Treasury Secretary James Baker both campaigned for Hargett in the district. Reagan cut two commercials for the GOP standard bearer. National Republican operatives were dispatched to Texas to work in the campaign. And on Election Day, Hargett finished first with 42 percent, or 29,814 out of 70,718 votes cast. But because he failed to garner 50 percent of the vote, he was forced into a runoff with second-place finisher Chapman, who drew 30 percent, or 21,370 votes. A runoff election was called for Aug. 3 between the low-key Hargett and the combative Chapman, a lawyer from Sulphur Springs.

National and Texas Democrats quickly rallied behind Chapman to try and overtake the Republicans, who already were united behind Hargett. Hargett attempted to play down his affiliation with the GOP, and focused his runoff campaign on his independent conservative credentials. He tried to paint Chapman as a liberal who would vote with Speaker Tip O'Neill and Eastern labor bosses more than he would for conservative East Texans.

Chapman, calling himself an "independent Democrat," focused on two key issues important to the poor and elderly residents of the district: protection of jobs and of Social Security benefits.

Although badly outspent, Chapman's message was more appealing to the voters. On Aug. 3, Chapman scratched out a 1,933-vote victory out of 103,407 ballots cast. Chapman garnered 50.9 percent, or 52,670 votes, while Hargett received 50,737.Using basic precinct organization, an aggressive absentee vote campaign and a 1,000-member volunteer army on Election Day, the Democrats had blunted political realignment, at least temporarily, in Texas.

Hargett aides conceded they were out-gunned, out-manned and out-organized. Grass-roots politics, including the use of a new no-excuse absentee voting law, would give Democrats another victory in a special election in 1989. This election would be called to fill the vacancy created by the resignation of a speaker of the U.S. House of Representatives.

Facing allegations that he violated House ethics rules numerous times, Speaker Jim Wright of Fort Worth gave up his long-coveted speakership in an impassioned speech before his colleagues on May 31, 1989. It was during that speech that Wright also offered to resign from tne 12th Congressional District in Tarrant County that he had represented for 34 years. That set up yet another nationally watched special election that Gov. Bill Clements would call for Aug. 12.

Republicans were eager to use the race as a demonstration of how much the GOP had grown in Texas. Democrats wanted to maintain the 12th District, which had been carefully drawn in previous redistricting sessions to protect Wright, as a demonstration of their respect for the disgraced speaker and party loyalist. Eight candidates entered the race, including four Democrats, three Republicans and one Libertarian.

Most GOP leaders put their money on political novice Dr. Bob Lanier, a pediatrician and host of a nationally syndicated TV show called "60-second House-call." Democrats were divided between lawyers Pete Geren and Jim Lane.

Lanier ran first with 39.4 percent, or 21,978 votes. Geren earned a runoff spot by finishing second with 31.8 percent, or 17,751 votes. Lane, who garnered 22 percent, and the other five hopefuls split the rest of the votes. On election night, Wright dramatically endorsed Geren, making the Sept. 12 runoff a referendum on how much influence the former speaker still had in his hometown.

Texas Democratic Party Chairman Bob Slagle said before the runoff: "It would be devastating to lose this from a public-image standpoint. If we lose it, the national press will take it out of context as a repudiation of Jim Wright."

Geren, a former aide to Texas Democratic U.S. Sen. Lloyd Bentsen, had lost a congressional bid in 1986 in the 6th District, but he campaigned as an experienced veteran.

On Election Day, Geren squeaked out a 51.03 percent victory.

The Democrat garnered 40,210 votes compared to Lanier's 38,590. Lanier had actually received more votes cast on Election Day, but Geren's victory came because of a well-orchestrated campaign to use the no-excuse absentee law. Geren got 9,261 absentee votes compared to Lanier's 6,244 election.

Democrats garnered another victory in another nationally watched special election. There was never any doubt that a Democrat would win a special election in Houston later in 1989. What made that congressional election special was that it was to replace the only black representative in the Texas congressional delegation.

The election was called after Rep. Mickey Leland of Houston was killed in an airplane crash in Ethiopia on Aug. 7 while on a mission to help the world's hungry. Worldwide attention was focused on the week-long search for Leland and eight other Americans who were in a twin-engine plane that crashed into a rugged mountainside.

When he paid his filing fee for the Nov. 7, 1989, election, State Sen. Craig Washington, a Houston Democrat, said the "world is watching" the race to replace Leland. "Because of the manner in which Mickey died, the world is watching this district.

"We're not just sending a person to Congress. We're sending someone who's expected to be a leader on constitutional rights as was Barbara Jordan and on civil rights as was Mickey Leland," Washington said. The 18th District was created in the 1971 redistricting session of the Legislature specifically for Ms. Jordan, who was then a state senator. Washington ultimately won the election in a Dec. 9 runoff against Houston City Councilman Anthony Hall with 57 percent, or 24,120 votes. Hall drew 18,473 votes. The two had finished one-two in the first election on Nov. 7 in a field of 11 candidates vying to represent the 18th Congressional District in Harris County.

In his acceptance speech, Washington said, "I claim this victory not for myself, but first for our brother who died on the side of a hill in Ethiopia." For residents of the district and for many Texans, it had, indeed, been a special election.

This article was written by Sam Attlesey, political writer for The Dallas Morning News.

Voting in a Man's World

Voting is taken for granted today by Texans. They can register to vote up to 30 days before an election. Every citizen, regardless of color or creed, has the right to vote. And once behind the curtain of a voting machine or within a small cubicle provided for privacy in marking a computer punch card, if you are a voter in most urban areas, your vote is secret

Still, fewer than 50 percent of the persons old enough to vote participate in most elections in Texas. That was not the case until the turn of the century, when a conscious attempt was made to reduce the size of the electorate and to limit voting by some racial and economic groups. Early Texans voted under much different circumstances than those in force today. Unfortunately, some voted both "early and often," as the old quip goes, a practice that cast a pall over many an election. Worse, it gave many Texans a very cynical view of the electoral process.

Little is known about the actual voting procedures in early Texas elections. Some extrapolation from practices in the United States is necessary, for early Texans brought the familiar voting procedures with them. The Republic's election laws were surprisingly progressive. Secret ballots were mandated in 1837, and a system of numbered ballots was instituted to prevent fraud and multiple voting. Beginning with the Constitution of the Republic, the method of elections by the people was directed to be "by ballot, unless Congress shall otherwise direct." That was a curious qualification, since presumably the Congress could direct use of a printed ballot or require a voice vote.

When Texas entered the Union, the voting procedures were transformed dramatically for a short time. Voters were required to express their opinions *viva voce*, or "with live voice." That had been the traditional method of voting in parts of the United States. All of Texas' early state constitutions called for voice vote by senators and representatives in the Legislature. The Constitution of 1845 also stated, "The privilege of free suffrage shall be supported by laws regulating elections, and prohibiting under adequate penalties, all undue influence thereon from power, bribery, tumult, or other improper practice." Maintenance of that ideal would have eliminated many of the election problems that future Texans faced. The military of the national government also was prohibited from voting in Texas elections.

No Secret Ballot

Except for the days of the Republic, the secret ballot was not in use in Texas until late in the 19th century. Whether voting by voice or written ballot, the voter lost anonymity. The ordinance calling the election to ratify secession in 1861 required the voting to be by ballot "For Secession" or "Against Secession." Votes by residents of Jack County were public knowledge. Secession lost 51-14, and the names of those for or against secession were public record. Peer pressure no doubt was influential in elections in which this procedure was used. How else could neighboring Palo Pinto County vote 113-0 "For Secession?" It is difficult to imagine 113 males in Texas agreeing on any one thing during the period, even if one disagreed out of pure cussedness alone.

Africans, their descendants and "Indians not taxed" were barred from voting through the Constitution of 1866, which is one reason federal Reconstruction authorities got tough with Texas after the Civil War. That constitution required members of the Senate to be "white males." Former male slaves got the right to vote in the Constitution of 1869, which was written by radical Republicans. It also required a system of voter registration for the first time.

When the current constitution was written in 1876, efforts were made to improve elections. The new charter, while prohibiting voter registration, directed the Legislature to provide for a system of numbered tickets (so called because the ballots resembled railroad tickets) to assure ballot security and to provide other laws to "preserve the purity of the ballot box." Access to the ballot was increased, too, when voting was allowed over a four-day period with polls open from 8 a.m. to 4 p.m. each day

Later in the century, voters got to choose privately printed ballots containing slates of candidates for the offices. On the Texas-Mexico border, where election manipulation and fraud became a science, and in East Texas, voters were given ballots printed on colored paper or irregularly shaped ballots. Both made voting easier for persons illiterate in the English language. They were particularly useful for persons who sold their votes and to political bosses who promoted a slate of candidates.

At the beginning of the 20th century, Texas, like the rest of the nation, went through a period of reform in which many questionable election practices were supposedly suppressed. Whatever the mind of man can conceive, however, the mind of man can circumvent. And nowhere does that observation apply better than to election law.

Through the early 19th century, the vote was limited to males 21 years of age and over with blacks and Indians barred from voting. Until after the Civil War, only white males could vote, and in some cases, property ownership requirements had to be met, usually when the subject of the vote cost tax dollars.

Voting rights for former slaves threw the Texas election system into a panic. Black voters made up a large percentage of the electorate in some counties and even a majority in a few. During Reconstruction, federal authorities saw that these newly endowed voters had an opportunity to participate in the election process.

Texas Democrats and former Confederates therefore pursued a policy of diluting the black voting strength by encouraging immigration, both from other states and from foreign countries. U.S. citizenship was not required for voting until the Constitution of 1866, and then only briefly. The radical Republican Constitution of 1869 specifically allowed aliens to vote, and the Constitution of 1876 required only that the alien declare his intention to become a U. S. citizen. The voter also was required to be a resident of the state for one year and of the county or district in which the election was held for six months.

Aliens Could Vote — Legally

Immigrants were needed after the Civil War for two reasons: Texas was a big, empty territory, and it needed people to settle and develop the land. And, there was a perceived, if not real, labor shortage after the war. Texas landowners were reluctant to contract with freed slaves, and white farm help was difficult to attract.

The liberal immigration policy therefore was envisioned as an attraction to white landowners and white farm laborers. Perhaps the policy-makers hoped that much of the immigration would come from the war-devastated states of the Old South, lending political stability by padding support for Democratic candidates.

Texas was not alone in offering the vote to newcomers; many frontier states did so. Texas, however, was the only one adjacent to a foreign border.

South Texas political bosses were quick to sign up Mexican nationals for their voting rolls. Initially, the voter, regardless of citizenship, had only to sign an oath declaring his intention to become a naturalized American citizen to be eligible to vote. In commenting on legislation in 1895 that would curb this practice, Jim Wells, the major political boss of the era, warned that if the Populists gained strength, he would "need every one of them," referring to the Mexican voters.

Early efforts to control alien voting were feeble. In the 1890s, for example, aliens were required to declare their intention to become citizens six months before the election. This usually only meant two trips across the Rio Grande rather than one.

Many tactics were used to get the Mexican nationals to the polls. Often they were transported across the river in wagons, treated to a barbeque and booze, taken to the polls, and after they cast the proper colored paper ballot, they were paid for their efforts and taken home.

While border aliens were pawns of the bosses, some other immigrants did not meet expectations either. German newcomers in the Hill Country, for example, indulged in a disturbing independence thought and action, often siding with Republicans rather than Democratic candidates.

Election reform was a major issue across the nation in the latter part of the 19th century. Kentucky and Massachusetts in 1888 led the way in the adoption of the so-called "blanket ballot," so named because it carried the names of all candidates from all parties. Texas adopted the blanket ballot in 1892, but its use was limited to cities of 10,000 or more population. A statewide Australian system, which included a secret ballot, was provided in the Terrell Election Law of 1905.

'Troublemakers' Targeted

Black and poor white farmers caused the Democratic establishment so much trouble during the agrarian revolt in the latter 19th century, efforts were made to curtail their participation in future elections. One bill in 1895 would have limited the aid that could be given to voters illiterate in English. That would have affected 82 percent of the black vote and 81 percent of the aliens, according to literacy figures compiled in the U.S. Census of 1900. Indeed, 15 percent of the entire electorate was illiterate at the time.

Candidates for local offices were selected in the infamous "white primaries," or "unofficial" official elections. Statewide candidates were chosen at a state convention. Attempts were made beginning in 1895 to clean up elections. Some controls were levied, but state Sen. Jim Wells, the South Texas political boss, blocked substantive reform.

After the turn of the century, several major changes were made in election law. In 1902, voters approved levy of a poll tax as a requisite for voting. For many years, state constitutions had directed that "The privilege of free suffrage shall be supported by laws regulating elections." And the Constitution of 1876 prohibited instituting a voter registration system, after one had been used by the hated radical Republicans. The change culminated an effort of almost 30 years by some conservative Democrats to reduce the size of the electorate.

Poor whites and black voters were hit the hardest by the new voting requirement. A poll tax is simply a head tax, and Texans had levied one during the Civil War. But tying the tax to the right to vote was an innovation of the early 20th century. Voter participation dropped dramatically after the tax was levied. For example, in 1896, when the Populist party was at its strongest in state politics, the gubernatorial election attracted 539,778 voters. That turnout represented about 84 percent of the voters qualified by age to participate. That turnout was not reached again in the governor's race until the Democratic primary of 1918, over 20 years later when the electorate, increased by the women's vote, was three times as large as in 1896. The total turnout represented only a 31.6 percent turnout of those eligible by age to participate. And the 1896 turnout was not surpassed in. the governor's race in the general election until 1924 when the electorate was more than four times the size of 1896.

'*All-White' Primary*

In addition, most counties instituted an "all-white" primary prior to the election. Only white persons were allowed to vote in these elections, and the winners often were unopposed on the general election ballot, giving black voters little say in the ultimate selection of public officials. Non-white votes could be excluded from this primary, it was argued, because the primary was function of a private organization, the political party. The practice was not overturned by the U.S. Supreme Court until 1944.

Not all the changes brought by the Terrell Election Law were bad, however. For the first time, the state's political parties were required to hold primaries so voters could select nominees in some standard fashion, rather that have the nominations brokered in the district or state conventions. Also, for the first time in Texas elections, the so-called Australian, or secret, ballot was adopted. Voters could privately mark their ballots. The Australian system was adopted in the 1880s in the United States, 30 years after its development in Australia, so Texas was slow in implementing this important change.

In 1913, a bill was passed requiring voters to be U.S. citizens and banning assistance to voters at the polls. The sponsor was honest about the intent of the law "to disqualify the Mexicans of the Western and Lower Rio Grande counties." Gov. Oscar Colquitt, an anti-prohibitionist, vetoed the bill, complaining that it also would have purged poor whites and blacks, along with Hispanics.

Deadline for the poll-tax payment was set in January of election years, six month before the election. The long period between qualification and participation successfully discouraged any last-minute interest from unregistered voters. And there was always the chance that a voter would lose his poll-tax receipt.

Adoption of modern voting technology in Texas has come slowly. Election machines had been used with varying degrees of success in the United States from the 1830s onward. The first laws regulating their use were passed in New York in 1892. Texas, however, did not change its laws to accommodate voting machines until 1930, and then their use was limited to the big cities. These machines provided privacy and supposed accuracy in counting votes in a precinct. There was still the chance of human error by a tired election judges — or an unscrupulous one — misreading vote totals on election night. While the machines speeded the vote-counting at the precinct level, the votes still had to be tabulated at the county level. And that could be time-consuming.

Other electronic voting devices introduced as early as 1951, were designed to speed this tabulation. After considerable controversy in the 1970s, punch-card machines were used in some Texas cities like Dallas. The 1980s saw development and refinement of a computer punch-card system that increased the speed of both voting and counting on the precinct level and tabulating on the county level.

Voting laws in Texas, though today codified and simplified to an extent, still can baffle the casual reader and confound even the most dedicated layman who is trying to live within their boundaries. The laws have been written over a long period of time, with each addition designed to prevent some action or promote another.

And still, election irregularities are charged after virtually every election in the state. Nevertheless today's elections are probably as pure and honest as any in the state's history — which is a somewhat troubling thought in itself.

This article was written by Mike Kingston, editor of the Texas Almanac.

Citizens at Last!

"We hold these truths to be self-evident, that all men are created equal..." —U.S. Declaration of Independence, 1776.

When the United States declared its independence from England, the sentence quoted above from the Declaration of Independence was taken literally. The word "men" was interpreted not as meaning "mankind" or all citizens, but males. Only men were able to vote.

Sixty years later, the Republic of Texas stated: "Every citizen of the republic who has attained the age of twenty-one years, and shall have resided six months within the district or county where the election is held, shall be entitled to vote for members of the general congress." In actual practice, however, women did not vote. The same document also stated that "every male citizen...shall be entitled to hold any office or place of honor, trust, or profit under the republic..."

In 1845, the newly annexed State of Texas was organized under a new state constitution. The first section of the Bill of Rights of that constitution declared: "All political power is inherent in the people..." Evidently "the people" did not include female people. Article III of that document granted the right to vote to "all free male persons over the age of twenty-one years, except Indians not taxed, Africans and descendants of Africans" who met certain residency requirements.

The right of women to vote was not prohibited only in Texas, however. All over the nation, women could not participate in choosing their government officials or in determining the policies under which their government would operate.

The first faltering steps toward woman suffrage in the United States were taken at a meeting of women and men in Seneca Falls, New York, in the summer of 1848. In this, the world's first women's rights convention, a series of resolutions was adopted. One of these resolutions outlined the right of women to vote.

The first apparent official interest in woman suffrage in Texas was in the Constitutional Convention of 1868, a convention that was also grappling with the enormous problems of Reconstruction following the Civil War. Delegate R. H. Mundine of Burleson County offered a resolution that all persons meeting age, residence and citizenship requirements be accepted as qualified voters "without distinction of sex." His resolution was referred to the committee on state affairs, which recommended its adoption. However, amid arguments that voting was "unwomanly" and that a true woman would shrink "from mingling in the busy noise of election days," the resolution was defeated in the full convention by a vote of 52 to 13.

In the 1875 Constitutional Convention, two woman suffrage resolutions were offered, both of which were referred to the committee on suffrage. Unswayed by the reasonableness of the resolutions, the committee recommended that the vote be extended to all males except minors, paupers, lunatics, felons, soldiers and sailors if they met residence, age and other requirements. Even aliens could vote if they had lived in the state for a year and declared their intentions to become citizens. Women were completely ignored. The resolution was adopted on Oct. 7, 1875, by a vote of 61 to 20.

There were intermittent outbreaks of agitation for woman suffrage in the nation, as well as in Texas, for the next couple of decades. And in the mid-1880s, the Woman's Christian Temperance Union endorsed woman suffrage, principally because it felt that women would vote for prohibition. In fact, many of the staunchest fighters in the battle for the right to vote came from the ranks of the WCTU.

In 1890, Wyoming became the first state in the union to allow women to vote. Colorado followed in 1893, and the campaign for woman suffrage in Texas began organizing in earnest that year.

And organizing was the key to the eventual success of the movement. To obtain the basic right to vote, the women of Texas finally were forced to mount a very comprehensive and sophisticated statewide political campaign. Their army of enthusiastic volunteers and their efficient organization might be the envy of many present-day candidates for public office.

The early efforts garnered few tangible results. Mrs. Rebecca Henry Hayes of Galveston called a convention of women and men in Dallas in 1893. Forty-eight delegates formed the Texas Equal Rights Association at the largely organizational meeting. Mrs. Hayes was elected president, and Mrs. S. L. Trumbull of Dallas was elected first vice president. Open to both men and women, the group was a chapter of the National American Woman Suffrage Association. Denison organized the first local affiliate in April 1893 with 13 members. In July, a group formed in Taylor, followed by one in Granger in November.

During the State Fair in Oct. 1893, a woman's congress was held in Dallas in the parlors of the Windsor Hotel with about 300 women attending. As a result, woman suffrage groups were organized in Dallas, Fort Worth, Belton and San Antonio in the spring of 1894.

The Texas suffragists realized that education of their members and of the public was vital to their cause. Local societies usually met once or twice a month, presenting speakers that informed the audiences about women's legal status, parliamentary law and the occupational oppression of women.

Polls Point 'Thumbs Down'

On March 20, 1894, The Dallas Morning News published the results of an opinion poll of 39 men who were prominent in Texas politics. The list included, but was not limited to, men who held statewide offices, both elected and appointed, or who were candidates for statewide offices. Of the total, 28 were opposed to woman suffrage, while 11 were in favor. Opponents argued that women were already adequately represented by men; that Southern women would not vote even if they could; that enfranchisement would break up the home and destroy chivalry; that it violated biblical teaching; and that women should not vote because they did not serve in the armed forces. Those in favor stated that women were mentally and morally qualified; that their participation would have a beneficial effect on politics; and that denying women the vote amounted to taxation without representation.

The San Antonio Express published the results of a poll of a group of women on the same subject in July 1894. Surprisingly, the women were split almost exactly down the middle: Of 21 women queried, 11 favored woman suffrage, but 10 were opposed. Those opposed said that they were willing to let men make the laws; they had enough rights already; they were too busy with household duties to bother; and that letting women vote would destroy chivalry and degrade womanhood. Said one: "God forbid that the day will come when we will see women turned loose upon the nation, a set of raving, tearing politicians, standing elbow to elbow with the rabble and the toughs; unsexing themselves to the detriment of the home and of all social and domestic relations." Those in favor echoed the reasons given by the men in Dallas: that enfranchisement would bring new dignity and honor to women and that women obeyed laws and paid taxes.

Ironically, at this time there was no constitutional prohibition of women holding most state or county offices. They could not be members of the Legislature, however, or hold municipal offices. Only qualified electors were eligible for those positions, and women were not electors. But women chose not to run for those statewide offices open to them; they preferred to devote their energies to working for voting rights for all women.

An effort in the summer of 1894 to make woman suffrage a part of each political party's platform was unsuccessful. Democrats, Republicans and Populists alike rejected the plank.

The first woman suffrage amendment to be introduced in the Texas Legislature was presented to the House of Representatives in the spring of 1895 by A. C. Tompkins of Hempstead. It was referred to the committee on constitutional amendments and was never heard of again. After 1895, the movement lost its momentum and went into a prolonged period of hibernation. By the end of 1896 the Texas Equal Rights Association was no longer active.

In February 1903, new life was breathed into the Texas woman suffrage movement when Annette Finnigan and her two sisters formed the Equal Suffrage League in Houston. The first meeting attracted 50 people. A chapter was organized in Galveston later that year with 25 members. The Houston group increased to 75 by December, when a statewide two-day convention was held in that city. Several hundred people attended the meeting, at which the Texas Woman Suffrage Association was resurrected.

When the Finnigan sisters left Texas in 1905, the state's suffrage movement again came to a temporary standstill for a lack of strong leadership. For several years the only active suffrage organization in Texas was the one in Austin, and it made no attempt to expand statewide.

But the need was still there, waiting for effective leadership to give it direction. In Feb. 1912, a group of 75 San Antonio women formed a suffrage society, the advance guard in the final, long push toward equality at the ballot box. Under the leadership of Eleanor Brackenridge, a prominent civic leader, the membership grew to 144 by the end of March; by November, the group was almost 400 strong. Suffrage clubs were also organized that year in Galveston, Waco, Dallas, Tyler and San Marcos.

The first Texas suffrage convention since 1904 was held at the St. Anthony Hotel in San Antonio in April 1913. Attending were 150 women and a few men. Delegates came from seven Texas cities: Galveston, San Antonio, Dallas, Houston, Austin, Temple and Del Rio. They urged the U. S. Congress to adopt a federal constitutional amendment for woman suffrage. After 1913, state conventions were held every year.

The 2,500 delegates attending the convention in Galveston in 1915 elected Minnie Fisher Cunningham of Galveston state president. In 1902, Cunningham was the first woman to receive a pharmacy degree from the University of Texas Medical School in Galveston. "Minnie Fish," as she was affectionately called by other suffragists, was elected president of the Galveston Equal Suffrage Association in 1910. Mrs. Cunningham led the statewide effort, sometimes reluctantly, from her election in 1915 to the successful conclusion of the campaign in 1920.

During the final stages of the suffrage fight, she also served as secretary of the National American Suffrage Association's congressional committee, dividing her time between Washington, D. C., and Texas. Mrs. Cunningham was also Texas chairman of the Liberty Loan Campaign, a public fund-raising drive to help finance the defense effort, during World War I. She was information editor for the Agricultural Extension Service of Texas A&M University from 1932 to 1942, moving to Washington to work with the United States Department of Agriculture during World War II (1942-43). She was a tireless political campaign worker until her death in 1964.

Jane McCallum of Austin was head of the ratification committee and was in charge of publicity. Mrs. McCallum, who studied journalism at the University of Texas, was an enthusiastic worker for suffrage and for prohibition. She persuaded almost all Texas daily newspapers to endorse woman suffrage. Mrs. McCallum was married to the superintendent of Austin public schools and was the mother of five children. She was an early "supermom," managing a household, attending her children's school functions, entertaining, organizing rallies, managing the campaign's press relations and lobbying legislators.

A Two-Front War

During World War I, suffragists joined other Texans in selling liberty bonds, planting victory gardens, and knitting and sewing for the troops. Since members of the armed forces could not vote at that time, the women also distributed literature reminding them: "You are disfranchised because you are a soldier. We are disfranchised because we are women. When the war is over you get your vote back. How about us?"

In 1916, the state organization changed its name to Texas Equal Suffrage Association and continued to grow. By May 1916, 80 locals had been formed, and the number reached 98 two years later.

The Texas suffrage leaders understood that they needed to know their facts, to maintain their dignity while presenting their arguments, and not to be side-tracked into discussions of other topics. They printed and circulated leaflets explaining why women wanted and deserved the vote. The local societies, as well as the state organization, held classes for their members on such subjects as the nature of politics and government, organizational methods and public speaking. They stressed the technique of not arguing with anti-suffragists. Members were told to listen politely to opponents, get their names and addresses, and send them literature answering their arguments.

Anti-suffragists finally organized in 1915. James B. Wells of Brownsville served as president of the Texas division of the National Association Opposed to Woman Suffrage. Wells, for whom Jim Wells County was named, was an influential and controversial — some say corrupt — South Texas political leader. Some of the literature his group distributed equated woman suffrage with socialism.

The first woman suffrage vote in the Texas Legislature came during the regular session in 1915. The resolution, introduced in the House of Representatives by Frank H. Burmeister and others, would "authorize females to vote." It was referred to the committee on constitutional amendments, which recommended its passage. The suffragists campaigned untiringly among the legislators. With their firm-hand-in-a-silken-glove approach, they thanked those lawmakers who had already expressed support for their cause, and they politely offered their literature to those who were opposed or undecided. In the debate preceding the House vote, Rep. W. T. Bagley said that woman suffrage was "contrary to the laws of nature" and that it would "lower" woman and "rob her of those modest charms so dear to us Southern men." Constitutional amendments require two-thirds majority of each house, and the vote in the lower house — 90 for, 32 against and 19 abstaining — was not enough.

In the next Legislative session, in Jan. 1917, Rep. Jesse Baker of Granbury introduced a resolution in the House, once more calling for a constitutional amendment. The resolution won a majority of the vote, 76 to 56, but again it was not the two-thirds necessary. This was despite Baker's impassioned plea: "Our present Constitution classes our women, as far as franchise is concerned, with children, idiots, lunatics, paupers and felony convicts. We are only asking you to submit an amendment of the Constitution to the qualified voters of the entire State, which shall take our women out of the above mentioned classes and lift them to a higher plane, where their intelligence and patriotism may have full play."

The following summer, Gov. James E. Ferguson, an opponent of woman suffrage, was impeached and convicted of certain questionable financial shenanigans and removed from office. The succession of Lt. Gov. William P. Hobby to the governor's office bolstered the suffragists hopes.

Texas suffrage leaders changed their focus in 1918. Gaining full suffrage was proving extremely tedious, since it required an amendment to the constitution. To be adopted, an amendment required not only approval of two-thirds of both houses of the Legislature, but also ratification by a majority of Texas voters. Since Texas was a one-party state at that time, the primary was where the real decisions among candidates were made. Primary suffrage could be obtained with a legislative act requiring only a simple majority, and it would be a foot in the door. In March 1918, Gov. Hobby called a special session of the Legislature for the purpose of amending the election laws to allow women to vote in primaries and in nominating conventions. C. B. Metcalfe of San Angelo submitted a resolution on March 12. It sailed through the House by a vote of 84 to 34. A few days later it passed the Senate by 18 to 4. With

Gov. Hobby's signature, primary suffrage became the law in Texas.

The primary suffrage law did not go into effect until June 26, and the primary was scheduled for July 27. A special provision of the new law exempted women from paying the poll tax in 1918 so they could be eligible to vote immediately, but they were required to register by 15 days before the election. In the 17 days before the registration deadline, Texas suffragists registered more than 300,000 women and educated the new voters about voting procedures, candidates' records and issues. Suffragists favored re-election of Gov. Hobby, and he won.

Success at the Polls

Women's rights advocates worked particularly hard to elect Annie Webb Blanton to the post of state superintendent of public instruction. Miss Blanton was an associate professor of English at North Texas State College in Denton from 1901 to 1918. She served as the first female president of the Texas State Teachers Association in 1916, and was vice president of the National Education Association from 1917 to 1921. She became the first woman to hold ·statewide elective office in Texas after a hard-fought campaign that was marked by smear tactics on the part of her male opponents. During her two terms in office, 1919-1923, teachers' pay increased 54 percent, and the state began providing free textbooks. Under her leadership, the state also improved rural schools and established schools for black children. After she left office, Miss Blanton became professor of rural education at The University of Texas, a post she held from 1923 to 1945, the year she died.

When the Legislature assembled in Jan. 1919, Gov. Hobby recommended changing the state elections laws to enfranchise women on equal terms with men. But he also recommended disenfranchising aliens. The two provisions were lumped together in one bill, which passed the Senate 28 to 0 and the House by 105 to 0. It was submitted to the voters on May 24, 1919. But since the election was not a primary, women could not vote. Aliens, on the other hand, could vote — on a proposal that would revoke their right to cast ballots.

Suffragists campaigned intensively, organizing mass meetings, walking from house to house circulating petitions, and distributing information and answering questions from booths set up in department stores and theater lobbies. Appeals were made to ministers to support woman suffrage in Mother's Day sermons. An estimated 1,500 speakers, both men and women, addressed groups and held public lectures across the state. The Texas Democrat, a suffrage newspaper edited by a man, Dr. A. Caswell Ellis of the University of Texas, published more than 200,000 copies. More than 3 million leaflets were distributed. U. S. President Woodrow Wilson sent a cable of support from Paris during a European trip. Both U. S. Senators from Texas, Charles A. Culberson and Morris Sheppard, supported the effort.

Gov. W. P. Hobby puts his signature to legislation giving women the right to vote in 1918. Texas was the first southern state to bring women into the electorate. The Democratic Party allowed women to vote in its primary even before the law was changed to allow them to vote in all elections. Photo courtesy McCallum Papers, Austin History Center, Austin Public Library.

The proposed amendment failed by 25,000 votes. Suffragists published a leaflet showing that, not surprisingly, counties with large alien populations returned large majorities against the amendment, since their right to vote was at stake.

In early June 1919, a scant month after the failure of the state amendment, a federal woman suffrage amendment was submitted to the states for ratification. In Congress, senators Culberson and Sheppard both supported the 19th Amendment. Of 18 members of the House of Representatives from Texas, 10 voted for it and one did not vote. Among the seven opposed were Sam Rayburn and John Nance Garner. Gov. Hobby called a special session of the Texas Legislature on June 23. The House resolution passed the next day by a vote of 96 to 21. The Senate resolution was adopted by voice vote on June 28, making Texas the ninth state in the union and the first in the South to ratify the 19th Amendment to the U. S. Constitution. The ratification amendment was signed by Gov. Hobby on August 25, 1920, who declared Sept. 4, 1920, to be a holiday honoring "the indomitable spirit of American womanhood." The 19th Amendment became part of the federal constitution when Tennessee ratified it in August 1920. The talent, time, money and energy of many women and a few good men had been required in order to add one deceptively simple sentence to the U. S. Constitution: "The right of citizens of the United States to vote shall not be denied or abridged by the United States or by any State on account of sex."

Jane McCallum wrote of the victory: "With high hopes and enthusiasm women stepped forth into a world in which they were citizens at last!"

Texas' ratification of the 19th Amendment ended suffrage activities in the state. But Jane McCallum realized that there was still much that

Newspaper cartoonists, like Bill DeOre of The Dallas Morning News, were quick to integrate the women's theme into their work. Here the governor reacts like almost any elected official at the suggestion of a tax hike.

could be done with the pool of educated, compassionate, energetic and talented volunteers that had been mobilized to secure women's voting rights. She led the formation of the Women's Joint Legislative Council, popularly known as the "Petticoat Lobby."

The Petticoat Lobby was a coalition of the Texas League of Women Voters, the Texas Federation of Women's Clubs, the Texas Congress of Mother and Parent-Teacher Associations, the Texas Woman's Christian Temperance Union, and the Texas Federation of Business and Professional Women. Each group had a slightly different focus for its own programs, but the coalition agreed to concentrate on a few fundamental measures, mainly prison reform, education, and maternal and infant health. By 1923, all six of their originally proposed measures passed, providing for revision and strengthening of prohibition laws, a survey of the conditions in Texas prisons, a survey of the conditions in public schools, an emergency appropriation for public schools, a system of registration of births and federal assistance for care of expectant mothers and newborns. The Petticoat Lobby used the same lady-like tactics that were effective in winning support in the suffrage movement.

Jane McCallum continued to work for civic and social causes, always cautioning women never to vote for a woman candidate simply because she was a woman, but to study all the candidates' stands on the issues. In Jan. 1927, Gov. Dan Moody appointed McCallum to the office of Secretary of State, the second woman to hold that post (she succeeded Mrs. Emma G. Meharg). His successor, Ross Sterling, reappointed her, and she served until 1933.

Legacy of Determination

Texas women made rapid strides in the field of politics and government in the decade following their right-to-vote victory. By the 1929-30 biennium, women held the following offices in the state: one state senator, two members of the state house of representatives (four had been elected for the next biennium), 109 county treasurers, 47 county school superintendents, 39 county clerks, 33 district clerks, 13 county tax collectors, seven county tax assessors, five constables, three justices of the peace and one county commissioner.

Because Texas women in the first two decades of this century were willing to risk ridicule and insults, because they were willing to challenge tradition and work against the established system for what they knew to be right, Texas women today can participate fully in the democratic process.

This chapter was written by Mary G. Crawford, associate editor of the Texas Almanac.

Laws Tailored to Please

When U.S. Sen. Lloyd Bentsen went to his hometown of Rio Grande City in October 1988, he followed an old Texas political adage. He voted early and often for himself. And he urged his fellow Texans to do likewise. It was all perfectly legal.

Voting several days before the November general election, Bentsen cast ballots for himself for vice president and for his re-election bid to the U.S. Senate. Bentsen was simply taking advantage of two of the most far-reaching election laws ever passed in Texas.

State and federal election statutes have changed the face of Texas politics throughout the years, but none has had any more impact than the LBJ Law and the no-excuse absentee voting legislation.

At the urging of Lyndon B. Johnson in 1959, the 56th Legislature amended the state Election Code. The amendment allowed candidates in Texas to run for president or vice president at the same time they were seeking another office. Johnson was able to run for president and seek re-election to his U.S. Senate seat simultaneously.

And when John F. Kennedy won the Democratic presidential nomination, he picked Johnson to be his running mate, creating the first Boston-to-Austin axis. In the 1960 general election, Johnson was on the ballot as the Democratic nominee for Senate and for vice president.

Supporters of the law say it encourages Texas politicians to seek national office. They note that without the law, Johnson would have forfeited his position of Senate Majority Leader. Numerous efforts have been made to repeal the peculiar law. Critics claim the LBJ law gives unfair advantage to the candidate seeking both offices.

According to associates of former GOP Gov. Bill Clements, campaign aides to George Bush attempted to get the governor to call a special session to repeal the law before the 1988 election. The aides to Bush were concerned that veteran Democratic U.S. Sen. Bentsen would use the law in the 1988 presidential race. And he did.

When Democratic presidential nominee Michael Dukakis of Massachusetts picked Bentsen as his running mate, Bentsen announced he would use the dual candidacy law to run for vice president and for re-election. It was the reincarnation of the 1960 Boston-to-Austin axis. Many observers believe that Bentsen would not have accepted the running-mate role if he could not have also run for re-election to the Senate.

Like Republican John Tower did against Johnson in 1960, Bentsen's GOP challenger Beau Boulter attempted to make the dual candidacy a campaign issue, telling voters to "strike Lloyd twice." But they didn't.

Although Bush beat the Dukakis-Bentsen ticket in Texas, Bentsen easily won re-election to his Senate seat. Supporters of the LBJ law noted that it had allowed Texans to vote for adopted Texan Bush for president and had kept Bentsen chairman of the powerful Senate Finance Committee. After the election, Bentsen said in an understatement, "This has been an unusual campaign, to say the least."

Some Republican legislators who originally wanted to repeal the law are now having second thoughts. They note that Texas' other U.S. Senator, Republican Phil Gramm, might be able to take advantage of it when he comes up for re-election in the presidential year of 1996.

The 1959 LBJ Law changed politics for the politicians, but a 1987 law revolutionized politics for the voters of Texas. Without fanfare and little publicity, the 70th Legislature repealed the Election Code restrictions on who could vote absentee.

In effect, the bill sponsored by State Rep. Bob Aikin and State Sen. Chet Edwards gave Texans a 17-day early voting period in which they could cast their ballots. They no longer needed excuses to vote absentee. It removed yet another barrier to voting that lawmakers have been trying to tear down since 1982 when they made it easier for senior citizens to vote absentee by mail.

Since the changes in the election laws, the increase in absentee — or early — voting has been dramatic.

A study conducted by Aikin's aide Shari Valentine showed that even though total voter turnout had declined in absolute numbers in selected counties since 1982, the absentee turnout has increased.

In the 1982 election in Harris County, the absentee vote was only 3.1 percent of the total turnout. But in the 1988 election, the absentee total had increased to 13.5 percent of the turnout. By 1990, some counties were reporting absentee totals ranging from 25 to 35 percent of the turnout.

"Its potential is even greater," said Aikin. He decided to author the no-excuse voting law after he won his first legislative race in 1986 because he had outpolled his opponent in absentee voting. "It's entirely possible that in future elections we will have absentee totals of 50 percent," Aikin said.

The early voting law spawned a cottage industry within the world of campaign consultants. Some political operatives now specialize in getting voters to turn out in the early voting period.

The impact of the no-excuse voting period was demonstrated in the 1989 special election in Congressional District 12 in Tarrant County. Democrat Pete Geren lost on Election Day, but he had a 3,000-vote lead in absentee voting. And that gave him a 1,600-vote margin of victory.

An extensive early voting program by Dallas County Democrats provided Ann Richards her margin of victory in the county in the 1990 governor's race. The early voting campaign gave Ms. Richards a 50.3 percent win in the county, making her the first Democratic gubernatorial candidate to carry the GOP stronghold since 1974.

"When we passed it, we realized it could be revolutionary," said Aikin. And on Election Night in 1990, ABC newsman David Brinkley said the no-excuse absentee law was the "most novel voting experiment in the country."

This article was written by Sam Attlesey, political writer for The Dallas Morning News.

Democrats in the 19th Century

The partisan tint that distinguished Texas' politics from early statehood onward was earned early by the national Democratic Party. It was Democrats who raised the issue of Texas' annexation to the Union, and Democrats ferried the legislation through Congress. The national party made Texas a campaign issue in the presidential election of 1844, and shortly thereafter, it started the procedural ball rolling to bring Texas into the fold.

In January 1845, one Texas editor rhapsodized, "We are all Democrats in Texas, since the glorious victory of that party, who fearlessly espoused our cause and nailed the 'Lone Star' to the top mast of their noble ship."

Realistically, it did not matter, on the state level, what political stripe the candidate carried for the first decade of Texas' statehood. The huge debt accumulated during nearly a decade of independence prior to annexation was a worrisome burden. Tied in part to the debt was the issue of setting state boundaries. The frontier, wherever it was placed, needed defense, and other issues of government organization had to be settled. None really lent itself to partisan politicking. So while most called themselves Democrats, a candidate would more likely be judged on whether he was pro-Sam Houston or an anti-Houston rather than by his party affiliation. Some candidates raised unique issues to attract attention. In 1845, Isaac Van Zandt of Marshall sought the first governor's chair by urging that Texas be divided into four more states. One political observer of the day noted that Van Zandt probably would have won the election, but he died in Houston of yellow fever before the election. The proposal to divide Texas was not raised again for several years.

By the mid-1850s, however, a political rival emerged that startled and frightened Democrats, and most important, moved them to organize in self-defense. The ogre was the Know-Nothing Party, the product of

alien sentiment and did so well it spread across the nation. Initially, the party preyed on anti-Catholic feelings, particularly against German and Irish immigrants, but adjusted its scope as it left its parochial birth-place and rippled across the nation.

The name derives from the response party members gave when asked about their secret activities: "I know nothing." This legendary answer evolved into the party's appellation.

Quietly, if not openly, Know-Nothings entered Texas in 1854. Within a year, candidates backed by the party carried municipal elections in Galveston and San Antonio, the state's two largest cities of the day. Buoyed by success, the party met in Washington-on-the-Brazos in June 1856 to nominate a slate of state and district candidates. Lt. Gov. D.C. Dickson was selected to challenge incumbent Democrat Gov. E. M. Pease.

Democratic Awakening

Usually passive Democrats took quick notice of the Know-Nothings. A convention system of sorts had been used in selecting congressional candidates since 1851 when Richardson Scurry of Clarksville got a convention endorsement to replace David Kaufman, who died in office. Richardson had some advantage in the convention because the method of calling a meeting was slipshod at best and only counties in the northern part of the First Congressional District, Scurry's home area, sent delegates to the meeting. The Second Congressional District (the western district) did not hold a convention until 1859, when Gen. T.N. Waul received the nomination. But Gen. Waul was defeated by A.J. Hamilton, running as an independent. The Know-Nothing threat prompted the Democrats to call the first convention to consider state-wide candidates. Meeting in Austin on June 16, 1855, the party named John Marshall as its first chairman and nominated Pease for a second term in the statehouse.

Know-Nothings exploited the periodic xenophobia that afflicts Americans. Early on, the party's spokesmen argued that German and Mexican immigrants were dangerous to the American way of life. In the trip from New York, Mexicans replaced Irish as a head on the Hydra targeted by the party's faithful. Both groups were heavily Roman Catholic. This strategic mistake sent Mexicans and Germans forthwith to the Democratic ranks, a move made in months, one Democrat noted, that otherwise would have taken years to accomplish.

Pease, who gained office with only 30 percent of the popular vote in 1853, handily outdistanced Dickson by more than 7,300 votes in a tough campaign. The Texas State Times in Austin complained about the tone of politics introduced into the state by the newcomers. At his inauguration, Gov. Pease, escorted to the capitol by a German immigrant, declared that the gubernatorial election of 1855 was "the first that had been decided by our citizens upon political issues alone."

Despite failing to capture the governor's chair, the Know-Nothings took several local offices and one congressional seat. The featured speaker at the party's victory bash a few months later was none other than Sam Houston. But the appearance may have cost him the 1857 gubernatorial election.

Regardless of their auspicious entry into Texas politics, the Know-Nothings had little staying power. The party fielded a slate of candidates for the 1856 election and then quietly faded from the scene. On the national level, Know-Nothings put Millard Fillmore, a former president, on the ballot to contest Democrat James Buchanan. But the challenger was no match for the Democrat, and the party, as quietly as it had appeared, slipped into history. In Texas, Democrats attracted delegates from 54 counties to their 1856 state convention, and state legislators were allowed to represent 37 more counties. Only eight counties did not have representation at this gathering, the largest convention of any kind held in Texas to that date. Buchanan easily won, but Fillmore got 30 percent of the vote in Texas that year.

Pro-Union leanings probably prompted the Know-Nothings to exit Texas, although it claimed to support slave holders. As the decade of the 1850s passed, the question of slavery grew larger in Texans' minds.

As a U.S. Senator, Sam Houston angered many Texans with a vote for the Kansas-Nebraska Act, which was unpopular in the state. The bill allowed settlers to vote on whether Kansas would be a free or slave state. When he returned to Texas to seek the governorship in 1857, that vote and his association with the secretive Know-Nothings worked against him.

At the Democratic convention in Waco that year, Democrats adopted the so-called two-thirds rule, requiring candidates to get two-thirds of the delegate vote to win the party's nomination in convention. National Democrats had used the rule for some time, and it had been used in the congressional district nominating conventions. The idea behind it was that only a truly strong candidate could attract a two-thirds vote. In practice, however, O.M. Roberts noted in commenting on the system 40 years later, the rule often worked to the disadvantage of the strongest candidate and allowed a lesser man to win the nomination. Roberts was well-qualified to evaluate the rule. He lost a congressional nomination when a compromise candidate sneaked into the considerations. But Roberts also benefited from the rule in 1878 when the Democratic convention deadlocked around incumbent governor Richard Hubbard and two other candidates. Roberts was selected as the compromise candidate despite not being present at the convention. As nominee, his first act was to borrow two bits from a friend to telegraph his acceptance of the nomination. Roberts served the usual two terms. The rule remained in effect for a half-century until replaced by the primary system as the vehicle for nominating candidates.

In 1857, Hardin R. Runnels, teamed with Francis R. Lubbock as a ticket for governor-lieutenant governor, handed Houston and his running mate, Edward Clark, a stunning defeat. It was the only election that Houston personally lost in Texas politics.

Houston's Revenge

By 1859, much of the state was in turmoil. Indians fought valiantly to save their hunting grounds from white settlers, and abolitionists were active on the national scene. Houston, again teamed with Clark, stumped the state criticizing the efforts at frontier defense and advocating a moderate support for the Union. Texans, for whatever reason, bought the position and gave Houston a handy victory over Runnels. Surprisingly enough, the state also elected two moderates to Congress, A.J. Hamilton and John H. Reagan, both of whom played major roles in later chapters of Texas history.

The legislature was not too sympathetic to the Union cause, however. Houston was replaced by Louis T. Wigfall in the U.S. Senate by the lawmakers. A rabid states' rights advocate, Wigfall was an embarrassment to Houston.

Events soon turned public sentiment to a harder line toward the national government. In October 1859, John Brown made his famous raid on Harper's Ferry, Va., and this was seen as a typical abolitionists' disregard for the law and the rights of slave owners. Coupled with continuing problems on the frontier and with raids along the Mexican border by the bandit-folk hero, Juan Cortina, which were blamed on abolitionists, public opinion in Texas changed dramatically. The federal government was not fulfilling its role of protector of law and order in the state. Drastic action was needed to protect the state, many Texans felt.

Texas delegates bolted the regular Democratic National Convention in 1860 to join other Southern states in Baltimore to nominate John C. Breckinridge for president. Republican Abraham Lincoln was not on the fall ballot, because there was no Republican Party in Texas at the time. Upon Lincoln's election, secessionists stepped up their demands for a quick exit from the Union.

As governor, Houston refused to call the legislature into session, so secessionists called a convention of their own. They argued that the federal government abrogated the annexation ordinance by failing to protect the frontier as promised. In a statewide vote, Texans approved secession from the Union, although there were pockets of opposition in North Texas and in the German areas of the state.

Houston left office after declining to take an oath of allegiance to the Confederacy, and Edward Clark replaced him in early 1861. (Houston argued that the secession vote in early 1861 did not authorize the state to join the Confederacy. He favored setting up a protectorate and annexing northern Mexico, after which Texas could return to its status as an independent nation.)

Clark sought election to a full term as governor after serving the final months of Houston's term. He faced Francis R. Lubbock, whom he had defeated for lieutenant governor two years earlier. Lubbock won by a mere 124 votes, the closest in the state's history in the three-way race in which T.J. Chambers ran a distant third. Lubbock, who met with Confederate President Jefferson Davis, was a staunch supporter of the war effort.

Two years later, Pendleton Murrah defeated Chambers in a race to replace Lubbock who opted for a more active role in the war. Murrah served until June 1864 when he left the state for Mexico where he died. A.J. Hamilton, the former congressman from Texas, was appointed provisional governor by President Andrew Johnson.

Reconstruction

For the next decade, Texas lived under the close, watchful eye of the federal government as the agonies of Reconstruction were played out on a people who felt they had not lost the war. Gubernatorial races became contests between "us-'n-them" with the "thems" being the former Unionists.

Many Texans were disqualified from voting because of their activities during the Civil War. One popularly elected Democratic governor, James W. Throckmorton, was removed from office by the military commander, and one unpopular radical Republican governor, E.J. Davis, was kept in office by little more than force of arms. The turmoil ended in 1873 when Democrat Richard Coke soundly defeated Davis at the polls and took office.

Through Reconstruction Democrats stuck together against common foes — the Republicans, the Unionists and the military authority. Despite the prohibitions that kept many former Confederates from the polls, the Democratic ranks grew, engorged with immigrants from other Southern states with similar political backgrounds. For many Southerners, Texas represented a new beginning, an avenue to escape the devastation of the Civil War and to live with people of similar cultural, political and racial attitudes.

On the dark side of Texas history, Democrats spent almost a century after the Civil War limiting the civil and human rights of the freed slaves. The first constitution written by Democrats after the Civil War denied full civil rights, including the right to vote, to the former slaves. Black males received the right to vote under the reconstruction Constitution of 1869 (women of any race, of course, were barred from voting). In some counties, the majority of qualified voters were black and controlled the politics of the county. The most common tactic of whites to limit black political power was terror and intimidation. Efforts also were

limit black political power was terror and intimidation. Efforts also were made to restrict the black vote by law.

Historically, Democrats, staunch states' righters, became the party of white supremacy in Texas and the South, and remained so into the 1960s. After the U.S. Congress lost interest in Reconstruction in the 1870s, it became easier for Democrats to control or discourage the black vote. This racist attitude thwarted attempts at reform by third parties over the closing decades of the 19th century.

Third parties, on the other hand, sought out the black vote, trying on occasion to break it away from its Republican base. Certainly many black farmers had the same economic problems as their white neighbors. Indeed, Texas generally suffered from economic problems that followed in the wake of the Civil War.

Invisible War Debt

As is the case with most wars, the Civil War was fought with borrowed money. Paper money replaced precious metals as the currency of the day in the United States. When demands for initial government expenditures were faced, more money was printed. At the war's end, $450 million in this paper money was in circulation in the states of the Union. With Confederate currency invalidated, the South was money poor. The result was inflation — fewer dollars chasing the same amount of goods.

To squeeze the inflation out of the economy, the Congress enacted a deflationary program. Silver was "demonetized" in 1873, and the country returned to the gold standard in 1879. Results were devastating to farmers in general and to the states of the old Confederacy in particular. Massachusetts alone had five times as much national bank circulation after the war than did the South. Northern mercantile houses provided goods to merchants on consignment. These merchants sold the consigned goods to farmers at a profit and under a lien system, charging high interest rates. A farmer agreed to put his crop under a lien in exchange for tools and goods to support his family through the growing season. To further secure his investment, the merchant would require the farmer to plant cotton. Even in the worst of years, there seldom was a total failure of a cotton crop, so the merchant was fairly sure of a return on his investment. But the practice meant an almost continuous excess of cotton that drove market prices down. Farmers had few choices than to deal with the merchants, for there were few banks in Texas, so the merchant was the only source of credit. Deal with him or don't deal at all. ·

Farmers slowly recognized their predicament and began to agitate for change. The first institution to direct the farmers' political energies was the Patrons of Husbandry, which was organized in Washington in 1867 and reached Texas in 1873. Although non-political, the Grange, as the organization came to be known, worked to raise farmers' awareness of their plight and of their place in the community. Local Granges could not participate in politics, so the Greenback Party became the vehicle to carry the political program. Initially, Greenbackers were concerned with the plight of the workers in the industrialized states, who faced many of the same problems with tight money as farmers did. By 1873, the party turned its attention to farmers.

Greenbacker Challenge

The party held its first Texas convention in Austin in 1878, nominating Gen. W.H. Hamman of Robertson Colony for governor, along with a full slate of other statewide candidates. Greenbackers called for the farmer to receive a fair portion of what was produced "by the sweat of his brow and the labor of his hands." The party's platform called for reinstituting the income tax (which the Union had levied in the North during the Civil War), a remonetization of silver and an issuance of "greenbacks," or paper money.

Results of the venture into Texas politics were encouraging to Greenbackers. Hamman out-polled the Republican candidate for second place behind the Democrat, and G. W. "Wash" Jones of Bastrop County was elected to Congress as a Greenbacker.

The party supported free immigration to attract foreign farmers and farm labor. Texas, as an enticement to immigration, had allowed aliens to vote. Many frontier states did this to integrate immigrants into the community as soon as possible.

Of 140 delegates attending the 1880 Greenback convention in Austin, 20 were black, a fact duly noted by the Democrats during the ensuing campaign. Two years later, interest in the party declined, so Greenbackers joined with Republicans to support G.W. Jones for governor. Jones polled 102,500 votes, the most until that time for a losing candidate for the top state office.

The last Greenback effort in Texas came in 1886 when A.B. Norton of Dallas was nominated for governor and attracted only a scattering of votes in Democrat John Ireland's landslide victory. (Ireland acquired the colorful nickname "Ox-cart John" because of his opposition to generous land grants to railroads for building new lines. As a legacy, the dying party had identified the economic injustices faced by farmers, and Democrats and Republicans absorbed some of its principals. But the farmers' lot was still far from ideal.

As the Grange passed from the scene, the Farmers Alliance gained attention. Organized in September 1877 at a meeting on the farm of J.R. Allen of Lampasas County, the Alliance soon became active in many issues, although it, too, was non-political.

One important idea to come from the Alliance was that of cooperative buying and selling by farmers. The plan was adopted by the Alliance

was to bargain large lots of cotton for higher prices than individual farmers could expect. Also, farm goods could be purchased cheaper in large lots, reducing the individual farmer's expenses. The plan was a step toward reducing over-production generated by the crop-lien system. Merchants usually dictated that farmers must grow cotton to attain supplies under a lien. Economically, it was smart, for there was seldom a total crop failure with cotton, so a merchant would always realize some return. But the practice had the effect of keeping market prices for cotton low, damaging the farmers' interests.

Populists Arise

In early 1887, Texas' Alliance sent speakers to other states to begin formation of a national alliance. The first national convention was held in Shreveport, La., in October 1887 with 10 states sending delegates. Texas had led farmers to the alliance.

From this organization evolved the People's Party, or Populists, of the 1890s.

It was difficult to politicize Texas farmers and to draw them away from the Democratic Party, the champion of white supremacy in the South. Most farmers wanted to work within the framework of the Democratic party. But when change proved to be impossible, they were more likely to turn to the Populist effort.

Black farmers' problems were aggravated by racism. While their difficulties might be the same as those of white farmers, the blacks were equally reluctant to abandon the Republican Party. They feared the farmers' revolt might fail, and they would be left without a political base.

Opponents of the Populists would point to the presence of blacks within the party as evidence of the impurity of the party's political stands. On a regional basis, opponents in the North would wave the "bloody shirt" at Populists for consorting with the enemies of their forefathers, a tactic also used by Democrats in the South to good effect. Efforts to work within the Democratic Party were dropped in 1891, and the radicals in the Farmers Alliance moved to create their own party.

Sul Ross easily won the 1888 and 1890 elections, continuing a line of distinguished politicians in the governors office. Ross was fortunate to preside over the first prosperous and peaceful period in the state since the Civil War. But just below the surface boiled a tempest that would put the party to its most severe test of the century.

To open the decade of the 1890s, Jim Hogg stepped into the Democratic spotlight, urging many reforms. Hogg, the first native Texan to become governor, was the first governor since 1859 who was not a Civil War veteran. He supported creation of a railroad commission to regulate the state's rail transportation and backed a host of other changes in government. Such innovations set off a revolt in the party. Conserva-

in government. Such innovations set off a revolt in the party. Conservatives led by George Clark fielded a separate Democratic ticket in the fall, seeking black support, as Hogg had done by setting up black voter clubs earlier in the campaign. It was the first time Democrats had openly courted the black vote, which was usually staunchly Republican.

Republican Split

Black Republicans, led by Norris Wright Cuney of Galveston, split with the Lily-white Republicans, who resented black leadership. Cuney forged an alliance with conservative Democrats in 1892 to back George Clark for governor.

For the entire decade of the 1890s, Populists ran strong races for governor in Texas behind T.L. Nugent in 1892 and 1894, and with J.C. Kearby heading the ticket in 1896. (Some historians feel the Populists may have out-polled Democrats in the latter election, only to have the results reversed by unscrupulous Democratic vote counters.)

Charles A. Culberson, a former attorney general and son of a long-time congressman, carried the Democratic banner in 1894 and 1896, and veteran congressman, Joseph D. Sayers, closed out the century on a winning note for the Democrats in 1898. E. M. House, a Houston businessman, engineered the election of both men, opening a political career that would eventually extend influence in national politics.

Chief among the Populist proposals was the creation of a subtreasury that would issue money, including remonetized silver. Farmers also could get loans on their crops from the institution. The basic problem with farmers was the lack of credit sources. Texas prohibited state-chartered banking until early in the 20th century, and although there were national banks and some private banks operating in the state, there were not enough banks competing for the farmers' loans. Texas Democrats had steadfastly opposed state-chartered banking since Andrew Jackson from his death bed sent a letter to the constitutional convention of 1845 urging that delegates do so. Though the national Democrats did not absorb the full Populist platform, they lined up well enough behind the campaigns of William Jennings Bryan and his loose money policies to satisfy many Populists, especially in Texas where a break with the Democratic party was much like losing one's wife. With the Democrats giving the farmers some support, the fledgling party slowly passed from the scene, although fielding gubernatorial candidates through 1904 in Texas. The Populists left a colorful legacy on the state's political record. Seldom have so many Texans so fervently and devoutly stood behind such a political effort.

The turmoil was not universally appreciated. Democrats for a time had flirted with loss of control of state government. That was enough to convince Texas Democrats in the late 19th century that some major changes were needed in the political system. So they made the changes

exclusivity in the party — all in the name of the reform movement that swept the nation in the early 20th century. It was the case of the politicians of the day deciding that if they could not satisfy the electorate they had, then they would create an electorate they could satisfy.

This article was written by Mike Kingston, editor of the Texas Almanac.

County Identification

See maps with numbered counties on pages 48 and 49.

1 Anderson	55 Culberson	109 Hill	163 Medina	217 Stonewall
2 Andrews	56 Dallam	110 Hockley	164 Menard	218 Sutton
3 Angelina	57 Dallas	111 Hood	165 Midland	219 Swisher
4 Aransas	58 Dawson	112 Hopkins	166 Milam	220 Tarrant
5 Archer	59 DeWitt	113 Houston	167 Mills	221 Taylor
6 Armstrong	60 Deaf Smith	114 Howard	168 Mitchell	222 Terrell
7 Atascosa	61 Delta	115 Hudspeth	169 Montague	223 Terry
8 Austin	62 Denton	116 Hunt	170 Montgomery	224 Throckmorton
9 Bailey	63 Dickens	117 Hutchinson	171 Moore	225 Titus
10 Bandera	64 Dimmit	118 Irion	172 Morris	226 Tom Green
11 Bastrop	65 Donley	119 Jack	173 Motley	227 Travis
12 Baylor	66 Duval	120 Jackson	174 Nacogdoches	228 Trinity
13 Bee	67 Eastland	121 Jasper	175 Navarro	229 Tyler
14 Bell	68 Ector	122 Jeff Davis	176 Newton	230 Upshur
15 Bexar	69 Edwards	123 Jefferson	177 Nolan	231 Upton
16 Blanco	70 Ellis	124 Jim Hogg	178 Nueces	232 Uvalde
17 Borden	71 El Paso	125 Jim Wells	179 Ochiltree	233 Val Verde
18 Bosque	72 Erath	126 Johnson	180 Oldham	234 Van Zandt
19 Bowie	73 Falls	127 Jones	181 Orange	235 Victoria
20 Brazoria	74 Fannin	128 Karnes	182 Palo Pinto	236 Walker
21 Brazos	75 Fayette	129 Kaufman	183 Panola	237 Waller
22 Brewster	76 Fisher	130 Kendall	184 Parker	238 Ward
23 Briscoe	77 Floyd	131 Kenedy	185 Parmer	239 Washington
24 Brooks	78 Foard	132 Kent	186 Pecos	240 Webb
25 Brown	79 Fort Bend	133 Kerr	187 Polk	241 Wharton
26 Burleson	80 Franklin	134 Kimble	188 Potter	242 Wheeler
27 Burnet	81 Freestone	135 King	189 Presidio	243 Wichita
28 Caldwell	82 Frio	136 Kinney	190 Rains	244 Wilbarger
29 Calhoun	83 Gaines	137 Kleberg	191 Randall	245 Willacy
30 Callahan	84 Galveston	138 Knox	192 Reagan	246 Williamson
31 Cameron	85 Garza	139 La Salle	193 Real	247 Wilson
32 Camp	86 Gillespie	140 Lamar	194 Red River	248 Winkler
33 Carson	87 Glasscock	141 Lamb	195 Reeves	249 Wise
34 Cass	88 Goliad	142 Lampasas	196 Refugio	250 Wood
35 Castro	89 Gonzales	143 Lavaca	197 Roberts	251 Yoakum
36 Chambers	90 Gray	144 Lee	198 Robertson	252 Young
37 Cherokee	91 Grayson	145 Leon	199 Rockwall	253 Zapata
38 Childress	92 Gregg	146 Liberty	200 Runnels	254 Zavala
39 Clay	93 Grimes	147 Limestone	201 Rusk	
40 Cochran	94 Guadalupe	148 Lipscomb	202 Sabine	
41 Coke	95 Hale	149 Live Oak	203 San Augustine	
42 Coleman	96 Hall	150 Llano	204 San Jacinto	
43 Collin	97 Hamilton	151 Loving	205 San Patricio	
44 Collingsworth	98 Hansford	152 Lubbock	206 San Saba	
45 Colorado	99 Hardeman	153 Lynn	207 Schleicher	
46 Comal	100 Hardin	154 McCulloch	208 Scurry	
47 Comanche	101 Harris	155 McLennan	209 Shackelford	
48 Concho	102 Harrison	156 McMullen	210 Shelby	
49 Cooke	103 Hartley	157 Madison	211 Sherman	
50 Coryell	104 Haskell	158 Marion	212 Smith	
51 Cottle	105 Hays	159 Martin	213 Somervell	
52 Crane	106 Hemphill	160 Mason	214 Starr	
53 Crockett	107 Henderson	161 Matagorda	215 Stephens	
54 Crosby	108 Hidalgo	162 Maverick	216 Sterling	

Texas

See Page 47 for a list of counties by number.

56	211	98	179	148	
103	171	117	197	106	
180	188	33	90	242	
59	191	6	65	44	
185	35	219	23	96	38
9	140	95	77	173	51
40	110	152	54	63	135
251	223	153	85	132	217
83	58	17	208	76	12
2	159	114	168	177	2

71

115   55   151   248   68   165   87   216   41   200

238   52   231   192   118   226   4

195

122   186   53   207   1

218   1

189   222   233   69   19

22   136

162

Counties

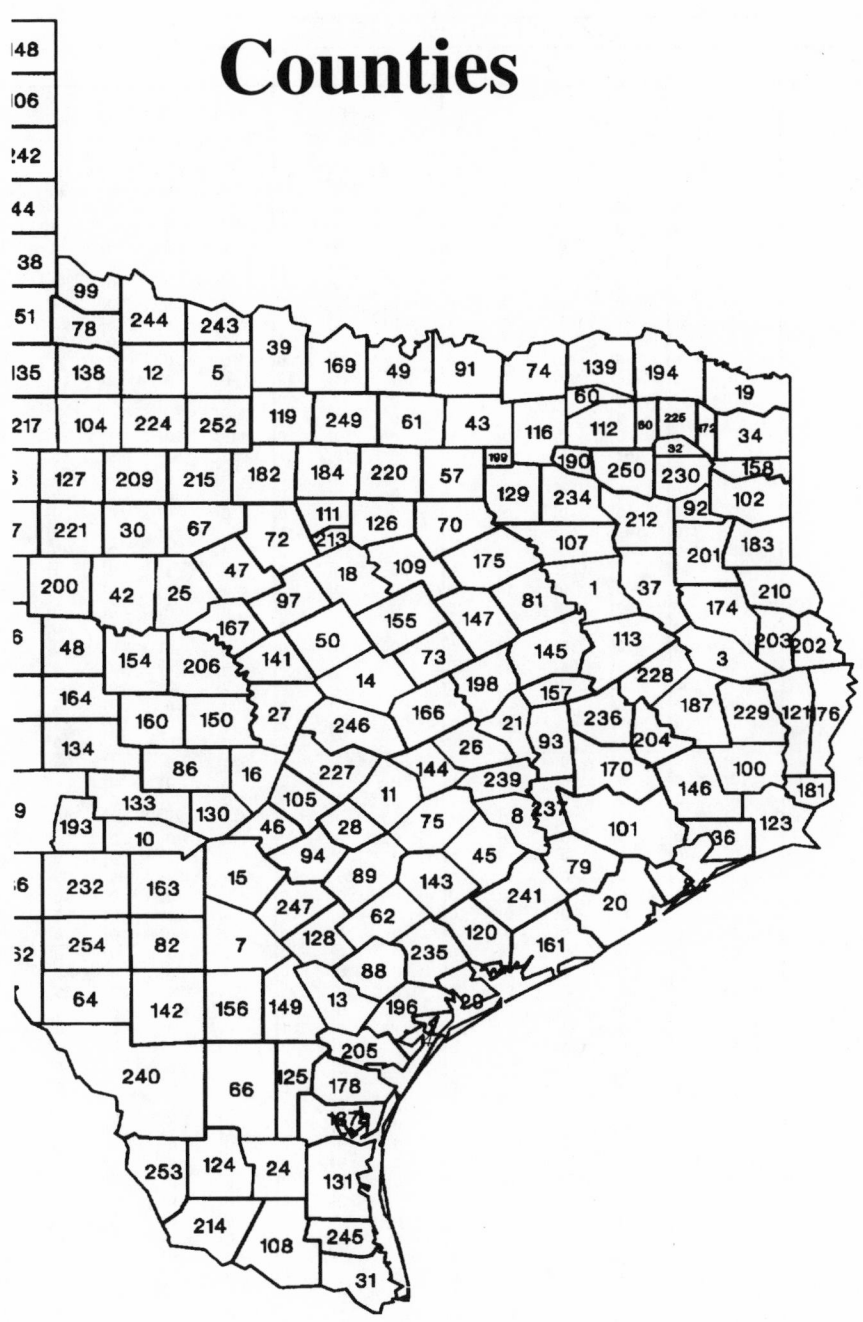

Table 1: Gubernatorial Races

General Elections, 1845-1851															
Year	1845		1847				1849			1851					
County	James P. Henderson	James B. Miller	George T. Wood	James B. Miller	Nicholas H. Darnell	J. J. Robinson	Peter H. Bell	George T. Wood	John T. Mills	Peter H. Bell	Middleton T. Johnson	John A. Greer	B. H. Epperson	Thomas J. Chambers
Anderson	0	0	115	11	28	27	18	130	194	52	126	192	91	22
Andrews	0	0	0	0	0	0	0	0	0	0	0	0	0	0
Angelina	0	0	0	0	0	0	7	61	4	0	0	0	0	0
Aransas	0	0	0	0	0	0	0	0	0	0	0	0	0	0
Archer	0	0	0	0	0	0	0	0	0	0	0	0	0	0
Armstrong	0	0	0	0	0	0	0	0	0	0	0	0	0	0
Atascosa	0	0	0	0	0	0	0	0	0	0	0	0	0	0
Austin	99	87	21	183	4	3	195	7	0	302	1	5	33	10
Bailey	0	0	0	0	0	0	0	0	0	0	0	0	0	0
Bandera	0	0	0	0	0	0	0	0	0	0	0	0	0	0
Bastrop	0	0	28	207	7	0	261	43	13	0	0	0	0	0
Baylor	0	0	0	0	0	0	0	0	0	0	0	0	0	0
Bee	0	0	0	0	0	0	0	0	0	0	0	0	0	0
Bell	0	0	0	0	0	0	0	0	0	148	20	11	6	8
Bexar	0	0	167	535	10	0	690	19	27	1,023	61	155	55	0
Blanco	0	0	0	0	0	0	0	0	0	0	0	0	0	0
Borden	0	0	0	0	0	0	0	0	0	0	0	0	0	0
Bosque	0	0	0	0	0	0	0	0	0	0	0	0	0	0
Bowie	299	110	199	64	71	2	7	58	112	64	16	15	57	9
Brazoria	96	146	41	235	1	3	302	18	2	188	1	2	43	2
Brazos	45	37	9	65	2	0	56	9	0	50	3	2	1	11
Brewster	0	0	0	0	0	0	0	0	0	0	0	0	0	0
Briscoe	0	0	0	0	0	0	0	0	0	0	0	0	0	0
Brooks	0	0	0	0	0	0	0	0	0	0	0	0	0	0
Brown	0	0	0	0	0	0	0	0	0	0	0	0	0	0
Burleson	0	0	9	104	1	15	115	41	2	98	8	17	0	74
Burnet	0	0	0	0	0	0	0	0	0	0	0	0	0	0
Caldwell	0	0	0	0	0	0	166	35	0	209	6	4	30	3
Calhoun	0	0	19	144	2	1	102	20	5	104	0	9	28	3
Callahan	0	0	0	0	0	0	0	0	0	0	0	0	0	0
Cameron	0	0	0	0	0	0	581	262	10	836	0	1	26	0
Camp	0	0	0	0	0	0	0	0	0	0	0	0	0	0
Carson	0	0	0	0	0	0	0	0	0	0	0	0	0	0
Cass	0	0	177	15	93	5	92	185	59	214	71	57	129	114
Castro	0	0	0	0	0	0	0	0	0	0	0	0	0	0
Chambers	0	0	0	0	0	0	0	0	0	0	0	0	0	0
Cherokee	0	0	0	0	0	0	118	386	100	365	334	198	93	77
Childress	0	0	0	0	0	0	0	0	0	0	0	0	0	0
Clay	0	0	0	0	0	0	0	0	0	0	0	0	0	0
Cochran	0	0	0	0	0	0	0	0	0	0	0	0	0	0
Coke	0	0	0	0	0	0	0	0	0	0	0	0	0	0
Coleman	0	0	0	0	0	0	0	0	0	0	0	0	0	0
Collin	0	0	0	0	0	0	123	30	105	22	188	22	39	30
Collingsworth	0	0	0	0	0	0	0	0	0	0	0	0	0	0
Colorado	218	25	60	99	35	24	111	7	1	0	0	0	0	0
Comal	0	0	23	120	10	0	137	54	0	141	1	1	1	41
Comanche	0	0	0	0	0	0	0	0	0	0	0	0	0	0
Concho	0	0	0	0	0	0	0	0	0	0	0	0	0	0
Cooke	0	0	0	0	0	0	12	0	21	2	37	0	0	0
Coryell	0	0	0	0	0	0	0	0	0	0	0	0	0	0
Cottle	0	0	0	0	0	0	0	0	0	0	0	0	0	0
Crane	0	0	0	0	0	0	0	0	0	0	0	0	0	0
Crockett	0	0	0	0	0	0	0	0	0	0	0	0	0	0
Crosby	0	0	0	0	0	0	0	0	0	0	0	0	0	0
Culberson	0	0	0	0	0	0	0	0	0	0	0	0	0	0
Dallam	0	0	0	0	0	0	0	0	0	0	0	0	0	0
Dallas	0	0	0	0	0	0	126	133	98	32	430	29	3	12
Dawson	0	0	0	0	0	0	0	0	0	0	0	0	0	0
Deaf Smith	0	0	0	0	0	0	0	0	0	0	0	0	0	0
Delta	0	0	0	0	0	0	0	0	0	0	0	0	0	0
Denton	0	0	0	0	0	0	39	33	8	10	78	0	0	26
DeWitt	0	0	0	0	0	0	100	25	1	140	8	5	2	0
Dickens	0	0	0	0	0	0	0	0	0	0	0	0	0	0
Dimmit	0	0	0	0	0	0	0	0	0	0	0	0	0	0
Donley	0	0	0	0	0	0	0	0	0	0	0	0	0	0

Table 1: Gubernatorial Races

County	General Elections, 1845-1851														
Year	1845		1847				1849			1851					
County	James P. Henderson	James B. Miller	George T. Wood	James B. Miller	Nicholas H. Darnell	J. J. Robinson	Peter H. Bell	George T. Wood	John T. Mills	Peter H. Bell	Middleton T. Johnson	John A. Greer	B. H. Epperson	Thomas J. Chambers
Duval	0	0	0	0	0	0	0	0	0	0	0	0	0	0
Eastland	0	0	0	0	0	0	0	0	0	0	0	0	0	0
Ector	0	0	0	0	0	0	0	0	0	0	0	0	0	0
Edwards	0	0	0	0	0	0	0	0	0	0	0	0	0	0
Ellis	0	0	0	0	0	0	0	0	0	36	43	11	14	6
El Paso	0	0	0	0	0	0	0	0	0	557	0	23	0	0
Erath	0	0	0	0	0	0	0	0	0	0	0	0	0	0
Falls	0	0	0	0	0	0	0	0	0	25	11	0	2	35
Fannin	0	0	565	11	21	33	184	76	201	49	217	102	50	12
Fayette	0	0	68	183	46	7	372	26	28	0	0	0	0	0
Fisher	0	0	0	0	0	0	0	0	0	0	0	0	0	0
Floyd	0	0	0	0	0	0	0	0	0	0	0	0	0	0
Foard	0	0	0	0	0	0	0	0	0	0	0	0	0	0
Fort Bend	23	121	5	213	4	1	201	2	0	162	0	0	27	2
Franklin	0	0	0	0	0	0	0	0	0	0	0	0	0	0
Freestone	0	0	0	0	0	0	0	0	0	34	42	34	3	18
Frio	0	0	0	0	0	0	0	0	0	0	0	0	0	0
Gaines	0	0	0	0	0	0	0	0	0	0	0	0	0	0
Galveston	334	13	240	111	5	4	299	165	25	259	4	14	124	20
Garza	0	0	0	0	0	0	0	0	0	0	0	0	0	0
Gillespie	0	0	0	0	0	0	203	2	0	138	1	3	0	1
Glasscock	0	0	0	0	0	0	0	0	0	0	0	0	0	0
Goliad	0	0	0	0	0	0	0	0	0	0	0	0	0	0
Gonzales	0	0	128	266	119	12	170	17	0	0	0	0	0	0
Gray	0	0	0	0	0	0	0	0	0	0	0	0	0	0
Grayson	0	0	0	0	0	0	58	46	103	15	210	33	22	38
Gregg	0	0	0	0	0	0	0	0	0	0	0	0	0	0
Grimes	0	0	0	0	0	0	75	258	14	102	55	120	96	19
Guadalupe	0	0	0	0	0	0	135	11	0	156	5	6	34	9
Hale	0	0	0	0	0	0	0	0	0	0	0	0	0	0
Hall	0	0	0	0	0	0	0	0	0	0	0	0	0	0
Hamilton	0	0	0	0	0	0	0	0	0	0	0	0	0	0
Hansford	0	0	0	0	0	0	0	0	0	0	0	0	0	0
Hardeman	0	0	0	0	0	0	0	0	0	0	0	0	0	0
Hardin	0	0	0	0	0	0	0	0	0	0	0	0	0	0
Harris	318	236	273	463	2	20	316	286	37	375	34	39	152	56
Harrison	0	0	518	83	43	15	118	464	121	599	63	43	200	75
Hartley	0	0	0	0	0	0	0	0	0	0	0	0	0	0
Haskell	0	0	0	0	0	0	0	0	0	0	0	0	0	0
Hays	0	0	0	0	0	0	44	10	1	39	2	2	1	13
Hemphill	0	0	0	0	0	0	0	0	0	0	0	0	0	0
Henderson	0	0	0	0	0	0	24	125	19	32	39	10	21	41
Hidalgo	0	0	0	0	0	0	0	0	0	0	0	0	0	0
Hill	0	0	0	0	0	0	0	0	0	0	0	0	0	0
Hockley	0	0	0	0	0	0	0	0	0	0	0	0	0	0
Hood	0	0	0	0	0	0	0	0	0	0	0	0	0	0
Hopkins	0	0	0	0	0	0	84	181	86	57	19	276	30	3
Houston	331	4	106	29	21	1	106	207	5	159	27	63	43	6
Howard	0	0	0	0	0	0	0	0	0	0	0	0	0	0
Hudspeth	0	0	0	0	0	0	0	0	0	0	0	0	0	0
Hunt	0	0	0	0	0	0	58	55	40	33	190	31	4	1
Hutchinson	0	0	0	0	0	0	0	0	0	0	0	0	0	0
Irion	0	0	0	0	0	0	0	0	0	0	0	0	0	0
Jack	0	0	0	0	0	0	0	0	0	0	0	0	0	0
Jackson	0	0	4	66	14	4	96	6	2	101	0	13	1	0
Jasper	0	0	138	5	33	14	70	65	1	41	96	47	50	23
Jeff Davis	0	0	0	0	0	0	0	0	0	0	0	0	0	0
Jefferson	0	0	119	33	3	2	14	104	2	200	3	22	1	5
Jim Hogg	0	0	0	0	0	0	0	0	0	0	0	0	0	0
Jim Wells	0	0	0	0	0	0	0	0	0	0	0	0	0	0
Johnson	0	0	0	0	0	0	0	0	0	0	0	0	0	0
Jones	0	0	0	0	0	0	0	0	0	0	0	0	0	0
Karnes	0	0	0	0	0	0	0	0	0	0	0	0	0	0
Kaufman	0	0	0	0	0	0	19	121	9	24	146	10	2	3
Kendall	0	0	0	0	0	0	0	0	0	0	0	0	0	0

Table 1: Gubernatorial Races

General Elections, 1845-1851														
Year	1845		1847				1849			1851				
County	James P. Henderson	James B. Miller	George T. Wood	James B. Miller	Nicholas H. Darnell	J. J. Robinson	Peter H. Bell	George T. Wood	John T. Mills	Peter H. Bell	Middleton T. Johnson	John A. Greer	B. H. Epperson	Thomas J. Chambers
Kenedy	0	0	0	0	0	0	0	0	0	0	0	0	0	0
Kent	0	0	0	0	0	0	0	0	0	0	0	0	0	0
Kerr	0	0	0	0	0	0	0	0	0	0	0	0	0	0
Kimble	0	0	0	0	0	0	0	0	0	0	0	0	0	0
King	0	0	0	0	0	0	0	0	0	0	0	0	0	0
Kinney	0	0	0	0	0	0	0	0	0	0	0	0	0	0
Kleberg	0	0	0	0	0	0	0	0	0	0	0	0	0	0
Knox	0	0	0	0	0	0	0	0	0	0	0	0	0	0
Lamar	331	3	192	221	8	9	273	148	151	119	135	144	127	14
Lamb	0	0	0	0	0	0	0	0	0	0	0	0	0	0
Lampasas	0	0	0	0	0	0	0	0	0	0	0	0	0	0
La Salle	0	0	0	0	0	0	0	0	0	0	0	0	0	0
Lavaca	0	0	0	0	0	0	0	0	0	221	10	0	0	6
Lee	0	0	0	0	0	0	0	0	0	0	0	0	0	0
Leon	0	0	0	0	0	0	49	47	36	74	22	96	69	2
Liberty	0	0	159	104	0	0	40	249	8	133	7	51	40	77
Limestone	0	0	0	0	0	0	211	51	31	22	62	119	1	4
Lips comb	0	0	0	0	0	0	0	0	0	0	0	0	0	0
Live Oak	0	0	0	0	0	0	0	0	0	0	0	0	0	0
Llano	0	0	0	0	0	0	0	0	0	0	0	0	0	0
Loving	0	0	0	0	0	0	0	0	0	0	0	0	0	0
Lubbock	0	0	0	0	0	0	0	0	0	0	0	0	0	0
Lynn	0	0	0	0	0	0	0	0	0	0	0	0	0	0
McCulloch	0	0	0	0	0	0	0	0	0	0	0	0	0	0
McLennan	0	0	0	0	0	0	0	0	0	64	20	8	35	3
McMullen	0	0	0	0	0	0	0	0	0	0	0	0	0	0
Madison	0	0	0	0	0	0	0	0	0	0	0	0	0	0
Marion	0	0	0	0	0	0	0	0	0	0	0	0	0	0
Martin	0	0	0	0	0	0	0	0	0	0	0	0	0	0
Mason	0	0	0	0	0	0	0	0	0	0	0	0	0	0
Matagorda	106	51	0	0	0	0	73	50	20	145	0	7	50	11
Maverick	0	0	0	0	0	0	0	0	0	0	0	0	0	0
Medina	0	0	0	0	0	0	50	5	0	124	0	3	6	0
Menard	0	0	0	0	0	0	0	0	0	0	0	0	0	0
Midland	0	0	0	0	0	0	0	0	0	0	0	0	0	0
Milam	152	52	30	92	67	4	205	64	5	0	0	0	0	0
Mills	0	0	0	0	0	0	0	0	0	0	0	0	0	0
Mitchell	0	0	0	0	0	0	0	0	0	0	0	0	0	0
Montague	0	0	0	0	0	0	0	0	0	0	0	0	0	0
Montgomery	541	199	137	114	1	8	29	208	9	157	31	26	66	2
Moore	0	0	0	0	0	0	0	0	0	0	0	0	0	0
Morris	0	0	0	0	0	0	0	0	0	0	0	0	0	0
Motley	0	0	0	0	0	0	0	0	0	0	0	0	0	0
Nacogdoches	0	0	317	21	50	24	58	480	28	84	110	305	22	134
Navarro	0	0	0	0	0	0	239	111	32	62	176	71	39	26
Newton	0	0	88	0	6	8	21	150	1	3	18	112	0	48
Nolan	0	0	0	0	0	0	0	0	0	0	0	0	0	0
Nueces	0	0	547	86	10	6	165	126	0	229	0	1	0	1
Ochiltree	0	0	0	0	0	0	0	0	0	0	0	0	0	0
Oldham	0	0	0	0	0	0	0	0	0	0	0	0	0	0
Orange	0	0	0	0	0	0	0	0	0	0	0	0	0	0
Palo Pinto	0	0	0	0	0	0	0	0	0	0	0	0	0	0
Panola	0	0	0	0	0	0	79	133	62	352	78	72	14	24
Parker	0	0	0	0	0	0	0	0	0	0	0	0	0	0
Parmer	0	0	0	0	0	0	0	0	0	0	0	0	0	0
Pecos	0	0	0	0	0	0	0	0	0	0	0	0	0	0
Polk	0	0	193	18	2	0	27	216	3	140	14	31	27	73
Potter	0	0	0	0	0	0	0	0	0	0	0	0	0	0
Presidio	0	0	0	0	0	0	0	0	0	0	0	0	0	0
Rains	0	0	0	0	0	0	0	0	0	0	0	0	0	0
Randall	0	0	0	0	0	0	0	0	0	0	0	0	0	0
Reagan	0	0	0	0	0	0	0	0	0	0	0	0	0	0
Real	0	0	0	0	0	0	0	0	0	0	0	0	0	0
Red River	0	0	291	16	53	4	124	142	224	67	112	128	136	16
Reeves	0	0	0	0	0	0	0	0	0	0	0	0	0	0

Table 1: Gubernatorial Races

General Elections, 1845-1851														
Year	1845		1847				1849			1851				
County	James P. Henderson	James B. Miller	George T. Wood	James B. Miller	Nicholas H. Darnell	J. J. Robinson	Peter H. Bell	George T. Wood	John T. Mills	Peter H. Bell	Middleton T. Johnson	John A. Greer	B. H. Epperson	Thomas J. Chambers
Refugio	0	0	0	42	0	0	51	5	0	69	3	2	0	1
Roberts	0	0	0	0	0	0	0	0	0	0	0	0	0	0
Robertson	276	54	149	234	54	9	94	19	0	101	3	16	5	37
Rockwall	0	0	0	0	0	0	0	0	0	0	0	0	0	0
Runnels	0	0	0	0	0	0	0	0	0	0	0	0	0	0
Rusk	271		457	13	42	20	310	301	232	350	600	87	179	86
Sabine	0	0	114	4	25	96	3	251	6	0	93	93	0	44
San Augustine	256	11	147	35	134	12	41	239	71	29	14	284	3	69
San Jacinto	0	0	0	0	0	0	0	0	0	0	0	0	0	0
San Patricio	111	10	1	11	0	0	41	3	0	36	0	0	0	7
San Saba	0	0	0	0	0	0	0	0	0	0	0	0	0	0
Schleicher	0	0	0	0	0	0	0	0	0	0	0	0	0	0
Scurry	0	0	0	0	0	0	0	0	0	0	0	0	0	0
Shackelford	0	0	0	0	0	0	0	0	0	0	0	0	0	0
Shelby	375	40	157	1	267	1	89	435	64	99	254	96	3	185
Sherman	0	0	0	0	0	0	0	0	0	0	0	0	0	0
Smith	0	0	0	0	0	0	76	255	26	188	156	57	96	133
Somervell	0	0	0	0	0	0	0	0	0	0	0	0	0	0
Starr	0	0	0	0	0	0	0	0	0	84	0	6	4	68
Stephens	0	0	0	0	0	0	0	0	0	0	0	0	0	0
Sterling	0	0	0	0	0	0	0	0	0	0	0	0	0	0
Stonewall	0	0	0	0	0	0	0	0	0	0	0	0	0	0
Sutton	0	0	0	0	0	0	0	0	0	0	0	0	0	0
Swisher	0	0	0	0	0	0	0	0	0	0	0	0	0	0
Tarrant	0	0	0	0	0	0	0	0	0	7	81	14	12	12
Taylor	0	0	0	0	0	0	0	0	0	0	0	0	0	0
Terrell	0	0	0	0	0	0	0	0	0	0	0	0	0	0
Terry	0	0	0	0	0	0	0	0	0	0	0	0	0	0
Throckmorton	0	0	0	0	0	0	0	0	0	0	0	0	0	0
Titus	0	0	142	10	11	7	136	242	72	77	40	250	149	40
Tom Green	0	0	0	0	0	0	0	0	0	0	0	0	0	0
Travis	185	30	18	324	9	1	324	93	13	461	98	35	27	3
Trinity	0	0	0	0	0	0	0	0	0	0	0	0	0	0
Tyler	0	0	0	0	0	0	35	152	2	52	78	20	1	35
Upshur	0	0	0	0	0	0	30	200	42	193	91	22	66	4
Upton	0	0	0	0	0	0	0	0	0	0	0	0	0	0
Uvalde	0	0	0	0	0	0	0	0	0	0	0	0	0	0
Val Verde	0	0	0	0	0	0	0	0	0	0	0	0	0	0
Van Zandt	0	0	0	0	0	0	20	83	4	32	55	22	5	3
Victoria	66	40	10	91	2	1	164	46	0	152	1	4	51	12
Walker	0	0	0	0	0	0	78	355	6	227	79	97	78	6
Waller	0	0	0	0	0	0	0	0	0	0	0	0	0	0
Ward	0	0	0	0	0	0	0	0	0	0	0	0	0	0
Washington	202	201	41	293	31	6	548	69	20	543	23	57	42	25
Webb	0	0	0	0	0	0	440	27	0	357	0	8	13	0
Wharton	0	0	0	0	0	0	76	6	1	116	0	2	0	17
Wheeler	0	0	0	0	0	0	0	0	0	0	0	0	0	0
Wichita	0	0	0	0	0	0	0	0	0	0	0	0	0	0
Wilbarger	0	0	0	0	0	0	0	0	0	0	0	0	0	0
Willacy	0	0	0	0	0	0	0	0	0	0	0	0	0	0
Williamson	0	0	0	0	0	0	116	20	7	211	30	0	20	2
Wilson	0	0	0	0	0	0	0	0	0	0	0	0	0	0
Winkler	0	0	0	0	0	0	0	0	0	0	0	0	0	0
Wise	0	0	0	0	0	0	0	0	0	0	0	0	0	0
Wood	0	0	0	0	0	0	0	0	0	0	0	0	0	0
Yoakum	0	0	0	0	0	0	0	0	0	0	0	0	0	0
Young	0	0	0	0	0	0	0	0	0	0	0	0	0	0
Zapata	0	0	0	0	0	0	0	0	0	0	0	0	0	0
Zavala	0	0	0	0	0	0	0	0	0	0	0	0	0	0
Official Totals	7,853	1,673	7,154	5,106	1,276	379	10,319	8,764	2,632	13,595	5,262	4,061	2,971	2,320
Unofficial Totals	4,635	1,470	6,222	4,975	1,347	464	10,319	8,764	2,632	12,573	5,090	3,973	2,900	2,058

Table 2: Gubernatorial Races

General Elections, 1853-1861																	
Year	1853						1855				1857		1859		1861		
County	E. M. Pease	W. B. Ochiltree	George T. Wood	L. D. Evans	T. J. Chambers	John Dancy	E. M. Pease	D. C. Dickson	M. T. Johnson	George T. Wood	H. R. Runnls (D)	Sam Houston	Sam Houston	H. R. Runnls (D)	F. R. Lubbock	Edward Clark	T. J. Chambers
Anderson	28	274	52	416	38	10	490	433	17	0	606	470	670	423	154	694	60
Andrews	0	0	0	0	0	0	0	0	0	0	0	0	0	0	0	0	0
Angelina	0	0	0	0	0	0	60	45	0	10	71	170	315	107	98	221	85
Aransas	0	0	0	0	0	0	0	0	0	0	0	0	0	0	0	0	0
Archer	0	0	0	0	0	0	0	0	0	0	0	0	0	0	0	0	0
Armstrong	0	0	0	0	0	0	0	0	0	0	0	0	0	0	0	0	0
Atascosa	0	0	0	0	0	0	0	0	0	0	106	95	148	77	80	31	27
Austin	291	59	18	0	45	3	374	233	0	0	424	273	405	507	249	279	210
Bailey	0	0	0	0	0	0	0	0	0	0	0	0	0	0	0	0	0
Bandera	0	0	0	0	0	0	0	0	0	0	0	0	17	28	10	27	1
Bastrop	261	168	25	7	81	8	433	292	0	0	415	248	363	406	30	20	374
Baylor	0	0	0	0	0	0	0	0	0	0	0	0	0	0	0	0	0
Bee	0	0	0	0	0	0	0	0	0	0	0	0	46	46	73	81	38
Bell	146	61	47	15	27	0	322	163	0	0	297	215	338	247	228	179	255
Bexar	1,430	199	56	36	15	4	1,682	619	0	0	927	521	1,038	723	1,025	289	170
Blanco	0	0	0	0	0	0	0	0	0	0	0	0	106	49	138	31	95
Borden	0	0	0	0	0	0	0	0	0	0	0	0	0	0	0	0	0
Bosque	0	0	0	0	0	0	15	45	0	0	104	45	146	31	129	74	120
Bowie	22	78	71	18	1	0	240	14	6	0	262	54	111	279	198	87	12
Brazoria	293	55	6	0	2	0	315	41	0	0	349	58	120	307	250	112	107
Brazos	42	24	23	0	10	0	15	98	0	0	73	149	201	78	133	80	52
Brewster	0	0	0	0	0	0	0	0	0	0	0	0	0	0	0	0	0
Briscoe	0	0	0	0	0	0	0	0	0	0	0	0	0	0	0	0	0
Brooks	0	0	0	0	0	0	0	0	0	0	0	0	0	0	0	0	0
Brown	0	0	0	0	0	0	0	0	0	0	12	4	24	1	62	23	0
Burleson	151	54	38	8	62	1	261	133	6	0	290	338	423	271	221	101	305
Burnet	77	24	16	1	0	1	73	152	0	0	130	104	294	70	155	63	72
Caldwell	120	140	139	17		47	324	254	0	0	345	277	283	289	249	14	188
Calhoun	136	83	12	2	12	0	174	96	0	0	185	156	193	138	192	110	40
Callahan	0	0	0	0	0	0	0	0	0	0	0	0	0	0	0	0	0
Cameron	530	0	3	0	109	0	203	100	0	0	670	76	97	332	587	46	16
Camp	0	0	0	0	0	0	0	0	0	0	0	0	0	0	0	0	0
Carson	0	0	0	0	0	0	0	0	0	0	0	0	0	0	0	0	0
Cass	248	284	14	17	37	0	438	357	12	9	587	369	578	626	107	239	214
Castro	0	0	0	0	0	0	0	0	0	0	0	0	0	0	0	0	0
Chambers	0	0	0	0	0	0	0	0	0	0	0	0	88	59	92	6	34
Cherokee	67	473	277	474	50	3	895	696	0	0	925	824	933	711	160	872	43
Childress	0	0	0	0	0	0	0	0	0	0	0	0	0	0	0	0	0
Clay	0	0	0	0	0	0	0	0	0	0	0	0	0	0	0	0	0
Cochran	0	0	0	0	0	0	0	0	0	0	0	0	0	0	0	0	0
Coke	0	0	0	0	0	0	0	0	0	0	0	0	0	0	0	0	0
Coleman	0	0	0	0	0	0	0	0	0	0	0	0	0	0	0	0	0
Collin	171	150	94	47	34	0	275	375	0	0	469	360	665	454	381	213	242
Collingsworth	0	0	0	0	0	0	0	0	0	0	0	0	0	0	0	0	0
Colorado	171	66	10	0	20	6	255	85	2	0	316	167	345	275	250	136	236
Comal	193	7	30	0	0	0	322	28	0	0	313	37	39	346	319	38	44
Comanche	0	0	0	0	0	0	0	0	0	0	68	49	89	10	3	106	3
Concho	0	0	0	0	0	0	0	0	0	0	0	0	0	0	0	0	0
Cooke	12	34	8	3	0	0	99	50	67	0	126	100	315	107	93	157	48
Coryell	0	0	0	0	0	0	222	137	0	0	167	138	216	52	40	58	47
Cottle	0	0	0	0	0	0	0	0	0	0	0	0	0	0	0	0	0
Crane	0	0	0	0	0	0	0	0	0	0	0	0	0	0	0	0	0
Crockett	0	0	0	0	0	0	0	0	0	0	0	0	0	0	0	0	0
Crosby	0	0	0	0	0	0	0	0	0	0	0	0	0	0	0	0	0
Culberson	0	0	0	0	0	0	0	0	0	0	0	0	0	0	0	0	0
Dallam	0	0	0	0	0	0	0	0	0	0	0	0	0	0	0	0	0
Dallas	253	163	67	53	42	0	309	221	0	0	569	404	545	429	263	452	218
Dawson	0	0	0	0	0	0	0	0	0	0	0	0	0	0	0	0	0
Deaf Smith	0	0	0	0	0	0	0	0	0	0	0	0	0	0	0	0	0
Delta	0	0	0	0	0	0	0	0	0	0	0	0	0	0	0	0	0
Denton	25	20	34	5	26	0	135	112	15	0	230	192	517	135	257	325	29
DeWitt	109	53	27	1	11	1	256	90	1	5	244	178	228	259	202	135	120
Dickens	0	0	0	0	0	0	0	0	0	0	0	0	0	0	0	0	0
Dimmit	0	0	0	0	0	0	0	0	0	0	0	0	0	0	0	0	0

Table 2: Gubernatorial Races

General Elections, 1853-1861																	
Year	1853						1855				1857		1859		1861		
County	E. M. Pease	W. B. Ochiltree	George T. Wood	L. D. Evans	T. J. Chambers	John Dancy	E. M. Pease	D. C. Dickson	M. T. Johnson	George T. Wood	H. R. Runnls (D)	Sam Houston	Sam Houston	H. R. Runnls (D)	F. R. Lubbock	Edward Clark	T. J. Chambers
Donley	0	0	0	0	0	0	0	0	0	0	0	0	0	0	0	0	0
Duval	0	0	0	0	0	0	0	0	0	0	0	0	0	0	0	0	0
Eastland	0	0	0	0	0	0	0	0	0	0	0	0	0	0	0	0	0
Ector	0	0	0	0	0	0	0	0	0	0	0	0	0	0	0	0	0
Edwards	0	0	0	0	0	0	0	0	0	0	0	0	0	0	0	0	0
Ellis	112	71	41	22	11	0	152	202	0	1	326	253	357	259	191	307	76
El Paso	814	0	0	0	0	0	760	0	0	0	898	14	65	465	537	88	1
Erath	0	0	0	0	0	0	0	0	0	0	29	33	250	13	65	212	24
Falls	51	30	13	0	38	0	0	0	0	0	113	214	237	109	69	56	107
Fannin	103	236	28	273	1	3	389	323	24	22	439	221	719	464	212	235	314
Fayette	268	162	29	5	114	119	509	368	0	0	601	467	604	526	304	44	771
Fisher	0	0	0	0	0	0	0	0	0	0	0	0	0	0	0	0	0
Floyd	0	0	0	0	0	0	0	0	0	0	0	0	0	0	0	0	0
Foard	0	0	0	0	0	0	0	0	0	0	0	0	0	0	0	0	0
Fort Bend	149	51	4	0	8	0	296	33	0	0	212	126	188	176	173	157	14
Franklin	0	0	0	0	0	0	0	0	0	0	0	0	0	0	0	0	0
Freestone	128	90	91	17	23	0	265	175	0	0	336	225	295	277	128	376	55
Frio	0	0	0	0	0	0	0	0	0	0	0	0	0	0	0	0	0
Gaines	0	0	0	0	0	0	0	0	0	0	0	0	0	0	0	0	0
Galveston	299	125	87	3	24	0	458	244	0	0	451	180	321	433	603	60	103
Garza	0	0	0	0	0	0	0	0	0	0	0	0	0	0	0	0	0
Gillespie	87	2	0	73	0	0	224	47	16	3	256	31	90	102	267	47	2
Glasscock	0	0	0	0	0	0	0	0	0	0	0	0	0	0	0	0	0
Goliad	94	30	13	4	1	0	96	135	0	0	126	152	226	137	117	167	12
Gonzales	281	118	35	5	11	6	396	411	0	0	479	390	493	407	250	255	238
Gray	0	0	0	0	0	0	0	0	0	0	0	0	0	0	0	0	0
Grayson	89	102	111	89	21	0	255	419	41	0	492	361	639	429	577	404	151
Gregg	0	0	0	0	0	0	0	0	0	0	0	0	0	0	0	0	0
Grimes	129	130	145	4	64	1	39	588	0	0	287	354	465	254	308	164	286
Guadalupe	218	109	22	30	5	1	340	252	0	0	354	255	251	287	127	77	224
Hale	0	0	0	0	0	0	0	0	0	0	0	0	0	0	0	0	0
Hall	0	0	0	0	0	0	0	0	0	0	0	0	0	0	0	0	0
Hamilton	0	0	0	0	0	0	0	0	0	0	0	0	43	2	17	85	11
Hansford	0	0	0	0	0	0	0	0	0	0	0	0	0	0	0	0	0
Hardeman	0	0	0	0	0	0	0	0	0	0	0	0	0	0	0	0	0
Hardin	0	0	0	0	0	0	0	0	0	0	0	0	0	0	75	43	45
Harris	230	232	205	0	51	4	415	426	0	0	685	474	829	626	1,629	297	306
Harrison	234	416	59	206	13	1	0	0	0	0	601	556	560	495	150	313	247
Hartley	0	0	0	0	0	0	0	0	0	0	0	0	0	0	0	0	0
Haskell	0	0	0	0	0	0	0	0	0	0	0	0	0	0	0	0	0
Hays	10	28	46	3	12	0	56	102	0	0	86	129	164	74	75	25	157
Hemphill	0	0	0	0	0	0	0	0	0	0	0	0	0	0	0	0	0
Henderson	2	87	7	119	36	0	37	210	63	0	289	145	0	0	33	252	40
Hidalgo	0	0	0	0	0	0	0	0	0	0	210	3	3	227	0	0	0
Hill	16	26	34	8	0	0	0	0	0	0	120	171	250	161	216	231	86
Hockley	0	0	0	0	0	0	0	0	0	0	0	0	0	0	0	0	0
Hood	0	0	0	0	0	0	0	0	0	0	0	0	0	0	0	0	0
Hopkins	69	124	69	291	0	7	0	0	0	0	600	348	584	500	144	380	147
Houston	64	56	161	69	59	1	0	0	0	0	422	313	450	354	142	90	403
Howard	0	0	0	0	0	0	0	0	0	0	0	0	0	0	0	0	0
Hudspeth	0	0	0	0	0	0	0	0	0	0	0	0	0	0	0	0	0
Hunt	101	54	60	112	3	0	282	151	34	32	386	257	403	440	244	143	24
Hutchinson	0	0	0	0	0	0	0	0	0	0	0	0	0	0	0	0	0
Irion	0	0	0	0	0	0	0	0	0	0	0	0	0	0	0	0	0
Jack	0	0	0	0	0	0	0	0	0	0	26	32	100	12	21	23	4
Jackson	64	33	17	0	2	1	0	0	0	0	74	115	143	60	88	23	92
Jasper	124	71	17	0	5	0	0	0	0	0	216	161	244	162	79	277	5
Jeff Davis	0	0	0	0	0	0	0	0	0	0	0	0	0	0	0	0	0
Jefferson	29	30	50	2	1	0	0	0	0	0	95	97	66	82	53	156	26
Jim Hogg	0	0	0	0	0	0	0	0	0	0	0	0	0	0	0	0	0
Jim Wells	0	0	0	0	0	0	0	0	0	0	0	0	0	0	0	0	0
Johnson	0	0	0	0	0	0	0	0	0	0	149	203	303	118	135	335	52
Jones	0	0	0	0	0	0	0	0	0	0	0	0	0	0	0	0	0
Karnes	0	0	0	0	0	0	0	0	0	0	121	143	165	67	50	176	29
Kaufman	29	93	68	73	4	0	0	0	0	0	249	219	383	266	130	424	64

Table 2: Gubernatorial Races

General Elections, 1853-1861																	
Year	1853						1855				1857		1859		1861		
County	E. M. Pease	W. B. Ochiltree	George T. Wood	L. D. Evans	T. J. Chambers	John Dancy	E. M. Pease	D. C. Dickson	M. T. Johnson	George T. Wood	H. R. Runnls (D)	Sam Houston	Sam Houston	H. R. Runnls (D)	F. R. Lubbock	Edward Clark	T. J. Chambers
Kendall	0	0	0	0	0	0	0	0	0	0	0	0	0	0	0	0	0
Kenedy	0	0	0	0	0	0	0	0	0	0	0	0	0	0	0	0	0
Kent	0	0	0	0	0	0	0	0	0	0	0	0	0	0	0	0	0
Kerr	0	0	0	0	0	0	0	0	0	0	33	20	47	11	65	76	12
Kimble	0	0	0	0	0	0	0	0	0	0	0	0	0	0	0	0	0
King	0	0	0	0	0	0	0	0	0	0	0	0	0	0	0	0	0
Kinney	0	0	0	0	0	0	0	0	0	0	0	0	0	0	0	0	0
Kleberg	0	0	0	0	0	0	0	0	0	0	0	0	0	0	0	0	0
Knox	0	0	0	0	0	0	0	0	0	0	0	0	0	0	0	0	0
Lamar	146	154	95	165	4	0	0	0	0	0	632	343	484	549	257	254	307
Lamb	0	0	0	0	0	0	0	0	0	0	0	0	0	0	0	0	0
Lampasas	0	0	0	0	0	0	0	0	0	0	0	0	221	65	100	81	22
La Salle	0	0	0	0	0	0	0	0	0	0	0	0	0	0	0	0	0
Lavaca	146	53	15	5	8	17	0	0	0	0	336	216	336	342	184	184	402
Lee	0	0	0	0	0	0	0	0	0	0	0	0	0	0	0	0	0
Leon	100	122	177	13	13	0	0	0	0	0	365	355	421	361	312	96	279
Liberty	101	50	100	0	51	1	199	121	0	0	259	176	152	210	181	67	151
Limestone	143	34	43	7	32	1	132	234	0	0	352	193	272	314	219	274	68
Lipscomb	0	0	0	0	0	0	0	0	0	0	0	0	0	0	0	0	0
Live Oak	0	0	0	0	0	0	0	0	0	0	68	64	58	43	48	100	3
Llano	0	0	0	0	0	0	0	0	0	0	70	23	89	43	52	55	23
Loving	0	0	0	0	0	0	0	0	0	0	0	0	0	0	0	0	0
Lubbock	0	0	0	0	0	0	0	0	0	0	0	0	0	0	0	0	0
Lynn	0	0	0	0	0	0	0	0	0	0	0	0	0	0	0	0	0
McCulloch	0	0	0	0	0	0	0	0	0	0	0	0	0	0	0	0	0
McLennan	26	50	54	12	59	0	0	0	0	0	260	291	408	190	96	119	487
McMullen	0	0	0	0	0	0	0	0	0	0	0	0	0	0	0	0	0
Madison	0	0	0	0	0	0	0	0	0	0	73	157	190	90	56	2	121
Marion	0	0	0	0	0	0	0	0	0	0	0	0	0	0	65	163	193
Martin	0	0	0	0	0	0	0	0	0	0	0	0	0	0	0	0	0
Mason	0	0	0	0	0	0	0	0	0	0	0	0	21	10	0	0	0
Matagorda	127	7	5	0	23	0	0	0	0	0	148	12	79	149	88	60	13
Maverick	0	0	0	0	0	0	0	0	0	0	0	0	0	0	0	0	0
Medina	147	6	2	0	0	0	0	0	0	0	125	46	54	197	57	48	38
Menard	0	0	0	0	0	0	0	0	0	0	0	0	0	0	0	0	0
Midland	0	0	0	0	0	0	0	0	0	0	0	0	0	0	0	0	0
Milam	49	63	40	6	101	2	0	0	0	0	213	256	330	218	93	130	349
Mills	0	0	0	0	0	0	0	0	0	0	0	0	0	0	0	0	0
Mitchell	0	0	0	0	0	0	0	0	0	0	0	0	0	0	0	0	0
Montague	0	0	0	0	0	0	0	0	0	0	0	0	75	8	129	24	43
Montgomery	85	121	88	0	20	0	0	0	0	0	161	290	299	153	106	46	244
Moore	0	0	0	0	0	0	0	0	0	0	0	0	0	0	0	0	0
Morris	0	0	0	0	0	0	0	0	0	0	0	0	0	0	0	0	0
Motley	0	0	0	0	0	0	0	0	0	0	0	0	0	0	0	0	0
Nacogdoches	139	396	131	3	81	2	0	0	0	0	441	592	715	308	240	392	151
Navarro	82	113	70	113	27	0	140	365	0	0	311	380	402	277	242	274	90
Newton	100	36	38	0	10	0	139	64	0	4	130	128	154	116	49	207	32
Nolan	0	0	0	0	0	0	0	0	0	0	0	0	0	0	0	0	0
Nueces	57	54	86	7	2	0	0	0	0	0	247	120	233	105	73	257	10
Ochiltree	0	0	0	0	0	0	0	0	0	0	0	0	0	0	0	0	0
Oldham	0	0	0	0	0	0	0	0	0	0	0	0	0	0	0	0	0
Orange	29	64	6	0	11	0	58	50	0	1	55	116	122	46	124	34	5
Palo Pinto	0	0	0	0	0	0	0	0	0	0	47	34	170	15	16	101	1
Panola	54	175	306	16	22	2	468	214	1	4	469	243	429	433	51	606	22
Parker	0	0	0	0	0	0	0	0	0	0	139	387	598	119	321	445	11
Parmer	0	0	0	0	0	0	0	0	0	0	0	0	0	0	0	0	0
Pecos	0	0	0	0	0	0	0	0	0	0	0	0	0	0	0	0	0
Polk	9	50	280	0	14	5	176	198	4	0	361	110	298	312	112	19	322
Potter	0	0	0	0	0	0	0	0	0	0	0	0	0	0	0	0	0
Presidio	0	0	0	0	0	0	0	0	0	0	0	0	0	0	0	0	0
Rains	0	0	0	0	0	0	0	0	0	0	0	0	0	0	0	0	0
Randall	0	0	0	0	0	0	0	0	0	0	0	0	0	0	0	0	0
Reagan	0	0	0	0	0	0	0	0	0	0	0	0	0	0	0	0	0
Real	0	0	0	0	0	0	0	0	0	0	0	0	0	0	0	0	0
Red River	92	189	158	7	7	5	310	267	2	0	398	327	474	405	312	108	337

Table 2: Gubernatorial Races

General Elections, 1853-1861																		
Year	1853						1855				1857		1859		1861			
County	E. M. Pease	W. B. Ochiltree	George T. Wood	L. D. Evans	T. J. Chambers	John Dancy	E. M. Pease	D. C. Dickson	M. T. Johnson	George T. Wood	H. R. Runnls (D)	Sam Houston	Sam Houston	H. R. Runnls (D)	F. R. Lubbock	Edward Clark	T. J. Chambers	
Reeves	0	0	0	0	0	0	0	0	0	0	0	0	0	0	0	0	0	
Refugio	57	2	32	1	0	0	93	48	0	0	108	59	82	77	15	83	5	
Roberts	0	0	0	0	0	0	0	0	0	0	0	0	0	0	0	0	0	
Robertson	41	54	84	7	24	0	43	206	0	0	162	199	259	160	130	123	28	
Rockwall	0	0	0	0	0	0	0	0	0	0	0	0	0	0	0	0	0	
Runnels	0	0	0	0	0	0	0	0	0	0	0	0	0	0	0	0	0	
Rusk	435	622	199	209	173	18	1,069	663	0	0	1,009	748	918	968	302	752	105	
Sabine	67	54	81	0	12	0	118	112	2	0	66	199	201	27	66	167	0	
San Augustine	192	91	38	0	48	1	270	93	0	0	162	194	273	109	59	266	12	
San Jacinto	0	0	0	0	0	0	0	0	0	0	0	0	0	0	0	0	0	
San Patricio	65	5	1	0	6	0	43	23	0	1	36	15	21	33	5	49	17	
San Saba	0	0	0	0	0	0	0	0	0	0	37	39	158	9	53	77	0	
Schleicher	0	0	0	0	0	0	0	0	0	0	0	0	0	0	0	0	0	
Scurry	0	0	0	0	0	0	0	0	0	0	0	0	0	0	0	0	0	
Shackelford	0	0	0	0	0	0	0	0	0	0	0	0	0	0	0	0	0	
Shelby	162	131	96	2	132	3	352	187	0	0	203	378	454	275	40	325	122	
Sherman	0	0	0	0	0	0	0	0	0	0	0	0	0	0	0	0	0	
Smith	46	250	40	584	75	8	502	263	366	0	828	558	801	466	201	869	8	
Somervell	0	0	0	0	0	0	0	0	0	0	0	0	0	0	0	0	0	
Starr	217	3	0	0	220	0	238	84	0	0	358	75	69	191	42	117	61	
Stephens	0	0	0	0	0	0	0	0	0	0	0	0	0	0	0	0	0	
Sterling	0	0	0	0	0	0	0	0	0	0	0	0	0	0	0	0	0	
Stonewall	0	0	0	0	0	0	0	0	0	0	0	0	0	0	0	0	0	
Sutton	0	0	0	0	0	0	0	0	0	0	0	0	0	0	0	0	0	
Swisher	0	0	0	0	0	0	0	0	0	0	0	0	0	0	0	0	0	
Tarrant	130	36	4	6	2	0	543	153	0	0	317	335	596	118	148	578	82	
Taylor	0	0	0	0	0	0	0	0	0	0	0	0	0	0	0	0	0	
Terrell	0	0	0	0	0	0	0	0	0	0	0	0	0	0	0	0	0	
Terry	0	0	0	0	0	0	0	0	0	0	0	0	0	0	0	0	0	
Throckmorton	0	0	0	0	0	0	0	0	0	0	0	0	0	0	0	0	0	
Titus	146	181	103	97	15	0	371	332	27	0	509	415	555	489	530	177	118	
Tom Green	0	0	0	0	0	0	0	0	0	0	0	0	0	0	0	0	0	
Travis	282	211	255	8	18	10	419	598	0	4	458	498	590	403	504	188	118	
Trinity	0	2	40	4	4	0	102	84	0	0	234	170	341	167	85	193	100	
Tyler	30	40	196	0	23	0	208	151	4	0	304	141	233	352	120	244	115	
Upshur	24	176	34	496	2	0	564	220	24	12	593	345	552	505	383	686	75	
Upton	0	0	0	0	0	0	0	0	0	0	0	0	0	0	0	0	0	
Uvalde	0	0	0	0	0	0	0	0	0	0	25	32	66	41	24	90	7	
Val Verde	0	0	0	0	0	0	0	0	0	0	0	0	0	0	0	0	0	
Van Zandt	4	18	4	187	0	0	12	109	107	19	282	113	210	165	67	215	7	
Victoria	126	62	16	3	9	0	180	105	0	0	190	108	123	181	89	97	199	
Walker	50	108	292	5	6	0	238	336	0	0	356	390	470	344	234	37	316	
Waller	0	0	0	0	0	0	0	0	0	0	0	0	0	0	0	0	0	
Ward	0	0	0	0	0	0	0	0	0	0	0	0	0	0	0	0	0	
Washington	425	273	149	2	46	6	497	458	0	0	643	548	745	607	458	77	625	
Webb	131	0	43	0	2	0	167	3	132	0	344	8	110	90	4	26	6	
Wharton	94	10	2	0	4	6	110	34	0	0	154	19	93	114	49	114	15	
Wheeler	0	0	0	0	0	0	0	0	0	0	0	0	0	0	0	0	0	
Wichita	0	0	0	0	0	0	0	0	0	0	0	0	0	0	0	0	0	
Wilbarger	0	0	0	0	0	0	0	0	0	0	0	0	0	0	0	0	0	
Willacy	0	0	0	0	0	0	0	0	0	0	0	0	0	0	0	0	0	
Williamson	165	109	92	19	14	0	245	281	0	1	289	293	488	187	193	122	151	
Wilson	0	0	0	0	0	0	0	0	0	0	0	0	0	0	63	55	46	
Winkler	0	0	0	0	0	0	0	0	0	0	0	0	0	0	0	0	0	
Wise	0	0	0	0	0	0	0	0	0	0	59	137	310	23	36	228	24	
Wood	0	28	9	165	0	0	184	38	51	107	0	0	403	250	274	307	28	
Yoakum	0	0	0	0	0	0	0	0	0	0	0	0	0	0	0	0	0	
Young	0	0	0	0	0	0	0	0	0	0	45	20	109	42	35	13	12	
Zapata	0	0	0	0	0	0	0	0	0	0	0	0	42	130	79	10	0	
Zavala	0	0	0	0	0	0	0	0	0	0	0	0	0	0	0	0	0	
Official	13,091		5,983		315		18,968		226		23,628		27,500		21,730			
Totals		9,178		4,677	2,449		26,336		809		32,552		36,227		21,854		13,759	
Unofficial	13,091		5,983		315		15,152		235		23,628		27,528		21,728			
Totals		9,178		4,677	2,449		21,346		921		32,472		36,189		21,573		13,759	

Table 3: Gubernatorial Races

General Elections, 1863-1880																
Year	1863		1866		1869			1873		1876		1878			1880		
County	Pendilton Murrah	T. J. Chambers	J. W. Throckmrtn	E. M. Pease	A. J. Hamilton	E. J. Davis	Hamilton Stuart	Richard Coke(D)	E. J. Davis (R)	Richard Coke (D)	William Chmbrs (R)	O. M. Roberts (D)	A. B. Norton (R)	W. H. Hmmn (GB)	O. M. Roberts (D)	E. J. Davis (R)	W. H. Hmmn (GB)
Anderson	228	271	910	23	603	803	0	1,135	916	1,529	995	1,416	946	118	1,576	1,270	0
Andrews	0	0	0	0	0	0	0	0	0	0	0	0	0	0	0	0	0
Angelina	0	0	273	124	225	72	0	462	116	642	6	636	96	2	768	0	2
Aransas	0	0	0	0	0	0	0	172	31	208	14	182	6	2	185	24	2
Archer	0	0	0	0	0	0	0	0	0	0	0	0	0	0	83	0	36
Armstrong	0	0	0	0	0	0	0	0	0	0	0	0	0	0	0	0	0
Atascosa	40	3	140	71	204	51	0	389	31	511	9	571	0	3	430	25	57
Austin	274	386	690	534	482	998	0	913	912	1,677	750	1,301	644	177	888	1,326	138
Bailey	0	0	0	0	0	0	0	0	0	0	0	0	0	0	0	0	0
Bandera	21	9	42	3	99	11	0	156	27	263	9	323	6	59	374	34	0
Bastrop	220	169	671	376	524	781	0	1,090	1,144	1,434	1,014	1,239	4	1,465	1,174	1,353	520
Baylor	0	0	0	0	0	0	0	0	0	0	0	0	0	0	142	0	0
Bee	40	24	75	11	43	11	0	114	7	276	6	369	0	9	307	17	0
Bell	172	131	495	113	411	50	1	1,862	198	2,702	22	2,699	41	310	2,840	148	394
Bexar	450	217	966	1,030	590	924	0	1,832	1,234	2,552	1,104	3,349	941	291	2,533	1,629	9
Blanco	72	44	93	50	53	38	0	202	64	425	65	440	28	109	453	21	132
Borden	0	0	0	0	0	0	0	0	0	0	0	0	0	0	0	0	0
Bosque	45	68	236	40	145	50	2	755	89	1,168	6	1,481	5	63	1,462	10	294
Bowie	50	80	322	6	177	264	0	530	268	873	46	959	515	171	983	775	110
Brazoria	278	108	336	34	434	603	1	1,092	336	413	1,060	669	1,071	5	324	1,142	1
Brazos	123	37	413	11	442	795	0	1,197	816	1,330	973	943	0	1,460	1,129	886	395
Brewster	0	0	0	0	0	0	0	0	0	0	0	0	0	0	0	0	0
Briscoe	0	0	0	0	0	0	0	0	0	0	0	0	0	0	0	0	0
Brooks	0	0	0	0	0	0	0	0	0	0	0	0	0	0	0	0	0
Brown	38	14	0	0	0	0	0	167	5	600	1	954	4	238	839	31	409
Burleson	179	116	494	113	434	385	0	1,085	581	912	556	549	0	903	787	666	226
Burnet	51	75	107	136	157	10	0	0	0	752	17	581	6	364	437	3	493
Caldwell	101	69	413	101	413	382	0	740	480	1,010	437	1,353	2	544	1,348	704	76
Calhoun	322	72	192	106	169	249	7	218	227	237	165	233	122	0	185	134	0
Callahan	0	0	0	0	0	0	0	0	0	0	0	263	0	1	407	0	34
Cameron	76	45	157	280	328	220	0	433	221	1,190	91	2,375	87	0	1,934	216	0
Camp	0	0	0	0	0	0	0	0	0	511	281	223	69	530	512	364	187
Carson	0	0	0	0	0	0	0	0	0	0	0	0	0	0	0	0	0
Cass	0	0	0	0	0	0	0	863	396	1,459	350	861	72	1,033	1,298	343	859
Castro	0	0	0	0	0	0	0	0	0	0	0	0	0	0	0	0	0
Chambers	55	31	59	0	65	73	0	208	149	221	105	243	0	15	275	97	9
Cherokee	260	327	1,046	93	909	247	1	1,486	527	1,896	333	1,585	368	676	1,791	602	392
Childress	0	0	0	0	0	0	0	0	0	0	0	0	0	0	0	0	0
Clay	0	9	0	0	0	0	0	76	0	313	0	528	0	187	615	9	320
Cochran	0	0	0	0	0	0	0	0	0	0	0	0	0	0	0	0	0
Coke	0	0	0	0	0	0	0	0	0	0	0	0	0	0	0	0	0
Coleman	0	0	0	0	0	0	0	0	0	90	0	352	0	74	452	0	100
Collin	268	195	1,044	121	723	28	0	1,690	288	3,131	35	3,195	106	887	3,960	364	442
Collingsworth	0	0	0	0	0	0	0	0	0	0	0	0	0	0	0	0	0
Colorado	198	62	582	329	728	1,175	0	0	0	1,376	1,441	1,169	28	1,394	1,056	1,769	71
Comal	16	101	190	363	255	360	0	363	345	437	354	481	326	11	321	343	0
Comanche	12	27	121	24	40	1	0	500	14	878	0	887	1	360	1,154	4	215
Concho	0	0	0	0	0	0	0	0	0	0	0	0	0	0	133	0	10
Cooke	196	14	512	28	404	9	3	1,028	57	2,038	8	2,739	14	67	2,489	231	533
Coryell	98	58	274	18	259	0	0	1,121	45	1,784	6	1,769	3	208	1,632	11	208
Cottle	0	0	0	0	0	0	0	0	0	0	0	0	0	0	0	0	0
Crane	0	0	0	0	0	0	0	0	0	0	0	0	0	0	0	0	0
Crockett	0	0	0	0	0	0	0	0	0	0	0	0	0	0	0	0	0
Crosby	0	0	0	0	0	0	0	0	0	0	0	0	0	0	0	0	0
Culberson	0	0	0	0	0	0	0	0	0	0	0	0	0	0	0	0	0
Dallam	0	0	0	0	0	0	0	0	0	0	0	0	0	0	0	0	0
Dallas	332	213	921	267	592	289	12	2,028	336	4,476	601	3,601	655	1,365	3,605	1,344	1,022
Dawson	0	0	0	0	0	0	0	0	0	0	0	0	0	0	0	0	0
Deaf Smith	0	0	0	0	0	0	0	0	0	0	0	0	0	0	0	0	0
Delta	0	0	0	0	0	0	0	391	54	610	5	635	7	103	682	50	260
Denton	224	74	654	142	305	14	2	1,249	118	2,055	3	2,386	90	189	2,656	212	310
DeWitt	163	45	408	95	222	367	4	545	553	883	451	1,238	207	165	803	696	11
Dickens	0	0	0	0	0	0	0	546	553	0	0	0	0	0	0	0	0
Dimmit	0	0	0	0	0	0	0	0	0	0	0	0	0	0	49	0	0
Donley	0	0	0	0	0	0	0	0	0	0	0	0	0	0	0	0	0

Table 3: Gubernatorial Races

County	1863 Pendlton Murrah	1863 T.J. Chambers	1866 J.W. Throckmrtn	1866 E.M. Pease	1869 A.J. Hamilton	1869 E.J. Davis	1869 Hamilton Stuart	1873 Richard Coke(D)	1873 E.J. Davis (R)	1876 Richard Coke (D)	1876 William Chmbrs (R)	1878 O.M. Roberts (D)	1878 A.B. Norton (R)	1878 W.H. Hmmn (GB)	1880 O.M. Roberts (D)	1880 E.J. Davis (R)	1880 W.H. Hmmn (GB)
Duval	0	0	0	0	0	0	0	0	0	0	0	360	15	0	359	206	1
Eastland	0	0	0	0	0	0	0	0	0	188	0	452	1	40	666	0	78
Ector	0	0	0	0	0	0	0	0	0	0	0	0	0	0	0	0	0
Edwards	0	0	0	0	0	0	0	0	0	0	0	0	0	0	0	0	0
Ellis	221	78	525	89	505	99	1	1,528	122	2,653	2	3,031	47	368	3,043	367	446
El Paso	0	0	0	0	122	336	0	447	46	628	19	355	176	0	308	244	0
Erath	42	75	224	131	115	13	0	476	58	1,065	8	1,535	6	112	1,519	3	475
Falls	45	80	373	38	594	362	0	834	738	1,573	1,076	1,112	3	1,113	1,530	76	1,481
Fannin	353	180	921	334	507	287	2	1,531	559	1,929	255	2,196	37	1,113	3,036	675	830
Fayette	272	261	696	606	526	1,174	126	1,677	1,551	2,480	1,530	2,470	1,777	396	1,973	2,549	130
Fisher	0	0	0	0	0	0	0	0	0	0	0	0	0	0	0	0	0
Floyd	0	0	0	0	0	0	0	0	0	0	0	0	0	0	0	0	0
Foard	0	0	0	0	0	0	0	0	0	0	0	0	0	0	0	0	0
Fort Bend	203	21	373	15	171	986	6	261	1,159	300	1,244	242	1,185	41	244	917	1
Franklin	0	0	0	0	0	0	0	0	0	714	0	538	0	289	605	0	273
Freestone	113	79	495	7	594	668	0	1,070	602	1,399	549	1,369	0	984	1,221	404	688
Frio	0	0	0	0	0	0	0	69	13	158	9	279	0	0	187	5	61
Gaines	0	0	0	0	0	0	0	0	0	0	0	0	0	0	0	0	0
Galveston	676	417	596	177	1,112	1,010	49	2,492	1,023	3,447	1,090	3,500	0	1,294	2,971	1,531	282
Garza	0	0	0	0	0	0	0	0	0	0	0	0	0	0	0	0	0
Gillespie	68	213	52	261	78	277	0	104	344	222	411	617	145	2	349	461	0
Glasscock	0	0	0	0	0	0	0	0	0	0	0	0	0	0	0	0	0
Goliad	392	147	195	181	130	172	0	132	169	592	180	744	22	130	555	317	0
Gonzales	229	146	0	0	513	476	0	1,054	415	1,841	313	2,008	15	410	1,565	490	215
Gray	0	0	0	0	0	0	0	0	0	0	0	0	0	0	0	0	0
Grayson	183	129	875	153	505	253	1	2,265	495	4,248	503	4,181	147	1,555	4,581	1,513	756
Gregg	0	0	0	0	0	0	0	308	154	764	433	587	322	471	523	688	217
Grimes	211	228	764	17	370	1,664	0	1,600	1,329	1,311	1,462	1,020	1,191	1,323	1,177	1,551	381
Guadalupe	218	58	458	206	328	516	0	890	810	840	713	1,215	183	602	1,172	895	49
Hale	0	0	0	0	0	0	0	0	0	0	0	0	0	0	0	0	0
Hall	0	0	0	0	0	0	0	0	0	0	0	0	0	0	0	0	0
Hamilton	30	10	129	2	44	0	0	187	6	698	0	926	0	84	966	8	105
Hansford	0	0	0	0	0	0	0	0	0	0	0	0	0	0	0	0	0
Hardeman	0	0	0	0	0	0	0	0	0	0	0	0	0	0	0	0	0
Hardin	0	0	73	34	58	0	0	136	20	107	19	118	6	25	203	3	17
Harris	1,027	206	1,398	132	908	1,426	0	2,966	2,169	3,426	2,368	2,661	45	2,306	2,741	2,282	127
Harrison	132	243	796	6	570	1,847	3	0	0	1,122	2,664	1,328	1,400	94	2,816	2,227	84
Hartley	0	0	0	0	0	0	0	0	0	0	0	0	0	0	0	0	0
Haskell	0	0	0	0	0	0	0	0	0	0	0	0	0	0	0	0	0
Hays	36	86	184	11	277	120	0	525	152	872	55	890	235	19	1,036	321	44
Hemphill	0	0	0	0	0	0	0	0	0	0	0	0	0	0	0	0	0
Henderson	100	73	463	84	335	193	0	763	249	951	279	960	6	404	988	243	134
Hidalgo	18	0	64	324	49	14	0	60	72	141	13	242	16	0	462	83	0
Hill	120	33	375	29	173	322	0	1,312	148	2,103	1	2,444	1	583	2,438	2	523
Hockley	0	0	0	0	0	0	0	0	0	0	0	0	0	0	0	0	0
Hood	0	0	0	0	289	1	3	773	32	821	0	1,076	1	21	1,088	0	63
Hopkins	116	200	1,058	134	609	134	4	1,871	193	1,987	124	2,166	44	273	2,007	150	429
Houston	206	269	582	181	478	790	3	1,014	1,058	1,276	986	1,132	162	669	1,427	1,163	34
Howard	0	0	0	0	0	0	0	0	0	0	0	0	0	0	0	0	0
Hudspeth	0	0	0	0	0	0	0	0	0	0	0	0	0	0	0	0	0
Hunt	43	239	712	54	504	1	0	1,469	136	2,205	58	2,214	51	299	2,446	120	557
Hutchinson	0	0	0	0	0	0	0	0	0	0	0	0	0	0	0	0	0
Irion	0	0	0	0	0	0	0	0	0	0	0	0	0	0	0	0	0
Jack	0	0	31	20	105	4	0	138	86	296	21	560	50	158	722	73	326
Jackson	74	26	134	36	57	197	17	164	244	220	240	214	223	3	222	249	0
Jasper	76	41	312	14	273	13	73	345	121	633	1	732	0	0	709	7	0
Jeff Davis	0	0	0	0	0	0	0	0	0	0	0	0	0	0	0	0	0
Jefferson	197	21	143	3	108	23	6	277	71	291	102	313	56	99	370	190	0
Jim Hogg	0	0	0	0	0	0	0	0	0	0	0	0	0	0	0	0	0
Jim Wells	0	0	0	0	0	0	0	0	0	0	0	0	0	0	0	0	0
Johnson	90	54	555	25	465	4	0	1,407	35	2,269	12	2,630	35	512	2,983	2	578
Jones	0	0	0	0	0	0	0	0	0	0	0	0	0	0	0	0	0
Karnes	99	7	192	3	135	31	0	185	88	331	0	514	0	42	371	49	3
Kaufman	188	57	698	44	450	105	0	1,070	142	1,860	45	1,847	79	695	2,028	212	776
Kendall	23	77	17	135	49	122	0	200	70	122	227	186	280	14	129	328	17

Table 3: Gubernatorial Races

General Elections, 1863-1880																
Year	1863		1866		1869			1873		1876		1878			1880		
County	Pendliton Murrah	T. J. Chambers	J. W. Throckmrtn	E. M. Pease	A. J. Hamilton	E. J. Davis	Hamilton Stuart	Richard Coke(D)	E. J. Davis (R)	Richard Coke (D)	William Chmbrs (R)	O. M. Roberts (D)	A. B. Norton (R)	W. H. Hmmn (GB)	O. M. Roberts (D)	E. J. Davis (R)	W. H. Hmmn (GB)
Kenedy	0	0	0	0	0	0	0	0	0	0	0	0	0	0	0	0	0
Kent	0	0	0	0	0	0	0	0	0	0	0	0	0	0	0	0	0
Kerr	40	17	65	41	76	60	0	143	77	205	68	217	86	33	243	105	24
Kimble	0	0	0	0	0	0	0	0	0	72	0	116	0	56	125	7	104
King	0	0	0	0	0	0	0	0	0	0	0	0	0	0	0	0	0
Kinney	0	0	0	0	15	0	0	94	114	203	25	455	53	36	423	99	0
Kleberg	0	0	0	0	0	0	0	0	0	0	0	0	0	0	0	0	0
Knox	0	0	0	0	0	0	0	0	0	0	0	0	0	0	0	0	0
Lamar	264	156	1,181	165	883	348	7	1,792	598	1,891	324	1,935	95	987	2,547	789	743
Lamb	0	0	0	0	0	0	0	0	0	0	0	0	0	0	0	0	0
Lampasas	28	81	89	80	116	7	0	375	13	667	1	477	1	353	542	1	305
La Salle	0	0	0	0	0	0	0	0	0	0	0	0	0	0	0	0	0
Lavaca	241	68	729	37	450	372	4	0	0	1,206	328	1,048	26	283	1,397	546	100
Lee	0	0	0	0	0	0	0	0	0	1,121	278	625	101	789	739	448	382
Leon	172	150	362	73	474	569	0	1,103	462	1,495	141	1,090	494	648	1,195	674	363
Liberty	121	75	333	8	249	255	0	0	0	413	367	486	0	249	430	352	4
Limestone	154	77	393	61	369	257	0	1,231	337	1,755	242	1,546	233	460	1,651	344	793
Lipscomb	0	0	0	0	0	0	0	0	0	0	0	0	0	0	0	0	0
Live Oak	68	1	91	7	83	1	0	115	13	262	3	347	3	14	251	7	0
Llano	74	30	98	21	75	1	0	108	7	413	2	325	3	104	497	3	270
Loving	0	0	0	0	0	0	0	0	0	0	0	0	0	0	0	0	0
Lubbock	0	0	0	0	0	0	0	0	0	0	0	0	0	0	0	0	0
Lynn	0	0	0	0	0	0	0	0	0	0	0	0	0	0	0	0	0
McCulloch	0	0	36	8	0	0	0	0	0	143	0	230	0	16	189	1	45
McLennan	168	170	639	85	606	797	0	1,631	878	2,041	906	2,514	12	1,746	2,376	1,029	269
McMullen	0	0	0	0	0	0	0	0	0	0	0	105	0	0	193	3	1
Madison	77	74	226	4	226	180	0	449	177	616	184	553	0	399	571	279	141
Marion	96	133	404	4	361	1,021	0	1,018	1,195	729	1,150	380	853	500	499	1,193	172
Martin	0	0	0	0	0	0	0	0	0	0	0	0	0	0	0	0	0
Mason	0	0	8	61	32	34	0	82	41	242	31	31	46	15	348	71	17
Matagorda	71	21	192	39	27	402	1	388	186	277	409	259	250	166	252	493	0
Maverick	0	0	0	0	17	35	0	71	65	312	74	436	16	1	290	142	0
Medina	28	42	19	217	10	230	0	326	76	234	297	610	93	23	318	412	16
Menard	0	0	0	0	0	0	0	74	54	79	0	146	2	1	183	14	0
Midland	0	0	0	0	0	0	0	0	0	0	0	0	0	0	0	0	0
Milam	129	233	520	14	0	0	0	997	138	2,305	55	1,817	135	882	1,932	427	583
Mills	0	0	0	0	0	0	0	0	0	0	0	0	0	0	0	0	0
Mitchell	0	0	0	0	0	0	0	0	0	0	0	0	0	0	0	0	0
Montague	40	91	110	30	102	2	0	526	51	973	0	1,324	1	117	1,255	0	547
Montgomery	180	88	538	41	356	379	0	689	708	827	814	0	0	0	749	319	650
Moore	0	0	0	0	0	0	0	0	0	0	0	0	0	0	0	0	0
Morris	0	0	0	0	0	0	0	0	0	672	19	437	0	341	545	321	123
Motley	0	0	0	0	0	0	0	0	0	0	0	0	0	0	0	0	0
Nacogdoches	177	165	666	22	411	498	0	987	395	1,236	368	1,395	438	36	1,386	2	411
Navarro	196	90	554	19	0	0	0	1,212	462	1,641	337	2,303	26	899	2,528	840	196
Newton	37	50	0	0	0	0	0	265	96	471	0	543	0	18	511	0	0
Nolan	0	0	0	0	0	0	0	0	0	0	0	0	0	0	0	0	0
Nueces	367	69	146	134	413	227	0	199	313	1,007	181	915	48	2	847	208	0
Ochiltree	0	0	0	0	0	0	0	0	0	0	0	0	0	0	0	0	0
Oldham	0	0	0	0	0	0	0	0	0	0	0	0	0	0	0	0	0
Orange	75	5	104	1	146	5	0	171	44	224	59	268	2	89	272	81	121
Palo Pinto	16	7	72	1	70	0	0	262	3	380	0	768	0	22	798	0	120
Panola	138	125	567	26	609	62	0	1,114	284	1,370	321	1,578	92	12	1,497	165	12
Parker	218	108	529	145	358	93	1	955	184	1,307	44	1,813	16	410	2,099	167	653
Parmer	0	0	0	0	0	0	0	0	0	0	0	0	0	0	0	0	0
Pecos	0	0	0	0	0	0	0	0	0	267	0	303	0	0	254	8	0
Polk	187	62	461	49	221	449	0	447	159	760	131	589	99	48	676	195	98
Potter	0	0	0	0	0	0	0	0	0	0	0	0	0	0	0	0	0
Presidio	0	0	0	0	15	19	0	0	0	239	22	351	0	0	0	0	0
Rains	0	0	0	0	0	0	0	251	40	382	2	351	0	91	355	0	162
Randall	0	0	0	0	0	0	0	0	0	0	0	0	0	0	0	0	0
Reagan	0	0	0	0	0	0	0	0	0	0	0	0	0	0	0	0	0
Real	0	0	0	0	0	0	0	0	0	0	0	0	0	0	0	0	0
Red River	189	350	1,057	48	506	780	0	1,321	939	1,446	875	1,541	983	176	1,787	1,187	117
Reeves	0	0	0	0	0	0	0	0	0	0	0	0	0	0	0	0	0

Table 3: Gubernatorial Races

General Elections, 1863-1880																	
Year	1863		1866		1869			1873		1876		1878			1880		
County	Pendlton Murrah	T. J. Chambers	J. W. Throckmrtn	E. M. Pease	A. J. Hamilton	E. J. Davis	Hamilton Stuart	Richard Coke (D)	E. J. Davis (R)	Richard Coke (D)	William Chmbrs (R)	O. M. Roberts (D)	A. B. Norton (R)	W. H. Hmmn (GB)	O. M. Roberts (D)	E. J. Davis (R)	W. H. Hmmn (GB)
Refugio	75	35	121	33	32	72	2	139	19	301	3	273	5	1	192	24	0
Roberts	0	0	0	0	0	0	0	0	0	0	0	0	0	0	0	0	0
Robertson	214	36	493	8	422	576	0	1,162	1,000	1,874	1,698	1,604	466	2,024	1,740	1,938	589
Rockwall	0	0	0	0	0	0	0	229	33	303	6	433	15	47	548	18	48
Runnels	0	0	0	0	0	0	0	0	0	0	0	0	0	0	176	0	0
Rusk	284	400	971	126	758	1,059	0	1,796	1,302	1,727	1,053	1,596	663	527	1,937	1,397	120
Sabine	88	19	186	27	333	3	0	340	114	454	147	540	0	145	543	81	0
San Augustine	83	55	286	8	332	157	1	0	0	495	385	486	0	431	583	336	0
San Jacinto	0	0	0	0	0	0	0	0	0	328	524	354	231	140	397	424	0
San Patricio	56	12	0	0	30	10	0	91	12	208	6	192	0	2	158	5	0
San Saba	58	42	130	11	111	0	0	291	2	574	0	596	0	293	476	0	262
Schleicher	0	0	0	0	0	0	0	0	0	0	0	0	0	0	0	0	0
Scurry	0	0	0	0	0	0	0	0	0	0	0	0	0	0	0	0	0
Shackelford	0	0	0	0	0	0	0	0	0	287	40	397	0	4	271	64	0
Shelby	71	78	435	120	201	248	0	676	402	757	305	836	1	508	1,324	0	57
Sherman	0	0	0	0	0	0	0	0	0	0	0	0	0	0	0	0	0
Smith	0	0	1,168	110	652	1,017	1	1,589	1,339	1,797	1,445	1,220	25	1,006	1,916	1,732	215
Somervell	0	0	0	0	0	0	0	0	0	390	0	349	0	39	707	0	72
Starr	23	0	287	29	82	14	0	100	97	248	70	361	45	0	286	318	0
Stephens	0	0	0	0	0	0	0	0	0	0	0	645	1	2	569	5	74
Sterling	0	0	0	0	0	0	0	0	0	0	0	0	0	0	0	0	0
Stonewall	0	0	0	0	0	0	0	0	0	0	0	0	0	0	0	0	0
Sutton	0	0	0	0	0	0	0	0	0	0	0	0	0	0	0	0	0
Swisher	0	0	0	0	0	0	0	0	0	0	0	0	0	0	0	0	0
Tarrant	274	127	628	121	568	54	0	1,820	138	2,593	45	3,471	138	756	3,189	384	1,023
Taylor	0	0	0	0	0	0	0	0	0	0	0	131	0	0	254	0	56
Terrell	0	0	0	0	0	0	0	0	0	0	0	0	0	0	0	0	0
Terry	0	0	0	0	0	0	0	0	0	0	0	0	0	0	0	0	0
Throckmorton	0	0	0	0	0	0	0	0	0	0	0	0	0	0	131	1	0
Titus	25	286	878	67	619	228	0	1,702	250	865	10	623	27	336	908	27	14
Tom Green	0	0	0	0	0	0	0	0	0	180	0	368	19	0	415	170	42
Travis	342	363	601	368	798	593	0	2,167	1,406	2,335	1,858	2,176	107	2,480	2,027	1,783	746
Trinity	98	67	347	27	153	136	0	450	70	564	120	517	4	179	595	109	31
Tyler	149	45	328	44	139	158	0	556	13	767	4	653	1	53	792	5	33
Upshur	129	144	888	7	537	402	0	1,166	605	1,139	213	983	346	318	1,106	267	412
Upton	0	0	0	0	0	0	0	0	0	0	0	0	0	0	0	0	0
Uvalde	26	9	46	27	29	8	0	148	22	252	3	303	0	13	388	17	15
Val Verde	0	0	0	0	0	0	0	0	0	0	0	0	0	0	0	0	0
Van Zandt	70	12	401	176	244	197	0	651	244	1,131	18	1,608	159	56	1,337	231	638
Victoria	164	29	275	125	202	338	23	450	517	656	423	807	1	421	609	633	0
Walker	243	159	601	3	431	1,028	0	774	877	798	891	805	0	1,087	700	13	939
Waller	0	0	0	0	0	0	0	433	672	656	774	527	880	84	539	1,125	47
Ward	0	0	0	0	0	0	0	0	0	0	0	0	0	0	0	0	0
Washington	414	318	982	252	959	2,035	16	1,697	2,324	2,201	2,600	1,733	1,148	1,625	1,935	2,770	132
Webb	185	0	0	0	110	23	0	91	512	646	6	1,314	35	0	1,330	109	0
Wharton	121	8	186	21	49	577	2	0	0	116	663	108	373	236	131	625	14
Wheeler	0	0	0	0	0	0	0	0	0	0	0	0	0	0	66	14	16
Wichita	0	0	0	0	0	0	0	0	0	0	0	0	0	0	0	0	0
Wilbarger	0	0	0	0	0	0	0	0	0	0	0	0	0	0	0	0	0
Willacy	0	0	0	0	0	0	0	0	0	0	0	0	0	0	0	0	0
Williamson	116	241	433	268	548	14	0	1,127	208	1,478	166	1,492	32	806	1,621	295	494
Wilson	70	30	0	0	105	151	1	330	93	886	137	1,121	74	28	1,027	176	49
Winkler	0	0	0	0	0	0	0	0	0	0	0	0	0	0	0	0	0
Wise	26	162	218	119	122	0	0	584	66	1,086	0	1,115	74	863	1,735	102	967
Wood	0	0	254	265	227	213	0	681	169	0	0	1,296	28	225	1,123	184	541
Yoakum	0	0	0	0	0	0	0	0	0	0	0	0	0	0	0	0	0
Young	24	18	0	0	0	0	0	0	0	276	0	666	2	10	647	21	125
Zapata	0	0	0	120	0	0	0	49	62	132	2	246	0	0	97	180	0
Zavala	0	0	0	0	0	0	0	0	0	0	0	0	0	0	0	0	0
Other	104	173	0	0	571	436	0	0	0	0	0	0	0	0	0	0	0
Official	17,511		48,631		39,092			85,549		150,581		158,302		55,002	64,382		
Totals		12,455		12,051		39,901	380		42,633		50,030		23,712			166,101	33,721
Unofficial	17,486		48,631		39,181			97,923		151,328		157,910		54,868	63,972		
Totals		12,254		12,051		39,730	386		46,494		50,004		23,539			166,082	33,771

Table 4: Gubernatorial Races

General Elections, 1882-1890

County	1882			1884			1886			1888		1890		
	John Ireland (D)	G.W. Jones (GB)	J.B. Robrtsn (ID)	John Ireland (D)	George W. Jones (GB)	A.B. Norton (R)	L.S. Ross (D)	A.M. Cochrn (R)	E.L. Dohny (P)	L.S. Ross (D)	Marion Martin (IF)	J.S. Hogg (D)	Webster Flangn (R)	E.C. Heath (P)
Anderson	1,671	1,343	0	1,976	1,653	2	1,667	1,010	0	1,628	0	1,594	903	0
Andrews	0	0	0	0	0	0	0	0	0	0	0	0	0	0
Angelina	834	117	0	898	59	36	1,021	32	0	1,031	191	1,199	78	6
Aransas	142	33	0	139	8	20	125	1	0	194	6	267	44	1
Archer	38	15	0	33	95	1	93	43	0	125	24	336	34	15
Armstrong	0	0	0	0	0	0	0	0	0	0	0	232	0	1
Atascosa	478	85	0	613	116	7	749	39	3	714	43	774	8	0
Austin	493	1,716	1	1,408	1,310	48	1,589	1,143	17	2,483	727	2,194	886	0
Bailey	0	0	0	0	0	0	0	0	0	0	0	0	0	0
Bandera	355	101	1	458	35	67	613	4	3	532	140	535	105	0
Bastrop	689	2,345	0	859	2,572	1	1,871	1,331	99	1,992	1,603	2,035	1,473	3
Baylor	291	13	0	269	26	3	320	2	0	229	10	436	22	0
Bee	222	32	0	238	4	11	304	0	3	455	58	731	80	0
Bell	2,273	953	20	4,146	771	21	3,541	158	1,310	4,601	1,036	5,109	517	0
Bexar	2,651	2,069	0	4,212	1,992	324	4,550	2,350	13	6,410	701	5,249	2,802	0
Blanco	440	245	0	553	292	19	830	76	41	649	170	794	76	0
Borden	0	0	0	0	0	0	0	0	0	0	0	0	0	0
Bosque	1,078	521	7	1,681	420	85	2,297	50	92	1,879	459	2,219	130	0
Bowie	1,040	702	0	1,257	70	617	1,607	1,001	177	2,024	1,390	1,852	1,116	4
Brazoria	271	1,214	0	0	0	0	382	1,073	3	450	455	413	1,133	0
Brazos	964	1,373	0	1,340	1,449	0	1,581	1,331	1	1,452	1,648	1,283	878	33
Brewster	0	0	0	0	0	0	0	0	0	274	0	275	1	0
Briscoe	0	0	0	0	0	0	0	0	0	0	0	0	0	0
Brooks	0	0	0	0	0	0	0	0	0	0	0	0	0	0
Brown	826	513	0	1,076	688	40	1,736	23	252	1,213	489	1,869	59	4
Burleson	579	1,294	6	957	1,111	0	1,181	950	65	1,113	1,172	1,325	1,026	12
Burnet	557	648	0	691	745	13	1,301	34	214	1,268	175	1,567	75	10
Caldwell	387	471	0	1,161	1,074	0	1,575	769	122	1,509	1,053	1,839	793	21
Calhoun	118	133	0	175	103	2	139	0	0	120	43	135	35	0
Callahan	392	177	0	710	0	15	638	18	151	583	195	885	38	18
Cameron	2,458	245	0	1,888	1,263	5	1,503	0	0	1,688	0	2,062	848	0
Camp	522	519	0	599	546	0	542	567	39	583	637	615	541	0
Carson	0	0	0	0	0	0	0	0	0	45	17	149	0	2
Cass	1,406	1,513	0	1,776	1,491	102	2,060	821	219	2,085	1,239	1,927	337	0
Castro	0	0	0	0	0	0	0	0	0	0	0	0	0	0
Chambers	200	106	0	278	45	90	261	127	4	266	142	222	116	0
Cherokee	1,559	1,162	0	2,124	584	128	2,009	885	305	2,336	1,168	1,916	660	1
Childress	0	0	0	0	0	0	0	0	0	82	0	0	0	0
Clay	670	156	0	655	316	22	876	71	43	742	237	1,122	90	27
Cochran	0	0	0	0	0	0	0	0	0	0	0	0	0	0
Coke	0	0	0	0	0	0	0	0	0	0	0	417	0	0
Coleman	455	131	10	525	298	9	866	0	32	877	31	1,214	5	0
Collin	3,494	547	0	4,328	406	595	4,580	260	441	5,510	1,497	5,067	772	168
Collingsworth	0	0	0	0	0	0	0	0	0	0	0	0	0	0
Colorado	795	1,828	0	1,332	1,753	1	1,526	1,578	17	1,876	1,781	1,699	1,418	0
Comal	472	545	0	567	403	1	615	315	3	1,116	6	615	212	0
Comanche	848	424	11	960	946	9	1,909	15	19	1,316	936	2,172	40	16
Concho	128	31	0	236	57	1	238	0	0	229	0	0	0	0
Cooke	2,566	861	1	3,395	408	285	3,220	844	319	3,361	679	3,282	376	9
Coryell	1,173	401	33	1,949	555	38	1,869	13	692	1,640	825	2,295	79	7
Cottle	0	0	0	0	0	0	0	0	0	0	0	0	0	0
Crane	0	0	0	0	0	0	0	0	0	0	0	0	0	0
Crockett	0	0	0	0	0	0	0	0	0	0	0	0	0	0
Crosby	0	0	0	0	0	0	51	1	19	226	17	181	1	27
Culberson	0	0	0	0	0	0	0	0	0	0	0	0	0	0
Dallam	0	0	0	0	0	0	0	0	0	0	0	0	0	0
Dallas	4,387	1,730	0	6,227	369	1,882	5,567	1,151	305	7,293	3,364	8,308	2,463	292
Dawson	0	0	0	0	0	0	0	0	0	0	0	0	0	0
Deaf Smith	0	0	0	0	0	0	0	0	0	0	0	91	0	0
Delta	744	280	0	937	160	115	999	1	221	1,470	134	1,301	132	15
Denton	2,364	690	0	2,968	501	235	2,922	337	416	2,455	1,322	2,707	451	50
DeWitt	545	855	0	917	718	11	936	500	50	1,221	376	1,498	827	0
Dickens	0	0	0	0	0	0	0	0	0	0	0	0	0	0
Dimmit	50	104	0	175	62	18	212	0	0	142	38	137	40	0
Donley	61	13	0	114	22	0	135	0	0	294	60	202	39	2

Table 4: Gubernatorial Races

General Elections, 1882-1890														
Year	1882			1884			1886			1888		1890		
County	John Ireland (D)	G.W. Jones (GB)	J.B. Robrtsn (ID)	John Ireland (D)	George W. Jones (GB)	A.B. Norton (R)	L.S. Ross (D)	A.M. Cochrn (R)	E.L. Dohny (P)	L.S. Ross (D)	Marion Martin (IF)	J.S. Hogg (D)	Webster Flangn (R)	E.C. Heath (P)
Duval	535	25	0	417	145	0	1,168	36	0	736	2	537	283	0
Eastland	650	306	0	698	676	21	982	11	339	1,140	325	1,740	50	18
Ector	0	0	0	0	0	0	0	0	0	0	0	0	0	0
Edwards	0	0	0	84	126	1	195	0	22	258	0	769	47	1
Ellis	3,304	763	0	4,312	515	184	4,077	419	311	4,707	1,206	4,690	572	52
El Paso	1,053	81	0	1,346	293	303	1,620	486	0	1,480	1,028	1,502	1,123	0
Erath	1,534	466	2	1,644	832	59	1,890	1	479	1,771	1,154	3,157	119	9
Falls	1,307	1,472	1	2,061	1,552	6	2,146	1,317	120	1,888	1,848	2,375	1,517	1
Fannin	2,538	812	0	3,724	911	99	2,159	141	216	4,923	1,862	2,549	380	7
Fayette	1,428	3,059	17	2,755	2,159	11	2,931	2,046	32	3,466	608	3,622	1,694	3
Fisher	0	0	0	0	0	0	0	0	0	216	10	498	0	23
Floyd	0	0	0	0	0	0	0	0	0	0	0	180	0	0
Foard	0	0	0	0	0	0	0	0	0	0	0	0	0	0
Fort Bend	180	1,267	0	305	1,284	302	252	1,532	0	540	1,971	308	575	0
Franklin	568	319	0	949	20	12	1,005	69	8	0	0	971	76	0
Freestone	1,016	976	0	1,497	1,133	0	1,361	745	18	1,726	1,126	1,357	907	4
Frio	194	211	0	230	219	0	379	1	104	426	20	480	72	0
Gaines	0	0	0	0	0	0	0	0	0	0	0	0	0	0
Galveston	3,318	2,325	0	4,232	1,543	297	4,699	1,229	2	3,924	2,134	4,778	1,587	0
Garza	0	0	0	0	0	0	0	0	0	0	0	0	0	0
Gillespie	248	648	1	348	308	163	830	175	0	1,152	33	963	274	0
Glasscock	0	0	0	0	0	0	0	0	0	0	0	0	0	0
Goliad	381	358	0	526	313	4	621	255	0	514	360	663	231	0
Gonzales	1,262	1,119	0	1,682	1,102	1	2,135	762	77	2,075	1,093	1,939	833	7
Gray	0	0	0	0	0	0	0	0	0	0	0	0	0	0
Grayson	4,011	2,073	0	5,465	1,111	1,421	5,184	1,239	842	6,074	2,111	6,568	1,811	95
Gregg	565	834	0	749	897	2	1,061	489	62	728	616	785	628	0
Grimes	982	1,897	1	1,448	896	691	1,643	1,905	18	1,672	2,142	1,702	1,673	0
Guadalupe	1,134	885	1	1,494	634	100	1,346	951	58	2,226	315	1,557	810	3
Hale	0	0	0	0	0	0	0	0	0	76	0	168	7	0
Hall	0	0	0	0	0	0	0	0	0	0	0	0	0	0
Hamilton	688	268	5	1,152	316	17	1,381	16	184	1,087	365	1,470	52	9
Hansford	0	0	0	0	0	0	0	0	0	0	0	21	16	0
Hardeman	0	0	0	0	0	0	304	0	0	251	37	717	30	7
Hardin	129	218	0	188	222	35	373	103	24	413	292	597	239	0
Harris	2,142	3,011	0	3,399	2,884	78	4,249	1,975	15	3,680	2,898	3,770	1,781	0
Harrison	1,000	1,081	0	2,691	661	5	3,018	816	25	4,200	348	3,087	862	0
Hartley	0	0	0	0	0	0	0	0	0	0	0	0	0	0
Haskell	0	0	0	0	0	0	152	0	0	186	0	352	0	0
Hays	812	599	0	1,116	534	22	1,336	374	301	1,185	695	1,530	411	32
Hemphill	0	0	0	0	0	0	0	0	0	173	15	127	22	0
Henderson	845	654	0	1,290	115	393	1,243	318	362	1,209	812	1,195	487	0
Hidalgo	510	72	0	602	7	0	934	39	0	723	0	506	109	0
Hill	2,281	802	13	3,205	690	161	3,791	132	286	3,258	1,513	4,129	303	104
Hockley	0	0	0	0	0	0	0	0	0	0	0	0	0	0
Hood	734	364	0	1,080	127	16	1,061	0	114	934	205	1,309	20	32
Hopkins	2,312	545	0	2,758	123	350	3,007	590	62	3,000	875	2,895	366	150
Houston	1,690	1,287	0	1,759	20	1,239	1,512	958	3	1,768	627	1,771	1,194	0
Howard	126	27	0	184	65	59	316	0	4	194	31	327	60	0
Hudspeth	0	0	0	0	0	0	0	0	0	0	0	0	0	0
Hunt	2,969	444	0	3,632	67	387	3,555	170	601	4,429	1,340	4,566	506	103
Hutchinson	0	0	0	0	0	0	0	0	0	0	0	0	0	0
Irion	0	0	0	0	0	0	0	0	0	0	0	184	1	4
Jack	536	379	0	1,023	516	3	921	335	90	852	462	1,440	153	7
Jackson	137	250	0	224	246	11	263	250	9	305	246	267	296	0
Jasper	369	9	0	427	200	84	668	0	0	508	281	568	333	0
Jeff Davis	0	0	0	0	0	0	0	0	0	155	0	90	145	0
Jefferson	411	302	0	565	316	0	490	260	5	581	333	729	437	0
Jim Hogg	0	0	0	0	0	0	0	0	0	0	0	0	0	0
Jim Wells	0	0	0	0	0	0	0	0	0	0	0	0	0	0
Johnson	2,475	641	0	3,204	302	76	3,079	9	498	2,949	1,295	3,646	81	62
Jones	105	4	0	283	55	6	381	0	11	415	96	723	13	0
Karnes	280	93	0	348	23	53	260	16	0	511	39	560	103	0
Kaufman	2,189	732	0	3,121	145	561	3,447	379	145	3,705	1,024	3,285	594	77
Kendall	93	377	0	233	17	328	216	383	0	333	2	317	283	0

Table 4: Gubernatorial Races

County	1882 John Ireland (D)	1882 G.W. Jones (GB)	1882 J.B. Robrtsn (ID)	1884 John Ireland (D)	1884 George W. Jones (GB)	1884 A.B. Norton (R)	1886 L.S. Ross (D)	1886 A.M. Cochm (R)	1886 E.L. Dohny (P)	1888 L.S. Ross (D)	1888 Marion Martin (IF)	1890 J.S. Hogg (D)	1890 Webster Flangn (R)	1890 E.C. Heath (P)
Kenedy	0	0	0	0	0	0	0	0	0	0	0	0	0	0
Kent	0	0	0	0	0	0	0	0	0	0	0	0	0	0
Kerr	210	262	0	354	141	9	492	117	2	526	100	581	124	0
Kimble	150	190	0	134	210	10	368	0	0	286	90	406	12	0
King	0	0	0	0	0	0	0	0	0	0	0	25	0	0
Kinney	275	351	0	426	310	8	379	79	0	233	5	265	217	0
Kleberg	0	0	0	0	0	0	0	0	0	0	0	0	0	0
Knox	0	0	0	0	0	0	116	0	0	153	7	242	3	0
Lamar	2,105	726	0	3,384	354	986	2,235	410	888	3,754	506	2,218	362	51
Lamb	0	0	0	0	0	0	0	0	0	0	0	0	0	0
Lampasas	528	456	0	911	640	10	1,031	33	460	813	480	1,097	77	85
La Salle	188	94	0	348	30	1	327	0	2	480	0	452	49	0
Lavaca	778	817	0	1,437	704	12	2,139	6	6	2,343	656	2,513	485	2
Lee	369	1,114	1	756	1,046	0	1,405	551	56	1,317	705	1,563	445	0
Leon	1,241	1,003	28	1,368	228	716	1,545	746	0	1,453	404	1,095	513	0
Liberty	352	379	0	514	4	305	345	264	0	491	369	514	318	0
Limestone	1,440	1,043	3	2,077	898	8	1,740	471	470	2,155	1,341	2,414	369	19
Lipscomb	0	0	0	0	0	0	0	0	0	149	60	116	52	0
Live Oak	245	57	0	317	1	1	342	0	0	331	1	322	1	0
Llano	517	474	0	794	407	3	1,169	0	15	915	139	1,211	7	0
Loving	0	0	0	0	0	0	0	0	0	0	0	0	0	0
Lubbock	0	0	0	0	0	0	0	0	0	0	0	0	0	0
Lynn	0	0	0	0	0	0	0	0	0	0	0	0	0	0
McCulloch	213	113	0	286	151	5	468	2	5	536	0	492	0	0
McLennan	1,550	905	104	2,992	1,459	77	3,064	940	400	4,124	2,864	2,384	329	31
McMullen	144	26	0	169	21	1	193	0	8	180	17	171	17	0
Madison	589	449	4	677	246	221	775	230	7	761	515	1,002	285	0
Marion	459	726	0	468	1,109	46	694	1,157	8	670	1,186	625	1,187	0
Martin	0	0	0	0	0	0	113	0	1	101	54	141	46	0
Mason	392	122	0	530	144	111	839	48	38	764	46	825	92	0
Matagorda	183	484	0	236	132	332	272	479	0	248	506	223	377	0
Maverick	196	216	0	179	239	1	376	183	0	387	282	264	364	0
Medina	312	445	0	403	298	66	676	251	7	961	76	851	292	0
Menard	192	19	0	184	65	0	261	0	1	274	1	223	5	0
Midland	0	0	0	0	0	0	139	33	3	125	55	273	39	0
Milam	1,640	1,508	22	2,539	1,146	168	2,642	759	366	2,733	843	3,159	957	0
Mills	0	0	0	0	0	0	0	0	0	614	149	951	15	0
Mitchell	221	125	0	244	343	15	505	0	55	277	142	452	77	0
Montague	1,579	565	0	2,050	860	52	2,565	1	125	2,093	821	3,263	119	13
Montgomery	834	1,009	0	970	1,051	1	0	0	0	1,243	880	1,312	833	0
Moore	0	0	0	0	0	0	0	0	0	0	0	0	0	0
Morris	553	466	0	574	404	33	715	412	8	780	473	862	109	0
Motley	0	0	0	0	0	0	0	0	0	0	0	0	0	0
Nacogdoches	1,398	332	0	1,687	456	75	2,069	0	5	2,560	54	2,043	588	0
Navarro	1,781	1,055	4	3,337	1,150	192	2,944	685	360	3,409	2,536	4,174	1,117	27
Newton	521	21	0	557	110	56	502	160	1	530	74	518	230	0
Nolan	178	93	0	265	126	8	189	0	7	219	51	329	1	3
Nueces	754	303	0	996	65	114	1,240	147	6	1,062	323	1,083	209	0
Ochiltree	0	0	0	0	0	0	0	0	0	0	0	50	14	0
Oldham	150	17	0	87	68	0	285	0	0	275	0	211	5	0
Orange	247	258	0	534	121	17	437	125	0	172	58	588	157	0
Palo Pinto	757	270	1	915	438	18	745	1	347	897	213	1,406	42	3
Panola	1,227	643	0	1,622	54	363	1,503	409	0	1,605	825	1,622	833	0
Parker	1,713	988	0	2,587	782	97	2,640	9	415	2,451	685	3,305	222	87
Parmer	0	0	0	0	0	0	258	15	0	0	0	0	0	0
Pecos	346	2	0	240	59	6	0	0	0	158	14	206	45	0
Polk	552	249	0	801	112	524	946	351	1	1,010	866	1,206	581	1
Potter	0	0	0	0	0	0	0	0	0	77	3	178	1	0
Presidio	543	131	0	465	43	196	321	33	0	429	0	645	53	0
Rains	344	221	0	473	92	33	704	2	3	490	358	590	74	92
Randall	0	0	0	0	0	0	0	0	0	0	0	67	0	0
Reagan	0	0	0	0	0	0	0	0	0	0	0	0	0	0
Real	0	0	0	0	0	0	0	0	0	0	0	0	0	0
Red River	1,446	1,022	0	1,908	32	1,070	1,515	456	158	2,625	50	2,069	1,095	5
Reeves	0	0	0	0	0	0	269	4	1	320	5	396	14	0

Table 4: Gubernatorial Races

General Elections, 1882-1890

County	1882 John Ireland (D)	1882 G.W. Jones (GB)	1882 J.B. Robrtsn (ID)	1884 John Ireland (D)	1884 George W. Jones (GB)	1884 A.B. Norton (R)	1886 L.S. Ross (D)	1886 A.M. Cochm (R)	1886 E.L. Dohny (P)	1888 L.S. Ross (D)	1888 Marion Martin (IF)	1890 J.S. Hogg (D)	1890 Webster Flangn (R)	1890 E.C. Heath (P)
Refugio	118	29	0	118	37	8	95	0	3	162	42	157	56	0
Roberts	0	0	0	0	0	0	0	0	0	0	0	73	18	0
Robertson	1,451	2,724	0	2,255	1,506	763	2,464	2,094	37	1,986	2,703	2,780	1,854	19
Rockwall	556	45	0	693	1	29	616	0	68	885	107	935	39	121
Runnels	193	10	0	228	92	1	377	26	6	440	24	575	32	2
Rusk	1,922	1,438	1	2,048	1,418	71	2,277	707	52	2,158	1,352	1,794	1,090	3
Sabine	375	217	0	545	86	74	532	134	1	642	35	725	149	0
San Augustine	517	295	0	630	56	327	723	388	0	830	5	695	286	0
San Jacinto	311	601	0	310	105	583	401	660	3	323	393	444	616	0
San Patricio	126	17	0	122	3	11	163	1	0	152	0	194	1	0
San Saba	437	400	0	636	414	19	976	0	76	632	267	973	59	27
Schleicher	0	0	0	0	0	0	0	0	0	0	0	0	0	0
Scurry	0	0	0	34	96	0	164	0	14	121	20	335	3	0
Shackelford	232	58	1	318	73	106	299	69	3	241	131	329	42	2
Shelby	1,104	432	0	1,540	48	15	1,661	110	0	1,948	262	1,414	201	0
Sherman	0	0	0	0	0	0	0	0	0	0	0	10	1	0
Smith	1,746	1,965	0	2,647	1,957	45	2,490	1,856	8	3,452	685	2,552	1,605	10
Somervell	225	196	0	403	143	0	517	0	33	287	155	557	6	0
Starr	4	544	0	363	253	1	546	39	0	480	0	738	544	0
Stephens	587	79	0	474	234	6	529	0	10	662	136	703	10	0
Sterling	0	0	0	0	0	0	0	0	0	0	0	0	0	0
Stonewall	0	0	0	0	0	0	0	0	0	0	0	226	0	0
Sutton	0	0	0	0	0	0	0	0	0	0	0	164	0	0
Swisher	0	0	0	0	0	0	0	0	0	0	0	51	0	0
Tarrant	2,858	1,472	8	4,230	2,155	19	4,086	1,008	1,244	4,331	2,674	4,178	889	12
Taylor	357	137	0	672	311	36	757	0	148	637	199	1,091	23	10
Terrell	0	0	0	0	0	0	0	0	0	0	0	0	0	0
Terry	0	0	0	0	0	0	0	0	0	0	0	0	0	0
Throckmorton	86	13	0	172	68	5	170	0	0	149	20	197	0	0
Titus	817	246	0	1,004	212	0	1,092	225	91	1,154	339	1,210	264	0
Tom Green	349	254	0	601	591	22	942	276	26	1,282	48	1,065	139	2
Travis	2,087	2,744	0	2,542	3,091	75	3,539	2,267	89	3,499	2,796	3,835	1,952	6
Trinity	553	208	0	901	207	27	912	258	1	995	109	1,046	335	0
Tyler	427	556	0	785	415	36	1,061	201	8	967	945	1,590	418	5
Upshur	1,165	591	0	1,335	604	105	1,419	582	137	1,412	408	1,555	565	0
Upton	0	0	0	0	0	0	0	0	0	0	0	0	0	0
Uvalde	420	107	0	540	113	6	633	43	17	506	29	626	119	0
Val Verde	0	0	0	0	0	0	274	80	0	433	85	131	39	0
Van Zandt	1,328	803	0	2,086	611	6	2,533	0	55	1,997	1,044	1,801	166	92
Victoria	446	739	0	0	0	0	731	734	7	748	725	773	737	0
Walker	522	1,049	0	723	1,204	2	869	854	15	871	1,049	1,011	457	0
Waller	407	1,011	0	790	40	1,160	632	1,175	39	1,085	268	874	1,089	0
Ward	0	0	0	0	0	0	0	0	0	0	0	0	0	0
Washington	1,354	3,575	7	2,414	2,987	264	2,214	1,986	52	2,970	1,878	2,568	2,036	0
Webb	762	251	0	1,375	33	352	1,724	43	0	883	2	1,699	161	0
Wharton	115	643	0	160	742	10	183	820	3	409	708	251	466	0
Wheeler	344	37	0	149	259	0	410	56	0	437	4	125	58	0
Wichita	86	39	0	340	81	76	339	55	0	405	18	666	180	0
Wilbarger	104	6	0	182	31	22	507	41	20	332	116	1,091	112	116
Willacy	0	0	0	0	0	0	0	0	0	0	0	0	0	0
Williamson	1,735	1,068	0	2,084	1,299	55	2,252	142	369	3,024	890	2,885	633	75
Wilson	945	284	0	902	357	11	1,590	166	1	1,455	321	1,654	157	0
Winkler	0	0	0	0	0	0	0	0	0	0	0	0	0	0
Wise	1,713	1,149	17	3,290	705	99	2,466	167	941	2,365	858	2,649	237	6
Wood	1,188	838	0	1,658	237	331	1,331	269	330	1,882	806	1,433	354	7
Yoakum	0	0	0	0	0	0	0	0	0	0	0	0	0	0
Young	542	151	0	628	183	23	620	39	3	634	119	861	47	29
Zapata	67	214	0	16	0	92	217	0	0	267	0	20	141	0
Zavala	0	0	0	121	42	0	190	0	24	175	1	169	5	0
Other	0	0	0	0	0	0	35	0	0	311	63	841	3	2
Official Totals	150,809	102,501	334	88,450	212,234	25,557	228,776	65,236	19,186	98,447	250,338	77,742	262,432	2,235
Unofficial Totals	150,820	107,293	332	89,306	210,109	23,300	229,302	66,996	19,326	102,816	250,078	77,777	265,894	2,523

Table 5: Gubernatorial Races

General Elections, 1892-1898																	
Year	1892					1894					1896			1898			
County	J. S. Hogg (D)	George Clark (D)	T. L. Nugent (PE)	A. J. Hustn (RR)	D. M. Prndrgst (P)	C. A. Culbrsn (D)	W. K. Makmsn (R)	J. B. Schmitz (LR)	T. L. Nugent (PE)	J. M. Dunn (P)	C. A. Culbrsn (D)	J. C. Kearby (PE)	Randolph Clark (P)	J. D. Sayers (D)	R. P. Bailey (P)	Barnett Gibbs (PE)	G. H. Royall (SL)
Anderson	1,389	1,022	1,033	2	8	1,662	198	0	1,971	25	2,866	2,175	2	2,765	68	893	0
Andrews	0	0	0	0	0	0	0	0	0	0	0	0	0	0	0	0	0
Angelina	847	87	591	1	4	1,077	49	0	750	9	1,225	992	6	1,406	16	526	0
Aransas	89	268	57	4	1	161	52	0	148	0	226	238	0	285	0	56	0
Archer	337	173	80	0	12	382	26	5	202	14	426	125	6	492	1	68	0
Armstrong	151	98	45	1	2	131	3	0	76	1	102	90	0	163	2	57	0
Atascosa	503	44	489	2	0	652	5	0	650	0	863	530	3	748	2	193	0
Austin	1,232	1,680	38	1	0	1,653	1,152	5	517	0	1,932	1,773	0	2,951	1	791	6
Bailey	0	0	0	0	0	0	0	0	0	0	0	0	0	0	0	0	0
Bandera	198	138	336	0	1	253	117	0	322	0	464	247	0	551	0	340	0
Bastrop	1,420	1,273	1,092	1	4	1,267	952	23	1,811	26	1,808	2,898	23	2,212	29	2,032	0
Baylor	317	180	115	0	3	279	11	1	141	0	363	125	2	264	1	13	0
Bee	383	476	208	0	4	754	75	0	375	1	1,146	391	3	999	1	251	0
Bell	3,480	1,298	2,284	2	30	3,536	184	162	3,026	47	4,860	3,988	23	4,104	17	1,549	6
Bexar	2,421	4,653	1,013	180	30	4,813	2,005	696	1,586	36	6,267	3,116	39	7,736	87	1,082	293
Blanco	214	352	380	5	0	426	6	90	463	1	449	484	0	515	5	358	0
Borden	53	18	62	0	0	66	0	0	30	0	50	48	0	99	0	37	0
Bosque	1,374	510	867	5	3	1,275	113	20	1,290	0	1,583	1,776	5	1,671	17	989	0
Bowie	1,429	965	1,263	0	11	1,907	331	0	1,700	15	2,413	2,189	0	2,714	0	1,111	0
Brazoria	970	887	69	1	8	0	0	0	0	0	1,261	1,667	9	2,636	4	324	0
Brazos	1,271	1,388	420	2	0	1,304	1,412	0	702	4	1,935	1,942	0	2,936	1	324	0
Brewster	103	130	1	0	0	192	71	2	2	0	232	58	0	420	0	4	2
Briscoe	89	8	55	1	0	96	0	2	73	2	72	96	0	137	0	70	0
Brooks	0	0	0	0	0	0	0	0	0	0	0	0	0	0	0	0	0
Brown	1,256	371	1,034	5	1	1,128	83	0	926	26	1,533	1,274	22	1,436	12	772	0
Burleson	1,154	745	862	0	4	1,073	746	0	1,272	2	1,699	1,613	4	2,336	11	466	0
Burnet	909	347	773	0	7	855	61	0	984	8	985	1,036	7	1,103	4	701	0
Caldwell	1,074	925	1,083	4	10	1,485	186	0	1,539	12	1,903	1,600	13	2,162	30	1,109	0
Calhoun	87	119	1	2	0	146	60	0	50	0	224	161	2	344	0	120	0
Callahan	451	300	505	0	13	553	1	28	635	1	827	637	0	821	0	489	0
Cameron	1,753	1,230	0	0	0	2,763	491	0	0	0	1,963	1,159	0	3,077	0	0	0
Camp	411	599	296	0	1	640	441	4	335	2	719	707	0	800	0	437	0
Carson	99	40	35	0	0	97	0	0	30	0	93	21	0	110	0	1	0
Cass	1,781	377	1,764	7	1	1,367	451	15	1,789	3	2,175	2,073	3	1,967	11	1,212	0
Castro	62	27	0	0	0	63	0	0	3	0	82	10	0	87	0	0	0
Chambers	160	106	163	0	0	281	100	0	123	0	317	189	0	338	0	104	0
Cherokee	1,805	848	1,232	1	12	1,614	270	1	1,803	5	1,882	2,250	12	2,142	0	1,765	0
Childress	311	82	71	0	1	219	9	0	157	1	284	86	1	343	0	64	0
Clay	853	381	555	3	16	943	9	51	808	9	1,035	686	3	1,162	78	332	0
Cochran	0	0	0	0	0	0	0	0	0	0	0	0	0	0	0	0	0
Coke	169	24	295	0	0	146	0	0	256	0	251	247	8	302	4	208	0
Coleman	797	228	487	1	7	690	37	0	514	0	949	614	10	925	1	385	0
Collin	4,566	1,392	2,238	16	32	4,061	518	9	2,793	62	5,708	3,855	44	3,614	57	1,458	0
Collingsworth	90	42	46	0	3	97	2	2	98	0	137	61	0	173	0	64	0
Colorado	1,091	1,458	462	1	1	1,234	1,278	0	938	2	1,726	2,257	0	3,783	0	353	0
Comal	90	900	42	0	0	759	176	215	84	0	1,186	174	0	1,343	0	8	0
Comanche	1,367	152	1,662	1	10	1,372	64	0	1,586	10	1,312	1,459	8	1,677	22	2,109	0
Concho	58	122	58	0	0	109	21	4	49	1	58	7	0	158	0	41	0
Cooke	2,264	961	1,075	3	19	2,399	154	12	1,439	40	3,404	1,764	20	2,082	24	440	0
Coryell	1,447	547	1,202	7	7	1,591	124	0	1,445	0	2,200	1,854	2	2,094	14	1,276	0
Cottle	60	11	10	3	0	74	2	0	61	0	93	29	0	114	0	33	0
Crane	0	0	0	0	0	0	0	0	0	0	0	0	0	0	0	0	0
Crockett	137	50	14	0	0	128	114	0	17	0	148	222	0	402	0	1	0
Crosby	76	69	17	0	4	77	0	0	53	0	93	19	0	0	0	0	0
Culberson	0	0	0	0	0	0	0	0	0	0	0	0	0	0	0	0	0
Dallam	14	22	6	0	0	27	2	0	10	0	36	7	0	35	0	0	0
Dallas	4,684	5,070	1,610	218	109	5,676	636	455	3,565	209	7,750	7,882	237	6,791	215	2,531	0
Dawson	0	0	0	0	0	0	0	0	0	0	0	0	0	0	0	0	0
Deaf Smith	81	24	12	0	0	75	0	0	11	0	81	28	0	104	0	3	0
Delta	616	231	1,089	3	7	657	96	1	1,230	10	980	1,320	0	1,222	5	1,475	0
Denton	2,279	1,133	775	53	51	2,246	126	372	1,083	73	3,781	1,659	23	1,983	11	330	0
DeWitt	666	1,149	773	4	2	1,621	610	1	1,132	9	1,696	2,126	1	2,191	7	1,065	0
Dickens	59	39	15	0	0	82	6	0	22	0	70	44	0	146	0	41	0
Dimmit	83	12	58	0	0	70	22	0	85	0	80	131	0	162	0	63	0

Table 5: Gubernatorial Races

General Elections, 1892-1898

County	1892					1894					1896			1898			
	J.S. Hogg (D)	George Clark (D)	T.L. Nugent (PE)	A.J. Hustn (RR)	D.M. Prndrgst (P)	C.A. Culbrsn (D)	W.K. Makmsn (R)	J.B. Schmitz (LR)	T.L. Nugent (PE)	J.M. Dunn (P)	C.A. Culbrsn (D)	J.C. Kearby (PE)	Randolph Clark (P)	J.D. Sayers (D)	R.P. Bailey (P)	Barnett Gibbs (PE)	G.H. Royall (SL)
Donley	83	186	71	2	3	172	14	21	120	13	198	131	3	322	5	103	0
Duval	446	170	0	0	0	307	493	0	1	0	340	794	0	977	0	0	0
Eastland	973	419	961	18	2	1,069	61	0	1,114	26	1,471	1,356	19	1,499	47	1,183	0
Ector	46	21	3	0	0	43	9	0	4	0	60	9	0	111	0	9	0
Edwards	216	51	121	6	0	143	66	12	180	0	281	219	0	384	0	134	0
Ellis	3,548	2,037	1,474	20	37	3,406	364	4	2,487	10	6,113	4,230	52	3,731	32	1,602	1
El Paso	428	2,188	96	34	2	1,660	1,075	17	127	0	2,126	1,585	0	2,272	0	23	0
Erath	1,769	584	1,998	0	21	1,859	179	0	2,140	44	2,176	3,070	32	2,407	96	2,010	0
Falls	2,528	1,005	915	0	6	2,154	711	19	1,810	25	3,567	2,847	0	3,482	0	1,780	0
Fannin	3,734	1,848	2,302	9	49	2,867	2,016	96	1,144	7	5,341	4,292	12	3,526	12	1,812	0
Fayette	1,670	3,416	556	9	3	0	0	0	0	0	4,236	2,454	0	4,731	0	1,258	9
Fisher	233	77	240	1	1	220	0	0	208	0	297	217	6	323	0	268	0
Floyd	166	63	94	0	0	133	5	0	153	16	177	120	0	185	0	86	0
Foard	153	16	142	0	0	154	8	0	139	8	136	164	0	187	0	129	0
Fort Bend	282	625	35	0	0	0	0	0	0	0	2,296	441	0	2,267	3	128	0
Franklin	729	43	329	0	0	647	3	0	482	3	937	525	2	739	2	225	0
Freestone	1,415	632	626	0	6	1,132	814	0	980	5	1,873	1,478	0	1,629	10	755	0
Frio	235	135	322	0	0	375	88	0	345	1	486	386	0	520	2	154	0
Gaines	0	0	0	0	0	0	0	0	0	0	0	0	0	0	0	0	0
Galveston	2,763	3,357	225	35	29	3,870	1,660	0	1,502	1	4,207	4,062	104	5,879	179	662	100
Garza	0	0	0	0	0	0	0	0	0	0	0	0	0	0	0	0	0
Gillespie	79	903	401	1	0	260	653	23	473	0	1,589	1,669	2	1,062	0	295	0
Glasscock	0	0	0	0	0	30	2	0	58	0	33	63	0	46	0	17	0
Goliad	237	471	438	4	0	497	344	20	530	0	551	854	0	812	0	457	0
Gonzales	1,230	591	1,764	0	4	1,698	300	0	2,226	12	1,923	2,530	0	2,313	11	2,088	0
Gray	0	0	0	0	0	0	0	0	0	0	0	0	0	0	0	0	0
Grayson	5,406	3,309	1,257	57	58	4,747	1,385	65	2,200	83	7,656	2,517	29	3,950	64	571	12
Gregg	752	547	351	0	9	593	236	0	637	1	1,399	686	0	846	0	361	0
Grimes	1,804	1,414	375	0	3	1,978	520	0	1,669	2	1,981	2,524	0	2,224	1	2,371	0
Guadalupe	1,246	1,092	583	7	1	1,382	777	203	677	0	0	0	0	2,500	0	712	0
Hale	237	67	50	0	3	191	6	7	79	5	204	89	1	210	0	74	0
Hall	241	81	30	0	0	149	10	0	128	3	227	66	0	264	17	58	0
Hamilton	771	270	844	0	11	884	82	0	1,019	3	1,131	1,189	29	1,144	37	1,091	0
Hansford	19	10	0	0	0	12	20	0	7	0	15	18	0	21	0	3	0
Hardeman	557	199	43	5	1	330	19	6	186	11	393	153	9	535	3	93	0
Hardin	154	460	188	0	0	355	42	0	555	0	703	247	0	702	5	42	0
Harris	3,642	2,878	107	98	22	4,675	1,381	351	1,328	1	6,473	5,335	29	6,275	180	610	72
Harrison	3,988	805	108	0	0	4,362	109	0	169	0	4,524	681	0	3,803	0	61	0
Hartley	33	75	24	0	2	102	6	0	30	0	80	35	0	111	0	12	0
Haskell	256	104	36	0	0	230	10	0	72	0	238	88	2	342	0	95	0
Hays	912	277	497	0	31	1,294	90	0	1,163	37	1,596	920	0	1,508	13	436	0
Hemphill	71	87	0	0	0	119	35	0	1	0	110	31	0	152	0	2	0
Henderson	1,106	278	767	1	6	1,038	242	0	1,165	2	1,658	1,568	0	1,764	0	801	0
Hidalgo	566	193	0	0	0	835	12	0	1	2	1,216	0	0	1,247	0	0	0
Hill	3,057	1,062	1,677	7	34	2,819	228	13	2,563	128	4,928	3,597	59	3,680	58	2,014	0
Hockley	0	0	0	0	0	0	0	0	0	0	0	0	0	0	0	0	0
Hood	627	249	605	2	21	748	51	0	624	21	900	737	88	908	5	620	0
Hopkins	1,678	574	1,607	0	59	1,877	86	2	2,002	41	2,503	2,295	62	2,374	44	1,751	0
Houston	162	260	132	0	4	1,655	299	0	1,900	0	2,533	2,065	3	1,935	1	491	0
Howard	1,086	829	1,520	0	22	227	36	2	177	0	200	183	0	295	0	134	0
Hudspeth	0	0	0	0	0	0	0	0	0	0	0	0	0	0	0	0	0
Hunt	3,465	1,371	1,711	17	41	3,464	196	137	2,605	48	5,207	3,214	17	3,303	17	1,380	0
Hutchinson	0	0	0	0	0	0	0	0	0	0	0	0	0	0	0	0	0
Irion	105	16	61	0	1	118	27	0	50	0	160	43	0	142	0	14	0
Jack	750	116	855	58	26	839	101	0	936	20	1,016	951	9	877	21	773	0
Jackson	152	379	78	0	0	276	247	0	203	0	425	643	0	574	0	441	0
Jasper	368	242	322	0	1	456	295	0	382	0	748	435	11	684	2	405	0
Jeff Davis	104	112	1	0	0	74	37	98	2	0	84	69	0	246	0	0	0
Jefferson	266	901	61	7	16	709	498	43	269	10	1,016	1,057	0	0	0	0	0
Jim Hogg	0	0	0	0	0	0	0	0	0	0	0	0	0	0	0	0	0
Jim Wells	0	0	0	0	0	0	0	0	0	0	0	0	0	0	0	0	0
Johnson	2,030	1,091	1,632	6	17	1,572	52	53	2,318	31	3,346	2,966	12	2,370	21	2,043	0
Jones	372	129	416	0	3	381	6	0	506	5	478	468	1	512	0	419	0
Karnes	359	272	406	0	0	567	114	1	613	1	885	857	0	850	2	476	0
Kaufman	2,520	1,382	481	1	12	2,494	133	23	1,114	25	3,618	2,175	10	2,882	13	776	0

Table 5: Gubernatorial Races

General Elections, 1892-1898																	
Year	1892					1894					1896			1898			
County	J. S. Hogg (D)	George Clark (D)	T. L. Nugent (PE)	A. J. Hustn (RR)	D. M. Prndrgst (P)	C. A. Culbrsn (D)	W. K. Makmsn (R)	J. B. Schmitz (LR)	T. L. Nugent (PE)	J. M. Dunn (P)	C. A. Culbrsn (D)	J. C. Kearby (PE)	Randolph Clark (P)	J. D. Sayers (D)	R. P. Bailey (P)	Barnett Gibbs (PE)	G. H. Royall (SL)
Kendall	82	360	213	7	7	155	213	158	198	1	275	441	0	508	0	229	0
Kenedy	0	0	0	0	0	0	0	0	0	0	0	0	0	0	0	0	0
Kent	0	0	0	0	0	34	0	0	85	0	81	63	0	95	1	49	0
Kerr	258	293	354	0	6	391	243	0	247	0	539	415	0	743	9	78	0
Kimble	153	109	215	0	0	136	38	0	200	0	261	166	0	229	2	165	0
King	70	28	5	0	0	68	0	0	10	0	84	10	0	102	0	1	0
Kinney	181	412	24	10	0	186	46	275	1	0	177	445	0	297	0	5	0
Kleberg	0	0	0	0	0	0	0	0	0	0	0	0	0	0	0	0	0
Knox	234	65	47	0	0	224	0	0	77	0	221	83	0	296	0	96	0
Lamar	3,237	2,523	1,364	83	6	3,619	730	26	2,524	7	4,567	3,498	0	3,200	6	1,336	0
Lamb	0	0	0	0	0	0	0	0	0	0	0	0	0	0	0	0	0
Lampasas	316	338	582	0	12	556	51	19	815	11	565	874	12	897	14	502	6
La Salle	198	258	21	0	0	340	109	0	25	0	205	144	0	361	21	21	0
Lavaca	1,252	1,083	1,013	0	1	1,707	384	5	2,133	8	2,777	1,937	1	3,221	2	1,406	0
Lee	551	846	704	0	2	796	718	3	853	10	962	1,661	8	1,326	7	1,177	0
Leon	1,103	720	708	0	2	1,138	254	0	1,162	0	1,475	1,583	0	1,549	0	1,081	0
Liberty	343	300	237	1	5	388	348	0	329	0	759	584	1	973	4	351	0
Limestone	1,819	1,075	1,205	0	45	1,808	277	19	2,034	50	3,507	2,763	35	2,729	30	1,664	0
Lipscomb	70	86	4	0	1	91	26	0	1	0	99	34	0	129	0	6	0
Live Oak	109	132	160	0	1	272	12	0	224	0	401	148	0	376	2	104	0
Llano	519	440	650	0	9	683	7	0	643	12	755	570	0	796	17	430	0
Loving	0	0	0	0	0	17	0	0	7	0	0	0	0	0	0	0	0
Lubbock	50	42	15	0	4	71	0	0	19	5	89	10	0	122	1	1	0
Lynn	0	0	0	0	0	0	0	0	0	0	0	0	0	0	0	0	0
McCulloch	301	126	262	1	1	333	13	18	244	0	367	322	0	477	1	207	3
McLennan	3,548	3,682	1,024	33	74	3,569	580	129	2,671	101	6,242	4,931	67	3,657	65	1,116	13
McMullen	51	96	59	0	1	105	18	2	55	0	140	59	0	195	0	9	0
Madison	533	248	551	0	0	510	79	0	978	12	873	746	2	748	3	690	0
Marion	925	801	330	7	2	852	612	47	509	1	1,167	902	0	429	1	454	0
Martin	80	52	6	0	0	87	6	0	15	6	90	27	0	113	0	6	0
Mason	384	249	339	0	1	382	130	74	333	1	451	557	0	624	1	397	0
Matagorda	491	167	27	0	0	134	274	0	44	0	471	520	0	627	0	67	0
Maverick	374	356	49	1	0	333	181	0	274	0	658	167	0	706	0	0	0
Medina	332	360	510	35	1	435	253	132	344	0	644	815	1	1,085	0	248	0
Menard	136	111	70	0	0	217	11	39	128	0	206	256	0	381	1	73	0
Midland	134	52	132	0	1	201	11	1	139	2	261	73	3	307	10	37	0
Milam	2,066	923	1,906	1	5	2,370	638	5	2,581	7	3,652	3,335	7	3,911	0	1,835	0
Mills	434	139	591	0	8	471	34	0	631	4	596	731	0	685	4	555	3
Mitchell	275	265	63	0	1	232	98	0	101	2	297	214	5	473	4	92	0
Montague	2,406	399	983	19	29	2,005	69	1	1,936	68	3,120	1,811	0	2,254	14	689	0
Montgomery	824	757	529	0	0	994	568	0	856	0	1,570	1,283	0	1,288	6	500	0
Moore	26	11	0	2	0	27	1	0	3	0	15	24	0	18	0	11	0
Morris	565	132	545	0	1	659	84	0	649	0	893	628	0	897	0	461	0
Motley	119	26	18	0	0	104	4	0	38	0	101	55	0	183	0	12	0
Nacogdoches	1,122	1,110	1,456	0	1	1,664	94	0	1,666	1	1,808	2,086	5	1,976	0	1,808	0
Navarro	2,440	1,183	2,533	4	23	2,852	414	30	3,475	44	4,225	3,952	50	3,932	43	2,323	0
Newton	355	271	172	1	2	413	228	50	129	18	585	370	13	919	7	115	0
Nolan	165	69	147	0	1	207	4	0	128	0	233	153	0	358	0	158	0
Nueces	635	825	124	0	1	1,297	318	5	163	0	1,483	584	0	1,866	0	110	0
Ochiltree	30	15	0	0	0	28	8	0	2	0	25	13	0	40	0	1	0
Oldham	10	63	0	0	0	63	0	0	1	0	64	15	0	92	0	0	0
Orange	494	270	184	3	6	426	231	22	228	0	803	490	7	770	14	314	0
Palo Pinto	668	310	703	1	0	755	12	1	780	16	976	1,085	10	1,057	44	787	0
Panola	1,361	241	585	0	0	1,126	63	0	673	0	2,236	510	0	1,376	0	226	0
Parker	2,230	656	1,420	32	44	1,766	3	112	2,127	53	2,820	2,261	36	2,342	13	1,631	0
Parmer	0	0	0	0	0	0	0	0	0	0	0	0	0	0	0	0	0
Pecos	90	230	6	5	6	201	38	19	33	0	193	63	0	266	0	0	0
Polk	650	618	806	0	0	943	349	2	958	0	1,284	1,153	2	1,283	8	903	0
Potter	141	175	36	0	0	168	13	0	162	0	215	131	0	264	0	56	1
Presidio	213	845	0	0	0	737	0	131	1	0	538	397	0	824	2	2	0
Rains	324	105	450	0	2	403	85	0	531	1	438	652	3	520	0	519	0
Randall	52	16	19	0	0	84	0	0	75	1	85	46	0	118	0	37	0
Reagan	0	0	0	0	0	0	0	0	0	0	0	0	0	0	0	0	0
Real	0	0	0	0	0	0	0	0	0	0	0	0	0	0	0	0	0
Red River	1,945	1,084	1,180	3	11	1,859	730	1	1,813	12	2,728	2,515	0	3,179	17	2,638	0

Table 5: Gubernatorial Races

General Elections, 1892-1898																
Year	1892					1894					1896			1898			
County	J.S. Hogg (D)	George Clark (D)	T.L. Nugent (PE)	A.J. Hustn (RR)	D.M. Prndrgst (P)	C.A. Culbrsn (D)	W.K. Makmsn (R)	J.B. Schmitz (LR)	T.L. Nugent (PE)	J.M. Dunn (P)	C.A. Culbrsn (D)	J.C. Kearby (PE)	Randolph Clark (P)	J.D. Sayers (D)	R.P. Bailey (P)	Barnett Gibbs (PE)	G.H. Royall (SL)
Reeves	302	132	43	0	0	455	40	0	160	0	576	76	0	483	0	13	0
Refugio	45	122	26	0	0	153	85	0	63	0	192	127	0	309	0	32	0
Roberts	48	27	0	0	0	65	17	0	3	0	116	40	0	169	0	33	0
Robertson	1,893	2,773	569	0	14	1,931	2,390	7	968	1	2,889	2,701	5	2,784	3	272	0
Rockwall	699	214	369	0	23	780	54	1	379	48	1,075	512	27	718	16	240	0
Runnels	379	222	141	0	1	382	17	0	247	6	415	316	4	452	10	266	2
Rusk	1,817	1,234	430	0	2	1,563	926	0	637	0	2,259	2,076	1	2,278	2	812	0
Sabine	190	82	588	0	2	389	2	0	620	1	404	567	7	630	4	554	0
San Augustine	217	311	688	0	1	545	99	0	745	0	657	848	0	566	0	756	0
San Jacinto	1,195	294	189	0	1	452	147	0	193	0	660	1,022	0	1,030	0	325	0
San Patricio	145	390	66	0	0	491	28	0	147	0	475	141	0	400	2	27	0
San Saba	516	178	571	0	10	566	66	0	503	0	630	675	1	871	2	524	0
Schleicher	0	0	0	0	0	0	0	0	0	0	0	0	0	0	0	0	0
Scurry	257	55	182	1	0	191	3	0	150	1	162	216	4	306	5	317	0
Shackelford	186	211	127	0	3	247	42	0	181	2	247	265	0	225	0	100	0
Shelby	1,535	349	601	44	1	1,576	0	0	0	0	2,097	1,121	30	1,371	66	370	0
Sherman	6	12	4	1	0	16	6	0	2	0	6	8	0	25	0	0	0
Smith	2,642	1,803	885	0	8	2,781	856	1	1,724	2	3,468	3,194	8	3,157	14	1,641	0
Somervell	134	118	315	0	0	240	0	0	394	0	356	364	4	328	0	357	0
Starr	4	1,638	0	0	1	1,247	567	0	0	0	1,467	298	0	1,138	0	14	0
Stephens	630	61	319	1	3	592	3	0	471	10	627	583	17	566	3	475	0
Sterling	136	31	83	0	0	94	2	0	74	1	106	105	0	97	0	111	0
Stonewall	100	41	58	0	0	92	6	0	78	0	117	94	0	0	0	0	0
Sutton	107	94	43	0	0	148	0	82	67	0	196	168	0	315	0	53	0
Swisher	113	33	80	1	0	107	5	0	95	0	111	98	0	127	0	68	0
Tarrant	3,209	2,800	1,906	81	27	0	0	0	0	0	6,142	3,995	51	3,904	30	1,101	0
Taylor	672	446	452	1	14	720	98	0	630	19	897	791	4	1,140	3	705	0
Terrell	0	0	0	0	0	0	0	0	0	0	0	0	0	0	0	0	0
Terry	0	0	0	0	0	0	0	0	0	0	0	0	0	0	0	0	0
Throckmorton	184	55	25	0	0	156	22	0	103	0	173	151	0	183	2	100	0
Titus	666	238	693	4	10	794	33	0	993	11	1,155	1,062	0	1,081	40	665	0
Tom Green	575	612	203	0	1	565	262	0	350	0	726	520	0	656	2	59	0
Travis	2,156	3,757	999	7	11	3,586	733	21	2,840	51	4,036	4,141	115	4,661	53	1,779	15
Trinity	552	283	615	0	1	671	166	1	661	0	922	763	0	910	1	566	0
Tyler	989	639	402	8	1	0	0	0	0	0	1,361	777	0	971	3	218	0
Upshur	1,208	120	808	0	13	1,088	123	0	1,066	10	1,539	1,257	6	0	0	0	0
Upton	0	0	0	0	0	0	0	0	0	0	0	0	0	0	0	0	0
Uvalde	480	303	177	4	2	490	150	2	211	0	515	534	0	602	0	302	3
Val Verde	180	548	0	0	0	408	338	31	41	0	475	176	0	674	1	15	0
Van Zandt	1,615	144	1,475	6	3	1,480	99	0	1,621	100	2,203	2,312	28	2,169	9	1,886	0
Victoria	612	1,040	72	1	1	801	870	0	284	0	860	1,298	0	2,002	1	445	0
Walker	808	511	943	0	0	864	484	0	1,004	0	1,251	1,318	1	1,552	0	762	0
Waller	614	738	520	2	1	610	917	0	731	0	1,486	1,334	0	2,417	1	361	0
Ward	30	47	9	0	1	79	13	0	25	0	78	93	0	161	0	73	0
Washington	2,360	2,016	92	3	2	2,356	1,939	57	834	4	2,711	3,167	3	3,519	9	249	0
Webb	127	1,667	0	0	0	1,452	920	1	134	0	1,194	1,758	0	1,850	0	3	0
Wharton	407	700	2	0	0	369	951	0	89	0	1,471	481	0	1,030	1	157	0
Wheeler	73	103	5	0	0	142	19	0	32	0	74	27	0	73	0	5	0
Wichita	746	585	98	1	1	666	104	0	418	10	621	330	11	948	22	130	0
Wilbarger	819	394	257	0	21	647	6	45	358	7	641	354	14	603	29	176	0
Willacy	0	0	0	0	0	0	0	0	0	0	0	0	0	0	0	0	0
Williamson	2,439	1,697	1,624	5	48	2,568	1,024	3	2,287	85	4,040	3,275	86	3,541	74	1,750	0
Wilson	801	244	1,049	0	0	907	85	0	1,285	0	1,290	1,221	1	1,686	0	1,019	0
Winkler	0	0	0	0	0	0	0	0	0	0	0	0	0	0	0	0	0
Wise	2,358	555	1,446	1	26	2,172	92	5	2,283	30	3,280	2,303	7	2,489	9	1,279	0
Wood	1,389	225	1,060	1	6	1,513	121	21	1,351	5	1,853	1,588	0	1,681	3	949	0
Yoakum	0	0	0	0	0	0	0	0	0	0	0	0	0	0	0	0	0
Young	555	116	281	0	3	640	28	0	405	0	764	443	0	743	4	215	0
Zapata	2	313	0	0	0	324	14	0	0	0	31	42	0	676	0	0	0
Zavala	106	22	41	0	0	116	4	0	32	1	115	30	0	105	0	15	0
Other	730	157	751	1	0	610	21	0	806	0							
Official Totals	190,486	133,395	108,483	1,322	1,592	206,141	54,520	5,026	152,731	2,196	298,643	238,325	1,846	291,548	2,437	114,955	552
Unofficial Totals	191,187	133,398	108,474	1,368	1,550	206,363	54,618	4,996	152,169	2,176	297,632	236,124	1,847	290,528	2,459	114,865	547

The Road to the White House

Texas has been a main avenue on the road to the White House. It has been a breeding ground for presidential candidates. It has been a gold mine for campaign contributions to contenders for chief executive. It has been host to national conventions. And it ranks third in the 50 states in the number of electoral votes with 32.

Neither the Democratic Party nor the Republican Party can afford to ignore the vote-rich state, because of the historical fact that no Democrat in modern times has won the presidency without carrying Texas.

The importance of the Lone Star State in presidential politics was never more evident than in 1988. The Republican nominee, George Bush, was an adopted Texan. The Democratic vice presidential nominee, Lloyd Bentsen, was a Texan. And the Libertarian Party presidential standard bearer, Ron Paul, was a Texan.

Five Texans have served as president or vice president: Bush served as vice president under President Ronald Reagan for two terms before being elected president in 1988. Lyndon B. Johnson was elected vice president in 1960, became president with the assassination of John F. Kennedy in Dallas in 1963 and was elected chief executive on his own right in 1964. Dwight D. Eisenhower, a native of Denison, Texas, served two terms as president from 1953-1961. John Nance Garner of Uvalde served as Franklin Roosevelt's vice president from 1933-1941, even though he said "becoming vice president was the only demotion I ever got" and that the job "isn't worth a bucket of warm spit."

Garner, Johnson and Bentsen were all vice presidential nominees, in part, because they were Texans who could help the presidential nominees carry Texas. That worked for Roosevelt and Kennedy, but Bentsen couldn't deliver Texas to Democratic nominee Michael Dukakis in 1988 because they were running against fellow Texan Bush.

Bentsen used the same law that Johnson used in 1960 to run for

Bentsen used the same law that Johnson used in 1960 to run for vice president and simultaneously seek re-election to his Senate seat. That so-called "LBJ Law" was adopted by the Texas Legislature in 1959 at the urging of Johnson. The Legislature also accommodated the presidential ambitions of Bentsen in 1975 when it passed a winner-take-all delegation selection primary bill. Observers said that the so-called "Bentsen Bill," was designed to guarantee the senator most of the Democratic delegates. Even as Bentsen was announcing for president on Feb. 17, 1975, a state House committee adopted the state's first presidential preference primary. But Bentsen's campaign was over before it started. Almost exactly one year after his announcement and before the Texas primary, he withdrew from the race after spending more than $2 million but failing to draw widespread popular support.

At least, Bentsen's aborted bid wasn't as expensive as the presidential campaign of former Gov. John Connally, a Democrat-turned-Republican. Connally sought the GOP presidential nomination in 1980. Despite spending $10 million, Connally won only one delegate, Ada Mills of Clarksville, Arkansas.

Texas conservatives had attempted to help Connally's presidential bid in 1979 when they tried to get a presidential primary bill through the Legislature. The bill would have established a separate presidential primary, allowing conservatives to vote for Connally for president but return to a regular primary to vote for Democratic candidates for legislative and courthouse offices. The effort was blunted when a dozen liberal senators known as the "Killer Bees" broke a quorum in the Senate by hiding out for nearly five days.

The Legislature was more successful in establishing a presidential primary in a special session in 1986. After much debate, lawmakers finally agreed to hold all of its primaries, including the presidential contest, on the second Tuesday of March in 1988. The purpose of moving the primaries from May to March was to give the Lone Star State more of a say in the selection of the Democratic and Republican nominees for president. Texas was one of several southern states that held its primaries on Super Tuesday that year.

Texas has twice played a major role in presidential politics by hosting national political party conventions. The first national convention held in the state was in 1928 when Houston's Sam Houston Hall was the site of the Democratic National Convention. The convention nominated Alfred Smith for president and Joseph Robinson as his running mate. The second convention was in Dallas in 1984 where Republicans re-nominated Ronald Reagan and George Bush as their ticket. A third national convention will be held in Houston in 1992 when Republicans convene at the Astrodome.

This article was written by Sam Attlesey, political writer for The Dallas Morning News.

Table 6: Presidential Races

	General Elections, 1848-1880													
Year	1848		1852		1856		1860		1872			1876		1880		
County	Lewis Cass (D)	Zachary Taylor (W)	Franklin Pierce (D)	Winfield Scott (W)	James C. Bchnan(D)	Millard Fillmore(W)	John C. Brkndg(D)	John Bell (CU)	Horace Greeley(D)	Ulysses S. Grant (R)	Charles OConr(LR)	Samuel J. Tilden (D)	Ruthrfrd B. Hayes (R)	Winfield S. Hncock (D)	James A. Grfield (R)	James B. Weavr(GB)
Anderson	229	83	412	150	612	325	853	113	1,094	910	0	1,212	1,043	1,468	1,127	0
Andrews	0	0	0	0	0	0	0	0	0	0	0	0	0	0	0	0
Angelina	0	0	56	28	114	77	213	122	313	120	0	233	40	770	0	1
Aransas	0	0	0	0	0	0	0	0	141	36	0	127	13	189	27	1
Archer	0	0	0	0	0	0	0	0	0	0	0	0	0	82	0	32
Armstrong	0	0	0	0	0	0	0	0	0	0	0	0	0	0	0	0
Atascosa	0	0	0	0	87	58	194	21	143	42	0	177	16	344	16	47
Austin	175	45	0	0	358	120	395	128	1,153	947	0	1,086	724	574	734	0
Bailey	0	0	0	0	0	0	0	0	0	0	0	0	0	0	0	0
Bandera	0	0	0	0	9	12	6	32	109	21	0	0	0	360	15	0
Bastrop	191	42	243	94	403	230	433	184	1,054	941	0	1,115	998	988	971	487
Baylor	0	0	0	0	0	0	0	0	0	0	0	0	148	0	0	0
Bee	0	0	0	0	0	0	121	24	82	0	0	164	0	312	17	0
Bell	0	0	157	26	312	151	487	192	438	154	0	2,064	149	2,870	121	364
Bexar	332	189	804	299	747	318	985	292	876	682	0	1,284	763	2,613	1,553	8
Blanco	0	0	0	0	0	0	135	28	160	36	0	252	28	66	1	68
Borden	0	0	0	0	0	0	0	0	0	0	0	0	0	0	0	0
Bosque	0	0	0	0	64	20	219	43	444	39	0	664	26	1,429	16	250
Bowie	0	0	0	0	171	88	324	126	352	309	0	601	184	1,103	802	74
Brazoria	172	83	0	0	225	51	390	65	244	1,019	0	317	923	324	1,144	0
Brazos	33	0	34	9	56	74	283	13	1,019	874	0	1,132	964	1,145	876	376
Brewster	0	0	0	0	0	0	0	0	0	0	0	0	0	0	0	0
Briscoe	0	0	0	0	0	0	0	0	0	0	0	0	0	0	0	0
Brooks	0	0	0	0	0	0	0	0	0	0	0	0	0	0	0	0
Brown	0	0	0	0	0	0	39	9	12	0	0	525	1	852	30	370
Burleson	64	9	103	19	261	168	506	110	671	257	0	651	438	693	412	225
Burnet	0	0	21	0	141	76	148	136	181	50	0	494	2	600	1	449
Caldwell	99	27	235	84	395	196	423	128	595	485	0	521	316	1,398	683	71
Calhoun	76	71	0	0	216	191	348	183	188	199	0	168	136	190	131	0
Callahan	0	0	0	0	0	0	0	0	0	0	0	0	0	412	0	29
Cameron	0	0	0	0	492	123	335	82	256	163	0	893	122	1,902	217	0
Camp	0	0	0	0	0	0	0	0	0	0	0	383	319	520	362	175
Carson	0	0	0	0	0	0	0	0	0	0	0	1,249	465	0	0	0
Cass	0	0	75	30	38	8	536	234	816	512	0	0	0	1,006	373	736
Castro	0	0	0	0	0	0	0	0	0	0	0	0	0	0	0	0
Chambers	0	0	0	0	0	0	106	19	134	69	0	150	11	275	99	9
Cherokee	302	110	696	248	844	514	908	158	968	372	0	1,101	451	1,490	598	148
Childress	0	0	0	0	0	0	0	0	0	0	0	0	0	0	0	0
Clay	0	0	0	0	0	0	0	0	0	0	0	87	9	683	0	210
Cochran	0	0	0	0	0	0	0	0	0	0	0	0	0	0	0	0
Coke	0	0	0	0	0	0	0	0	0	0	0	0	0	0	0	0
Coleman	0	0	0	0	0	0	0	0	0	0	0	123	0	414	0	74
Collin	99	43	133	58	564	302	667	402	667	176	0	2,139	229	3,396	335	292
Collingsworth	0	0	0	0	0	0	0	0	0	0	0	0	0	0	0	0
Colorado	68	20	92	30	252	133	569	394	1,150	1,175	0	1,036	1,322	1,103	1,738	71
Comal	105	14	112	6	284	26	201	22	381	186	0	176	260	337	506	0
Comanche	0	0	0	0	40	11	104	9	264	0	0	96	0	1,184	3	195
Concho	0	0	0	0	0	0	0	0	0	0	0	0	0	132	0	13
Cooke	0	0	14	3	97	39	264	136	387	32	0	1,468	36	3,155	234	388
Coryell	0	0	0	0	118	69	248	85	554	21	0	1,059	6	1,676	11	83
Cottle	0	0	0	0	0	0	0	0	0	0	0	3,029	808	0	0	0
Crane	0	0	0	0	0	0	0	0	0	0	0	0	0	0	0	0
Crockett	0	0	0	0	0	0	0	0	0	0	0	0	0	0	0	0
Crosby	0	0	0	0	0	0	0	0	0	0	0	0	0	0	0	0
Culberson	0	0	0	0	0	0	0	0	0	0	0	0	0	0	0	0
Dallam	0	0	0	0	0	0	0	0	0	0	0	0	0	0	0	0
Dallas	209	57	383	108	603	245	868	274	1,097	403	0	0	0	3,957	1,352	800
Dawson	0	0	0	0	0	0	0	0	0	0	0	0	0	0	0	0
Deaf Smith	0	0	0	0	0	0	0	0	0	0	0	0	0	0	0	0
Delta	0	0	0	0	0	0	0	0	229	59	0	477	61	697	50	221
Denton	46	7	37	0	308	132	586	189	502	56	0	1,498	75	0	0	0
DeWitt	81	16	0	0	253	107	491	83	386	224	0	724	230	739	644	9
Dickens	0	0	0	0	0	0	0	0	0	0	0	0	0	0	0	0
Dimmit	0	0	0	0	0	0	0	0	0	0	0	0	0	49	0	0
Donley	0	0	0	0	0	0	0	0	0	0	0	0	0	0	0	0

Table 6: Presidential Races

	General Elections, 1848-1880															
Year	1848		1852		1856		1860		1872			1876		1880		
County	Lewis Cass (D)	Zachary Taylor (W)	Franklin Pierce (D)	Winfield Scott (W)	James C. Bchnan(D)	Millard Fillmore(W)	John C. Brknrdg(D)	John Bell (CU)	Horace Greeley(D)	Ulysses S. Grant (R)	Charles OConr(LR)	Samuel J. Tilden (D)	Ruthrfrd B. Hayes (R)	Winfield S. Hncock (D)	James A. Grfield (R)	James B. Weavr(GB)
Duval	0	0	0	0	0	0	0	0	0	0	0	0	0	501	30	1
Eastland	0	0	0	0	0	0	0	0	0	0	0	175	1	367	0	30
Ector	0	0	0	0	0	0	0	0	0	0	0	0	0	0	0	0
Edwards	0	0	0	0	0	0	0	0	0	0	0	0	0	0	0	0
Ellis	0	0	90	43	239	176	416	206	616	76	0	1,782	3	3,101	370	350
El Paso	0	0	0	0	1,022	0	1,042	11	0	0	0	121	56	184	306	0
Erath	0	0	0	0	0	0	214	19	246	16	0	892	4	1,684	1	410
Falls	0	0	0	0	158	74	161	85	842	866	0	1,182	277	1,125	89	855
Fannin	245	88	208	63	577	229	778	377	617	351	0	1,620	395	3,204	703	584
Fayette	175	92	341	165	567	399	745	442	1,193	1,144	0	1,514	1,407	1,903	2,284	108
Fisher	0	0	0	0	0	0	0	0	0	0	0	0	0	0	0	0
Floyd	0	0	0	0	0	0	0	0	0	0	0	0	0	0	0	0
Foard	0	0	0	0	0	0	0	0	0	0	0	0	0	0	0	0
Fort Bend	135	39	86	31	196	136	317	38	216	1,006	0	187	1,037	266	918	0
Franklin	0	0	0	0	0	0	0	0	0	0	0	472	6	639	0	255
Freestone	0	0	0	0	341	0	568	69	813	602	0	1,113	149	1,250	404	679
Frio	0	0	0	0	0	0	0	0	48	0	0	42	7	171	6	63
Gaines	0	0	0	0	0	0	0	0	0	0	0	0	0	0	0	0
Galveston	235	217	324	141	431	314	730	283	2,412	1,252	0	2,888	1,053	0	0	0
Garza	0	0	0	0	0	0	0	0	0	0	0	0	0	0	0	0
Gillespie	0	0	74	2	115	25	66	70	215	183	0	133	132	350	458	2
Glasscock	0	0	0	0	0	0	0	0	0	0	0	0	0	0	0	0
Goliad	34	27	0	0	93	135	237	136	321	235	0	304	111	520	0	3
Gonzales	92	58	208	112	515	363	647	215	871	473	0	1,129	390	1,561	485	212
Gray	0	0	0	0	0	0	0	0	0	0	0	0	0	0	0	0
Grayson	0	0	198	48	415	182	776	441	710	321	0	3,017	759	4,967	1,456	597
Gregg	0	0	0	0	0	0	0	0	0	0	0	691	516	540	874	209
Grimes	186	53	142	54	323	260	604	203	1,047	1,508	0	702	1,182	1,158	1,553	571
Guadalupe	72	31	143	68	359	258	243	139	721	589	0	597	445	996	713	25
Hale	0	0	0	0	0	0	0	0	0	0	0	0	0	0	0	0
Hall	0	0	0	0	0	0	0	0	0	0	0	0	0	0	0	0
Hamilton	0	0	0	0	0	0	108	8	120	2	0	455	0	767	2	48
Hansford	0	0	0	0	0	0	0	0	0	0	0	0	0	0	0	0
Hardeman	0	0	0	0	0	0	0	0	0	0	0	0	0	0	0	0
Hardin	0	0	0	0	0	0	231	16	34	17	0	36	9	212	2	0
Harris	443	289	468	195	645	449	1,011	382	1,889	2,150	0	2,373	1,681	3,068	2,124	65
Harrison	381	364	400	283	565	505	681	388	775	2,374	0	1,299	2,947	2,231	2,528	68
Hartley	0	0	0	0	0	0	0	0	0	0	0	0	0	0	0	0
Haskell	0	0	0	0	0	0	0	0	0	0	0	0	0	0	0	0
Hays	43	12	55	21	130	128	164	132	406	191	0	504	165	1,053	305	46
Hemphill	0	0	0	0	0	0	0	0	0	0	0	0	0	0	0	0
Henderson	0	0	74	23	292	75	464	120	713	229	0	628	224	980	244	139
Hidalgo	0	0	0	0	169	0	64	0	79	57	0	100	35	462	83	0
Hill	0	0	0	0	175	131	391	130	785	152	0	1,623	4	2,491	2	393
Hockley	0	0	0	0	0	0	0	0	0	0	0	0	0	0	0	0
Hood	0	0	0	0	0	0	0	0	442	0	0	571	3	1,099	0	47
Hopkins	0	0	0	0	530	227	812	271	592	161	0	1,337	202	2,029	153	418
Houston	161	24	125	46	400	176	432	128	806	757	0	1,036	958	1,295	1,060	12
Howard	0	0	0	0	0	0	0	0	0	0	0	0	0	0	0	0
Hudspeth	0	0	0	0	0	0	0	0	0	0	0	0	0	0	0	0
Hunt	66	11	121	19	392	138	712	235	495	74	0	1,545	94	2,508	120	521
Hutchinson	0	0	0	0	0	0	0	0	0	0	0	0	0	0	0	0
Irion	0	0	0	0	0	0	0	0	0	0	0	0	0	0	0	0
Jack	0	0	0	0	0	0	101	35	100	101	0	97	43	756	74	306
Jackson	61	13	90	33	93	88	181	115	114	201	0	160	186	227	247	0
Jasper	113	53	121	30	185	0	268	88	305	241	0	308	0	627	45	0
Jeff Davis	0	0	0	0	0	0	0	0	0	0	0	0	0	0	0	0
Jefferson	0	0	0	0	109	49	257	85	127	64	0	169	60	373	188	0
Jim Hogg	0	0	0	0	0	0	0	0	0	0	0	0	0	0	0	0
Jim Wells	0	0	0	0	0	0	0	0	0	0	0	0	0	0	0	0
Johnson	0	0	0	0	186	78	446	59	921	1	0	1,701	33	2,970	3	533
Jones	0	0	0	0	0	0	0	0	0	0	0	0	0	0	0	0
Karnes	0	0	0	0	103	119	160	65	173	28	0	277	1	306	0	0
Kaufman	0	0	0	0	191	63	663	164	634	177	0	1,326	77	2,137	228	742
Kendall	0	0	0	0	0	0	0	0	68	94	0	61	153	135	325	15

Table 6: Presidential Races

	General Elections, 1848-1880															
Year	1848		1852		1856		1860		1872			1876		1880		
County	Lewis Cass (D)	Zachary Taylor (W)	Franklin Pierce (D)	Winfield Scott (W)	James C. Bchnan(D)	Millard Fillmore(W)	John C. Brknrdg(D)	John Bell (CU)	Horace Greeley(D)	Ulysses S. Grant (R)	Charles OConr(LR)	Samuel J. Tilden (D)	Ruthrfrd B. Hayes (R)	Winfield S. Hncock (D)	James A. Grfield (R)	James B. Weavr(GB)
Kenedy	0	0	0	0	0	0	0	0	0	0	0	0	0	0	0	0
Kent	0	0	0	0	0	0	0	0	0	0	0	0	0	0	0	0
Kerr	0	0	0	0	16	9	86	31	129	53	0	89	33	233	107	17
Kimble	0	0	0	0	0	0	0	0	0	0	0	9	0	94	6	75
King	0	0	0	0	0	0	0	0	0	0	0	0	0	0	0	0
Kinney	0	0	0	0	0	0	0	0	55	147	0	144	28	436	123	0
Kleberg	0	0	0	0	0	0	0	0	0	0	0	0	0	0	0	0
Knox	0	0	0	0	0	0	0	0	0	0	0	0	0	0	0	0
Lamar	358	186	189	57	555	0	791	332	884	455	0	2,169	867	2,630	805	669
Lamb	0	0	0	0	0	0	0	0	0	0	0	0	0	0	0	0
Lampasas	0	0	0	0	77	61	80	72	161	8	0	474	5	548	1	292
La Salle	0	0	0	0	0	0	0	0	0	0	0	0	0	0	0	0
Lavaca	34	13	85	33	360	116	596	110	800	353	0	1,015	367	1,406	513	99
Lee	0	0	0	0	0	0	0	0	0	0	0	770	155	752	433	376
Leon	142	26	124	48	337	227	576	138	928	485	0	961	194	1,102	110	205
Liberty	144	68	87	40	180	103	345	6	268	274	0	332	173	434	313	0
Limestone	0	0	176	38	401	119	482	40	1,019	445	0	427	241	1,365	343	618
Lipscomb	0	0	0	0	0	0	0	0	0	0	0	0	0	0	0	0
Live Oak	0	0	0	0	19	16	133	11	121	1	0	155	2	262	7	0
Llano	0	0	0	0	55	23	153	48	147	2	0	82	0	470	2	224
Loving	0	0	0	0	0	0	0	0	0	0	0	0	0	0	0	0
Lubbock	0	0	0	0	0	0	0	0	0	0	0	0	0	0	0	0
Lynn	0	0	0	0	0	0	0	0	0	0	0	0	0	0	0	0
McCulloch	0	0	0	0	0	0	0	0	0	0	0	127	0	169	0	41
McLennan	0	0	45	5	293	201	524	202	1,353	1,116	0	2,005	826	2,754	1,028	204
McMullen	0	0	0	0	0	0	0	0	0	0	0	0	0	0	0	0
Madison	0	0	0	0	113	125	232	26	379	222	0	518	62	579	279	130
Marion	0	0	0	0	0	0	446	184	772	1,041	0	652	1,019	527	1,188	119
Martin	0	0	0	0	0	0	0	0	0	0	0	0	0	0	0	0
Mason	0	0	0	0	0	0	17	1	95	61	0	71	17	342	71	17
Matagorda	79	69	74	30	111	43	195	8	134	365	0	209	166	255	424	0
Maverick	0	0	0	0	0	0	0	0	110	94	0	81	61	292	138	0
Medina	45	0	42	2	136	39	146	44	40	144	0	114	66	244	358	14
Menard	0	0	0	0	0	0	0	0	0	0	0	0	0	159	18	2
Midland	0	0	0	0	0	0	0	0	0	0	0	0	0	0	0	0
Milam	119	38	119	55	211	196	474	174	835	182	0	1,619	292	1,488	362	373
Mills	0	0	0	0	0	0	0	0	0	0	0	0	0	0	0	0
Mitchell	0	0	0	0	0	0	0	0	0	0	0	0	0	0	0	0
Montague	0	0	0	0	0	0	120	32	123	28	0	464	8	1,658	0	418
Montgomery	163	59	120	74	179	163	265	113	526	623	0	576	506	760	311	734
Moore	0	0	0	0	0	0	0	0	0	0	0	0	0	0	0	0
Morris	0	0	0	0	0	0	0	0	0	0	0	342	168	540	304	0
Motley	0	0	0	0	0	0	0	0	0	0	0	0	0	0	0	0
Nacogdoches	313	97	312	79	557	182	381	191	772	419	0	858	453	1,205	2	398
Navarro	0	0	0	0	300	210	491	171	1,123	439	0	1,659	578	2,411	704	76
Newton	0	0	111	16	138	79	100	12	157	90	0	268	0	485	0	0
Nolan	0	0	0	0	0	0	0	0	0	0	0	0	0	0	0	0
Nueces	56	66	52	21	128	0	125	44	373	272	0	603	169	890	169	0
Ochiltree	0	0	0	0	0	0	0	0	0	0	0	0	0	0	0	0
Oldham	0	0	0	0	0	0	0	0	0	0	0	0	0	0	0	0
Orange	0	0	39	23	73	60	129	6	85	55	0	79	29	222	77	53
Palo Pinto	0	0	0	0	0	0	152	6	137	5	0	187	0	779	0	122
Panola	194	43	0	0	458	130	519	131	892	3	0	1,198	29	1,391	110	0
Parker	0	0	0	0	333	25	775	166	468	111	0	1,014	77	1,823	168	573
Parmer	0	0	0	0	0	0	0	0	0	0	0	0	0	0	0	0
Pecos	0	0	0	0	0	0	0	0	0	0	0	122	19	201	8	0
Polk	107	56	0	0	285	64	562	62	258	134	0	275	0	682	182	89
Potter	0	0	0	0	0	0	0	0	0	0	0	0	0	0	0	0
Presidio	0	0	0	0	0	0	0	0	0	0	0	128	43	0	0	0
Rains	0	0	0	0	0	0	0	0	302	25	0	304	9	365	0	150
Randall	0	0	0	0	0	0	0	0	0	0	0	0	0	0	0	0
Reagan	0	0	0	0	0	0	0	0	0	0	0	0	0	0	0	0
Real	0	0	0	0	0	0	0	0	0	0	0	0	0	0	0	0
Red River	0	0	233	86	388	235	514	310	761	790	0	1,223	867	1,383	848	50
Reeves	0	0	0	0	0	0	0	0	0	0	0	0	0	0	0	0

Table 6: Presidential Races

	General Elections, 1848-1880															
Year	1848		1852		1856		1860		1872			1876		1880		
County	Lewis Cass (D)	Zachary Taylor (W)	Franklin Pierce (D)	Winfield Scott (W)	James C. Bchnan(D)	Millard Fillmore(W)	John C. Brknrdg(D)	John Bell (CU)	Horace Greeley(D)	Ulysses S. Grant (R)	Charles OConr(LR)	Samuel J. Tilden (D)	Ruthrfrd B. Hayes (R)	Winfield S. Hncock (D)	James A. Grfield (R)	James B. Weavr(GB)
Refugio	0	0	0	0	82	37	161	32	176	8	0	163	3	180	18	0
Roberts	0	0	0	0	0	0	0	0	0	0	0	0	0	0	0	0
Robertson	57	5	94	53	222	96	341	96	1,188	1,084	0	1,458	1,459	1,620	1,930	513
Rockwall	0	0	0	0	0	0	0	0	0	0	0	222	22	558	40	19
Runnels	0	0	0	0	0	0	0	0	0	0	0	0	0	176	0	0
Rusk	455	202	588	242	1,154	669	1,149	519	1,372	1,335	0	1,630	1,022	1,313	868	111
Sabine	181	38	81	13	118	80	232	12	229	150	0	341	0	500	71	0
San Augustine	234	70	158	29	182	72	219	34	270	377	0	311	318	557	323	0
San Jacinto	0	0	0	0	0	0	0	0	308	440	0	146	342	409	542	0
San Patricio	26	5	30	0	49	0	64	3	79	8	0	46	1	160	3	0
San Saba	0	0	0	0	48	21	115	39	142	6	0	288	1	425	0	236
Schleicher	0	0	0	0	0	0	0	0	0	0	0	0	0	0	0	0
Scurry	0	0	0	0	0	0	0	0	0	0	0	0	0	0	0	0
Shackelford	0	0	0	0	0	0	0	0	0	0	0	132	1	287	63	0
Shelby	0	0	106	19	308	76	425	89	485	240	0	716	42	1,328	0	20
Sherman	0	0	0	0	0	0	0	0	0	0	0	0	0	0	0	0
Smith	0	0	0	0	810	370	1,155	348	1,228	1,302	0	1,738	1,496	1,929	1,742	194
Somervell	0	0	0	0	0	0	0	0	0	0	0	209	2	402	0	70
Starr	0	0	0	0	347	17	40	106	128	149	0	46	65	250	319	0
Stephens	0	0	0	0	0	0	0	0	0	0	0	0	0	684	4	57
Sterling	0	0	0	0	0	0	0	0	0	0	0	0	0	0	0	0
Stonewall	0	0	0	0	0	0	0	0	0	0	0	0	0	0	0	0
Sutton	0	0	0	0	0	0	0	0	0	0	0	0	0	0	0	0
Swisher	0	0	0	0	0	0	0	0	0	0	0	0	0	0	0	0
Tarrant	0	0	60	1	490	92	618	208	572	115	0	1,633	138	3,369	391	884
Taylor	0	0	0	0	0	0	0	0	0	0	0	0	0	260	0	42
Terrell	0	0	0	0	0	0	0	0	0	0	0	0	0	0	0	0
Terry	0	0	0	0	0	0	0	0	0	0	0	0	0	0	0	0
Throckmorton	0	0	0	0	0	0	0	0	0	0	0	0	0	127	2	0
Titus	296	123	240	100	502	257	884	278	740	227	0	512	126	892	23	0
Tom Green	0	0	0	0	0	0	0	0	0	0	0	0	0	351	159	18
Travis	249	29	370	118	551	467	589	421	1,274	1,193	0	1,947	1,309	1,842	1,551	649
Trinity	0	0	17	0	161	106	218	27	327	113	0	232	57	592	123	0
Tyler	0	0	0	0	234	33	496	8	279	117	0	337	28	790	3	25
Upshur	0	0	0	0	683	255	945	334	808	596	0	678	364	1,129	268	380
Upton	0	0	0	0	0	0	0	0	0	0	0	0	0	0	0	0
Uvalde	0	0	0	0	18	22	81	20	95	6	0	184	11	285	17	10
Val Verde	0	0	0	0	0	0	0	0	0	0	0	0	0	0	0	0
Van Zandt	68	26	43	0	223	37	335	29	543	253	0	735	156	1,442	238	538
Victoria	86	87	96	84	141	117	234	93	476	414	0	382	193	578	562	0
Walker	207	119	228	72	387	343	499	161	774	979	0	397	1	634	83	733
Waller	0	0	0	0	0	0	0	0	0	0	0	600	767	557	1,127	33
Ward	0	0	0	0	0	0	0	0	0	0	0	0	0	0	0	0
Washington	373	123	519	199	653	481	908	171	1,813	2,359	0	1,682	2,256	1,977	2,843	168
Webb	0	0	0	0	382	0	76	1	0	0	0	243	39	1,339	109	0
Wharton	51	26	59	17	76	40	213	21	109	728	0	39	404	99	622	12
Wheeler	0	0	0	0	0	0	0	0	0	0	0	0	0	65	0	16
Wichita	0	0	0	0	0	0	0	0	0	0	0	0	0	0	0	0
Wilbarger	0	0	0	0	0	0	0	0	0	0	0	0	0	0	0	0
Willacy	0	0	0	0	0	0	0	0	0	0	0	0	0	0	0	0
Williamson	41	16	143	62	307	240	487	225	494	170	0	1,165	172	1,804	306	565
Wilson	0	0	0	0	0	0	47	40	0	0	0	297	95	231	18	10
Winkler	0	0	0	0	0	0	0	0	0	0	0	0	0	0	0	0
Wise	0	0	0	0	67	0	169	89	164	39	0	583	27	1,970	105	809
Wood	0	0	0	0	335	124	516	252	611	253	0	825	224	1,157	205	500
Yoakum	0	0	0	0	0	0	0	0	0	0	0	0	0	0	0	0
Young	0	0	0	0	39	11	98	11	0	0	0	252	22	706	22	72
Zapata	0	0	0	0	0	0	151	0	38	61	0	46	64	60	51	0
Zavala	0	0	0	0	0	0	0	0	0	0	0	0	0	0	0	0
Other	0	0	0	0	0	0	0	0	0	0	0	0	0	0	0	0
Official	8,801		11,519		32,460		47,887		66,435		2,580	44,800		57,893		
Totals		3,777		4,187		15,472		15,527		47,426	104,755		156,428		27,405	
Unofficial	8,801		11,515		31,852		47,949		66,455		0	44,729		57,845		
Totals		3,777		4,185		15,130		15,529		47,426	1064,180		156,228		27,405	

Table 7: Presidential Races

General Elections, 1884-1896

County	1884 Grover Clevlnd (D)	James G. Blaine (R)	Benjamin F. Butler(GB)	John P. St. John(P)	1888 Grover Clevlnd (D)	Benjamin Harrison (R)	Alson J. Streetr (UL)	Clinton B. Fisk (P)	1892 Grover Clevlnd (D)	Benjamin Harrisn (R)	James B. Weavr (PE)	Unknown	John Bidwell (P)	1896 William J. Bryan (D)	William J. Bryan (PE)	William McKinly (R)	John McA. Palmer(ND)	Joshua Levring (P)
Anderson	1,994	1,649	0	1	1,635	1,368	179	18	1,703	840	899	0	5	2,723	365	1,956	0	3
Andrews	0	0	0	0	0	0	0	0	0	0	0	0	0	0	0	0	0	0
Angelina	951	57	0	0	1,050	82	95	7	841	53	549	69	7	1,318	559	344	0	7
Aransas	156	26	0	0	172	34	0	0	252	91	15	0	1	309	14	160	8	1
Archer	84	38	0	5	109	52	2	4	416	0	79	39	13	0	0	0	0	0
Armstrong	0	0	0	0	0	0	0	0	243	4	42	4	3	128	62	8	0	0
Atascosa	710	40	4	0	645	4	0	9	536	2	547	0	0	1,004	286	96	3	6
Austin	1,349	1,566	0	6	2,049	1,132	40	13	2,012	904	36	0	0	1,545	118	2,183	83	0
Bailey	0	0	0	0	0	0	0	0	0	0	0	0	0	0	0	0	0	0
Bandera	464	88	0	0	461	212	0	0	277	50	290	0	1	478	150	152	1	0
Bastrop	1,724	1,581	0	6	2,079	1,408	143	0	1,435	1,267	1,085	0	12	1,732	975	2,013	10	41
Baylor	296	5	0	7	238	1	0	2	460	30	113	0	2	398	26	72	2	2
Bee	228	13	0	3	422	84	0	7	760	89	21	0	5	1,202	116	228	11	0
Bell	4,480	471	0	76	4,596	466	491	64	4,317	510	0	0	34	5,433	1,628	1,735	114	0
Bexar	3,965	2,636	41	4	4,335	2,809	9	17	4,883	1,234	801	386	48	5,870	297	4,989	162	29
Blanco	605	217	0	21	613	156	35	8	509	30	382	18	0	414	243	241	55	2
Borden	0	0	0	0	0	0	0	0	62	0	60	0	0	81	19	8	0	0
Bosque	1,830	172	139	6	1,864	193	319	26	1,688	191	816	9	2	1,737	717	875	30	3
Bowie	1,256	871	0	14	2,110	1,297	39	0	1,664	852	1,138	0	16	2,108	503	1,922	20	9
Brazoria	430	1,128	0	0	0	0	0	0	599	1,229	97	0	10	1,260	103	1,564	9	8
Brazos	1,474	1,349	0	5	1,469	1,457	145	15	1,403	1,207	373	0	0	1,636	274	2,003	0	0
Brewster	0	0	0	0	223	51	0	0	218	15	0	0	0	219	1	79	0	0
Briscoe	0	0	0	0	0	0	0	0	98	0	0	1	0	93	82	2	0	0
Brooks	0	0	0	0	0	0	0	0	0	0	0	0	0	0	0	0	0	0
Brown	1,636	62	0	85	1,198	38	440	5	1,486	110	1,001	0	14	1,753	736	328	12	23
Burleson	1,080	958	0	56	1,212	1,039	118	28	1,083	685	652	0	6	1,628	168	1,605	10	4
Burnet	1,079	70	25	101	1,222	140	0	117	1,173	87	740	0	22	1,210	435	268	8	1
Caldwell	1,463	790	0	7	1,491	741	272	169	1,653	390	1,018	2	15	1,928	724	778	38	16
Calhoun	179	115	0	0	119	47	0	0	158	45	0	5	0	275	21	89	0	2
Callahan	839	23	0	0	619	58	100	0	707	58	479	0	15	899	409	123	13	0
Cameron	1,889	1,271	0	0	1,432	424	0	0	1,971	995	0	0	0	1,732	0	1,374	0	0
Camp	604	543	0	0	597	559	59	17	444	576	259	0	2	536	0	825	12	0
Carson	0	0	0	0	58	16	0	0	134	11	0	3	0	97	6	7	0	0
Cass	2,144	1,113	0	0	2,034	1,070	246	14	1,580	549	1,764	25	0	1,658	743	1,731	0	5
Castro	0	0	0	0	0	0	0	0	84	5	47	0	0	80	0	8	0	0
Chambers	299	117	0	0	267	136	7	0	241	31	110	25	2	325	93	201	15	0
Cherokee	2,130	877	0	32	2,394	1,077	40	31	1,926	715	1,240	0	15	1,995	352	1,610	60	14
Childress	0	0	0	0	80	0	0	0	380	22	63	0	0	300	35	27	10	0
Clay	820	197	0	22	718	114	158	10	1,059	179	516	0	23	1,145	333	237	27	5
Cochran	0	0	0	0	0	0	0	0	0	0	0	0	0	0	0	0	0	0
Coke	0	0	0	0	0	0	0	0	197	0	254	0	0	292	180	33	0	8
Coleman	715	10	0	2	895	38	6	1	902	49	460	0	5	1,003	400	159	31	5
Collin	4,823	620	122	128	5,647	556	467	125	4,988	976	2,081	1	47	6,161	1,430	1,936	167	46
Collingsworth	0	0	0	0	0	0	0	0	141	8	36	0	3	143	53	3	4	0
Colorado	1,359	1,700	0	0	1,855	1,629	154	3	1,369	1,169	429	35	1	1,598	340	2,052	7	0
Comal	453	516	0	0	692	435	0	0	680	299	35	11	15	252	16	1,083	14	0
Comanche	1,826	90	4	4	1,327	46	846	0	1,482	51	1,613	6	0	1,361	1,179	158	8	10
Concho	253	49	0	0	193	46	0	0	151	28	52	0	0	40	2	17	8	1
Cooke	3,638	500	0	13	3,354	594	282	85	2,806	391	1,026	0	25	3,502	875	828	41	15
Coryell	2,419	74	0	0	1,700	78	742	21	1,848	126	1,160	13	9	2,229	1,255	488	56	5
Cottle	0	0	0	0	0	0	0	0	69	0	7	2	0	104	12	5	0	0
Crane	0	0	0	0	0	0	0	0	0	0	0	0	0	0	0	0	0	0
Crockett	0	0	0	0	0	0	0	0	178	0	1	15	0	160	0	215	0	0
Crosby	0	0	0	0	223	0	0	15	141	5	12	0	7	99	5	4	3	0
Culberson	0	0	0	0	0	0	0	0	0	0	0	0	0	0	0	0	0	0
Dallam	0	0	0	0	0	0	0	0	14	0	0	0	0	36	0	7	0	0
Dallas	6,066	2,221	73	160	7,059	3,029	679	223	7,858	1,975	1,407	249	147	9,203	863	5,657	379	147
Dawson	0	0	0	0	0	0	0	0	0	0	0	0	0	0	0	0	0	0
Deaf Smith	0	0	0	0	0	0	0	0	101	0	10	1	0	100	8	3	0	0
Delta	987	121	88	11	1,475	163	0	70	753	124	1,053	3	14	961	718	307	0	3
Denton	3,073	527	180	163	2,709	509	476	81	2,894	0	714	126	60	3,944	489	949	96	21
DeWitt	916	765	0	1	1,114	841	84	16	1,311	497	768	0	5	1,775	292	1,777	15	4
Dickens	0	0	0	0	0	0	0	0	91	3	17	0	0	83	13	12	5	0
Dimmit	207	33	0	0	146	49	0	0	0	0	49	0	0	78	73	65	0	0
Donley	125	12	0	0	273	52	9	4	227	50	60	0	4	196	84	66	10	5

Table 7: Presidential Races

County	1884				1888				1892					1896				
	Grover Clevlnd (D)	James G. Blaine (R)	Benjamin F. Butler(GB)	John P. St. John(P)	Grover Clevlnd (D)	Benjamin Harrison (R)	Alson J. Streetr (UL)	Clinton B. Fisk (P)	Grover Clevlnd (D)	Benjamin Harrisn (R)	James B. Weavr (PE)	Unknown	John Bidwell (P)	William J. Bryan (D)	William J. Bryan (PE)	William McKinly (R)	John McA. Palmer(ND)	Joshua Levring (P)
Duval	363	128	0	0	369	371	0	0	554	63	0	3	0	421	0	790	0	0
Eastland	1,202	73	147	2	1,163	74	223	7	1,310	91	890	0	36	1,591	985	237	36	15
Ector	0	0	0	0	0	0	0	0	53	17	2	0	0	68	0	8	0	0
Edwards	65	2	0	0	223	80	0	0	248	31	106	0	0	339	39	130	0	0
Ellis	4,390	709	0	52	4,763	732	361	174	4,785	761	1,317	30	52	6,501	1,989	1,763	231	61
El Paso	1,167	805	0	0	1,418	1,028	19	7	1,737	760	55	31	3	2,307	0	1,244	69	0
Erath	2,060	52	345	112	1,806	36	1,006	29	2,125	214	1,912	0	38	2,460	1,805	924	21	29
Falls	2,173	1,424	0	6	1,892	1,299	510	42	2,295	1,290	835	5	18	3,185	437	2,734	74	0
Fannin	3,800	919	0	83	5,114	1,175	485	63	4,650	1,172	2,148	0	24	5,702	1,494	2,329	76	14
Fayette	2,723	2,063	0	3	3,279	1,685	179	28	3,408	1,690	556	0	2	2,597	505	3,473	36	9
Fisher	0	0	0	0	213	1	0	1	313	1	228	0	1	303	151	44	0	9
Floyd	0	0	0	0	0	0	0	0	220	5	93	1	0	198	83	18	0	1
Foard	0	0	0	0	0	0	0	0	167	5	137	1	1	145	113	42	4	0
Fort Bend	317	1,588	0	0	552	1,971	0	0	390	524	41	0	0	847	45	2,228	11	0
Franklin	938	37	0	27	979	58	146	1	285	25	290	0	0	973	391	76	0	3
Freestone	1,562	994	0	0	1,769	1,088	0	2	1,301	774	597	0	4	1,509	521	1,345	29	0
Frio	288	69	0	2	342	76	0	2	300	46	290	0	1	620	53	197	8	0
Gaines	0	0	0	0	0	0	0	0	0	1,713	0	0	0	0	0	0	0	0
Galveston	4,262	2,081	24	0	3,837	2,178	76	11	4,361	0	174	85	39	4,406	187	4,613	199	36
Garza	0	0	0	0	0	0	0	0	0	0	0	0	0	0	0	0	0	0
Gillespie	469	479	0	0	759	392	0	0	618	351	377	21	2	349	109	1,064	14	0
Glasscock	0	0	0	0	0	0	0	0	0	0	0	0	0	38	5	49	0	0
Goliad	527	332	0	0	467	430	0	15	453	286	422	0	0	566	241	637	1	0
Gonzales	1,893	882	0	30	2,037	689	459	34	1,576	204	1,772	0	10	2,292	1,522	644	38	0
Gray	0	0	0	0	0	0	0	0	0	0	0	136	0	0	0	0	0	0
Grayson	5,664	2,155	320	219	5,822	2,297	364	107	6,542	2,074	1,123	0	69	7,743	1,158	3,354	104	29
Gregg	754	867	0	27	633	471	262	6	691	640	252	0	9	658	193	881	0	3
Grimes	1,677	1,847	0	3	0	0	0	0	1,811	1,337	375	0	1	1,752	715	2,017	48	0
Guadalupe	1,235	998	0	0	1,346	989	200	0	1,663	391	549	300	2	1,199	111	2,229	56	2
Hale	0	0	0	0	81	0	0	0	0	0	39	0	0	220	55	23	0	0
Hall	0	0	0	0	0	0	0	0	0	0	0	0	0	261	22	23	0	0
Hamilton	1,420	25	1	15	1,179	8	234	14	998	46	800	6	20	1,181	773	353	18	20
Hansford	0	0	0	0	0	0	0	0	16	10	2	0	0	15	1	17	0	0
Hardeman	0	0	0	0	259	4	16	6	602	38	51	1	6	480	27	49	11	2
Hardin	324	52	0	0	352	160	185	0	446	189	154	0	0	660	62	244	1	0
Harris	3,501	3,053	0	4	3,571	2,817	216	18	4,493	1,323	91	774	20	6,103	72	5,766	86	34
Harrison	1,153	1,588	0	29	1,937	786	0	0	1,047	1,440	103	15	2	2,076	54	1,720	11	26
Hartley	0	0	0	0	0	0	0	0	111	2	15	0	3	91	6	19	1	0
Haskell	0	0	0	0	179	0	0	0	346	10	33	0	0	275	41	16	0	2
Hays	1,191	401	0	35	1,304	393	155	39	1,349	291	493	0	67	1,609	204	692	76	15
Hemphill	0	0	0	0	141	50	0	0	116	34	0	0	0	111	3	39	8	0
Henderson	1,305	406	70	20	1,188	288	705	3	1,059	307	765	0	7	1,665	881	664	7	1
Hidalgo	318	1	0	0	513	45	0	0	678	81	0	0	0	1,083	0	149	0	0
Hill	3,611	315	97	5	3,389	367	923	147	3,706	406	1,541	10	92	4,948	2,177	1,185	122	58
Hockley	0	0	0	0	0	0	0	0	0	0	0	0	0	0	0	0	0	0
Hood	1,106	22	1	121	958	12	65	85	802	16	545	57	25	0	0	0	0	0
Hopkins	2,114	382	61	11	3,080	453	41	253	1,988	344	1,586	0	62	2,424	517	1,472	56	86
Houston	1,759	1,244	0	0	1,728	1,272	13	6	1,459	601	1,410	0	10	2,419	866	1,296	26	6
Howard	223	87	0	0	187	81	17	0	351	0	131	23	4	267	68	110	0	0
Hudspeth	0	0	0	0	0	0	0	0	0	0	0	0	0	0	0	0	0	0
Hunt	3,661	392	0	2	4,369	552	455	134	4,146	756	1,624	3	49	5,328	986	1,827	52	70
Hutchinson	0	0	0	0	0	0	0	0	0	0	0	0	0	0	0	0	0	0
Irion	0	0	0	0	0	0	0	0	117	6	56	0	1	157	0	45	0	0
Jack	1,266	169	0	69	800	136	336	5	809	48	842	71	29	1,004	714	223	9	16
Jackson	258	271	0	0	312	304	0	0	232	300	76	0	0	418	188	458	10	0
Jasper	553	246	0	0	511	257	8	2	407	97	319	113	5	573	252	366	0	11
Jeff Davis	0	0	0	0	152	206	0	0	103	110	0	0	0	48	0	102	6	0
Jefferson	583	319	0	0	482	361	100	0	661	534	57	6	17	1,038	123	941	0	8
Jim Hogg	0	0	0	0	0	0	0	0	0	0	0	0	0	0	0	0	0	0
Jim Wells	0	0	0	0	0	0	0	0	0	0	0	0	0	0	0	0	0	0
Johnson	3,139	171	189	86	2,966	114	1,050	116	2,878	197	1,456	36	25	3,736	1,628	869	61	12
Jones	312	10	0	13	365	16	42	5	494	9	410	0	3	536	360	44	6	0
Karnes	348	70	0	0	444	39	22	1	458	121	0	0	1	840	529	389	3	0
Kaufman	3,349	564	90	81	3,701	676	296	85	3,133	759	471	2	22	3,734	0	0	47	17
Kendall	184	398	0	0	251	446	0	0	211	224	207	12	0	216	51	515	6	0

Table 7: Presidential Races

| County | General Elections, 1884-1896 | | | | | | | | | | | | | | | | | |
| | 1884 | | | | 1888 | | | | 1892 | | | | | 1896 | | | | |
	Grover Clevlnd (D)	James G. Blaine (R)	Benjamin F. Butler(GB)	John P. St. John(P)	Grover Clevlnd (D)	Benjamin Harrison (R)	Alson J. Streeter (UL)	Clinton B. Fisk (P)	Grover Clevlnd (D)	Benjamin Harrisn (R)	James B. Weavr (PE)	Unknown	John Bidwell (P)	William J. Bryan (D)	William J. Bryan (PE)	William McKinly (R)	John McA. Palmer(ND)	Joshua Levring (P)
Kenedy	0	0	0	0	0	0	0	0	0	0	0	0	0	0	0	0	0	0
Kent	0	0	0	0	0	0	0	0	0	0	0	0	0	92	38	5	0	0
Kerr	370	146	0	0	331	211	84	0	452	108	327	0	7	485	108	393	2	0
Kimble	284	17	0	0	324	10	0	10	217	47	202	0	0	325	0	98	0	0
King	0	0	0	0	0	0	0	0	76	0	5	0	0	88	0	1	0	0
Kinney	438	295	0	0	193	313	0	0	356	236	36	0	0	149	0	467	2	0
Kleberg	0	0	0	0	0	0	0	0	0	0	0	0	0	0	0	0	0	0
Knox	0	0	0	0	157	0	0	0	282	1	54	0	0	237	55	18	2	0
Lamar	3,465	1,272	125	63	3,667	1,537	129	68	4,322	1,412	996	129	8	4,621	1,350	2,191	143	0
Lamb	0	0	0	0	0	0	0	0	0	0	0	0	0	0	0	0	0	0
Lampasas	1,150	79	80	160	837	167	145	153	582	78	505	0	18	677	473	290	13	16
La Salle	300	72	0	0	0	0	0	0	302	85	17	54	0	243	0	260	0	0
Lavaca	1,607	502	0	0	2,451	564	1	10	2,016	357	974	0	1	2,099	1,206	1,476	26	2
Lee	1,039	769	0	29	1,401	493	130	5	1,038	391	685	0	2	960	267	1,328	69	9
Leon	1,580	831	0	0	1,454	761	113	7	1,241	638	663	0	0	1,518	537	1,012	8	1
Liberty	476	369	0	0	373	291	198	0	332	283	204	60	6	700	190	464	0	3
Limestone	2,186	446	308	18	2,116	571	707	98	2,365	576	1,052	0	45	3,153	1,787	0	82	37
Lipscomb	0	0	0	0	132	76	3	1	100	57	3	0	1	98	2	30	0	0
Live Oak	300	8	0	1	322	0	0	3	218	15	162	0	2	417	89	50	1	0
Llano	985	5	0	59	905	42	0	0	861	12	620	65	16	858	297	149	1	13
Loving	0	0	0	0	0	0	0	0	0	0	0	0	0	0	0	0	0	0
Lubbock	0	0	0	0	0	0	0	0	84	5	13	0	3	87	6	7	2	1
Lynn	0	0	0	0	0	0	0	0	0	0	0	0	0	0	0	0	0	0
McCulloch	387	19	0	3	453	78	1	0	411	12	246	4	1	384	180	132	0	0
McLennan	3,170	1,410	0	112	4,023	1,789	951	253	5,105	1,769	885	76	111	6,511	873	4,126	158	86
McMullen	157	21	0	0	177	4	13	0	148	7	44	0	1	141	7	53	3	0
Madison	877	283	0	0	772	226	341	0	617	0	530	77	0	790	622	298	12	0
Marion	534	1,265	0	4	0	0	0	0	597	1,181	249	2	0	611	93	1,409	0	0
Martin	0	0	0	0	97	58	0	0	123	14	4	0	0	97	0	22	0	0
Mason	623	141	0	9	617	184	0	3	470	154	344	0	1	496	222	293	5	0
Matagorda	248	476	0	0	250	505	0	0	192	470	76	0	0	449	0	561	3	0
Maverick	184	239	0	0	334	382	0	0	491	234	11	0	0	517	1	319	4	0
Medina	440	371	0	0	702	330	0	1	749	0	464	82	1	792	84	580	0	1
Menard	201	43	0	0	251	26	0	0	231	19	67	0	0	294	55	124	0	0
Midland	0	0	0	0	120	32	8	8	175	21	118	0	3	272	17	45	0	3
Milam	2,828	916	0	147	2,733	796	467	33	2,140	824	1,917	0	2	369	984	1,902	51	22
Mills	0	0	0	0	638	49	61	25	559	27	571	0	8	604	537	180	0	1
Mitchell	394	209	0	22	279	96	30	10	428	109	63	0	1	338	30	147	7	5
Montague	2,650	80	0	13	0	0	0	0	2,632	123	959	0	33	3,547	1,063	375	51	25
Montgomery	1,030	980	0	5	1,047	888	168	33	975	602	115	0	0	1,489	454	933	1	0
Moore	0	0	0	0	0	0	0	0	35	2	0	2	0	24	12	3	0	0
Morris	579	395	0	0	760	486	15	0	614	101	532	0	2	0	0	0	0	0
Motley	0	0	0	0	0	0	0	0	135	11	16	0	0	134	23	7	0	0
Nacogdoches	1,675	505	0	0	2,063	596	5	4	1,263	280	1,333	0	0	1,763	1,128	760	37	11
Navarro	3,468	1,174	35	4	3,865	1,320	574	574	2,867	929	2,224	5	43	3,885	2,103	2,113	136	64
Newton	558	189	0	0	527	87	0	6	464	133	133	0	1	508	117	345	0	15
Nolan	351	33	0	5	216	7	0	4	217	3	126	2	2	263	93	25	2	0
Nueces	975	219	0	0	1,091	347	0	0	1,129	273	92	0	0	1,524	10	554	16	0
Ochiltree	0	0	0	0	0	0	0	0	36	9	0	0	0	28	1	9	0	0
Oldham	0	0	0	0	247	24	170	0	64	0	0	0	0	69	6	2	1	0
Orange	540	157	0	0	0	0	0	0	553	65	189	48	5	795	60	426	3	7
Palo Pinto	1,211	23	0	0	925	0	0	0	947	69	673	0	3	1,154	728	196	10	3
Panola	1,621	409	0	0	1,646	747	60	0	1,317	349	498	0	0	2,219	376	291	0	20
Parker	2,627	266	272	126	2,405	363	237	97	2,590	278	1,392	51	75	3,108	1,330	638	33	0
Parmer	0	0	0	0	0	0	0	0	0	0	0	0	0	0	0	0	0	0
Pecos	227	70	0	0	156	17	0	0	275	50	2	6	0	196	1	60	0	0
Polk	926	536	0	0	989	625	207	0	870	445	760	1	0	1,272	624	587	15	2
Potter	0	0	0	0	69	3	0	0	270	38	37	0	0	228	71	52	5	0
Presidio	461	243	0	0	376	80	0	0	852	211	0	0	0	517	0	418	4	0
Rains	542	43	0	0	490	0	400	7	353	70	448	0	0	581	247	215	0	0
Randall	0	0	0	0	0	0	0	0	64	5	18	0	0	94	30	1	1	0
Reagan	0	0	0	0	0	0	0	0	0	0	0	0	0	0	0	0	0	0
Real	0	0	0	0	0	0	0	0	0	0	0	0	0	0	0	0	0	0
Red River	1,936	1,095	0	30	2,576	1,285	0	26	2,051	962	1,167	9	11	2,900	731	1,560	16	0
Reeves	0	0	0	0	308	14	0	0	398	33	39	0	0	605	12	45	0	0

Table 7: Presidential Races

General Elections, 1884-1896

Year	1884				1888				1892					1896				
County	Grover Clevlnd (D)	James G. Blaine (R)	Benjamin F. Butler(GB)	John P. St. John(P)	Grover Clevlnd (D)	Benjamin Harrison (R)	Alson J. Streetr (UL)	Clinton B. Fisk (P)	Grover Clevlnd (D)	Benjamin Harrisn (R)	James B. Weavr (PE)	Unknown	John Bidwell (P)	William J. Bryan (D)	William J. Bryan (PE)	William McKinly (R)	John McA. Palmer(ND)	Joshua Levring (P)
Refugio	90	37	0	0	161	68	0	0	142	29	21	0	0	173	6	147	9	0
Roberts	0	0	0	0	0	0	0	0	58	21	0	0	0	123	15	19	0	0
Robertson	2,072	2,078	0	0	1,918	2,198	298	109	1,665	2,705	518	0	28	2,447	422	2,660	13	5
Rockwall	692	32	0	0	1,020	41	29	39	839	19	318	0	44	1,144	139	267	52	36
Runnels	302	6	0	0	0	0	0	0	554	52	133	0	0	418	197	109	7	5
Rusk	2,097	1,440	0	0	2,216	1,477	8	18	1,805	1,305	385	0	1	2,181	473	1,674	78	1
Sabine	545	87	0	0	680	0	0	0	357	0	583	0	2	378	504	32	0	7
San Augustine	612	351	0	0	802	0	1	0	425	111	677	0	1	657	592	265	10	0
San Jacinto	391	606	22	0	369	594	223	0	291	406	202	123	6	710	215	766	0	0
San Patricio	124	13	0	0	149	0	0	0	486	54	60	0	0	0	0	0	0	0
San Saba	934	96	0	8	783	96	18	12	653	51	547	0	0	711	471	118	14	1
Schleicher	0	0	0	0	0	0	0	0	0	0	0	0	0	0	0	0	0	0
Scurry	110	16	0	2	117	2	14	7	302	8	182	0	0	177	156	39	1	6
Shackelford	387	108	0	1	245	86	40	0	326	68	127	0	6	286	107	117	9	0
Shelby	1,520	35	0	2	1,927	195	22	14	1,465	155	547	28	1	2,164	882	186	1	35
Sherman	0	0	0	0	0	0	0	0	10	6	3	1	2	6	0	8	0	0
Smith	2,649	1,926	50	1	2,714	1,977	207	19	2,827	1,515	881	0	9	3,395	622	2,606	36	8
Somervell	471	0	27	41	292	0	144	0	258	3	301	0	0	390	312	23	0	2
Starr	385	254	0	0	474	0	0	0	689	952	0	0	0	1,035	0	732	0	0
Stephens	775	7	0	11	676	0	82	0	667	2	300	0	2	672	490	13	29	0
Sterling	0	0	0	0	0	0	0	0	165	4	77	2	0	113	85	22	0	85
Stonewall	0	0	0	0	0	0	0	0	144	0	35	0	0	0	0	0	0	0
Sutton	0	0	0	0	0	0	0	0	177	21	43	0	0	175	0	186	4	2
Swisher	0	0	0	0	0	0	0	0	150	0	64	4	0	115	78	15	1	1
Tarrant	5,018	1,270	5	201	4,129	1,068	1,676	69	4,746	1,153	1,174	145	51	6,882	1,093	2,294	136	37
Taylor	853	123	0	10	656	86	51	33	943	125	465	12	13	868	458	247	16	5
Terrell	0	0	0	0	0	0	0	0	0	0	0	0	0	0	0	0	0	0
Terry	0	0	0	0	0	0	0	0	0	0	0	0	0	0	0	0	0	0
Throckmorton	226	19	0	0	135	34	0	2	192	15	17	33	0	0	0	0	0	0
Titus	997	203	0	0	1,162	237	139	0	771	118	664	0	12	1,129	742	345	0	0
Tom Green	757	444	15	0	878	418	0	0	0	0	0	0	0	740	37	464	18	37
Travis	3,119	2,532	55	8	3,178	2,735	108	63	3,631	1,929	898	35	23	3,733	292	4,133	180	65
Trinity	916	228	0	0	992	98	35	1	6,443	202	602	0	1	762	508	447	3	0
Tyler	978	326	0	1	957	450	823	0	1,218	426	338	11	0	1,273	278	478	0	0
Upshur	0	0	0	0	1,237	510	294	31	1,119	229	795	0	13	1,466	452	822	6	1
Upton	0	0	0	0	0	0	0	0	0	0	0	0	0	0	0	0	0	0
Uvalde	547	133	0	1	510	147	0	2	706	86	160	0	2	535	2	515	4	0
Val Verde	0	0	0	0	308	198	0	0	419	334	6	0	0	408	0	200	0	0
Van Zandt	3,258	346	0	115	2,001	0	952	16	1,672	104	1,457	11	3	2,392	1,230	687	9	35
Victoria	654	775	0	0	723	844	0	2	916	742	50	0	0	844	39	1,332	41	0
Walker	898	1,031	0	0	722	332	865	0	838	477	942	0	2	1,205	256	1,057	17	0
Waller	820	1,187	0	0	787	1,349	4	1	573	814	480	0	2	1,107	221	1,491	0	1
Ward	0	0	0	0	0	0	0	0	59	12	7	0	1	92	9	71	0	0
Washington	2,351	3,119	5	37	2,595	2,241	0	12	2,359	1,797	73	69	5	1,654	40	4,198	70	3
Webb	1,376	391	0	0	765	138	0	0	1,551	233	0	0	0	1,183	1	2,067	3	0
Wharton	164	756	0	0	332	1,153	0	0	283	784	0	0	0	844	46	1,166	0	0
Wheeler	347	49	0	4	357	90	0	0	141	39	1	0	0	77	4	23	0	0
Wichita	381	126	0	2	339	99	0	1	480	234	102	0	20	719	80	165	3	5
Wilbarger	218	23	0	0	286	101	42	5	1,090	115	256	0	16	743	129	137	9	14
Willacy	0	0	0	0	0	0	0	0	0	0	0	0	0	0	0	0	0	0
Williamson	2,635	726	0	113	2,682	815	230	105	3,176	781	1,662	37	73	3,919	1,164	2,151	4	100
Wilson	1,139	251	0	0	1,479	63	225	12	963	90	1,137	0	0	1,716	586	189	15	2
Winkler	0	0	0	0	0	0	0	0	0	0	0	0	0	0	0	0	0	0
Wise	3,568	375	168	90	2,318	263	568	37	2,605	304	1,360	0	41	3,581	1,446	540	16	14
Wood	1,709	444	159	4	1,543	447	886	0	1,401	108	545	45	6	1,750	816	778	3	4
Yoakum	0	0	0	0	0	0	0	0	0	0	0	0	0	0	0	0	0	0
Young	764	77	0	1	648	53	49	15	637	42	256	142	3	809	305	99	10	1
Zapata	66	103	0	0	196	0	0	0	0	0	0	0	0	14	0	250	0	0
Zavala	143	2	0	0	163	12	0	0	146	3	16	0	0	119	18	20	4	0
Other	0	0	0	0	265	16	75	1	834	35	682	0	0	0	0	0	0	0
Official	225,309		3,321		234,883		29,459		239,148		99,688		2,165	78,926			4,853	
Totals		93,141		3,534		88,422		4,749		77,478			3,968		234,298	158,863		1,722
Unofficial	225,883		3,347		232,106		29,177		244,346		97,303		2,199	77,740			4,991	
Totals		92,743		3,459		88,504		4,738		74,572			4,161		285,263	162,766		1,911

Table 8: Presidential Races

General Elections, 1900-1924																
Year	1900		1904		1908		1912		1916			1920		1924		
County	William J. Bryan (D)	William McKinly (R)	Alton B. Parker (D)	Theodore Roosvit (R)	William J. Bryan (D)	William H. Taft (R)	Woodrow Wilson (D)	William H. Taft (R)	Woodrow Wilson (D)	Charles E. Hughes (R)	Allan L. Benson (S)	James M. Cox (D)	Warren G. Harding (R)	John W. Davis (D)	Calvin Coolidge (R)	Robert M. LaFlitt (PR)
Anderson	2,462	1,471	1,708	924	1,601	697	1,737	444	1,984	501	187	2,355	323	374	562	255
Andrews	0	0	0	0	0	0	97	1	71	0	0	74	9	60	7	4
Angelina	1,381	456	940	226	1,089	197	1,071	45	1,344	75	335	1,661	205	3,914	333	172
Aransas	205	113	153	50	193	33	188	7	179	24	6	146	49	195	75	8
Archer	465	85	323	74	331	63	458	25	527	104	34	449	169	883	146	88
Armstrong	197	41	216	17	252	32	274	32	353	43	7	405	87	426	106	24
Atascosa	836	291	704	104	614	142	593	34	635	119	44	531	218	869	303	217
Austin	1,864	1,094	1,392	600	1,394	572	1,168	244	960	673	10	538	568	2,600	457	569
Bailey	0	0	0	0	0	0	0	0	0	0	0	0	0	166	63	21
Bandera	551	348	536	128	449	284	413	158	537	168	44	311	249	426	442	57
Bastrop	2,194	1,828	1,035	70	1,225	522	1,022	216	1,335	550	21	1,088	484	2,711	494	247
Baylor	471	88	446	32	600	53	553	15	711	47	74	632	145	1,012	135	16
Bee	1,051	301	655	149	533	137	476	35	584	152	29	545	283	988	944	146
Bell	4,584	1,211	2,507	287	3,067	480	3,036	128	3,615	356	162	3,595	483	7,272	1,632	552
Bexar	5,272	3,762	3,589	1,574	3,890	3,549	4,863	1,007	7,008	5,483	186	6,926	9,131	10,841	9,898	3,963
Blanco	524	385	488	215	438	259	447	127	628	235	19	426	378	586	317	175
Borden	130	30	187	5	135	5	128	1	84	1	3	89	4	86	10	0
Bosque	1,729	609	1,091	361	1,394	268	1,221	64	1,561	179	73	1,556	569	2,534	403	80
Bowie	0	0	1,549	1,010	1,676	705	1,542	317	1,941	414	273	2,396	1,032	3,455	740	269
Brazoria	967	165	432	341	567	405	747	263	1,033	581	80	1,184	1,234	1,761	1,114	119
Brazos	1,786	1,616	1,022	281	876	138	763	142	1,027	273	3	1,281	277	0	0	0
Brewster	256	198	252	63	283	34	333	30	207	43	7	210	125	366	113	21
Briscoe	217	31	217	31	117	7	148	2	260	4	22	262	39	397	53	26
Brooks	0	0	0	0	0	0	402	13	101	63	1	127	37	205	59	4
Brown	1,685	632	712	312	1,557	346	1,466	115	1,986	181	104	1,708	397	3,467	396	100
Burleson	1,601	1,351	909	461	1,201	365	992	228	1,208	262	23	981	142	2,496	224	24
Burnet	1,283	522	764	814	857	270	624	85	913	115	23	795	241	1,723	277	58
Caldwell	2,167	909	1,970	817	1,227	197	1,068	56	1,216	225	15	1,240	269	2,194	399	204
Calhoun	0	0	72	16	219	71	356	36	388	84	64	363	95	686	181	35
Callahan	820	288	570	112	866	102	783	45	959	74	83	804	213	1,614	244	88
Cameron	1,564	1,562	1,089	74	1,217	971	2,146	149	1,260	420	25	920	910	2,225	1,266	176
Camp	591	687	509	302	569	324	492	155	721	206	35	661	156	1,186	187	43
Carson	103	22	135	19	159	41	199	19	326	78	7	428	242	611	306	35
Cass	1,373	1,714	1,136	940	1,551	996	1,284	402	1,505	707	124	1,563	1,446	2,125	997	89
Castro	116	24	172	21	110	8	171	18	176	69	5	158	113	219	68	82
Chambers	318	207	280	126	323	275	219	4	239	101	43	240	278	315	239	11
Cherokee	1,930	1,528	1,591	446	1,575	211	1,684	145	2,002	241	245	2,233	478	4,384	666	90
Childress	380	54	393	35	595	92	714	34	948	31	77	1,206	162	1,117	178	71
Clay	1,199	271	599	119	1,115	242	1,005	54	1,324	177	54	1,324	403	1,402	318	113
Cochran	0	0	0	0	0	0	0	0	0	0	0	0	0	59	9	4
Coke	0	0	395	57	356	56	301	7	484	29	42	444	57	673	80	13
Coleman	1,433	228	712	63	1,170	135	1,281	52	1,700	96	178	1,445	355	2,763	502	76
Collin	5,081	1,750	3,437	958	3,797	792	3,184	342	4,141	594	190	4,045	1,337	7,215	1,981	169
Collingsworth	201	13	250	14	398	26	415	14	589	31	54	640	307	731	234	23
Colorado	2,019	1,190	1,107	357	1,116	486	1,024	106	1,041	358	76	765	478	2,104	681	376
Comal	722	501	875	246	626	509	602	156	432	743	38	181	765	330	312	1,823
Comanche	2,204	586	1,609	294	2,236	292	1,659	68	1,494	148	301	1,633	930	276	456	114
Concho	206	75	280	58	228	36	326	16	418	36	53	405	151	668	90	23
Cooke	3,211	516	1,952	421	2,439	523	1,780	206	2,273	353	106	2,170	1,003	3,170	525	391
Coryell	2,178	10	1,235	26	1,653	201	1,270	66	1,802	188	72	1,542	444	2,890	429	70
Cottle	157	29	136	14	157	18	297	8	455	12	67	472	125	580	59	19
Crane	0	0	0	0	0	0	0	0	65	0	0	0	0	0	0	0
Crockett	170	173	124	136	65	13	53	5	0	16	5	89	80	0	0	0
Crosby	0	0	158	7	148	1	247	7	456	31	46	572	146	1,242	278	34
Culberson	0	0	0	0	0	0	0	0	124	2	1	40	8	93	15	9
Dallam	26	2	167	32	285	94	247	18	363	81	39	478	195	506	254	285
Dallas	8,253	3,405	5,933	1,321	7,329	2,067	7,925	590	13,410	2,554	184	14,390	4,983	30,207	8,618	1,012
Dawson	0	0	0	0	96	6	94	7	288	14	10	296	75	1,079	185	35
DeWitt	1,701	1,286	1,433	786	966	853	1,080	219	1,056	1,068	23	971	1,277	2,131	868	792
Deaf Smith	185	29	128	31	273	48	221	21	356	77	16	459	205	538	192	33
Delta	1,420	613	971	171	946	131	905	57	1,254	72	115	1,081	316	2,186	479	51
Denton	3,305	956	2,406	553	2,739	493	2,290	189	2,844	451	157	1,257	900	4,708	712	385
Dickens	192	6	195	21	195	28	279	11	389	15	39	433	109	849	161	10
Dimmit	144	114	136	78	151	101	292	131	193	74	0	231	108	289	180	24
Donley	325	122	344	47	410	36	388	11	636	42	54	766	206	903	273	68

Table 8: Presidential Races

General Elections, 1900-1924

County	1900		1904		1908		1912		1916			1920		1924		
	William J. Bryan (D)	William McKinly (R)	Alton B. Parker (D)	Theodore Roosvlt (R)	William J. Bryan (D)	William H. Taft (R)	Woodrow Wilson (D)	William H. Taft (R)	Woodrow Wilson (D)	Charles E. Hughes (R)	Allan L. Benson (S)	James M. Cox (D)	Warren G. Harding (R)	John W. Davis (D)	Calvin Coolidge (R)	Robert M. LaFlitt (PR)
Duval	338	481	161	219	692	605	917	0	597	37	3	387	86	0	0	0
Eastland	0	0	1,680	222	1,856	229	1,498	66	1,486	146	294	2,942	941	4,548	972	162
Ector	0	0	165	7	136	5	89	3	120	2	0	100	24	138	12	5
Edwards	268	257	245	175	208	232	133	114	299	73	5	201	297	204	346	14
El Paso	2,492	1,007	1,706	789	2,302	1,019	2,914	291	3,603	1,770	111	4,143	4,070	0	0	0
Ellis	5,659	1,095	3,563	395	4,413	594	3,484	293	4,718	324	74	4,081	819	7,678	1,220	142
Erath	2,880	1,169	1,290	941	2,074	504	1,569	156	2,024	184	287	1,914	358	3,396	406	152
Falls	2,968	2,541	2,200	1,641	1,791	503	1,663	353	2,037	729	232	1,878	585	2,817	440	191
Fannin	5,560	1,869	3,191	799	3,192	614	2,661	227	3,493	471	235	3,461	1,103	5,596	653	213
Fayette	3,546	2,043	2,777	1,240	2,247	1,235	2,016	461	1,902	1,212	40	932	1,121	3,851	1,450	1,154
Fisher	431	113	398	42	776	62	572	21	950	46	229	143	152	1,653	302	58
Floyd	265	50	224	50	292	16	381	22	600	48	78	841	167	1,197	166	29
Foard	232	69	257	23	302	38	429	18	475	41	88	491	101	585	95	35
Fort Bend	628	967	546	661	550	353	681	276	788	329	15	27	79	1,690	356	204
Franklin	0	0	616	82	650	72	573	19	684	62	42	0	0	1,157	118	61
Freestone	1,460	1,173	940	348	1,186	302	1,305	475	1,575	637	97	1,463	378	2,484	608	80
Frio	507	235	445	155	397	112	418	25	410	55	4	421	101	637	158	13
Gaines	0	0	0	0	93	7	68	0	80	0	4	134	9	342	37	62
Galveston	3,401	2,133	2,094	666	2,185	849	2,464	332	3,543	1,264	72	2,933	1,620	5,068	1,912	639
Garza	0	0	0	0	67	4	144	7	330	14	14	392	28	588	331	25
Gillespie	434	1,147	312	1,003	281	1,332	307	219	405	1,463	12	137	1,270	352	768	1,582
Glasscock	16	5	95	15	75	6	60	0	96	8	4	91	25	89	14	6
Goliad	727	685	595	436	397	644	500	425	605	548	59	448	512	733	438	162
Gonzales	2,489	1,282	1,499	600	1,441	609	1,326	318	1,675	649	51	1,299	748	2,499	463	328
Gray	0	0	135	12	338	82	272	13	482	69	35	529	251	0	0	0
Grayson	6,440	2,464	3,522	1,131	4,506	1,388	3,937	410	5,092	1,024	285	5,241	2,125	7,413	1,973	949
Gregg	737	970	595	428	565	273	590	129	820	159	25	1,050	257	1,286	177	208
Grimes	1,594	82	915	125	974	88	939	35	1,108	108	25	1,027	214	2,136	177	32
Guadalupe	1,605	1,844	1,091	1,460	1,044	1,621	1,126	1,070	830	1,812	7	560	1,990	831	1,657	1,601
Hale	280	46	379	33	406	41	554	26	908	80	43	1,279	351	1,446	507	88
Hall	324	10	174	13	508	56	774	24	925	49	88	922	194	1,060	229	64
Hamilton	1,239	532	1,050	374	1,123	222	992	67	1,231	201	46	1,075	422	2,035	202	90
Hansford	22	24	95	12	98	26	93	12	166	47	14	124	54	263	76	24
Hardeman	561	95	528	45	663	108	855	36	932	94	123	967	251	1,099	256	53
Hardin	578	333	767	241	809	234	979	101	1,279	158	92	999	202	1,416	645	117
Harris	5,527	2,524	4,131	1,383	5,074	1,722	6,422	726	10,131	3,009	433	14,808	7,725	20,648	8,953	2,878
Harrison	1,234	1,122	1,104	832	2,161	289	1,141	140	1,374	172	60	2,134	377	2,573	463	226
Hartley	110	17	179	23	150	30	115	16	161	30	1	144	81	156	61	26
Haskell	416	72	584	71	1,245	145	1,015	45	1,200	95	369	1,127	254	2,050	428	128
Hays	1,397	489	1,158	210	871	133	939	60	995	123	10	1,075	242	1,616	394	79
Hemphill	150	55	146	41	172	77	313	61	496	141	23	417	253	405	167	71
Henderson	1,627	919	643	11	1,143	255	1,370	137	1,790	268	354	1,684	538	3,819	405	80
Hidalgo	1,397	426	475	37	554	36	1,203	39	1,364	260	29	2,409	1,108	3,662	996	214
Hill	4,427	1,159	2,857	376	3,331	414	2,674	129	3,951	382	86	3,254	1,022	5,778	807	103
Hockley	0	0	0	0	0	0	0	0	0	0	0	0	0	69	20	5
Hood	1,086	366	559	147	945	162	674	38	693	64	84	697	175	1,074	122	60
Hopkins	2,516	1,097	1,762	262	2,184	271	1,999	146	2,568	218	231	2,548	837	4,156	557	121
Houston	1,913	1,297	1,641	924	1,310	493	1,458	342	1,730	373	155	1,475	385	2,692	457	38
Howard	351	103	301	21	504	52	3,530	22	747	30	99	703	107	1,101	186	161
Hudspeth	0	0	0	0	0	0	0	0	0	0	0	97	37	84	34	24
Hunt	4,691	1,229	3,600	613	3,806	518	3,410	225	4,242	424	155	4,397	880	6,828	836	146
Hutchinson	0	0	0	0	134	30	91	16	114	28	6	135	106	159	69	6
Irion	156	0	172	30	102	5	132	0	150	5	11	148	45	205	73	10
Jack	0	0	0	0	782	268	752	84	862	121	115	566	254	1,154	290	26
Jackson	440	334	320	161	298	139	325	35	403	123	63	562	355	758	354	57
Jasper	518	587	614	315	695	187	628	40	906	75	41	793	89	1,526	176	17
Jeff Davis	93	155	112	67	121	83	129	62	234	74	1	91	41	117	49	18
Jefferson	0	0	1,623	794	1,962	821	1,700	187	3,082	488	155	4,246	1,110	5,925	4,348	483
Jim Hogg	0	0	0	0	0	0	0	0	187	11	0	70	23	139	19	0
Jim Wells	0	0	0	0	0	0	241	24	335	100	35	304	168	654	213	125
Johnson	3,586	1,057	2,178	328	2,747	339	2,487	109	3,040	275	166	3,041	661	4,600	851	310
Jones	747	142	740	80	1,754	206	1,301	63	1,798	114	214	1,792	270	3,010	566	101
Karnes	993	203	1,006	144	631	170	710	66	889	238	5	642	481	1,727	531	235
Kaufman	0	0	2,272	330	2,205	387	2,043	250	2,780	427	172	3,070	573	5,574	884	74
Kendall	266	485	140	545	148	537	201	119	232	590	5	142	846	136	689	407

Table 8: Presidential Races

	General Elections, 1900-1924														
Year	1900		1904		1908		1912		1916			1920		1924		
County	William J. Bryan (D)	William McKinly (R)	Alton B. Parker (D)	Theodore Roosvit (R)	William J. Bryan (D)	William H. Taft (R)	Woodrow Wilson (D)	William H. Taft (R)	Woodrow Wilson (D)	Charles E. Hughes (R)	Allan L. Benson (S)	James M. Cox (D)	Warren G. Harding (R)	John W. Davis (D)	Calvin Coolidge (R)	Robert M. LaFlitt (PR)
Kenedy	0	0	0	0	0	0	0	0	0	0	0	0	0	67	7	1
Kent	169	29	126	4	194	17	135	7	212	2	25	214	45	386	80	8
Kerr	558	238	565	231	453	327	576	126	621	272	30	612	464	735	892	182
Kimble	288	158	335	125	181	60	133	19	223	13	13	299	150	465	223	19
King	119	6	102	0	69	1	77	2	47	3	0	157	0	83	4	0
Kinney	179	190	218	192	171	274	76	97	233	201	7	98	137	144	158	13
Kleberg	0	0	0	0	0	0	0	0	427	106	44	455	172	721	226	208
Knox	413	34	442	68	797	92	644	32	884	64	105	773	159	1,399	455	81
La Salle	180	323	97	171	328	224	339	21	340	40	96	252	53	458	73	10
Lamar	4,187	1,619	2,536	724	2,866	482	2,289	206	3,412	309	4	3,765	639	5,224	596	159
Lamb	0	0	0	0	13	5	52	6	150	14	31	264	136	356	121	30
Lampasas	848	439	713	209	746	296	517	66	848	113	3	778	227	1,596	228	22
Lavaca	2,868	966	2,463	491	1,674	866	1,438	267	1,784	936	241	1,249	100	3,290	746	1,235
Lee	1,184	1,125	977	395	820	509	687	134	571	836	82	712	322	1,561	271	452
Leon	1,680	1,062	990	372	861	351	856	191	979	335	162	1,124	220	2,004	311	79
Liberty	956	486	675	312	539	248	583	81	704	235	82	0	0	1,506	639	44
Limestone	3,143	1,114	1,636	213	1,773	247	1,667	153	2,188	225	107	2,165	408	4,868	523	43
Lipscomb	135	60	116	46	169	60	251	47	350	116	47	350	425	430	405	114
Live Oak	406	57	375	30	320	80	308	26	397	119	51	234	108	596	323	93
Llano	748	362	828	131	485	116	432	29	716	72	23	665	184	928	88	61
Loving	0	0	0	0	0	0	0	0	0	0	0	0	0	12	2	0
Lubbock	165	41	238	14	224	26	366	16	633	34	27	1,180	204	1,740	411	192
Lynn	0	0	133	8	258	15	122	6	331	15	8	538	76	1,131	313	57
Madison	953	500	534	178	540	123	379	37	730	120	41	650	63	1,592	146	5
Marion	390	789	273	486	594	414	339	85	445	166	1	430	392	620	397	84
Martin	83	11	172	24	234	27	125	4	125	14	22	136	33	353	92	7
Mason	602	339	370	118	429	322	472	150	386	157	32	304	294	384	171	163
Matagorda	347	259	328	90	590	167	712	107	748	252	79	992	968	1,353	893	128
Maverick	407	416	291	211	258	287	185	141	192	246	2	173	296	196	261	31
McCulloch	512	220	387	111	651	184	593	41	847	61	117	780	210	1,322	495	22
McLennan	4,868	1,988	3,677	694	3,778	741	3,836	296	4,979	940	122	4,975	1,656	7,882	2,384	455
McMullen	158	64	86	28	85	35	50	9	115	29	0	72	34	109	111	3
Medina	881	535	590	436	578	695	649	220	758	650	26	519	772	981	816	477
Menard	312	167	356	58	151	36	109	15	267	44	32	197	203	304	247	27
Midland	275	76	36	18	304	30	215	10	339	24	7	271	68	398	44	4
Milam	3,406	1,479	1,118	943	2,073	460	1,939	244	2,198	576	230	2,598	371	5,085	930	317
Mills	690	331	453	128	567	201	572	91	640	129	106	669	247	1,284	175	51
Mitchell	451	142	467	73	635	73	573	19	803	39	80	694	89	1,243	169	35
Montague	3,052	347	2,700	212	2,048	329	1,534	151	1,803	245	242	714	474	2,235	586	447
Montgomery	1,380	897	943	420	752	308	614	120	880	197	141	935	203	1,498	186	23
Moore	27	7	85	3	97	12	57	5	103	6	0	101	13	82	9	1
Morris	0	4	569	235	646	142	191	89	689	163	52	669	164	0	0	0
Motley	263	4	239	10	123	13	195	8	393	9	28	345	40	454	62	10
Nacogdoches	1,897	1,094	1,375	276	1,478	186	1,616	94	1,766	92	141	1,794	238	3,418	204	47
Navarro	4,062	1,911	2,510	439	2,879	618	2,585	165	3,527	294	100	3,328	820	6,401	996	77
Newton	769	350	469	318	357	94	278	11	493	34	23	420	58	689	145	21
Nolan	395	120	518	80	733	104	656	60	1,048	91	79	923	176	1,421	337	82
Nueces	1,140	461	575	152	831	253	910	85	1,830	404	142	1,246	381	0	0	0
Ochiltree	22	10	81	18	142	47	93	0	238	41	8	281	135	352	155	55
Oldham	82	21	65	13	40	15	92	22	138	42	0	139	52	187	71	14
Orange	842	393	604	190	534	119	553	26	758	92	0	1,055	179	1,515	509	39
Palo Pinto	1,366	341	971	160	1,483	268	1,234	68	1,431	124	282	1,645	342	1,926	473	232
Panola	1,764	678	1,178	345	1,242	266	1,207	82	1,228	125	71	1,086	268	2,088	119	26
Parker	2,571	552	1,833	518	2,061	314	1,700	135	1,797	173	240	1,765	496	2,391	438	150
Parmer	0	0	0	0	96	31	108	6	194	64	10	189	140	214	91	36
Pecos	0	0	231	64	154	100	256	76	394	96	2	386	394	440	192	30
Polk	1,137	888	503	55	627	243	615	41	918	107	113	810	255	1,838	272	31
Potter	331	97	119	0	803	158	800	41	1,288	166	99	1,374	358	2,393	831	586
Presidio	258	420	121	250	233	135	188	86	245	27	0	238	122	0	0	0
Rains	548	454	190	139	416	61	445	67	509	71	289	462	189	803	151	48
Randall	216	48	285	34	233	44	269	21	341	63	6	360	183	627	154	64
Reagan	0	0	0	0	52	3	34	0	242	14	25	49	4	187	300	10
Real	0	0	0	0	0	0	0	0	59	2	0	177	134	111	31	2
Red River	2,602	848	1,586	637	1,813	587	1,497	255	2,021	356	141	2,263	798	3,183	311	49
Reeves	559	46	320	20	316	24	278	8	346	43	5	457	91	387	96	29

Table 8: Presidential Races

General Elections, 1900-1924

Year	1900		1904		1908		1912		1916			1920		1924		
County	William J. Bryan (D)	William McKinly (R)	Alton B. Parker (D)	Theodore Roosvlt (R)	William J. Bryan (D)	William H. Taft (R)	Woodrow Wilson (D)	William H. Taft (R)	Woodrow Wilson (D)	Charles E. Hughes (R)	Allan L. Benson (S)	James M. Cox (D)	Warren G. Harding (R)	John W. Davis (D)	Calvin Coolidge (R)	Robert M. LaFlitt (PR)
Refugio	192	84	148	86	138	178	206	118	408	232	47	227	357	0	0	0
Roberts	213	79	100	20	125	31	183	16	220	27	3	173	60	241	104	2
Robertson	1,867	1,247	1,265	196	1,233	394	1,052	153	1,313	218	44	1,634	225	1,969	226	64
Rockwall	1,140	121	639	50	734	38	643	0	828	27	0	873	104	1,367	93	7
Runnels	612	74	224	39	981	103	1,117	58	1,487	195	133	1,197	331	2,555	458	140
Rusk	2,243	1,627	1,973	1,641	1,595	871	1,450	488	1,849	521	196	1,555	745	3,097	651	67
Sabine	0	0	644	224	467	54	426	19	681	22	54	637	97	1,148	61	7
San Augustine	673	383	426	213	423	87	375	12	682	18	51	658	121	0	0	0
San Jacinto	862	524	471	543	371	299	379	0	442	255	1	320	7	585	104	11
San Patricio	460	40	184	36	273	115	553	175	594	130	65	620	308	1,077	987	79
San Saba	1,082	341	838	149	744	124	692	39	935	66	90	874	180	1,811	187	16
Schleicher	0	0	209	26	126	9	124	3	163	10	1	211	81	246	118	1
Scurry	376	161	440	119	722	84	663	31	994	40	78	801	151	1,291	269	49
Shackelford	230	73	164	23	266	30	246	18	378	51	36	342	116	729	727	0
Shelby	0	0	1,536	188	1,727	182	1,505	76	1,767	131	175	1,700	150	3,407	160	130
Sherman	24	9	22	0	158	37	96	22	152	39	9	170	77	188	87	25
Smith	2,706	2,470	2,387	1,204	2,089	863	1,936	485	2,422	773	270	2,965	707	4,469	1,079	171
Somervell	380	143	365	40	251	39	241	12	278	20	83	198	92	403	42	24
Starr	1,249	857	905	325	901	411	674	252	516	115	0	418	89	756	23	0
Stephens	735	45	376	16	692	34	462	11	572	12	103	643	142	2,182	372	105
Sterling	141	44	129	15	148	5	165	4	205	6	0	152	17	0	0	0
Stonewall	305	107	328	23	329	14	342	7	502	21	119	356	134	778	171	118
Sutton	176	158	240	27	79	10	62	12	130	13	0	190	104	143	124	2
Swisher	148	50	230	25	239	26	280	24	381	62	10	443	149	575	212	34
Tarrant	5,277	1,746	3,988	852	6,403	1,500	7,219	533	10,269	1,550	329	12,431	3,485	13,638	5,859	2,619
Taylor	1,253	440	1,056	120	1,706	177	1,536	59	3,134	120	118	1,932	300	3,693	441	62
Terrell	0	0	0	0	110	62	118	36	181	59	2	155	95	106	122	85
Terry	0	0	123	6	167	8	96	6	146	1	0	270	39	823	160	18
Throckmorton	250	54	237	22	223	33	251	4	333	10	76	399	72	539	174	6
Titus	956	445	632	142	960	199	943	70	1,164	189	95	1,094	509	1,670	0	0
Tom Green	602	235	736	125	920	113	907	50	1,243	92	63	1,264	256	2,115	554	124
Travis	4,194	2,601	2,402	810	2,445	1,196	2,741	468	3,682	690	71	3,541	1,203	7,548	1,909	345
Trinity	1,110	517	916	419	602	156	657	112	906	156	91	643	124	1,504	146	42
Tyler	1,215	522	630	102	665	122	534	32	635	24	31	1,066	115	928	90	25
Upshur	0	0	809	344	898	287	895	168	1,346	198	121	1,222	616	2,611	258	42
Upton	0	0	0	0	0	0	28	2	42	6	1	46	25	35	4	1
Uvalde	558	280	452	78	748	320	601	53	728	92	24	143	247	1,313	351	52
Val Verde	571	227	462	121	362	182	298	196	446	135	5	418	296	434	457	107
Van Zandt	2,276	855	1,540	347	1,626	179	1,790	110	2,040	232	648	1,958	728	3,958	0	0
Victoria	0	0	856	352	567	328	689	100	897	476	35	686	781	1,653	459	306
Walker	1,299	1,131	706	605	614	441	629	323	763	315	24	788	404	1,809	201	3
Waller	971	760	794	545	698	349	595	144	636	182	6	674	167	1,239	203	19
Ward	0	0	144	21	234	30	147	6	178	23	8	181	79	203	42	26
Washington	1,811	1,371	1,343	640	1,543	798	1,109	546	1,119	1,306	3	796	684	3,568	496	73
Webb	1,103	1,770	535	1,007	233	1,109	654	888	676	472	0	633	467	1,316	429	52
Wharton	778	535	607	462	746	433	792	108	948	351	85	836	852	2,020	858	111
Wheeler	0	0	200	11	384	55	403	35	554	56	83	516	198	908	197	46
Wichita	907	215	655	157	806	256	1,125	108	2,108	347	94	3,812	1,487	5,832	2,189	461
Wilbarger	626	138	302	58	780	110	993	44	1,242	99	116	1,118	335	1,223	269	87
Willacy	0	0	0	0	0	0	102	5	110	10	0	53	9	306	110	17
Williamson	3,673	1,812	2,253	614	2,424	723	2,018	245	2,701	656	80	2,677	818	6,338	934	320
Wilson	1,800	477	984	278	858	252	785	95	869	346	24	753	821	1,635	495	326
Winkler	0	0	0	0	0	0	26	0	21	0	0	17	2	15	1	0
Wise	2,993	703	1,638	344	2,253	350	1,842	156	2,023	263	9	2,031	579	0	0	0
Wood	1,623	933	1,329	451	1,330	375	1,442	147	1,719	248	416	1,643	798	3,026	342	132
Yoakum	0	0	0	0	36	4	40	0	85	1	1	79	9	95	9	8
Young	858	158	891	94	813	89	922	35	1,175	71	71	1,214	209	1,999	322	51
Zapata	102	462	28	369	0	424	0	199	26	214	0	50	98	300	197	1
Zavala	126	35	146	11	123	29	241	42	229	43	17	264	101	325	95	32
Official	267,432		199,799		224,110		221,589		286,514		18,969	114,538		128,240		
Totals		130,651		65,823		70,458		228,863		64,999			288,767		484,605	42,541
Unofficial	**267,317**		**199,303**		**226,995**		**222,670**		**287,415**		**1,932**	**114,335**		**128,860**		
Totals		126,728		65,630		69,184		28,310		65,000			286,734		478,425	42,535

Table 9: Presidential Races

General Elections, 1928-1948

Year	1928		1932		1936		1940		1944			1948		
County	Alfred E. Smith (D)	Herbert C. Hoover (R)	Franklin D. Roosvlt (D)	Herbert C. Hoover (R)	Franklin D. Roosvlt (D)	Alfred M. Landon (R)	Franklin D. Roosvlt (D)	Wendell L. Willkie (R)	Franklin D. Roosvlt (D)	Thomas E. Dewey (R)	Texas Regulars	Harry S. Truman (D)	Thomas E. Dewey (R)	J. Strom Thrmd (SR)
Anderson	1,747	1,814	4,354	259	3,749	289	5,289	688	4,342	467	660	3,242	1,199	735
Andrews	25	66	186	6	287	18	440	26	329	48	21	816	101	35
Angelina	2,305	1,209	4,962	287	3,943	342	6,001	369	4,387	1,001	508	4,377	1,000	928
Aransas	152	161	268	39	206	60	536	141	456	150	13	418	235	26
Archer	865	799	1,555	97	1,672	146	1,904	276	1,674	194	227	1,599	191	58
Armstrong	373	316	813	63	897	33	902	86	623	132	44	686	97	31
Atascosa	682	888	2,101	192	2,041	285	1,901	405	1,757	685	202	0	0	0
Austin	2,129	466	2,806	142	1,635	290	1,424	1,400	1,316	619	1,248	1,252	1,260	345
Bailey	142	410	851	104	788	191	1,041	330	943	358	153	1,115	234	93
Bandera	317	936	883	359	720	431	891	435	532	634	92	445	570	107
Bastrop	1,534	850	3,077	180	2,395	198	2,404	490	2,604	385	299	2,518	443	265
Baylor	784	491	1,437	55	1,541	100	1,668	138	1,568	102	118	1,522	101	47
Bee	1,043	1,189	2,180	534	1,462	603	1,756	948	1,306	848	250	1,441	801	123
Bell	3,079	3,366	7,607	724	6,119	475	7,443	1,043	6,960	763	1,216	7,548	1,069	436
Bexar	16,626	16,477	37,765	7,466	35,781	12,951	38,200	18,268	35,024	23,588	1,697	35,970	26,202	3,418
Blanco	539	615	1,233	127	1,056	313	1,042	520	846	533	133	1,003	497	66
Borden	73	98	242	7	220	26	339	39	237	34	36	203	18	9
Bosque	1,235	1,526	3,214	272	2,283	350	3,087	596	2,502	504	324	2,303	501	141
Bowie	0	0	5,269	541	5,030	472	6,934	1,097	7,045	790	1,063	7,028	1,161	2,096
Brazoria	1,086	1,588	2,948	617	2,284	462	3,781	799	5,543	850	1,286	4,783	2,133	1,408
Brazos	1,480	738	2,588	195	2,610	45	4,151	617	3,358	464	550	3,459	1,533	522
Brewster	273	406	875	130	828	151	995	244	864	237	83	940	312	82
Briscoe	336	301	977	42	849	64	909	154	615	80	131	0	0	0
Brooks	332	160	608	86	365	117	769	201	403	142	86	1,029	217	30
Brown	1,992	2,033	4,024	330	3,971	448	4,413	663	2,426	430	675	5,059	1,071	327
Burleson	1,558	339	2,423	119	1,466	135	1,999	327	1,992	158	256	2,051	240	135
Burnet	467	936	1,904	144	1,583	111	1,877	223	1,697	228	184	0	0	0
Caldwell	1,211	1,189	3,317	291	3,019	247	3,574	691	2,916	704	266	0	0	0
Calhoun	375	333	834	100	685	92	835	152	732	158	176	0	0	0
Callahan	940	979	0	0	1,739	245	2,046	277	1,962	224	276	1,844	258	104
Cameron	3,202	3,544	7,146	1,785	5,887	2,160	6,045	3,341	5,998	5,309	510	6,778	4,689	342
Camp	640	494	1,416	73	939	78	1,345	200	977	180	210	0	0	0
Carson	592	891	0	0	1,568	147	1,636	362	1,216	446	97	1,301	413	32
Cass	1,698	1,323	3,135	224	2,461	169	3,126	454	2,866	541	331	2,540	457	878
Castro	384	319	949	66	950	65	1,000	224	838	222	143	1,158	189	20
Chambers	242	256	843	91	984	134	1,279	218	1,038	179	111	787	302	299
Cherokee	1,938	1,933	4,125	233	3,908	302	5,269	795	3,918	598	621	3,079	1,154	544
Childress	726	1,438	2,072	153	2,076	209	2,729	335	2,295	299	199	2,415	273	94
Clay	1,160	1,327	2,365	151	2,168	196	2,258	383	2,307	311	358	2,131	332	107
Cochran	109	197	345	31	683	58	765	122	716	123	157	971	119	94
Coke	0	0	983	57	888	68	988	95	824	65	69	909	65	30
Coleman	1,459	1,645	2,881	235	2,900	269	3,257	454	2,887	498	312	2,695	545	176
Collin	3,377	3,476	6,059	589	5,669	531	7,255	1,029	6,574	974	784	5,516	1,155	543
Collingsworth	608	1,179	1,753	115	2,012	158	2,034	307	1,725	261	168	1,779	198	98
Colorado	1,787	891	2,715	331	1,435	372	1,674	1,166	1,517	638	931	1,316	900	930
Comal	1,893	508	2,211	176	1,611	554	852	1,851	787	2,021	178	1,212	1,752	105
Comanche	1,311	1,483	3,134	192	2,587	355	3,226	610	2,941	356	484	2,915	408	164
Concho	426	446	1,126	44	1,089	76	1,266	189	1,090	151	123	1,156	174	12
Cooke	1,924	2,262	3,775	470	3,686	686	4,482	1,358	3,270	919	739	0	0	0
Coryell	1,306	1,123	3,347	191	2,064	150	3,155	649	2,518	413	228	2,350	310	88
Cottle	451	473	1,196	38	1,265	86	1,504	251	2,551	130	94	1,318	102	32
Crane	159	127	416	37	622	25	815	68	552	58	25	0	0	0
Crockett	64	291	329	168	231	75	389	126	323	112	57	400	127	18
Crosby	728	1,004	1,590	108	1,711	153	1,705	276	1,691	201	230	1,731	168	158
Culberson	85	0	285	18	239	23	280	40	200	17	34	244	38	22
Dallam	539	618	1,935	341	1,436	220	1,538	425	1,118	323	167	1,504	399	28
Dallas	17,437	27,272	37,363	8,919	42,153	7,204	49,431	16,574	60,909	21,099	11,781	47,464	35,664	10,162
Dawson	427	1,448	1,659	153	1,829	156	2,808	360	2,149	472	244	2,605	393	136
DeWitt	1,594	1,142	3,206	309	1,977	616	2,056	1,735	1,884	1,879	419	1,808	1,612	214
Deaf Smith	411	570	1,307	198	1,236	142	1,282	423	1,117	508	176	1,496	535	42
Delta	958	753	2,013	87	1,466	82	2,214	190	1,706	133	148	0	0	0
Denton	2,384	2,587	5,115	520	5,021	476	6,333	873	5,558	771	739	4,549	1,531	824
Dickens	415	741	1,491	63	1,445	115	1,732	254	1,617	141	117	1,492	115	83
Dimmit	258	626	843	241	704	296	1,061	474	554	328	95	863	384	60
Donley	491	1,092	1,626	141	1,515	133	1,575	213	1,170	280	108	1,372	241	71

Table 9: Presidential Races

County	General Elections, 1928-1948													
Year	**1928**		**1932**		**1936**		**1940**		**1944**			**1948**		
	Alfred E. Smith (D)	Herbert C. Hoover (R)	Franklin D. Roosvlt (D)	Herbert C. Hoover (R)	Franklin D. Roosvlt (D)	Alfred M. Landon (R)	Franklin D. Roosvlt (D)	Wendell L. Willkie (R)	Franklin D. Roosvlt (D)	Thomas E. Dewey (R)	Texas Regulars	Harry S. Truman (D)	Thomas E. Dewey (R)	J. Strom Thrmd (SR)
Duval	1,245	434	1,566	30	2,901	163	3,280	201	3,353	136	28	3,551	117	11
Eastland	2,501	3,233	4,958	598	4,659	724	5,821	1,077	4,607	643	809	0	0	0
Ector	151	168	530	37	816	81	2,783	451	2,265	432	384	4,305	1,145	231
Edwards	59	546	575	224	354	157	565	175	348	187	48	0	0	0
El Paso	6,114	6,050	11,336	527	11,920	1,773	12,575	3,764	11,426	2,072	2,202	15,341	5,544	395
Ellis	4,399	3,569	7,033	2,841	5,644	319	7,881	692	7,065	666	564	0	0	0
Erath	1,372	1,923	3,319	284	2,694	290	3,459	646	3,330	411	415	0	0	0
Falls	2,484	877	3,896	181	3,411	140	3,949	961	3,191	377	648	3,385	546	271
Fannin	2,525	2,122	5,338	460	5,242	368	7,479	792	5,984	677	496	6,132	553	364
Fayette	3,647	689	4,985	245	2,820	595	2,608	2,424	3,156	1,611	1,254	3,106	1,737	429
Fisher	837	1,259	1,395	105	2,068	155	2,268	199	2,041	154	135	2,063	149	66
Floyd	666	1,176	1,976	145	1,863	217	1,880	484	1,756	370	320	2,174	344	119
Foard	466	430	882	53	928	74	997	142	925	84	69	751	90	32
Fort Bend	1,724	631	3,109	148	2,588	176	3,029	746	2,781	442	752	2,058	1,016	519
Franklin	713	386	1,305	56	925	90	1,621	183	1,336	147	110	1,236	146	135
Freestone	1,318	1,178	2,481	170	1,929	134	3,504	481	2,427	277	312	2,265	460	483
Frio	258	673	998	142	1,019	193	1,012	235	951	293	124	898	345	91
Gaines	140	312	510	44	680	42	1,313	198	1,173	173	118	1,465	207	107
Galveston	5,951	4,401	10,491	2,011	9,370	1,666	11,162	2,452	11,751	1,542	1,761	12,491	4,857	1,266
Garza	285	794	812	87	807	132	1,073	209	842	144	169	861	176	63
Gillespie	1,174	1,447	2,642	662	1,016	1,422	487	3,105	333	2,950	287	593	2,741	77
Glasscock	34	124	212	42	252	29	269	41	185	34	48	188	69	16
Goliad	468	554	1,542	170	1,184	323	708	613	641	609	95	0	0	0
Gonzales	1,319	1,112	3,384	337	2,674	352	3,048	757	2,805	841	338	2,612	666	305
Gray	986	1,871	3,446	505	4,347	464	4,315	1,215	3,067	1,739	172	3,699	1,594	384
Grayson	4,600	6,277	9,631	1,317	10,627	947	12,527	1,342	11,636	1,372	1,044	10,991	2,174	953
Gregg	996	646	5,204	341	6,489	621	9,331	1,640	6,401	1,412	1,249	5,104	2,477	2,917
Grimes	1,175	701	2,065	153	1,851	136	2,154	295	1,559	137	274	901	336	476
Guadalupe	1,872	1,442	3,751	691	2,962	1,266	2,181	2,708	1,583	2,556	200	2,119	2,502	259
Hale	1,098	2,143	3,029	369	3,109	451	3,407	906	3,066	712	594	3,995	1,013	269
Hall	493	1,409	2,114	91	2,195	126	2,216	167	1,812	164	126	2,122	174	76
Hamilton	989	927	2,474	164	1,929	202	2,263	635	1,790	344	363	0	0	0
Hansford	319	417	803	67	826	74	725	150	590	203	49	895	206	17
Hardeman	910	1,333	1,985	145	1,991	207	2,453	362	1,756	223	192	1,654	226	86
Hardin	1,032	951	2,783	161	2,351	119	2,997	226	2,632	243	234	2,233	196	595
Harris	21,536	27,188	46,886	8,604	59,205	8,083	73,520	20,797	71,077	11,843	21,095	58,488	43,117	19,934
Harrison	2,023	1,776	4,057	528	3,400	302	4,515	681	3,588	619	782	2,504	946	2,106
Hartley	163	179	586	74	560	40	544	110	484	26	10	477	83	5
Haskell	1,532	1,430	2,330	154	2,713	156	2,914	286	2,573	261	249	2,735	181	77
Hays	620	1,088	1,822	220	1,964	286	2,370	453	1,690	495	241	2,239	555	176
Hemphill	317	489	918	133	1,008	121	868	170	792	274	70	930	201	34
Henderson	1,726	1,128	3,522	219	3,259	260	4,111	803	3,219	427	566	3,669	540	197
Hidalgo	4,043	4,285	9,695	2,969	6,782	2,962	7,467	4,786	4,080	865	0	0	0	0
Hill	2,413	2,446	5,297	360	4,710	366	6,002	627	4,876	516	582	0	0	0
Hockley	235	765	1,513	76	1,731	90	2,382	261	2,641	319	400	3,071	346	199
Hood	479	640	1,119	106	988	102	1,325	175	1,203	146	120	1,273	169	56
Hopkins	1,845	1,767	4,891	261	2,753	261	4,965	547	3,981	533	348	3,885	479	284
Houston	1,336	763	3,087	165	2,458	99	3,579	474	2,329	233	584	2,014	532	541
Howard	665	812	2,733	149	3,094	230	4,333	367	3,588	334	404	4,179	561	285
Hudspeth	117	123	341	31	363	24	426	54	333	35	28	437	49	10
Hunt	3,510	3,009	6,856	465	5,801	335	8,120	896	6,200	714	1,105	5,082	1,195	763
Hutchinson	730	1,115	1,976	505	2,478	392	3,019	1,101	2,760	864	196	4,527	1,382	84
Irion	119	259	398	47	476	49	536	74	363	54	35	366	63	9
Jack	450	1,068	1,429	189	1,113	183	2,046	305	1,484	217	258	1,426	265	110
Jackson	473	572	1,030	182	952	171	1,506	296	1,708	344	244	1,343	488	122
Jasper	898	611	1,990	93	1,500	109	2,168	220	1,850	341	235	1,777	284	450
Jeff Davis	112	157	252	46	291	33	374	50	331	51	35	0	0	0
Jefferson	7,006	9,209	17,129	3,584	18,187	2,544	19,694	4,659	22,066	4,525	2,447	22,475	5,749	5,108
Jim Hogg	263	109	428	51	712	48	810	100	620	77	16	0	0	0
Jim Wells	747	423	1,449	162	1,691	338	2,120	914	1,908	1,113	167	3,781	1,402	101
Johnson	1,981	3,181	4,858	530	4,281	337	5,531	649	4,757	546	582	4,042	707	434
Jones	1,563	1,995	2,934	224	3,396	305	3,688	401	3,417	361	336	3,599	432	132
Karnes	1,052	855	2,458	186	2,067	371	1,987	610	1,920	692	340	2,198	592	176
Kaufman	2,657	1,718	4,116	268	3,943	229	5,125	509	4,251	430	441	3,479	764	629
Kendall	377	663	1,185	416	405	693	420	1,321	309	1,337	114	511	1,207	65

Table 9: Presidential Races

	General Elections, 1928-1948												
Year	1928		1932		1936		1940		1944			1948		
County	Alfred E. Smith (D)	Herbert C. Hoover (R)	Franklin D. Roosvlt (D)	Herbert C. Hoover (R)	Franklin D. Roosvlt (D)	Alfred M. Landon (R)	Franklin D. Roosvlt (D)	Wendell L. Willkie (R)	Franklin D. Roosvlt (D)	Thomas E. Dewey (R)	Texas Regulars	Harry S. Truman (D)	Thomas E. Dewey (R)	J. Strom Thrmd (SR)
Kenedy	118	12	123	5	96	30	38	68	16	60	5	45	31	5
Kent	163	363	561	23	533	31	705	67	572	31	55	479	33	22
Kerr	570	1,575	2,165	623	1,586	994	1,634	1,113	1,377	1,358	204	1,505	1,520	162
Kimble	157	660	890	121	681	151	1,113	210	880	225	142	851	303	95
King	45	85	224	4	211	13	264	25	228	13	15	231	6	4
Kinney	200	182	678	89	357	175	418	156	401	200	1	0	0	0
Kleberg	695	751	1,727	198	1,488	156	1,631	429	1,473	421	59	2,083	697	70
Knox	784	992	1,600	102	1,823	171	1,699	253	1,785	156	199	1,792	157	52
La Salle	479	327	810	375	704	74	716	103	692	127	41	0	0	0
Lamar	2,163	2,887	5,911	271	5,621	308	7,673	789	6,283	725	732	6,306	1,018	1,015
Lamb	0	0	2,978	120	2,320	300	3,241	508	2,407	616	415	3,286	475	173
Lampasas	567	899	1,824	92	1,462	134	2,006	244	1,693	212	160	1,459	276	72
Lavaca	2,842	911	4,378	224	2,204	403	2,419	1,407	3,406	960	580	3,046	1,165	265
Lee	1,176	449	1,831	110	1,155	271	954	1,150	953	771	463	1,540	465	109
Leon	862	543	1,958	108	1,748	92	2,349	252	1,569	140	189	0	0	0
Liberty	918	1,070	2,527	247	2,813	244	3,457	497	2,561	336	551	0	0	0
Limestone	2,608	1,642	4,416	213	3,857	196	4,784	559	4,299	239	514	3,289	688	510
Lipscomb	331	776	865	349	973	273	774	425	551	396	76	668	354	18
Live Oak	383	484	1,070	114	874	231	888	499	642	548	212	945	479	131
Llano	1,514	439	1,229	108	1,302	107	1,484	238	1,199	198	140	0	0	0
Loving	10	6	187	27	118	21	98	10	60	18	6	62	29	4
Lubbock	1,979	3,079	5,330	596	6,425	622	8,112	1,283	7,654	1,169	2,021	11,114	2,837	1,202
Lynn	754	1,268	1,930	110	1,983	169	2,618	255	1,968	263	256	2,179	224	120
Madison	452	364	1,344	20	1,127	45	1,434	127	1,115	65	125	801	134	188
Marion	640	443	861	84	919	129	1,253	166	1,057	219	104	703	200	159
Martin	213	330	694	44	775	70	1,044	136	758	131	97	945	77	52
Mason	244	807	828	309	787	359	1,025	622	822	420	248	836	498	14
Matagorda	829	1,194	2,039	408	1,700	459	2,156	643	1,854	412	798	1,628	1,016	640
Maverick	180	311	847	199	890	166	850	166	787	302	30	695	270	22
McCulloch	741	1,294	2,006	265	1,772	323	2,373	443	2,088	463	251	0	0	0
McLennan	5,330	5,744	11,972	1,108	12,489	1,116	15,952	2,178	15,336	1,668	1,592	16,034	3,088	913
McMullen	94	96	258	12	265	37	336	77	223	106	45	222	61	17
Medina	1,400	1,243	2,516	515	2,050	969	1,749	1,480	1,469	1,607	311	1,875	1,492	144
Menard	234	589	901	150	734	135	1,153	246	776	96	250	0	0	0
Midland	350	347	1,245	136	1,229	190	1,921	646	1,688	302	938	2,032	1,410	370
Milam	2,842	1,270	4,676	264	3,546	123	4,083	1,110	3,537	623	803	3,261	646	359
Mills	442	774	1,434	133	1,005	165	1,612	322	1,428	172	216	1,135	205	69
Mitchell	746	1,099	1,490	148	2,035	192	2,401	251	2,215	218	138	0	0	0
Montague	452	1,519	3,090	262	0	0	3,449	530	2,900	429	375	2,872	475	194
Montgomery	905	613	1,971	126	2,443	186	3,347	408	2,902	219	494	1,795	544	984
Moore	124	87	549	56	583	47	959	224	999	313	80	1,748	323	27
Morris	780	287	1,253	38	1,220	52	7,752	82	1,269	122	85	1,164	143	247
Motley	349	450	900	34	867	64	938	103	744	107	79	774	75	48
Nacogdoches	1,879	822	3,603	117	4,075	209	4,988	440	3,226	319	619	0	0	0
Navarro	3,648	3,341	6,392	512	5,815	293	7,665	721	6,298	449	640	4,679	1,188	587
Newton	564	397	1,586	46	1,111	93	1,716	173	910	187	124	957	110	316
Nolan	1,035	1,475	2,453	219	2,913	268	3,322	463	3,071	322	349	3,408	552	99
Nueces	2,985	2,481	6,659	967	6,597	1,234	9,678	3,057	11,087	3,819	834	15,240	5,577	754
Ochiltree	270	556	1,097	183	1,111	109	1,213	294	863	307	136	0	0	0
Oldham	157	172	432	61	437	20	416	82	277	93	36	339	100	18
Orange	1,247	919	2,830	244	2,281	190	3,011	358	4,500	910	421	4,957	987	851
Palo Pinto	1,161	2,001	2,722	392	2,738	371	3,599	506	3,291	416	410	3,736	977	297
Panola	1,312	420	2,630	50	2,425	95	3,135	188	2,106	221	164	1,751	256	792
Parker	1,110	2,178	3,074	372	2,493	375	3,617	562	3,503	59	476	3,061	806	180
Parmer	315	620	1,154	148	936	135	1,188	370	810	415	157	1,091	280	45
Pecos	562	524	1,261	180	1,330	167	1,569	317	1,226	305	120	0	0	0
Polk	994	508	2,117	110	1,618	141	2,642	280	1,817	154	280	1,422	317	518
Potter	2,637	3,627	6,366	1,233	6,496	1,018	7,203	2,285	6,519	2,759	783	9,622	4,110	414
Presidio	315	254	863	112	938	106	901	184	648	211	165	0	0	0
Rains	544	202	937	41	676	63	1,080	251	628	137	149	739	111	90
Randall	659	733	1,394	231	1,656	142	1,779	382	1,439	409	263	0	0	0
Reagan	229	387	681	124	477	66	520	88	426	53	40	444	112	21
Real	98	479	335	89	210	55	361	123	326	163	59	446	156	12
Red River	1,666	1,172	3,181	145	2,685	199	3,980	541	2,991	466	361	2,987	323	637
Reeves	394	344	1,085	122	1,127	100	1,305	247	1,157	201	149	1,383	309	95

Table 9: Presidential Races

County	1928 Alfred E. Smith (D)	1928 Herbert C. Hoover (R)	1932 Franklin D. Roosvlt (D)	1932 Herbert C. Hoover (R)	1936 Franklin D. Roosvlt (D)	1936 Alfred M. Landon (R)	1940 Franklin D. Roosvlt (D)	1940 Wendell L. Willkie (R)	1944 Franklin D. Roosvlt (D)	1944 Thomas E. Dewey (R)	1944 Texas Regulars	1948 Harry S. Truman (D)	1948 Thomas E. Dewey (R)	1948 J. Strom Thrmd (SR)
Refugio	671	383	1,201	172	1,058	242	1,484	395	991	376	96	1,637	489	64
Roberts	104	243	451	36	426	27	408	55	289	89	37	317	76	25
Robertson	1,487	751	2,396	148	2,633	86	3,364	284	2,681	126	231	0	0	0
Rockwall	850	289	1,237	62	1,168	26	1,510	95	1,153	98	98	947	117	164
Runnels	1,494	1,645	2,975	235	2,985	313	3,087	926	2,657	685	438	2,954	526	117
Rusk	1,732	1,033	5,074	483	6,107	433	7,911	748	5,232	637	973	4,322	1,294	1,730
Sabine	807	0	1,789	57	1,216	108	1,624	161	1,169	203	75	0	0	0
San Augustine	0	0	1,802	19	1,054	64	1,325	119	1,176	102	0	858	137	249
San Jacinto	503	296	828	16	564	67	764	1,119	522	53	145	509	106	153
San Patricio	579	1,388	2,142	407	2,213	482	2,964	981	2,712	878	242	2,649	963	181
San Saba	752	682	1,904	122	1,505	147	2,298	223	2,109	177	104	2,050	184	65
Schleicher	137	227	516	76	469	78	601	117	520	84	89	495	107	43
Scurry	462	1,597	1,604	105	1,746	162	2,303	280	1,761	285	130	2,040	201	55
Shackelford	533	558	1,316	117	1,153	152	1,521	229	1,007	135	194	892	211	43
Shelby	1,961	676	3,594	120	3,167	136	4,610	334	2,927	428	205	3,051	307	666
Sherman	137	248	515	91	568	34	528	82	454	97	32	479	98	10
Smith	2,343	3,493	7,424	750	7,116	660	9,209	1,544	6,671	936	1,921	6,473	3,181	1,600
Somervell	136	241	561	43	532	57	532	138	406	87	127	446	91	46
Starr	736	79	754	32	2,289	320	1,232	66	1,312	68	15	1,996	179	10
Stephens	1,163	1,789	2,684	256	2,380	681	2,750	471	2,104	217	479	2,132	572	164
Sterling	167	122	354	13	384	14	423	16	330	18	10	244	17	7
Stonewall	500	442	976	50	1,001	59	1,182	156	902	89	89	968	65	28
Sutton	92	290	372	113	398	64	571	84	449	118	69	433	131	58
Swisher	374	887	1,448	166	1,453	140	1,432	298	1,275	331	208	1,670	307	57
Tarrant	9,208	20,481	27,836	5,251	29,791	3,781	35,615	7,474	36,791	4,113	10,161	36,325	17,157	6,932
Taylor	1,891	4,050	5,235	639	6,169	678	7,830	982	7,975	602	1,149	8,184	1,658	478
Terrell	85	364	479	133	324	84	417	138	329	156	17	0	0	0
Terry	407	622	1,448	87	1,619	87	2,206	145	2,304	273	203	2,283	236	152
Throckmorton	304	703	932	95	949	132	996	138	970	76	135	1,026	63	30
Titus	1,149	469	2,523	75	1,872	77	3,686	255	2,612	265	226	2,339	379	332
Tom Green	1,528	2,618	4,957	739	4,803	627	6,443	1,055	6,272	1,125	891	6,777	1,822	481
Travis	4,487	4,847	11,718	1,532	12,092	1,154	17,311	3,130	14,384	2,324	2,496	19,598	5,994	1,252
Trinity	686	456	1,514	65	1,196	151	1,892	205	1,132	127	287	905	150	250
Tyler	666	298	1,450	44	1,076	1,116	1,720	241	1,037	219	162	895	177	466
Upshur	1,553	649	2,900	129	0	0	3,580	518	2,369	446	548	2,118	555	485
Upton	189	270	1,012	92	728	81	988	157	742	105	67	811	155	55
Uvalde	747	1,224	1,759	422	1,743	354	1,871	560	1,322	858	166	0	0	0
Val Verde	620	854	1,412	421	1,262	504	1,357	533	1,210	676	98	1,242	672	63
Van Zandt	1,789	1,502	4,203	190	3,257	245	4,987	729	3,139	503	540	3,264	578	463
Victoria	1,710	663	2,777	190	2,081	352	2,491	956	2,331	936	415	2,435	1,262	328
Walker	747	488	1,811	83	1,715	69	1,618	147	1,638	145	254	1,439	570	542
Waller	504	376	1,192	89	889	111	1,166	301	1,007	190	234	812	448	359
Ward	256	216	678	70	1,113	98	1,931	335	1,449	268	100	2,119	414	118
Washington	2,491	275	3,443	99	1,993	176	1,449	1,868	1,387	534	2,101	1,647	1,904	190
Webb	1,615	767	4,299	657	3,594	696	4,147	774	4,742	776	47	4,595	1,004	53
Wharton	1,545	1,151	3,357	405	3,034	307	4,007	780	3,754	529	754	2,811	1,354	484
Wheeler	750	1,038	2,263	165	2,415	277	2,609	517	1,869	511	228	2,010	370	67
Wichita	4,853	7,226	8,889	1,479	9,428	1,327	11,672	2,206	11,392	1,597	1,609	12,235	2,887	683
Wilbarger	1,447	1,590	3,397	199	3,279	316	3,249	697	3,382	1,517	513	2,963	529	295
Willacy	396	0	1,042	259	1,002	376	1,173	740	846	754	133	1,139	676	99
Williamson	3,689	1,833	6,783	418	4,995	375	3,364	1,142	5,284	1,239	886	5,638	1,094	258
Wilson	1,499	622	2,435	174	2,573	286	2,749	605	2,666	676	185	2,313	593	108
Winkler	310	162	642	78	903	63	1,330	172	1,004	120	68	1,588	296	90
Wise	1,093	2,141	2,681	286	2,737	348	3,754	495	3,114	444	413	3,064	448	254
Wood	1,645	1,161	3,308	189	2,751	192	3,659	585	3,045	485	503	2,590	629	642
Yoakum	66	86	245	11	227	13	885	134	646	106	86	861	119	32
Young	1,275	1,826	3,156	320	3,065	304	3,264	423	3,183	327	596	0	0	0
Zapata	296	19	271	24	282	34	784	495	501	43	3	632	414	1
Zavala	229	571	783	166	788	209	763	282	696	342	90	618	306	58
Official	341,032		760,348		734,485		840,151		821,605		135,439	282,240		
Totals		367,036		97,959		103,711		199,152		191,425		750,700		106,909
Unofficial	340,082		767,585		734,391		911,066		821,580		135,539	282,240		
Totals		367,036		97,852		104,869		212,684		191,925		750,700		106,909

Table 10: Presidential Races

	General Elections, 1952-1968													
Year	1952		1956			1960		1964			1968		
County	Adlai E. Stevnsn (D)	Dwight D. Eisnhwr (R)	Adlai E. Stevnsn (D)	Dwight D. Eisnhwr (R)	T. Coleman Andrews (C)	John F. Kennedy (D)	Richard M. Nixon (R)	Lyndon B. Johnson (D)	Barry Goldwtr (R)	Joseph B. Lightbrn (C)	Hubert H. Humphny (D)	Richard M. Nixon (R)	George C. Wallace (A)
Anderson	3,462	4,637	2,710	4,181	23	3,296	3,642	4,809	3,362	10	3,447	2,828	3,196
Andrews	920	805	968	1,131	14	1,821	1,550	2,133	1,442	10	922	1,400	1,312
Angelina	6,224	4,705	4,781	5,274	41	7,046	5,169	8,194	5,262	28	5,174	4,645	6,111
Aransas	503	818	425	757	7	948	792	1,492	602	7	1,222	1,076	417
Archer	1,272	937	1,067	825	7	1,341	680	1,766	441	0	1,308	636	413
Armstrong	425	562	422	372	4	730	877	544	365	0	301	434	206
Atascosa	2,124	2,148	1,492	1,804	11	2,544	1,812	3,224	1,283	9	2,522	1,805	771
Austin	1,445	2,964	1,215	2,501	10	1,725	1,978	2,365	1,545	5	1,299	1,971	1,084
Bailey	1,039	1,118	1,274	871	6	1,064	1,180	1,503	1,056	3	820	1,174	563
Bandera	358	1,350	336	1,083	5	539	942	876	762	1	535	842	423
Bastrop	3,148	1,540	2,504	1,531	10	2,866	1,208	3,912	1,130	7	2,687	1,455	975
Baylor	1,142	879	1,047	715	4	1,199	713	1,403	389	2	1,064	657	443
Bee	1,583	2,536	1,929	2,401	15	2,557	2,220	3,314	1,509	9	2,957	1,995	589
Bell	9,484	4,862	9,603	4,285	44	10,651	4,606	14,557	2,938	17	11,893	5,705	3,547
Bexar	50,260	65,391	46,790	65,901	640	75,373	63,934	108,658	53,469	393	95,325	72,951	16,598
Blanco	697	919	615	796	7	830	557	1,197	290	1	620	614	223
Borden	210	182	240	127	1	230	166	266	152	1	157	117	112
Bosque	1,940	1,982	1,670	1,654	7	1,852	1,653	2,690	1,024	7	1,817	1,377	727
Bowie	10,437	6,501	7,675	6,823	104	9,198	5,927	10,368	7,018	24	6,468	5,966	7,165
Brazoria	8,386	8,360	7,137	9,536	208	10,561	10,880	15,917	8,477	103	11,439	10,631	8,026
Brazos	4,213	4,681	3,463	4,942	31	5,907	4,553	7,998	4,003	18	6,299	6,839	2,437
Brewster	609	1,096	479	837	8	716	736	1,251	635	1	958	790	342
Briscoe	508	692	648	357	3	570	533	966	348	3	528	411	219
Brooks	1,577	809	1,108	802	10	1,934	567	2,299	402	2	1,904	534	166
Brown	3,778	4,635	3,195	3,664	21	3,720	3,512	5,214	2,070	9	3,999	2,997	1,606
Burleson	2,347	1,052	1,726	1,173	16	2,466	672	2,527	617	3	1,678	891	694
Burnet	1,431	1,270	1,422	1,163	5	1,770	1,189	2,585	821	4	1,876	1,459	643
Caldwell	2,887	2,052	2,513	1,747	5	2,729	1,482	3,580	1,046	3	2,889	1,402	837
Calhoun	813	1,406	1,067	1,912	13	1,961	1,599	3,398	1,031	5	2,612	1,672	1,065
Callahan	1,502	1,431	1,199	1,140	14	1,559	1,261	2,178	849	10	1,437	921	737
Cameron	7,559	14,018	8,829	11,952	241	12,416	10,190	16,056	9,531	72	15,726	11,759	2,042
Camp	1,535	951	1,053	958	18	1,307	873	1,841	729	7	1,272	555	1,074
Carson	1,071	1,471	976	1,061	7	1,009	1,387	1,574	1,044	3	904	1,211	570
Cass	3,160	2,502	2,395	2,970	44	2,934	2,322	3,603	2,681	8	2,536	1,930	2,883
Castro	825	1,169	1,305	697	4	1,544	810	1,865	626	3	1,181	1,033	623
Chambers	1,116	1,497	860	1,520	13	1,524	1,260	1,921	1,023	12	1,217	1,061	1,329
Cherokee	3,868	3,825	2,912	4,022	27	4,544	3,233	5,485	3,043	9	3,242	2,575	3,791
Childress	1,879	1,890	1,503	1,268	9	1,189	1,571	1,977	952	2	1,093	1,045	621
Clay	2,044	1,272	1,813	990	5	1,692	1,019	2,357	659	4	1,573	936	665
Cochran	906	780	923	599	1	1,028	646	1,260	497	4	633	548	449
Coke	736	576	690	549	6	799	575	900	366	3	563	387	208
Coleman	1,824	2,555	1,577	2,247	17	1,835	2,127	2,670	1,434	1	1,449	1,507	1,153
Collin	5,906	4,037	5,280	3,823	34	5,229	3,865	7,833	3,341	19	5,918	6,494	3,850
Collingsworth	1,321	1,334	1,229	815	11	691	1,084	1,145	724	3	746	712	475
Colorado	2,043	3,237	1,648	2,691	28	2,299	1,909	3,650	1,918	6	1,976	2,296	1,163
Comal	1,252	3,350	1,140	3,397	20	1,845	3,082	3,644	2,223	8	2,338	3,646	724
Comanche	2,181	2,411	1,962	1,900	16	1,979	1,828	2,851	962	6	1,980	1,436	708
Concho	708	808	567	574	1	718	522	948	307	1	502	411	197
Cooke	2,657	4,385	2,272	4,164	37	3,168	3,983	4,083	3,117	11	2,711	3,799	1,412
Coryell	2,432	1,658	2,372	1,509	2	2,700	1,477	3,679	877	8	2,987	1,698	1,172
Cottle	1,368	494	1,138	329	2	986	370	1,122	230	1	742	268	266
Crane	857	621	707	626	15	848	678	919	637	3	498	493	712
Crockett	306	654	305	702	2	517	635	799	409	3	571	509	279
Crosby	1,550	1,053	1,804	704	6	1,783	889	2,278	611	3	1,574	865	401
Culberson	252	331	269	324	3	343	300	473	314	0	330	298	145
Dallam	1,197	1,464	1,074	1,018	11	835	961	1,058	700	1	588	990	430
Dallas	69,394	118,218	65,472	125,361	1,862	88,876	149,369	166,472	137,065	621	123,809	184,193	55,552
Dawson	2,093	2,388	2,049	1,615	6	2,063	2,161	3,171	1,691	6	1,522	2,091	900
DeWitt	1,934	4,075	1,435	3,401	13	2,253	2,763	3,286	2,283	4	1,871	2,589	784
Deaf Smith	1,006	2,468	1,361	1,685	9	1,299	2,024	2,094	1,793	10	1,545	2,474	691
Delta	1,585	707	1,262	605	10	1,360	460	1,619	339	2	1,037	370	475
Denton	5,289	5,840	4,972	5,350	24	5,366	5,724	9,137	4,335	22	7,463	8,222	3,178
Dickens	1,249	782	1,243	565	0	1,075	521	1,324	339	4	811	428	295
Dimmit	503	954	427	705	7	886	648	1,184	501	3	896	584	177

Table 10: Presidential Races

	General Elections, 1952-1968													
Year	1952		1956			1960		1964			1968		
County	Adlai E. Stevnsn (D)	Dwight D. Eisnhwr (R)	Adlai E. Stevnsn (D)	Dwight D. Eisnhwr (R)	T. Coleman Andrews (C)	John F. Kennedy (D)	Richard M. Nixon (R)	Lyndon B. Johnson (D)	Barry Goldwtr (R)	Joseph B. Lightbm (C)	Hubert H. Humphry (D)	Richard M. Nixon (R)	George C. Wallace (A)
Donley	900	1,150	903	826	2	764	951	1,068	708	0	543	816	268
Duval	3,316	672	3,110	1,459	6	3,803	809	4,432	353	4	3,978	384	121
Eastland	3,370	4,518	2,512	3,580	16	3,058	3,359	4,692	2,049	11	2,884	2,453	1,013
Ector	5,270	8,259	5,109	8,805	194	8,996	11,145	10,826	11,497	63	5,312	10,557	8,671
Edwards	210	586	133	533	3	168	463	337	371	4	148	409	82
El Paso	14,595	20,005	15,157	18,532	193	26,027	21,551	35,050	20,687	190	32,658	30,347	5,111
Ellis	6,275	4,183	5,211	3,585	24	5,841	3,666	7,278	2,779	5	5,431	3,794	2,838
Erath	2,664	3,249	2,377	2,775	19	2,490	2,696	3,851	1,642	5	2,915	2,209	935
Falls	3,287	1,962	2,674	1,819	14	3,399	1,559	3,933	1,216	2	2,990	1,345	1,364
Fannin	5,363	2,099	4,504	1,910	6	4,282	1,844	5,976	1,219	5	3,931	1,585	1,661
Fayette	2,557	4,240	2,282	3,574	48	3,462	2,213	3,630	2,036	11	1,833	2,380	1,562
Fisher	1,405	952	1,664	673	6	1,966	679	2,108	454	5	1,560	555	268
Floyd	1,463	2,066	1,767	1,445	9	1,437	1,580	2,383	1,229	9	1,305	1,465	847
Foard	830	418	687	243	2	723	270	833	146	1	594	216	168
Fort Bend	3,241	3,974	2,464	3,779	73	4,335	3,301	6,186	3,493	20	4,493	4,573	2,447
Franklin	1,358	564	1,082	556	3	1,148	620	1,520	424	0	1,001	481	507
Freestone	2,902	1,707	1,813	1,627	15	1,997	1,629	2,816	1,074	2	2,066	958	1,069
Frio	983	1,011	886	825	10	1,068	713	1,507	607	3	1,330	795	307
Gaines	1,540	1,350	1,527	1,244	8	1,498	1,520	2,045	1,153	3	1,087	1,401	1,037
Galveston	19,058	15,715	15,603	17,567	336	23,940	16,373	30,672	12,365	136	26,041	16,229	10,322
Garza	797	742	786	628	1	829	737	1,254	567	6	662	615	383
Gillespie	300	3,687	240	3,070	5	816	2,687	2,264	1,695	1	725	2,945	432
Glasscock	197	235	174	224	0	207	152	179	183	1	106	169	172
Goliad	452	1,065	338	902	7	711	741	990	549	2	690	707	156
Gonzales	2,563	2,249	2,260	1,767	10	2,730	1,554	3,348	1,190	7	1,930	1,476	983
Gray	3,367	5,467	3,034	5,047	72	2,802	6,197	3,633	5,011	6	2,374	5,994	2,427
Grayson	10,435	7,736	8,876	7,402	52	9,866	7,312	14,207	5,500	21	10,379	8,007	4,615
Gregg	7,969	10,583	4,881	9,440	198	7,765	10,679	8,741	11,761	82	5,733	9,278	8,109
Grimes	1,362	1,557	1,079	1,281	14	1,713	1,053	2,229	1,014	4	1,473	1,076	976
Guadalupe	2,330	4,396	2,099	4,296	30	3,116	3,657	4,568	2,731	9	3,529	4,332	1,241
Hale	3,351	4,858	3,848	3,804	11	3,695	4,784	5,910	3,666	18	3,293	4,696	2,309
Hall	1,744	1,253	1,487	687	5	1,192	939	1,785	667	1	1,038	753	434
Hamilton	1,313	2,130	1,124	1,709	10	1,136	1,592	2,048	1,006	2	1,116	1,266	452
Hansford	456	1,234	545	919	1	512	1,322	860	1,193	3	392	1,359	437
Hardeman	1,242	1,571	1,281	1,119	9	1,182	1,472	1,835	697	0	1,145	873	531
Hardin	3,423	1,653	2,371	2,130	19	4,315	2,115	5,143	1,987	16	2,894	1,986	3,979
Harris	107,604	146,665	93,961	155,555	5,033	148,275	168,170	227,819	154,401	765	182,546	202,079	86,412
Harrison	4,516	4,708	2,668	5,048	79	5,108	4,613	6,351	5,568	11	4,959	3,668	5,324
Hartley	402	468	448	353	2	397	413	565	437	1	299	597	264
Haskell	2,481	1,290	2,340	993	8	2,776	866	2,903	512	6	1,888	713	610
Hays	2,070	2,135	2,017	1,873	14	2,916	1,606	3,780	1,279	5	3,546	1,993	643
Hemphill	590	892	401	620	1	333	847	649	563	1	400	699	201
Henderson	4,439	2,534	3,065	2,479	25	3,411	2,521	4,697	1,988	29	3,119	2,315	2,497
Hidalgo	9,251	15,303	9,804	13,270	253	18,663	13,628	22,110	11,563	83	20,087	14,455	2,569
Hill	4,504	3,242	4,199	2,487	21	4,340	2,226	5,130	1,557	9	3,415	1,809	1,751
Hockley	2,962	2,651	3,175	2,001	10	3,169	2,159	4,049	1,674	10	2,426	2,265	1,456
Hood	1,356	780	1,095	751	6	1,238	943	1,661	423	3	1,155	593	411
Hopkins	3,750	2,460	3,118	2,206	23	3,228	2,117	4,133	1,518	0	2,700	1,860	1,932
Houston	2,900	2,222	1,998	1,941	19	2,703	1,591	3,681	1,675	10	2,782	1,391	2,062
Howard	4,779	3,412	4,506	3,051	14	4,844	3,403	6,083	3,272	12	3,897	3,812	2,789
Hudspeth	262	355	368	316	8	409	267	438	224	3	289	285	132
Hunt	4,953	5,614	4,051	4,508	33	4,116	4,084	6,567	3,302	10	4,785	4,651	3,469
Hutchinson	5,083	5,369	4,184	5,110	42	3,295	6,432	4,625	5,358	17	2,416	4,813	2,919
Irion	282	268	178	252	2	246	238	351	199	0	187	211	92
Jack	1,130	1,406	997	1,327	23	1,079	1,342	1,594	847	3	1,133	966	512
Jackson	1,584	2,113	1,571	2,259	22	2,268	1,670	2,775	1,168	9	1,698	1,438	1,145
Jasper	2,595	1,946	1,856	2,430	22	3,004	2,102	3,600	1,919	18	2,438	1,839	2,906
Jeff Davis	183	306	165	239	3	195	182	304	174	1	239	191	66
Jefferson	29,384	25,363	25,057	30,102	270	40,533	29,395	44,584	28,771	239	30,032	26,007	21,824
Jim Hogg	1,053	309	617	282	7	1,255	224	1,375	152	3	1,276	223	53
Jim Wells	3,745	3,592	2,752	3,348	22	5,330	2,773	6,849	1,988	0	6,304	2,827	913
Johnson	4,496	3,985	3,560	3,750	30	3,844	4,510	6,381	3,251	10	5,330	4,372	2,709
Jones	2,680	2,941	2,594	2,073	10	2,772	2,196	3,622	1,295	3	2,372	1,676	931
Karnes	1,884	2,374	1,636	1,764	17	2,556	1,526	3,178	993	6	2,271	1,342	686
Kaufman	3,762	2,964	2,902	2,816	32	3,008	2,717	4,766	1,922	6	3,311	2,431	2,350

Table 10: Presidential Races

General Elections, 1952-1968													
Year	1952		1956			1960		1964			1968		
County	Adlai E. Stevnsn (D)	Dwight D. Eisnhwr (R)	Adlai E. Stevnsn (D)	Dwight D. Eisnhwr (R)	T. Coleman Andrews (C)	John F. Kennedy (D)	Richard M. Nixon (R)	Lyndon B. Johnson (D)	Barry Goldwtr (R)	Joseph B. Lightbrn (C)	Hubert H. Humphry (D)	Richard M. Nixon (R)	George C. Wallace (A)
Kendall	370	1,786	341	1,519	13	549	1,544	970	1,200	3	538	1,569	364
Kenedy	14	108	10	125	0	78	74	115	30	1	100	76	7
Kent	526	259	519	234	2	491	205	563	115	0	303	143	188
Kerr	1,337	3,683	1,025	3,555	14	1,323	3,252	2,894	2,706	8	1,878	3,692	1,073
Kimble	525	1,077	484	821	2	550	699	862	520	1	463	640	264
King	189	66	177	46	1	133	39	180	34	0	109	44	71
Kinney	306	384	289	368	3	358	211	439	155	0	333	198	68
Kleberg	3,193	2,037	2,436	2,121	15	3,773	2,092	4,568	1,652	10	4,633	2,713	670
Knox	1,556	1,033	1,262	835	3	1,365	729	1,773	439	4	1,222	580	325
La Salle	816	565	574	449	1	718	326	988	223	1	645	324	112
Lamar	5,524	3,929	4,202	4,154	25	5,084	3,964	6,303	2,594	8	4,635	3,395	2,903
Lamb	2,748	2,913	3,325	1,840	12	3,089	2,764	4,318	2,022	9	2,267	2,595	1,460
Lampasas	1,199	1,478	1,134	1,308	5	1,372	1,222	2,224	744	2	1,423	935	460
Lavaca	2,750	3,599	2,412	2,509	20	4,002	1,507	4,031	1,480	6	2,165	1,698	1,451
Lee	1,389	1,316	1,061	1,200	13	1,369	1,048	1,884	923	2	1,283	1,075	631
Leon	1,842	1,266	1,260	1,079	7	1,803	868	2,373	642	7	1,536	659	880
Liberty	3,632	4,106	2,318	4,129	56	3,902	3,361	5,357	2,884	16	3,469	2,746	3,393
Limestone	4,132	2,485	3,067	2,097	7	3,472	2,023	3,777	1,478	8	2,796	1,485	1,402
Lipscomb	204	1,174	345	806	3	267	939	589	763	0	279	1,079	187
Live Oak	573	1,443	521	1,077	41	770	1,048	1,423	795	8	922	938	484
Llano	1,102	840	1,034	672	3	1,131	704	1,727	655	2	1,282	1,079	464
Loving	24	71	36	55	0	46	42	46	32	1	18	23	40
Lubbock	11,650	16,137	12,540	13,970	66	15,340	20,065	22,057	17,372	34	15,430	25,646	9,078
Lynn	1,762	1,351	1,800	861	6	1,872	953	2,281	745	4	1,333	1,005	544
Madison	1,152	692	713	733	12	909	607	1,298	644	3	994	608	765
Marion	970	877	709	1,126	13	904	742	1,372	927	4	1,260	637	957
Martin	952	562	903	318	6	831	350	892	402	3	373	343	539
Mason	606	1,069	504	885	1	575	833	941	590	4	560	789	169
Matagorda	2,101	4,122	1,944	3,927	78	2,971	2,975	4,143	2,407	5	3,595	3,094	1,777
Maverick	962	839	820	721	19	1,498	639	2,113	545	3	1,570	771	165
McCulloch	1,623	1,788	1,158	1,292	5	1,579	1,165	2,100	655	6	1,353	947	359
McLennan	17,251	14,974	16,181	15,561	111	20,100	14,926	28,429	10,892	25	22,388	15,958	8,268
McMullen	156	290	185	226	2	240	241	267	175	1	160	169	99
Medina	1,840	3,204	1,516	2,668	17	2,325	2,028	3,408	1,583	1	2,471	2,058	722
Menard	399	843	318	614	0	491	608	588	397	0	362	491	118
Midland	3,244	7,956	3,468	8,287	86	5,842	11,343	8,646	11,906	53	4,756	12,789	5,675
Milam	3,227	2,539	2,969	2,486	11	3,640	1,898	4,368	1,334	7	3,269	1,614	1,525
Mills	875	1,089	735	912	1	869	1,012	1,228	495	0	722	645	296
Mitchell	2,031	1,417	1,891	1,091	0	2,131	1,208	2,420	737	2	1,589	893	499
Montague	3,012	2,367	2,358	2,003	11	2,346	2,101	3,746	1,106	4	2,555	1,736	914
Montgomery	3,432	2,969	2,572	3,360	42	3,510	3,309	4,989	3,167	40	4,021	4,353	4,879
Moore	2,114	1,909	2,219	1,820	10	1,547	2,463	2,393	1,762	4	1,359	2,378	1,258
Morris	1,722	890	1,592	1,463	20	1,952	1,569	2,366	1,218	10	1,701	1,064	1,323
Motley	513	675	511	411	4	439	480	678	324	2	397	415	295
Nacogdoches	3,556	2,891	2,855	3,285	25	3,522	3,042	4,524	2,976	19	3,449	3,235	3,196
Navarro	8,745	3,592	4,723	3,193	15	5,540	3,361	6,811	2,139	3	5,296	2,845	2,245
Newton	1,630	917	1,037	1,030	9	1,815	756	2,211	738	6	1,476	555	1,509
Nolan	3,123	2,907	2,535	2,232	13	3,247	2,421	3,540	1,610	12	2,784	1,969	1,185
Nueces	20,156	19,124	19,912	19,985	162	29,361	18,907	40,426	14,048	84	39,025	21,307	7,159
Ochiltree	426	1,755	512	1,209	19	521	1,870	920	1,814	3	432	2,208	492
Oldham	280	341	294	284	0	326	313	397	269	4	237	320	230
Orange	6,403	4,491	5,910	5,501	51	9,078	5,483	9,390	6,216	39	6,485	5,886	8,845
Palo Pinto	2,876	3,029	2,369	2,818	12	3,022	2,695	3,791	1,748	2	3,552	2,627	1,257
Panola	2,897	2,080	2,225	2,538	73	2,187	2,264	2,608	2,818	11	1,711	1,586	2,650
Parker	3,434	3,523	3,165	3,390	33	3,629	3,467	5,270	2,175	13	4,301	3,068	1,934
Parmer	663	1,503	1,362	1,028	14	1,090	1,674	1,556	1,216	7	833	1,539	730
Pecos	1,076	1,573	931	1,425	11	1,724	1,412	2,068	1,393	12	1,592	1,524	900
Polk	2,238	1,454	1,465	1,663	16	2,037	1,268	2,492	1,199	9	1,841	1,013	1,712
Potter	9,259	14,931	8,720	11,943	49	8,989	14,202	12,850	11,505	64	8,238	13,338	5,486
Presidio	621	770	517	494	8	866	376	1,156	431	1	969	481	132
Rains	588	500	524	427	1	680	401	893	272	3	558	340	306
Randall	1,905	4,305	2,774	4,609	17	3,282	6,958	6,016	7,843	22	4,060	11,400	3,128
Reagan	460	533	384	669	1	621	489	614	406	2	370	454	288
Real	303	450	191	350	0	273	377	487	255	1	277	290	136
Red River	3,484	1,964	2,567	1,956	11	2,850	1,527	3,391	1,257	6	2,245	1,305	1,554

Table 10: Presidential Races

	General Elections, 1952-1968													
Year	1952		1956			1960		1964			1968		
County	Adlai E. Stevnsn (D)	Dwight D. Eisnhwr (R)	Adlai E. Stevnsn (D)	Dwight D. Eisnhwr (R)	T. Coleman Andrews (C)	John F. Kennedy (D)	Richard M. Nixon (R)	Lyndon B. Johnson (D)	Barry Goldwtr (R)	Joseph B. Lightbrn (C)	Hubert H. Humphry (D)	Richard M. Nixon (R)	George C. Wallace (A)
Reeves	1,385	1,727	1,356	1,492	8	2,235	1,549	2,340	1,251	4	1,456	1,310	743
Refugio	1,401	1,427	1,188	1,355	9	1,777	1,062	2,319	772	0	1,699	1,114	486
Roberts	91	379	118	279	2	104	339	198	297	0	90	311	113
Robertson	2,626	1,378	2,212	1,285	11	2,669	935	3,350	895	2	2,833	965	944
Rockwall	1,175	602	920	657	6	917	652	1,305	445	5	778	614	582
Runnels	1,853	2,622	1,442	2,416	5	1,938	2,128	2,645	1,480	7	1,448	1,707	668
Rusk	5,694	5,634	3,381	5,140	52	4,390	6,001	6,528	5,488	17	4,078	3,739	4,729
Sabine	1,573	729	913	801	1	1,208	619	1,801	428	1	1,078	455	935
San Augustine	1,359	730	1,086	900	11	1,269	638	1,173	760	7	817	506	1,137
San Jacinto	1,043	494	755	565	9	1,115	448	1,680	343	3	1,235	381	693
San Patricio	3,315	3,220	3,728	3,302	22	5,246	3,129	7,176	2,188	20	6,818	3,717	1,876
San Saba	1,752	900	1,419	797	6	1,251	849	1,859	418	0	1,140	535	465
Schleicher	421	628	336	471	4	351	455	514	388	1	378	396	178
Scurry	2,480	2,620	2,691	2,250	8	3,020	2,235	3,381	1,741	15	2,031	1,745	1,084
Shackelford	776	1,057	555	849	5	713	684	934	487	3	673	557	277
Shelby	4,249	1,792	3,403	1,988	49	3,266	1,679	3,487	2,220	4	2,511	1,127	3,285
Sherman	317	669	383	481	5	305	686	462	629	1	297	723	376
Smith	8,450	10,947	6,468	12,255	69	8,494	12,042	12,474	12,960	38	8,897	12,079	9,595
Somervell	450	494	309	467	5	345	441	641	210	3	384	313	204
Starr	3,055	620	2,727	547	0	4,051	280	4,056	678	8	3,922	1,374	71
Stephens	1,471	2,272	1,126	1,832	13	1,357	1,664	1,753	1,119	2	1,239	1,287	525
Sterling	158	277	150	223	0	193	182	243	140	1	151	170	54
Stonewall	836	319	829	306	3	864	306	978	219	2	635	213	262
Sutton	351	581	290	546	2	474	437	694	357	0	351	412	147
Swisher	1,074	1,843	1,802	876	6	1,777	1,310	2,410	815	5	1,760	1,177	623
Tarrant	45,968	63,680	43,922	66,329	946	59,385	72,813	97,092	56,593	473	79,705	81,786	29,256
Taylor	7,936	10,260	7,177	9,488	34	9,347	12,258	13,366	9,220	34	9,107	12,218	4,289
Terrell	295	426	217	350	2	352	291	364	294	0	201	250	149
Terry	2,105	1,823	2,050	1,473	3	2,237	1,908	3,034	1,592	6	1,625	1,948	854
Throckmorton	728	586	656	466	5	689	442	883	247	0	618	317	126
Titus	3,142	1,887	2,031	1,971	33	2,701	2,216	3,528	1,687	4	2,317	1,572	1,886
Tom Green	5,797	9,698	4,923	9,070	40	7,031	8,176	9,767	6,664	12	6,774	9,682	3,074
Travis	19,155	20,850	19,982	23,551	98	27,022	22,107	44,058	19,838	62	39,667	34,309	8,424
Trinity	1,725	958	1,091	865	11	1,521	707	1,654	763	11	1,146	636	997
Tyler	1,304	1,466	797	1,734	10	1,242	1,401	1,818	1,216	3	1,204	1,120	1,462
Upshur	3,040	2,391	1,995	2,737	32	3,248	2,262	4,027	2,222	13	2,480	1,519	2,886
Upton	850	940	834	999	7	930	798	958	636	10	463	664	459
Uvalde	1,230	2,805	994	2,449	20	1,324	2,214	2,358	1,963	5	1,736	2,252	768
Val Verde	1,647	1,725	1,598	1,660	9	2,049	1,551	3,555	1,346	1	3,205	1,914	573
Van Zandt	3,911	2,279	2,919	2,142	9	2,825	2,120	4,047	1,614	15	2,706	1,954	2,091
Victoria	3,128	4,306	3,280	5,596	28	5,779	4,591	8,141	4,201	25	6,042	6,352	2,336
Walker	2,078	1,897	1,287	1,991	48	1,832	1,750	2,877	1,557	2	2,391	1,946	1,452
Waller	1,264	1,487	929	1,426	42	1,101	1,115	2,167	980	2	1,684	958	797
Ward	1,840	1,994	1,638	1,772	22	2,018	1,763	2,221	1,730	3	1,331	1,552	1,382
Washington	1,354	3,519	933	2,975	15	1,864	2,613	2,938	2,019	5	1,686	3,244	677
Webb	6,208	2,784	5,827	2,744	16	10,059	1,802	10,073	1,094	15	9,419	2,103	304
Wharton	4,022	5,232	3,439	4,714	50	5,004	3,387	6,234	2,775	11	4,304	3,773	1,882
Wheeler	1,551	1,645	1,252	1,178	13	1,011	1,428	1,440	1,138	2	812	1,176	570
Wichita	13,505	12,197	12,726	12,181	41	14,587	12,587	19,131	8,585	14	15,387	11,937	6,087
Wilbarger	2,646	3,019	2,347	2,230	10	2,319	2,796	3,200	1,539	3	1,996	1,909	1,292
Willacy	1,324	2,244	1,261	1,656	31	2,109	1,367	2,152	1,230	6	1,930	1,243	465
Williamson	5,010	3,646	4,402	2,947	18	5,410	2,429	7,430	1,766	6	5,528	2,923	1,669
Wilson	2,187	1,823	2,149	1,519	10	2,905	1,248	3,472	718	5	2,336	1,321	542
Winkler	1,508	1,550	1,287	1,471	19	1,642	1,562	2,059	1,617	3	938	1,391	1,249
Wise	3,121	2,309	2,443	2,058	23	2,470	2,562	3,852	1,386	3	2,774	1,983	1,107
Wood	3,026	2,748	2,199	2,508	15	2,633	2,400	3,528	2,068	10	2,192	2,046	2,020
Yoakum	873	858	989	923	3	994	1,207	1,415	859	6	615	1,123	724
Young	2,536	2,649	2,028	2,083	19	2,419	2,067	3,395	1,600	1	2,482	1,860	1,004
Zapata	616	526	886	637	1	675	260	1,009	135	3	909	251	52
Zavala	677	1,043	528	896	3	706	761	1,784	598	3	1,307	693	214
Official	969,228		859,958			1,167,932		1,663,185		5,060	1,227,844		
Totals		1,102,878		1,080,619	14,591		1,121,699		958,566		1,266,804		584,269
Unofficial	969,228		859,728			1,167,932		1,663,185		5,060	1,227,844		
Totals		1,102,879		1,080,619	14,591		1,121,699		958,566		1,266,804		584,269

Table 11: Presidential Races

	General Elections, 1972-1988										
Year	1972		1976			1980			1984		1988	
County	George McGvrn (D)	Richard Nixon (R)	Jimmy Carter (D)	Gerald Ford (R)	Eugene J. McCrthy (I)	Jimmy Carter (D)	Ronald Reagan (R)	John Andrsn (I)	Walter Mondle (D)	Ronald Reagan (R)	Michael Dukaks (D)	George Bush (R)
Anderson	2,233	5,826	5,499	4,172	17	5,163	5,970	137	4,747	8,634	6,128	7,858
Andrews	677	2,615	1,777	2,127	7	1,155	2,800	39	820	3,918	1,122	3,052
Angelina	4,970	11,453	9,750	7,223	47	10,140	9,900	232	9,054	14,685	10,849	12,738
Aransas	844	2,037	2,136	1,985	29	1,800	3,081	134	1,696	4,352	2,305	3,858
Archer	632	1,494	1,577	966	7	1,444	1,804	30	1,089	2,487	1,627	2,010
Armstrong	177	768	513	506	1	333	709	9	238	791	314	720
Atascosa	1,804	3,400	4,565	2,415	19	3,980	4,364	93	3,547	5,279	4,657	4,777
Austin	1,043	3,084	2,313	2,686	10	1,893	3,734	87	1,941	4,872	2,593	4,524
Bailey	465	1,837	1,356	1,255	9	800	1,809	26	684	1,888	876	1,459
Bandera	434	1,796	1,183	1,554	14	894	2,373	64	771	3,152	1,251	3,435
Bastrop	1,906	3,097	4,788	2,383	31	4,716	3,768	205	4,744	6,439	8,004	5,991
Baylor	598	1,190	1,335	783	10	1,183	1,098	14	1,019	1,314	1,153	914
Bee	2,067	3,779	3,690	2,953	42	3,606	4,171	125	3,659	5,377	4,616	4,620
Bell	6,848	17,525	17,499	15,126	143	15,823	20,729	934	13,322	31,117	17,751	29,382
Bexar	91,662	137,572	146,581	121,176	1,621	137,729	159,578	9,467	136,947	203,319	174,036	193,192
Blanco	460	1,215	923	1,015	9	794	1,434	52	700	1,957	1,012	1,680
Borden	96	330	234	150	3	131	279	3	140	325	169	283
Bosque	1,014	2,947	2,954	1,912	6	2,431	2,908	62	2,046	3,923	2,670	3,458
Bowie	5,227	14,722	12,445	9,590	81	11,339	13,942	244	10,077	18,244	12,331	15,454
Brazoria	11,350	21,045	21,711	19,475	172	18,253	27,614	1,205	18,609	39,166	23,436	34,028
Brazos	5,692	14,243	10,628	15,685	175	9,856	17,798	1,453	12,348	34,733	14,885	29,369
Brewster	904	1,524	1,227	1,368	15	1,271	1,496	89	1,462	2,066	1,569	1,708
Briscoe	349	642	823	285	7	561	562	13	471	538	574	464
Brooks	1,657	1,117	2,782	641	3	2,488	780	43	2,702	896	2,859	608
Brown	2,171	5,990	5,577	4,483	7	4,867	6,515	102	4,070	8,468	4,763	6,810
Burleson	1,361	1,762	2,924	1,142	7	2,615	1,943	33	2,578	3,076	3,085	2,242
Burnet	1,227	3,438	3,818	2,777	22	3,711	4,033	132	2,983	5,895	4,343	5,120
Caldwell	1,974	3,171	3,647	2,235	29	3,155	2,879	112	3,401	4,315	4,649	3,553
Calhoun	1,936	3,614	3,642	2,377	29	3,034	3,312	136	2,586	4,434	3,314	3,183
Callahan	665	2,223	2,241	1,581	13	2,002	2,284	29	1,305	3,538	2,017	2,887
Cameron	13,340	20,816	25,310	16,448	199	23,200	22,041	801	26,394	29,545	30,972	24,263
Camp	1,041	1,599	2,146	1,133	4	2,052	1,531	19	1,917	2,238	2,121	1,908
Carson	561	1,868	1,542	1,269	2	1,006	1,888	26	826	2,412	1,034	2,100
Cass	1,981	5,303	5,134	3,712	15	5,578	4,993	60	5,053	6,677	5,941	5,305
Castro	751	1,685	2,033	1,007	13	1,199	1,955	44	1,009	2,026	1,436	1,604
Chambers	1,206	2,390	2,927	1,835	16	2,517	3,140	96	2,632	4,322	3,035	3,694
Cherokee	2,467	5,743	6,509	3,921	16	5,726	5,629	92	4,494	8,187	5,604	7,520
Childress	729	1,716	1,578	1,043	2	1,222	1,443	33	900	1,574	1,060	1,201
Clay	1,023	1,893	2,568	1,200	7	2,233	1,824	40	1,844	2,569	2,288	2,043
Cochran	415	1,106	1,031	701	6	513	1,064	23	557	1,117	681	771
Coke	358	761	844	517	4	838	708	10	532	1,060	674	863
Coleman	721	2,386	2,264	1,669	12	1,719	2,228	33	1,420	2,790	1,978	2,340
Collin	4,783	17,667	14,039	21,608	153	15,187	36,559	1,559	13,604	61,095	22,934	67,776
Collingsworth	501	1,250	1,169	629	2	798	1,020	18	742	1,396	809	872
Colorado	1,502	3,495	3,028	2,991	35	2,377	3,520	58	2,428	4,528	2,847	3,723
Comal	1,823	6,761	4,068	6,377	55	3,554	9,758	324	4,179	13,452	5,716	13,994
Comanche	1,176	2,608	3,414	1,297	8	2,550	1,977	40	2,248	2,678	2,622	2,120
Concho	350	709	715	474	2	702	700	8	580	821	643	617
Cooke	1,702	6,317	4,483	4,804	28	3,842	6,760	129	3,278	8,260	4,217	7,196
Coryell	1,235	5,077	4,710	4,140	45	4,097	5,494	228	3,113	9,056	4,026	7,461
Cottle	571	564	1,047	311	1	732	511	9	623	507	690	379
Crane	349	1,123	664	963	20	607	1,310	23	392	1,473	596	1,219
Crockett	329	851	804	802	0	595	885	10	589	1,094	881	932
Crosby	1,021	1,503	2,176	897	11	1,408	1,361	17	1,212	1,376	1,435	1,121
Culberson	238	555	407	373	3	423	541	7	407	509	557	417
Dallam	327	1,271	1,029	936	17	632	965	33	496	1,594	645	1,205
Dallas	129,662	305,112	196,303	263,081	2,594	190,459	306,682	14,271	203,592	405,444	243,198	347,094
Dawson	846	3,247	2,162	2,474	13	1,867	3,267	55	1,781	3,685	2,155	3,154
DeWitt	1,357	3,755	2,540	2,754	20	2,044	3,450	66	1,882	4,401	2,579	3,628
Deaf Smith	1,240	3,690	2,613	2,776	21	1,666	4,073	77	1,485	4,762	1,930	3,744
Delta	581	957	1,563	421	2	1,347	767	18	973	1,024	1,244	849
Denton	9,720	19,138	18,887	20,440	290	17,381	29,908	1,953	16,772	52,865	26,204	57,444
Dickens	534	708	1,222	343	2	912	554	13	692	594	696	435
Dimmit	1,078	1,172	1,721	890	5	2,102	1,173	25	2,546	1,338	2,735	900
Donley	350	1,229	1,095	704	3	751	1,106	22	529	1,297	661	1,043

Table 11: Presidential Races

General Elections, 1972-1988												
Year	1972		1976			1980			1984		1988	
County	George McGvrn (D)	Richard Nixon (R)	Jimmy Carter (D)	Gerald Ford (R)	Eugene J. McCrthy (I)	Jimmy Carter (D)	Ronald Reagan (R)	John Andrsn (I)	Walter Mondale (D)	Ronald Reagan (R)	Michael Dukaks (D)	George Bush (R)
Duval	3,729	623	4,267	661	10	3,706	1,012	28	3,748	1,201	4,177	907
Eastland	1,630	4,106	4,320	2,340	18	3,346	3,442	37	2,522	4,841	3,215	3,929
Ector	5,449	21,386	10,802	18,973	177	9,069	26,188	636	8,913	31,228	10,825	23,155
Edwards	109	520	258	412	2	237	575	11	159	626	368	556
El Paso	32,435	49,981	45,477	42,697	721	40,082	53,276	5,096	51,917	66,114	62,622	55,573
Ellis	3,839	8,779	9,991	6,996	28	9,219	10,046	214	8,029	16,873	11,169	16,422
Erath	1,648	4,777	4,821	2,925	33	4,156	3,981	92	3,234	6,122	4,113	5,427
Falls	1,825	3,017	4,277	2,261	7	3,328	2,606	51	2,834	3,133	2,877	2,344
Fannin	2,295	3,826	5,845	2,102	12	5,284	3,196	74	4,399	4,692	5,163	4,024
Fayette	1,400	3,882	3,428	3,030	16	2,590	4,104	77	2,379	5,711	3,390	4,551
Fisher	933	1,207	1,993	573	5	1,564	838	23	1,384	965	1,516	721
Floyd	841	2,181	1,991	1,402	15	1,477	2,043	24	1,023	2,092	1,391	1,741
Foard	312	369	706	240	1	617	349	7	448	472	513	306
Fort Bend	4,541	10,475	11,264	17,354	93	11,583	25,366	1,005	18,729	41,370	23,351	39,818
Franklin	546	1,059	1,636	758	6	1,487	1,105	14	1,104	1,836	1,453	1,439
Freestone	1,283	2,459	2,679	1,674	1	2,739	2,468	33	2,489	3,624	2,916	3,159
Frio	1,588	1,904	2,598	1,280	14	2,849	1,753	47	2,656	2,003	3,016	1,505
Gaines	669	1,923	1,880	1,643	7	1,182	2,390	46	797	2,714	1,310	2,265
Galveston	22,565	30,936	37,873	25,251	331	30,778	29,527	1,955	36,092	40,262	38,633	34,913
Garza	446	1,153	957	755	11	677	1,188	22	521	1,219	989	1,183
Gillespie	526	3,490	1,260	3,541	32	1,170	4,736	90	1,137	5,496	1,588	5,662
Glasscock	75	288	190	218	3	116	416	2	128	403	143	384
Goliad	464	1,018	875	846	3	1,081	1,170	22	836	1,540	1,358	1,427
Gonzales	1,164	2,707	3,219	1,789	12	2,896	2,931	61	2,196	3,962	2,897	2,983
Gray	1,367	7,968	3,872	6,010	38	2,786	7,187	103	2,003	8,955	2,460	7,259
Grayson	6,952	16,769	17,015	11,981	72	13,807	16,811	532	11,803	22,554	14,347	18,825
Gregg	5,325	19,927	9,827	17,582	78	10,219	23,399	311	10,700	29,697	12,486	26,465
Grimes	1,116	2,243	2,656	1,473	6	2,440	2,087	42	2,370	3,365	2,735	2,820
Guadalupe	3,404	8,287	6,054	6,766	53	5,049	9,901	407	5,060	14,382	7,111	13,265
Hale	2,135	7,051	5,580	5,390	19	3,610	7,277	123	3,202	7,670	3,502	6,284
Hall	607	1,303	1,633	671	2	1,057	1,141	13	984	1,058	1,029	714
Hamilton	685	1,931	1,981	1,176	22	1,526	1,683	30	1,130	2,118	1,355	1,718
Hansford	202	1,947	983	1,401	9	518	2,046	17	259	2,213	443	1,967
Hardeman	614	1,357	1,403	805	7	1,174	1,056	28	927	1,238	1,143	855
Hardin	2,952	5,190	6,558	4,046	39	7,358	6,087	200	6,782	8,380	8,245	6,897
Harris	215,916	365,672	321,897	357,536	4,023	274,061	416,655	22,917	334,135	536,029	342,919	464,217
Harrison	4,333	9,600	7,796	7,787	23	7,746	9,328	125	7,773	12,618	8,974	11,957
Hartley	206	946	774	811	6	470	1,248	28	356	1,419	505	1,229
Haskell	950	1,744	2,512	838	4	1,951	1,447	22	1,434	1,701	1,715	1,193
Hays	4,068	5,406	7,005	5,714	117	6,013	6,517	590	6,663	12,467	11,187	11,716
Hemphill	214	942	707	858	10	592	1,152	21	413	1,650	527	1,170
Henderson	2,741	6,263	8,245	4,658	18	8,199	7,903	134	7,302	12,725	9,819	11,005
Hidalgo	18,366	22,920	35,021	19,199	172	34,542	25,808	1,063	44,147	35,059	54,330	29,246
Hill	1,882	4,481	5,327	2,680	10	4,688	4,113	73	3,420	5,344	4,381	4,796
Hockley	1,625	4,084	3,949	3,137	28	2,447	4,599	90	2,044	5,462	2,850	4,368
Hood	949	1,743	3,181	1,857	14	3,001	3,755	109	3,063	6,817	4,255	7,400
Hopkins	1,710	3,903	4,992	2,556	16	4,344	3,834	93	3,707	5,772	4,984	5,133
Houston	1,844	3,317	3,179	2,229	5	4,181	2,889	47	3,275	4,542	3,846	3,882
Howard	2,714	7,343	6,984	4,899	39	4,451	6,658	158	4,115	7,519	4,445	6,024
Hudspeth	250	467	479	395	5	394	471	14	362	557	406	405
Hunt	3,655	9,535	8,543	6,676	57	8,773	9,283	327	6,971	14,303	8,820	12,331
Hutchinson	1,405	7,411	3,691	6,137	44	2,935	7,439	170	2,052	9,078	2,950	7,526
Irion	111	363	297	302	2	239	427	2	199	619	326	539
Jack	775	1,719	1,814	1,049	5	1,349	1,482	29	945	1,825	1,521	1,542
Jackson	1,163	2,743	2,524	1,884	14	1,826	2,540	66	1,804	3,661	2,141	2,954
Jasper	2,746	4,575	5,422	3,167	10	5,707	4,396	98	5,787	5,965	6,613	4,985
Jeff Davis	202	382	309	288	5	300	409	10	299	511	325	524
Jefferson	29,909	45,819	47,581	32,451	272	45,642	36,763	1,664	54,846	45,124	55,649	35,754
Jim Hogg	848	765	1,645	429	0	1,437	535	23	1,703	608	1,630	510
Jim Wells	4,404	5,283	7,961	3,547	34	7,267	4,606	102	7,795	5,896	8,495	4,335
Johnson	3,968	10,042	10,864	7,194	27	10,542	11,411	333	9,148	18,254	12,507	17,509
Jones	1,050	3,202	3,318	2,072	13	3,043	2,765	45	2,343	4,017	2,898	3,000
Karnes	1,780	2,639	2,996	1,675	22	2,284	2,719	52	1,802	3,068	2,529	2,383
Kaufman	2,795	5,100	6,302	3,867	21	6,266	5,852	110	5,554	9,343	7,358	8,466
Kendall	484	2,681	1,190	2,543	37	1,075	3,890	88	938	4,568	1,446	4,875

Table 11: Presidential Races

	General Elections, 1972-1988										
Year	**1972**		**1976**			**1980**			**1984**		**1988**	
County	George McGvrn (D)	Richard Nixon (R)	Jimmy Carter (D)	Gerald Ford (R)	Eugene J. McCrthy (I)	Jimmy Carter (D)	Ronald Reagan (R)	John Andrsn (I)	Walter Mondle (D)	Ronald Reagan (R)	Michael Dukaks (D)	George Bush (R)
Kenedy	88	124	139	65	1	106	76	2	110	96	119	76
Kent	223	465	474	171	2	351	339	0	253	332	398	274
Kerr	1,511	6,039	3,767	6,021	52	3,387	9,090	259	3,102	11,829	3,587	11,207
Kimble	266	971	759	846	12	608	1,011	22	442	1,333	551	1,061
King	75	143	100	96	0	55	144	5	53	141	64	111
Kinney	234	425	516	318	5	472	543	23	486	774	669	771
Kleberg	4,481	5,312	5,803	3,771	56	5,125	4,608	231	4,924	5,712	5,367	4,443
Knox	638	1,148	1,498	551	8	1,163	783	17	921	1,027	1,013	765
La Salle	567	1,073	1,294	677	4	1,442	773	19	1,504	1,007	7,553	693
Lamar	2,865	7,736	8,601	4,443	17	7,178	6,094	148	5,504	9,273	2,230	8,021
Lamb	1,350	3,981	3,374	2,413	11	2,132	3,723	51	1,919	3,892	1,954	3,064
Lampasas	688	2,251	2,376	1,563	9	1,979	2,323	56	1,356	3,285	1,651	3,000
Lavaca	1,429	3,288	3,458	2,466	23	2,678	3,254	54	2,464	5,058	3,531	4,377
Lee	920	1,877	1,937	1,348	14	1,581	1,803	59	1,659	2,967	2,527	2,513
Leon	863	1,699	2,085	1,161	2	2,190	1,821	19	1,821	3,207	2,316	2,778
Liberty	3,311	6,111	7,086	4,552	19	6,810	6,470	163	6,292	10,504	8,343	8,524
Limestone	1,452	2,949	3,825	2,045	10	3,403	2,835	45	3,228	4,063	3,476	3,257
Lipscomb	156	1,226	644	911	8	338	1,343	28	241	1,461	377	1,111
Live Oak	610	1,745	1,656	1,287	5	1,380	2,193	32	1,260	2,481	1,573	2,277
Llano	766	2,164	2,361	1,947	8	2,130	2,866	72	1,894	4,042	2,629	3,550
Loving	7	55	35	47	0	22	50	0	16	57	23	54
Lubbock	15,353	43,564	24,797	38,478	307	18,732	46,711	1,952	18,793	57,151	22,202	50,760
Lynn	697	1,766	1,575	1,166	7	1,236	1,603	28	1,009	1,617	1,086	1,279
Madison	561	1,540	1,885	1,062	4	1,583	1,389	32	1,384	2,158	1,835	1,896
Marion	1,106	1,680	1,860	1,291	5	2,015	1,666	28	2,111	2,336	2,255	1,857
Martin	287	935	907	698	3	605	1,093	15	512	1,218	632	1,017
Mason	369	1,096	814	805	11	630	966	17	570	1,168	671	975
Matagorda	2,473	5,003	4,971	3,679	30	4,585	5,545	146	5,201	8,452	5,675	6,787
Maverick	1,710	1,477	2,840	924	11	2,932	1,370	39	3,063	1,783	4,395	1,592
McCulloch	753	1,769	1,888	1,300	9	1,750	1,572	24	1,433	2,060	1,665	1,618
McLennan	15,947	33,377	30,091	25,370	149	26,305	31,968	964	23,206	42,232	27,545	38,606
McMullen	88	304	194	217	0	122	271	4	61	337	94	302
Medina	1,507	4,059	3,681	3,252	30	3,034	4,742	84	3,053	5,737	4,227	5,722
Menard	273	644	543	441	5	489	548	11	394	725	614	552
Midland	4,388	18,905	7,725	19,178	106	6,839	25,027	586	7,214	33,706	8,487	30,618
Milam	2,159	3,554	4,871	2,404	22	4,230	3,251	111	3,734	4,384	4,865	3,512
Mills	388	1,089	1,012	684	9	1,028	985	24	688	1,262	842	1,043
Mitchell	699	1,790	1,730	1,058	7	1,446	1,455	12	1,332	2,007	1,773	1,596
Montague	1,285	3,463	4,087	2,182	7	3,233	3,143	59	2,602	4,406	3,689	3,475
Montgomery	4,358	15,067	13,718	15,739	96	12,593	26,237	819	13,293	41,230	18,394	40,360
Moore	863	3,620	2,767	2,759	26	1,743	3,736	67	1,129	4,649	1,537	3,710
Morris	1,162	2,699	3,071	1,843	11	3,105	2,133	27	2,925	2,778	3,522	2,104
Motley	230	657	522	428	3	341	573	7	282	533	262	429
Nacogdoches	3,656	8,757	6,697	7,315	101	5,981	8,626	422	5,694	13,063	6,886	11,767
Navarro	3,246	6,039	6,995	4,012	22	6,988	5,400	126	5,672	7,816	6,749	6,445
Newton	1,636	1,946	3,468	1,011	7	3,284	1,379	24	3,296	2,123	3,640	1,659
Nolan	1,338	3,634	3,094	2,431	8	2,796	2,781	87	2,524	3,608	2,853	2,734
Nueces	33,277	41,682	52,755	32,797	518	43,424	40,586	2,045	46,721	54,333	49,209	46,337
Ochiltree	298	2,861	1,084	2,471	11	594	3,032	52	419	3,492	579	2,928
Oldham	173	666	554	354	2	290	557	9	226	762	303	691
Orange	7,172	13,234	15,177	9,147	61	14,928	12,389	395	16,816	15,386	17,834	11,959
Palo Pinto	2,181	5,058	5,170	2,684	21	4,244	4,068	98	3,349	5,701	3,930	4,649
Panola	1,511	4,324	3,731	3,218	21	3,637	4,022	58	3,179	5,676	4,123	4,642
Parker	3,184	7,152	8,186	4,692	58	7,336	8,505	189	6,050	13,647	8,517	14,090
Parmer	495	2,304	1,914	1,487	8	707	2,640	30	567	2,524	764	2,061
Pecos	847	2,419	1,971	2,234	10	1,602	2,723	37	1,596	3,451	1,960	2,483
Polk	1,760	3,048	4,384	2,529	19	4,213	3,771	80	3,898	5,987	5,943	5,831
Potter	6,264	18,891	11,917	13,819	158	9,633	16,327	545	8,365	20,396	9,563	16,400
Presidio	674	785	1,232	687	7	1,039	723	22	992	837	1,176	586
Rains	532	865	1,339	510	3	1,174	813	18	1,027	1,560	1,448	1,281
Randall	3,470	18,557	9,074	17,115	141	7,323	23,136	677	6,044	30,249	8,492	27,986
Reagan	244	703	563	666	2	414	917	14	243	1,079	418	935
Real	150	483	510	448	6	603	832	14	360	1,004	483	795
Red River	1,361	3,112	3,670	1,852	6	3,501	2,225	31	2,518	2,979	3,165	2,475
Reeves	1,510	2,427	2,613	1,711	11	2,138	2,315	52	2,396	2,461	2,812	1,724

Table 11: Presidential Races

General Elections, 1972-1988												
Year	1972		1976			1980			1984		1988	
County	George McGvrn (D)	Richard Nixon (R)	Jimmy Carter (D)	Gerald Ford (R)	Eugene J. McCrthy (I)	Jimmy Carter (D)	Ronald Reagan (R)	John Andrsn (I)	Walter Mondale (D)	Ronald Reagan (R)	Michael Dukakis (D)	George Bush (R)
Refugio	1,060	1,937	2,218	1,537	6	2,224	1,944	57	1,559	2,421	1,831	1,883
Roberts	71	467	202	350	2	150	482	4	106	539	135	441
Robertson	1,976	1,977	3,741	1,244	2	3,572	1,661	33	3,339	2,663	3,630	2,184
Rockwall	610	1,890	1,828	2,087	8	1,985	4,036	113	1,639	6,688	2,659	7,214
Runnels	739	2,752	2,068	2,203	5	1,648	2,532	36	1,179	2,968	1,720	2,417
Rusk	2,867	8,179	6,063	6,800	31	5,582	8,705	116	4,599	11,081	5,140	9,117
Sabine	936	1,333	2,391	904	1	1,983	1,387	15	1,940	2,045	2,053	1,925
San Augustine	753	1,508	1,817	1,047	2	1,674	1,397	14	1,583	1,937	2,118	1,946
San Jacinto	1,020	1,296	2,406	1,094	5	2,376	1,726	42	2,466	3,174	2,972	2,691
San Patricio	5,097	7,179	9,469	5,853	49	8,627	8,326	280	8,838	11,074	9,920	9,159
San Saba	567	1,106	1,408	582	5	1,405	948	23	1,070	1,566	1,165	1,099
Schleicher	250	630	468	516	2	444	672	6	326	854	494	653
Scurry	1,223	3,777	2,639	2,797	18	2,003	3,745	53	1,564	5,028	2,119	3,749
Shackelford	331	909	764	748	3	606	959	9	415	1,181	681	865
Shelby	1,792	4,292	4,680	2,695	7	4,215	3,500	71	3,610	4,863	4,261	3,999
Sherman	169	996	718	679	12	286	1,128	28	246	1,269	340	1,145
Smith	8,041	23,671	16,856	22,238	108	14,838	28,236	414	15,227	40,740	18,719	34,658
Somervell	284	703	1,054	332	1	1,015	792	21	635	1,422	983	1,304
Starr	3,320	2,389	4,646	664	10	4,782	1,389	50	5,047	1,658	6,958	1,218
Stephens	678	2,259	1,796	1,621	8	1,372	2,161	34	1,046	2,898	1,519	2,342
Sterling	94	286	174	202	2	218	364	2	129	577	188	464
Stonewall	394	662	812	252	3	719	488	6	643	599	724	421
Sutton	245	705	768	831	4	485	1,000	13	465	1,251	571	996
Swisher	1,300	1,790	2,811	753	9	1,854	1,450	50	1,642	1,611	1,893	1,271
Tarrant	69,187	151,596	122,287	124,433	1,265	121,068	173,466	7,818	120,147	248,050	151,310	242,660
Taylor	6,024	22,417	14,453	19,822	118	13,245	22,961	620	9,628	34,444	13,073	28,563
Terrell	124	467	321	317	2	260	411	14	289	407	390	296
Terry	1,099	3,057	2,859	2,113	12	1,945	3,178	45	1,535	3,181	1,941	2,645
Throckmorton	348	568	658	356	1	455	444	7	388	586	534	455
Titus	1,703	3,671	4,205	2,603	10	3,872	3,747	44	3,631	5,069	4,357	4,247
Tom Green	6,082	15,784	11,064	12,316	107	9,892	16,555	661	8,981	23,847	12,283	21,463
Travis	54,157	70,561	78,585	71,031	2,129	75,028	73,151	9,796	94,124	124,944	127,783	105,915
Trinity	826	1,467	2,100	1,042	0	2,510	1,503	32	2,115	2,599	2,657	2,448
Tyler	1,321	2,955	3,322	1,965	13	3,540	2,545	70	3,119	3,638	4,198	3,070
Upshur	1,879	4,736	4,902	3,272	15	4,894	4,836	78	4,614	7,325	5,242	5,991
Upton	256	1,186	686	869	5	485	1,169	13	380	1,603	544	1,189
Uvalde	1,438	3,883	2,299	3,103	19	2,402	3,887	62	2,482	4,790	3,684	4,266
Val Verde	2,049	4,052	4,603	3,476	24	4,116	5,055	145	3,857	5,909	5,044	5,109
Van Zandt	1,939	4,839	6,449	3,385	33	5,707	5,495	78	4,506	8,474	6,153	7,371
Victoria	4,226	11,246	7,326	9,594	65	7,382	13,392	347	7,037	18,787	8,923	15,056
Walker	2,940	5,082	5,105	4,974	56	4,869	5,657	274	4,263	8,809	5,826	8,473
Waller	1,538	2,263	2,828	1,992	10	3,329	3,019	76	3,828	4,116	3,957	3,607
Ward	1,049	2,687	2,046	2,123	27	1,405	2,912	50	1,188	3,474	1,858	2,709
Washington	1,323	3,862	2,635	3,820	24	2,518	4,821	95	2,483	6,506	2,960	6,041
Webb	8,435	6,011	10,362	4,222	73	11,856	5,421	242	12,308	8,582	16,227	7,528
Wharton	3,481	6,271	5,914	4,682	26	5,138	6,598	160	5,072	8,495	5,935	6,978
Wheeler	502	1,766	1,598	1,273	6	1,090	1,626	16	805	2,251	1,067	1,703
Wichita	10,948	25,197	22,017	19,024	122	17,657	22,884	847	16,009	28,932	17,956	23,324
Wilbarger	1,139	3,183	3,280	2,145	11	2,347	3,031	53	2,011	3,644	2,248	2,669
Willacy	1,384	2,317	2,984	1,542	12	3,047	1,995	38	3,037	2,340	3,165	1,750
Williamson	3,806	6,998	9,355	7,481	90	10,408	15,035	946	9,911	25,774	19,589	27,322
Wilson	2,072	2,953	3,973	1,926	0	3,097	3,443	73	2,829	4,588	3,953	4,436
Winkler	602	2,467	1,382	1,842	11	1,021	2,160	35	752	2,213	947	1,656
Wise	1,741	4,230	5,133	2,856	7	4,674	4,350	108	3,856	6,958	5,288	6,064
Wood	1,842	4,746	4,107	3,076	9	4,033	4,515	74	3,449	7,144	4,553	6,216
Yoakum	457	1,952	1,181	1,477	5	715	1,937	28	456	2,204	727	1,762
Young	1,486	3,353	3,473	2,652	11	2,740	4,153	84	2,203	5,282	3,007	4,156
Zapata	768	695	1,216	462	0	1,218	874	19	1,577	1,214	2,171	958
Zavala	1,122	1,288	1,822	735	5	2,621	831	69	2,937	924	3,338	628
Official	1,154,289		2,082,319		20,118	2,510,705			1,949,276		2,352,748	
Totals		2,298,896		1,953,300			1,881,147			111,613		3,433,428	3,036,829
Unofficial	1,154,290		2,082,319		20,118	2,510,705			1,949,276		2,352,748	
Totals		2,298,896		1,953,300			1,881,147			111,613		3,433,428	3,036,829

Put Your Money On Reagan County

A betting man would look to Reagan County in West Texas to see how sentiment in a presidential election runs. Since the county began holding presidential elections, it has backed the national winner 86 percent of the time, regardless of how the rest of the state voted. Upton and Terrell counties, also in West Texas, are only a percentage point behind at 85 percent. These counties have an advantage in the sweepstakes because they all are relatively new counties, participating in 21 or less of 33 presidential elections held since Texas joined the Union.

Fort Bend County on the Gulf Coast is the champion of the older counties, backing the winner 79 percent of the time.

Two counties have tied as having the best record for voting Democratic in presidential elections. Neither Brooks nor Jim Hogg counties, both in South Texas, has ever voted Republican. Brooks has participated in 20 presidential elections and Jim Hogg, 18. Forty-two Texas counties have voted 90 percent of the time for Democratic presidential candidates.

Kendall County in West Texas is the champion Republican county, supporting the party's nominee for president 93 per cent of the time in 27 elections. Runner-up was Gillespie, also in West Central Texas, with a 66 percent support record for Republicans. Ten counties have voted for Republican presidential candidates more than 50 percent of the time.

Third parties have not fared well in Texas. George Wallace in 1968 carried 21 counties for the best showing. Champion supporter of third-party presidential nominees is Bandera, voting three times with third-party candidates. Here is how counties voted:

Table 12: Election Analysis

		Presidential Voting Success Summary																
Area Covered		Historic Performance Since 1848										Since 1964				Backed Winner		
County	Geographic Region	Democrats Won	Democrats Rank	Republicans Won	Republicans Rank	Others Won	Others Rank	Total Elections	Democrat Pct.	Republican Pct	Democrats Won	Republicans Won	Others Won	Winners Backed	% Backing Winners	Back Winners Rank
Anderson	North Texas	25	141	9	112	0	112	34	0.74	0.26	3	4	0	21	0.62	107
Andrews	West Texas	12	218	8	36	0	89	20	0.60	0.40	1	6	0	16	0.80	6
Angelina	East Texas	28	63	4	201	1	14	33	0.85	0.12	3	3	1	18	0.55	175
Aransas	South Texas	23	131	7	122	0	235	30	0.77	0.23	3	4	0	19	0.63	84
Archer	North Central	23	65	4	182	0	182	27	0.85	0.15	3	4	0	16	0.59	124
Armstrong	Panhandle	18	152	7	98	0	98	25	0.72	0.28	2	5	0	16	0.64	82
Atascosa	South Texas	23	142	7	120	1	38	31	0.74	0.23	3	4	0	18	0.58	153
Austin	Upper Gulf	19	220	13	33	0	97	32	0.59	0.41	1	6	0	19	0.59	131
Bailey	Panhandle	9	238	8	15	0	196	17	0.53	0.47	2	5	0	14	0.82	4
Bandera	West Central	15	244	13	30	3	1	31	0.48	0.42	1	6	0	15	0.48	232
Bastrop	Central Texas	31	26	3	221	0	222	34	0.91	0.09	5	2	0	17	0.50	222
Baylor	North Central	26	17	2	233	0	233	28	0.93	0.07	5	2	0	14	0.50	217
Bee	South Texas	24	126	7	125	0	242	31	0.77	0.23	3	4	0	19	0.61	113
Bell	Central Texas	28	71	5	184	0	184	33	0.85	0.15	3	4	0	19	0.58	144

Table 12: Election Analysis

		Presidential Voting Success Summary														
Area Covered		Historic Performance Since 1848									Since 1964			Backed Winner		
County	Geographic Region	Democrats Won	Democrats Rank	Republicans Won	Republicans Rank	Others Won	Others Rank	Total Elections	Democrat Pct.	Republican Pct	Democrats Won	Republicans Won	Others Won	Winners Backed	% Backing Winners	Back Winners Rank
Bexar	South Texas	27	116	7	134	0	134	34	0.79	0.21	3	4	0	21	0.62	106
Blanco	Central Texas	22	159	8	108	1	31	31	0.71	0.26	2	5	0	18	0.58	138
Borden	Panhandle	20	112	5	138	0	138	25	0.80	0.20	3	4	0	16	0.64	79
Bosque	North Central	26	101	6	149	0	149	32	0.81	0.19	3	4	0	19	0.59	128
Bowie	East Texas	25	86	4	195	1	44	30	0.83	0.13	2	4	1	17	0.57	158
Brazoria	Upper Gulf	18	223	13	31	0	105	31	0.58	0.42	3	4	0	21	0.68	44
Brazos	Central Texas	22	183	9	101	2	7	33	0.67	0.27	1	6	0	19	0.58	140
Brewster	West Texas	17	193	9	57	0	75	26	0.65	0.35	2	5	0	16	0.62	110
Briscoe	Panhandle	20	84	4	168	0	168	24	0.83	0.17	4	3	0	14	0.58	141
Brooks	South Texas	20	1	0	253	0	253	20	1.00	0.00	7	0	0	10	0.50	216
Brown	West Central	24	125	7	124	0	124	31	0.77	0.23	3	4	0	19	0.61	114
Burleson	Central Texas	32	15	2	241	0	241	34	0.94	0.06	5	2	0	16	0.47	241
Burnet	Central Texas	26	109	6	147	0	142	32	0.81	0.19	3	4	0	19	0.59	125
Caldwell	Central Texas	31	6	2	240	0	240	33	0.94	0.06	5	2	0	15	0.45	251
Calhoun	Upper Gulf	25	100	6	144	0	148	31	0.81	0.19	4	3	0	18	0.58	137
Callahan	West Central	22	108	5	142	0	147	27	0.81	0.19	3	4	0	16	0.59	132
Cameron	South Texas	27	78	5	174	0	174	32	0.84	0.16	5	2	0	18	0.56	167
Camp	East Texas	23	89	5	156	0	156	28	0.82	0.18	5	2	0	14	0.50	213
Carson	Panhandle	17	194	9	58	0	78	26	0.65	0.35	2	5	0	17	0.65	70
Cass	East Texas	25	121	5	170	2	4	32	0.78	0.16	4	2	1	18	0.56	170
Castro	Panhandle	20	113	5	137	0	137	25	0.80	0.20	3	4	0	16	0.64	75
Chambers	East Texas	22	156	8	107	1	29	31	0.71	0.26	2	4	1	20	0.65	65
Cherokee	East Texas	29	68	4	198	1	30	34	0.85	0.12	3	3	1	18	0.53	188
Childress	Panhandle	19	146	7	103	0	103	26	0.73	0.27	3	4	0	16	0.62	108
Clay	North Central	26	38	3	214	0	209	29	0.90	0.10	5	2	0	15	0.52	203
Cochran	Panhandle	12	158	5	92	0	92	17	0.71	0.29	3	4	0	13	0.76	14
Coke	West Central	19	85	3	196	1	16	23	0.83	0.13	4	3	0	13	0.57	159
Coleman	West Central	20	171	9	78	0	135	29	0.69	0.31	2	5	0	19	0.66	62
Collin	North Central	27	117	7	131	0	131	34	0.79	0.21	1	6	0	19	0.56	161
Collingsworth	Panhandle	18	150	7	97	0	169	25	0.72	0.28	3	4	0	16	0.64	71
Colorado	Upper Gulf	22	188	11	67	0	106	33	0.67	0.33	2	5	0	24	0.73	22
Comal	South Texas	15	251	17	5	1	8	33	0.45	0.52	1	6	0	18	0.55	177
Comanche	North Central	26	107	5	169	1	35	32	0.81	0.16	5	2	0	17	0.53	185
Concho	West Central	23	95	5	160	0	160	28	0.82	0.18	5	2	0	17	0.61	115
Cooke	North Central	22	174	10	81	0	81	32	0.69	0.31	1	6	0	19	0.59	127
Coryell	Central Texas	28	48	4	197	0	197	32	0.88	0.13	3	4	0	17	0.53	187
Cottle	Panhandle	25	5	1	250	0	250	26	0.96	0.04	7	0	0	12	0.46	248
Crane	West Texas	10	205	5	75	1	22	16	0.63	0.31	1	5	1	11	0.69	38
Crockett	West Texas	12	243	12	9	0	67	24	0.50	0.50	3	4	0	19	0.79	7
Crosby	Panhandle	22	54	3	202	0	214	25	0.88	0.12	5	2	0	14	0.56	162
Culberson	West Texas	14	143	5	111	0	111	19	0.74	0.26	4	3	0	14	0.74	18
Dallam	Panhandle	17	177	8	71	0	113	25	0.68	0.32	2	5	0	17	0.68	47
Dallas	North Central	23	163	10	85	0	85	33	0.70	0.30	1	6	0	20	0.61	116
Dawson	Panhandle	12	224	9	28	0	118	21	0.57	0.43	1	6	0	15	0.71	30
DeWitt	South Texas	14	228	11	26	0	123	25	0.56	0.44	1	6	0	16	0.64	74
Deaf Smith	Panhandle	19	204	10	63	1	34	30	0.63	0.33	1	6	0	17	0.57	155
Delta	North Central	30	8	2	247	0	247	32	0.94	0.06	5	2	0	15	0.47	239
Denton	North Central	21	196	12	51	0	54	33	0.64	0.36	1	6	0	19	0.58	143
Dickens	Panhandle	23	19	2	232	0	232	25	0.92	0.08	6	1	0	13	0.52	205
Dimmit	South Texas	23	90	4	186	1	18	28	0.82	0.14	6	1	0	15	0.54	179
Donley	Panhandle	19	167	8	88	0	88	27	0.70	0.30	2	5	0	18	0.67	57
Duval	South Texas	23	60	4	180	0	180	27	0.85	0.15	7	0	0	16	0.59	121
Eastland	West Central	19	165	8	90	0	90	27	0.70	0.30	3	4	0	17	0.63	83
Ector	West Texas	13	236	11	19	0	102	24	0.54	0.46	0	7	0	16	0.67	53
Edwards	West Central	12	249	14	4	0	170	26	0.46	0.54	0	7	0	19	0.73	20
El Paso	West Texas	27	74	5	177	0	177	32	0.84	0.16	4	3	0	19	0.59	136
Ellis	North Central	25	87	5	163	0	163	30	0.83	0.17	3	4	0	17	0.57	157
Erath	North Central	23	127	7	118	0	236	30	0.77	0.23	4	3	0	16	0.53	193
Falls	Central Texas	29	34	3	222	0	227	32	0.91	0.09	5	2	0	16	0.50	226
Fannin	North Central	32	9	2	246	0	246	34	0.94	0.06	5	2	0	16	0.47	243
Fayette	Upper Gulf	24	157	10	91	0	91	34	0.71	0.29	2	5	0	24	0.71	33
Fisher	West Central	23	47	3	207	0	208	26	0.88	0.12	6	1	0	14	0.54	181
Floyd	Panhandle	17	176	8	68	0	107	25	0.68	0.32	2	5	0	17	0.68	45

Table 12: Election Analysis

| Area Covered | | Historic Performance Since 1848 | | | | | | | | | Since 1964 | | | Backed Winner | | |
County	Geographic Region	Democrats Won	Democrats Rank	Republicans Won	Republicans Rank	Others Won	Others Rank	Total Elections	Democrat Pct.	Republican Pct	Democrats Won	Republicans Won	Others Won	Winners Backed	% Backing Winners	Back Winners Rank
Foard	North Central	23	20	2	230	0	230	25	0.92	0.08	5	2	0	13	0.52	210
Fort Bend	Upper Gulf	16	247	17	7	0	121	33	.48	.52	1	6	0	26	0.79	9
Franklin	North Central	24	43	2	234	1	28	27	0.89	0.07	5	2	0	13	0.48	236
Freestone	North Central	29	25	3	224	0	228	32	0.91	0.09	4	3	0	16	0.50	221
Frio	South Texas	27	37	3	213	0	207	30	0.90	0.10	6	1	0	15	0.50	219
Gaines	Panhandle	14	197	8	56	0	74	22	0.64	0.36	2	5	0	15	0.68	51
Galveston	Upper Gulf	29	55	4	203	0	204	33	0.88	0.12	5	2	0	18	0.55	171
Garza	Panhandle	16	137	5	115	0	201	21	0.76	0.24	3	4	0	15	0.71	31
Gillespie	West Central	9	253	21	2	2	3	32	0.28	0.66	1	6	0	20	0.63	97
Glasscock	West Texas	13	237	10	29	1	40	24	0.54	0.42	0	6	1	16	0.67	54
Goliad	South Texas	19	222	12	42	1	43	32	0.59	0.38	2	5	0	21	0.66	63
Gonzales	South Texas	29	66	4	199	1	13	34	0.85	0.12	3	4	0	17	0.50	223
Gray	Panhandle	10	250	11	10	1	10	22	0.45	0.50	0	7	0	15	0.68	48
Grayson	North Central	28	61	5	181	0	181	33	0.85	0.15	3	4	0	19	0.58	149
Gregg	East Texas	15	234	13	18	0	101	28	0.54	0.46	0	7	0	18	0.64	78
Grimes	Upper Gulf	23	155	9	99	0	99	32	0.72	0.28	4	3	0	22	0.69	40
Guadalupe	South Texas	15	252	19	3	0	192	34	0.44	0.56	1	6	0	21	0.62	101
Hale	Panhandle	17	192	8	77	1	20	26	0.65	0.31	2	5	0	16	0.62	102
Hall	Panhandle	20	81	4	167	0	167	24	0.83	0.17	4	3	0	14	0.58	147
Hamilton	North Central	22	148	8	102	0	176	30	0.73	0.27	2	5	0	17	0.57	156
Hansford	Panhandle	12	246	13	8	0	186	25	0.48	0.52	0	7	0	18	0.72	28
Hardeman	North Central	21	98	5	145	0	145	26	0.81	0.19	5	2	0	14	0.54	178
Hardin	East Texas	28	41	2	237	1	9	31	0.90	0.06	4	2	1	14	0.45	249
Harris	Upper Gulf	23	181	11	73	0	115	34	0.68	0.32	1	6	0	21	0.62	104
Harrison	East Texas	22	185	10	83	1	46	33	0.67	0.30	2	4	1	21	0.64	81
Hartley	Panhandle	16	200	9	53	0	61	25	0.64	0.36	1	6	0	16	0.64	76
Haskell	West Central	24	18	2	231	0	231	26	0.92	0.08	5	2	0	13	0.50	227
Hays	Central Texas	28	92	6	157	0	157	34	0.82	0.18	3	4	0	20	0.59	126
Hemphill	Panhandle	16	210	10	44	0	55	26	0.62	0.38	1	6	0	17	0.65	64
Henderson	North Central	30	22	3	223	0	224	33	0.91	0.09	4	3	0	17	0.52	201
Hidalgo	South Texas	27	58	4	189	0	189	31	0.87	0.13	6	1	0	16	0.52	207
Hill	North Central	27	57	4	190	0	190	31	0.87	0.13	4	3	0	16	0.52	206
Hockley	Panhandle	12	161	5	93	0	161	17	0.71	0.29	3	4	0	13	0.76	17
Hood	North Central	24	79	5	162	0	162	29	0.83	0.17	3	4	0	17	0.59	123
Hopkins	North Central	29	32	3	219	0	219	32	0.91	0.09	4	3	0	16	0.50	220
Houston	East Texas	31	28	3	228	0	223	34	0.91	0.09	4	3	0	17	0.50	218
Howard	West Texas	22	102	5	153	0	153	27	0.81	0.19	3	4	0	17	0.63	91
Hudspeth	West Texas	13	154	5	100	0	100	18	0.72	0.28	4	3	0	13	0.72	25
Hunt	North Central	28	93	6	158	0	158	34	0.82	0.18	3	4	0	20	0.59	120
Hutchinson	Panhandle	10	245	11	6	0	140	21	0.48	0.52	0	7	0	15	0.71	29
Irion	West Central	17	178	8	70	0	108	25	0.68	0.32	1	6	0	17	0.68	49
Jack	North Central	19	189	9	76	1	19	29	0.66	0.31	3	4	0	18	0.62	109
Jackson	Upper Gulf	21	195	12	52	0	60	33	0.64	0.36	3	4	0	23	0.70	35
Jasper	East Texas	29	64	4	200	1	12	34	0.85	0.12	4	2	1	18	0.53	189
Jeff Davis	West Texas	14	227	11	24	0	76	25	0.56	0.44	3	4	0	19	0.76	15
Jefferson	East Texas	28	35	3	211	0	203	31	0.90	0.10	6	1	0	16	0.52	209
Jim Hogg	South Texas	18	2	0	254	0	254	18	1.00	0.00	7	0	0	8	0.44	252
Jim Wells	South Texas	18	40	2	210	0	202	20	0.90	0.10	6	1	0	12	0.60	119
Johnson	North Central	25	120	7	129	0	129	32	0.78	0.22	3	4	0	18	0.56	160
Jones	West Central	22	106	5	150	0	150	27	0.81	0.19	4	3	0	17	0.63	85
Karnes	South Texas	26	103	5	176	1	51	32	0.81	0.16	4	3	0	17	0.53	190
Kaufman	North Central	28	36	3	212	0	205	31	0.90	0.10	4	3	0	16	0.52	204
Kendall	West Central	2	254	27	1	0	127	29	0.07	0.93	0	7	0	20	0.69	37
Kenedy	South Texas	12	160	5	94	0	94	17	0.71	0.29	6	1	0	9	0.53	192
Kent	Panhandle	21	50	3	193	0	193	24	0.88	0.13	5	2	0	13	0.54	180
Kerr	West Central	20	207	12	47	0	59	32	0.63	0.38	1	6	0	19	0.59	133
Kimble	West Central	19	191	10	60	0	79	29	0.66	0.34	1	6	0	18	0.62	103
King	West Central	20	114	5	136	0	136	25	0.80	0.20	3	4	0	16	0.64	72
Kinney	South Texas	15	241	14	13	0	195	29	0.52	0.48	3	4	0	23	0.79	10
Kleberg	South Texas	16	72	3	175	0	175	19	0.84	0.16	5	2	0	12	0.63	100
Knox	North Central	23	51	3	205	0	206	26	0.88	0.12	5	2	0	14	0.54	182
La Salle	South Texas	30	27	3	229	0	229	33	0.91	0.09	6	1	0	16	0.48	229
Lamar	North Central	19	83	4	164	0	164	23	0.83	0.17	4	3	0	14	0.61	117

Table 12: Election Analysis

Presidential Voting Success Summary																
Area Covered		Historic Performance Since 1848									Since 1964			Backed Winner		
County	Geographic Region	Democrats Won	Democrats Rank	Republicans Won	Republicans Rank	Others Won	Others Rank	Total Elections	Democrat Pct.	Republican Pct	Democrats Won	Republicans Won	Others Won	Winners Backed	% Backing Winners	Back Winners Rank
Lamb	Panhandle	23	118	6	132	0	132	29	0.79	0.21	2	5	0	19	0.66	59
Lampasas	Central Texas	18	173	8	82	0	82	26	0.69	0.31	3	4	0	20	0.77	11
Lavaca	South Texas	28	91	6	155	0	155	34	0.82	0.18	3	4	0	20	0.59	134
Lee	Central Texas	22	136	7	116	0	116	29	0.76	0.24	4	3	0	15	0.52	200
Leon	Central Texas	30	31	3	225	0	225	33	0.91	0.09	4	3	0	16	0.48	230
Liberty	Upper Gulf	25	122	7	127	0	252	32	0.78	0.22	4	3	0	20	0.63	94
Limestone	North Central	31	16	2	245	0	245	33	0.94	0.06	5	2	0	16	0.48	234
Lipscomb	Panhandle	14	232	12	16	0	194	26	0.54	0.46	0	7	0	17	0.65	69
Live Oak	South Texas	23	151	9	96	0	96	32	0.72	0.28	2	5	0	20	0.63	90
Llano	Central Texas	27	56	4	191	0	191	31	0.87	0.13	3	4	0	16	0.52	194
Loving	West Texas	9	240	7	32	1	32	17	0.53	0.41	1	5	1	13	0.76	13
Lubbock	Panhandle	15	217	10	37	0	64	25	0.60	0.40	1	6	0	17	0.68	50
Lynn	Panhandle	17	130	5	119	0	119	22	0.77	0.23	3	4	0	15	0.68	46
Madison	Central Texas	25	59	4	188	0	188	29	0.86	0.14	4	3	0	16	0.55	173
Marion	East Texas	28	62	5	179	0	179	33	0.85	0.15	5	2	0	19	0.58	148
Martin	West Texas	21	124	5	141	1	49	27	0.78	0.19	2	4	1	17	0.63	88
Mason	Central Texas	22	170	9	95	1	36	32	0.69	0.28	2	5	0	19	0.59	130
Matagorda	Upper Gulf	16	229	13	22	0	77	29	0.55	0.45	3	4	0	20	0.69	39
Maverick	South Texas	20	132	6	121	0	237	26	0.77	0.23	7	0	0	15	0.58	151
McCulloch	West Central	25	88	5	166	0	166	30	0.83	0.17	5	2	0	16	0.53	191
McLennan	Central Texas	23	164	10	86	0	141	33	0.70	0.30	3	4	0	21	0.64	73
McMullen	South Texas	17	221	12	34	0	69	29	0.59	0.41	1	6	0	19	0.66	60
Medina	South Texas	23	179	11	69	0	104	34	0.68	0.32	3	4	0	23	0.68	42
Menard	West Central	18	186	9	64	0	93	27	0.67	0.33	3	4	0	18	0.67	58
Midland	West Texas	16	208	10	46	0	57	26	0.62	0.38	0	7	0	15	0.58	154
Milam	Central Texas	30	24	3	216	0	216	33	0.91	0.09	5	2	0	16	0.48	237
Mills	Central Texas	18	169	7	104	1	15	26	0.69	0.27	4	3	0	15	0.58	146
Mitchell	West Central	22	70	4	178	0	178	26	0.85	0.15	4	3	0	15	0.58	145
Montague	North Central	26	39	3	215	0	215	29	0.90	0.10	5	2	0	14	0.48	233
Montgomery	Upper Gulf	26	135	7	130	1	26	34	0.76	0.21	1	5	1	19	0.56	163
Moore	Panhandle	19	133	6	117	0	117	25	0.76	0.24	2	5	0	15	0.60	118
Morris	East Texas	25	4	1	248	0	248	26	0.96	0.04	6	1	0	13	0.50	214
Motley	Panhandle	17	182	8	72	0	72	25	0.68	0.32	2	5	0	17	0.68	41
Nacogdoches	East Texas	26	115	6	154	1	45	33	0.79	0.18	2	5	0	16	0.48	235
Navarro	North Central	30	13	2	243	0	243	32	0.94	0.06	5	2	0	15	0.47	246
Newton	East Texas	31	7	1	251	0	25	33	0.94	0.03	5	1	1	15	0.45	250
Nolan	West Central	24	44	3	209	0	210	27	0.89	0.11	5	2	0	16	0.56	168
Nueces	South Texas	29	49	3	220	1	41	33	0.88	0.09	5	2	0	18	0.55	176
Ochiltree	Panhandle	13	235	11	20	0	133	24	0.54	0.46	0	7	0	15	0.63	92
Oldham	Panhandle	19	149	7	105	0	199	26	0.73	0.27	2	5	0	18	0.69	36
Orange	East Texas	30	10	1	252	1	24	32	0.94	0.03	5	1	1	15	0.47	245
Palo Pinto	North Central	25	96	6	143	0	144	31	0.81	0.19	4	3	0	18	0.58	152
Panola	East Texas	25	134	7	133	1	23	33	0.76	0.21	1	5	1	16	0.48	238
Parker	North Central	25	119	7	128	0	128	32	0.78	0.22	3	4	0	20	0.63	86
Parmer	Panhandle	13	211	8	43	0	65	21	0.62	0.38	2	5	0	16	0.76	12
Pecos	West Texas	19	168	8	87	0	87	27	0.70	0.30	2	5	0	17	0.63	87
Polk	East Texas	30	33	3	218	0	218	33	0.91	0.09	5	2	0	16	0.48	231
Potter	Panhandle	16	209	10	45	0	56	26	0.62	0.38	1	6	0	17	0.65	66
Presidio	West Texas	22	69	4	185	0	185	26	0.85	0.15	6	1	0	15	0.58	139
Rains	North Central	27	42	2	235	1	11	30	0.90	0.07	5	2	0	13	0.43	254
Randall	Panhandle	13	233	11	17	0	187	24	0.54	0.46	0	7	0	15	0.63	93
Reagan	West Texas	11	242	10	11	0	220	21	0.52	0.48	1	6	0	18	0.86	1
Real	West Central	10	239	9	14	0	198	19	0.53	0.47	2	5	0	15	0.79	8
Red River	East Texas	30	29	3	227	0	221	33	0.91	0.09	5	2	0	17	0.52	196
Reeves	West Texas	21	105	5	151	0	151	26	0.81	0.19	4	3	0	16	0.62	105
Refugio	South Texas	24	129	7	123	0	234	31	0.77	0.23	4	3	0	20	0.65	67
Roberts	Panhandle	14	225	11	27	0	120	25	0.56	0.44	0	7	0	16	0.64	77
Robertson	Central Texas	26	97	6	148	0	143	32	0.81	0.19	6	1	0	16	0.50	211
Rockwall	North Central	24	80	5	165	0	165	29	0.83	0.17	2	5	0	15	0.52	199
Runnels	West Central	17	206	10	50	0	53	27	0.63	0.37	1	6	0	18	0.67	56
Rusk	East Texas	26	139	7	135	1	21	34	0.76	0.21	1	5	1	17	0.50	215
Sabine	East Texas	28	53	2	242	2	6	32	0.88	0.06	5	2	0	14	0.44	253
San Augustine	East Texas	26	110	4	192	2	2	32	0.81	0.13	4	2	1	17	0.53	186

Table 12: Election Analysis

		Presidential Voting Success Summary														
Area Covered		Historic Performance Since 1848									Since 1964			Backed Winner		
County	Geographic Region	Democrats Won	Democrats Rank	Republicans Won	Republicans Rank	Others Won	Others Rank	Total Elections	Democrat Pct.	Republican Pct	Democrats Won	Republicans Won	Others Won	Winners Backed	% Backing Winners	Back Winners Rank
San Jacinto	Upper Gulf	19	190	10	61	0	83	29	0.66	0.34	5	2	0	17	0.59	129
San Patricio	South Texas	30	21	3	217	0	217	33	0.91	0.09	5	2	0	17	0.52	208
San Saba	Central Texas	30	12	2	244	0	244	32	0.94	0.06	5	2	0	15	0.47	244
Schleicher	West Central	12	231	10	23	0	126	22	0.55	0.45	1	6	0	16	0.73	24
Scurry	West Central	20	145	7	109	0	109	27	0.74	0.26	2	5	0	17	0.63	96
Shackelford	West Central	22	138	7	114	0	114	29	0.76	0.24	3	4	0	19	0.66	61
Shelby	East Texas	29	23	2	236	1	39	32	0.91	0.06	4	2	1	16	0.50	212
Sherman	Panhandle	14	226	11	25	0	122	25	0.56	0.44	1	6	0	18	0.72	26
Smith	East Texas	20	202	12	48	0	58	32	0.63	0.38	0	7	0	19	0.59	122
Somervell	North Central	21	153	7	113	1	42	29	0.72	0.24	4	3	0	16	0.55	172
Starr	South Texas	27	76	4	194	1	33	32	0.84	0.13	7	0	0	15	0.47	247
Stephens	North Central	19	180	9	74	0	125	28	0.68	0.32	2	5	0	19	0.68	43
Sterling	West Central	16	187	8	66	0	66	24	0.67	0.33	1	6	0	17	0.71	34
Stonewall	West Central	23	3	1	249	0	249	24	0.96	0.04	6	1	0	12	0.50	224
Sutton	West Central	15	215	10	39	0	70	25	0.60	0.40	1	6	0	19	0.76	16
Swisher	Panhandle	22	46	3	206	0	212	25	0.88	0.12	6	1	0	14	0.56	166
Tarrant	North Central	23	162	10	84	0	84	33	0.70	0.30	1	6	0	20	0.61	111
Taylor	West Central	18	199	10	54	0	62	28	0.64	0.36	1	6	0	18	0.64	80
Terrell	West Texas	12	216	8	38	0	63	20	0.60	0.40	3	4	0	17	0.85	3
Terry	Panhandle	16	147	6	106	0	200	22	0.73	0.27	2	5	0	16	0.73	19
Throckmorton	North Central	24	45	3	208	0	213	27	0.89	0.11	5	2	0	15	0.56	169
Titus	East Texas	32	11	2	239	0	239	34	0.94	0.06	5	2	0	16	0.47	240
Tom Green	West Central	17	201	10	49	0	52	27	0.63	0.37	1	6	0	17	0.63	95
Travis	Central Texas	28	94	6	159	0	159	34	0.82	0.18	5	2	0	20	0.59	135
Trinity	East Texas	31	14	2	238	0	238	33	0.94	0.06	5	2	0	16	0.48	228
Tyler	East Texas	25	123	6	139	1	48	32	0.78	0.19	4	2	1	15	0.47	242
Upshur	East Texas	24	82	4	187	1	17	29	0.83	0.14	3	3	1	15	0.52	197
Upton	West Texas	11	230	9	21	0	130	20	0.55	0.45	1	6	0	17	0.85	2
Uvalde	South Texas	19	213	11	59	1	50	31	0.61	0.35	1	6	0	18	0.58	142
Val Verde	West Central	18	172	8	79	0	139	26	0.69	0.31	3	4	0	19	0.73	21
Van Zandt	North Central	31	30	3	226	0	226	34	0.91	0.09	4	3	0	17	0.50	225
Victoria	Upper Gulf	20	203	11	62	1	37	32	0.63	0.34	1	6	0	23	0.72	27
Walker	Upper Gulf	24	140	6	140	2	5	32	0.75	0.19	3	4	0	18	0.56	164
Waller	Upper Gulf	18	198	10	55	0	73	28	0.64	0.36	5	2	0	17	0.61	112
Ward	West Texas	16	184	8	65	0	95	24	0.67	0.33	1	6	0	17	0.71	32
Washington	Upper Gulf	16	248	16	12	1	27	33	0.48	0.48	1	6	0	18	0.55	174
Webb	South Texas	26	77	5	172	0	172	31	0.84	0.16	7	0	0	16	0.52	198
Wharton	Upper Gulf	20	214	13	40	0	71	33	0.61	0.39	3	4	0	24	0.73	23
Wheeler	Panhandle	19	166	8	89	0	154	27	0.70	0.30	2	5	0	18	0.67	52
Wichita	North Central	22	99	5	146	0	146	27	0.81	0.19	3	4	0	17	0.63	99
Wilbarger	North Central	20	144	7	110	0	110	27	0.74	0.26	3	4	0	17	0.63	98
Willacy	South Texas	17	67	3	183	0	183	20	0.85	0.15	6	1	0	13	0.65	68
Williamson	Central Texas	30	52	4	204	0	211	34	0.88	0.12	3	4	0	18	0.53	184
Wilson	South Texas	24	111	5	161	1	47	30	0.80	0.17	3	4	0	16	0.53	183
Winkler	West Texas	12	219	8	35	0	86	20	0.60	0.40	1	6	0	16	0.80	5
Wise	North Central	26	73	5	173	0	173	31	0.84	0.16	4	3	0	16	0.52	195
Wood	North Central	26	75	5	171	0	171	31	0.84	0.16	3	4	0	18	0.58	150
Yoakum	Panhandle	13	212	8	41	0	68	21	0.62	0.38	1	6	0	14	0.67	55
Young	North Central	23	128	7	126	0	251	30	0.77	0.23	3	4	0	19	0.63	89
Zapata	South Texas	20	175	9	80	0	80	29	0.69	0.31	7	0	0	15	0.52	202
Zavala	South Texas	22	104	5	152	0	152	27	0.81	0.19	6	1	0	15	0.56	165

Republicans Had a Rocky Start

As the decade of the 1990s opened, Texas Republicans were poised to bring true two-party politics to the state for the first time in more than a century. It was more than 100 years between the time the first Republican governor, E.J. Davis, left office in 1874 near the end of Reconstruction and the second one, William P. (Bill) Clements Jr., took the oath as Texas' chief executive in 1979.

In the interim, the party suffered debilitating losses in its black-based electorate, founded in intraparty and interracial bickering and finally lapsed into what historian V. O. Key called a "wavering somewhat between an esoteric cult on the order of a lodge and a conspiracy for plunder . . ."

The party's history is intriguing, however. No Texan, for example, voted for the first successful Republican presidential candidate, Abraham Lincoln, in 1860 because he was not on the ballot. The Republican Party, in fact, did not exist as an official organization in Texas until 1867, although A.J. Hamilton, who was appointed provincial governor of the state by President Andrew Johnson in 1865, is often called the state's first Republican governor. Hamilton, a Unionist, was elected to the U.S. Congress in 1859 as an Independent Democrat and had served as a Democratic elector. He migrated north during the Civil War to serve in the Union army.

Texas' economy suffered more from neglect and the absence of thousands of young men who fought for the Confederacy. At the end of the Civil War, production of cotton, which was the only cash crop and the economic base of the state, was only a fraction of its pre-war level. And the state was suffering the social and economic upheaval of the freeing of an estimated 250,000 slaves.

President Andrew Johnson's limited reconstruction program placed few limitations on voting or on office-holding by former Confederates, who controlled the 1866 constitutional convention in Texas. John H. Reagan's advice that the freed slaves should be given full rights with the vote was ignored. But the predictions of the former postmaster general for the Confederacy were prophetic. The constitution approved in this convention did little to improve the status of the former slaves, other than recognizing their freedom from bondage. Basic rights of blacks were restricted. For example, a black man could not sue a white person or testify against a white person in court. This type of denial of basic political rights prompted the U.S. Congress to become involved in a harsher reconstruction.

Under congressional reconstruction, however, more severe restrictions were placed on the electorate, and much of the work accomplished under the unreconstructed Democrats was overthrown. Military rule was imposed, and E.M. Pease, a former governor and a Unionist, was named governor in 1867 by the state's military commander to replace J. W. Throckmorton, who had been elected under the Constitution of 1866.

Dissidents Came First

The fledgling Republican Party, which was an an amalgamation of pre-war dissidents including Unionists, Know-Nothings, Whigs and Independent Democrats, controlled the second Reconstruction constitutional convention that met in 1868 and 1869 to write a state charter more acceptable to the U.S. Congress. The political split in the convention was dramatized by the Hamilton family. Morgan C. Hamilton nominated E.J. Davis, leader of the radical wing of the Republican party, for chairman of the convention, while his brother, A.J. Hamilton, put C. Caldwell's name before the gathering. Davis won, 43-31, in a division that reflected the strengths of the two factions. The new constitution provided for full constitutional rights, including the right to vote, for the freed slaves and mandated free public education for all children in Texas — black, white and brown.

A.J. Hamilton led the conservative Republican faction at the convention. It was hardly distinguishable from the antebellum Democrats who had been disenfranchised under Reconstruction. And Davis defeated Hamilton by only 800 votes for the governorship in 1869 in an election in which most former Confederates and their supporters were still disenfranchised. With that election the party factions were defined for more than a decade. Davis is the most vilified governor in the state's history, although he was a scrupulously honest and personably likable man, according to contemporaries. But many of his administration's policies were anathema to unreconstructed Texans.

His most obnoxious act, according to historians, was the creation of a state police force to crack down on the growing violence in the state. Nearly 1,000 Texans, half of them freed slaves, had been murdered between 1865 and 1868. About 40 percent of the special force was made up of blacks. Many former Unionists, who had suffered indignities at the hands of other Texans during the Civil War, joined the force. Davis also received authority from the Legislature to call out the militia in some circumstances.

In addition, the Davis administration backed creation of a public school system in which the county superintendents were appointed by the governor. The cost of government rose from about one-half million dollars to $2 million annually under the Republican governor.

Many Texans were concerned that the expense of state government was diverting much-needed capital from economic development, and they were outraged at the thought of educating former slaves, who they felt would not continue to work in the fields if they learned to read and write.

The Republican-dominated Legislature also issued bonds — eventually about $6 million worth — to encourage railroad construction in the state, reversing the long-established state policy of giving land grants, not cash, to attract railroad development.

Republicans lost control of the Legislature in 1871 when a large surge of white immigrants from other Southern states swelled the number of Democrats on the voters rolls, and the new set of lawmakers began dismantling the radical Republican program in Austin the following year. In 1873, Democrat Richard Coke defeated Davis, and the Republican Party in Texas began a long decline that kept it from the seats of power in state government for more than a century.

Patronage a Goal

With state patronage beyond their control, Republicans were dependent on the federal government positions available to the party holding the White House. Even after Davis left the governor's office, he remained the party leader for many years, and through that position usually had considerable say in the dispensation of patronage. However, he fell out with U.S. Sen. Morgan C. Hamilton, A.J.' s brother, who funnelled federal positions to conservative Republicans for several years.

Davis took the chairmanship of the state party in 1875, and in the interest of harmony stayed out of the debates of the constitutional convention later that year. He did launch the career of a young black man, Norris Wright Cuney, who became leader of the Republican party and one of the leading lights of Texas politics for the next two decades. Wright was named to a position at the Galveston customshouse.

In 1876, the Texas delegation to the Republican National Convention first supported Sen. Oliver P. Morton of Indiana for the presidential nomination, but later switched to Rutherford B. Hayes, the eventual winner of the election.

With Hayes, Texas Republicans faced a patronage problem that would become all too common in the years ahead. President Hayes thought the best way to foster growth in the Republican party in the

South was to wean conservatives from the Democratic party. When vacancies arose in Texas, Hayes would counsel with conservative Democratic leaders, like Guy M. Bryan, or Republicans, like E.M. Pease. He even removed Cuney from the customshouse. One Republican worker lamented that there were 1,000 post offices in Texas and only 100 Republican postmasters. "How can opposition to democracy succeed with all the state and most of the federal offices in the hands of the democrats," the worker wondered. Davis himself was no happier, noting that no Texas Republican was respectable to Northern Republicans unless nincompoop enough to curry favor with the Democrats and to get their endorsement. Even on the state level, Republicans had problems. Pease was criticized for naming a Democrat and a Greenbacker as assistants after he was appointed customs collector at Galveston. In recompense, he named Cuney customs inspector.

Cuney Takes Command

After Davis' death, Cuney gained control of the state party, and he and Richard Allen, another young black, were selected as delegates-at-large to the national convention. Afterward, whites protested black domination of the party and organized Republican clubs in several towns including Fort Worth, Dallas and Waco. This initiated a rift that eventually destroyed the party as a viable political force.

By 1886, Cuney had firm control of the party and was the most powerful Republican in the state. A Texas attorney, E.H. Terrell of San Antonio, gave a seconding speech for Benjamin Harrison at the party's national convention that year. After Harrison's election, Terrell was named ambassador to Belgium, and Cuney returned to the Galveston customshouse as collector of customs.

On protecting black voting rights in the South, President Harrison got a variety of advice. Terrell said the "Southern question" would resolve itself without "irritating legislation" as blacks got better educated. S.J. Wright, a Lily-white Republican and a former Unionist, saw the answer in building the party with the "white man in front."

Pressure grew from the Lily-white faction within the party for a greater say in its activities, although blacks still made up the vast majority of Republicans in Texas. After a rump convention in 1890, the Lily-whites' gubernatorial nominee called for a war against Negro domination of the party and a reorganization on the basis of segregated primaries.

Throughout this agitation, Cuney kept a firm grip on the party, but the Lily-white faction was growing more vocal. In 1892, it called a reform convention in conjunction with the state League of Republican Clubs. A.J. Houston, the youngest son of Sam Houston, was nominated for governor, teaming with J.P. Newcomb for lieutenant governor. The pair polled only 1,300 votes. Harrison lost the presidency in the same

Texas has had only two Republican governors since joining in 1845. William P. Clements Jr., left, took office in 1979, almost exactly 105 years after Edmund J. Davis, right, left the state's highest office.Pictures from Associated Press and the Texas State Library.

election, closing doors on patronage from Washington.

In 1896, Cuney lost an internal political battle over support for William McKinley and with it control of the party. He remained active, but died in 1898. Lily-whites gained control of the shell of the party, which became little more than a patronage dispenser for half a century, despite periodic voting successes.

Democrats, who had their hands full with challenges by Green-backers and Populists in the last quarter of the 19th century, were concerned about the rowdy element that challenged their control in the Texas electorate. State Sen. A.W. Terrell of Austin had unsuccessfully attempted to have a poll tax levied as a voting requisite in the Constitution of 1876. The farmers who controlled the convention saw that poor members of their class would be barred from the polls, as well as blacks, at whom the senator had aimed the law.

Sen. Terrell was nothing if not persistent. In 1902, he returned to the legislature and authored a series of election reforms that effectively closed the polls to blacks and poor whites. The Terrell Election Law of 1902, which levied the poll tax, decimated the Republicans' black-voter base and further reduced the party's clout in statewide elections. In 1912 and 1914, for example, even the tiny Socialist Party outpolled state Republicans.

In some defense of Terrell, Texans in general had tired of cheating in elections, and there was a substantial reform movement under way that had lobbied for registration of voters, if not for a poll tax.

that had lobbied for registration of voters, if not for a poll tax.

With its principal bloc vote disenfranchised and with personal ambition placed ahead of party success, the Republican party in Texas dozed into an extended slumber in elections.

Behind the scenes, however, the intrigue would have done justice to a daytime soap opera.

In 1920, historian Roger Olien noted in *From Token to Triumph,* four Texans attended the inaugural celebrations of Warren Harding in Washington. Each of the quartet had a role to play in the dramatics of Republican politics in the new decade. Henry F. McGregor was a wealthy Houston businessman and long-time national committeeman from Texas. Rentfro B. Creager of Brownsville was an up-and-coming young attorney who already had tempered his political talents in parries with Archer Parr and Jim Wells in the rough and tumble politics of the Lower Rio Grande Valley. Frank E. Scobey was a San Antonio business-man and a long-time friend of Harding's who had migrated to Texas from Ohio. Harry M. Wurzbach of Sequin was "the" Republican con-gressman from Texas. From this group would emerge a power struggle for control of the state party that would seal its fate for 30 years.

McGregor had the unfortunate luck to support not only one, but two candidates for the Republican nomination for president and neither was Harding. So despite his seniority within the party, he was on the bubble, as they say, as a dispenser of patronage. Creager and Scobey had salvaged 19 and one-half delegate votes from Texas for Harding on the ninth and deciding ballot.

Emergence of Creager

Scobey had taken Creager under his wing before the convention and they had worked in Harding's behalf throughout the nomination process. Scobey sought to use his friendship with Harding, in Ohio along with the service dispensed at the national convention, to become a patronage disperser, and, of course, Creager hoped that the last-minute effort for Harding at the convention would pay off in patronage for him, too. Scobey and Creager were early winners. Scobey success-fully backed Creager for the state vice-chairmanship of the party, and worked his way in with Harding as an advisor and political informant. When McGregor died in 1923, Creager was poised to move into the national committee seat, which he held until his death in 1950.

Scobey did not fare so well. He successfully strong-armed a post-master nomination from Harding over Wurzbach's opposition. But while he won the battle, he lost the war, for Harding was embarrassed by the maneuvering.

Wurzbach, a former Guadalupe County judge who had sneaked away with the congressional seat in San Antonio, believed that the con-gressman from a region should be the arbitrator for patronage. He had been a surprise winner in 1920. As congressman, Wurzbach supported pork-barrel projects for his district. But he also was the only Texas congressman to support the Dyer anti-lynching bill

When the postmaster post opened again, Scobey tried the same tactics to get his man appointed, but this time, Creager supported Wurzbach's nominee, who got the position. Creager then eased his mentor out of politics until 1928, when Scobey tried to blacken Creager's name during the battle for delegates to the national convention.

Creager proved invulnerable, however, and maintained a star-crossed life, though political opponents, muckraking journalists and others tried over the years to reduce his influence and loosen his control of the state party.

A Move to Dallas

A new age in Texas politics opened with Creager, for he opened the first full-time, fully staffed party headquarters in the state. William E. Talbot of Dallas was the director of the facility located in his hometown. The headquarters was financed by party officeholders, who signed two-year unsecured personal notes ranging from $25 to $5,000, which usually were discounted to banks. Legality of the unique form of support was often questioned, but no one could prove that the federal employees were threatened with the loss of their jobs if they did not sign notes.

Creager also usurped the authority of the state executive committee by appointing county chairmen when vacancies occurred in areas with thin Republican participation. Often the chairmen were beneficiaries of Republican patronage. In 1928, 36 county chairmen were postmasters, and 32 others were married to postmasters.

Most Republican support in these days — as also is the case today — came from newcomers to Texas. A survey of voters in the Dallas County Republican primary in 1926 revealed that 69 percent had been born outside Texas, while only 25 percent of the county's total population was not native to the state.

Briefly in 1928, the party stirred from its lethargy long enough to participate in generating the first majority in history for a Republican presidential candidate in Texas. Herbert Hoover appealed to the instincts of those conservative Texans who featured themselves dedicated to good government. And, of course, the Democrats, holding their national convention in Houston, nominated Al Smith, a Catholic, an Easterner and a perceived citified dandy, as their standard bearer, and Protestant Texas could abide none of the three shortcomings.

The victory gave Creager ammunition to refute critics, like Wurzbach, who claimed he deliberately weakened the party to ensure his control of patronage. Democrats for the first time broke with the national party, and several groups of Democrats campaigned for Hoover, some using an anti-Catholic theme. But this participation was not all good news, for although the Democrats raised about $60,000 for the Hoover campaign, they left many unpaid bills for the Republican party to pick up after the election.

Wurzbach lost his congressional seat to Democrat August McCloskey in 1928, but contested the race that was marred by many charges of fraud. "Corrected" returns kept flooding in to the secretary of state's office for weeks after the election. Bee County's final returns did not arrive until mid-January 1929. McCloskey was charged with vote fraud, but acquitted. The U.S. House Committee on Elections #3, however, seated Wurzbach in February of 1930.

Never one to be outdone, Creager charged during a congressional investigation that Wurzbach had received illegal campaign contributions from federal employees. Wurzbach was promptly indicted in March 1929. And just as quickly, the charge was quashed by the justice department. But Creager kept lobbying for reindictment until Wurzbach's death in November 1931.

In 1930, the Republican Party was required to hold its first primary, since its gubernatorial candidate had polled more than 100,000 votes in the previous election year. For Creager, it was a major challenge, for his control of the party was maintained by back-room manipulations, not by democratic procedures. George Butte won the gubernatorial nomination, but declined to run in the general election. So the Creager-controlled state convention placed William Talbot, the first party director hired by Creager, on the ballot. Talbot ran a fine public-relations campaign, but polled less than 20 percent of the total vote statewide.

Two years later, Orville Bullington, former director of the University of Texas Exes organization, ran a brilliant campaign, polling 200,000 votes more than the national ticket, but still not winning. Democrats tied the Great Depression around Herbert Hoover's neck so tightly that he polled less than 100,000 votes in a state he carried only four years earlier. Bullington's effort was the last good race by a Republican candidate in a statewide race for two decades. With Democrats firmly in control in Washington and in Austin, there was no patronage to attract the party faithful.

The New Republicans

During this period, however, a new breed of Republican developed: the wealthy ex-Democrat who broke with the New-Deal policies of President Franklin D. Roosevelt. One of the first was Marrs McLean of San Antonio, who came aboard as a fund-raiser in 1936 and held that position until 1952. This was of no help to state and local candidates. But these former Democrats were not upset with the way the state government, and particularly the railroad commission that controlled oil and gas production, was run. Republicans bided their time, while accepting the support of these "Presidential Republicans" in presidential election years.

The longer FDR stayed in office, of course, the larger grew the ranks of the disgruntled. In 1944, a serious split took place within the Democratic Party of Texas. Opponents of a fourth term for President Roosevelt split the state convention, and the national party seated a loyalist delegation led by Congressman Sam Rayburn. The so-called "Texas Regulars" fielded a slate of electors in the general election but polled only 12 percent of the vote, while FDR attracted 65 percent.

The low point in Republican history probably came in the 1942 gubernatorial election when the party's candidate polled less than 10,000 votes to the Democrats' 290,000.

But disenchantment with Franklin Roosevelt's New Deal and Harry Truman's Fair Deal began moving conservative Democrats into the Republican camp. That transition, plus immigration from the North and Midwest during World War II, brought fresh blood to the party. The new members were more intent on electing public officials than on simply controlling patronage, which had been the only goal of long-time Texas Republicans.

Lyndon B. Johnson's 87-vote victory over Coke Stevenson in the 1948 runoff for the U.S. senatorial nomination angered many conservatives and appeared to open the door for Republican gains in the state. H. J. "Jack" Porter, an independent oilman from Houston, got the job of finding a candidate. The popular former governor and U.S. Senator W. Lee O'Daniel, who broke with the Democratic Party, was one possibility, but he did not want the job. So Porter took the nomination himself and ran surprisingly well. He ran ahead of the national ticket and carried two of the state's largest oil towns, Tyler and Midland. These results convinced the energetic Porter that Texas Republicans might become effective if they had strong candidates, adequate financing and aggressive leadership.

Creager maintained party unity with his back-room machinations, but he died in October 1950. And a new era opened for the Texas Republican party. Porter sought the national committee post but lost to Henry Zweifel. But it was only a minor setback.

The Eisenhower Years

The Legislature provided some help for Republicans in 1951 by rewriting the laws governing state political conventions. The previous year, Ben Guill of Pampa pulled off a major political upset by defeating an array of Democratic candidates for the remaining months of the congressional term of Eugene Worley, who resigned to take a federal judgeship. In those days, a candidate needed only a plurality to win a special election.

Until 1952, most of the state Republican energies were dissipated in intraparty disputes. Only a handful of Republicans were elected to the Texas Legislature. Julius Real of Kerrville, the most prominent, served five terms in the State Senate. Harry Wurzbach served six terms in Congress before his defeat in 1930, and he figured prominently in patronage fights with Creager. Between 1931 and 1961, however, few Republicans served in the Texas Legislature, and after Wurzbach's defeat in 1930, it was 20 years before another Republican, Guill, won a seat temporarily in a special election in 1950, representing the Texas Panhandle in Congress.

In 1952, Texas Republicans came of age. The vehicle was an old-fashioned, knock-down, drag-out political battle between U.S. Sen. Robert Taft and war hero Dwight D. Eisenhower for the party's presidential nomination.

Sen. Taft was the favorite of the old guard in Texas with support dating back to 1936, when he first entered the Senate. And these Republicans were in control of the party machinery. Eisenhower's backers were younger, more brash and more energetic. They brought to the Republican process of selecting delegates an energy and dedication that the party had not seen in decades. Old-timers were not convinced of the righteousness of the cause of the hundreds of New Republicans who were flooding the convention process. And Texas law shined little light on when a person became a party member. Party designations were not required when a citizen bought a poll tax. Not until a voter signed in at a primary polling place was any party designation connected to their participation. When the combatants clashed at precinct conventions, the Eisenhower forces won hands down. The Taft forces used the tactic of "rump" conventions, holding separate meetings to select delegates for county and state conventions and hoping that the national credentials committee would look favorably on their complaints.

When delegates were chosen for the national convention, Sen. Taft's supporters prevailed. Eisenhower's supporters were enraged and journeyed to the national convention to contest the seating of the usurper's delegates.

Texans were ready for a rowdy floor fight over seating Taft delegates from the state and turned down proposed compromises. But the issue never came to a floor fight because on an early vote on seating Georgia's Eisenhower delegates, Sen. Taft saw how the vote would go and capitulated to the Eisenhower backers.

Nominating a candidate and electing him, however, were two entirely different jobs. And it was doubly tough in Texas. Only Herbert Hoover in 1928 had carried the state as a Republican presidential nominee before Eisenhower claimed consecutive victories in 1952 and 1956. And in 1952, Bruce Alger was elected to Congress from Dallas County.

In the Eisenhower campaign, many Texas Democrats enlisted their support. Even Gov. Allan Shivers led a campaign, while also running as the Republican candidate for governor in the only election in the state's history in which cross-filing in both parties was allowed.

When the smoke settled and Eisenhower had Texas' electoral votes in his pocket, Republicans waited in vain for the patronage that was expected. Many of the top posts, like secretary of the treasury went to Texans alright, but to Democrats who had supported the general. Without patronage, party workers became demoralized, and the party was hindered in the development of new candidates. Of course with Sam Rayburn leading the U.S. House as Speaker and Johnson serving as the majority leader in the Senate, Eisenhower had to respect the concerns of Texas Democrats if he was going to be successful in dealing with either house. Throughout his presidency, this lack of patronage was a critical point with Texas Republicans. When in his second term, President Eisenhower started talking about the New Republicanism, which sounded a lot like old New-Dealism to Texans, supporters became disenchanted, indeed. Some Republicans still look upon the Eisenhower years as yet another period of marking time, awaiting an opportunity to develop a true two-party system of government in Texas.

Women Step Forward

A new element entered Republican politics as the 1950s opened: women. Women became the political sinew of the party. Women prepared the mailing lists, canvassed neighborhoods, manned the phone banks on election day. Across the state, women organized clubs. Of the 28 clubs operating in 1952 and 1954, 14 were in Dallas County. These organizations became a force to be reckoned with in the party. They brought energy and organizational know-how to the party, and in most races, gave it an advantage over Democrats, which were notorious for their lack of organization, if not election victories.

Women played a major role in the election of Congressman Bruce Alger of Dallas in 1954, handling the many details that are needed for the success of the candidate.

As national committeeman, Jack Porter ran as tight a ship as Creager, almost to the exclusion of the state executive committee. He believed in selective challenges of Democrats. The main focus of the state party, he thought, should be candidate recruitment and fund raising. Organizational details were best kept on the local level.

When Thad Hutcheson of Houston became state chairman in 1956, party enthusiasm at the local level became a major concern. Hutcheson thought that Republicans' unenthusiastic efforts in the special election for Price Daniel's senatorial seat were a factor in liberal Democrat Ralph Yarborough's victory in the race.

A few other successes followed in the 1950s and early 1960s. Most important was John Tower's victory in a special election in 1961 for the U.S. Senate seat Lyndon Johnson abandoned to become Vice President

A young John Tower takes the oath of office for the U.. S. Senate from his predecessor, Vice President Lyndon B. Johnson, in 1961. Tower won a special election for the seat vacated by Johnson upon his election as vice president. Tower became a national spokesman for the conservative political cause and an authority on defense. His election marks the beginning of a new political era in Texas. Dallas Morning News Photo.

of the United States. Ed Foreman was elected to Congress from West Texas in 1962 to join Alger, and Jack Cox fought a tight battle for the governorship before losing to Democrat John Connally, also in 1962. And nine Republicans were serving in the Legislature in 1963.

As 1963 opened, Texas Republicans had every hope of inflicting serious harm on Democrats in Texas. Sen. Barry Goldwater of Arizona, "Mr. Conservative" to most Republicans, was seeking support for a presidential nomination, and Texas had plenty of enthusiastic support for him. Republicans also captured some legislative seats in special elections in Dallas County in the summer, and Democrats seemed to be on the brink of yet another serious split, with loyalists and conservatives at each other's throats. But the assassin's bullets that killed President John F. Kennedy in Dallas, were as fatal to Republican hopes for any successes in Texas in 1964. Rather than running against an unpopular incumbent president with liberal political credentials, Texas Republicans found themselves facing a popular native son in the White House. The democratic surge behind President Lyndon Johnson in 1964 swept most Texas Republicans from office. All GOP congressmen in Texas were defeated, and only one Republican was elected to the Legislature. The work of a decade was in shambles.

Throughout the remainder of the 1960s, the party made a few gains in the Legislature, but failed in statewide elections, usually because rural Texans, unlike their city counterparts, refused to break Democratic voting traditions. Republican candidates also usually suffered from underfinanced campaigns, and in a state as large as Texas with the media so important to carrying a candidate's message, the lack of funds can be fatal.

Voting patterns that began in the 1930s with the immigration of white-collar management types into the urban areas, where they brought their Republican credentials, continued. But cracks began to show in the straight-Democratic voting propensities of the rural areas. Republicans could count on the urban vote where their organizational superiority and energetic women workers could make a difference. Things were not so easy in rural areas, where the basic partisan political apparatus, the county courthouse, was under Democrats' undisputed control. The rural vote in 1960 gave John F. Kennedy the presidency, and that same bloc in 1968 gave Hubert Humphrey a fighting chance against Richard Nixon.

These patterns did begin to weaken in the 1970s, however. In 1972, Republican President Richard Nixon devastated Democrat nominee George McGovern, carrying 246 of 254 counties including rural counties that had never voted Republican. The step was taken, the die cast: Rural Texans had voted Republican and did not drop dead nor raise Democratic ancestors from their graves. A psychological barrier was broken.

In 1976, Jimmy Carter attracted the rural vote back into the Democratic column and that carried him to a statewide victory despite losing the cities to Republican incumbent Gerald Ford.

For Republicans, the frustrating pattern in state races also began changing in 1978. Dallas oilman W. P. Clements Jr. defeated a divided Democratic party led by former attorney general John Hill. Clement's well-financed campaign cut his losses in rural areas and made him the state's first Republican governor since Davis more than a century before. Clements proved to be the most surprising governor in the state's history.

That Surprising Clements

The fiesty Clements surprised pundits when he won in 1978, and they were equally taken aback when former secretary of state Mark White of Houston beat him in 1982. Clements evened the score in 1986 by making an amazing comeback and becoming, after Miriam Ferguson, the second governor in the state's history to be voted out of office and then regain it. Clements announced in 1989 that he would not seek re-election.

When the rural areas abandoned Carter in 1980, giving the state's electoral votes to Republican Ronald Reagan, Republican hopes were raised that the Democratic tradition in these areas might be permanently broken. Certainly nothing in 1984 or 1988 did anything to discourage those hopes. Reagan won a surprisingly easy re-election, and George Bush, who moved to Texas after World War II and made it home, did almost as well, even though the Democratic ticket was strengthened by the presence of Texas Sen. Lloyd Bentsen as the vice-presidential candidate. Bush has solidified his hold on the state by providing Texans with many important jobs within his administration, including appointment of Houston attorney James Baker as Secretary of State in an administration that has scored many victories in foreign policy in its early years.

On down the ballot, Republicans made substantial gains. From a handful of seats in the early 1980s, Republicans held 57 house seats and nine senate seats in the 72nd Texas Legislature. As important, however, is the fact that Republican candidates are taken seriously on the local level. Republicans now hold the majorities on the commissioners courts in more than 20 counties — including the state's two largest, Harris and Dallas — and they regularly elect justices of the peace and constables as well as countywide officers like county clerks and tax assessors-collectors. A survey of county clerks by the Texas Almanac in the fall of 1991 found that there are about 420 Republican officials in county government across the state. That is a little over 10 percent of the 4,004 total county officials. About one-third of the state judiciary — 159 of 314 district and appellate judges — is Republican. Add to that 66 members of the legislature and nine members of Congress, and there are 654 elected Republican officials in the state, about 14 percent of the total.

Some clouds are on the horizon, however. After a banner year in 1988, Republican leaders saw in 1990 a chance to elect a governor and perhaps gain control of the Texas House. Both were prime targets since the 72nd Legislature was charged with redistricting the state, and without Republican control of one house or the governorship, Democrats could gerrymander both legislative and congressional seats to their advantage.

While Democratic gubernatorial candidates cut each other up in another in a line of their bloody primary battles, Republicans basked in the rising of a new political star in Texas: West Texas oilman Clayton Williams. He launched a television blitz that carried him to an easy victory in the Republican primary. Democratic State Treasurer Ann Richards emerged from her party's primary and runoff against Attorney General Jim Mattox a little bruised but still feisty.

The Big Flop

On Labor Day, Williams held a double-digit lead in the polls over Ms. Richards, and it appeared his biggest problem would be planning the inauguration festivities. Then the Republican candidate launched a series of gaffes that were unparalleled in Texas politics, which has had its share of gaffes over the years. Each time he opened his mouth, it seemed, he put his foot in it, particularly in making crude and insulting remarks about rape, which probably cost him the women's vote. Williams' biggest mistake, however, probably was in relying on the media to carry his message and ignoring the use of phone banks to get out his vote.

Nevertheless, Ann Richards emerged victorious on election day, become Texas' second woman governor, in one of the great political upsets of all time in the state. And she did it by carrying the big cities, while losing the rural areas, which once was the Republicans' formula for success in statewide races. Republican hopes of winning big in the legislative races also were dashed. But the party did elect two down-ballot state officials, State Treasurer Kay Hutchinson and Agriculture Commissioner Rick Perry.

With the gains the party has made on the local level in the large and medium sized counties, it is possible that the Republicans will become the dominant party in the state, though it has a long way to go in rural Texas where officials remain steadfast in their loyalty to the Democratic Party, if only in word, not action. But it is doubtful that they will remain in control as long as the Democrats. The bottom line is that Texas has developed into a two-party state in the past quarter century.

This chapter was written by Mike Kingston, editor of the Texas Almanac.

U.S. Senate: A Steady Job

No job in Texas is more secure than that of U.S. Senator. In 26 general elections, three special elections, and a double handful of primaries in both parties, incumbent senators have been beaten only three times since 1916 when the office became elective.

Charles A. Culberson was the first senator to run afoul the electorate. He was appointed to the Senate by the Texas Legislature in 1899 and stood for re-election in the primaries of 1904, 1906 and 1910 without opposition. But in 1916, he ran behind Gov. Oscar Colquitt in the first Democratic primary before rallying to win the second primary. Six years later, Culberson ran third in the primary behind Earle Mayfield, who won, and Jim Ferguson.

Mayfield, recipient of Ku Klux Klan support, served one term and was ousted in 1928 by Tom Connally, who went on to serve 23 years, 10 months. Connally won four general elections before retiring in 1952.

Ralph Yarborough, an outspoken liberal, also lost attempting to win a third term. Yarborough surprised political pundits in 1957 by outdistancing 22 opponents in a special election to fill the unexpired term of Price Daniel, who left the Senate to run for governor. Yarborough was twice elected to the Senate in general elections before losing in the Democratic primary to Lloyd Bentsen in 1970.

Bentsen stands with Tom Connally and Morris Sheppard, who each won four general elections without defeat in their careers.

Sheppard, who served 28 years in the Senate, the longest of any Texan, was the first man to gain the Senate office by virtue of an election. Early in the century, the Democratic Party required all candidates for public office to stand for election in the primary. Even senators, who did not normally face voters, had to run. Incumbent Joe Bailey, with scandal nipping at his heels, chose not to run. And in the 1912 primary, Sheppard won a plurality vote against five opponents.

At the time, senators still were appointed by the Legislature, and when the lawmakers met the following year, R. M. Johnson, a Houston newspaper publisher, was backed by Gov. Colquitt for the post. Sheppard's supporters immediately kicked off a campaign to replace Johnson. At stake, they claimed, was important seniority that could give Sheppard and Texas an advantage in the Senate. Johnson resigned, Colquitt relented, and Sheppard took office on Feb. 13, 1913, to begin his 28-year tenure.

Ironically, Sheppard's record service is bookended by the two shortest tenures by Texans in the Senate. Johnson served only 28 days, and A. J. Houston, Sam Houston's youngest son, was appointed as interim Senator by Gov. W. Lee O'Daniel and served only 24 days in June 1941.

O'Daniel won a narrow plurality for the office in a special election against 28 other candidates, including a young congressman named Lyndon B. Johnson. Johnson's campaign workers claimed the election was stolen from them by faulty vote counting. But nothing came of the charge at the time.

Special elections for the Senate always draw a crowd. Twenty-nine sought the office in 1941, and 23 were on the ballot in 1957 when Ralph Yarborough won the office. But the largest turnout was in 1961 when 71 candidates littered the ballot. John Tower won the runoff that year, defeating William A. Blakley and the hoard of others. Tower was the first Republican senator from Texas since Reconstruction and proved tough to beat in winning three subsequent general elections.

Blakely is the only man to hold seats in both the Sam Houston and Thomas J. Rusk successions, named for Texas' first two U.S. Senators. Blakely was appointed to the office in the Rusk succession in 1957 by new governor Price Daniel, but lost the special election to Yarborough. Daniel again appointed Blakely in 1961 when Lyndon B. Johnson left the Houston succession seat in the Senate to become vice president of the United States. Tower beat Blakely in the runoff, which was added to special elections after Yarborough's victory in 1957.

For ambitious politicans in the modern era, the Senate is the prime launching pad for a national political career. Lyndon B. Johnson gained a national following and a place on the 1960 Democratic ticket from the Senate, and Lloyd Bentsen followed suit in 1988, although not as successfully. John Tower became a national conservative spokesman from the Senate, and his successor, Phil Gramm, reportedly has national ambitions.

Texans in the 20th century have been patient with many shortcomings in their Senators. And those who lost usually had quit listening to constituents for too long to be tolerated.

Following are the primary and general election results that are available for U.S. Senate elections in Texas:

Table 13: Senatorial Races

Year	1912				1924			1928						Runoff	
County	Jacob F. Wolters	Morris Sheppard	Choice B. Randall	Matthew Zollner	Morris Sheppard	John F. Maddox	Fred W. Davis	Thomas L. Blanton	Tom Connally	Minnie F. Cunningham	Earle B. Mayfield	Jeff McLemore	Alvin Owsley	Tom Connally	Earle B. Mayfield
Anderson	884	1,478	234	91	3,369	382	1,269	268	988	218	2,119	38	738	1,973	2,852
Andrews	18	102	21	1	83	13	44	65	37	5	73	0	10	31	46
Angelina	684	984	243	35	2,516	540	1,625	525	1,160	454	1,754	32	1,057	2,494	2,505
Aransas	104	116	6	0	253	22	27	55	61	11	161	6	34	170	191
Archer	305	370	70	11	658	171	261	233	278	58	238	14	512	745	502
Armstrong	73	304	94	4	566	25	129	76	173	23	266	3	116	226	242
Atascosa	375	381	139	30	977	252	350	628	369	61	538	43	264	1,090	1,083
Austin	1,647	144	82	11	1,193	475	1,215	360	774	47	560	180	1,358	1,188	297
Bailey	0	0	0	0	233	37	71	211	81	27	121	14	152	309	311
Bandera	117	105	24	1	240	103	123	0	0	0	0	0	0	0	0
Bastrop	993	889	147	20	1,662	313	1,090	254	756	119	1,469	48	374	627	649
Baylor	370	554	93	5	917	159	595	389	258	55	193	14	496	1,165	662
Bee	360	442	155	15	908	5	28	121	89	24	323	10	39	0	0
Bell	2,228	3,028	522	31	6,264	973	1,613	586	5,613	117	939	57	768	4,724	1,211
Bexar	7,194	1,688	1,023	201	18,327	4,365	3,003	3,419	6,983	570	7,148	487	3,819	7,409	2,670
Blanco	291	176	26	2	328	161	207	102	129	13	163	12	184	79	66
Borden	70	126	18	0	148	15	55	117	35	10	47	3	32	36	44
Bosque	777	1,473	226	20	2,338	359	938	540	1,823	68	763	33	313	2,298	1,249
Bowie	408	2,241	113	6	4,225	306	837	997	860	374	1,799	97	1,729	3,463	2,630
Brazoria	432	451	29	6	1,279	133	144	90	193	45	423	12	199	381	326
Brazos	609	689	103	13	1,699	197	534	136	1,066	85	908	29	480	1,557	1,007
Brewster	107	59	20	5	411	98	140	141	176	46	262	19	150	184	139
Briscoe	94	158	32	8	412	56	212	201	144	37	352	8	131	326	388
Brooks	254	55	4	0	205	29	25	42	42	4	87	4	55	36	42
Brown	916	1,410	349	55	2,256	416	1,245	2,257	709	339	418	14	390	2,690	1,433
Burleson	906	609	143	16	1,418	609	855	253	743	50	670	37	744	1,477	720
Burnet	542	635	170	21	1,071	259	599	919	460	36	338	18	186	799	679
Caldwell	820	1,056	56	5	1,506	553	510	430	735	709	1,026	19	622	747	683
Calhoun	287	238	27	18	514	248	228	150	300	41	292	20	146	149	72
Callahan	663	685	78	15	1,117	340	586	1,499	270	44	221	50	181	1,352	778
Cameron	1,411	206	30	3	2,582	221	350	797	1,214	155	1,518	59	627	2,281	1,807
Camp	189	726	36	0	1,157	153	469	356	417	129	451	20	288	916	475
Carson	64	157	64	23	723	107	158	240	234	77	471	18	298	537	815
Cass	651	1,561	53	17	1,938	175	1,234	513	442	91	1,049	12	477	1,489	1,980
Castro	61	138	44	12	225	22	93	257	139	19	235	10	95	317	283
Chambers	246	90	106	7	425	64	79	96	103	28	205	11	83	0	0
Cherokee	720	1,680	297	28	3,556	329	1,319	668	801	471	1,550	32	1,583	2,313	2,183
Childress	266	635	179	8	1,499	166	441	508	444	136	836	21	548	1,242	1,279
Clay	436	928	133	9	1,508	303	673	684	445	89	763	41	682	1,279	1,144
Cochran	0	0	0	0	25	1	3	51	41	14	98	2	22	42	43
Coke	128	301	141	7	607	191	223	474	154	27	108	30	86	378	257
Coleman	590	1,739	142	54	1,789	579	1,219	2,073	809	53	379	13	444	2,082	987
Collin	788	2,328	2,070	34	5,980	591	3,479	717	1,012	394	2,003	39	1,763	3,243	3,399
Collingsworth	99	610	70	15	1,142	115	443	423	593	54	615	27	345	911	668
Colorado	1,132	288	77	6	1,390	1,024	438	288	771	61	562	38	618	1,091	605
Comal	1,264	26	21	5	255	372	354	106	466	11	166	57	356	349	115
Comanche	804	1,624	195	10	2,554	510	966	1,767	925	133	448	22	303	2,199	1,713
Concho	265	300	86	15	645	129	327	873	154	23	51	9	111	877	545
Cooke	922	1,226	287	14	2,135	593	1,979	457	1,062	121	1,048	55	1,060	2,191	1,750
Coryell	1,138	1,395	187	17	2,214	292	1,294	400	2,351	43	456	17	198	1,923	649
Cottle	143	257	50	5	771	90	346	381	252	48	319	12	369	590	436
Crane	0	0	0	0	0	0	0	58	94	7	89	15	68	144	132
Crockett	77	68	20	2	207	21	46	124	92	25	110	0	41	40	28
Crosby	114	206	38	3	1,095	160	365	527	514	53	527	13	197	1,034	842
Culberson	90	51	18	1	105	8	5	74	26	11	34	1	25	78	39
Dallam	137	161	39	5	647	50	311	168	291	44	495	17	117	139	123
Dallas	4,664	5,507	1,853	190	23,335	3,040	4,343	2,109	6,840	621	8,500	97	10,995	16,345	13,616
Dawson	55	176	35	0	874	112	523	653	294	183	371	16	236	933	1,118
DeWitt	1,905	303	62	25	2,332	895	1,194	516	575	57	909	132	758	516	280
Deaf Smith	41	228	56	3	539	81	170	197	300	48	237	5	252	619	348
Delta	230	1,460	160	8	1,736	163	963	419	538	80	850	23	469	1,001	953
Denton	1,165	1,636	560	29	3,203	241	2,196	785	694	144	1,198	33	2,876	3,140	2,754
Dickens	105	218	48	5	923	114	340	473	391	119	488	30	161	1,043	733
Dimmit	33	101	5	1	214	31	53	184	91	27	118	22	85	0	0
Donley	175	413	80	2	841	52	342	278	617	57	698	29	256	959	925

Table 13: Senatorial Races

	Democratic Primaries, 1912-1928														
Year	1912				1924			1928						Runoff	
County	Jacob F. Wolters	Morris Sheppard	Choice B. Randall	Matthew Zollner	Morris Sheppard	John F. Maddox	Fred W. Davis	Thomas L. Blanton	Tom Connally	Minnie F. Cunningham	Earle B. Mayfield	Jeff McLemore	Alvin Owsley	Tom Connally	Earle B. Mayfield
Duval	688	5	5	0	1,244	2	2	6	8	0	1,173	4	4	6	700
Eastland	611	1,523	222	18	4,267	801	1,355	3,600	1,120	174	812	32	584	3,732	2,501
Ector	97	67	13	1	150	21	75	109	106	11	96	8	87	273	139
Edwards	0	0	0	0	143	8	35	150	17	7	33	0	4	32	46
El Paso	2,911	1,196	324	102	5,871	417	681	1,182	2,164	397	1,619	132	2,944	4,050	1,769
Ellis	1,993	3,588	427	64	5,474	658	1,398	547	1,500	205	2,609	47	2,004	3,598	4,062
Erath	888	1,979	409	47	2,126	374	1,874	862	1,317	140	1,068	68	661	2,713	1,856
Falls	1,298	1,513	343	53	2,709	500	810	201	3,492	46	353	10	164	3,211	594
Fannin	792	2,085	1,848	10	3,555	470	3,101	736	1,124	374	1,874	98	1,429	2,852	3,443
Fayette	3,110	274	53	18	1,002	1,255	1,276	894	1,275	56	817	116	1,821	2,611	1,186
Fisher	274	673	103	13	1,485	221	689	848	584	64	410	18	198	1,261	950
Floyd	134	391	107	6	1,124	236	510	617	538	65	378	9	252	951	540
Foard	115	319	117	6	560	108	315	482	213	63	215	11	368	563	330
Fort Bend	652	310	38	5	973	274	307	266	632	143	1,020	60	592	1,412	1,528
Franklin	275	906	51	6	1,028	94	830	155	857	56	434	26	182	1,241	676
Freestone	518	1,066	285	32	2,192	283	951	363	977	84	671	19	397	1,676	1,523
Frio	157	421	58	2	721	81	297	454	108	27	346	34	154	172	141
Gaines	41	92	14	3	291	20	119	164	50	29	203	5	42	160	317
Galveston	2,200	1,917	256	127	5,196	1,067	1,229	331	2,577	802	1,689	299	1,163	1,617	678
Garza	46	160	48	3	1,027	103	191	475	149	47	313	7	184	429	706
Gillespie	759	74	13	4	365	180	241	81	146	10	89	42	187	25	21
Glasscock	57	75	18	4	120	20	38	61	23	10	22	1	14	0	0
Goliad	373	122	9	0	583	82	117	9	84	9	54	7	27	0	0
Gonzales	1,147	1,239	61	9	1,781	426	1,285	564	880	122	906	48	490	570	322
Gray	50	241	47	5	684	32	197	438	550	119	622	32	403	1,110	1,129
Grayson	1,038	1,989	3,771	11	6,488	625	2,836	1,129	1,740	286	2,849	71	1,674	4,342	4,105
Gregg	203	765	47	1	1,732	90	246	242	379	122	801	7	485	915	1,295
Grimes	560	858	50	11	1,175	191	207	122	488	77	699	19	174	422	445
Guadalupe	1,149	391	36	7	485	309	290	79	101	9	109	32	278	0	0
Hale	196	653	131	7	1,870	140	317	873	604	206	1,087	19	301	1,319	1,175
Hall	208	744	143	15	1,431	142	441	231	368	97	849	40	291	534	842
Hamilton	698	1,006	223	16	1,568	292	735	462	1,353	95	327	36	197	1,310	641
Hansford	0	0	0	0	284	28	139	127	46	51	187	7	115	113	136
Hardeman	198	766	143	6	1,167	260	589	308	825	87	747	37	613	1,405	918
Hardin	555	634	81	13	1,606	204	430	181	429	80	961	23	401	613	594
Harris	8,327	2,734	722	43	22,391	6,391	2,765	2,292	6,487	1,188	10,493	449	2,765	12,317	9,141
Harrison	682	1,179	228	9	3,288	352	851	413	757	569	1,557	41	930	707	436
Hartley	41	75	21	3	210	28	84	76	106	10	172	8	51	0	0
Haskell	468	934	130	13	2,020	292	968	1,275	748	240	1,176	54	576	2,613	2,024
Hays	513	806	93	2	1,479	104	575	197	649	84	673	20	149	543	397
Hemphill	44	103	50	2	464	32	106	316	87	45	118	6	61	117	81
Henderson	680	1,012	347	32	2,604	532	1,626	654	622	343	1,393	43	1,376	2,289	2,476
Hidalgo	571	312	12	3	3,516	65	275	209	571	71	3,852	8	224	416	1,465
Hill	1,801	3,145	318	42	4,379	812	1,497	749	1,979	129	2,100	70	1,061	3,324	3,084
Hockley	0	0	0	0	119	43	76	474	173	72	278	8	123	494	620
Hood	294	753	234	15	927	228	473	310	308	48	203	12	368	755	533
Hopkins	637	2,756	199	30	3,441	493	2,004	587	824	177	2,125	40	862	2,028	3,066
Houston	755	1,389	230	26	2,337	377	1,141	306	652	123	950	37	808	1,236	1,719
Howard	254	479	73	4	1,146	117	596	580	239	31	527	26	340	999	967
Hudspeth	0	0	0	0	138	15	40	124	52	13	67	3	44	0	0
Hunt	966	2,998	1,165	94	6,004	926	3,015	752	2,333	238	2,895	45	1,301	4,436	3,324
Hutchinson	16	11	8	0	23	0	1	164	293	64	300	10	251	1,030	721
Irion	104	105	43	0	275	66	75	170	70	24	61	14	52	124	80
Jack	325	687	105	6	990	496	191	412	349	45	480	48	196	823	733
Jackson	234	260	40	3	769	205	211	252	221	79	364	16	172	178	111
Jasper	413	435	76	5	1,132	222	490	174	268	160	1,040	38	387	408	904
Jeff Davis	8	16	0	0	157	24	37	75	43	4	28	0	10	52	57
Jefferson	1,567	1,374	150	8	6,761	676	1,457	797	3,615	623	6,277	178	1,866	5,806	6,625
Jim Hogg	0	0	0	0	113	5	22	8	143	5	13	12	5	279	25
Jim Wells	123	135	35	1	574	263	214	105	249	15	223	89	126	186	70
Johnson	1,040	2,577	611	28	4,210	359	1,265	566	1,301	215	1,887	30	938	2,686	2,925
Jones	605	1,528	169	14	2,725	462	1,044	2,087	522	80	785	43	367	1,654	1,388
Karnes	943	467	55	15	1,547	1,130	345	354	370	39	735	33	1,057	601	429
Kaufman	1,108	2,090	337	78	3,688	585	1,867	684	728	177	1,531	24	769	2,167	2,106
Kendall	306	37	22	4	138	31	52	21	2	1	13	9	41	0	0

Table 13: Senatorial Races

| | Democratic Primaries, 1912-1928 | | | | | | | | | | | | | | |
| Year | 1912 | | | | 1924 | | | 1928 | | | | | | Runoff | |
County	Jacob F. Wolters	Morris Sheppard	Choice B. Randall	Matthew Zollner	Morris Sheppard	John F. Maddox	Fred W. Davis	Thomas L. Blanton	Tom Connally	Minnie F. Cunningham	Earle B. Mayfield	Jeff McLemore	Alvin Owsley	Tom Connally	Earle B. Mayfield
Kenedy	0	0	0	0	104	0	2	0	8	1	49	0	33	49	30
Kent	118	142	37	8	412	26	240	479	59	19	137	7	42	339	415
Kerr	320	244	9	3	669	52	157	179	161	9	204	4	120	104	154
Kimble	228	131	27	6	484	95	261	672	99	29	163	20	76	417	809
King	22	41	10	5	74	24	42	60	24	8	46	0	36	114	118
Kinney	31	13	4	0	106	4	18	23	57	1	16	1	17	34	6
Kleberg	0	0	0	0	1,139	101	116	221	285	48	686	33	129	238	438
Knox	326	527	133	5	1,572	402	483	540	339	109	758	31	447	1,001	929
La Salle	293	93	15	2	366	31	60	78	253	11	60	13	126	213	44
Lamar	959	3,705	309	35	4,122	464	2,937	804	1,640	326	2,312	93	1,426	3,057	3,131
Lamb	0	0	0	0	425	52	138	611	287	73	447	14	179	174	210
Lampasas	363	619	84	10	1,307	154	505	1,351	361	58	200	11	121	1,452	716
Lavaca	2,351	343	68	7	2,690	1,373	1,157	272	1,377	95	1,125	67	2,255	3,167	1,517
Lee	882	259	55	6	905	555	513	183	445	61	753	68	710	678	418
Leon	386	1,027	120	17	1,126	193	502	181	600	67	659	9	517	769	582
Liberty	573	470	49	19	1,451	191	424	220	404	159	939	110	268	620	681
Limestone	808	1,828	298	25	3,683	656	1,317	498	3,095	184	1,355	36	641	3,286	1,803
Lipscomb	25	58	12	2	148	12	98	82	41	9	70	2	26	226	206
Live Oak	30	49	5	2	477	40	67	293	118	43	442	33	299	481	677
Llano	497	364	105	6	781	149	511	531	316	21	180	10	90	403	174
Loving	0	0	0	0	0	0	0	0	0	0	0	0	0	0	0
Lubbock	154	352	120	6	2,567	273	812	811	1,259	282	1,989	29	566	2,357	2,096
Lynn	44	176	19	2	1,249	297	414	738	457	93	578	19	362	1,484	974
Madison	288	714	137	13	1,305	276	365	744	107	122	260	16	434	960	768
Marion	75	404	10	2	318	65	247	172	76	13	129	10	55	228	79
Martin	86	112	7	5	376	32	94	379	100	36	137	5	84	359	343
Mason	233	200	44	4	461	104	494	420	94	19	108	10	438	206	477
Matagorda	569	484	49	5	835	62	86	128	140	27	263	8	89	256	144
Maverick	36	35	9	1	144	26	29	43	12	2	69	12	50	24	87
McCulloch	409	605	52	8	1,077	273	1,007	1,508	476	37	253	10	266	543	452
McLennan	3,121	3,340	1,123	26	7,490	690	1,847	486	8,762	127	1,481	406	848	7,529	2,025
McMullen	41	38	9	3	117	19	48	64	46	6	76	17	57	174	125
Medina	511	237	18	1	733	222	433	196	74	20	222	23	466	51	49
Menard	211	66	31	4	492	101	245	219	118	9	48	9	121	104	83
Midland	142	203	20	1	466	61	188	354	161	22	131	13	141	484	207
Milam	1,599	1,515	403	22	3,076	1,832	1,545	316	2,301	184	1,442	102	1,362	1,735	697
Mills	323	550	78	7	996	194	503	806	215	62	350	20	110	716	635
Mitchell	198	767	82	9	1,370	107	400	828	389	75	360	9	232	1,053	620
Montague	814	1,305	523	17	1,764	289	1,538	706	658	166	804	39	767	1,834	1,586
Montgomery	496	541	122	21	1,335	421	367	406	490	437	954	74	276	1,181	1,435
Moore	30	57	20	5	139	23	45	45	45	10	109	3	36	87	70
Morris	247	787	34	2	837	94	557	253	227	194	567	13	257	736	826
Motley	79	202	47	8	569	55	285	268	333	33	254	4	116	561	477
Nacogdoches	669	1,477	377	28	2,650	494	1,113	673	829	298	1,825	159	877	1,896	2,377
Navarro	1,470	2,467	748	31	4,724	803	2,294	665	2,138	262	2,392	45	1,512	4,421	3,709
Newton	217	323	58	16	593	121	294	329	129	37	543	29	201	423	824
Nolan	310	754	130	16	1,981	214	439	1,491	340	62	514	31	438	1,603	1,380
Nueces	491	312	109	12	3,582	477	467	895	1,394	89	1,474	198	439	1,504	1,368
Ochiltree	50	71	25	5	331	25	129	420	22	50	60	3	37	130	70
Oldham	44	12	3	0	172	13	78	46	102	20	114	16	63	201	203
Orange	424	442	47	7	1,638	223	357	166	706	98	796	57	386	556	488
Palo Pinto	781	1,042	137	7	1,023	1,738	193	1,280	473	124	944	27	361	1,285	1,641
Panola	659	962	217	12	1,683	350	934	337	363	98	720	22	462	1,766	1,799
Parker	836	1,913	204	49	2,343	337	832	728	663	135	1,440	27	511	1,692	1,980
Parmer	62	60	21	8	245	222	133	241	52	44	147	6	79	0	0
Pecos	64	87	13	1	163	22	45	106	69	4	70	0	36	128	127
Polk	510	710	153	6	1,301	235	516	420	597	185	887	34	249	657	829
Potter	412	912	185	15	2,520	149	487	435	1,499	308	1,985	36	1,449	2,632	2,413
Presidio	151	82	9	0	362	17	110	174	133	23	143	17	113	105	69
Rains	132	297	251	47	561	119	470	115	104	92	423	26	221	649	464
Randall	148	210	21	2	775	97	197	389	239	55	349	6	328	536	329
Reagan	36	24	6	0	163	13	58	229	234	13	132	5	54	477	250
Real	0	0	0	0	84	6	27	45	6	8	19	3	3	0	0
Red River	537	2,571	182	20	3,006	341	1,105	1,123	800	175	1,346	40	748	933	713
Reeves	114	325	67	3	536	26	164	198	137	33	155	8	95	218	143

Table 13: Senatorial Races

| | Democratic Primaries, 1912-1928 | | | | | | | | | | | | | | |
| County | 1912 | | | | 1924 | | | 1928 | | | | | | Runoff | |
	Jacob F. Wolters	Morris Sheppard	Choice B. Randall	Matthew Zollner	Morris Sheppard	John F. Maddox	Fred W. Davis	Thomas L. Blanton	Tom Connally	Minnie F. Cunningham	Earle B. Mayfield	Jeff McLemore	Alvin Owsley	Tom Connally	Earle B. Mayfield
Refugio	112	50	6	2	358	142	86	19	25	25	57	21	74	0	0
Roberts	29	74	18	1	320	21	66	90	70	22	105	1	48	71	63
Robertson	728	1,057	190	26	1,918	241	418	177	1,419	78	593	24	260	1,780	964
Rockwall	276	646	59	175	1,197	103	390	135	345	26	471	7	542	453	273
Runnels	690	1,108	141	10	1,803	690	1,143	2,127	619	54	355	19	412	1,513	806
Rusk	833	1,663	113	29	3,062	272	846	401	563	454	2,028	21	501	1,716	2,967
Sabi ne	284	422	214	11	601	215	367	300	388	44	532	104	475	1,046	983
SanAugustine	395	306	195	130	783	326	555	418	227	50	404	39	897	940	1,024
San Jacinto	219	321	50	3	488	122	151	163	51	89	180	8	37	334	588
San Patricio	208	91	13	1	1,485	84	141	418	408	52	748	56	236	429	414
San Saba	384	956	90	8	1,222	279	665	1,094	247	47	401	7	352	1,138	834
Schleicher	96	136	18	1	270	61	125	247	99	15	69	7	102	119	39
Scurry	329	808	125	11	1,293	106	750	1,053	336	102	543	47	327	1,155	1,229
Shackelford	140	261	54	4	659	157	357	1,144	133	25	92	5	71	568	148
Shelby	903	1,601	360	22	2,440	342	2,146	485	647	329	1,508	205	1,527	2,541	2,471
Sherman	33	94	24	3	221	25	39	86	30	15	66	0	26	0	0
Smith	683	1,872	559	24	4,181	192	1,232	523	793	216	3,137	33	1,391	2,289	4,665
Somervell	187	239	34	6	362	61	196	123	112	19	145	9	260	390	394
Starr	535	1	0	1	587	7	0	4	874	1	3	0	18	294	4
Stephens	325	458	101	6	2,003	269	906	1,418	637	142	464	12	410	2,042	1,005
Sterling	76	142	36	1	273	69	81	130	63	10	77	1	38	108	53
Stonewall	167	307	85	9	665	56	452	761	131	34	179	10	225	661	508
Sutton	81	104	24	6	263	59	94	152	95	21	45	2	84	62	56
Swisher	110	269	77	8	647	260	88	495	321	39	441	12	133	805	536
Tarrant	4,328	5,301	968	119	14,491	1,730	3,528	2,964	7,918	1,067	8,454	170	7,711	14,499	12,432
Taylor	739	1,615	171	16	3,152	407	790	4,503	500	57	688	39	392	1,898	1,345
Terrell	33	9	2	0	112	3	18	18	7	1	14	0	10	0	0
Terry	43	131	48	4	529	64	542	488	194	54	387	9	133	542	647
Throckmorton	130	333	50	4	666	68	214	680	105	26	179	8	155	643	579
Titus	320	1,256	107	7	1,620	171	986	217	561	165	834	99	659	1,735	1,425
Tom Green	715	872	194	6	2,616	494	574	1,374	1,364	261	571	17	734	2,821	1,554
Travis	2,747	2,191	373	30	5,817	741	2,856	988	3,791	436	3,164	72	637	4,733	3,633
Trinity	518	508	60	25	869	195	425	301	288	98	611	18	260	809	1,066
Tyler	440	492	95	2	798	147	357	188	318	58	440	17	316	549	624
Upshur	389	1,618	255	18	1,892	238	1,250	554	1,125	114	987	81	594	2,284	1,430
Upton	31	36	9	0	46	13	22	140	148	29	133	23	117	0	0
Uvalde	281	544	56	17	1,369	125	502	668	279	59	506	67	168	1,290	792
Val Verde	71	69	13	1	1,011	75	134	175	148	18	204	6	75	202	122
Van Zandt	579	1,732	142	34	3,254	426	1,557	839	631	299	1,397	48	821	2,118	2,163
Victoria	1,200	345	50	1	1,576	627	404	243	621	57	501	72	797	331	239
Walker	497	534	90	6	1,141	299	237	145	279	725	630	11	147	1,053	861
Waller	474	389	55	7	870	129	86	105	263	60	457	68	209	278	213
Ward	78	168	26	5	279	16	51	148	95	21	142	5	71	95	63
Washington	1,903	212	80	7	1,574	1,082	810	138	1,829	24	341	16	568	1,321	157
Webb	364	36	12	1	662	15	43	39	560	6	64	50	81	593	44
Wharton	703	526	53	3	1,398	540	335	542	541	107	784	36	723	1,063	773
Wheeler	119	331	112	20	853	140	307	328	523	55	475	27	220	1,101	705
Wichita	544	836	203	20	6,355	1,142	877	825	2,733	377	2,205	48	2,257	4,594	2,954
Wilbarger	534	740	245	10	1,762	207	772	648	576	94	610	45	576	2,013	1,659
Willacy	73	0	0	0	156	12	29	114	229	36	269	7	76	209	174
Williamson	1,967	2,015	363	47	4,276	1,074	1,581	286	1,950	367	1,364	52	1,019	3,422	2,163
Wilson	1,082	615	63	42	818	931	487	313	1,128	53	386	80	639	898	149
Winkler	29	31	9	0	22	1	6	81	137	12	75	5	86	0	0
Wise	794	2,350	194	29	2,352	321	1,196	807	690	87	943	23	560	789	834
Wood	862	1,483	184	45	2,013	217	1,731	417	296	79	1,079	17	753	1,518	2,305
Yoakum	24	55	27	2	134	17	61	115	32	11	12	2	18	40	43
Young	285	1,085	82	8	1,893	164	482	1,131	660	135	557	14	338	1,297	769
Zapata	0	0	0	0	192	0	0	1	270	0	0	0	0	120	0
Zavala	0	0	0	0	387	28	108	285	48	31	193	26	98	0	0
Official	146,214		3,960		80,070			126,758		28,944		9,244		320,071	
Totals		182,907	40,693		440,511		159,663	178,091		200,246			131,755		257,747
Unofficial	146,206		3,962		80,104			126,734		28,933		9,254		320,080	
Totals		182,928	40,693		440,555		159,003	178,084		200,346			132,148		257,746

Table 14: Senatorial Races

	Democratic Primaries, 1930-1940											
Year	1930			1936						1940		
County	Morris Sheppard	C.A. Mitchner	Robert L. Henry	Morris Sheppard	Guy B. Fisher	Richard C. Bush	Joseph H. Price	Joe H. Eagle	J. Edward Glenn	Tom Connally	A.P. Belcher	Guy B. Fisher
Anderson	4,176	203	1,314	4,017	1,182	136	158	626	117	5,562	503	655
Andrews	133	13	28	224	16	5	18	20	29	384	72	35
Angelina	3,720	194	1,351	3,528	1,228	86	77	626	228	5,205	253	2,316
Aransas	395	14	63	239	29	71	10	46	11	682	30	65
Archer	1,220	92	377	1,319	178	41	189	84	87	1,805	172	153
Armstrong	665	20	97	755	108	41	39	24	17	950	70	43
Atascosa	1,250	90	370	1,712	175	138	43	284	37	2,314	110	343
Austin	1,549	255	1,395	1,724	242	50	17	1,094	53	2,606	230	282
Bailey	626	39	72	741	109	78	66	53	46	1,205	177	112
Bandera	182	14	62	186	38	7	32	64	11	1,000	195	129
Bastrop	1,844	287	586	2,252	545	68	174	460	49	3,039	143	284
Baylor	1,095	94	407	1,565	202	60	85	106	72	1,856	157	153
Bee	627	40	96	1,975	212	70	93	317	54	2,731	89	191
Bell	5,959	477	1,949	6,860	511	640	636	848	229	8,614	439	440
Bexar	18,737	937	7,680	23,169	3,821	1,478	669	10,749	476	39,317	1,580	5,117
Blanco	364	28	139	549	76	19	18	63	23	705	77	75
Borden	218	20	57	258	17	10	24	11	20	333	25	21
Bosque	2,614	213	747	2,378	322	200	169	272	1,061	3,841	375	210
Bowie	4,622	138	855	4,783	884	203	115	312	55	6,529	608	838
Brazoria	1,152	54	592	1,180	94	141	27	471	22	3,216	115	227
Brazos	2,116	108	486	2,591	213	68	48	641	34	4,113	124	355
Brewster	681	118	75	1,008	75	119	35	86	40	1,267	80	95
Briscoe	599	35	138	832	145	38	50	68	34	1,128	130	90
Brooks	243	9	46	453	13	5	1	48	5	679	55	61
Brown	3,696	341	891	3,842	455	189	692	501	205	5,295	672	445
Burleson	1,736	112	784	1,988	248	85	124	532	133	2,780	171	337
Burnet	1,311	128	425	1,702	152	64	93	120	70	2,257	174	198
Caldwell	2,546	119	868	2,736	257	75	151	591	98	4,039	161	284
Calhoun	731	43	221	830	68	26	19	143	30	1,273	57	107
Callahan	1,523	161	609	1,209	218	102	160	187	105	2,279	389	157
Cameron	3,566	165	1,058	6,304	463	547	107	721	175	6,296	488	795
Camp	1,126	73	425	1,168	397	36	46	79	45	1,571	142	247
Carson	967	42	183	1,339	140	34	70	108	41	1,735	113	34
Cass	2,796	138	918	2,789	342	59	139	256	48	3,860	134	400
Castro	880	40	129	792	92	35	41	32	37	1,098	118	105
Chambers	418	10	182	800	86	13	13	325	20	1,489	47	206
Cherokee	3,722	157	1,054	4,048	1,229	122	201	465	87	5,891	235	1,294
Childress	2,046	215	382	1,944	336	93	181	174	118	2,435	244	189
Clay	1,663	130	576	1,957	277	44	248	181	78	2,021	247	290
Cochran	229	20	80	583	91	61	42	30	41	897	131	101
Coke	698	208	164	664	108	29	134	103	65	742	101	151
Coleman	2,554	289	978	2,892	357	132	229	375	186	3,814	306	193
Collin	4,576	314	1,581	4,888	1,149	308	354	550	79	6,659	462	623
Collingsworth	1,978	74	256	1,608	232	75	129	118	166	2,043	145	151
Colorado	1,533	130	1,008	1,952	269	38	19	535	66	2,592	209	347
Comal	500	20	533	1,345	251	94	42	658	52	1,937	326	420
Comanche	2,498	326	780	2,059	357	158	479	574	294	3,360	1,042	225
Concho	970	151	230	907	118	50	47	160	71	1,242	118	151
Cooke	2,625	246	1,141	3,305	664	147	250	301	139	4,758	285	441
Coryell	2,361	154	1,058	2,447	398	288	141	277	174	4,260	264	144
Cottle	1,195	64	249	1,018	217	38	88	183	57	1,705	280	202
Crane	461	56	137	399	61	22	45	95	21	781	67	60
Crockett	329	95	47	451	22	6	21	24	7	299	24	19
Crosby	1,530	88	356	1,651	156	79	107	95	146	2,083	241	135
Culberson	167	8	53	248	17	6	22	34	23	328	13	11
Dallam	978	110	152	1,030	329	349	47	63	15	1,459	85	264
Dallas	24,421	1,096	8,737	27,289	2,823	1,113	4,378	4,554	696	36,001	2,227	3,229
Dawson	1,974	167	317	1,983	252	145	143	143	153	2,803	230	175
DeWitt	1,939	300	986	2,107	465	76	52	643	73	3,608	220	538
Deaf Smith	1,110	40	124	1,082	130	120	29	38	24	1,439	97	92
Delta	1,818	143	681	1,265	320	32	117	896	46	2,422	260	267
Denton	3,999	210	937	3,946	657	272	606	423	227	6,043	349	620
Dickens	1,610	91	411	1,480	138	39	80	129	107	1,991	245	154
Dimmit	663	20	110	810	105	144	23	155	40	991	96	82
Donley	1,480	64	291	1,303	226	81	103	121	61	179	129	179

Table 14: Senatorial Races

Democratic Primaries, 1930-1940												
Year	1930			1936						1940		
County	Morris Sheppard	C.A. Mitchner	Robert L. Henry	Morris Sheppard	Guy B. Fisher	Richard C. Bush	Joseph H. Price	Joe H. Eagle	J. Edward Glenn	Tom Connally	A.P. Belcher	Guy B. Fisher
Duval	1,531	1	31	2,601	8	4	4	30	3	3,820	28	40
Eastland	3,719	374	1,447	4,162	509	251	633	639	581	6,014	984	427
Ector	388	29	109	727	55	33	64	58	43	2,603	281	233
Edwards	150	21	43	490	55	14	26	53	19	747	44	53
El Paso	7,587	338	1,119	8,601	542	223	435	850	196	10,007	490	661
Ellis	5,737	179	1,304	4,849	401	336	349	628	93	7,791	189	313
Erath	2,890	346	1,020	2,829	445	110	268	288	827	3,208	2,322	179
Falls	2,684	389	1,366	2,678	550	733	109	559	118	4,983	435	181
Fannin	4,179	303	1,606	5,828	702	99	248	456	150	8,711	376	444
Fayette	2,694	575	2,092	3,506	743	170	86	1,430	131	4,668	357	833
Fisher	1,671	125	348	1,721	224	47	125	177	193	2,142	344	142
Floyd	2,181	109	359	1,527	190	98	149	203	165	2,071	329	267
Foard	913	78	329	888	82	117	80	97	39	1,071	101	122
Fort Bend	1,612	144	1,435	1,192	235	30	33	1,338	92	2,929	179	525
Franklin	717	60	287	1,210	269	146	175	187	37	1,866	136	215
Freestone	2,393	102	691	2,554	431	166	101	326	135	3,656	145	291
Frio	612	62	172	811	232	75	44	105	31	1,158	60	102
Gaines	496	35	70	530	60	32	61	65	67	1,486	181	91
Galveston	4,693	626	2,498	5,564	448	204	189	3,284	217	10,648	415	675
Garza	962	60	151	853	105	44	87	110	58	1,132	139	109
Gillespie	248	21	183	516	150	34	168	202	67	875	50	130
Glasscock	170	49	22	246	31	7	13	17	12	231	39	34
Goliad	326	13	106	164	8	14	1	37	0	470	16	44
Gonzales	2,482	181	868	3,197	285	145	97	427	42	3,477	239	502
Gray	1,844	122	529	3,030	371	321	339	254	70	4,103	393	528
Grayson	7,323	460	1,757	9,129	1,243	211	448	753	223	11,743	544	821
Gregg	1,977	47	337	7,091	990	192	344	860	223	7,946	288	835
Grimes	1,095	49	356	1,340	77	29	12	748	16	2,400	84	188
Guadalupe	445	28	392	1,278	295	329	45	516	28	1,333	61	319
Hale	2,245	113	504	2,580	245	129	169	247	73	3,575	420	279
Hall	2,095	151	303	1,681	287	216	210	204	61	2,272	221	135
Hamilton	1,601	136	664	1,948	223	138	95	165	450	2,624	428	160
Hansford	588	36	76	664	89	109	28	23	16	672	32	47
Hardeman	1,474	149	514	1,857	418	159	158	191	48	2,222	237	163
Hardin	2,064	113	739	2,189	399	34	41	335	67	2,458	91	559
Harris	21,015	619	13,146	28,431	1,504	982	731	31,456	267	64,260	1,721	6,025
Harrison	3,601	147	875	4,486	369	51	101	363	106	5,323	187	589
Hartley	329	41	73	455	51	69	19	38	9	545	53	47
Haskell	2,173	166	837	2,823	246	208	140	288	221	3,364	444	258
Hays	1,667	110	316	2,074	216	64	114	214	70	2,830	160	102
Hemphill	691	30	110	837	127	99	24	39	20	924	75	58
Henderson	3,333	460	971	3,125	657	392	284	463	287	5,456	398	520
Hidalgo	1,982	75	425	6,237	449	1,153	149	863	237	8,573	337	589
Hill	4,435	364	1,203	4,879	549	385	235	433	560	6,361	405	411
Hockley	1,104	66	193	1,461	173	238	123	101	131	2,507	311	238
Hood	1,029	78	284	1,086	155	49	197	67	200	1,252	682	92
Hopkins	3,590	208	1,238	3,115	635	73	204	604	174	5,148	390	812
Houston	2,387	139	924	2,454	323	66	180	930	42	4,324	280	353
Howard	1,843	164	481	2,636	316	121	223	362	223	4,468	343	243
Hudspeth	246	14	61	461	24	7	22	22	16	413	33	26
Hunt	4,965	318	1,719	5,405	1,003	130	444	654	310	8,427	371	829
Hutchinson	1,295	147	418	1,714	424	184	139	148	84	3,090	97	296
Irion	238	254	42	359	105	44	45	64	29	504	63	110
Jack	1,342	132	358	1,073	485	74	149	83	48	1,912	226	339
Jackson	694	123	293	1,042	134	31	27	219	49	1,646	202	212
Jasper	1,597	83	567	1,946	358	36	32	116	116	1,540	97	1,265
Jeff Davis	224	13	17	301	33	5	6	36	8	360	15	18
Jefferson	9,130	372	5,549	11,743	1,618	620	367	2,440	265	19,258	949	1,978
Jim Hogg	195	5	76	468	23	6	12	22	12	824	9	18
Jim Wells	618	481	206	1,144	150	38	37	189	48	2,060	158	212
Johnson	4,143	282	761	3,699	407	116	772	388	603	5,286	399	378
Jones	2,811	193	592	2,960	240	75	296	262	124	3,866	364	224
Karnes	1,197	123	1,025	1,667	319	283	100	780	138	2,974	161	318
Kaufman	3,777	300	986	3,553	634	332	238	390	109	4,601	324	622
Kendall	54	7	72	89	19	4	6	74	3	286	17	29

Table 14: Senatorial Races

	Democratic Primaries, 1930-1940											
Year	1930			1936						1940		
County	Morris Sheppard	C.A. Mitchner	Robert L. Henry	Morris Sheppard	Guy B. Fisher	Richard C. Bush	Joseph H. Price	Joe H. Eagle	J. Edward Glenn	Tom Connally	A.P. Belcher	Guy B. Fisher
Kenedy	75	8	19	103	7	1	0	4	4	100	0	11
Kent	604	50	149	561	79	22	42	67	57	820	105	57
Kerr	474	20	178	388	32	4	9	227	14	2,055	112	135
Kimble	810	114	329	921	144	29	62	125	53	1,286	155	190
King	143	12	50	196	28	3	17	9	18	224	32	32
Kinney	108	4	31	110	12	2	3	15	0	154	7	4
Kleberg	1,375	56	230	1,411	107	116	22	312	34	1,277	47	106
Knox	1,560	110	402	1,842	190	53	112	143	113	1,893	250	103
La Salle	490	6	70	513	21	3	4	33	6	704	13	34
Lamar	5,053	316	1,209	5,648	825	152	561	935	437	8,489	865	1,500
Lamb	1,971	109	516	2,246	235	84	132	165	115	3,128	371	209
Lampasas	1,491	132	334	1,576	193	106	61	94	104	2,119	185	153
Lavaca	2,610	665	1,697	2,332	647	111	385	934	159	4,226	396	593
Lee	1,263	270	669	1,354	268	187	102	266	53	1,770	131	410
Leon	1,757	54	507	1,526	183	58	142	513	74	2,815	101	206
Liberty	1,758	136	772	2,155	419	68	160	841	60	3,986	135	547
Limestone	4,454	213	1,407	4,114	769	645	148	530	249	5,571	274	308
Lipscomb	233	10	30	347	55	21	25	11	5	581	21	65
Live Oak	804	47	212	1,225	203	112	100	207	69	1,574	124	202
Llano	765	58	259	1,371	150	46	64	110	63	1,481	147	162
Loving	0	0	0	92	5	5	10	12	5	91	7	6
Lubbock	285	635	3,857	5,956	474	338	346	526	250	8,506	562	403
Lynn	1,842	121	383	1,931	197	203	168	195	142	2,782	314	232
Madison	1,455	74	314	1,365	207	25	21	476	43	1,914	98	264
Marion	433	19	166	538	53	16	17	61	3	955	37	113
Martin	643	82	137	792	88	39	55	79	47	1,048	117	108
Mason	772	138	270	924	133	84	124	112	41	1,240	166	177
Matagorda	1,091	55	350	1,025	106	32	17	242	18	2,259	91	190
Maverick	218	4	57	589	45	37	94	141	31	764	99	110
McCulloch	1,849	202	392	1,655	267	76	97	481	111	2,658	253	190
McLennan	8,746	821	4,195	8,229	1,180	3,775	237	2,232	429	17,273	450	1,067
McMullen	221	6	50	241	32	32	11	100	15	304	26	43
Medina	425	20	328	882	211	28	38	207	29	1,931	77	155
Menard	668	120	184	911	108	23	50	210	51	1,182	228	142
Midland	1,145	90	252	1,517	78	34	98	104	48	2,112	164	130
Milam	3,436	265	962	3,832	687	353	119	1,182	197	5,780	335	732
Mills	1,201	130	318	993	195	55	78	118	79	1,853	225	121
Mitchell	1,891	206	378	1,803	133	119	139	176	84	2,206	262	274
Montague	2,109	247	849	2,598	473	84	300	147	605	3,798	281	314
Montgomery	1,683	112	629	2,304	326	72	61	1,335	127	3,558	208	677
Moore	195	6	22	494	55	21	20	26	10	1,096	69	71
Morris	1,155	54	318	1,123	99	47	78	119	19	1,631	76	178
Motley	744	61	185	814	90	40	56	55	71	746	115	117
Nacogdoches	3,267	148	916	3,401	1,239	45	66	711	143	4,458	166	2,225
Navarro	5,491	268	1,840	5,616	790	871	654	758	237	8,208	274	559
Newton	789	80	319	1,042	447	53	28	126	131	854	124	1,149
Nolan	2,340	207	406	2,545	190	84	326	357	214	3,280	653	240
Nueces	3,921	157	1,599	4,730	537	541	584	1,324	234	10,846	767	459
Ochiltree	670	24	119	600	102	190	18	24	5	1,050	79	194
Oldham	275	26	47	283	48	38	13	28	8	499	29	41
Orange	1,809	103	525	1,787	603	43	168	349	63	2,698	107	939
Palo Pinto	2,337	566	189	2,235	430	117	390	306	224	2,647	1,724	153
Panola	2,539	143	776	2,621	806	103	175	240	64	3,275	400	833
Parker	2,600	180	521	2,241	383	59	616	399	121	3,450	420	231
Parmer	578	31	108	844	128	52	54	94	45	1,212	171	118
Pecos	846	129	247	1,533	151	35	71	139	66	1,817	183	240
Polk	1,585	776	434	1,509	465	80	98	650	45	2,491	118	405
Potter	4,114	288	874	5,114	593	402	485	476	173	7,149	473	552
Presidio	620	36	88	721	93	19	40	96	35	589	26	50
Rains	757	73	239	622	495	67	66	69	28	1,188	127	235
Randall	1,341	79	294	1,390	158	69	75	135	28	1,967	101	141
Reagan	429	189	148	472	73	8	41	50	30	560	39	35
Real	90	6	25	344	34	8	9	36	17	490	38	43
Red River	3,595	131	707	3,046	412	94	152	417	214	4,392	361	481
Reeves	965	60	160	1,137	60	53	77	123	37	1,550	76	74

Table 14: Senatorial Races

Democratic Primaries, 1930-1940											
Year	1930			1936						1940		
County	Morris Sheppard	C.A. Mitchner	Robert L. Henry	Morris Sheppard	Guy B. Fisher	Richard C. Bush	Joseph H. Price	Joe H. Eagle	J. Edward Glenn	Tom Connally	A.P. Belcher	Guy B. Fisher
Refugio	269	24	95	387	25	13	4	159	8	1,077	53	100
Roberts	371	22	63	413	25	11	10	21	4	443	19	37
Robertson	1,703	105	432	2,287	360	316	208	513	78	3,537	167	210
Rockwall	1,189	74	347	1,218	185	30	60	128	30	1,681	94	141
Runnels	2,154	35	969	2,569	369	116	196	452	203	3,736	265	396
Rusk	2,635	171	942	4,878	1,667	543	384	971	351	8,616	490	1,558
Sabine	1,265	108	396	1,167	728	32	20	230	54	1,188	84	1,348
San Augustine	1,281	141	624	616	1,733	33	77	77	57	723	81	2,011
San Jacinto	607	46	253	623	117	17	19	280	40	985	60	176
San Patricio	1,846	58	303	2,343	200	144	59	295	70	3,723	197	258
San Saba	1,442	171	395	1,310	216	102	105	326	77	2,303	229	188
Schleicher	396	117	84	563	49	7	26	32	25	664	44	114
Scurry	1,673	165	427	1,744	173	117	167	203	186	2,334	295	128
Shackelford	1,041	85	295	983	91	42	175	86	75	1,472	267	152
Shelby	3,396	406	1,062	2,918	2,293	76	154	409	118	3,374	160	262
Sherman	202	24	28	422	43	14	19	16	10	524	35	33
Smith	5,615	195	1,190	6,928	926	456	413	908	194	9,649	893	1,138
Somervell	562	47	176	316	92	18	99	36	197	609	206	54
Starr	479	2	30	2,551	2	0	2	11	1	976	3	4
Stephens	2,448	186	622	2,419	242	75	265	182	30	2,412	739	259
Sterling	272	51	49	328	16	10	20	45	13	373	22	35
Stonewall	821	66	243	941	188	44	181	95	79	1,101	220	148
Sutton	336	85	53	400	34	11	21	78	19	511	81	42
Swisher	1,026	124	210	1,249	169	63	141	126	63	1,496	135	104
Tarrant	20,524	1,646	5,328	21,379	2,224	1,323	5,649	4,935	486	34,993	2,027	2,346
Taylor	4,770	295	937	6,160	424	178	367	506	209	7,623	781	472
Terrell	130	14	18	368	22	6	13	53	8	314	19	21
Terry	996	95	214	1,296	136	196	147	105	99	2,124	235	121
Throckmorton	849	64	222	875	167	42	124	61	97	1,131	206	95
Titus	1,798	203	623	2,169	671	39	104	198	57	3,567	445	564
Tom Green	3,618	796	883	4,156	666	313	663	854	230	5,655	421	968
Travis	9,079	256	1,987	11,620	748	458	492	1,769	509	19,807	696	1,072
Trinity	1,266	78	435	1,042	291	89	39	509	77	1,864	111	592
Tyler	840	88	412	1,052	232	45	65	249	49	1,531	98	539
Upshur	2,395	156	993	2,979	989	120	213	336	167	4,638	242	601
Upton	618	197	170	758	129	41	51	136	47	1,067	102	88
Uvalde	1,255	90	336	1,648	132	46	102	201	72	2,193	121	197
Val Verde	711	85	308	1,124	115	104	60	169	33	1,702	244	114
Van Zandt	3,742	203	919	3,688	915	104	337	366	234	5,168	406	974
Victoria	1,536	70	386	2,279	146	22	27	449	45	2,943	147	269
Walker	1,402	130	441	1,611	190	42	18	769	46	2,594	96	331
Waller	799	51	389	656	95	20	14	846	32	1,470	57	182
Ward	496	39	134	909	96	38	67	70	55	1,717	190	133
Washington	1,404	407	1,125	1,099	155	210	61	1,165	37	3,902	152	383
Webb	1,365	30	154	2,627	27	15	45	107	8	3,116	130	99
Wharton	2,297	149	1,191	3,085	382	56	43	879	72	3,628	908	516
Wheeler	1,435	195	257	1,628	310	224	103	219	52	2,377	293	354
Wichita	6,774	488	1,342	8,915	616	188	581	757	248	11,599	512	751
Wilbarger	2,625	152	820	3,285	314	226	170	350	55	3,708	203	237
Willacy	716	37	190	1,152	140	129	52	149	68	1,611	220	240
Williamson	4,958	375	2,031	4,288	493	288	142	1,506	293	7,475	267	615
Wilson	670	83	1,035	2,240	307	131	64	568	168	3,472	214	269
Winkler	592	100	188	656	90	58	98	65	58	1,439	159	125
Wise	3,040	251	512	2,669	545	95	441	235	203	4,062	280	382
Wood	2,279	197	912	2,661	757	78	209	289	124	3,554	344	538
Yoakum	222	27	58	224	19	20	39	16	26	764	114	107
Young	2,282	147	470	2,648	365	60	218	201	112	3,605	316	386
Zapata	128	11	7	336	0	0	0	4	0	420	28	8
Zavala	579	28	230	845	68	24	33	119	50	939	50	92
Official Totals	526,293	40,130	174,260	616,293	89,215	37,842	45,919	136,718	28,641	923,219	66,962	98,125
Unofficial Totals	525,383	40,287	175,921	616,292	89,215	37,842	45,922	136,708	28,641	923,219	66,962	98,125

Table 15: Senatorial Races

Democratic Primaries, 1942-1946											
Year	1942				Runoff		1946				
County	James V. Allred	Dan Moody	W. Lee O'Daniel	Floyd E. Ryan	James V. Allred	W. Lee O'Daniel	Tom Connally	Cyclone Davis	Floyd E. Ryan	Terrell Sledge	Laverne Somerville
Anderson	2,166	1,244	3,509	71	3,325	3,387	4,820	841	608	340	224
Andrews	104	41	276	4	112	214	521	51	79	26	30
Angelina	1,884	906	4,552	103	2,585	4,224	5,583	672	1,145	279	228
Aransas	229	132	491	14	311	413	604	55	61	30	21
Archer	736	237	1,400	29	797	1,294	1,485	147	142	78	173
Armstrong	314	76	369	12	394	357	643	81	31	20	35
Atascosa	468	487	1,809	27	729	1,512	1,804	227	232	244	62
Austin	858	250	2,048	34	897	1,961	2,348	157	364	174	105
Bailey	260	95	727	15	290	668	825	104	134	30	32
Bandera	346	167	777	13	286	564	437	32	78	37	17
Bastrop	983	460	1,562	38	1,306	1,327	2,644	100	271	686	98
Baylor	590	338	1,234	26	816	1,057	1,496	143	155	68	87
Bee	612	602	1,386	15	1,086	1,328	2,129	173	327	169	63
Bell	3,004	932	3,348	79	3,084	3,742	8,708	530	562	408	176
Bexar	8,026	5,328	9,287	324	11,235	10,330	18,863	4,307	1,454	2,296	1,990
Blanco	322	139	500	10	469	545	653	49	64	124	17
Borden	108	58	252	10	0	0	274	21	20	6	3
Bosque	1,155	590	2,393	73	1,739	2,361	2,628	299	274	193	136
Bowie	1,638	1,223	3,655	54	2,112	3,395	6,884	699	759	381	252
Brazoria	1,784	434	1,855	39	2,156	1,979	3,291	188	481	263	62
Brazos	1,398	1,093	1,962	45	2,204	1,850	4,634	214	278	281	126
Brewster	352	379	310	10	522	253	990	38	31	59	63
Briscoe	354	148	656	29	490	613	812	91	96	36	27
Brooks	362	74	351	5	391	226	661	26	56	36	8
Brown	1,705	1,237	2,545	66	2,450	2,496	4,562	950	313	416	316
Burleson	1,164	263	1,414	17	1,171	1,077	2,546	155	492	192	101
Burnet	701	402	1,100	38	1,049	1,048	2,019	105	76	230	60
Caldwell	961	841	1,866	30	1,506	1,614	3,110	168	240	524	57
Calhoun	426	133	840	14	357	617	1,125	83	138	58	31
Callahan	817	557	1,462	53	1,184	1,421	2,151	199	180	102	94
Cameron	2,391	1,219	3,499	86	3,313	3,255	6,946	435	419	235	536
Camp	354	281	1,132	17	529	975	1,342	168	216	79	83
Carson	689	232	844	19	817	765	1,092	91	119	72	52
Cass	1,217	692	2,537	65	1,861	2,720	3,115	354	411	140	133
Castro	404	134	730	17	410	539	862	89	86	39	46
Chambers	556	154	796	13	473	543	1,169	80	302	41	25
Cherokee	1,371	1,078	3,432	95	2,044	3,388	4,396	335	334	166	644
Childress	1,146	442	1,799	45	1,478	1,551	2,049	193	175	209	113
Clay	1,062	441	2,081	60	1,309	2,034	2,071	185	111	190	173
Cochran	244	152	781	27	493	787	888	103	161	43	48
Coke	253	280	600	4	361	480	839	81	80	49	34
Coleman	1,215	771	2,622	71	1,889	2,574	3,819	414	300	278	189
Collin	1,803	1,101	4,914	68	2,950	5,110	5,286	509	443	197	449
Collingsworth	615	268	1,650	15	739	1,461	1,578	168	176	78	103
Colorado	889	271	1,776	30	1,013	1,823	2,090	209	440	201	116
Comal	831	338	1,523	13	1,013	1,400	1,944	129	125	422	106
Comanche	1,219	655	2,760	51	1,704	2,731	3,172	455	439	341	240
Concho	407	239	697	20	558	619	889	47	77	39	28
Cooke	1,464	1,130	3,152	76	1,898	2,463	3,594	363	406	252	252
Coryell	1,019	650	2,127	48	1,518	2,125	3,334	250	108	183	143
Cottle	517	165	1,095	21	580	881	1,369	141	102	45	77
Crane	449	114	280	15	472	270	631	51	100	24	34
Crockett	170	208	216	20	320	262	492	22	18	21	24
Crosby	641	249	1,408	29	851	1,396	1,862	171	175	72	80
Culberson	71	69	36	2	149	31	344	14	11	12	3
Dallam	720	139	644	27	694	505	1,107	170	68	80	56
Dallas	12,290	12,242	14,536	632	21,450	15,201	37,627	2,832	1,330	5,492	2,360
Dawson	998	373	1,818	42	1,125	1,675	2,383	371	330	127	145
DeWitt	1,243	411	2,492	35	1,202	2,135	2,358	284	499	490	104
Deaf Smith	533	177	788	14	700	640	1,426	98	142	35	58
Delta	645	311	1,561	12	928	1,528	2,029	185	103	90	119
Denton	1,652	1,916	3,198	33	3,145	3,385	5,879	454	220	394	359
Dickens	664	259	1,307	48	811	1,230	1,334	183	187	86	74
Dimmit	282	143	396	5	364	396	902	70	117	91	41
Donley	665	197	916	9	759	885	1,193	125	131	52	65

Table 15: Senatorial Races

	Democratic Primaries, 1942-1946										
Year	1942				Runoff		1946				
County	James V. Allred	Dan Moody	W. Lee O'Daniel	Floyd E. Ryan	James V. Allred	W. Lee O'Daniel	Tom Connally	Cyclone Davis	Floyd E. Ryan	Terrell Sledge	Laverne Somerville
Duval	2,777	26	148	2	2,770	115	4,561	4	5	0	4
Eastland	1,480	1,325	3,492	70	2,514	3,472	5,184	495	504	541	335
Ector	1,145	442	994	55	991	736	2,522	306	377	153	187
Edwards	198	266	395	9	289	222	476	37	43	44	13
El Paso	4,761	3,528	1,788	93	6,183	1,410	10,099	552	613	495	195
Ellis	2,514	1,774	3,458	132	4,103	3,494	6,762	571	405	291	476
Erath	1,595	937	3,110	74	2,405	3,207	4,093	483	405	278	263
Falls	1,549	628	2,454	53	2,147	2,272	4,112	523	255	602	223
Fannin	2,060	1,193	5,922	98	3,129	5,492	6,138	499	569	295	285
Fayette	1,784	610	3,432	41	2,307	2,984	4,663	580	1,213	641	326
Fisher	594	586	1,380	40	1,081	1,361	2,070	150	145	160	139
Floyd	730	331	1,707	30	934	1,710	2,164	220	81	78	128
Foard	373	187	820	26	493	805	882	135	60	68	59
Fort Bend	1,102	359	1,515	20	1,391	1,575	2,072	175	322	165	61
Franklin	529	327	1,746	24	682	1,381	1,563	306	197	105	86
Freestone	805	994	1,809	53	1,765	1,913	2,992	274	242	236	161
Frio	291	232	584	4	537	554	957	78	80	188	28
Gaines	476	174	753	28	617	778	1,295	164	202	79	96
Galveston	5,393	1,122	3,032	220	5,700	3,126	11,323	441	1,305	1,138	404
Garza	372	170	937	22	504	891	900	94	147	57	50
Gillespie	170	418	982	11	274	1,098	509	56	66	52	17
Glasscock	112	37	103	6	107	95	186	16	10	11	15
Goliad	165	71	352	3	158	308	746	56	130	133	30
Gonzales	1,108	722	2,515	31	1,670	2,403	3,298	264	431	344	154
Gray	1,385	671	2,271	96	1,712	2,214	3,074	360	408	167	218
Grayson	4,078	2,498	6,497	126	6,335	6,289	9,893	915	830	1,166	519
Gregg	2,221	1,777	4,686	94	3,204	4,013	6,368	634	853	638	380
Grimes	610	407	1,001	13	1,007	1,047	1,324	56	125	69	56
Guadalupe	421	288	1,392	7	604	1,557	1,666	108	188	294	36
Hale	1,260	584	1,946	46	1,858	1,983	3,330	290	253	127	157
Hall	798	348	1,648	34	975	1,452	1,753	161	179	159	79
Hamilton	757	509	1,867	38	1,112	1,839	2,205	223	278	171	217
Hansford	279	49	281	6	288	212	365	15	26	18	15
Hardeman	701	338	1,172	26	890	1,083	1,576	167	159	153	74
Hardin	920	207	2,030	39	827	1,384	2,643	225	524	220	83
Harr is	31,408	8,190	22,111	642	32,100	23,401	57,149	3,522	13,025	4,211	2,089
Harrison	922	1,852	2,113	54	2,198	1,842	4,056	432	443	206	177
Hartley	220	67	249	9	207	172	376	36	34	16	10
Haskell	1,046	746	2,343	65	1,700	2,295	2,644	423	172	161	134
Hays	683	718	1,185	19	1,116	1,198	2,179	58	84	835	25
Hemphill	455	151	662	13	413	456	648	38	85	15	24
Henderson	1,334	618	3,128	44	1,826	2,899	4,743	488	324	467	316
Hidalgo	3,032	1,750	5,041	48	4,037	4,406	8,224	396	950	449	217
Hill	2,089	1,270	3,445	75	3,236	3,280	5,259	367	374	270	376
Hockley	1,025	457	1,985	42	1,281	1,842	2,217	252	330	95	122
Hood	337	288	740	7	558	755	1,335	170	154	115	83
Hopkins	1,507	952	3,569	62	2,344	3,310	4,263	1,103	274	147	424
Houston	1,229	784	3,079	69	1,782	2,909	3,611	288	445	176	134
Howard	1,635	766	1,680	44	2,230	1,658	3,181	273	261	570	166
Hudspeth	158	131	190	5	0	0	395	18	7	16	6
Hunt	2,789	1,380	4,222	91	3,863	4,039	7,661	513	335	294	303
Hutchinson	1,242	240	934	50	1,165	714	2,895	284	360	872	143
Irion	166	139	358	11	226	287	385	40	24	26	30
Jack	686	469	1,477	33	977	1,421	1,359	156	145	93	131
Jackson	878	210	1,418	18	920	1,261	1,497	109	301	121	59
Jasper	724	415	1,637	25	924	1,440	1,893	407	255	115	80
Jeff Davis	145	121	111	6	144	31	322	20	19	19	5
Jefferson	7,948	2,458	6,302	345	8,105	5,191	20,034	1,287	2,464	1,594	552
Jim Hogg	721	88	118	5	578	86	557	15	31	22	9
Jim Wells	1,116	314	1,741	24	1,348	1,690	2,213	135	103	130	69
Johnson	1,922	1,426	2,437	991	3,112	2,535	3,875	367	310	285	261
Jones	1,097	1,081	2,012	55	1,965	1,945	3,211	389	296	187	156
Karnes	718	459	1,877	63	1,201	1,652	2,502	154	394	272	69
Kaufman	1,296	1,283	2,915	65	2,522	2,908	4,085	365	265	233	343
Kendall	94	56	306	3	139	456	210	21	28	25	6

Texas Political History

Table 15: Senatorial Races

County	1942 James V. Allred	1942 Dan Moody	1942 W. Lee O'Daniel	1942 Floyd E. Ryan	Runoff James V. Allred	Runoff W. Lee O'Daniel	1946 Tom Connally	1946 Cyclone Davis	1946 Floyd E. Ryan	1946 Terrell Sledge	1946 Laverne Somerville
Kenedy	29	67	8	3	27	61	70	1	2	1	0
Kent	294	125	687	23	402	667	539	52	85	21	12
Kerr	340	738	977	9	761	916	1,462	142	167	115	35
Kimble	382	407	826	19	513	530	1,012	202	86	90	44
King	81	37	226	3	77	141	189	25	21	11	6
Kinney	72	67	54	0	123	53	133	10	7	13	1
Kleberg	583	337	346	7	672	488	1,304	90	186	49	38
Knox	779	321	1,419	35	907	1,218	1,761	114	135	71	81
La Salle	367	50	252	2	418	246	680	28	46	39	13
Lamar	2,205	1,009	5,306	56	3,158	4,882	6,178	813	1,033	304	316
Lamb	1,051	415	2,428	55	1,360	2,325	2,966	439	380	145	204
Lampasas	763	427	1,417	36	915	1,021	1,806	104	113	84	43
Lavaca	2,048	367	2,980	48	1,987	2,590	3,399	377	599	328	223
Lee	515	171	1,590	13	623	1,409	1,818	107	146	306	166
Leon	574	719	1,196	18	1,168	1,079	2,146	135	223	130	44
Liberty	1,270	471	2,372	38	1,252	1,778	3,405	325	815	216	106
Limestone	1,959	888	2,787	106	2,847	2,852	5,257	448	250	317	356
Lipscomb	218	40	289	7	245	278	403	17	67	13	27
Live Oak	323	223	979	14	485	830	1,280	143	187	114	49
Llano	374	551	1,020	32	783	868	1,325	110	64	154	61
Loving	21	15	44	7	37	39	58	10	5	2	2
Lubbock	3,157	1,745	2,852	50	4,455	2,761	9,831	632	745	474	228
Lynn	877	364	1,524	26	1,203	1,463	2,553	162	107	71	96
Madison	605	443	1,112	22	939	1,030	1,487	85	193	106	75
Marion	184	238	446	6	400	505	587	60	76	41	13
Martin	319	117	638	15	363	598	819	108	119	79	60
Mason	408	243	1,087	13	444	750	1,138	193	81	81	74
Matagorda	736	308	1,572	10	963	1,588	1,669	102	239	218	40
Maverick	177	64	208	6	428	170	755	69	95	59	27
McCulloch	814	553	1,647	25	1,048	1,323	2,528	194	313	131	131
McLennan	6,367	2,583	6,433	169	7,961	5,795	14,611	1,693	858	1,419	786
McMullen	69	87	267	5	121	215	203	14	23	21	4
Medina	351	218	936	6	601	1,230	966	90	120	59	61
Menard	424	236	926	30	454	666	1,028	135	157	109	67
Midland	617	517	959	34	864	833	2,191	232	240	129	120
Milam	1,788	746	3,485	52	2,124	3,080	4,643	416	251	375	208
Mills	573	296	1,268	53	830	1,321	1,442	140	94	79	148
Mitchell	673	607	1,571	63	1,276	1,495	2,263	320	94	44	111
Montague	1,495	549	2,780	32	1,832	2,870	2,721	287	340	433	219
Montgomery	1,403	436	2,616	65	1,670	2,680	3,263	346	1,051	150	150
Moore	399	107	323	11	394	258	1,042	85	125	47	43
Morris	391	244	1,093	10	662	1,005	1,456	159	233	72	80
Motley	309	157	653	12	435	558	763	53	58	29	71
Nacogdoches	1,496	911	3,262	89	2,361	3,219	4,525	471	776	271	161
Navarro	1,897	1,985	3,843	117	3,552	3,959	7,675	636	600	387	358
Newton	606	212	1,008	21	571	744	1,109	113	225	65	69
Nolan	1,275	817	1,718	91	2,013	1,668	3,314	307	328	194	176
Nueces	4,320	2,186	4,106	61	5,836	4,327	11,473	526	483	445	519
Ochiltree	275	86	405	6	381	404	738	50	70	35	35
Oldham	134	54	243	10	121	174	352	31	28	20	18
Orange	1,425	565	2,094	124	1,417	1,513	4,484	543	454	243	120
Palo Pinto	1,364	955	2,334	102	2,144	2,408	3,102	394	393	333	287
Panola	898	859	2,050	90	1,667	2,126	3,090	507	564	187	182
Parker	1,186	966	2,922	69	2,141	3,033	3,910	369	173	261	348
Parmer	313	77	763	18	384	756	807	105	139	39	47
Pecos	656	504	957	73	1,120	1,082	1,349	146	196	82	76
Polk	741	411	1,876	39	748	1,455	2,280	152	438	102	79
Potter	2,751	947	1,851	53	3,320	1,943	5,799	414	273	367	512
Presidio	352	227	350	16	238	180	844	70	96	44	30
Rains	320	186	1,225	27	522	1,223	915	250	101	76	99
Randall	717	305	574	26	950	541	1,585	102	119	70	60
Reagan	175	212	185	7	360	199	492	37	27	18	14
Real	136	110	555	5	209	543	446	38	51	41	27
Red River	870	770	3,140	26	1,539	2,981	3,633	351	387	97	199
Reeves	345	299	302	16	542	256	1,299	107	115	71	51

Table 15: Senatorial Races

	Democratic Primaries, 1942-1946										
Year	1942				Runoff		1946				
County	James V. Allred	Dan Moody	W. Lee O'Daniel	Floyd E. Ryan	James V. Allred	W. Lee O'Daniel	Tom Connally	Cyclone Davis	Floyd E. Ryan	Terrell Sledge	Laverne Somerville
Refugio	319	158	461	5	474	491	505	24	22	21	3
Roberts	133	75	222	6	173	164	336	17	27	15	5
Robertson	1,101	463	1,803	44	1,210	1,296	3,189	186	190	336	110
Rockwall	484	352	1,105	76	764	898	1,402	158	155	141	153
Runnels	1,018	729	2,018	64	1,588	1,911	3,041	250	145	177	215
Rusk	2,259	2,103	4,657	166	3,890	4,414	7,041	804	1,212	520	371
Sabine	581	229	1,261	46	535	878	1,495	186	300	48	172
San Augustine	688	169	1,705	39	750	1,338	1,625	277	248	99	122
San Jacinto	228	87	823	16	275	690	713	91	211	47	39
San Patricio	1,268	700	1,651	38	1,537	1,451	3,041	223	358	243	92
San Saba	663	549	1,601	47	1,159	1,574	1,904	172	230	105	71
Schleicher	224	224	365	6	322	255	663	33	51	23	17
Scurry	828	539	1,631	51	1,380	1,644	2,186	238	209	104	118
Shackelford	287	445	947	22	596	949	1,269	101	80	69	119
Shelby	1,296	756	3,742	86	1,820	3,251	3,877	723	971	200	341
Sherman	285	23	173	3	339	204	237	18	33	6	7
Smith	2,131	2,256	5,105	102	3,934	4,852	9,269	865	571	706	658
Somervell	199	89	553	14	241	534	503	79	90	43	0
Starr	959	13	30	1	982	32	2,357	10	21	51	13
Stephens	829	544	1,703	56	1,111	1,550	2,302	191	199	90	108
Sterling	193	94	122	11	220	87	346	14	12	19	4
Stonewall	382	261	862	28	540	761	860	101	154	27	56
Sutton	185	248	288	11	278	159	645	33	9	14	35
Swisher	564	219	879	28	752	846	1,446	150	75	81	86
Tarrant	12,101	8,902	9,330	603	17,640	10,184	33,398	3,094	2,872	4,440	2,112
Taylor	2,227	2,808	3,086	86	4,543	3,092	7,966	581	281	282	242
Terrell	120	93	56	6	122	60	473	30	33	26	8
Terry	850	280	1,347	21	887	1,166	2,366	173	188	115	94
Throckmorton	276	147	1,008	22	331	818	976	87	128	55	83
Titus	1,356	510	2,221	46	1,760	2,004	2,946	422	541	194	152
Tom Green	2,059	2,089	2,778	90	3,700	2,888	5,975	519	241	324	229
Travis	5,349	7,215	5,137	93	10,800	5,688	20,281	956	655	3,881	339
Trinity	629	164	1,368	13	578	1,066	1,621	149	239	91	122
Tyler	431	275	1,430	25	665	1,473	1,694	122	191	73	63
Upshur	870	854	3,521	54	1,776	3,363	3,939	338	656	239	209
Upton	499	176	434	17	481	365	892	76	104	39	47
Uvalde	496	531	1,131	22	813	1,149	1,829	161	89	163	62
Val Verde	624	299	469	18	825	327	1,211	107	60	62	34
Van Zandt	1,754	745	4,095	107	2,481	3,816	4,378	671	509	382	383
Victoria	1,341	215	1,441	16	1,423	1,401	3,561	155	321	125	282
Walker	890	384	1,464	30	1,036	1,199	2,263	130	468	68	177
Waller	518	184	956	12	579	743	1,350	106	361	131	50
Ward	533	406	544	50	719	496	1,630	163	125	37	84
Washington	510	486	2,252	8	726	2,579	3,987	123	289	287	73
Webb	2,646	121	283	2	4,254	291	5,004	25	55	26	22
Wharton	2,197	472	1,997	131	2,135	1,778	3,491	382	524	400	140
Wheeler	844	331	1,990	42	932	1,598	1,604	141	109	44	165
Wichita	5,029	1,521	4,910	133	5,225	4,739	8,517	761	646	735	845
Wilbarger	1,110	912	2,439	45	1,677	2,475	3,506	298	291	154	171
Willacy	330	270	1,366	16	461	1,217	1,004	170	200	88	74
Williamson	1,778	1,768	3,558	65	3,322	3,478	6,815	323	218	556	207
Wilson	931	380	2,457	33	1,092	1,804	2,766	134	233	132	103
Winkler	440	377	532	35	582	484	1,208	144	155	59	79
Wise	1,168	838	2,505	61	1,742	2,570	3,236	391	390	239	267
Wood	1,247	1,047	3,185	99	2,025	3,072	3,392	486	388	259	221
Yoakum	160	183	438	9	292	314	748	83	92	43	46
Young	1,115	678	2,334	65	1,729	2,555	2,962	333	158	242	221
Zapata	436	1	30	1	615	23	415	1	2	4	3
Zavala	246	156	697	5	284	428	849	78	170	59	29
Official Totals	317,501	178,471	475,541	12,213	433,203	451,359	823,818	74,252	85,292	66,947	42,290
Unofficial Totals	317,501	178,471	475,541	13,113	432,238	452,321	824,280	74,336	85,344	66,960	42,353

Table 16: Senatorial Races

| County | Democratic Primary, 1948 | | | | | | | | | | | Runoff | |
| | 1948 | | | | | | | | | | | | |
	Otis C. Myers	F.B. Clark	Roscoe Collier	Coke Stevenson	Cyclone Davis	Frank Cortez	Jesse Saunders	George Peddy	Lyndo B. Johnson	Terrell Sledge	James Alford	Coke Stevenson	Lyndon B. Johnson
Anderson	120	43	76	2,928	86	19	22	2,084	1,228	30	98	3,171	2,563
Andrews	26	16	12	551	13	7	8	57	416	5	27	539	491
Angelina	55	152	34	3,591	44	20	66	2,591	2,539	26	52	4,418	3,640
Aransas	23	9	15	408	11	10	3	147	373	11	8	471	561
Archer	52	13	20	701	17	1	6	215	1,120	2	16	787	1,224
Armstrong	7	1	1	334	3	2	0	87	266	0	2	256	197
Atascosa	44	20	6	1,316	16	270	4	335	1,298	6	18	1,126	1,072
Austin	68	20	8	1,502	19	3	4	756	581	7	38	2,635	1,168
Bailey	28	15	16	573	24	3	4	131	400	2	16	412	392
Bandera	6	3	3	706	3	4	4	119	156	4	1	741	250
Bastrop	24	11	9	911	8	8	8	286	2,797	88	26	1,185	3,036
Baylor	9	9	24	889	12	3	6	291	835	30	6	832	1,113
Bee	37	10	18	1,249	16	140	12	667	1,054	19	29	1,150	902
Bell	170	71	77	4,175	85	39	55	1,782	3,791	30	86	3,839	4,346
Bexar	420	592	801	23,471	911	3,891	577	6,348	11,994	730	325	15,511	15,610
Blanco	1	0	2	194	0	0	0	38	698	0	0	296	946
Borden	2	1	2	99	0	1	17	17	62	1	0	72	55
Bosque	82	42	40	1,685	33	6	18	663	1,255	3	35	1,707	1,519
Bowie	209	72	102	4,458	124	15	125	1,837	2,197	23	16	4,021	4,013
Brazoria	20	70	2	2,054	41	6	10	2,037	962	14	19	2,373	2,040
Brazos	19	356	78	1,695	76	20	11	1,621	1,894	21	28	1,815	2,442
Brewster	29	6	17	782	6	66	31	160	552	3	12	380	367
Briscoe	9	1	8	491	9	2	1	102	212	2	4	269	142
Brooks	21	6	0	275	5	142	5	118	566	14	11	150	438
Brown	52	26	49	3,248	54	3	18	1,087	2,154	12	25	3,644	2,184
Burleson	33	46	15	679	15	7	8	623	1,761	5	21	837	1,286
Burnet	3	2	10	460	5	0	3	114	1,970	2	3	530	1,882
Caldwell	16	11	6	901	15	15	10	320	2,571	28	21	1,000	2,605
Calhoun	11	5	2	312	6	1	1	193	106	1	6	287	230
Callahan	11	8	37	978	20	10	12	348	1,048	4	8	682	833
Cameron	34	47	42	3,424	78	1,008	52	1,842	4,706	45	68	5,204	7,276
Camp	37	4	23	766	35	13	16	589	543	4	28	1,172	997
Carson	18	4	9	697	11	1	9	180	290	19	3	467	259
Cass	112	68	45	1,746	51	5	16	706	1,131	14	73	2,017	2,346
Castro	25	2	14	811	9	1	4	110	486	2	11	518	300
Chambers	38	17	19	802	10	9	23	521	370	1	38	552	380
Cherokee	135	27	34	2,614	62	11	22	1,415	1,301	11	57	2,742	2,027
Childress	27	33	44	1,229	43	11	7	378	1,122	37	16	1,390	1,454
Clay	28	7	28	976	13	1	5	410	1,285	13	31	809	1,045
Cochran	58	12	26	644	28	8	9	160	458	7	31	704	676
Coke	16	5	4	593	7	2	2	75	511	3	5	534	644
Coleman	51	18	27	1,818	49	2	11	388	1,456	5	16	1,353	1,129
Collin	58	14	69	2,978	162	4	186	1,468	2,063	11	15	3,950	3,159
Collingsworth	34	3	11	955	13	0	5	304	781	2	7	761	746
Colorado	33	26	27	1,106	22	7	9	1,162	864	9	22	1,125	828
Comal	19	23	5	1,572	4	24	5	373	887	22	12	1,771	1,145
Comanche	41	15	23	1,548	15	4	7	1,093	1,052	1	7	1,806	1,649
Concho	8	5	3	578	8	4	2	68	663	2	2	504	707
Cooke	111	19	42	2,633	57	10	17	852	1,041	11	40	1,779	985
Coryell	14	10	28	1,198	17	1	3	499	1,467	8	15	834	989
Cottle	36	10	16	721	21	4	9	185	622	7	17	660	702
Crane	42	14	10	596	11	1	4	100	412	5	14	510	440
Crockett	1	1	6	391	7	7	2	27	176	1	1	144	99
Crosby	27	9	8	686	15	1	4	282	1,211	5	16	843	1,509
Culberson	13	5	2	208	2	13	3	25	121	2	1	173	144
Dallam	19	7	71	935	13	5	6	84	341	4	7	511	439
Dallas	978	274	769	29,928	637	128	350	14,436	21,682	1,559	184	26,263	17,649
Dawson	27	8	118	1,425	60	12	11	442	1,502	5	44	1,614	1,966
DeWitt	69	9	10	1,869	13	21	13	697	1,052	41	23	1,562	981
Deaf Smith	14	4	13	1,187	4	3	3	234	416	5	9	680	315
Delta	64	15	36	1,159	33	21	28	595	917	18	14	1,398	1,272
Denton	68	32	84	3,582	123	2	19	1,442	1,897	20	75	3,397	2,487
Dickens	30	7	10	544	17	3	6	171	664	3	11	557	837
Dimmit	5	8	5	565	8	77	10	206	445	8	5	646	765
Donley	22	3	15	897	13	0	2	300	498	8	12	978	644

Table 16: Senatorial Races

County	Otis C. Myers	F.B. Clark	Roscoe Collier	Coke Stevenson	Cyclone Davis	Frank Cortez	Jesse Saunders	George Peddy	Lyndo B. Johnson	Terrell Sledge	James Alford	Coke Stevenson	Lyndon B. Johnson
Duval	1	0	0	66	12	1	1	20	3,707	0	2	40	4,622
Eastland	59	28	92	2,624	62	13	29	1,321	2,271	41	24	2,645	2,317
Ector	118	40	55	2,556	40	19	13	347	1,915	19	45	1,927	1,743
Edwards	11	5	2	475	2	0	1	114	208	2	3	328	194
El Paso	347	187	248	6,427	140	825	236	1,580	5,729	111	527	3,129	6,439
Ellis	74	51	102	2,999	51	26	21	1,843	2,214	6	11	3,860	3,008
Erath	129	39	84	2,149	70	9	16	1,132	1,480	10	35	2,570	2,085
Falls	114	56	47	1,809	49	15	23	992	1,433	11	33	2,170	1,950
Fannin	97	51	120	3,366	122	37	74	1,532	3,589	17	92	3,945	4,475
Fayette	117	63	28	1,956	29	14	198	1,145	2,102	20	65	1,901	2,003
Fisher	47	13	37	939	33	3	10	444	1,216	3	22	766	1,348
Floyd	33	18	22	1,368	38	2	16	352	1,004	6	20	1,518	1,303
Foard	16	5	29	500	8	4	3	102	280	0	13	318	216
Fort Bend	17	71	10	720	8	4	11	1,021	690	9	17	1,170	969
Franklin	60	16	45	824	47	10	27	528	668	2	29	1,114	1,054
Freestone	103	33	33	1,743	49	5	11	991	1,068	22	55	2,294	1,861
Frio	4	1	13	741	25	99	7	180	587	6	2	953	966
Gaines	55	27	33	1,063	28	7	13	189	598	10	30	1,034	843
Galveston	71	137	126	8,621	219	112	85	2,115	3,149	101	168	7,985	5,992
Garza	38	11	20	734	17	13	8	217	384	5	13	690	664
Gillespie	2	0	0	762	1	0	0	217	262	0	0	1,014	250
Glasscock	5	0	0	198	5	0	0	17	97	3	2	155	121
Goliad	26	8	2	626	12	6	6	214	221	10	13	443	241
Gonzales	46	21	12	2,077	19	25	10	622	1,364	22	29	2,169	1,732
Gray	102	29	36	2,714	52	31	31	661	1,022	20	39	2,233	1,086
Grayson	340	61	93	5,763	127	21	37	2,079	4,153	29	79	3,378	3,797
Gregg	206	42	72	3,591	205	21	33	1,321	3,958	76	38	4,221	1,978
Grimes	13	28	6	650	14	3	5	713	394	8	11	778	802
Guadalupe	0	4	9	773	3	7	2	121	488	6	3	1,237	598
Hale	70	17	49	2,654	40	7	20	842	1,453	7	47	2,052	1,550
Hall	44	18	18	1,090	22	4	8	384	959	4	22	772	820
Hamilton	63	19	35	1,362	18	3	13	554	768	8	16	1,202	821
Hansford	11	2	4	425	7	1	2	175	97	3	5	0	0
Hardeman	40	7	36	677	13	2	8	308	633	3	7	513	612
Hardin	71	28	90	1,368	38	11	55	857	1,118	20	89	1,038	812
Harris	454	234	418	31,477	402	199	267	44,289	21,400	303	1,198	51,495	37,377
Harrison	173	26	16	2,593	39	18	18	1,162	2,640	7	55	2,619	2,760
Hartley	11	2	10	277	2	0	0	15	84	0	3	122	64
Haskell	58	18	30	1,264	56	27	38	651	1,406	11	33	1,159	1,844
Hays	7	0	10	578	3	11	6	158	2,583	27	2	634	2,215
Hemphill	5	5	9	492	64	2	9	88	369	2	8	185	108
Henderson	51	46	45	2,531	142	13	36	1,822	2,001	53	31	3,441	3,905
Hidalgo	354	80	62	4,378	89	1,010	37	1,710	5,392	38	139	6,851	10,412
Hill	110	44	40	2,470	65	20	15	1,573	2,453	19	42	3,283	3,222
Hockley	84	35	36	1,310	52	11	15	280	1,689	10	23	1,371	1,972
Hood	86	20	35	1,018	24	4	14	465	487	16	18	1,306	1,065
Hopkins	28	25	51	2,779	121	10	58	1,287	1,792	33	37	3,436	2,868
Houston	70	27	34	1,740	55	11	27	1,604	904	6	57	2,564	2,550
Howard	84	22	37	2,439	31	23	10	144	1,048	14	29	2,411	2,635
Hudspeth	21	2	3	223	5	11	7	44	186	2	7	87	117
Hunt	152	42	65	3,184	70	13	92	1,437	1,703	14	49	3,215	2,137
Hutchinson	72	23	39	2,339	34	14	13	420	1,389	591	35	2,076	1,454
Irion	5	4	3	289	3	0	8	39	214	0	3	215	224
Jack	64	9	14	841	10	3	11	428	902	1	26	894	879
Jackson	3	11	2	437	6	6	4	815	547	0	19	757	1,174
Jasper	122	26	25	1,361	37	14	125	1,163	608	4	42	2,333	1,651
Jeff Davis	1	3	4	197	2	16	1	67	97	1	5	154	100
Jefferson	237	119	2,431	9,075	182	81	457	3,794	9,701	240	221	11,801	15,670
Jim Hogg	10	3	0	266	1	36	0	43	312	2	7	211	796
Jim Wells	21	22	20	1,357	14	245	11	543	1,881	7	26	770	1,988
Johnson	59	31	86	2,457	57	26	13	842	1,565	18	15	2,112	1,813
Jones	60	13	32	1,614	43	5	9	484	2,078	11	25	1,415	2,152
Karnes	69	22	31	1,240	14	94	9	456	1,578	13	21	1,133	1,492
Kaufman	47	27	74	2,738	148	13	35	1,168	1,796	45	21	3,039	2,734
Kendall	1	1	0	213	0	0	0	62	131	1	2	290	139

Table 16: Senatorial Races

	Democratic Primary, 1948												
Year	1948											Runoff	
County	Otis C. Myers	F.B. Clark	Roscoe Collier	Coke Stevenson	Cyclone Davis	Frank Cortez	Jesse Saunders	George Peddy	Lyndo B. Johnson	Terrell Sledge	James Alford	Coke Stevenson	Lyndon B. Johnson
Kenedy	6	0	1	46	0	0	0	7	7	0	0	52	8
Kent	18	5	6	213	8	4	3	51	278	0	10	147	235
Kerr	32	6	6	1,824	16	25	3	335	1,224	6	23	1,218	855
Kimble	7	4	0	1,201	5	6	1	69	418	2	3	1,115	493
King	11	1	5	101	10	0	2	28	119	2	6	135	160
Kinney	1	0	1	131	3	23	1	3	61	1	2	0	0
Kleberg	29	12	26	1,380	13	281	18	560	1,039	18	16	1,289	1,677
Knox	43	12	84	873	9	5	7	322	923	5	13	592	869
La Salle	3	3	0	358	1	24	2	86	514	1	2	302	605
Lamar	379	65	99	3,900	101	39	87	979	2,795	15	89	5,010	4,155
Lamb	79	13	27	1,531	40	14	68	345	1,462	11	34	807	900
Lampasas	27	3	14	823	7	0	6	287	946	3	2	677	801
Lavaca	30	272	5	1,863	106	7	10	1,189	1,293	32	47	1,225	1,324
Lee	3	14	3	800	6	2	5	259	1,730	17	11	956	1,389
Leon	26	21	24	875	11	1	7	655	649	2	7	803	957
Liberty	84	45	27	1,799	62	11	28	2,318	671	17	109	2,160	1,573
Limestone	89	24	59	1,991	52	11	14	1,266	1,993	21	64	1,940	2,072
Lipscomb	2	4	5	372	9	9	1	25	178	5	4	134	78
Live Oak	43	11	7	861	14	41	9	339	539	6	20	860	724
Llano	3	7	2	657	8	0	3	183	1,090	4	1	736	1,077
Loving	6	2	0	49	1	0	0	4	14	0	1	22	15
Lubbock	141	37	77	4,193	77	18	17	1,375	6,285	14	73	3,218	6,445
Lynn	69	13	24	1,173	34	6	19	378	1,069	4	12	726	966
Madison	25	36	14	626	27	4	10	564	356	6	26	764	830
Marion	57	12	1	529	9	11	9	155	790	13	28	208	615
Martin	45	8	19	587	17	1	8	156	441	4	9	677	721
Mason	1	4	13	1,146	7	3	4	60	510	0	3	846	402
Matagorda	17	28	5	721	16	7	0	559	336	5	16	928	625
Maverick	24	7	3	336	5	96	1	86	388	4	20	425	671
McCulloch	21	17	9	1,324	7	13	8	219	1,957	1	6	1,245	1,461
McLennan	192	129	193	7,371	288	117	108	3,532	8,760	50	98	8,663	10,178
McMullen	6	2	0	158	3	1	1	38	135	0	1	166	144
Medina	10	7	8	820	11	51	10	333	548	16	22	798	729
Menard	14	5	21	790	13	12	5	92	518	3	16	916	652
Midland	25	16	27	1,837	51	20	9	636	921	19	79	1,233	796
Milam	31	110	17	2,210	56	81	59	1,136	1,689	51	43	2,271	1,949
Mills	34	20	18	711	18	24	3	275	794	2	7	652	519
Mitchell	7	15	64	1,282	22	5	0	316	830	4	6	603	703
Montague	81	17	38	1,494	40	5	19	621	1,586	19	26	1,917	2,101
Montgomery	44	27	71	1,786	114	17	37	2,227	694	45	91	2,407	1,955
Moore	48	17	23	1,244	19	9	14	84	461	96	15	872	400
Morris	39	8	13	656	19	3	4	588	666	4	29	671	850
Motley	3	5	5	597	7	1	5	82	271	2	4	366	295
Nacogdoches	129	19	37	2,090	42	14	57	3,494	929	14	157	3,525	3,485
Navarro	59	33	47	3,420	107	10	39	1,609	2,013	63	58	2,713	1,870
Newton	34	22	24	692	70	10	75	627	273	21	26	1,155	1,125
Nolan	121	36	195	1,658	86	9	21	466	1,686	14	51	1,508	2,139
Nueces	170	61	112	4,745	54	846	33	2,677	8,428	36	47	4,118	7,598
Ochiltree	43	8	8	809	8	0	6	138	268	1	3	996	439
Oldham	3	0	2	220	1	0	3	35	246	1	1	163	173
Orange	136	24	105	3,313	53	28	955	1,788	1,052	19	26	3,636	2,504
Palo Pinto	42	40	34	1,356	35	6	44	683	802	12	12	1,426	1,086
Panola	91	19	22	739	40	9	31	2,969	914	27	39	874	1,615
Parker	68	71	35	1,854	56	4	22	663	1,223	22	17	2,060	1,780
Parmer	29	5	27	782	16	3	5	173	325	1	12	390	222
Pecos	58	17	8	1,289	23	98	8	112	681	5	35	1,265	831
Polk	68	29	22	1,281	28	5	39	1,038	645	3	91	1,726	1,361
Potter	33	29	67	6,604	170	22	56	987	3,290	39	33	6,418	3,959
Presidio	8	8	8	550	9	215	9	69	280	3	15	556	437
Rains	17	9	17	453	20	11	21	350	480	2	9	563	655
Randall	6	6	19	1,697	38	1	9	255	789	1	5	1,415	696
Reagan	5	1	1	228	2	0	0	34	165	3	7	179	166
Real	9	1	6	394	6	4	3	53	242	1	2	401	308
Red River	43	79	53	2,326	72	68	24	1,161	1,374	18	66	2,870	2,594
Reeves	52	16	30	914	21	55	10	188	500	10	17	889	885

Table 16: Senatorial Races

	Democratic Primary, 1948													
Year	1948											Runoff	
County	Otis C. Myers	F.B. Clark	Roscoe Collier	Coke Stevenson	Cyclone Davis	Frank Cortez	Jesse Saunders	George Peddy	Lyndo B. Johnson	Terrell Sledge	James Alford	Coke Stevenson	Lyndon B. Johnson
Refugio	2	0	0	190	1	0	0	184	175	3	3	294	312
Roberts	5	1	1	351	4	0	2	40	38	0	2	181	12
Robertson	91	113	41	1,242	49	16	19	1,133	1,104	20	63	1,386	1,828
Rockwall	47	9	30	867	31	3	2	440	567	10	10	802	513
Runnels	46	14	15	1,980	47	7	35	518	1,638	7	21	1,959	2,228
Rusk	230	71	71	5,488	72	18	45	2,347	1,733	32	174	6,573	3,362
Sabine	23	13	19	532	15	22	44	1,315	370	2	26	1,332	1,434
San Augustine	27	20	0	635	25	16	75	1,063	543	1	24	784	1,559
San Jacinto	33	15	10	329	11	2	7	412	209	2	34	446	435
San Patricio	27	17	46	1,333	12	124	9	623	2,047	11	33	1,743	2,198
San Saba	21	6	15	892	9	3	4	357	1,222	8	16	868	1,228
Schleicher	7	0	0	333	3	0	0	68	304	0	2	339	290
Scurry	80	19	28	1,061	25	3	10	505	798	4	37	983	1,190
Shackelford	11	5	16	694	12	2	4	200	375	1	1	349	291
Shelby	66	18	22	558	29	9	54	4,238	357	23	77	1,639	2,259
Sherman	19	4	6	409	5	1	4	29	135	0	4	104	40
Smith	37	32	85	4,919	91	18	19	2,864	3,634	19	31	6,135	4,077
Somervell	35	9	9	366	10	1	2	232	190	1	6	358	316
Starr	33	10	5	93	4	65	1	115	2,571	1	20	170	3,038
Stephens	32	20	67	1,402	59	17	20	457	1,105	23	33	1,285	1,020
Sterling	0	0	1	126	3	0	1	16	138	0	0	70	124
Stonewall	29	14	17	365	5	10	74	99	558	1	8	442	778
Sutton	0	0	2	364	0	32	1	33	134	0	0	281	157
Swisher	43	8	6	1,043	9	2	5	220	500	4	16	788	420
Tarrant	1,233	278	428	23,063	350	84	140	6,957	16,873	108	237	22,741	18,092
Taylor	26	42	35	3,505	50	26	13	786	5,115	20	20	3,078	4,651
Terrell	13	5	10	304	8	36	8	135	104	0	1	116	47
Terry	28	13	8	781	25	2	5	214	1,091	4	14	740	1,114
Throckmorton	14	3	12	398	14	3	3	206	590	7	5	287	539
Titus	91	27	53	1,598	88	7	19	804	1,250	8	40	1,926	2,003
Tom Green	35	37	18	4,063	45	52	11	672	3,666	51	10	3,510	3,913
Travis	35	59	94	7,298	34	79	35	2,839	17,477	59	55	8,525	17,981
Trinity	10	25	23	1,025	17	14	15	787	373	6	35	943	783
Tyler	29	17	35	801	10	3	42	780	425	4	12	1,238	754
Upshur	145	31	43	1,623	49	13	31	1,075	1,815	17	83	1,594	1,249
Upton	33	8	8	582	3	2	2	65	406	3	21	374	350
Uvalde	16	3	11	1,729	11	58	10	295	708	19	8	898	474
Val Verde	8	8	8	1,011	16	203	4	117	462	5	17	515	361
Van Zandt	45	30	74	1,483	122	7	23	1,832	2,183	12	17	2,616	3,136
Victoria	5	8	0	929	10	33	3	437	504	0	5	1,017	681
Walker	14	12	15	1,330	20	10	14	911	921	11	22	1,453	1,472
Waller	2	14	13	503	3	5	18	844	365	10	33	867	811
Ward	80	28	34	1,403	33	10	14	222	779	9	31	1,293	974
Washington	5	6	6	1,768	13	0	3	651	2,545	3	7	1,540	1,727
Webb	1	8	6	531	6	25	5	531	6,476	4	2	1,179	5,554
Wharton	44	46	11	1,519	18	13	12	1,202	1,430	37	51	1,424	1,183
Wheeler	21	9	32	1,067	68	3	9	280	600	10	11	854	666
Wichita	2	9	3	4,846	12	16	5	1,191	7,326	1	0	4,188	5,913
Wilbarger	92	14	183	1,758	45	5	9	450	1,203	7	19	1,907	1,607
Willacy	71	20	22	1,048	24	205	15	443	758	8	40	1,467	1,274
Williamson	34	13	12	1,822	13	5	17	406	4,828	11	24	2,531	4,949
Wilson	7	47	6	1,515	17	105	5	310	1,835	4	5	1,784	1,901
Winkler	29	15	32	1,253	28	3	12	187	617	19	35	1,030	753
Wise	14	13	47	1,359	37	2	14	1,019	1,375	5	31	1,101	1,625
Wood	23	18	74	1,973	56	14	25	1,104	1,603	29	19	2,424	2,065
Yoakum	39	11	23	566	18	3	8	75	387	6	18	592	574
Young	53	29	36	1,308	28	4	7	487	1,953	11	20	972	1,584
Zapata	0	10	0	28	0	8	0	5	580	0	0	71	669
Zavala	22	9	1	478	6	45	6	151	492	15	13	395	425
Official Totals	15,330	7,420	12,327	477,077	10,871	13,344	7,401	237,195	405,617	6,692	9,117	494,104	494,191
Unofficial Totals	15,330	7,420	12,327	477,077	10,871	13,334	7,401	237,195	405,617	6,692	9,117	494,104	494,191

Table 17: Senatorial Races

County	Democratic Primaries, 1952-1966										
Year	1952			1954		1958		1964		1966	
County	Price Daniel	Lindley Beckworth	E.W. Napier	Dudley T. Dougherty	Lyndon B. Johnson	William A. Blakley	Ralph W. Yarborough	Ralph W. Yarborough	Gordon McLendon	John R. Willoughby	Waggoner Carr
Anderson	4,220	1,797	256	2,553	4,696	2,648	3,985	3,774	4,769	980	3,611
Andrews	1,024	373	110	352	1,202	995	1,432	1,709	1,578	559	2,511
Angelina	7,132	3,162	280	3,022	6,430	3,488	6,613	7,595	6,826	2,618	9,473
Aransas	744	188	43	357	531	462	883	1,074	798	220	737
Archer	1,150	269	611	440	1,296	668	1,174	1,332	539	257	1,622
Armstrong	737	82	73	106	638	191	437	427	342	97	583
Atascosa	2,653	431	147	1,298	2,011	1,205	2,281	1,823	1,240	508	2,117
Austin	3,052	524	64	1,085	2,070	1,231	1,164	1,304	1,093	508	2,317
Bailey	1,439	239	154	313	1,423	653	913	721	654	228	1,070
Bandera	1,284	187	47	417	816	774	609	737	794	349	1,193
Bastrop	2,894	859	146	854	2,976	1,178	2,706	2,639	1,288	638	2,514
Baylor	1,393	195	413	411	1,358	563	932	832	380	185	1,626
Bee	3,008	467	148	2,824	1,361	1,321	2,008	2,159	1,531	756	2,728
Bell	9,420	2,643	460	2,804	8,087	2,851	7,460	8,940	4,327	922	6,028
Bexar	25,469	5,245	3,123	18,685	26,412	25,698	35,532	50,264	26,145	13,284	55,734
Blanco	347	87	10	173	616	212	309	357	249	110	616
Borden	285	31	27	87	268	194	201	211	151	77	356
Bosque	2,527	762	142	1,166	2,387	1,128	1,936	1,601	1,360	460	2,204
Bowie	8,495	2,776	465	2,975	8,706	3,875	6,555	6,939	5,615	997	4,294
Brazoria	9,330	2,639	404	2,174	5,914	5,008	6,083	9,265	6,458	2,083	6,822
Brazos	4,746	1,472	125	1,847	4,593	2,459	4,928	5,447	3,294	1,499	6,678
Brewster	1,031	167	16	268	844	468	754	1,029	714	220	1,002
Briscoe	862	63	65	207	892	348	687	786	378	45	450
Brooks	1,034	221	111	580	914	476	1,556	1,374	1,045	309	1,425
Brown	5,021	1,537	214	1,985	4,038	2,825	3,743	3,293	2,236	673	3,098
Burleson	2,369	841	168	707	2,916	1,012	2,169	1,942	942	472	2,251
Burnet	2,056	280	99	474	2,031	892	1,473	1,667	1,119	291	1,413
Caldwell	3,141	613	94	1,048	2,772	1,262	2,191	2,101	1,298	438	2,416
Calhoun	1,728	142	41	468	1,498	1,042	1,718	2,107	1,450	779	2,588
Callahan	1,639	658	219	570	1,831	896	1,160	1,543	906	434	1,955
Cameron	7,590	1,088	860	3,917	7,515	7,247	6,850	7,818	6,304	1,516	6,939
Camp	996	1,541	19	396	1,844	1,021	1,330	1,205	894	368	1,552
Carson	1,239	353	106	281	1,327	484	876	1,112	560	245	1,097
Cass	3,669	965	83	929	3,723	2,190	2,740	1,855	2,573	923	3,076
Castro	1,346	252	72	241	1,381	476	1,100	998	372	332	1,011
Chambers	1,695	275	53	431	1,233	955	1,103	1,760	1,219	432	1,218
Cherokee	4,438	2,597	246	1,664	4,446	2,040	3,663	4,886	3,503	865	3,214
Childress	2,230	487	567	482	2,318	718	1,221	1,495	1,086	220	1,648
Clay	1,692	358	689	516	1,992	849	1,814	1,638	840	409	1,909
Cochran	1,353	200	142	327	969	571	885	750	714	167	1,158
Coke	1,010	286	64	223	776	453	930	413	281	170	927
Coleman	2,961	817	253	962	2,683	1,445	1,646	1,832	1,473	444	2,577
Collin	4,870	1,491	385	1,887	5,443	2,346	4,561	4,501	3,705	961	5,486
Collingsworth	1,976	208	271	360	1,726	655	1,196	917	731	177	1,233
Colorado	3,845	481	128	1,494	2,687	1,958	2,294	2,743	2,078	634	2,512
Comal	3,258	381	84	1,157	2,539	1,304	1,193	1,900	1,417	631	2,179
Comanche	2,539	1,293	355	1,328	2,684	967	1,978	1,939	1,500	377	1,895
Concho	1,048	257	55	213	802	418	616	735	418	127	559
Cooke	4,188	902	407	1,663	2,857	2,298	2,603	2,535	3,307	918	4,372
Coryell	2,515	798	110	968	2,507	1,194	2,076	1,600	1,237	472	3,118
Cottle	1,066	198	239	232	1,239	359	990	892	371	111	947
Crane	1,040	259	124	360	980	418	717	676	596	183	747
Crockett	648	149	53	300	748	296	324	500	480	203	936
Crosby	1,570	359	223	501	1,716	476	1,334	1,418	835	207	1,836
Culberson	362	100	21	90	410	234	183	331	403	110	537
Dallam	1,806	264	171	293	1,404	591	819	592	533	214	1,057
Dallas	43,430	18,501	2,260	20,323	40,873	41,203	43,395	56,470	65,288	11,884	45,775
Dawson	3,486	402	205	818	2,321	1,270	1,716	2,104	1,604	323	2,025
DeWitt	3,517	251	55	1,830	2,756	1,964	1,647	2,165	2,387	392	2,400
Deaf Smith	2,280	335	152	368	1,779	761	934	1,395	1,071	383	1,982
Delta	1,379	621	95	481	1,638	586	1,080	969	805	198	1,229
Denton	5,528	2,197	432	2,485	5,298	2,930	3,997	4,712	3,645	624	2,437
Dickens	1,413	272	263	338	1,307	499	1,117	946	523	92	681
Dimmit	1,076	178	52	383	848	614	646	418	1,032	247	1,362

Table 17: Senatorial Races

Democratic Primaries, 1952-1966											
Year	1952			1954		1958		1964		1966	
County	Price Daniel	Lindley Beckworth	E.W. Napier	Dudley T. Dougherty	Lyndon B. Johnson	William A. Blakley	Ralph W. Yarborough	Ralph W. Yarborough	Gordon McLendon	John R. Willoughby	Waggoner Carr
Donley	1,433	204	161	293	1,303	481	724	915	802	152	1,117
Duval	2,822	198	41	1,445	2,926	674	2,594	3,990	240	60	3,807
Eastland	4,672	1,885	538	1,976	4,041	2,300	3,055	3,150	2,467	701	3,637
Ector	6,569	1,441	492	1,890	4,936	3,371	2,709	4,179	4,504	1,443	5,434
Edwards	677	50	28	306	465	417	199	240	485	107	531
El Paso	14,563	4,114	582	2,058	12,822	6,014	10,474	16,131	9,259	4,925	15,594
Ellis	5,201	1,933	283	2,179	4,105	1,824	2,693	3,208	2,618	654	4,025
Erath	2,743	1,415	228	1,397	3,191	1,483	2,609	2,466	1,911	485	3,208
Falls	1,796	876	84	1,360	2,810	1,312	2,217	2,837	1,634	431	2,392
Fannin	5,085	1,806	684	1,753	5,074	1,358	3,932	4,074	2,454	578	3,183
Fayette	3,925	523	436	1,785	4,011	2,094	2,380	2,301	1,804	697	2,445
Fisher	1,762	526	285	370	1,778	678	1,580	1,502	797	354	1,562
Floyd	2,500	330	211	616	2,059	952	1,409	1,282	1,062	120	629
Foard	837	135	192	237	846	331	724	361	134	56	583
Fort Bend	3,293	727	125	1,118	2,401	2,055	2,333	4,338	3,661	1,881	4,889
Franklin	1,281	669	53	597	1,441	713	1,169	1,109	700	254	1,354
Freestone	3,081	671	155	1,258	2,734	1,538	2,193	2,035	1,688	533	2,595
Frio	1,367	160	93	622	947	688	1,109	1,047	1,017	270	1,402
Gaines	1,933	461	282	571	1,914	901	1,594	1,347	1,128	189	1,152
Galveston	13,250	3,099	989	3,074	14,895	6,522	13,019	14,728	8,622	4,908	15,534
Garza	1,094	225	163	378	1,033	484	729	934	716	203	1,228
Gillespie	1,525	69	16	447	574	653	284	310	428	87	751
Glasscock	321	64	33	128	310	200	162	102	122	20	136
Goliad	512	36	16	697	654	563	569	642	373	105	570
Gonzales	2,322	284	68	945	1,807	1,433	1,999	1,725	1,607	220	1,496
Gray	3,285	455	316	1,297	3,388	2,307	2,369	1,742	1,348	741	3,498
Grayson	8,297	3,369	816	2,646	8,385	2,614	5,581	7,807	5,543	1,597	7,377
Gregg	4,908	6,456	157	2,686	6,983	6,275	4,472	3,885	7,276	2,218	7,289
Grimes	1,250	197	30	441	1,491	682	1,044	1,946	1,178	493	2,377
Guadalupe	1,212	116	59	872	1,452	1,026	1,354	1,694	1,254	596	2,702
Hale	3,403	466	185	923	2,923	2,151	2,936	3,167	2,632	481	2,937
Hall	1,951	296	227	303	1,936	431	1,377	1,323	759	136	986
Hamilton	2,357	439	181	1,133	1,907	995	1,100	1,272	1,614	419	1,861
Hansford	780	91	43	220	979	500	427	207	261	138	782
Hardeman	1,915	317	322	719	1,550	863	1,033	1,444	967	216	1,352
Hardin	3,574	1,138	127	976	3,207	1,210	3,590	4,839	2,118	1,336	5,051
Harris	86,211	28,108	3,537	26,700	60,922	54,711	74,211	92,805	67,734	23,386	82,346
Harrison	4,078	2,672	166	1,341	5,707	4,612	2,839	3,130	4,192	1,355	6,136
Hartley	606	90	49	85	530	297	309	264	239	84	682
Haskell	2,015	796	576	807	2,843	950	2,176	2,141	1,164	532	2,196
Hays	1,719	324	66	723	2,555	1,109	1,562	2,750	1,534	661	2,891
Hemphill	835	123	96	162	963	351	563	569	445	117	668
Henderson	3,714	2,464	507	1,659	5,095	1,426	4,168	4,411	2,810	1,402	4,912
Hidalgo	12,837	1,135	755	5,573	10,077	7,982	9,319	10,595	10,484	3,642	10,461
Hill	5,690	1,225	262	2,037	4,723	2,373	4,394	3,570	2,416	345	2,667
Hockley	3,229	862	547	979	2,965	1,781	2,752	2,395	1,735	464	2,695
Hood	1,338	474	161	548	1,349	551	1,306	999	746	259	1,367
Hopkins	3,833	1,709	168	1,506	3,769	1,957	3,168	2,558	2,537	700	3,381
Houston	3,115	1,157	121	1,067	3,075	1,364	2,470	3,311	2,101	799	3,266
Howard	4,200	1,664	305	1,256	4,479	1,650	3,313	4,663	2,882	827	4,523
Hudspeth	442	123	32	75	527	217	337	379	316	86	469
Hunt	5,663	1,721	219	2,731	5,136	2,774	3,579	4,492	4,126	987	4,396
Hutchinson	4,467	1,136	416	1,407	3,656	1,729	3,279	3,357	2,262	1,106	3,144
Irion	432	108	30	150	365	307	220	235	237	97	420
Jack	1,425	367	358	592	1,261	920	1,232	1,105	927	276	1,618
Jackson	2,493	524	112	944	2,378	1,348	1,664	1,785	1,656	901	5,293
Jasper	3,129	801	93	1,023	3,474	1,444	3,340	3,474	1,952	1,174	3,682
Jeff Davis	335	78	23	79	238	109	176	132	89	103	281
Jefferson	17,877	9,008	1,398	7,430	19,435	11,520	18,474	32,092	21,033	6,387	18,506
Jim Hogg	556	66	13	304	647	214	875	1,123	460	155	730
Jim Wells	4,777	762	202	3,281	3,028	1,666	4,096	4,894	3,235	1,549	4,713
Johnson	3,761	1,110	214	1,996	4,178	1,609	2,768	4,006	3,602	570	2,788
Jones	3,040	1,134	483	896	3,122	1,342	2,014	2,370	1,624	362	2,439
Karnes	3,447	253	68	1,688	1,943	1,516	2,353	1,950	1,495	396	2,186
Kaufman	3,878	1,964	179	1,545	3,304	2,092	2,751	3,175	2,724	1,269	4,534

Table 17: Senatorial Races

Democratic Primaries, 1952-1966											
Year	**1952**			**1954**		**1958**		**1964**		**1966**	
County	Price Daniel	Lindley Beckworth	E.W. Napier	Dudley T. Dougherty	Lyndon B. Johnson	William A. Blakley	Ralph W. Yarborough	Ralph W. Yarborough	Gordon McLendon	John R. Willoughby	Waggoner Carr
Kendall	341	42	9	230	346	321	178	174	185	44	234
Kenedy	66	17	1	112	22	69	18	31	79	24	85
Kent	476	241	52	149	590	285	569	458	232	95	665
Kerr	3,337	463	106	1,134	2,301	1,972	1,462	1,262	1,328	446	1,791
Kimble	1,024	181	79	674	862	563	403	633	653	141	786
King	108	20	16	40	185	67	139	129	93	21	175
Kinney	119	32	5	152	246	206	341	270	211	90	417
Kleberg	2,671	858	152	1,064	1,897	919	2,339	3,063	2,075	1,239	3,479
Knox	1,465	485	304	400	1,777	607	1,058	953	491	154	1,280
LaS alle	897	112	41	182	644	365	671	530	457	171	706
Lamar	6,941	1,396	427	2,547	6,280	3,079	4,397	4,566	3,668	1,329	4,882
Lamb	3,341	459	380	917	3,246	1,281	2,438	2,102	1,590	414	2,583
Lampasas	1,843	323	61	707	1,583	874	1,210	1,242	1,003	253	1,206
Lavaca	3,337	414	132	1,416	3,084	1,207	2,612	2,773	1,806	638	2,683
Lee	1,981	341	79	604	1,841	707	1,716	1,270	771	394	1,448
Leon	2,036	656	47	585	2,268	1,150	1,885	1,549	1,047	248	833
Liberty	5,593	915	213	1,437	3,644	2,243	2,824	3,539	2,600	1,535	2,996
Limestone	4,701	1,077	199	1,546	4,089	1,719	3,011	2,512	2,201	632	2,745
Lipscomb	523	66	50	79	508	342	549	470	475	92	663
Live Oak	1,841	168	72	1,194	778	824	859	984	1,134	347	1,385
Llano	1,470	251	63	285	935	443	852	1,050	815	253	1,034
Loving	53	7	4	11	63	48	46	25	43	10	54
Lubbock	12,042	2,363	1,457	3,636	9,874	6,588	7,676	10,441	9,346	1,929	9,941
Lynn	2,069	383	232	516	1,698	788	1,242	1,193	1,201	237	1,814
Madison	1,502	255	105	432	1,439	615	1,261	1,252	889	266	1,436
Marion	1,170	670	66	225	1,359	983	696	598	880	335	1,249
Martin	1,086	300	91	251	937	319	491	447	356	78	477
Mason	1,287	170	58	546	832	525	654	676	601	130	705
Matagorda	4,028	467	157	1,591	3,372	1,534	1,870	2,472	2,426	1,073	3,007
Maverick	1,046	95	32	163	809	540	920	1,303	992	407	1,876
McCulloch	2,497	375	154	691	2,681	1,020	1,335	1,264	954	310	1,476
McLennan	15,716	5,235	806	6,548	16,092	7,851	15,291	18,919	8,802	2,193	11,345
McMullen	327	46	9	274	211	234	240	136	168	83	250
Medina	879	120	20	513	1,075	896	1,386	1,308	966	290	1,799
Menard	954	243	71	332	723	482	503	219	183	144	587
Midland	4,719	1,031	283	2,074	4,011	3,482	2,357	3,433	4,498	940	4,526
Milam	3,670	801	238	1,650	3,078	2,094	3,613	2,945	1,674	708	2,923
Mills	1,392	510	88	646	1,273	601	1,006	998	901	196	883
Mitchell	2,130	824	181	704	2,114	887	1,673	1,260	668	238	2,020
Montague	3,465	638	795	1,130	2,920	1,353	2,252	2,594	1,688	436	1,872
Montgomery	4,587	795	246	1,917	4,314	1,960	3,593	3,892	3,693	2,462	5,923
Moore	2,158	728	152	471	1,912	869	1,564	1,857	1,243	577	2,281
Morris	1,567	975	57	573	2,356	1,341	1,519	1,789	1,655	473	2,324
Motley	909	99	134	208	795	433	552	481	457	103	768
Nacogdoches	4,521	1,607	337	1,521	4,528	2,095	3,865	4,112	4,254	1,307	5,051
Navarro	5,355	1,724	289	1,866	5,008	2,137	3,938	3,829	2,277	1,337	4,367
Newton	1,860	396	93	514	1,558	678	1,986	1,812	862	594	2,243
Nolan	3,728	908	825	846	3,247	1,517	2,394	2,693	1,947	472	3,169
Nueces	17,391	4,465	1,342	8,408	13,797	7,740	15,417	19,867	10,602	5,439	18,457
Ochiltree	1,404	138	90	262	881	766	753	333	565	173	679
Oldham	424	94	31	68	499	226	329	254	183	82	427
Orange	7,694	1,620	314	2,036	7,245	2,766	5,901	7,698	5,076	2,279	6,453
Palo Pinto	2,870	1,302	306	1,261	2,420	1,720	2,258	2,300	2,134	497	2,990
Panola	2,358	3,314	79	1,114	4,842	2,774	1,883	1,744	3,235	789	2,263
Parker	3,429	1,174	432	1,542	4,306	1,593	2,679	3,233	2,539	754	3,305
Parmer	1,018	134	85	283	1,173	714	1,090	835	626	162	1,135
Pecos	1,894	371	158	607	1,942	1,117	1,275	1,133	1,101	186	1,052
Polk	2,718	712	149	700	2,017	1,383	1,990	2,549	1,623	822	2,488
Potter	5,148	1,050	286	1,904	8,867	3,962	4,514	7,710	4,214	947	4,097
Presidio	806	161	51	252	875	353	516	777	549	203	899
Rains	1,016	212	25	287	871	269	661	602	413	196	757
Randall	3,044	483	221	673	3,078	2,160	2,028	2,930	2,290	490	2,031
Reagan	693	147	47	277	910	564	683	520	473	109	641
Real	508	65	37	129	240	298	334	219	224	27	169
Red River	3,630	1,261	236	1,265	3,769	1,600	2,560	2,242	2,133	447	2,519

Table 17: Senatorial Races

Democratic Primaries, 1952-1966											
Year	1952			1954		1958		1964		1966	
County	Price Daniel	Lindley Beckworth	E.W. Napier	Dudley T. Dougherty	Lyndon B. Johnson	William A. Blakley	Ralph W. Yarborough	Ralph W. Yarborough	Gordon McLendon	John R. Willoughby	Waggoner Carr
Reeves	1,904	477	110	441	1,950	920	1,219	1,490	1,278	289	1,961
Refugio	1,528	220	57	784	907	557	1,089	1,273	917	269	1,198
Roberts	193	17	14	122	298	176	109	94	87	34	365
Robertson	2,237	739	89	972	2,736	1,011	2,385	2,348	1,113	550	2,180
Rockwall	1,281	449	86	398	837	685	985	887	773	161	1,162
Runnels	1,938	413	103	823	2,193	1,549	1,418	1,600	1,499	265	1,224
Rusk	4,300	5,330	470	2,047	6,276	4,229	4,259	2,866	4,619	746	4,252
Sabine	1,959	408	106	446	1,899	717	1,481	1,509	843	417	1,457
San Augustine	1,711	522	199	505	1,096	786	1,421	1,290	1,090	492	1,696
San Jacinto	759	170	36	268	765	205	542	1,349	661	541	1,074
San Patricio	3,458	877	106	2,143	2,909	1,861	3,762	4,582	2,827	1,573	3,915
San Saba	1,309	425	86	655	1,764	614	1,339	1,410	830	205	1,252
Schleicher	907	141	51	255	755	385	422	318	306	130	747
Scurry	3,419	912	355	760	2,609	1,827	2,375	2,471	2,130	622	3,470
Shackelford	1,340	328	154	399	916	717	609	766	667	220	1,156
Shelby	4,337	2,657	178	1,890	5,071	2,335	3,720	3,356	3,291	1,376	4,042
Sherman	634	102	54	129	699	325	358	295	321	97	587
Smith	7,560	7,966	130	4,387	10,907	6,057	7,228	8,268	6,958	2,432	8,600
Somervell	716	149	45	300	632	389	601	553	416	131	533
Starr	3,451	256	21	328	3,783	265	3,102	3,707	434	102	3,022
Stephens	2,627	629	194	1,017	2,115	1,177	1,252	1,349	1,405	312	1,841
Sterling	300	55	20	80	273	224	167	71	101	13	113
Stonewall	769	202	173	254	966	383	835	803	514	138	1,000
Sutton	404	78	6	210	578	322	263	236	278	60	299
Swisher	2,029	199	99	281	1,656	605	1,764	1,745	608	157	1,009
Tarrant	43,983	13,573	3,808	18,406	40,528	23,808	31,991	44,128	32,549	12,073	35,080
Taylor	8,953	3,013	822	1,872	7,368	5,425	4,679	7,970	7,041	1,846	8,596
Terrell	143	55	8	168	368	189	249	172	195	47	299
Terry	2,919	369	364	594	1,957	1,032	1,794	2,060	1,699	397	2,442
Throckmorton	819	278	225	295	995	304	724	814	409	148	895
Titus	3,294	1,717	158	1,258	3,051	1,617	2,709	2,095	2,088	400	1,925
Tom Green	7,887	2,106	720	2,780	7,272	4,409	5,137	5,685	4,714	1,734	7,272
Travis	22,923	5,614	1,023	8,057	20,970	12,587	17,759	26,645	16,396	7,616	23,991
Trinity	1,538	452	160	653	1,611	735	1,582	1,573	1,014	632	1,874
Tyler	2,277	307	49	718	2,010	1,422	1,591	1,540	1,211	535	1,704
Upshur	1,516	4,486	51	802	5,254	2,470	3,139	3,100	2,774	1,222	2,346
Upton	1,154	251	78	427	1,117	560	787	552	600	204	811
Uvalde	2,462	248	87	1,160	1,738	1,526	1,690	1,553	2,094	506	1,919
Val Verde	1,677	281	61	520	2,103	1,026	1,360	2,427	1,078	671	2,556
Van Zandt	2,194	4,044	116	1,334	4,529	1,631	3,451	2,891	1,968	913	3,444
Victoria	3,867	605	167	2,098	4,100	2,112	3,638	4,211	3,277	1,195	5,923
Walker	2,679	416	102	1,330	2,353	1,283	2,116	2,419	1,674	587	2,288
Waller	1,972	274	67	512	1,219	778	1,088	1,340	806	509	2,040
Ward	2,086	622	202	900	2,197	1,112	1,347	1,399	1,206	457	2,080
Washington	2,552	374	59	1,356	3,049	1,714	1,185	1,105	781	384	1,844
Webb	6,105	71	20	516	7,156	2,576	6,468	6,528	1,087	424	8,010
Wharton	6,086	851	298	2,143	4,749	2,639	3,778	3,582	2,227	1,682	4,208
Wheeler	1,624	330	224	497	1,865	848	1,311	775	607	247	1,577
Wichita	8,117	2,531	4,976	3,400	9,870	5,345	8,164	12,468	5,022	2,059	7,645
Wilbarger	3,188	673	794	890	3,021	1,940	2,219	2,487	1,727	358	2,594
Willacy	2,462	310	199	801	2,093	1,130	875	1,445	1,419	580	2,175
Williamson	4,567	879	210	1,533	4,969	2,241	3,496	4,612	2,228	1,077	4,814
Wilson	2,900	475	119	1,434	2,191	1,066	2,385	2,360	1,296	419	3,094
Winkler	1,775	341	138	576	1,783	721	1,099	1,548	1,692	313	1,551
Wise	3,641	914	533	1,069	3,784	1,339	2,857	2,068	1,668	238	1,037
Wood	2,086	2,575	63	1,311	3,342	1,848	3,226	2,509	1,962	669	2,568
Yoakum	1,048	161	138	391	1,224	615	1,273	1,133	950	340	1,794
Young	2,809	554	423	836	2,076	1,367	2,157	2,356	1,628	323	2,458
Zapata	398	13	12	14	559	73	668	823	158	27	953
Zavala	1,199	109	33	481	938	664	873	1,357	1,600	582	1,538
Official Totals	940,770	285,842	70,132	354,188	883,264	535,418	761,511	905,011	672,573	226,598	899,523
Unofficial Totals	940,770	285,843	70,232	354,188	882,454	525,418	760,511	905,041	672,573	226,568	902,223

Table 18: Senatorial Races

	General Elections, 1916-1924										
Year	1916				1918			1922		1924	
County	Charles A. Culbrsn (D)	Alex W. Atchsn (R)	E. H. Conibear (P)	T. A. Hickey (S)	Morris Shepprd (D)	J. Webster Flangn (R)	M. A. Smith (S)	Earle B. Mayfld (D)	George E. B. Peddy (R)	Morris Shepprd (D)	T. M. Kennrly (R)
Anderson	2,045	481	4	188	1,241	254	13	1,964	569	4,117	488
Andrews	72	0	0	1	40	0	0	48	9	66	7
Angelina	1,373	52	27	342	679	27	9	2,195	1,182	4,462	275
Aransas	182	20	2	6	151	5	0	235	47	216	61
Archer	415	47	4	38	304	8	0	503	333	1,168	83
Armstrong	856	33	5	8	172	10	1	350	61	489	50
Atascosa	677	70	6	55	317	10	0	458	284	1,236	249
Austin	1,412	250	0	9	826	305	23	444	2,152	3,288	361
Bailey	0	0	0	0	0	0	0	83	26	220	30
Bandera	546	159	3	45	362	58	10	339	280	625	384
Bastrop	1,436	443	5	22	781	175	0	1,259	790	3,059	426
Baylor	727	28	4	77	380	11	5	480	263	1,198	98
Bee	510	105	6	23	587	61	5	947	508	2,156	560
Bell	3,825	222	36	175	2,215	142	13	3,038	1,037	7,710	1,454
Bexar	9,207	3,226	48	143	3,224	1,433	38	8,154	7,030	17,772	8,324
Blanco	703	164	4	18	495	111	3	608	464	852	278
Borden	105	1	0	1	29	0	0	56	12	121	9
Bosque	1,600	142	5	73	1,002	162	3	1,160	1,052	2,887	272
Bowie	1,988	350	9	280	1,179	56	7	1,508	482	3,874	502
Brazoria	1,062	530	37	83	521	267	13	1,126	543	2,258	960
Brazos	1,082	228	6	4	900	242	2	1,124	270	2,252	239
Brewster	219	37	0	8	111	3	0	187	79	439	81
Briscoe	259	3	0	22	114	1	1	222	93	422	34
Brooks	106	58	2	1	70	4	0	67	51	236	53
Brown	1,991	153	7	101	894	45	8	1,097	908	3,635	344
Burleson	1,163	249	2	21	587	109	0	919	472	2,569	170
Burnet	940	87	8	24	493	66	3	687	205	1,901	223
Caldwell	1,499	171	2	19	581	80	1	1,130	519	2,497	285
Calhoun	413	65	4	64	255	14	3	460	243	798	159
Callahan	974	48	13	77	547	18	3	0	0	1,823	176
Cameron	1,310	361	12	26	791	39	0	1,020	608	2,668	0
Camp	732	198	1	32	375	78	2	524	204	1,264	144
Carson	347	58	4	5	150	9	0	360	286	821	187
Cass	1,541	683	0	131	1,072	218	9	748	474	2,410	839
Castro	189	46	6	5	138	19	1	97	143	324	0
Chambers	247	105	21	24	129	32	0	175	112	432	164
Cherokee	2,041	224	3	250	1,444	141	21	1,882	715	4,964	398
Childress	957	28	3	76	381	10	1	845	574	1,256	110
Clay	1,354	156	5	54	811	0	0	1,197	510	1,888	205
Cochran	0	0	0	0	0	0	0	0	0	88	2
Coke	489	25	4	43	180	5	2	297	234	756	63
Coleman	1,722	81	6	200	815	36	10	1,198	783	3,118	448
Collin	4,109	584	16	185	2,215	286	20	4,806	1,631	7,715	1,690
Collingsworth	712	31	5	65	300	19	2	536	375	989	145
Colorado	1,200	207	9	66	653	165	26	907	1,315	2,698	564
Comal	817	348	0	28	386	268	21	227	1,224	1,297	731
Comanche	1,515	103	27	311	955	158	25	1,164	1,007	3,102	282
Concho	425	27	2	57	206	19	1	275	230	840	50
Cooke	2,405	270	5	108	1,285	124	4	2,384	993	3,668	407
Coryell	1,882	111	5	76	998	48	9	1,368	624	3,326	259
Cottle	451	9	4	69	169	0	0	387	281	639	35
Crane	0	0	0	0	0	0	0	0	0	0	0
Crockett	64	11	0	7	30	2	0	61	31	144	44
Crosby	467	22	0	45	312	7	3	484	366	1,143	203
Culberson	118	1	0	1	42	1	0	56	24	120	6
Dallam	387	63	7	39	151	24	4	490	188	864	223
Dallas	13,663	2,128	134	183	4,115	387	17	15,668	5,510	33,000	6,496
Dawson	292	8	2	14	148	5	3	201	87	1,446	110
DeWitt	1,747	381	4	22	542	79	4	1,097	1,852	3,023	635
Deaf Smith	355	75	5	15	175	24	0	246	172	607	173
Delta	1,272	74	10	109	593	26	0	1,187	422	2,295	336
Denton	2,864	387	13	163	1,659	252	0	2,366	915	5,324	622
Dickens	393	9	0	40	237	8	1	412	193	948	91
Dimmit	201	68	5	6	109	18	0	119	41	341	169

Table 18: Senatorial Races

	General Elections, 1916-1924										
Year	1916				1918			1922		1924	
County	Charles A. Culbrsn (D)	Alex W. Atchsn (R)	E. H. Conibear (P)	T. A. Hickey (S)	Morris Shepprd (D)	J. Webster Flangn (R)	M. A. Smith (S)	Earle B. Mayfld (D)	George E.B. Peddy (R)	Morris Shepprd (D)	T. M. Kenrry (R)
Donley	637	36	7	55	303	11	0	877	262	1,063	211
Duval	604	30	0	3	278	5	0	437	98	986	81
Eastland	1,492	122	14	305	834	55	18	2,348	1,441	5,116	796
Ector	121	1	0	0	69	0	0	69	45	154	3
Edwards	309	67	2	5	245	16	2	161	62	303	254
El Paso	4,208	1,195	30	102	689	36	1	5,679	2,373	0	0
Ellis	4,753	417	7	33	2,223	298	10	3,755	1,115	8,083	1,002
Erath	1,984	138	31	288	1,146	89	14	1,292	819	3,571	351
Falls	2,352	488	12	244	2,086	223	8	1,162	886	3,414	239
Fannin	3,501	456	10	234	1,928	189	15	3,507	424	5,977	603
Fayette	2,465	684	6	42	1,232	640	22	550	4,364	5,064	1,637
Fisher	949	31	7	234	370	9	2	699	825	1,849	200
Floyd	611	42	6	77	435	13	11	453	441	1,311	148
Foard	479	41	2	89	308	21	5	308	220	490	58
Fort Bend	937	318	6	15	422	80	1	612	741	2,425	322
Franklin	671	63	0	42	439	48	2	496	110	1,293	106
Freestone	1,575	636	1	97	980	521	11	1,722	511	2,724	573
Frio	440	28	3	4	193	4	0	883	109	728	120
Gaines	81	1	0	4	73	1	0	145	25	306	23
Galveston	3,824	1,006	46	67	1,257	357	8	1,861	2,185	6,727	1,407
Garza	331	12	0	14	145	5	0	282	163	925	104
Gillespie	593	1,297	3	12	296	670	96	0	0	1,400	890
Glasscock	99	5	0	4	52	0	1	71	37	122	11
Goliad	659	500	5	60	206	15	4	653	765	1,105	399
Gonzales	1,798	534	13	51	1,042	191	3	1,058	671	2,901	468
Gray	511	35	7	35	221	23	2	390	322	742	220
Grayson	5,177	945	33	271	2,750	466	17	4,715	1,561	9,000	1,772
Gregg	831	0	0	0	379	51	3	824	165	1,544	131
Grimes	1,152	63	1	28	596	24	3	967	350	2,215	169
Guadalupe	1,324	1,328	4	6	798	1,072	15	480	1,986	1,510	0
Hale	922	69	8	43	387	23	1	948	500	1,606	419
Hall	924	42	5	91	558	9	6	990	177	1,215	148
Hamilton	1,343	141	1	30	662	79	1	772	628	2,235	194
Hansford	169	44	5	14	67	7	1	0	0	314	53
Hardeman	942	77	5	126	422	27	8	894	262	1,150	174
Hardin	1,324	128	6	85	408	29	4	1,045	146	1,844	465
Harris	11,353	1,815	63	409	5,858	953	91	14,003	5,964	28,648	5,781
Harrison	1,341	135	7	55	569	46	3	1,216	657	2,969	274
Hartley	159	24	0	7	24	2	0	112	38	208	45
Haskell	1,220	65	338	2	635	24	28	1,024	372	2,454	285
Hays	1,026	99	4	8	500	14	0	972	204	1,878	281
Hemphill	508	128	15	25	198	28	1	292	129	506	129
Henderson	1,794	262	3	358	1,269	203	30	1,345	758	3,940	383
Hidalgo	1,399	231	6	33	1,060	71	5	2,485	591	4,041	911
Hill	4,021	280	15	77	2,214	208	6	3,138	1,017	6,575	569
Hockley	0	0	0	0	0	0	0	51	23	179	11
Hood	699	59	1	82	442	27	0	543	181	1,201	108
Hopkins	2,572	208	12	226	1,767	115	14	3,127	288	4,293	518
Houston	1,750	373	0	162	1,108	183	9	1,354	360	3,341	422
Howard	748	28	2	106	337	6	0	790	149	1,358	160
Hudspeth	0	0	0	0	58	0	0	71	28	133	12
Hunt	4,241	417	16	155	2,606	184	18	5,530	362	8,018	756
Hutchinson	159	23	3	6	81	11	3	195	42	170	67
Irion	153	1	11	1	96	0	0	115	58	283	23
Jack	871	107	4	104	451	56	15	810	445	1,336	276
Jackson	412	116	6	65	259	33	12	646	431	922	366
Jasper	917	65	3	38	400	15	2	879	140	1,588	161
Jeff Davis	237	65	2	1	78	0	0	163	8	173	17
Jefferson	3,200	357	23	149	1,716	129	16	3,471	931	8,066	3,125
Jim Hogg	187	10	0	0	41	3	0	40	17	144	17
Jim Wells	400	43	3	34	224	8	3	380	121	840	180
Johnson	3,116	235	8	159	1,630	0	0	0	0	4,724	671
Jones	1,802	101	7	216	847	46	6	1,382	520	3,393	498
Karnes	917	116	4	8	345	32	1	1,222	918	2,234	430
Kaufman	2,790	409	2	177	1,483	250	4	2,317	700	5,866	624

Table 18: Senatorial Races

	General Elections, 1916-1924										
Year	1916				1918			1922		1924	
County	Charles A. Culbrsn (D)	Alex W. Atchsn (R)	E. H. Conibear (P)	T. A. Hickey (S)	Morris Shepprd (D)	J. Webster Flangn (R)	M. A. Smith (S)	Earle B. Mayfld (D)	George E.B. Peddy (R)	Morris Shepprd (D)	T. M. Kennrly (R)
Kendall	391	440	1	6	205	462	5	254	755	383	724
Kenedy	0	0	0	0	0	0	0	9	42	72	72
Kent	222	2	0	26	94	0	0	151	41	424	48
Kerr	751	238	5	29	216	52	2	428	252	1,142	629
Kimble	199	14	0	12	140	1	2	374	81	660	882
King	47	3	0	0	13	0	0	53	69	66	4
Kinney	236	59	1	7	127	76	0	189	102	213	151
Kleberg	472	78	2	52	273	19	3	698	230	1,030	165
Knox	918	36	3	99	429	21	4	783	252	1,645	338
La Salle	346	35	2	3	168	4	0	160	30	487	51
Lamar	3,425	294	6	96	1,358	69	6	3,025	491	5,755	403
Lamb	156	9	5	3	84	7	0	0	0	400	91
Lampasas	865	95	4	31	457	71	2	628	328	1,677	180
Lavaca	2,182	509	9	255	989	301	10	843	2,283	4,870	684
Lee	1,089	312	0	81	883	285	13	847	1,269	2,095	283
Leon	997	311	0	169	635	248	7	777	334	1,776	392
Liberty	721	200	4	78	363	122	5	825	319	1,896	465
Limestone	2,219	192	6	103	1,469	208	7	1,859	506	5,053	376
Lipscomb	343	114	16	49	292	98	22	211	277	531	373
Live Oak	425	90	6	48	267	0	0	421	227	773	328
Llano	755	31	2	21	340	14	0	358	267	997	63
Loving	0	0	0	0	0	0	0	0	0	13	21
Lubbock	644	27	5	27	433	12	1	933	246	2,711	385
Lynn	333	11	0	9	177	3	0	347	168	1,336	206
Madison	725	112	5	45	405	122	2	500	140	1,627	135
Marion	448	162	2	1	217	46	0	339	317	777	251
Martin	124	13	0	23	60	1	0	108	89	415	56
Mason	456	102	1	33	216	13	5	202	180	566	131
Matagorda	776	225	14	80	426	82	4	1,168	584	1,516	947
Maverick	205	235	1	2	117	36	0	135	121	292	240
McCulloch	856	48	2	120	441	14	3	731	244	1,672	342
McLennan	5,221	657	15	119	1,847	210	7	4,535	2,143	9,178	1,711
McMullen	121	18	0	0	64	4	1	82	34	176	41
Medina	841	556	11	26	583	383	12	707	1,324	1,671	651
Menard	285	245	1	34	70	1	0	154	103	489	78
Midland	344	19	0	7	126	7	1	164	57	432	25
Milam	2,311	361	4	244	1,348	109	37	1,803	1,522	5,792	553
Mills	756	79	4	108	480	42	6	0	0	1,321	155
Mitchell	804	35	1	80	295	12	2	579	284	1,367	151
Montague	1,904	231	8	242	1,078	49	24	1,495	454	2,629	250
Montgomery	893	177	3	139	543	96	4	737	117	1,651	160
Moore	104	3	1	0	44	0	0	25	6	90	5
Morris	704	81	0	2	457	39	1	477	141	975	79
Motley	388	3	25	1	162	0	0	243	50	500	23
Nacogdoches	1,783	81	4	147	1,055	48	9	1,274	834	3,418	149
Navarro	3,539	293	7	102	2,677	315	22	2,974	1,191	7,059	770
Newton	497	20	8	33	247	7	0	299	64	923	114
Nolan	1,073	73	3	77	373	21	0	839	323	1,847	234
Nueces	1,893	306	20	126	762	74	9	1,431	914	3,882	640
Ochiltree	246	32	0	7	240	6	1	231	46	416	131
Oldham	129	39	4	0	94	21	0	139	43	232	49
Orange	775	66	7	43	392	20	4	921	200	1,736	359
Palo Pinto	1,454	102	11	285	796	47	15	1,685	556	2,443	321
Panola	1,230	114	0	73	964	117	0	721	295	2,146	87
Parker	1,840	140	14	243	1,125	50	32	1,506	473	2,939	345
Parmer	190	58	9	10	119	12	0	188	48	261	68
Pecos	411	89	2	1	174	13	1	174	176	573	145
Polk	955	84	0	111	536	24	4	770	119	1,929	133
Potter	1,321	117	8	97	457	50	5	0	0	3,443	480
Presidio	265	14	1	0	229	6	1	150	111	0	0
Rains	542	65	1	294	394	30	15	737	133	1,012	47
Randall	354	40	11	5	185	8	0	286	229	756	120
Reagan	61	1	0	0	40	0	0	267	28	151	11
Real	242	14	1	24	153	12	9	71	20	264	249
Red River	2,037	331	8	143	1,325	68	7	1,616	770	3,385	271

Table 18: Senatorial Races

General Elections, 1916-1924										
Year	**1916**				**1918**			**1922**		**1924**	
County	Charles A. Culbrsn (D)	Alex W. Atchsn (R)	E. H. Conibear (P)	T. A. Hickey (S)	Morris Shepprd (D)	J. Webster Flangn (R)	M. A. Smith (S)	Earle B. Mayfld (D)	George E.B. Peddy (R)	Morris Shepprd (D)	T. M. Kennrly (R)
Reeves	358	31	2	3	187	3	0	286	116	472	76
Refugio	412	220	10	51	230	54	11	374	371	0	0
Roberts	218	17	1	3	83	10	1	191	30	282	63
Robertson	1,342	183	1	45	582	46	1	995	318	2,303	194
Rockwall	837	26	12	10	446	13	4	656	301	1,443	85
Runnels	1,547	129	8	137	663	102	10	1,174	844	2,911	352
Rusk	1,857	514	4	198	1,149	500	2	1,572	368	3,334	506
Sabine	684	16	9	53	349	8	1	442	202	1,411	47
San Augustine	682	12	3	50	246	10	2	479	409	1,630	58
San Jacinto	444	258	1	11	192	37	1	267	67	664	108
San Patricio	620	110	10	67	538	36	6	1,029	380	1,569	601
San Saba	840	45	8	101	505	83	1	482	402	1,813	149
Schleicher	164	7	0	1	92	3	0	130	78	327	59
Scurry	1,008	28	6	78	295	3	5	845	146	1,535	197
Shackelford	393	41	1	38	159	11	3	283	395	781	63
Shelby	1,737	132	5	199	1,510	95	4	1,824	1,134	3,657	120
Sherman	159	29	4	10	106	5	0	121	15	246	63
Smith	2,450	741	16	283	1,914	314	25	2,960	634	5,167	943
Somervell	298	17	0	87	142	19	0	168	107	448	28
Starr	525	108	0	0	339	0	0	345	31	762	19
Stephens	561	11	1	102	211	10	1	731	471	2,326	275
Sterling	208	3	0	0	118	6	0	189	35	284	6
Stonewall	519	21	9	119	193	2	4	273	173	294	113
Sutton	132	5	0	0	137	4	0	82	84	231	73
Swisher	401	46	3	11	154	12	0	389	166	696	149
Tarrant	10,667	1,189	76	318	4,532	276	36	10,379	3,620	19,073	3,588
Taylor	2,149	101	120	5	774	11	3	1,868	403	3,998	337
Terrell	181	57	0	2	107	15	0	82	55	199	80
Terry	146	0	0	0	86	1	0	210	69	906	125
Throckmorton	360	9	1	69	233	4	0	339	77	683	77
Titus	1,176	128	20	71	657	74	2	636	344	1,770	0
Tom Green	1,184	71	10	62	496	44	5	1,162	575	2,609	398
Travis	4,052	631	29	70	1,702	202	12	3,344	1,531	9,365	1,454
Trinity	948	135	94	3	459	31	10	562	237	1,623	107
Tyler	642	32	0	21	414	16	13	303	118	1,103	51
Upshur	1,365	179	9	121	866	46	15	907	465	827	140
Upton	47	2	0	1	0	0	0	12	15	44	0
Uvalde	742	75	1	24	343	16	0	526	132	1,547	290
Val Verde	472	109	2	5	193	10	1	273	130	784	232
Van Zandt	2,085	184	11	645	1,464	91	37	1,998	508	4,070	0
Victoria	1,088	281	7	33	358	104	2	417	1,033	2,126	348
Walker	766	306	1	25	499	178	14	557	171	1,872	160
Waller	693	136	0	4	363	83	0	587	386	1,285	149
Ward	186	14	1	8	107	5	1	85	138	254	20
Washington	1,977	410	1	3	570	250	6	1,780	864	3,825	291
Webb	716	430	0	0	459	47	0	563	394	1,376	388
Wharton	1,018	321	24	88	562	158	11	1,181	884	2,291	821
Wheeler	569	49	9	83	328	39	3	489	321	1,026	130
Wichita	2,168	300	11	134	812	64	10	2,471	1,105	7,552	1,515
Wilbarger	1,361	60	1	107	568	12	8	1,181	273	1,649	189
Willacy	114	6	0	0	42	0	0	111	164	397	125
Williamson	3,367	372	17	73	1,463	248	8	2,483	1,848	7,221	701
Wilson	961	248	5	22	512	43	2	366	861	2,146	338
Winkler	21	0	0	0	7	0	0	6	14	15	0
Wise	2,304	214	18	151	1,207	95	9	2,379	623	3,202	468
Wood	1,720	219	13	421	1,302	190	43	1,796	321	3,558	316
Yoakum	85	1	0	1	22	0	0	87	22	112	5
Young	1,187	55	11	127	715	18	10	1,357	617	2,204	228
Zapata	31	214	0	0	77	12	0	247	91	320	211
Zavala	233	34	2	16	155	6	4	186	66	437	64
Official Totals	301,905	48,775	2,313	18,616	155,158	22,183	1,587	264,260	130,744	592,057	101,252
Unofficial Totals	303,755	49,009	2,313	18,557	155,140	22,201	1,591	264,263	131,133	582,768	98,962

Table 19: Senatorial Races

	General Elections, 1928-1934											
Year	1928				1930				1934			
County	Tom Connlly(D)	T.M. Kennrly (R)	John Rust (CM)	David Curran (S)	Morris Shepprd (D)	D.J. Haesly (R)	Guy L. Smith (S)	W.A. Berry (CM)	Tom Connlly (D)	U.S. Goen (R)	W.B. Starr (S)	L.C. Keel (CM)
Anderson	3,177	332	0	6	1,992	125	7	1	2,625	33	5	0
Andrews	72	13	0	0	74	2	1	0	189	0	1	0
Angelina	3,188	333	0	3	0	0	0	0	2,083	14	11	0
Aransas	220	77	0	0	150	16	0	0	139	14	11	0
Archer	991	216	0	0	627	67	2	0	139	2	3	0
Armstrong	617	75	1	0	371	23	1	0	905	9	5	0
Atascosa	1,277	330	0	1	861	78	5	1	511	5	0	0
Austin	2,388	234	0	1	1,057	144	3	3	1,139	13	6	1
Bailey	388	152	1	2	548	17	1	0	1,495	33	2	0
Bandera	414	688	1	0	585	288	2	1	484	16	5	0
Bastrop	2,059	283	0	0	944	105	4	0	979	109	10	2
Baylor	1,182	108	0	2	397	25	4	0	1,428	32	5	1
Bee	1,312	639	1	3	1,252	257	18	27	1,164	38	3	1
Bell	5,703	645	1	4	2,308	134	4	1	6,533	35	9	0
Bexar	25,625	9,372	9	27	19,719	4,004	85	37	17,404	824	99	27
Blanco	752	404	1	3	781	342	0	3	1,098	115	5	0
Borden	161	13	0	1	91	3	0	0	123	0	0	0
Bosque	2,083	519	0	2	1,091	199	2	1	1,640	55	2	0
Bowie	4,148	883	0	17	1,779	91	11	0	3,759	50	16	0
Brazoria	1,458	904	0	5	1,148	312	4	1	903	63	2	1
Brazos	2,061	140	0	0	986	24	1	0	1,344	15	0	0
Brewster	499	140	1	1	347	15	0	0	646	6	1	2
Briscoe	549	78	0	4	0	0	0	0	413	0	0	0
Brooks	405	83	0	0	313	4	0	0	621	8	0	0
Brown	3,414	545	0	0	1,459	134	2	3	1,779	26	5	3
Burleson	1,809	114	0	0	964	53	0	0	1,081	17	0	0
Burnet	1,103	238	0	1	682	75	0	1	951	31	0	0
Caldwell	2,179	194	0	0	1,194	110	0	1	1,452	0	0	0
Calhoun	605	104	0	2	0	0	0	0	906	9	5	0
Callahan	1,696	225	0	0	805	75	0	0	890	6	0	0
Cameron	4,388	1,844	1	9	3,088	684	4	2	3,239	191	2	1
Camp	967	154	0	0	330	32	0	0	760	8	0	0
Carson	933	484	0	0	383	71	0	0	1,227	29	5	1
Cass	2,294	652	0	0	1,172	223	3	5	1,583	40	5	0
Castro	585	103	0	0	306	42	1	0	496	5	0	0
Chambers	391	142	0	0	449	84	1	0	336	9	1	0
Cherokee	3,243	424	2	0	1,932	206	3	0	2,632	43	8	0
Childress	1,745	319	0	1	680	37	0	0	1,048	25	12	1
Clay	2,086	388	0	0	830	92	3	0	1,227	10	3	0
Cochran	266	38	0	2	296	4	1	0	425	4	5	0
Coke	678	91	0	3	462	26	3	0	606	10	11	0
Coleman	2,696	354	0	9	1,318	139	3	0	2,425	24	16	0
Collin	5,286	1,451	1	19	2,614	497	7	1	3,121	101	10	0
Collingsworth	1,420	299	0	0	502	50	0	0	895	14	2	0
Colorado	2,181	464	2	10	782	139	7	0	1,300	61	3	1
Comal	1,965	346	0	2	1,566	633	5	3	1,007	56	3	0
Comanche	2,155	294	0	5	0	0	0	0	1,556	36	7	2
Concho	780	98	0	3	433	40	0	0	552	6	0	0
Cooke	3,432	702	2	3	1,844	201	4	0	619	77	8	0
Coryell	2,103	278	0	2	1,024	135	3	0	1,550	26	3	0
Cottle	833	71	0	2	358	14	4	1	648	8	3	0
Crane	250	23	0	0	222	21	1	0	421	1	1	0
Crockett	268	49	0	0	194	4	1	0	139	0	0	0
Crosby	1,537	189	1	2	595	14	0	0	1,010	4	0	0
Culberson	149	7	0	0	154	3	0	0	114	1	0	0
Dallam	888	253	1	6	1,026	47	9	1	794	17	9	1
Dallas	33,933	10,177	8	62	9,057	1,387	38	2	27,162	876	162	11
Dawson	1,386	399	0	0	518	50	2	0	773	7	5	0
DeWitt	2,380	355	0	1	1,458	300	1	1	1,235	37	2	1
Deaf Smith	791	199	0	0	345	49	0	0	569	25	3	0
Delta	1,450	215	1	1	820	32	1	0	1,549	17	1	0
Denton	4,289	667	0	13	1,722	160	12	0	2,919	72	12	0
Dickens	1,034	113	0	5	461	43	1	0	1,646	0	0	0
Dimmit	600	256	0	0	220	60	1	0	562	28	1	0
Donley	0	0	0	0	534	41	1	0	845	11	5	1

Table 19: Senatorial Races

County	General Elections, 1928-1934											
Year	1928				1930				1934			
County	Tom Connlly(D)	T.M. Kennrly (R)	John Rust (CM)	David Curran (S)	Morris Shepprd (D)	D.J. Haesly (R)	Guy L. Smith (S)	W.A. Berry (CM)	Tom Connlly (D)	U.S. Goen (R)	W.B. Starr (S)	L.C. Keel (CM)
Duval	1,251	438	0	0	1,741	118	0	0	3,006	3	0	0
Eastland	4,570	1,087	0	0	0	0	0	0	2,224	71	41	37
Ector	226	58	0	0	177	7	0	0	201	2	0	0
Edwards	216	251	1	3	476	147	2	0	606	7	3	0
El Paso	8,952	2,273	0	9	4,336	551	11	3	5,034	158	12	2
Ellis	6,945	969	0	10	0	0	0	0	2,874	46	4	0
Erath	2,762	539	0	4	1,336	200	5	0	1,744	29	14	2
Falls	0	0	0	0	0	0	0	0	2,053	0	0	0
Fannin	3,913	684	1	2	1,911	240	1	0	2,710	79	5	1
Fayette	3,934	380	0	1	2,121	251	2	4	3,268	119	4	0
Fisher	1,770	278	0	0	596	43	1	0	1,071	10	3	3
Floyd	1,591	210	0	0	702	62	2	0	1,077	22	2	0
Foard	785	130	0	5	315	35	0	0	506	12	5	0
Fort Bend	2,100	193	0	0	1,096	50	4	0	1,432	14	2	0
Franklin	1,018	113	0	0	330	63	2	0	623	29	2	0
Freestone	2,134	346	0	1	1,168	187	2	0	1,462	31	2	0
Frio	736	157	0	0	503	24	0	0	614	7	1	0
Gaines	367	79	0	4	204	9	4	0	268	1	0	0
Galveston	8,073	2,098	4	9	2,683	645	10	8	4,248	166	8	1
Garza	884	160	0	4	297	55	1	0	455	0	0	0
Gillespie	1,491	1,071	1	1	1,064	1,564	6	9	1,783	937	24	9
Glasscock	131	8	0	1	87	9	1	0	123	1	2	0
Goliad	734	285	0	2	750	492	5	3	1,142	185	6	5
Gonzales	2,017	304	0	1	2,155	129	1	0	1,451	20	2	2
Gray	2,022	785	0	4	2,177	0	0	0	1,865	31	23	3
Grayson	8,453	2,279	0	12	4,660	654	12	0	5,149	156	12	1
Gregg	1,423	173	0	2	1,001	94	0	0	2,234	23	4	0
Grimes	1,728	145	0	1	779	33	1	0	1,222	9	3	0
Guadalupe	2,058	1,229	2	7	1,682	2,105	13	2	3,038	1,061	3	3
Hale	2,643	552	0	1	921	163	2	0	1,523	30	12	0
Hall	1,653	228	0	1	691	47	2	0	951	13	2	0
Hamilton	1,535	256	0	0	811	120	1	1	1,050	40	2	0
Hansford	509	159	0	0	769	42	3	3	385	5	12	0
Hardeman	1,776	281	0	0	695	43	0	0	1,040	13	1	0
Hardin	1,695	257	0	1	623	26	3	0	986	8	0	0
Harris	38,085	10,366	16	44	10,046	1,003	41	14	40,439	543	128	30
Harrison	3,396	340	0	3	1,103	25	0	2	1,488	17	5	0
Hartley	265	60	0	0	0	0	0	0	557	8	0	0
Haskell	2,693	250	1	7	823	43	4	1	1,372	24	8	1
Hays	1,346	170	0	0	896	28	1	0	1,308	10	1	0
Hemphill	657	128	0	0	717	46	1	0	795	20	1	0
Henderson	2,470	308	0	6	1,541	264	7	0	2,156	34	8	0
Hidalgo	4,841	3,256	0	0	5,449	3,485	25	12	8,259	504	28	3
Hill	4,221	554	2	3	2,344	189	3	0	2,741	38	2	0
Hockley	656	278	0	7	437	31	3	0	815	8	27	0
Hood	902	205	0	2	403	68	0	0	642	14	7	0
Hopkins	2,921	429	0	6	1,754	132	6	3	2,206	42	3	0
Houston	1,949	269	0	0	1,219	160	5	0	2,280	78	2	0
Howard	1,090	207	0	1	1,118	36	3	1	1,264	4	2	0
Hudspeth	195	29	0	1	76	54	15	30	216	3	2	0
Hunt	5,617	813	0	0	2,359	229	3	3	2,816	13	3	1
Hutchinson	1,067	698	0	0	1,236	54	0	0	1,816	32	15	1
Irion	344	32	0	0	172	7	2	0	207	1	11	1
Jack	1,117	337	0	1	626	112	3	1	971	27	3	0
Jackson	775	249	0	0	456	48	3	1	603	15	2	1
Jasper	1,338	139	0	0	703	20	1	0	1,003	11	1	0
Jeff Davis	231	23	0	1	189	5	1	0	136	1	1	0
Jefferson	12,374	4,045	6	2	2,674	401	7	0	4,681	106	36	5
Jim Hogg	336	23	0	0	363	84	0	0	223	14	0	0
Jim Wells	990	183	1	0	984	43	2	1	771	14	3	0
Johnson	4,017	1,015	1	3	1,607	271	1	1	1,834	46	2	0
Jones	2,730	562	1	8	1,163	92	6	1	1,809	23	9	4
Karnes	1,760	314	0	0	1,183	119	2	1	1,484	29	1	0
Kaufman	3,795	484	0	6	1,840	186	1	0	2,119	45	2	1
Kendall	395	365	0	1	442	676	1	6	801	335	11	10

Table 19: Senatorial Races

County	1928				1930				1934			
	Tom Connlly(D)	T.M. Kennrly (R)	John Rust (CM)	David Curran (S)	Morris Sheppd (D)	D.J. Haesly (R)	Guy L. Smith (S)	W.A. Berry (CM)	Tom Connlly (D)	U.S. Goen (R)	W.B. Starr (S)	L.C. Keel (CM)
Kenedy	127	3	0	0	83	3	0	0	126	3	0	0
Kent	423	41	0	3	189	7	0	0	336	2	3	0
Kerr	1,326	788	2	4	1,456	377	13	2	2,219	362	17	7
Kimble	603	170	1	1	248	17	0	0	343	8	0	0
King	115	8	0	0	67	0	0	0	123	0	0	0
Kinney	269	98	0	0	325	85	1	7	604	31	1	0
Kleberg	1,265	210	1	1	545	26	0	0	1,342	5	4	0
Knox	1,371	261	0	4	551	39	0	0	906	16	9	0
La Salle	721	86	0	0	390	70	0	0	585	3	0	1
Lamar	4,356	490	2	6	1,860	108	3	0	3,842	121	12	1
Lamb	1,196	442	0	0	438	52	4	2	1,043	13	11	0
Lampasas	1,227	147	1	1	655	75	0	0	912	17	0	0
Lavaca	3,491	399	1	4	1,676	194	6	0	2,119	56	10	0
Lee	1,390	175	2	1	833	245	2	0	1,024	57	1	0
Leon	1,237	212	3	0	791	116	11	0	1,181	19	5	0
Liberty	1,582	359	0	1	698	66	9	0	990	13	12	0
Limestone	3,872	380	0	0	2,014	72	2	1	2,034	13	1	0
Lipscomb	603	501	0	9	634	293	6	0	826	155	13	0
Live Oak	737	114	0	0	578	49	6	1	557	20	10	0
Llano	863	76	0	0	637	30	0	0	1,025	16	0	0
Loving	0	0	0	0	0	0	0	0	128	1	0	0
Lubbock	4,325	671	1	2	1,237	136	4	0	2,420	43	18	8
Lynn	1,600	300	0	5	604	51	1	2	923	23	4	0
Madison	778	67	0	2	665	65	0	0	1,088	7	0	0
Marion	694	344	0	0	309	47	0	0	364	14	0	0
Martin	472	63	0	0	264	32	0	0	410	4	4	0
Mason	823	159	0	2	331	40	0	0	872	38	3	0
Matagorda	1,395	589	0	6	655	159	5	0	884	42	4	0
Maverick	302	189	0	0	215	42	1	0	481	14	0	0
McCulloch	1,538	335	0	0	897	96	2	1	973	15	2	1
McLennan	9,593	1,524	1	11	4,702	354	17	1	5,901	100	53	15
McMullen	155	13	0	0	147	4	0	0	211	2	0	0
Medina	1,825	681	1	3	1,280	708	1	5	2,591	370	7	7
Menard	643	123	0	4	262	25	1	1	403	12	1	1
Midland	554	99	0	3	· 424	18	0	0	390	6	0	0
Milam	3,803	290	1	0	1,647	161	6	2	2,897	30	5	0
Mills	831	182	0	0	558	152	6	0	650	30	5	0
Mitchell	1,666	233	0	1	0	0	0	0	1,058	18	0	0
Montague	2,289	417	0	0	938	146	9	1	1,574	37	11	0
Montgomery	1,389	107	0	0	1,496	30	2	1	1,307	17	5	0
Moore	183	26	0	0	138	8	1	0	291	5	2	0
Morris	1,016	71	1	0	469	24	0	0	677	7	1	1
Motley	674	64	0	0	267	16	0	0	416	4	1	0
Nacogdoches	2,551	147	0	5	1,276	57	4	0	1,811	20	4	0
Navarro	6,123	833	0	0	3,162	244	0	0	4,228	72	0	0
Newton	839	112	0	1	413	20	0	0	677	18	3	0
Nolan	2,189	361	0	2	833	78	1	0	1,228	26	1	0
Nueces	4,326	1,108	1	3	2,921	247	2	1	4,077	216	11	2
Ochiltree	470	261	0	3	336	28	2	0	905	13	9	0
Oldham	218	74	0	0	169	5	0	0	237	3	0	0
Orange	1,950	252	1	2	906	15	1	1	1,130	7	0	0
Palo Pinto	2,536	656	2	6	959	119	7	1	1,399	37	12	0
Panola	1,638	84	0	3	890	21	0	0	1,474	7	11	0
Parker	2,713	530	0	18	1,177	111	12	0	1,993	0	0	0
Parmer	576	280	0	7	0	0	0	0	594	31	4	0
Pecos	878	192	1	7	498	30	0	0	874	10	1	2
Polk	1,380	151	2	2	674	51	0	4	1,323	15	6	1
Potter	4,840	1,304	0	11	1,313	157	7	2	3,489	118	12	4
Presidio	472	54	0	0	218	6	1	1	534	7	0	0
Rains	667	83	0	3	441	54	4	0	492	18	4	0
Randall	1,053	222	0	1	463	32	0	0	786	14	1	11
Reagan	500	104	0	1	411	17	0	0	390	7	0	0
Real	227	328	0	1	328	69	1	4	289	5	1	9
Red River	2,527	355	3	3	1,267	94	1	0	1,681	32	3	0
Reeves	655	81	0	0	326	31	0	0	377	7	1	1

Table 19: Senatorial Races

General Elections, 1928-1934											
Year	1928				1930				1934			
County	Tom Connlly(D)	T.M. Kennrly (R)	John Rust (CM)	David Curran (S)	Morris Sheppard (D)	D.J. Haesly (R)	Guy L. Smith (S)	W.A. Berry (CM)	Tom Connlly (D)	U.S. Goen (R)	W.B. Starr (S)	L.C. Keel (CM)
Refugio	827	236	0	3	695	161	8	11	1,198	74	3	7
Roberts	290	70	0	0	145	15	1	0	192	10	0	0
Robertson	2,005	241	0	1	851	76	0	2	1,270	12	0	0
Rockwall	1,071	80	0	0	659	20	0	0	550	7	0	0
Runnels	2,799	352	1	8	1,075	126	3	0	1,534	21	6	0
Rusk	2,484	352	0	0	1,092	87	2	0	2,351	18	7	0
Sabine	1,171	59	0	4	730	14	5	2	1,051	14	8	1
San Augustine	1,190	1,192	0	0	852	25	3	0	918	0	0	0
San Jacinto	706	73	1	0	307	17	0	0	429	6	0	0
San Patricio	1,356	531	1	1	844	123	0	0	1,053	24	9	0
San Saba	1,204	178	0	0	707	77	1	0	1,321	16	2	0
Schleicher	307	42	0	0	0	0	0	0	239	6	1	0
Scurry	1,434	347	0	1	0	0	0	0	997	11	1	0
Shackelford	952	112	0	1	446	33	2	2	588	14	2	0
Shelby	2,486	159	0	11	1,318	49	2	1	297	18	59	0
Sherman	258	108	0	0	172	16	0	0	274	9	0	0
Smith	4,239	1,056	0	5	2,349	314	7	1	3,061	57	13	2
Somervell	0	0	0	0	187	24	6	2	233	5	4	0
Starr	769	44	0	0	793	7	0	0	657	1	0	0
Stephens	2,279	574	0	0	875	134	4	5	1,690	36	5	22
Sterling	276	14	0	0	169	3	0	0	199	2	0	0
Stonewall	802	130	0	4	336	14	0	0	525	8	1	0
Sutton	334	36	0	0	94	12	1	1	115	4	1	0
Swisher	843	315	0	0	420	57	1	1	810	14	6	0
Tarrant	21,255	7,233	0	0	5,100	559	17	1	20,292	347	100	8
Taylor	4,730	998	0	7	2,538	166	2	2	2,271	26	6	0
Terrell	186	231	2	1	0	0	0	0	172	4	0	0
Terry	767	210	0	0	340	44	0	0	715	5	6	0
Throckmorton	759	168	0	0	357	5	1	0	631	19	1	0
Titus	1,535	125	0	0	676	68	1	0	984	11	0	0
Tom Green	3,563	496	1	2	1,894	112	3	0	1,956	32	62	1
Travis	8,290	1,168	1	10	4,125	252	8	1	6,141	87	24	3
Trinity	1,152	99	1	1	434	19	0	0	840	23	0	0
Tyler	878	55	0	0	587	9	1	0	1,004	12	2	0
Upshur	2,067	194	0	5	1,152	104	7	0	1,321	23	5	0
Upton	0	0	0	0	369	19	1	2	382	7	1	1
Uvalde	1,614	328	0	0	655	51	0	0	1,048	25	3	0
Val Verde	955	474	0	0	837	135	3	0	824	50	0	0
Van Zandt	2,916	397	0	16	0	0	0	0	2,196	38	34	0
Victoria	2,131	246	0	0	674	91	0	1	1,859	45	3	1
Walker	1,137	96	0	0	650	69	0	1	1,098	4	1	0
Waller	817	79	1	0	411	32	0	1	697	7	3	0
Ward	385	72	0	0	0	0	0	0	334	8	0	0
Washington	2,636	124	0	0	939	79	1	0	1,326	15	2	0
Webb	1,815	426	1	1	1,298	174	0	0	2,468	72	3	4
Wharton	2,033	595	0	0	2,662	147	6	4	1,641	33	17	1
Wheeler	1,372	363	2	3	742	122	1	0	1,031	40	16	0
Wichita	9,023	2,980	0	7	2,591	364	9	0	3,116	58	20	0
Wilbarger	2,570	419	0	1	844	49	1	0	1,428	16	3	0
Willacy	620	139	0	0	403	46	0	0	595	75	0	0
Williamson	5,047	465	2	5	1,997	174	3	1	3,154	27	1	2
Wilson	1,828	318	0	0	1,340	282	2	2	1,368	23	1	0
Winkler	414	47	0	0	401	25	3	0	423	14	1	0
Wise	2,246	949	0	2	1,135	159	1	0	1,440	44	2	0
Wood	2,120	433	0	0	1,287	118	8	0	1,779	45	9	0
Yoakum	129	20	0	0	192	1	1	0	146	0	1	0
Young	0	0	0	0	0	0	0	0	1,482	21	3	0
Zapata	300	15	0	0	208	16	0	0	408	4	0	0
Zavala	532	265	0	1	452	35	0	0	555	6	1	0
Official Totals	556,139	129,910	114	690	265,054	38,910	808	294	439,375	12,895	1,828	310
Unofficial Totals	566,139	130,172	114	690	266,560	39,055	809	293	436,754	12,959	1,837	310

Table 20: Senatorial Races

General Elections, 1936-1941											
Year	1936				1940			1941 Spl.			
County	Morris Shepprd (D)	Carlos G. Watsn (R)	W.D. Starr (S)	Gertrude Wilson(U)	Tom Connally (D)	George L. Shann(R)	Homer Brooks (CM)	Martin Dies	Lyndon B. Johnson	Gerald C. Mann	W. Lee O'Daniel
Anderson	3,917	124	1	0	5,887	167	1	502	696	915	1,112
Andrews	295	10	0	0	458	10	0	35	54	43	76
Angelina	4,160	120	4	0	6,433	134	1	1,445	375	323	1,138
Aransas	229	40	2	4	0	0	0	17	86	40	88
Archer	1,726	83	0	6	2,093	72	0	43	379	214	410
Armstrong	914	20	0	1	963	15	0	22	115	64	171
Atascosa	2,175	1	0	0	2,281	83	2	233	438	195	585
Austin	1,817	127	2	0	2,647	136	1	98	329	797	810
Bailey	871	96	1	18	1,310	62	0	67	115	149	249
Bandera	785	312	3	10	1,160	135	2	210	81	95	238
Bastrop	2,508	85	2	0	2,952	67	0	41	1,654	230	822
Baylor	1,618	58	1	0	1,787	32	0	29	283	300	330
Bee	1,837	212	3	7	2,708	76	1	200	395	431	395
Bell	6,136	192	0	9	8,320	198	1	491	1,896	1,198	1,757
Bexar	41,314	7,258	36	145	46,566	9,809	63	2,335	10,257	3,274	6,238
Blanco	1,177	221	1	3	1,436	171	2	16	654	124	279
Borden	230	13	1	0	416	7	0	29	46	47	66
Bosque	2,419	191	5	2	3,555	120	0	132	672	631	716
Bowie	5,240	268	7	8	7,707	308	0	683	766	803	1,620
Brazoria	2,037	299	2	18	4,351	236	0	401	987	532	1,052
Brazos	2,700	45	1	0	4,664	119	0	309	612	981	597
Brewster	933	66	0	0	1,235	52	0	69	245	83	75
Briscoe	878	29	0	2	1,045	22	1	25	112	180	226
Brooks	418	70	0	0	883	27	3	36	188	28	96
Brown	4,243	244	4	18	5,082	132	2	290	756	1,106	878
Burleson	1,647	65	0	0	2,271	73	0	67	950	230	677
Burnet	1,658	60	1	0	2,394	58	1	45	1,326	144	336
Caldwell	3,156	106	0	16	4,091	84	0	179	1,203	649	674
Calhoun	723	51	1	0	986	28	0	0	154	136	271
Callahan	1,853	141	5	0	0	0	0	141	581	436	533
Cameron	6,704	1,366	6	56	8,674	848	4	1,170	1,355	601	993
Camp	973	49	0	1	1,501	48	0	113	80	392	356
Carson	1,634	93	0	0	1,918	108	0	89	161	208	198
Cass	2,523	115	0	0	0	0	0	293	456	720	1,000
Castro	985	52	1	5	1,191	38	0	16	102	167	194
Chambers	1,073	69	1	1	1,451	59	0	216	200	114	204
Cherokee	4,139	131	2	3	5,970	142	2	420	414	1,281	1,322
Childress	2,201	100	5	0	3,010	74	0	68	328	516	549
Clay	2,276	85	0	5	2,703	93	0	147	437	371	634
Cochran	700	31	8	0	860	28	0	53	101	95	194
Coke	923	37	6	1	1,051	15	3	54	283	98	212
Coleman	3,063	155	3	0	3,653	125	0	188	692	565	940
Collin	5,638	340	28	4	8,009	401	1	509	894	2,031	2,073
Collingsworth	2,057	119	2	0	2,233	75	0	36	204	321	556
Colorado	1,575	198	4	1	2,623	216	0	177	416	672	844
Comal	1,784	293	0	5	2,214	300	6	128	319	808	541
Comanche	2,587	0	0	0	3,770	77	1	247	533	674	1,102
Concho	1,112	58	0	0	1,436	51	0	31	373	148	239
Cooke	4,042	360	5	5	5,486	363	0	472	685	1,170	1,354
Coryell	2,144	69	0	4	3,545	82	0	79	770	640	913
Cottle	1,272	53	4	5	1,678	71	0	59	173	262	318
Crane	638	8	0	0	867	25	0	37	158	91	44
Crockett	272	29	0	0	510	31	0	16	82	87	45
Crosby	1,784	82	0	0	1,953	41	0	103	143	329	387
Culberson	258	13	0	0	362	15	0	19	100	8	14
Dallam	1,518	127	1	38	1,899	110	1	34	211	230	298
Dallas	44,032	5,305	110	119	57,569	8,273	36	3,524	5,404	12,572	5,925
Dawson	1,897	89	1	2	3,102	76	0	323	266	418	575
DeWitt	2,288	225	3	2	0	0	0	249	599	690	996
Deaf Smith	1,306	80	0	6	1,595	125	0	46	144	212	285
Delta	1,495	46	0	0	0	0	0	118	291	605	580
Denton	5,284	283	7	11	7,012	302	0	273	1,036	1,687	1,299
Dickens	1,559	61	1	0	1,939	47	0	64	170	348	331
Dimmit	852	155	0	10	1,003	78	0	53	129	127	239

Table 20: Senatorial Races

General Elections, 1936-1941											
Year	1936				1940			1941 Spl.			
County	Morris Shepprd (D)	Carlos G. Watsn (R)	W.D. Starr (S)	Gertrude Wilson(U)	Tom Connlly (D)	George L. Shannn(R)	Homer Brooks (CM)	Martin Dies	Lyndon B. Johnson	Gerald C. Mann	W. Lee O'Daniel
Donley	1,583	75	1	12	1,842	5	0	52	211	265	375
Duval	2,920	129	0	2	3,353	52	0	11	1,506	35	65
Eastland	5,010	398	16	6	6,658	305	2	397	1,143	1,016	1,430
Ector	886	31	0	3	3,116	0	0	118	285	259	190
Edwards	446	75	0	3	710	35	0	61	151	93	160
El Paso	12,458	1,050	19	67	14,857	1,215	5	630	2,588	555	507
Ellis	5,759	214	6	3	8,341	171	0	883	1,429	1,751	1,877
Erath	2,843	178	3	3	4,314	167	0	255	692	895	1,110
Falls	3,521	83	1	1	4,749	234	0	118	845	851	1,106
Fannin	5,314	270	5	0	7,931	301	3	320	1,126	1,343	2,359
Fayette	3,210	279	2	3	4,702	340	1	204	953	984	1,654
Fisher	2,140	60	4	0	2,448	41	0	105	494	375	493
Floyd	1,963	124	1	6	2,308	79	10	109	186	382	567
Foard	950	52	1	1	1,100	42	0	0	144	152	219
Fort Bend	2,705	80	3	0	3,750	120	0	296	938	450	984
Franklin	950	52	1	0	1,732	70	0	47	110	470	556
Freestone	1,979	84	2	0	3,841	138	0	418	404	686	661
Frio	1,097	117	0	0	1,197	52	1	129	181	95	177
Gaines	701	21	2	0	1,646	60	0	66	156	164	244
Galveston	10,074	963	12	25	12,806	842	6	960	2,596	654	1,246
Garza	863	81	1	3	1,203	22	1	131	115	147	242
Gillespie	1,170	1,204	6	46	1,934	1,315	9	37	166	916	803
Glasscock	269	20	1	0	318	6	0	23	44	73	29
Goliad	1,234	281	0	0	1,194	222	0	103	123	157	193
Gonzales	2,914	138	0	0	3,634	89	0	362	605	712	927
Gray	4,528	320	4	18	5,109	403	1	143	227	409	512
Grayson	10,990	593	11	4	13,365	604	1	648	3,212	1,902	2,682
Gregg	6,688	340	4	1	10,002	940	9	702	710	1,679	1,241
Grimes	1,941	48	2	1	2,443	44	0	125	518	420	504
Guadalupe	3,305	996	5	4	3,736	1,084	4	177	276	561	1,229
Hale	3,229	244	4	2	4,118	185	0	157	408	700	777
Hall	2,222	66	5	10	2,396	56	0	56	276	294	530
Hamilton	2,062	95	1	1	2,794	84	0	119	382	664	745
Hansford	865	46	6	8	830	46	0	17	66	110	116
Hardeman	2,075	113	2	0	0	0	0	64	230	408	353
Hardin	2,375	0	0	0	3,179	59	0	1,037	187	71	537
Harris	63,167	4,134	75	53	89,065	4,936	23	6,945	14,037	5,411	8,162
Harrison	3,570	101	5	0	0	0	0	470	1,312	643	694
Hartley	583	34	0	1	626	37	0	20	47	75	89
Haskell	2,776	89	6	2	3,242	114	0	92	518	644	693
Hays	2,127	100	0	12	2,772	79	0	183	1,153	326	425
Hemphill	1,094	77	0	5	0	0	0	18	210	142	220
Henderson	3,407	125	3	0	0	0	0	339	407	654	1,133
Hidalgo	7,818	2,018	12	155	11,178	1,182	0	1,457	1,213	1,352	1,475
Hill	4,853	147	0	0	0	0	0	396	1,568	928	1,248
Hockley	1,730	55	9	1	2,605	64	0	146	286	344	580
Hood	1,048	58	0	0	1,441	61	0	91	211	277	376
Hopkins	2,869	159	2	0	5,245	152	0	293	498	1,628	1,265
Houston	2,469	68	1	0	3,885	120	0	530	465	421	1,100
Howard	3,123	105	3	3	4,714	96	1	261	933	641	454
Hudspeth	384	10	0	0	478	11	0	19	106	28	36
Hunt	5,924	232	3	5	8,668	365	63	1,587	929	1,727	1,628
Hutchinson	2,617	272	6	0	3,818	312	1	155	266	351	376
Irion	521	18	4	0	611	11	4	38	127	49	100
Jack	1,303	103	3	2	2,247	96	0	69	373	446	466
Jackson	1,002	100	0	3	1,750	57	1	135	289	343	430
Jasper	1,531	63	2	0	2,336	56	0	895	169	129	578
Jeff Davis	327	6	0	0	0	0	0	14	95	23	23
Jefferson	19,387	1,369	30	18	23,677	1,166	16	6,825	2,066	824	1,262
Jim Hogg	730	28	0	0	906	32	0	9	119	35	21
Jim Wells	1,910	152	2	4	2,882	98	1	257	322	220	344
Johnson	4,452	180	3	9	5,945	166	0	546	1,035	1,109	1,063
Jones	3,531	176	5	0	4,132	63	0	181	842	736	777
Karnes	2,363	153	0	2	2,563	69	0	374	530	321	567
Kaufman	4,028	149	0	0	5,335	186	1	387	621	1,510	1,195

Table 20: Senatorial Races

General Elections, 1936-1941											
Year	1936				1940			1941 Spl.			
County	Morris Shepprd (D)	Carlos G. Watsn (R)	W.D. Starr (S)	Gertrude Wilson(U)	Tom Connlly (D)	George L. Shannn(R)	Homer Brooks (CM)	Martin Dies	Lyndon B. Johnson	Gerald C. Mann	W. Lee O'Daniel
Kendall	477	606	1	4	1,133	552	3	74	97	161	330
Kenedy	119	7	0	0	0	0	0	5	10	35	41
Kent	554	9	1	0	790	10	0	23	66	123	150
Kerr	1,917	656	1	5	2,337	328	0	179	414	205	460
Kimble	739	55	0	0	1,288	49	0	83	278	100	415
King	211	13	0	0	284	3	1	15	23	42	72
Kinney	441	127	0	0	529	62	1	20	78	24	28
Kleberg	1,596	71	2	39	2,024	49	0	138	317	189	259
Knox	1,888	96	3	0	0	0	0	64	307	422	470
LaSalle	742	46	0	0	808	13	0	26	216	27	108
Lamar	5,741	197	7	6	8,345	167	1	449	1,251	1,272	2,393
Lamb	2,408	192	5	4	3,604	166	0	100	396	480	874
Lampasas	1,520	50	0	0	2,201	56	0	50	523	377	525
Lavaca	2,478	185	2	2	3,693	189	0	268	649	810	1,146
Lee	1,334	110	1	0	1,904	154	0	27	566	309	831
Leon	1,764	62	0	0	0	0	0	101	480	298	619
Liberty	2,895	151	10	0	3,808	157	0	1,026	281	242	582
Limestone	3,943	97	1	1	5,282	77	1	265	943	869	918
Lipscomb	1,032	225	3	3	1,023	171	0	27	80	101	149
Live Oak	1,047	123	2	13	1,334	64	0	109	182	178	333
Llano	1,269	56	0	0	1,695	39	1	116	622	143	366
Loving	132	9	0	0	116	2	0	2	28	10	9
Lubbock	7,139	616	4	4	9,124	292	4	428	825	1,153	783
Lynn	2,083	93	6	4	2,799	86	0	139	259	531	497
Madison	1,162	24	0	0	0	0	0	71	293	249	355
Marion	958	96	0	0	1,192	94	0	50	335	256	315
Martin	814	44	1	5	1,158	34	1	45	188	171	238
Mason	981	115	1	0	1,459	109	3	23	174	295	345
Matagorda	1,871	272	1	0	2,646	145	0	483	391	271	621
Maverick	959	98	1	31	1,101	48	1	45	62	151	103
McCulloch	1,979	147	6	2	0	0	0	154	666	377	573
McLennan	12,896	643	28	69	17,314	640	0	411	4,341	2,417	2,597
McMullen	284	19	0	0	0	0	0	37	83	31	102
Medina	2,338	708	0	1	0	0	0	130	224	298	635
Menard	811	80	0	4	1,364	48	0	33	238	108	201
Midland	1,337	90	0	3	2,476	116	0	236	284	322	262
Milam	3,546	123	10	4	5,128	121	3	415	975	709	1,597
Mills	1,048	85	0	0	1,885	50	0	43	299	292	456
Mitchell	2,087	141	3	1	2,657	58	3	152	504	381	375
Montague	0	0	0	0	3,779	117	4	154	518	672	975
Montgomery	2,565	63	1	0	3,687	81	0	400	638	270	691
Moore	601	33	1	0	1,156	54	2	35	60	121	100
Morris	1,231	31	0	0	0	0	0	52	130	420	380
Motley	891	37	0	0	1,041	24	0	57	91	223	222
Nacogdoches	4,198	88	2	0	5,239	121	1	861	425	445	830
Navarro	5,943	153	1	1	8,171	231	0	723	1,175	1,355	1,507
Newton	1,160	66	0	0	1,920	42	0	795	67	52	287
Nolan	3,046	147	1	7	3,729	91	0	260	746	538	537
Nueces	7,254	491	7	64	12,301	595	5	597	4,217	1,495	1,378
Ochiltree	1,164	65	1	36	0	0	0	21	132	120	301
Oldham	455	12	0	5	489	9	0	24	66	48	68
Orange	2,283	85	3	2	3,329	69	1	1,458	102	62	272
Palo Pinto	2,911	181	10	4	3,959	135	0	227	750	768	890
Panola	2,425	95	22	1	3,065	35	0	445	347	304	497
Parker	2,671	187	11	5	4,053	203	2	316	595	708	1,086
Parmer	989	98	2	2	443	117	0	44	115	164	395
Pecos	1,432	90	1	2	1,869	79	2	61	318	163	120
Polk	1,703	60	0	0	0	0	0	620	266	186	627
Potter	6,891	597	9	100	8,661	827	3	533	1,077	794	1,149
Presidio	1,024	33	1	3	1,073	41	2	36	164	49	42
Rains	715	41	2	0	1,226	83	0	64	103	298	319
Randall	1,757	61	1	3	2,083	81	1	82	190	347	266
Reagan	510	30	0	0	593	14	0	48	178	57	40
Real	229	39	0	0	546	37	0	13	70	78	155
Red River	2,796	93	0	0	4,181	169	0	201	389	1,069	1,211

Table 20: Senatorial Races

	General Elections, 1936-1941										
Year	**1936**				**1940**			**1941 Spl.**			
County	Morris Sheppard (D)	Carlos G. Watsn (R)	W.D. Starr (S)	Gertrude Wilson(U)	Tom Connlly (D)	George L. Shann(R)	Homer Brooks (CM)	Martin Dies	Lyndon B. Johnson	Gerald C. Mann	W. Lee O'Daniel
Reeves	1,197	46	1	0	1,521	49	0	43	230	216	59
Refugio	1,115	193	0	0	1,959	136	3	100	244	157	213
Roberts	434	23	0	0	458	13	0	33	36	84	58
Robertson	2,686	46	0	0	3,342	50	0	65	991	397	762
Rockwall	1,177	14	0	0	1,597	14	0	79	123	516	283
Runnels	3,147	159	4	6	3,787	126	26	138	701	574	860
Rusk	5,737	248	1	2	8,446	242	0	926	684	1,173	1,075
Sabine	1,281	45	1	0	1,665	38	0	488	125	82	269
San Augustine	0	0	0	0	0	0	0	683	112	83	347
San Jacinto	606	20	0	0	856	30	0	77	136	73	240
San Patricio	2,422	218	2	15	385	136	1	241	634	723	535
San Saba	1,585	71	0	0	2,491	32	0	84	661	277	587
Schleicher	528	35	1	0	0	0	0	34	266	54	133
Scurry	1,863	68	1	0	0	0	0	180	329	442	487
Shackelford	0	0	0	0	1,699	44	0	72	196	253	307
Shelby	3,241	71	8	0	4,986	92	0	1,144	249	229	957
Sherman	581	24	0	0	0	0	0	11	62	62	65
Smith	7,450	379	5	1	10,622	363	1	443	957	2,093	1,838
Somervell	341	35	2	1	583	23	0	41	92	151	234
Starr	2,315	290	5	2	1,253	16	0	7	615	10	12
Stephens	2,518	145	4	5	3,153	95	2	224	295	508	550
Sterling	397	9	0	0	438	8	0	39	140	70	46
Stonewall	1,028	34	1	0	1,294	43	0	57	168	154	267
Sutton	425	37	0	0	642	26	0	32	225	40	81
Swisher	1,517	80	0	2	1,662	66	0	59	127	235	299
Tarrant	31,445	2,207	41	7	41,849	1,902	7	2,690	8,155	3,626	3,505
Taylor	6,515	315	3	3	8,538	219	0	427	2,451	967	1,145
Terrell	371	44	0	0	496	44	0	15	90	49	31
Terry	1,648	51	1	5	2,215	42	0	101	313	341	471
Throckmorton	1,028	44	0	0	1,118	24	0	89	103	129	343
Titus	1,903	52	2	1	0	0	0	224	572	621	637
Tom Green	5,101	382	13	30	7,218	341	0	448	1,832	732	1,103
Travis	12,457	515	23	113	20,040	685	2	500	7,477	2,720	2,716
Trinity	1,313	56	1	0	2,027	56	0	196	234	208	603
Tyler	1,150	44	0	6	1,861	35	0	657	61	116	340
Upshur	0	0	0	0	3,996	236	0	204	313	614	898
Upton	791	47	0	0	0	0	0	48	230	74	86
Uvalde	1,891	200	0	1	2,350	109	2	201	258	331	379
Val Verde	1,500	274	1	3	1,979	262	0	219	230	165	141
Van Zandt	3,357	160	11	8	5,583	177	1	259	531	1,285	1,266
Victoria	2,206	190	0	1	3,043	296	1	293	376	646	554
Walker	1,719	22	2	2	2,355	34	0	259	336	265	419
Waller	944	45	1	1	1,387	62	0	93	308	146	368
Ward	1,136	83	0	2	2,139	77	3	70	254	302	118
Washington	2,095	74	3	0	3,235	96	0	57	1,128	377	1,746
Webb	3,945	398	0	0	4,722	237	2	77	978	81	257
Wharton	3,211	181	5	4	4,586	168	0	572	1,185	716	827
Wheeler	2,490	175	5	1	2,786	181	1	105	299	429	570
Wichita	9,906	744	20	11	13,116	709	0	403	2,277	1,259	1,652
Wilbarger	3,474	119	3	12	3,852	128	0	201	349	627	747
Willacy	1,152	220	0	11	0	0	0	347	66	110	326
Williamson	5,238	185	3	4	7,439	277	3	115	2,863	875	1,749
Wilson	2,710	150	3	0	3,268	90	2	76	1,003	324	997
Winkler	939	54	4	3	1,477	52	1	81	108	130	57
Wise	2,872	209	3	1	4,112	132	1	182	662	635	982
Wood	2,837	138	6	1				174	390	1,194	940
Yoakum	237	15	2	3	0	0	0	42	78	159	150
Young	3,181	171	2	3	4,046	116	0	149	593	726	815
Zapata	291	27	0	0	0	0	0	1	273	5	21
Zavala	906	112	2	2	980	55	0	61	84	161	152
Official Totals	774,975	59,491	958	1,836	978,095	59,340	408	80,551	174,279	140,807	175,590
Unofficial Totals	775,019	59,491	958	1,773	987,991	59,615	404	78,551	174,279	140,707	175,602

Table 21: Senatorial Races

County	1942 W. Lee O'Daniel (D)	1942 Dudley Lawson (R)	1942 Charles L. Smvll(PUP)	1946 Tom Connally (D)	1946 Murray C. Sells (R)	1948 Lyndon B. Johnson(D)	1948 Jack Porter (R)	1948 Sam Morris (P)	1952 Price Daniel (D)	1952 Price Daniel (R)	1954 Lyndon B. Johnson(D)	1954 Carlos G. Watson(R)	1954 Fred T. Spnglr (CO)	1957 Spl. Martin Dies	1957 Spl. Thad Hutcheson	1957 Spl. Ralph W. Yarborough
Anderson	1,561	23	0	1,571	79	3,394	1,741	61	7,485	451	2,513	151	2	1,394	338	1,380
Andrews	256	3	0	259	12	776	133	12	1,271	191	756	36	2	197	170	497
Angelina	1,020	22	2	1,270	81	0	0	0	8,796	1,444	2,890	139	1	2,646	356	2,556
Aransas	124	8	3	190	36	383	267	19	986	253	260	47	1	111	173	242
Archer	457	22	0	569	28	1,523	267	14	7,758	175	659	51	0	159	116	465
Armstrong	227	6	0	265	22	658	133	5	793	134	399	26	0	102	38	181
Atascosa	612	20	0	1,005	121	0	0	0	3,538	598	160	1,062	6	600	400	860
Austin	886	28	0	1,017	104	0	0	0	3,765	590	1,000	96	1	743	410	338
Bailey	182	11	0	306	72	1,104	268	18	1,535	409	450	74	0	156	119	391
Bandera	984	44	1	336	106	394	703	26	1,241	469	413	133	2	232	282	109
Bastrop	712	16	0	989	49	2,908	626	9	3,842	356	1,353	81	0	360	258	1,336
Baylor	372	1	0	1,048	12	1,452	181	8	1,651	136	594	24	0	203	95	401
Bee	532	25	1	0	0	1,339	1,009	42	4,231	0	1,953	200	1	697	468	500
Bell	1,633	23	1	2,221	145	7,310	1,455	97	11,043	1,356	3,567	157	2	1,512	657	4,082
Bexar	7,126	1,221	189	9,091	5,503	33,255	28,026	994	57,114	47,817	20,794	6,997	786	10,521	19,017	18,161
Blanco	942	48	3	996	187	0	0	0	1,002	516	829	153	1	109	223	277
Borden	96	0	0	95	4	175	46	8	290	43	160	5	0	52	25	109
Bosque	885	33	3	1,100	64	0	0	0	3,155	397	1,158	107	0	544	262	830
Bowie	1,379	24	1	2,176	139	7,269	2,238	117	14,579	1,336	3,655	205	2	2,701	624	2,408
Brazoria	739	36	6	1,647	161	4,733	3,145	61	11,820	4,314	3,804	1,004	21	1,983	2,212	3,864
Brazos	793	35	1	1,360	43	3,559	1,772	15	7,387	1,160	2,133	228	0	903	759	1,379
Brewster	249	14	1	398	48	976	341	0	1,240	333	673	64	1	237	160	208
Briscoe	231	1	1	203	22	0	0	0	934	152	376	39	0	119	47	237
Brooks	204	6	3	230	13	1,042	256	7	2,114	282	1,033	60	1	162	275	590
Brown	1,017	24	1	1,646	118	4,170	2,024	51	5,964	1,246	2,187	212	4	1,217	743	1,621
Burleson	658	7	0	694	13	2,037	349	5	3,242	176	966	24	0	382	122	692
Burnet	550	18	1	661	58	2,077	265	8	1,989	385	939	58	1	196	302	748
Caldwell	2,352	15	0	1,217	119	2,839	750	27	3,903	362	1,519	120	0	439	300	1,090
Calhoun	298	4	1	540	32	572	427	21	2,038	0	660	97	1	286	303	443
Callahan	0	0	0	817	54	1,748	350	40	2,231	370	775	46	1	387	168	549
Cameron	2,681	98	37	2,637	435	7,201	4,513	45	14,961	5,748	3,385	980	9	2,467	2,545	2,880
Camp	527	4	1	1,288	40	0	0	0	1,983	202	557	35	0	386	49	488
Carson	362	19	2	687	104	1,248	498	10	1,818	595	868	108	2	270	232	662
Cass	977	17	0	1,088	73	2,568	896	46	4,688	594	1,678	92	0	1,323	187	1,025
Castro	257	7	0	522	55	1,046	273	9	1,769	0	636	83	24	198	107	521
Chambers	285	8	0	317	18	798	484	8	2,133	341	605	50	0	662	218	361
Cherokee	1,352	30	1	1,705	65	0	0	0	6,625	802	3,140	195	2	1,673	331	1,632
Childress	528	17	0	786	100	2,309	354	60	2,820	379	1,205	77	3	434	120	563
Clay	787	17	0	922	51	2,076	434	28	2,497	272	983	94	1	195	164	704
Cochran	185	5	2	298	25	902	225	5	1,460	131	554	33	0	143	68	228
Coke	299	3	0	296	5	884	109	8	1,1	77	424	12	1	205	85	303
Coleman	1,117	15	1	1,158	64	2,516	819	52	3,336	726	2,263	109	2	701	237	727
Collin	1,999	50	0	2,213	188	5,314	1,673	37	7,098	1,824	2,631	243	1	1,513	712	2,397
Collingsworth	507	17	3	677	70	1,753	287	28	1,865	497	870	108	1	356	102	515
Colorado	578	31	2	812	120	1,448	1,578	10	4,397	765	1,566	216	3	657	733	616
Comal	697	55	4	927	317	1,213	1,892	6	3,561	1,082	1,264	320	0	580	895	405
Comanche	1,117	27	7	1,617	82	2,738	706	43	3,459	509	1,483	143	0	612	250	1,021
Concho	359	18	1	460	37	1,090	211	16	1,216	151	447	40	0	132	68	354
Cooke	1,380	52	3	1,320	155	2,992	1,810	32	5,346	1,136	1,683	225	0	1,391	403	842
Coryell	778	27	2	823	30	2,221	478	24	3,200	283	1,169	41	0	428	178	958
Cottle	260	15	0	583	59	1,274	142	13	1,046	134	743	47	0	178	62	468
Crane	271	12	1	165	11	736	146	25	1,079	157	807	22	1	146	94	286
Crockett	130	2	1	106	6	402	134	1	739	144	268	48	1	122	87	95
Crosby	450	2	0	737	24	0	0	0	1,853	285	681	37	1	199	84	844
Culberson	81	0	0	179	13	239	49	2	448	76	246	13	2	114	57	52
Dallam	305	13	9	418	76	1,400	463	14	1,896	518	939	117	0	237	201	513
Dallas	9,108	1,125	628	11,580	4,892	46,464	43,951	606	85,298	86,163	33,015	14,868	893	32,564	30,709	25,886
Dawson	575	12	0	792	96	2,480	550	36	3,420	619	1,531	115	0	412	197	550
DeWitt	834	28	1	1,147	373	0	0	0	4,965	817	1,580	231	2	821	769	503
Deaf Smith	349	10	1	660	156	1,422	599	21	2,445	781	1,047	227	1	324	303	526
Delta	524	6	0	609	9	1,546	278	48	1,851	174	736	19	0	351	43	424
Denton	0	0	0	2,291	129	4,315	2,399	30	8,432	962	2,323	400	2	1,424	891	1,679
Dickens	429	11	3	592	26	1,453	176	29	1,579	124	786	37	2	144	110	575
Dimmit	264	11	0	370	55	0	0	0	1,160	246	525	52	0	148	185	205

Table 21: Senatorial Races

Year	1942			1946		1948			1952		1954			1957 Spl.		
County	W. Lee O'Daniel (D)	Dudley Lawson (R)	Charles L. Smrvll(PUP)	Tom Connally (D)	Murray C. Sells (R)	Lyndon B. Johnson(D)	Jack Porter (R)	Sam Morris (P)	Price Daniel (D)	Price Daniel (R)	Lyndon B. Johnson(D)	Carlos G. Watson(R)	Fred T. Spnglr (CO)	Martin Dies	Thad Hutcheson	Ralph W. Yarborough
Donley	354	11	3	654	105	1,285	342	20	1,615	315	702	69	0	231	101	297
Duval	2,126	0	0	4,150	7	3,545	126	9	3,928	148	2,662	52	6	764	462	974
Eastland	1,810	49	6	1,847	194	4,593	1,833	86	5,817	1,098	2,269	293	1	1,245	494	1,339
Ector	531	23	5	643	114	4,054	213	7	11,168	2,703	2,383	679	31	1,429	1,081	1,174
Edwards	184	5	1	195	20	314	213	4	612	159	261	66	0	100	133	59
El Paso	1,603	361	51	2,916	502	16,708	4,130	20	25,667	6,673	9,907	1,430	15	3,592	3,398	6,840
Ellis	1,720	48	1	2,228	99	5,572	1,857	41	7,569	1,235	2,428	386	0	1,725	471	2,272
Erath	1,124	34	0	1,451	140	2,986	0	0	4,229	879	1,615	235	0	888	376	988
Falls	1,258	20	10	0	0	3,228	909	27	4,185	463	1,487	83	0	757	210	1,002
Fannin	1,783	50	1	1,901	87	6,143	836	42	5,706	670	2,367	132	0	717	233	1,741
Fayette	1,483	64	1	1,927	198	3,007	2,198	12	5,825	1,039	2,142	183	3	1,081	717	862
Fisher	991	10	3	686	19	1,988	219	9	1,755	172	926	20	0	237	89	694
Floyd	561	14	2	700	45	1,899	629	48	2,754	469	1,239	104	1	471	158	635
Foard	303	3	2	326	14	728	133	0	909	110	346	17	0	115	35	245
Fort Bend	944	19	1	1,057	99	2,180	1,417	14	6,041	927	1,731	242	2	1,660	669	988
Franklin	760	6	0	683	21	0	0	0	1,367	148	597	23	0	231	69	506
Freestone	1,145	18	0	1,119	36	2,205	863	30	3,695	373	1,278	80	0	834	201	869
Frio	312	8	0	423	58	892	409	14	1,672	230	542	75	1	187	206	473
Gaines	427	5	0	394	19	1,346	355	23	2,069	163	694	33	2	422	130	584
Galveston	3,106	265	51	3,145	582	13,024	5,170	64	21,524	9,761	7,483	1,571	68	3,546	4,232	7,118
Garza	255	13	0	362	18	844	188	21	1,223	195	387	46	0	146	80	231
Gillespie	1,914	453	7	1,307	1,327	484	2,941	3	1,255	2,887	1,386	779	7	229	822	92
Glasscock	67	1	0	84	9	169	98	8	337	73	168	19	0	87	42	46
Goliad	767	60	1	344	82	0	0	0	1,251	387	347	77	0	137	186	89
Gonzales	917	15	4	1,238	79	2,442	983	36	4,175	478	2,657	160	3	726	280	797
Gray	1,602	72	7	1,703	530	3,224	2,046	52	5,708	2,657	3,137	512	4	1,088	799	1,323
Grayson	2,934	183	27	3,688	288	10,762	2,843	25	12,570	2,524	4,114	564	3	1,799	1,155	3,464
Gregg	1,163	146	33	1,711	463	4,732	5,063	97	10,314	5,541	3,068	761	44	3,976	854	1,959
Grimes	569	3	0	651	21	1,107	587	14	2,430	358	682	58	1	367	179	763
Guadalupe	2,507	466	13	3,240	1,434	2,019	2,974	17	4,057	2,754	2,963	783	4	509	1,063	670
Hale	981	24	1	1,138	125	3,730	1,405	51	5,752	1,621	1,620	220	0	918	571	1,202
Hall	520	5	1	962	31	0	0	0	2,338	244	1,108	48	0	301	87	672
Hamilton	730	0	25	910	79	0	0	0	2,732	432	914	142	3	692	184	511
Hansford	165	5	5	291	27	0	0	0	1,137	485	590	107	0	204	139	200
Hardeman	408	12	0	580	38	1,572	339	14	2,146	370	739	38	0	460	133	446
Hardin	606	9	0	741	34	2,374	465	58	4,173	564	1,233	59	0	974	189	1,392
Harris	29,693	1,074	170	41,990	4,702	60,108	57,454	378	168,064	71,567	72,753	20,684	576	36,482	46,248	51,054
Harrison	597	4	1	0	0	3,197	1,834	73	7,477	1,384	2,317	129	1	1,928	287	902
Hartley	169	1	0	188	20	159	21	0	671	131	350	29	1	113	67	176
Haskell	979	3	0	870	29	2,675	259	15	3,010	291	1,111	55	0	467	116	819
Hays	855	10	1	781	41	2,395	547	22	3,307	467	1,080	89	0	412	335	855
Hemphill	230	14	1	407	69	0	0	0	1,015	326	624	63	1	218	122	291
Henderson	1,403	42	1	3,866	135	3,594	861	9	4,900	671	2,369	125	0	879	283	1,830
Hidalgo	2,832	112	32	4,553	624	9,927	6,173	107	16,673	7,324	8,553	1,888	14	3,448	3,516	4,497
Hill	1,683	25	3	1,734	82	0	0	0	5,544	686	2,582	153	4	1,108	278	1,694
Hockley	500	14	0	853	62	2,855	621	33	4,216	744	1,114	93	1	588	359	1,243
Hood	339	14	0	456	40	1,193	242	20	1,726	189	699	16	0	215	119	477
Hopkins	1,397	43	0	1,504	76	3,843	727	36	4,783	541	1,923	102	0	989	219	1,221
Houston	1,088	12	0	1,060	26	2,134	862	76	4,301	452	1,224	103	0	714	281	1,021
Howard	641	20	6	1,040	54	3,769	1,175	29	6,176	809	1,968	104	1	752	466	1,406
Hudspeth	60	2	0	108	3	422	57	1	405	145	363	10	0	126	40	81
Hunt	2,319	30	4	1,969	139	4,866	1,950	37	8,486	1,352	2,779	211	1	1,840	550	1,373
Hutchinson	443	89	5	1,432	340	4,327	1,539	26	6,503	2,619	3,321	570	21	893	782	1,606
Irion	193	2	1	167	11	0	0	0	430	78	172	12	0	74	52	77
Jack	534	20	1	570	55	1,305	382	56	1,980	245	797	118	1	367	179	416
Jackson	434	11	1	590	65	1,305	587	31	2,971	633	849	64	1	507	272	457
Jasper	477	6	0	727	16	1,836	497	40	3,934	448	1,194	73	1	1,289	196	967
Jeff Davis	212	0	1	111	6	0	0	0	308	69	208	24	1	48	34	47
Jefferson	2,373	176	34	9,036	633	24,707	7,916	154	33,016	17,811	10,352	1,730	90	9,892	4,836	11,039
Jim Hogg	224	17	0	544	52	716	111	0	1,267	70	580	7	0	156	53	131
Jim Wells	597	15	3	3,841	125	3,423	1,840	29	6,579	737	4,128	210	10	512	758	1,185
Johnson	1,167	42	0	1,418	133	3,783	1,235	41	5,739	1,131	2,268	347	2	1,069	564	1,499
Jones	1,236	22	8	1,449	57	3,519	356	71	4,082	709	1,473	80	0	749	287	1,158
Karnes	953	17	0	1,338	72	0	0	0	3,908	264	1,611	104	0	591	308	612
Kaufman	1,579	36	2	1,599	79	3,391	1,324	27	5,467	893	2,024	127	0	1,311	374	1,263

Table 21: Senatorial Races

General Elections, 1942-1957																
Year	1942			1946		1948			1952		1954			1957 Spl.		
County	W. Lee O'Daniel (D)	Dudley Lawson (R)	Charles L. Smrvll(PUP)	Tom Connally (D)	Murray C. Sells (R)	Lyndon B. Johnson(D)	Jack Porter (R)	Sam Morris (P)	Price Daniel (D)	Price Daniel (R)	Lyndon B. Johnson(D)	Carlos G. Watson(R)	Fred T. Spnglr (CO)	Martin Dies	Thad Hutcheson	Ralph W. Yarborough
Kendall	982	257	3	541	610	505	1,304	11	731	1,426	936	477	6	183	483	102
Kenedy	95	1	0	58	5	14	63	0	95	25	85	12	0	23	76	6
Kent	268	1	0	204	10	441	46	6	624	42	456	10	0	135	22	194
Kerr	500	66	7	589	322	1,437	1,633	29	3,287	1,572	1,802	442	5	622	1,015	437
Kimble	341	7	0	443	36	706	514	6	1,095	392	440	76	0	335	296	345
King	84	0	0	117	1	225	8	0	146	14	133	1	0	29	8	80
Kinney	141	26	26	386	64	0	0	0	594	100	102	30	0	69	43	85
Kleberg	332	10	10	498	45	2,016	770	36	4,086	616	1,069	81	0	402	535	931
Knox	494	9	9	689	19	1,753	237	16	2,110	196	803	43	0	271	87	555
La Salle	280	1	0	0	0	637	189	12	1,167	144	401	14	1	179	64	253
Lamar	1,562	19	11	1,639	96	6,180	1,739	78	7,934	942	2,542	151	0	1,368	385	1,205
Lamb	511	15	0	1,236	74	3,013	679	42	4,238	808	1,113	99	2	493	430	1,407
Lampasas	518	16	0	505	33	0	0	0	2,067	291	720	98	1	342	173	469
Lavaca	1,240	31	5	1,514	153	2,886	1,526	26	5,480	813	2,004	159	0	1,059	441	637
Lee	681	17	0	649	40	1,501	592	9	2,314	289	794	37	1	238	215	614
Leon	606	12	2	799	16	1,283	343	17	2,575	240	786	28	0	520	81	525
Liberty	1,962	10	0	908	59	2,194	1,339	94	6,080	995	1,554	180	0	1,717	456	1,027
Limestone	1,492	19	6	1,531	69	3,251	1,100	41	4,241	1,882	1,990	98	0	910	234	1,682
Lipscomb	308	48	2	411	99	644	370	27	977	480	553	118	0	98	132	150
Live Oak	336	2	0	493	78	893	586	28	1,721	302	669	59	0	221	274	242
Llano	909	9	1	748	48	1,389	350	11	1,398	208	606	43	3	131	152	518
Loving	40	2	0	79	6	55	21	0	67	20	46	4	1	18	12	23
Lubbock	1,310	81	9	2,780	304	0	0	0	20,022	5,567	5,364	680	0	2,804	2,129	3,811
Lynn	438	7	0	858	29	2,011	398	45	2,287	352	838	31	0	333	128	535
Madison	386	8	1	382	7	817	260	30	1,491	178	570	16	0	289	97	345
Marion	262	11	0	340	41	982	280	21	1,202	554	598	26	1	432	81	141
Martin	119	3	3	328	26	873	129	31	1,099	37	692	15	0	123	36	240
Mason	273	17	0	0	0	762	536	20	1,241	338	481	103	0	107	260	247
Matagorda	654	19	0	757	100	1,611	1,523	16	5,296	878	1,273	240	0	844	837	709
Maverick	210	10	1	240	23	697	272	9	1,369	342	457	46	0	156	133	523
McCulloch	550	9	0	767	67	2,080	501	11	2,653	466	1,080	73	0	472	246	539
McLennan	2,692	114	54	3,109	316	15,873	3,625	269	22,540	4,934	7,754	648	19	4,151	2,453	7,686
McMullen	229	1	0	157	11	189	101	5	372	57	222	18	0	90	52	55
Medina	1,601	121	7	1,424	578	2,509	1,032	30	3,114	1,765	1,145	371	5	597	626	605
Menard	317	5	1	352	39	679	328	15	918	231	342	61	0	103	129	142
Midland	482	25	3	532	185	1,760	1,900	42	5,911	4,823	2,385	686	34	1,595	2,123	752
Milam	1,466	38	4	1,285	81	3,126	936	38	4,980	459	1,913	141	2	785	305	1,334
Mills	460	8	0	460	24	0	0	0	1,522	270	543	62	1	248	111	317
Mitchell	791	8	0	796	32	2,057	337	29	2,425	379	1,020	50	3	371	185	729
Montague	1,080	21	2	2,966	168	0	0	0	3,911	622	1,323	158	1	668	243	986
Montgomery	1,185	21	0	1,042	25	2,285	1,014	50	5,477	248	1,811	175	2	974	478	1,120
Moore	178	8	0	496	25	1,611	430	12	2,856	749	1,274	168	5	360	356	989
Morris	382	7	0	560	16	1,195	282	16	2,255	145	811	41	0	609	95	613
Motley	225	1	0	288	12	744	132	14	863	169	399	29	0	204	33	137
Nacogdoches	1,097	17	1	1,151	62	3,321	1,060	57	5,443	631	1,876	107	0	1,505	253	1,545
Navarro	2,306	22	6	2,337	86	4,359	1,972	99	7,478	487	2,549	136	3	1,441	481	2,248
Newton	484	8	2	360	17	0	0	0	2,234	0	762	27	1	601	77	529
Nolan	1,084	37	0	941	85	3,312	698	17	4,883	678	1,372	71	0	520	346	1,041
Nueces	2,037	126	45	5,798	667	0	0	0	26,989	9,717	7,149	1,261	64	3,784	4,397	6,924
Ochiltree	279	15	2	498	56	0	0	0	1,386	733	1,040	133	4	333	160	161
Oldham	144	11	1	173	24	403	120	0	416	124	295	49	0	69	73	189
Orange	647	12	2	3,976	101	0	0	0	8,570	1,869	2,354	227	2	2,478	682	2,425
Palo Pinto	945	19	2	1,099	124	3,310	1,532	84	4,296	874	1,565	276	3	844	414	1,107
Panola	749	6	0	764	14	2,162	491	42	4,399	358	1,635	26	0	1,245	88	715
Parker	1,187	30	5	1,327	101	2,632	1,297	81	4,685	1,144	1,930	253	0	599	595	1,222
Parmer	274	40	0	0	0	979	392	33	1,662	388	576	145	0	296	148	356
Pecos	406	21	0	364	44	1,331	402	18	2,417	0	823	82	0	356	248	365
Polk	596	8	2	1,158	22	0	0	0	3,262	286	1,017	66	0	747	140	697
Potter	1,107	158	24	3,617	832	0	0	0	13,890	8,271	7,017	1,212	11	2,346	2,011	3,308
Presidio	291	4	0	299	31	868	259	8	962	407	462	32	0	157	90	107
Rains	350	3	0	376	8	742	148	4	893	88	363	23	0	175	59	180
Randall	366	19	5	878	121	1,932	791	24	3,898	1,948	2,204	336	1	781	816	961
Reagan	222	6	0	155	16	429	137	0	741	143	323	25	1	140	58	140
Real	167	10	1	177	19	406	186	9	587	137	223	29	0	71	129	96
Red River	1,027	11	1	960	26	3,062	727	49	4,749	330	1,622	78	0	917	163	1,104

Table 21: Senatorial Races

County	1942 W. Lee O'Daniel (D)	1942 Dudley Lawson (R)	1942 Charles L. Smrvll(PUP)	1946 Tom Connally (D)	1946 Murray C. Sells (R)	1948 Lyndon B. Johnson(D)	1948 Jack Porter (R)	1948 Sam Morris (P)	1952 Price Daniel (D)	1952 Price Daniel (R)	1954 Lyndon B. Johnson(D)	1954 Carlos G. Watson(R)	1954 Fred T. Spnglr (CO)	1957 Spl. Martin Dies	1957 Spl. Thad Hutcheson	1957 Spl. Ralph W. Yarborough
Reeves	224	11	0	460	52	0	0	0	2,137	334	813	81	1	415	173	307
Refugio	574	22	5	973	89	0	0	0	2,356	418	485	53	0	368	270	349
Roberts	92	6	2	155	25	214	173	1	290	144	258	25	1	96	74	61
Robertson	770	6	0	750	26	0	0	0	3,993	287	1,029	44	0	489	185	1,266
Rockwall	661	7	2	494	12	918	268	32	1,396	199	554	22	2	349	78	355
Runnels	782	26	0	861	67	2,786	733	27	3,530	559	1,114	78	0	1,430	562	1,308
Rusk	2,101	53	1	2,120	106	4,419	2,834	93	7,536	2,832	4,049	256	18	2,416	394	1,097
Sabine	433	2	1	574	11	1,147	178	54	1,963	209	705	27	0	407	61	340
San Augustine	640	6	1	509	11	996	173	38	1,859	182	795	17	0	427	29	420
San Jacinto	247	3	0	896	9	542	171	36	1,297	175	459	29	0	140	52	392
San Patricio	761	42	11	974	103	2,336	1,171	66	4,817	1,636	1,405	171	0	847	720	1,469
San Saba	651	12	0	731	28	1,972	249	33	1,994	193	1,021	36	0	216	102	675
Schleicher	179	0	0	160	15	478	149	6	865	103	419	34	0	140	187	178
Scurry	899	11	0	883	40	1,973	292	24	4,114	454	1,171	107	0	597	285	626
Shackelford	414	12	4	392	35	825	294	19	1,453	215	373	37	0	246	118	229
Shelby	1,024	22	0	1,292	35	3,277	550	64	5,382	204	1,935	95	0	1,403	109	1,178
Sherman	96	8	0	77	4	466	102	6	666	211	356	43	1	119	54	172
Smith	2,655	82	7	2,450	388	5,480	5,487	93	15,183	3,603	5,317	531	9	3,694	1,880	3,319
Somervell	493	3	2	226	26	380	139	11	761	132	274	32	0	101	62	163
Starr	617	0	0	1,967	15	0	0	0	3,636	136	2,348	15	0	53	80	1,335
Stephens	974	12	0	837	83	0	0	0	2,815	449	1,474	149	1	592	333	487
Sterling	122	4	0	134	7	0	0	0	339	68	135	13	0	82	32	52
Stonewall	327	1	2	500	18	0	0	0	913	90	307	8	0	82	37	285
Sutton	139	10	0	533	11	406	195	0	568	285	215	53	0	126	156	81
Swisher	350	15	2	563	59	1,509	455	12	2,047	733	864	119	0	170	166	847
Tarrant	20,366	873	92	11,320	2,494	33,083	23,214	446	72,827	22,355	26,078	6,861	35	19,486	11,645	17,940
Taylor	1,934	66	16	2,392	128	7,670	2,352	198	11,495	3,394	3,154	344	0	2,700	1,650	2,835
Terrell	73	8	0	97	30	165	92	1	486	166	261	49	0	64	84	83
Terry	391	4	1	610	55	2,166	407	28	3,416	372	922	60	0	283	157	619
Throckmorton	356	8	0	620	4	1,001	112	2	1,087	100	465	222	0	114	53	350
Titus	692	6	1	3,084	94	2,273	646	23	3,964	470	1,188	75	2	734	161	939
Tom Green	1,279	60	6	1,859	215	6,606	2,253	40	11,665	3,015	3,317	479	2	1,879	1,499	1,823
Travis	3,100	167	50	6,986	529	20,714	5,876	83	27,587	8,463	11,562	1,104	12	3,041	5,665	10,174
Trinity	981	8	0	437	15	1,011	328	0	2,425	194	504	39	0	333	95	590
Tyler	427	1	0	541	24	978	278	74	2,389	261	956	40	0	867	169	447
Upshur	1,005	50	0	1,027	48	2,043	954	35	4,325	625	1,813	54	0	930	171	922
Upton	293	5	4	252	12	771	220	12	1,418	234	1,102	50	7	365	194	380
Uvalde	463	9	0	603	162	1,367	1,025	25	2,480	1,357	796	187	0	427	635	430
Val Verde	319	37	0	553	135	1,200	722	20	2,429	691	654	111	1	377	335	312
Van Zandt	1,453	41	1	1,363	82	3,198	996	60	4,770	504	1,854	109	2	815	273	1,377
Victoria	633	35	0	869	69	2,247	1,777	21	5,929	1,162	1,343	195	2	822	948	919
Walker	568	9	0	602	22	0	0	0	3,463	341	1,546	79	0	526	253	811
Waller	283	1	0	464	28	868	673	11	2,165	416	672	82	2	451	228	419
Ward	300	15	0	482	76	1,964	600	15	2,872	286	941	102	0	555	337	570
Washington	777	12	0	1,367	59	1,807	1,964	2	4,372	559	1,010	108	0	581	521	412
Webb	976	16	0	2,447	88	4,708	905	10	8,551	518	5,401	109	4	4,238	396	948
Wharton	807	28	2	1,126	83	2,799	1,760	22	7,158	1,650	2,319	254	0	1,285	872	1,545
Wheeler	594	39	3	878	131	1,865	459	45	2,438	506	1,099	148	0	281	163	542
Wichita	1,857	94	14	3,019	369	0	0	0	17,609	3,432	9,306	893	5	2,306	2,341	5,273
Wilbarger	826	6	0	901	59	2,832	837	28	4,727	324	1,160	108	1	937	337	534
Willacy	519	15	2	474	78	1,119	735	34	3,004	512	575	93	4	679	319	359
Williamson	1,744	47	0	2,080	135	5,596	1,344	29	6,550	954	2,563	152	0	875	493	1,856
Wilson	742	18	3	1,343	260	2,224	767	8	3,588	518	1,500	151	3	260	425	1,008
Winkler	231	20	1	262	32	1,449	465	47	2,393	276	779	91	0	437	191	521
Wise	1,081	38	3	1,158	102	2,957	660	44	4,175	598	1,569	234	0	553	342	1,033
Wood	1,179	20	0	1,370	106	2,523	1,196	28	4,564	770	1,548	129	0	998	269	1,168
Yoakum	162	8	2	275	9	809	164	13	1,299	204	672	47	7	290	131	420
Young	1,010	11	1	1,099	62	3,082	714	36	3,436	890	1,308	132	0	565	334	969
Zapata	701	333	0	307	7	629	417	0	765	522	874	602	1	93	220	337
Zavala	279	11	1	454	51	617	250	7	1,410	275	459	44	2	192	201	254
Official	260,629	1,934		43,750		349,665			1,425,007		538,417	3,025		219,591		
Totals		12,064		336,931		702,985		8,913		469,594		95,033		290,803		364,605
Unofficial	260,629	1,975		43,619		349,665			1,430,974		538,425	3,026		219,591		
Totals		12,054		336,891		702,785		8,913		469,594		94,903		290,869		364,838

Table 22: Senatorial Races

County	1958 Ralph W. Yarbrgh (D)	1958 Roy Whtmbg (R)	1958 Bard A. Logan (CO)	1960 Lyndon B. Johnsn(D)	1960 John G. Tower(R)	1961 Spl. William A. Blakley	1961 Spl. John G. Tower	1964 Ralph W. Yarbrgh(D)	1964 George Bush (R)	1964 Jack Carswll(CO)	1966 Waggoner Carr (D)	1966 John G. Tower (R)	1966 Jas. Barker Hollnd (CO)
Anderson	1,998	383	8	4,012	2,840	1,563	1,282	4,700	3,457	6	1,680	2,143	4
Andrews	805	130	8	2,095	1,163	530	482	1,795	1,784	11	753	1,040	6
Angelina	3,755	436	12	7,279	4,338	2,545	1,872	7,301	6,158	8	3,041	4,027	24
Aransas	311	39	2	1,068	709	247	272	1,328	730	7	530	530	3
Archer	1,084	62	3	1,489	525	641	282	1,593	614	1	950	547	2
Armstrong	228	119	1	486	323	187	140	477	415	1	299	338	2
Atascosa	959	87	4	2,689	1,446	853	797	3,006	1,506	6	849	1,054	4
Austin	911	168	6	2,104	1,515	671	855	2,228	1,677	1	988	1,249	0
Bailey	629	196	2	1,243	1,085	435	545	1,168	1,368	0	567	866	3
Bandera	323	114	2	688	824	252	402	809	825	3	374	669	2
Bastrop	1,437	128	2	3,599	932	1,402	614	3,644	1,369	10	1,572	1,096	5
Baylor	516	54	1	1,348	531	506	234	1,278	499	3	711	492	0
Bee	842	197	5	2,814	1,953	732	930	3,019	1,804	8	1,196	1,282	7
Bell	4,291	424	5	11,787	3,360	3,801	1,640	13,420	4,043	16	4,199	3,555	68
Bexar	19,707	10,132	709	77,249	543	22,821	27,161	95,141	64,711	380	44,415	52,319	1,118
Blanco	784	175	3	997	487	371	310	978	499	1	466	456	1
Borden	166	13	0	270	122	121	71	238	172	0	123	158	0
Bosque	1,253	196	7	2,202	1,303	984	597	2,496	1,223	5	1,198	899	3
Bowie	3,225	447	29	10,663	4,209	2,622	2,007	10,408	6,746	145	3,765	4,396	14
Brazoria	5,265	1,414	215	10,988	9,330	3,748	4,650	13,818	10,220	99	5,918	7,912	177
Brazos	4,145	514	14	6,957	3,296	2,114	1,540	7,216	4,782	13	3,492	3,763	23
Brewster	435	92	1	929	574	301	346	1,162	711	1	420	485	2
Briscoe	274	80	0	723	352	201	154	883	411	4	443	310	1
Brooks	842	58	4	2,147	525	596	255	2,217	487	3	1,360	386	1
Brown	2,160	354	3	4,559	2,782	1,609	1,171	4,654	2,595	8	1,740	1,856	13
Burleson	927	28	3	2,653	495	1,021	343	2,462	665	3	990	530	5
Burnet	912	121	6	2,115	891	925	538	2,290	1,095	2	969	859	2
Caldwell	1,421	124	0	3,127	1,051	1,168	599	3,316	1,269	5	1,491	1,137	5
Calhoun	797	124	13	2,309	1,379	674	567	2,998	1,401	2	1,013	1,186	7
Callahan	746	84	2	1,764	1,023	808	457	1,983	1,047	6	965	795	1
Cameron	3,957	1,608	52	13,828	9,213	5,020	5,104	14,993	10,441	69	6,243	7,614	49
Camp	671	99	4	1,580	676	455	266	1,790	778	4	777	509	0
Carson	478	270	1	1,329	1,173	406	455	1,390	1,223	3	877	929	1
Cass	1,843	218	6	3,533	1,689	1,114	747	3,416	2,754	7	1,425	1,788	8
Castro	694	170	2	1,758	607	592	293	1,668	813	4	703	879	2
Chambers	634	70	6	1,850	927	464	405	1,709	1,203	7	541	808	3
Cherokee	2,940	332	9	5,067	2,739	1,701	1,349	5,233	3,293	18	1,931	2,238	13
Childress	741	163	0	1,565	1,137	661	396	1,789	1,132	4	827	876	2
Clay	902	100	1	1,896	801	858	418	2,182	821	3	1,145	746	3
Cochran	540	71	3	1,190	483	503	313	1,027	734	2	620	554	0
Coke	585	57	1	919	441	360	201	783	474	1	399	283	1
Coleman	1,295	203	3	2,162	1,815	967	831	2,398	1,681	3	1,019	1,313	3
Collin	2,685	375	2	6,516	2,586	2,719	1,150	6,958	3,934	12	3,199	2,987	5
Collingsworth	557	166	2	1,053	745	508	368	1,056	806	5	638	603	1
Colorado	1,154	185	26	2,745	1,804	955	988	3,402	2,176	4	1,191	1,576	3
Comal	1,384	512	5	2,264	2,676	812	1,367	2,970	2,849	10	1,101	2,067	8
Comanche	1,187	151	3	2,379	1,361	978	622	2,595	1,192	8	1,302	764	4
Concho	338	61	0	717	365	362	194	956	399	1	308	320	1
Cooke	1,774	399	3	3,752	2,991	1,192	1,132	3,708	3,490	6	1,502	2,151	7
Coryell	1,720	154	3	3,058	1,045	1,224	478	3,359	1,182	5	2,136	1,228	6
Cottle	521	51	0	1,120	232	464	135	1,066	287	3	566	247	0
Crane	501	85	17	947	570	261	247	828	721	2	332	453	2
Crockett	277	59	2	654	466	160	182	688	509	2	303	359	0
Crosby	798	83	3	2,027	614	581	402	1,938	934	3	961	686	5
Culberson	205	36	0	422	207	125	145	419	366	0	303	279	2
Dallam	479	215	2	1,113	758	244	333	930	821	1	519	624	6
Dallas	61,489	50,445	1,256	98,761	128,504	44,506	57,044	136,002	162,421	968	57,906	105,725	1,164
Dawson	1,000	141	2	2,549	1,590	808	793	2,568	2,270	7	1,014	1,404	1
DeWitt	991	393	11	2,486	2,258	811	1,214	2,891	2,652	6	985	1,682	1
Deaf Smith	621	324	0	1,608	1,703	474	712	1,834	2,037	16	1,155	1,790	8
Delta	602	28	5	1,542	285	675	112	1,557	375	2	571	225	2
Denton	3,821	743	13	6,459	4,598	2,458	1,724	8,047	5,373	8	2,861	4,058	10
Dickens	604	58	3	1,254	359	462	216	1,206	445	2	615	299	0
Dimmit	390	75	2	1,037	536	411	277	952	725	2	689	474	1

Table 22: Senatorial Races

General Elections, 1958-1966												
Year	1958			1960		1961 Spl.		1964			1966		
County	Ralph W. Yarbrgh (D)	Roy Whtnbg (R)	Bard A. Logan (CO)	Lyndon B. Johnsn(D)	John G. Tower(R)	William A. Blakley	John G. Tower	Ralph W. Yarbrgh(D)	George Bush (R)	Jack Carswll(CO)	Waggoner Carr (D)	John G. Tower (R)	Jas. Barker Hollnd (CO)
Donley	408	104	1	958	705	314	286	968	813	2	507	598	2
Duval	3,660	75	3	3,881	738	2,326	323	4,394	396	4	3,381	193	0
Eastland	1,995	417	3	3,731	2,793	1,666	1,132	4,321	2,409	9	1,658	1,695	2
Ector	2,444	1,398	296	9,204	9,310	2,212	4,027	8,606	13,228	66	3,441	8,590	66
Edwards	246	107	2	272	407	75	198	284	420	3	106	309	1
El Paso	11,735	2,311	127	26,135	19,977	7,119	11,342	31,429	23,936	215	12,949	20,151	150
Ellis	3,562	468	10	6,827	2,794	2,498	1,016	6,620	3,445	12	2,868	2,228	7
Erath	1,669	256	4	3,067	2,007	1,222	855	3,604	1,891	10	1,524	1,368	1
Falls	1,508	180	3	3,588	1,158	1,634	607	3,739	1,411	0	1,763	1,097	1
Fannin	2,128	170	3	4,858	1,285	2,019	456	5,740	1,446	1	2,165	900	3
Fayette	1,844	196	12	4,021	1,721	1,551	1,087	3,461	2,273	6	1,603	1,526	2
Fisher	1,566	80	1	2,117	959	713	231	2,002	552	4	739	507	6
Floyd	868	198	3	1,907	1,216	633	545	2,056	1,611	1	802	1,169	3
Foard	347	31	0	794	199	271	70	794	181	0	373	173	2
Fort Bend	1,887	356	35	4,911	3,050	1,663	1,896	5,564	4,036	25	3,345	3,468	19
Franklin	596	42	3	1,369	446	500	151	1,443	479	0	696	330	0
Freestone	1,103	195	5	2,408	1,198	894	456	2,728	1,163	4	1,244	756	8
Frio	512	80	0	1,215	591	528	340	1,406	727	5	681	634	8
Gaines	1,745	170	3	1,866	1,129	543	431	1,579	1,589	5	680	1,067	3
Galveston	9,215	2,393	444	22,586	13,791	6,560	7,534	27,002	15,136	146	9,875	11,203	319
Garza	365	75	0	1,022	514	286	286	1,001	800	5	497	563	7
Gillespie	859	873	2	1,228	2,462	279	1,167	1,748	2,199	1	451	1,543	1
Glasscock	164	28	2	263	124	96	88	155	214	0	96	150	1
Goliad	240	75	1	800	716	244	373	933	601	3	253	332	3
Gonzales	1,278	83	1	3,003	1,156	1,030	547	2,953	1,603	3	1,092	906	2
Gray	1,771	1,175	10	3,906	5,044	1,044	2,151	3,194	5,820	7	2,015	4,593	12
Grayson	4,515	669	10	11,513	5,611	3,812	2,003	12,953	6,502	9	5,462	4,679	19
Gregg	2,794	1,533	76	8,431	8,627	2,443	3,359	7,607	12,272	88	3,479	7,825	127
Grimes	810	70	6	1,896	841	1,041	577	2,093	1,127	5	946	893	1
Guadalupe	2,755	812	18	3,537	3,280	903	1,613	3,948	3,336	6	2,094	2,885	13
Hale	1,717	468	5	4,652	3,897	1,446	1,562	4,619	4,917	19	2,079	2,896	7
Hall	695	141	3	1,513	613	593	208	1,655	801	1	771	560	1
Hamilton	877	151	1	1,513	1,280	750	615	1,758	1,301	1	625	838	1
Hansford	233	319	1	795	1,044	166	390	685	1,365	3	466	944	1
Hardeman	653	106	1	1,539	1,027	431	385	1,597	935	3	687	663	4
Hardin	1,590	112	4	4,820	1,471	1,431	571	5,045	2,077	14	1,858	1,950	6
Harris	73,548	29,711	8,120	150,752	149,844	40,215	78,479	198,112	179,900	971	94,164	144,033	1,292
Harrison	1,770	508	23	6,047	2,574	1,634	1,187	6,126	5,759	9	3,773	4,228	28
Hartley	192	111	1	505	328	155	149	501	499	3	342	455	0
Haskell	1,238	57	2	2,985	619	1,043	257	2,722	688	3	1,053	598	2
Hays	1,150	122	0	3,277	1,262	1,212	798	3,421	1,620	5	1,647	1,625	10
Hemphill	469	191	5	489	689	170	257	568	633	1	501	495	1
Henderson	2,071	186	7	3,851	2,084	1,519	1,058	4,522	2,142	13	1,657	1,534	10
Hidalgo	7,375	2,626	64	19,550	12,718	6,483	7,695	20,097	12,939	74	7,927	10,400	67
Hill	2,158	140	35	5,063	1,556	2,313	664	4,729	1,944	7	1,872	1,256	1
Hockley	1,417	249	4	3,416	1,642	1,220	873	3,239	2,472	10	1,353	1,696	7
Hood	590	56	3	1,654	543	402	207	1,458	510	3	554	344	2
Hopkins	1,766	141	1	3,563	1,649	1,593	592	3,680	1,936	2	1,528	1,071	2
Houston	1,106	124	8	3,046	1,293	920	619	3,480	1,768	4	1,659	1,388	4
Howard	2,178	370	3	5,649	2,600	1,414	1,198	5,713	3,636	7	2,217	3,034	14
Hudspeth	230	23	1	483	204	165	131	399	258	1	230	170	0
Hunt	2,421	404	11	5,349	3,065	1,951	1,182	5,901	3,887	6	2,331	2,367	4
Hutchinson	1,939	1,167	12	4,548	5,221	1,119	1,986	3,963	6,025	18	2,637	4,720	27
Irion	208	43	0	285	200	199	112	259	233	2	306	220	1
Jack	693	135	11	1,285	1,066	563	527	1,434	1,023	3	912	859	4
Jackson	902	92	22	2,548	1,299	713	522	2,475	1,459	11	926	911	2
Jasper	1,827	123	5	3,491	1,591	1,026	695	3,459	2,064	13	1,209	1,677	10
Jeff Davis	114	23	3	256	147	76	83	291	188	1	216	173	0
Jefferson	32,350	7,409	436	41,693	24,166	12,919	11,984	40,667	31,025	285	13,844	25,098	278
Jim Hogg	601	10	2	1,302	181	231	69	1,341	187	0	869	176	0
Jim Wells	1,533	293	4	5,248	2,295	1,383	1,050	6,342	2,491	8	3,168	2,411	15
Johnson	2,076	445	11	4,888	3,567	1,964	1,477	5,642	3,984	3	1,929	2,413	8
Jones	1,469	180	0	3,419	1,644	1,360	672	3,247	1,633	6	1,248	1,146	1
Karnes	1,247	98	3	2,494	983	1,161	611	2,929	1,220	2	1,224	865	1
Kaufman	1,755	297	7	3,614	2,098	1,602	699	4,453	2,208	5	1,948	1,340	9

Table 22: Senatorial Races

General Elections, 1958-1966															
Year	1958			1960		1961 Spl.		1964			1966			
County	Ralph W. Yarbrgh (D)	Roy Whtthbg (R)	Bard A. Logan (CO)	Lyndon B. Johnsn(D)	John G. Tower(R)	William A. Blakley	John G. Tower	Ralph W. Yarbrgh(D)	George Bush (R)	Jack Carswll(CO)	Waggoner Carr (D)	John G. Tower (R)	Jas. Barker Hollnd (CO)
Kendall	720	488	7	482	720	181	675	828	1,340	3	283	1,079	3
Kenedy	77	15	0	91	64	51	60	97	49	1	70	54	0
Kent	441	11	0	524	138	282	66	486	184	0	312	155	0
Kerr	1,555	677	10	1,826	2,909	697	1,513	2,550	3,011	3	972	2,539	6
Kimble	396	129	2	636	648	327	351	793	599	0	297	437	1
King	119	11	0	147	32	84	25	166	50	0	94	58	0
Kinney	134	50	1	403	177	89	110	409	180	0	486	187	2
Kleberg	1,193	170	4	4,088	1,752	1,000	914	4,192	2,036	6	1,438	1,969	9
Knox	667	39	1	1,621	496	616	236	1,067	596	2	818	518	5
La Salle	439	24	5	834	254	294	125	892	308	2	438	200	0
Lamar	2,274	325	5	6,166	2,651	2,101	883	5,866	3,010	3	2,482	2,126	1
Lamb	1,434	211	2	3,772	2,007	1,135	1,032	3,558	2,780	6	1,569	1,894	4
Lampasas	598	123	3	1,747	830	612	483	1,810	847	2	688	813	2
Lavaca	1,647	167	9	4,260	1,193	1,892	720	3,838	1,645	3	1,487	1,190	5
Lee	685	62	4	1,650	717	635	577	1,767	1,041	4	848	814	13
Leon	2,272	79	4	1,901	625	714	234	2,307	710	4	853	449	3
Liberty	2,356	246	27	4,595	2,613	1,509	1,273	4,949	3,120	15	1,887	2,092	7
Limestone	2,696	209	17	3,810	1,466	1,389	548	3,520	1,723	2	1,544	1,073	5
Lipscomb	296	184	3	496	678	113	302	485	863	1	462	686	1
Live Oak	391	72	1	911	944	362	502	1,307	939	4	487	615	3
Llano	526	59	1	1,315	516	587	351	1,463	871	3	587	688	2
Loving	74	12	2	52	25	16	20	38	39	1	35	29	2
Lubbock	5,354	2,238	17	18,964	15,992	5,783	7,867	15,692	23,525	41	10,505	14,518	28
Lynn	797	113	0	2,173	656	735	336	1,826	1,197	1	871	761	2
Madison	586	32	6	1,036	454	375	163	1,244	666	6	519	467	0
Marion	543	94	1	1,175	502	279	218	1,375	952	1	623	594	2
Martin	559	36	2	999	236	359	115	777	513	1	339	382	3
Mason	351	151	0	705	726	291	483	835	707	1	356	513	1
Matagorda	1,531	260	34	3,572	2,508	983	1,235	3,818	2,799	13	1,504	2,083	8
Maverick	696	68	1	1,650	528	762	261	2,037	638	3	1,688	621	11
McCulloch	808	126	2	1,892	876	730	457	1,962	826	0	725	644	2
McLennan	8,406	1,360	25	23,814	11,314	9,223	5,195	25,812	13,655	38	10,646	10,413	38
McMullen	131	13	1	276	204	115	117	239	204	2	154	135	0
Medina	1,631	455	11	2,234	1,550	714	985	3,094	1,909	3	930	1,324	2
Menard	327	96	2	597	523	191	262	545	439	0	240	346	0
Midland	2,482	2,166	177	6,702	9,238	2,094	5,440	6,427	13,893	64	4,395	9,721	90
Milam	2,029	243	6	4,181	1,495	1,624	714	4,082	1,620	4	1,574	1,337	7
Mills	539	71	1	1,139	682	469	420	1,069	643	5	424	410	2
Mitchell	1,060	71	1	2,521	837	924	384	2,276	876	4	857	683	4
Montague	1,338	162	7	3,030	1,555	1,190	705	3,338	1,499	5	1,441	1,097	2
Montgomery	2,430	207	34	3,958	2,429	991	1,052	4,603	3,521	43	2,660	3,055	34
Moore	750	390	3	2,194	1,944	420	667	2,024	2,128	6	1,357	1,760	13
Morris	958	159	2	2,474	1,095	850	448	2,259	1,317	10	1,023	1,028	5
Motley	374	51	1	647	273	251	139	553	441	2	402	351	2
Nacogdoches	2,248	268	17	4,208	2,454	1,352	763	4,182	3,293	11	1,685	2,328	7
Navarro	2,417	440	5	6,309	2,509	2,338	1,046	6,362	2,568	4	2,602	1,744	6
Newton	1,164	23	3	2,060	548	509	241	2,197	754	5	756	579	4
Nolan	1,596	309	5	3,762	1,786	1,396	925	3,693	1,993	6	1,317	1,371	8
Nueces	10,957	2,637	262	29,186	16,868	8,282	7,766	35,363	18,076	91	16,616	16,849	208
Ochiltree	518	439	3	730	1,638	168	570	690	2,038	0	368	1,312	4
Oldham	218	125	1	414	230	144	144	300	356	4	214	257	1
Orange	3,747	412	9	10,859	3,959	2,625	1,774	8,514	7,013	31	3,340	5,082	32
Palo Pinto	1,623	339	13	3,391	1,971	1,207	854	3,506	2,002	4	1,374	1,429	6
Panola	1,340	198	21	2,801	1,685	1,022	453	2,592	2,801	9	1,350	1,542	7
Parker	1,715	297	4	4,463	2,795	1,488	1,131	4,855	2,586	6	2,110	2,107	9
Parmer	672	275	3	1,522	1,227	487	573	1,262	1,507	4	651	1,078	1
Pecos	875	162	11	1,916	1,188	732	511	1,797	1,654	7	640	1,086	1
Polk	1,435	84	4	2,303	893	655	346	2,345	1,283	6	936	795	4
Potter	4,269	4,140	24	11,665	11,124	2,998	4,705	10,470	13,738	71	5,406	8,981	35
Presidio	406	49	1	1,042	311	246	202	1,126	460	2	478	339	0
Rains	342	21	0	720	278	282	99	835	310	2	361	197	0
Randall	1,547	1,751	8	4,561	5,663	1,291	2,456	4,699	9,036	32	2,963	6,511	34
Reagan	403	43	3	722	262	378	133	540	471	1	225	312	1
Real	182	43	2	346	323	129	148	454	287	1	296	212	1
Red River	1,650	162	9	3,220	972	1,160	355	3,232	1,373	6	1,303	935	5

Table 22: Senatorial Races

General Elections, 1958-1966														
Year	1958			1960		1961 Spl.		1964			1966			
County	Ralph W. Yarbrgh (D)	Roy Whtnbg (R)	Bard A. Logan (CO)	Lyndon B. Johnsn(D)	John G. Tower(R)	William A. Blakley	John G. Tower	Ralph W. Yarbrgh(D)	George Bush (R)	Jack Carswll(CO)	Waggoner Carr (D)	John G. Tower (R)	Jas. Barker Hollnd (CO)
Reeves	644	202	6	2,431	1,172	789	595	1,956	1,584	10	997	1,008	6
Refugio	958	121	2	2,573	910	684	444	2,106	992	1	678	760	6
Roberts	82	97	0	149	294	85	144	171	320	1	170	262	0
Robertson	1,385	162	7	2,907	748	1,054	284	3,218	913	0	1,615	744	12
Rockwall	462	46	1	1,101	453	511	161	1,185	541	1	564	325	0
Runnels	1,072	192	4	2,443	1,582	863	853	2,284	1,588	7	825	1,198	1
Rusk	2,426	715	36	4,250	5,120	1,736	2,413	5,937	5,629	15	2,289	3,808	18
Sabine	649	19	1	1,366	474	406	178	1,752	454	3	541	375	0
San Augustine	676	22	2	1,289	500	399	324	1,122	821	7	455	674	3
San Jacinto	402	20	5	1,049	306	357	156	1,672	344	2	661	293	2
San Patricio	1,852	266	17	5,923	2,709	1,767	1,115	6,481	2,711	17	2,336	2,337	11
San Saba	878	67	2	1,483	633	710	277	1,724	543	2	720	440	1
Schleicher	277	73	0	451	372	216	248	477	424	0	267	307	0
Scurry	1,263	182	3	3,343	1,772	1,111	724	2,883	2,260	13	1,098	1,332	6
Shackelford	526	73	3	848	548	360	226	803	622	0	358	440	0
Shelby	1,909	87	10	3,789	1,121	928	384	3,473	2,287	10	1,452	1,110	5
Sherman	192	192	0	468	511	131	241	401	685	1	320	568	0
Smith	4,252	1,768	31	10,262	10,594	3,352	5,363	11,393	13,879	37	5,034	9,662	46
Somervell	435	60	2	475	329	195	125	607	240	3	220	142	3
Starr	2,265	15	0	4,051	284	2,087	101	3,835	855	10	2,835	803	4
Stephens	841	242	2	1,631	1,377	716	600	1,597	1,257	5	621	968	1
Sterling	160	24	0	243	118	125	61	204	174	0	81	111	0
Stonewall	376	21	2	957	208	331	75	907	290	1	301	210	0
Sutton	330	126	9	566	375	179	202	612	430	3	235	295	1
Swisher	857	192	2	1,747	808	533	412	2,202	1,024	3	1,127	789	0
Tarrant	28,408	8,934	431	72,862	57,718	22,702	26,652	83,457	69,531	354	29,251	47,147	233
Taylor	4,166	1,177	18	12,650	10,330	4,093	4,060	11,252	11,196	42	5,041	7,978	10
Terrell	284	63	0	377	258	123	116	341	312	0	159	234	2
Terry	1,238	186	0	2,525	1,544	820	763	2,345	2,270	6	1,091	1,451	5
Throckmorton	338	28	0	769	327	313	143	842	292	0	429	218	1
Titus	1,162	159	5	3,333	1,600	996	468	3,391	1,804	4	1,096	1,251	4
Tom Green	4,226	1,255	9	8,403	6,661	3,436	3,579	8,553	7,849	16	3,295	6,016	12
Travis	13,157	3,214	101	33,137	17,261	14,224	12,030	36,677	27,216	82	15,576	25,151	76
Trinity	634	47	5	1,570	550	426	305	1,574	832	7	632	523	4
Tyler	912	121	6	1,473	1,147	565	582	1,726	1,290	1	662	1,024	3
Upshur	2,149	189	2	3,809	1,568	1,000	562	3,907	2,288	9	1,504	1,554	4
Upton	636	90	5	1,040	647	268	251	803	800	5	420	605	4
Uvalde	839	225	3	1,599	2,001	522	997	2,142	2,165	1	567	1,439	3
Val Verde	657	202	2	2,336	1,307	581	609	3,352	1,542	3	993	1,045	3
Van Zandt	1,851	170	2	3,249	1,664	1,409	686	3,735	1,914	8	1,578	1,223	3
Victoria	1,808	423	17	6,276	4,316	1,898	2,000	6,858	5,482	32	3,081	4,099	15
Walker	894	129	8	2,225	1,360	590	623	2,727	1,700	0	1,108	1,397	6
Waller	693	88	25	1,261	1,021	522	511	2,113	1,044	1	1,489	955	8
Ward	827	160	14	2,297	1,411	716	705	1,931	2,009	3	1,261	1,595	9
Washington	1,087	144	3	2,314	2,133	590	1,215	2,657	2,248	2	1,072	1,401	5
Webb	3,474	208	10	10,346	1,611	3,881	848	9,757	1,407	9	5,751	1,463	10
Wharton	2,861	359	28	5,469	2,284	2,162	1,708	5,742	3,265	11	2,228	2,675	12
Wheeler	978	366	2	1,575	1,076	490	499	1,325	1,238	1	898	941	1
Wichita	5,626	1,127	14	16,584	10,130	5,922	5,334	16,974	10,810	17	9,230	11,019	31
Wilbarger	1,465	242	1	2,782	1,931	846	621	2,886	1,872	3	1,287	1,383	7
Willacy	747	165	9	2,366	1,228	1,107	790	2,044	1,335	3	856	956	4
Williamson	2,309	270	1	6,275	1,778	2,778	1,168	6,790	2,383	7	2,972	2,632	12
Wilson	1,097	119	2	3,087	966	1,146	505	3,295	933	1	1,212	734	2
Winkler	799	134	16	1,924	1,267	459	624	1,774	1,897	4	875	1,239	7
Wise	1,822	246	7	2,949	1,928	1,136	774	3,580	1,684	3	1,226	1,120	4
Wood	1,648	233	4	3,026	1,955	1,253	872	3,332	2,251	7	1,373	1,433	6
Yoakum	608	102	0	1,354	424	376	405	1,048	1,219	4	561	869	1
Young	1,356	278	1	2,774	1,858	1,180	785	3,073	1,930	1	1,688	1,520	2
Zapata	389	34	0	693	240	137	118	991	149	1	821	88	1
Zavala	449	69	3	795	750	253	308	1,485	868	2	755	650	6
Official Totals	587,030	185,926	14,172	926,653 1,306,625		448,217 437,874		1,134,337 1,463,958		5,542	643,855 842,501		6,778
Unofficial Totals	587,030	185,926	14,172	871,493 1,305,108		448,217 437,874		1,134,337 1,463,958		5,542	643,855 842,501		6,778

Table 23: Senatorial Races

	General Elections, 1970-1976									
Year	1970		1972				1976			
County	Lloyd Bentsen(D)	George Bush (R)	Barefoot Sanders(D)	John G. Tower (R)	Flores Amaya (RZ)	Tom Leonard (S)	Lloyd Bentsn(D)	Alan Steelmn (R)	Marjorie P. Gallion (A)	Pedro Vasqs (SW)
Anderson	3,553	2,537	3,542	4,396	16	7	6,050	3,099	10	3
Andrews	1,326	1,123	1,356	1,956	24	4	1,796	1,882	9	7
Angelina	6,706	3,616	8,773	7,777	15	13	11,619	4,770	85	22
Aransas	951	754	1,133	1,516	26	3	2,357	1,676	32	14
Archer	1,363	435	1,042	1,014	3	2	1,883	558	2	0
Armstrong	409	342	370	567	1	0	637	327	2	0
Atascosa	2,363	1,119	2,187	2,667	263	8	4,759	1,556	13	35
Austin	1,662	1,675	1,760	2,337	2	4	2,780	2,082	10	4
Bailey	920	854	767	1,521	54	2	1,532	957	0	3
Bandera	987	701	849	1,353	10	0	1,439	1,124	11	2
Bastrop	2,424	1,203	2,313	2,554	47	7	4,827	1,821	7	24
Baylor	1,306	442	951	943	1	0	1,538	499	2	0
Bee	2,662	1,724	2,189	3,086	588	24	4,246	2,073	25	65
Bell	9,504	4,506	9,787	14,013	538	29	18,323	12,292	101	66
Bexar	82,408	57,449	100,515	110,774	10,266	1,056	156,097	99,364	1,950	2,450
Blanco	652	430	644	1,002	5	4	1,094	706	7	0
Borden	199	124	212	236	3	0	274	104	0	2
Bosque	2,003	1,015	1,774	2,178	3	1	2,898	1,769	7	0
Bowie	7,295	4,418	8,243	11,333	33	39	14,798	6,657	102	38
Brazoria	12,031	11,289	16,420	15,292	345	47	25,342	15,096	392	164
Brazos	5,158	6,076	8,398	11,123	265	56	11,441	14,302	229	170
Brewster	986	687	763	1,165	490	5	1,610	894	12	29
Briscoe	574	217	585	413	0	2	888	175	0	3
Brooks	1,925	556	1,501	836	266	3	2,729	411	3	33
Brown	3,356	2,049	3,317	4,797	91	2	5,401	4,301	21	3
Burleson	1,884	585	1,821	1,244	15	1	2,955	889	8	4
Burnet	1,957	1,406	1,804	2,681	8	7	3,883	2,523	9	3
Caldwell	2,351	1,113	2,378	2,349	357	12	3,769	1,748	19	32
Calhoun	2,079	1,375	3,017	2,252	237	8	3,792	1,838	15	34
Callahan	1,553	638	1,316	1,637	1	1	2,499	1,221	16	0
Cameron	13,102	9,408	13,525	16,904	1,456	199	25,168	13,545	151	187
Camp	1,434	598	1,519	1,036	3	0	2,203	897	2	0
Carson	1,205	924	1,120	1,356	4	0	1,762	963	4	0
Cass	3,447	1,480	2,884	4,087	2	4	5,529	2,613	7	2
Castro	1,297	705	1,206	1,168	55	2	2,021	929	15	13
Chambers	1,433	1,029	1,953	1,640	6	11	3,341	1,358	64	8
Cherokee	4,093	2,042	3,915	4,291	1	11	6,978	3,074	10	4
Childress	1,444	729	1,127	1,301	1	5	1,727	726	1	0
Clay	1,780	732	1,568	1,391	1	2	2,664	834	0	8
Cochran	659	380	722	776	21	2	1,198	404	2	0
Coke	686	227	534	601	4	1	980	364	7	0
Coleman	1,737	830	1,266	1,850	23	2	2,546	1,259	8	1
Collin	7,202	5,426	8,599	13,814	96	15	15,473	19,393	240	54
Collingsworth	900	476	779	920	2	2	1,268	421	1	0
Colorado	1,883	1,774	2,283	2,672	15	5	3,630	2,107	28	6
Comal	2,428	2,884	2,614	5,619	234	11	5,128	4,974	31	30
Comanche	2,211	917	1,833	1,946	14	3	3,369	1,174	1	1
Concho	569	220	450	571	14	2	963	209	1	1
Cooke	3,100	2,442	3,207	4,811	11	4	4,315	4,800	11	2
Coryell	3,376	1,190	2,293	3,675	32	0	4,104	4,367	18	6
Cottle	933	225	781	361	1	0	1,091	192	7	0
Crane	636	489	606	837	11	4	847	513	204	13
Crockett	507	306	340	684	125	2	1,041	393	1	33
Crosby	1,498	519	1,234	1,140	115	2	2,328	559	6	26
Culberson	399	272	311	422	31	0	449	214	1	18
Dallam	780	620	692	860	7	3	1,129	724	7	1
Dallas	117,076	143,393	175,613	249,699	2,060	3,461	178,931	262,947	1,940	1,153
Dawson	1,833	1,419	1,475	2,505	87	2	2,746	1,624	3	12
DeWitt	2,006	1,790	2,016	2,961	46	4	2,994	2,249	4	8
Deaf Smith	1,697	1,549	1,930	2,742	149	11	1,474	2,146	15	26
Delta	1,100	253	839	641	4	3	17,307	478	1	0
Denton	7,279	6,898	13,665	14,505	234	71	2,868	20,852	108	161
Dickens	944	260	668	550	4	0	1,194	258	2	3
Dimmit	1,192	535	1,001	853	365	9	1,895	533	5	30
Donley	823	552	614	961	0	1	1,178	507	3	1
Duval	3,435	269	3,769	576	43	4	4,236	532	2	14

Table 23: Senatorial Races

General Elections, 1970-1976									
Year	**1970**		**1972**				**1976**			
County	Lloyd Bentsen(D)	George Bush (R)	Barefoot Sanders(D)	John G. Tower (R)	Flores Amaya (RZ)	Tom Leonard (S)	Lloyd Bentsn(D)	Alan Steelmn (R)	Marjorie P. Gallion (A)	Pedro Vasqs (SW)
Eastland	3,128	1,556	2,563	3,201	10	5	4,489	1,955	15	1
Ector	7,323	8,471	8,535	17,692	732	151	14,572	14,637	404	154
Edwards	244	198	171	438	5	0	385	231	0	0
El Paso	27,131	21,948	32,766	41,848	4,804	246	10,132	28,596	1,033	3,482
Ellis	5,456	2,843	5,753	6,101	58	9	57,759	6,286	45	14
Erath	2,838	1,675	2,535	3,872	9	10	5,045	2,533	16	4
Falls	2,352	919	2,493	2,223	50	3	4,240	1,790	13	7
Fannin	3,847	1,160	3,885	2,438	3	3	5,986	1,777	5	1
Fayette	2,632	1,981	2,090	3,138	11	2	4,102	2,014	13	3
Fisher	1,292	325	1,196	888	11	2	1,742	436	4	5
Floyd	1,644	977	1,276	1,699	32	2	2,229	990	3	11
Foard	550	154	452	244	1	1	758	148	0	1
Fort Bend	4,441	4,384	6,383	8,272	227	24	13,879	13,350	53	68
Franklin	1,156	301	815	694	3	0	1,718	567	1	0
Freestone	1,925	768	1,599	1,919	1	0	2,262	1,154	4	0
Frio	1,238	463	1,423	1,290	511	13	2,516	891	9	34
Gaines	1,382	881	1,132	1,722	31	9	2,098	1,271	5	5
Galveston	19,736	16,678	28,468	23,244	674	316	39,327	19,985	310	351
Garza	826	465	714	734	12	1	1,050	472	1	3
Gillespie	1,151	1,736	871	3,121	4	2	2,044	2,670	21	3
Glasscock	184	120	144	232	0	0	244	159	1	0
Goliad	730	496	622	779	40	2	1,017	580	0	3
Gonzales	2,040	1,009	1,691	2,050	33	12	3,218	1,237	6	11
Gray	3,353	4,490	2,983	6,297	8	17	4,810	4,649	15	3
Grayson	10,188	5,675	12,220	11,394	56	15	16,945	10,668	40	31
Gregg	6,762	8,545	8,028	16,577	30	269	10,743	14,936	81	30
Grimes	1,488	1,014	1,600	1,659	10	7	2,782	1,113	15	4
Guadalupe	3,995	3,430	4,797	6,511	397	23	6,501	5,717	31	26
Hale	3,701	3,301	3,234	5,683	136	21	6,161	4,267	10	35
Hall	1,185	486	944	942	0	0	1,739	465	2	1
Hamilton	1,268	776	1,055	1,518	3	2	1,781	1,251	5	0
Hansford	620	869	591	1,577	5	0	1,255	1,119	0	0
Hardeman	1,304	559	882	1,072	5	0	1,530	572	1	0
Hardin	3,924	1,899	4,119	3,583	13	8	7,094	3,012	40	4
Harris	142,400	215,750	273,800	291,416	5,215	2,273	337,970	295,074	2,588	3,044
Harrison	5,866	4,213	5,051	8,114	42	124	8,542	5,100	43	18
Hartley	516	388	474	689	0	0	950	563	2	1
Haskell	1,943	412	1,436	1,290	8	3	2,644	605	2	5
Hays	2,553	2,111	3,987	4,471	767	46	7,179	4,646	30	86
Hemphill	462	567	404	743	2	1	882	570	0	2
Henderson	3,665	2,010	4,210	4,738	7	5	8,067	4,298	15	4
Hidalgo	18,478	12,486	15,844	18,348	4,501	394	34,389	15,460	189	273
Hill	3,474	1,396	2,932	3,501	17	2	5,276	2,391	12	0
Hockley	2,763	1,573	2,672	2,985	85	7	4,629	2,117	2	21
Hood	1,198	435	1,356	1,288	2	4	3,059	1,712	11	4
Hopkins	3,356	1,294	3,028	2,609	5	5	5,070	2,205	10	1
Houston	3,091	1,242	2,754	2,333	4	10	3,648	1,249	7	7
Howard	4,255	2,883	4,196	5,683	209	5	7,438	4,197	16	16
Hudspeth	457	120	292	369	15	4	604	162	1	0
Hunt	5,796	3,573	6,106	7,117	46	25	8,319	6,149	34	19
Hutchinson	3,251	3,688	3,236	5,919	4	4	4,604	4,901	26	5
Irion	192	161	179	283	9	2	380	158	4	3
Jack	1,323	748	1,171	1,351	4	2	2,010	685	3	1
Jackson	1,921	1,344	1,884	1,937	18	5	2,635	1,546	9	11
Jasper	2,670	1,580	3,842	3,342	0	1	5,736	2,457	12	1
Jeff Davis	218	157	199	289	59	1	356	177	5	18
Jefferson	28,491	23,871	36,407	36,985	234	192	53,405	25,597	324	257
Jim Hogg	1,033	402	691	759	130	4	1,656	239	0	0
Jim Wells	4,685	2,184	4,922	3,759	445	13	8,459	2,571	15	36
Johnson	5,368	3,598	5,773	7,454	32	13	10,687	6,287	36	4
Jones	2,287	955	2,132	2,286	19	0	3,561	1,602	8	5
Karnes	2,123	874	2,079	1,959	194	8	3,264	1,178	15	14
Kaufman	3,813	1,838	4,226	3,867	9	5	6,388	3,456	7	2
Kendall	671	1,281	803	2,348	21	2	1,638	1,901	18	10
Kenedy	129	27	98	93	7	2	145	50	0	0

Table 23: Senatorial Races

General Elections, 1970-1976										
Year	1970		1972				1976			
County	Lloyd Bentsen(D)	George Bush (R)	Barefoot Sanders(D)	John G. Tower (R)	Flores Amaya (RZ)	Tom Leonard (S)	Lloyd Bentsn(D)	Alan Steelmn (R)	Marjorie P. Gallion (A)	Pedro Vasqs (SW)
Kent	414	92	362	318	1	0	491	121	0	0
Kerr	2,358	2,930	2,445	5,215	39	7	4,445	4,967	94	20
Kimble	653	374	471	739	16	0	1,002	385	5	6
King	138	25	107	115	0	0	128	52	0	0
Kinney	483	131	320	281	22	1	590	190	0	4
Kleberg	3,550	2,195	4,492	4,288	852	17	5,985	3,195	15	65
Knox	1,404	333	976	818	0	2	1,641	311	0	0
La Salle	920	265	674	656	585	1	8,003	391	8	19
Lamar	4,910	2,665	5,723	5,199	6	10	3,734	4,330	14	1
Lamb	2,299	1,774	2,221	3,026	94	10	2,256	1,703	4	19
Lampasas	1,329	644	1,150	1,772	4	3	1,074	1,466	9	5
Lavaca	2,385	1,308	2,416	2,138	4	4	3,879	1,786	11	1
Lee	1,300	745	1,226	1,527	6	3	2,153	804	3	2
Leon	1,630	519	1,201	1,260	1	4	2,084	811	6	0
Liberty	3,446	2,625	5,167	4,227	10	14	7,568	3,451	34	4
Limestone	2,834	1,095	2,198	1,999	7	2	3,839	1,818	10	2
Lipscomb	565	785	363	978	0	2	848	596	0	0
Live Oak	1,255	692	934	1,296	59	3	1,862	941	6	7
Llano	1,274	1,055	1,092	1,878	2	0	2,471	1,695	6	1
Loving	45	24	24	41	0	0	40	25	0	0
Lubbock	16,617	18,043	21,486	35,587	1,819	112	32,723	27,617	89	331
Lynn	1,303	626	1,101	1,265	57	0	1,973	665	0	7
Madison	990	630	976	1,075	2	1	1,982	748	7	1
Marion	1,138	632	1,280	1,331	1	0	2,020	813	3	0
Martin	605	333	524	695	13	0	1,030	440	3	2
Mason	588	568	507	927	23	1	964	577	7	3
Matagorda	3,211	2,591	3,611	3,344	123	7	5,429	2,874	39	23
Maverick	1,364	482	1,376	1,107	474	5	2,930	560	4	29
McCulloch	1,443	624	1,132	1,331	30	3	2,125	784	9	6
McLennan	20,996	12,125	23,136	25,593	675	80	30,595	23,741	124	86
McMullen	228	135	146	235	5	1	237	154	1	0
Medina	2,260	1,313	2,014	3,208	403	4	4,324	2,270	24	14
Menard	497	316	372	515	23	0	680	261	3	7
Midland	5,770	10,503	6,645	16,344	196	139	10,033	15,281	178	71
Milam	3,159	1,313	2,948	2,750	39	3	5,126	1,904	8	4
Mills	783	383	612	849	1	0	957	669	1	0
Mitchell	1,459	596	1,192	1,261	24	3	1,823	877	0	0
Montague	2,635	1,187	2,064	2,663	3	0	3,917	1,743	154	21
Montgomery	5,298	5,706	8,395	11,070	23	30	15,328	12,649	5	2
Moore	1,852	1,659	1,781	2,721	10	5	3,357	1,940	7	4
Morris	2,013	825	1,762	2,047	0	1	3,219	1,366	3	1
Motley	425	305	378	522	4	0	621	272	4	2
Nacogdoches	4,025	2,368	5,542	6,670	58	42	7,255	6,095	33	40
Navarro	5,051	2,059	5,029	4,270	10	8	7,212	3,264	8	11
Newton	1,746	576	2,142	1,241	5	9	3,372	717	5	3
Nolan	2,635	1,221	2,278	2,705	36	6	3,423	1,949	2	3
Nueces	24,596	16,332	33,529	35,625	4,239	341	54,940	27,339	292	409
Ochiltree	946	1,351	841	2,327	2	1	1,727	1,645	5	1
Oldham	354	278	421	440	1	1	519	266	9	0
Orange	8,149	5,620	10,784	9,585	18	15	16,202	7,338	92	6
Palo Pinto	3,976	1,984	2,576	4,560	23	8	5,320	2,367	27	5
Panola	2,584	1,357	2,472	3,249	8	7	4,354	2,103	8	0
Parker	4,925	2,716	4,503	5,685	27	3	8,281	4,275	47	5
Parmer	1,156	1,013	1,015	1,817	17	0	2,133	1,147	2	1
Pecos	1,768	1,151	1,305	1,857	148	6	2,421	1,505	38	40
Polk	2,031	959	2,759	1,978	1	3	4,458	1,803	32	2
Potter	8,937	9,405	10,087	14,781	161	65	14,692	10,337	230	102
Presidio	1,094	346	658	598	172	0	1,191	371	3	26
Rains	705	248	700	582	3	0	1,262	466	0	0
Randall	5,558	8,434	7,377	15,323	63	36	13,012	12,766	170	60
Reagan	524	305	420	510	11	1	783	402	1	1
Real	288	188	246	372	7	1	616	244	1	7
Red River	3,100	750	2,146	2,002	3	1	3,779	1,153	1	0
Reeves	1,515	907	1,419	1,905	403	7	2,416	1,258	11	88
Refugio	1,331	771	1,464	1,410	79	1	2,441	1,011	6	11
Roberts	215	257	177	368	0	0	278	252	2	0

Table 23: Senatorial Races

Year	1970		1972				1976			
County	Lloyd Bentsen(D)	George Bush (R)	Barefoot Sanders(D)	John G. Tower (R)	Flores Amaya (RZ)	Tom Leonard (S)	Lloyd Bentsn(D)	Alan Steelmn (R)	Marjorie P. Gallion (A)	Pedro Vasqs (SW)
Robertson	2,610	796	2,408	1,415	27	2	3,691	1,011	10	3
Rockwall	1,243	606	1,102	1,418	7	5	1,827	1,995	1	2
Runnels	1,743	995	1,426	2,085	119	2	2,727	1,198	1	0
Rusk	4,510	3,247	4,215	6,268	16	16	6,086	5,016	36	11
Sabine	1,391	400	1,244	941	4	0	2,464	608	2	1
San Augustine	1,048	365	1,058	1,147	1	5	2,012	651	4	0
San Jacinto	926	495	1,342	871	1	2	2,386	821	11	1
San Patricio	5,579	2,576	6,034	5,836	389	133	9,753	5,003	33	52
San Saba	1,075	384	837	850	6	1	1,426	514	4	1
Schleicher	411	281	356	503	7	1	638	305	8	5
Scurry	2,351	1,273	2,249	2,702	65	7	3,106	2,123	5	8
Shackelford	668	370	561	679	0	1	850	524	7	1
Shelby	3,023	947	2,965	3,111	3	1	5,472	1,473	3	1
Sherman	371	434	398	752	0	0	844	500	6	0
Smith	10,576	11,536	11,565	19,701	37	35	17,042	19,977	48	25
Somervell	441	186	476	457	7	1	1,002	361	3	0
Starr	3,306	2,215	3,363	1,938	212	6	4,630	474	4	7
Stephens	1,316	885	1,230	1,714	9	0	1,810	1,361	3	2
Sterling	215	103	151	228	1	0	247	121	0	0
Stonewall	752	152	625	436	4	0	862	182	2	0
Sutton	323	261	352	513	45	0	1,013	449	10	22
Swisher	1,717	695	1,838	1,245	22	1	2,867	590	3	1
Tarrant	67,073	66,698	89,521	125,936	564	2,586	125,385	109,663	1,440	660
Taylor	10,217	7,783	10,519	17,371	286	43	16,506	15,708	70	44
Terrell	197	211	195	350	44	0	406	185	4	1
Terry	1,753	1,206	1,762	2,257	113	4	3,235	1,468	2	15
Throckmorton	632	222	493	416	2	0	746	227	2	0
Titus	2,804	1,149	2,798	2,641	0	5	4,267	2,021	5	0
Tom Green	6,872	6,724	7,872	13,151	783	20	13,788	9,130	154	104
Travis	32,754	35,189	59,652	60,819	3,514	764	76,818	66,422	1,389	4,180
Trinity	1,176	579	1,236	1,008	1	1	2,311	566	12	1
Tyler	1,839	1,129	2,177	2,029	1	5	3,416	1,418	14	1
Upshur	3,404	1,712	2,952	3,575	4	9	4,884	2,664	9	4
Upton	701	521	494	910	26	5	900	571	7	12
Uvalde	1,916	1,372	1,860	2,910	547	4	3,090	2,028	11	37
Val Verde	2,959	1,161	2,398	2,809	816	12	5,494	2,252	22	26
Van Zandt	3,140	1,570	3,351	3,471	3	4	6,410	3,180	9	6
Victoria	6,331	4,810	6,794	7,955	472	19	7,952	8,406	49	92
Walker	2,105	1,979	4,515	4,062	96	30	5,560	3,902	43	40
Waller	1,424	950	1,985	1,704	3	1	3,106	1,469	17	5
Ward	1,972	1,158	1,550	1,906	172	1	2,159	1,814	11	12
Washington	2,042	2,097	2,190	2,973	3	9	3,826	2,377	8	5
Webb	6,985	2,228	8,256	4,102	1,223	19	10,359	2,453	33	139
Wharton	3,839	3,179	4,974	4,562	90	6	6,464	3,737	3	2
Wheeler	1,035	830	808	1,355	1	1	1,655	1,015	3	2
Wichita	17,227	10,032	15,480	21,294	198	30	25,647	14,321	68	41
Wilbarger	2,828	1,173	2,010	2,501	14	2	3,886	1,213	20	2
Willacy	2,027	974	1,337	1,802	376	22	3,178	1,096	1	19
Williamson	4,597	2,195	4,760	5,675	401	16	9,690	6,219	31	44
Wilson	2,199	779	2,466	2,140	209	6	3,934	1,432	11	6
Winkler	1,618	1,251	1,240	1,691	28	4	1,846	1,220	8	13
Wise	2,907	1,474	2,694	3,153	18	2	5,351	2,387	9	1
Wood	2,956	1,690	3,152	3,344	8	10	4,147	2,815	23	3
Yoakum	895	807	920	1,457	33	1	1,486	1,048	5	8
Young	2,746	1,374	2,304	2,597	2	0	3,924	1,988	12	1
Zapata	727	433	684	454	188	1	1,260	306	4	5
Zavala	1,134	504	1,009	901	1,886	19	1,467	429	6	36
Official Totals	1,226,568	1,071,234	1,511,985	1,822,877	63,543	14,464	2,199,956	1,636,370	17,355	20,549
Unofficial Totals	1,193,814	1,036,045	1,511,985	1,822,877	63,543	14,464	2,199,955	1,636,370	17,298	20,496

Table 24: Senatorial Races

General Elections, 1978-1984										
Year	1978				1982				1984	
County	Robert Krueger (D)	John G. Tower (R)	Luis A. Diaz deLen (RZ)	Miguel Pends (SW)	Lloyd Bentsen(D)	Jim Collins (R)	John E. Ford (LT)	Lineaus H. Lorett (CO)	Lloyd Doggett (D)	Phil Gramm (R)
Anderson	4,168	2,610	4	6	5,303	3,389	25	4	5,570	7,747
Andrews	936	1,190	3	2	1,328	1,337	17	4	1,058	3,660
Angelina	4,946	3,466	0	0	10,145	4,444	246	13	10,381	13,462
Aransas	1,087	1,316	11	5	2,059	1,670	30	5	1,948	4,008
Archer	985	609	0	0	1,380	1,025	6	0	1,371	2,173
Armstrong	341	359	1	0	456	404	5	1	299	725
Atascosa	2,023	2,067	27	2	3,589	2,153	13	5	3,981	4,710
Austin	1,673	1,787	3	1	2,589	1,845	17	1	2,247	4,467
Bailey	624	886	16	0	1,219	813	3	0	838	1,562
Bandera	1,053	1,558	1	4	1,102	1,499	14	4	1,019	2,866
Bastrop	2,555	1,901	13	6	4,638	2,038	42	10	5,534	5,547
Baylor	762	523	0	0	1,051	610	7	1	1,142	1,158
Bee	1,370	1,815	52	3	3,339	1,947	62	6	3,955	4,899
Bell	9,398	9,179	193	27	12,382	9,256	278	26	15,754	27,911
Bexar	84,569	79,889	2,013	771	112,538	78,403	1,086	425	151,535	178,958
Blanco	698	775	3	0	964	835	9	2	921	1,706
Borden	145	158	1	0	205	129	1	0	148	310
Bosque	1,932	1,635	4	0	2,592	1,644	11	1	2,395	3,583
Bowie	5,816	5,671	45	10	10,328	6,180	286	17	12,098	16,350
Brazoria	11,645	10,964	88	21	18,186	12,737	210	28	22,343	36,487
Brazos	7,267	7,479	152	31	10,718	8,153	361	26	13,595	33,786
Brewster	743	713	12	2	1,262	816	19	2	1,587	1,835
Briscoe	452	295	1	0	709	234	3	0	542	477
Brooks	1,230	408	22	2	2,537	370	8	3	2,760	684
Brown	3,657	2,777	0	1	5,306	2,851	13	4	4,461	8,031
Burleson	1,696	674	8	1	2,547	824	15	1	2,829	2,786
Burnet	2,563	2,228	10	3	3,481	2,163	20	2	3,558	4,817
Caldwell	2,191	1,711	40	9	3,697	1,633	20	6	3,901	3,741
Calhoun	2,072	1,446	35	2	3,402	1,880	30	1	3,116	3,884
Callahan	1,504	1,212	0	0	1,908	1,265	14	2	1,554	3,275
Cameron	11,813	11,093	407	88	21,236	12,127	207	77	27,781	26,010
Camp	1,018	641	2	0	1,860	846	7	1	2,094	2,006
Carson	964	850	1	0	1,301	1,103	12	1	998	2,229
Cass	3,394	2,534	3	2	5,517	2,416	23	3	5,402	5,938
Castro	1,343	1,093	42	1	1,633	879	8	1	1,153	1,824
Chambers	1,351	1,080	8	3	2,893	1,368	30	7	3,168	4,000
Cherokee	3,549	2,340	5	1	5,139	2,676	17	8	5,143	7,165
Childress	881	675	1	0	1,098	686	6	0	997	1,449
Clay	1,509	841	0	0	2,380	1,083	2	0	2,106	2,281
Cochran	597	596	6	1	952	491	11	1	648	957
Coke	777	443	0	0	751	430	8	0	611	965
Coleman	1,157	1,173	1	1	1,989	1,017	10	0	1,659	2,509
Collin	8,299	12,101	45	20	14,853	22,775	301	41	17,673	56,349
Collingsworth	707	520	2	2	898	454	3	0	810	1,219
Colorado	1,581	1,553	7	1	2,637	1,647	18	1	2,639	3,966
Comal	3,552	4,502	19	5	4,337	5,715	144	12	5,146	12,478
Comanche	1,711	954	2	2	2,785	980	10	0	2,430	2,504
Concho	594	342	2	2	759	301	0	0	679	702
Cooke	2,493	2,875	5	1	4,126	3,382	25	3	3,794	7,592
Coryell	2,311	2,609	8	2	3,607	2,343	17	1	4,130	2,920
Cottle	508	323	2	0	743	215	13	1	661	466
Crane	503	503	0	1	773	788	9	0	501	1,338
Crockett	449	440	8	1	486	394	5	0	566	1,051
Crosby	1,256	837	34	1	1,537	428	11	3	1,319	1,242
Culberson	315	368	17	4	611	278	4	0	400	457
Dallam	524	614	2	1	696	650	7	3	596	1,455
Dallas	117,076	142,290	2,011	484	150,799	145,968	2,002	310	229,649	371,128
Dawson	1,772	1,909	110	11	2,451	1,349	16	1	1,855	3,465
DeWitt	1,531	1,801	11	2	2,276	2,013	8	1	2,093	4,063
Deaf Smith	1,459	1,926	53	6	2,196	2,210	14	5	1,751	4,379
Delta	751	330	0	0	1,177	323	2	3	1,070	888
Denton	10,375	10,826	93	22	15,210	17,793	455	73	20,915	48,325
Dickens	728	314	7	0	894	221	1	0	749	508
Dimmit	1,316	840	34	4	2,240	628	3	3	2,598	1,171

Table 24: Senatorial Races

General Elections, 1978-1984											
Year	1978				1982				1984		
County	Robert Krueger (D)	John G. Tower (R)	Luis A. Diaz deLen (RZ)	Miguel Pends (SW)	Lloyd Bentsen(D)	Jim Collins (R)	John E. Ford (LT)	Lineaus H. Lorett (CO)	Lloyd Doggett (D)	Phil Gramm (R)	
Donley	603	579	0	2	776	491	7	1	608	1,179	
Duval	2,324	535	35	2	3,395	417	27	12	3,756	1,037	
Eastland	2,198	1,789	9	3	3,603	1,848	17	2	2,808	4,518	
Ector	7,446	11,007	255	33	9,627	13,633	210	51	10,644	29,352	
Edwards	236	303	0	2	243	315	3	1	209	545	
El Paso	28,233	25,324	0	0	44,793	24,387	866	154	59,741	57,696	
Ellis	4,902	4,009	10	2	8,212	4,898	43	4	8,983	15,832	
Erath	2,395	2,240	4	2	4,291	2,226	25	1	3,785	5,574	
Falls	2,474	1,448	6	4	3,046	1,183	10	2	3,117	2,733	
Fannin	4,233	1,863	5	2	5,577	1,704	16	2	4,895	4,130	
Fayette	2,072	1,753	3	3	3,346	2,035	11	2	2,906	4,934	
Fisher	1,051	629	7	0	1,564	337	6	1	1,427	903	
Floyd	1,244	984	4	0	1,396	763	5	0	1,158	1,922	
Foard	581	216	1	0	610	175	1	1	492	398	
Fort Bend	7,508	11,229	156	24	14,325	13,347	168	38	21,701	37,425	
Franklin	690	378	0	0	1,275	550	10	0	1,207	1,703	
Freestone	1,522	1,144	1	1	2,478	1,280	11	0	2,697	3,407	
Frio	1,561	1,286	202	7	2,374	937	7	4	2,673	1,800	
Gaines	1,266	1,244	16	4	1,157	960	17	3	1,047	2,453	
Galveston	17,560	12,469	305	73	29,875	13,187	891	91	38,525	36,266	
Garza	478	471	4	0	653	393	5	0	597	1,097	
Gillespie	1,076	2,444	6	2	1,631	2,817	21	5	1,457	5,239	
Glasscock	166	249	1	0	210	225	2	0	153	372	
Goliad	548	565	3	1	1,044	727	8	0	891	1,402	
Gonzales	1,540	1,321	6	0	2,282	1,294	16	0	2,420	3,541	
Gray	2,657	3,703	6	2	3,168	4,409	36	9	2,454	8,408	
Grayson	7,278	6,144	30	13	13,588	7,237	496	28	13,886	20,327	
Gregg	6,557	9,920	63	12	10,464	13,079	609	28	12,346	27,004	
Grimes	1,983	1,184	12	1	2,259	1,043	11	0	2,502	3,148	
Guadalupe	3,565	5,050	38	3	6,293	5,677	47	7	6,191	12,961	
Hale	3,023	3,430	76	13	4,050	3,471	34	4	3,292	7,150	
Hall	739	471	1	0	1,230	412	4	0	1,044	894	
Hamilton	1,074	985	0	0	1,554	915	9	0	1,354	1,882	
Hansford	487	989	0	0	751	943	4	1	365	2,073	
Hardeman	1,112	691	4	0	1,109	466	6	0	960	1,034	
Hardin	5,146	3,065	4	4	7,179	2,809	43	3	7,453	7,706	
Harris	155,075	192,381	2,277	800	270,753	195,718	3,360	669	367,293	493,518	
Harrison	3,913	4,369	54	12	7,153	4,565	180	13	8,161	11,566	
Hartley	584	627	2	0	648	687	3	0	424	1,341	
Haskell	1,404	937	0	0	1,824	501	8	3	1,528	1,540	
Hays	3,460	2,600	56	10	5,683	3,303	78	37	8,684	10,435	
Hemphill	379	545	0	1	662	638	5	0	496	1,498	
Henderson	4,558	3,408	9	1	7,789	3,840	43	3	8,492	11,380	
Hidalgo	16,321	13,730	581	84	34,482	13,597	236	94	44,702	31,792	
Hill	2,551	1,965	7	0	4,301	2,073	14	3	3,690	5,095	
Hockley	2,503	1,931	28	4	2,639	1,708	36	9	2,535	4,980	
Hood	1,714	1,516	1	1	3,475	2,450	16	1	3,489	6,398	
Hopkins	2,557	1,618	3	0	4,398	1,815	18	1	3,975	5,416	
Houston	2,893	1,119	2	0	3,809	1,457	15	1	3,593	4,065	
Howard	2,997	3,226	95	9	5,216	3,046	49	6	4,676	6,944	
Hudspeth	218	231	9	0	338	204	4	1	387	439	
Hunt	4,139	3,583	7	2	7,917	4,627	59	10	8,293	12,795	
Hutchinson	2,946	3,571	4	2	3,362	4,092	41	7	2,633	8,400	
Irion	195	172	1	0	300	226	4	0	266	544	
Jack	859	664	2	0	1,338	714	5	0	1,097	1,653	
Jackson	1,664	1,231	7	0	2,494	1,476	11	3	2,085	3,230	
Jasper	2,723	1,833	2	1	5,231	1,829	19	2	6,363	5,228	
Jeff Davis	225	226	3	0	296	244	2	0	306	409	
Jefferson	23,599	16,582	116	69	41,329	16,623	399	49	58,903	41,322	
Jim Hogg	995	628	18	1	1,572	179	2	2	1,791	442	
Jim Wells	3,269	2,117	62	10	6,717	2,135	53	4	8,124	5,233	
Johnson	5,682	4,572	6	4	10,462	6,159	70	5	10,335	17,174	
Jones	2,352	1,656	12	2	2,987	1,367	13	0	2,636	3,687	
Karnes	1,353	1,408	14	3	2,139	1,296	4	3	1,960	2,771	
Kaufman	3,392	2,332	3	4	6,426	3,209	45	2	6,456	8,329	
Kendall	1,165	2,074	5	1	1,231	2,479	22	1	1,196	4,367	

Table 24: Senatorial Races

General Elections, 1978-1984										
Year	1978				1982				1984	
County	Robert Krueger (D)	John G. Tower (R)	Luis A. Diaz deLen (RZ)	Miguel Pends (SW)	Lloyd Bentsen(D)	Jim Collins (R)	John E. Ford (LT)	Lineaus H. Lorett (CO)	Lloyd Doggett (D)	Phil Gramm (R)
Kenedy	70	58	0	0	168	27	0	0	110	83
Kent	307	180	2	0	454	134	2	0	273	309
Kerr	2,937	4,690	6	0	3,570	5,441	35	1	3,701	10,897
Kimble	574	604	3	2	610	494	5	0	474	1,271
King	51	90	0	0	127	74	1	0	69	124
Kinney	232	311	1	0	634	333	6	1	569	616
Kleberg	2,531	2,117	134	9	4,254	1,955	75	15	5,014	5,218
Knox	826	467	2	0	1,150	344	2	1	1,055	875
La Salle	1,153	658	67	4	1,768	516	5	1	1,526	827
Lamar	5,054	2,587	5	3	7,183	2,755	18	7	6,650	7,979
Lamb	1,953	2,006	29	5	2,441	1,357	21	1	2,163	3,533
Lampasas	1,178	1,277	5	1	1,786	1,110	6	1	1,624	2,994
Lavaca	2,101	1,461	4	1	2,982	1,810	8	0	2,891	4,488
Lee	976	802	1	0	1,884	915	6	1	2,004	2,582
Leon	1,186	736	2	0	1,850	852	7	2	1,992	2,957
Liberty	3,453	2,734	5	1	6,954	3,269	48	5	7,071	9,490
Limestone	2,397	1,659	0	0	3,412	1,463	9	1	3,393	3,861
Lipscomb	309	590	0	0	487	632	5	0	346	1,321
Live Oak	797	1,008	3	0	1,300	1,084	5	3	1,404	2,280
Llano	1,679	1,489	3	0	2,493	1,837	11	1	2,270	3,628
Loving	20	36	0	0	25	31	0	0	15	55
Lubbock	15,068	20,473	506	63	22,216	22,276	344	41	22,779	53,612
Lynn	1,122	824	14	2	1,378	632	7	1	1,167	1,446
Madison	877	608	4	6	1,465	638	5	0	1,532	1,954
Marion	1,033	753	1	1	1,872	908	13	1	2,248	2,066
Martin	443	560	5	2	623	468	3	2	569	1,142
Mason	629	695	1	3	564	614	2	0	627	1,097
Matagorda	2,529	2,243	10	1	4,172	2,437	40	4	5,792	7,752
Maverick	1,582	603	46	4	2,877	553	23	12	3,117	1,495
McCulloch	1,182	905	2	1	1,850	824	4	0	1,519	1,959
McLennan	17,241	16,526	87	12	24,619	16,501	191	35	26,289	39,067
McMullen	126	204	1	0	153	157	2	1	67	325
Medina	1,947	2,717	26	2	3,188	2,592	26	5	3,416	5,223
Menard	479	290	1	0	508	298	1	0	454	504
Midland	5,448	12,672	116	19	7,119	14,581	204	26	8,281	32,078
Milam	2,892	1,579	8	3	4,177	1,587	16	3	4,251	3,798
Mills	682	518	1	1	941	509	6	3	730	1,016
Mitchell	1,142	645	2	1	1,581	670	12	1	1,506	1,788
Montague	1,978	1,406	1	1	3,232	1,505	17	6	2,855	4,117
Montgomery	6,349	8,116	36	14	14,850	13,965	187	36	15,704	38,188
Moore	1,430	1,465	3	0	1,805	1,849	15	2	1,419	4,303
Morris	1,491	1,174	1	0	3,035	1,075	7	1	3,086	2,545
Motley	281	379	2	0	401	268	3	2	324	475
Nacogdoches	3,449	2,901	24	14	5,456	3,779	138	13	6,705	12,079
Navarro	3,939	2,639	5	2	5,899	2,549	24	5	6,177	7,231
Newton	1,401	497	1	1	2,987	560	10	1	3,538	1,791
Nolan	1,654	1,867	8	0	2,787	1,388	20	1	2,664	3,319
Nueces	24,306	22,076	750	116	42,713	19,817	399	143	49,232	49,784
Ochiltree	462	1,316	1	0	891	1,841	8	1	558	3,304
Oldham	339	337	0	0	385	302	3	0	295	662
Orange	7,465	4,503	3	5	14,874	5,470	153	9	18,156	13,647
Palo Pinto	2,512	1,982	0	1	4,378	2,144	24	3	3,865	5,161
Panola	2,055	1,631	1	0	3,277	1,960	17	4	3,689	4,995
Parker	4,158	3,622	6	1	7,247	4,697	79	8	7,274	12,309
Parmer	954	1,376	4	0	1,094	1,324	6	0	723	2,340
Pecos	1,495	1,158	23	1	1,567	1,448	20	4	1,934	3,034
Polk	2,156	1,419	4	1	4,084	1,802	121	2	4,457	5,416
Potter	7,133	7,343	101	19	9,638	8,547	337	29	9,824	19,273
Presidio	505	388	24	13	955	375	9	1	963	737
Rains	594	375	0	0	1,349	510	15	1	1,235	1,316
Randall	5,882	9,794	40	5	8,746	12,972	109	26	7,774	28,578
Reagan	436	363	2	0	574	436	2	0	322	989
Real	482	414	20	1	699	578	8	1	462	847
Red River	1,634	1,008	1	1	3,122	946	2	2	2,756	2,559
Reeves	1,701	1,211	269	35	2,548	1,047	29	10	2,504	2,228

Table 24: Senatorial Races

General Elections, 1978-1984										
Year	1978				1982				1984	
County	Robert Krueger (D)	John G. Tower (R)	Luis A. Diaz deLen (RZ)	Miguel Pends (SW)	Lloyd Bentsen(D)	Jim Collins (R)	John E. Ford (LT)	Lineaus H. Lorett (CO)	Lloyd Doggett (D)	Phil Gramm (R)
Refugio	1,741	1,127	16	5	1,605	791	5	2	1,738	2,147
Roberts	153	231	0	0	208	244	4	0	138	498
Robertson	1,980	767	1	2	2,954	800	12	2	3,470	2,489
Rockwall	1,219	1,541	1	1	2,197	2,813	23	4	2,090	6,172
Runnels	1,464	1,345	2	3	1,780	1,162	9	3	1,464	2,653
Rusk	2,679	3,422	14	15	4,659	4,610	33	13	5,481	10,042
Sabine	1,002	544	2	1	1,742	654	6	0	2,106	1,816
San Augustine	1,082	601	2	0	1,573	601	5	2	1,764	1,667
San Jacinto	1,011	701	1	1	2,419	803	26	1	2,605	2,852
San Patricio	4,138	4,057	145	23	7,629	3,840	230	26	9,160	10,327
San Saba	918	586	5	0	1,190	471	2	0	1,195	1,406
Schleicher	397	380	4	0	461	342	2	0	394	771
Scurry	1,440	1,907	20	4	2,076	1,802	28	4	1,753	4,829
Shackelford	517	486	0	0	650	481	5	0	496	1,087
Shelby	2,177	1,479	3	1	3,359	1,362	10	0	4,023	4,278
Sherman	451	499	1	0	420	580	4	1	333	1,148
Smith	10,161	13,481	33	15	14,471	17,667	142	12	18,261	37,613
Somervell	700	365	2	0	939	364	8	1	826	1,159
Starr	3,192	856	28	4	4,921	567	12	5	5,194	1,290
Stephens	913	1,012	2	0	1,548	1,155	17	0	1,164	2,750
Sterling	191	163	0	0	258	213	0	0	185	488
Stonewall	436	230	1	0	774	170	5	2	695	519
Sutton	455	470	3	1	614	503	5	0	503	1,195
Swisher	1,892	790	7	2	2,310	583	11	0	1,817	1,370
Tarrant	62,725	69,124	528	235	115,079	93,376	1,248	260	135,541	228,117
Taylor	9,801	11,906	58	19	13,936	13,136	136	21	11,771	32,290
Terrell	182	231	5	2	359	218	3	0	315	357
Terry	1,550	1,486	17	2	2,037	1,389	14	4	1,551	3,056
Throckmorton	397	216	0	1	475	213	1	0	421	557
Titus	1,997	1,511	1	0	4,150	1,914	10	1	4,143	4,466
TomGreen	7,191	6,280	38	8	10,998	7,972	84	19	11,111	21,840
Travis	45,754	40,610	1,197	366	82,431	41,124	2,131	1,006	117,518	101,337
Trinity	1,240	639	0	0	2,387	681	10	5	2,380	2,238
Tyler	1,633	1,049	1	0	2,916	1,151	13	1	3,398	3,286
Upshur	2,387	1,983	3	2	4,540	2,447	21	0	5,315	6,473
Upton	479	522	3	0	557	472	6	0	522	1,361
Uvalde	1,699	2,646	59	4	3,083	2,413	10	1	2,778	4,309
Val Verde	2,569	2,059	14	1	3,870	1,894	14	2	4,405	5,065
Van Zandt	3,618	2,508	4	2	5,602	3,241	37	4	5,307	7,564
Victoria	5,062	6,084	142	16	7,537	7,682	172	22	7,579	17,241
Walker	2,751	2,569	4	2	4,881	2,753	51	5	4,964	7,998
Waller	1,649	1,387	5	4	2,940	1,710	15	3	4,133	3,843
Ward	1,147	1,202	11	3	1,509	1,486	18	9	1,478	3,257
Washington	1,821	2,024	3	2	3,901	2,711	13	2	2,970	5,964
Webb	5,498	2,703	428	27	10,847	2,494	95	3	15,032	6,370
Wharton	3,447	3,103	18	3	6,471	3,217	23	3	5,876	7,630
Wheeler	837	809	0	0	1,144	957	3	0	954	2,024
Wichita	10,226	10,280	37	18	16,537	10,068	739	35	18,986	25,856
Wilbarger	1,608	1,375	2	0	2,928	1,469	15	3	2,287	3,264
Willacy	1,287	1,163	27	6	2,652	1,110	19	1	3,128	2,077
Williamson	5,828	6,092	33	10	10,870	7,895	161	34	13,434	21,931
Wilson	1,746	1,533	7	2	2,686	1,797	6	0	3,150	4,044
Winkler	1,199	1,129	16	2	1,128	1,021	6	4	860	2,083
Wise	2,452	1,888	2	1	4,460	2,103	25	2	4,523	6,260
Wood	2,397	2,013	5	5	3,865	2,930	17	0	4,026	6,454
Yoakum	721	867	13	0	893	889	19	1	656	1,996
Young	1,967	1,720	3	1	2,867	2,259	14	2	2,627	4,823
Zapata	747	414	6	0	1,391	427	5	2	1,723	962
Zavala	1,303	676	2,088	4	1,912	369	4	0	2,849	712
Official Totals	1,139,149	1,151,376	17,869	4,018	1,818,223	1,256,759	23,494	4,564	2,202,557	3,111,348
Unofficial Totals	1,139,149	1,151,376	17,869	4,018	1,818,223	1,256,759	23,494	4,564	2,202,556	3,111,248

Table 25: Senatorial Races

	General Elections, 1988-1990					
Year	1988			1990		
County	Lloyd Bentsen (D)	Beau Boulter (R)	Jeffi Daiell (LT)	Phil Gramm (R)	Hugh Parmer (D)	Gary Johnsn (LT)
Anderson	8,506	5,378	114	6,263	3,826	167
Andrews	2,034	2,281	30	2,152	530	48
Angelina	15,044	8,153	405	9,522	6,828	259
Aransas	3,340	2,780	49	3,229	1,416	112
Archer	2,042	1,543	5	1,813	1,194	42
Armstrong	474	542	9	523	209	25
Atascosa	5,978	3,251	110	3,920	2,622	210
Austin	3,758	3,174	29	3,890	1,706	78
Bailey	1,186	1,074	9	1,163	530	24
Bandera	1,996	2,483	55	2,474	985	176
Bastrop	10,067	3,367	148	4,842	5,206	335
Baylor	1,327	699	6	669	733	15
Bee	5,811	3,282	45	3,814	2,838	103
Bell	23,442	20,841	463	18,596	12,590	631
Bexar	211,845	139,956	3,288	124,138	87,040	7,174
Blanco	1,516	1,071	19	1,441	790	87
Borden	229	200	1	258	109	6
Bosque	3,369	2,611	23	2,891	2,167	59
Bowie	17,490	9,318	358	10,211	6,935	474
Brazoria	32,467	23,914	935	27,430	14,763	1,141
Brazos	25,490	17,774	383	22,233	9,120	663
Brewster	2,088	1,084	42	1,328	819	77
Briscoe	724	319	2	403	401	8
Brooks	3,115	333	26	592	1,463	34
Brown	6,783	4,764	67	5,651	3,333	115
Burleson	3,844	1,341	23	2,219	1,956	42
Burnet	5,794	3,323	53	4,254	3,359	146
Caldwell	5,612	2,127	69	2,903	3,140	173
Calhoun	4,276	2,187	56	3,392	2,118	89
Callahan	2,729	1,888	14	2,636	1,319	51
Cameron	33,574	17,304	324	18,211	14,367	914
Camp	2,769	1,136	10	1,496	1,345	24
Carson	1,563	1,526	3	1,661	921	53
Cass	7,660	3,070	25	3,885	3,355	63
Castro	1,838	1,180	11	1,362	742	27
Chambers	4,310	2,379	78	2,986	1,809	107
Cherokee	7,839	4,755	64	5,774	3,262	124
Childress	1,205	1,027	8	965	668	12
Clay	2,543	1,571	8	1,709	1,506	30
Cochran	894	537	5	643	361	30
Coke	971	523	4	787	395	20
Coleman	2,633	1,579	5	1,921	1,018	24
Collin	39,508	50,602	768	54,151	15,516	2,125
Collingsworth	1,021	638	1	630	495	9
Colorado	3,850	2,552	18	3,380	1,850	74
Comal	8,561	10,911	292	10,193	4,093	626
Comanche	3,225	1,413	9	1,773	1,773	50
Concho	895	339	3	577	357	15
Cooke	5,621	5,350	51	5,359	2,651	170
Coryell	6,008	5,334	74	4,666	3,340	176
Cottle	777	299	1	260	474	14
Crane	955	810	9	1,218	419	20
Crockett	1,213	486	8	752	245	18
Crosby	1,677	794	4	1,008	725	24
Culberson	664	216	5	369	225	15
Dallam	903	907	11	910	453	34
Dallas	322,712	256,302	4,997	254,951	153,363	11,660
Dawson	2,902	2,070	18	2,611	994	42
DeWitt	3,266	2,774	35	3,056	1,327	60
Deaf Smith	2,879	2,806	42	2,896	1,158	91
Delta	1,514	518	9	753	678	10
Denton	39,661	43,263	889	41,751	17,132	2,010
Dickens	790	328	5	406	474	7
Dimmit	2,843	571	16	1,266	2,012	44

Table 25: Senatorial Races

General Elections, 1988-1990					
Year	1988			1990		
County	Lloyd Bentsen (D)	Beau Boulter (R)	Jeffj Daiell (LT)	Phil Gramm (R)	Hugh Parmer (D)	Gary Johnsn (LT)
Donley	863	818	11	814	484	18
Duval	4,272	598	21	797	2,895	36
Eastland	4,055	2,802	34	3,429	2,096	98
Ector	17,166	17,706	244	17,238	5,521	463
Edwards	436	342	3	581	184	15
El Paso	84,022	34,393	1,155	45,185	29,033	2,046
Ellis	15,658	11,750	161	14,227	7,751	530
Erath	5,549	3,770	42	4,279	2,645	143
Falls	3,102	1,769	10	1,963	2,399	38
Fannin	6,422	2,611	49	2,859	3,239	111
Fayette	4,896	2,819	28	4,630	2,456	119
Fisher	1,636	409	5	742	965	16
Floyd	1,622	1,498	8	1,608	745	11
Foard	583	237	3	232	379	2
Fort Bend	35,925	27,068	447	32,115	15,310	797
Franklin	1,939	828	9	1,255	896	29
Freestone	3,623	2,327	24	2,729	1,838	53
Frio	3,305	1,087	23	1,252	1,279	43
Gaines	2,024	1,715	32	1,666	647	41
Galveston	48,452	24,095	570	26,576	24,138	1,241
Garza	1,177	817	10	829	429	17
Gillespie	2,604	4,567	71	4,284	1,297	207
Glasscock	269	240	3	407	95	6
Goliad	1,601	994	14	1,306	601	24
Gonzales	3,708	1,845	39	2,546	1,379	48
Gray	3,732	6,020	103	6,043	1,942	203
Grayson	19,825	13,258	301	13,551	8,910	543
Gregg	18,383	17,874	534	18,485	1,850	530
Grimes	3,621	1,756	27	2,361	1,565	61
Guadalupe	10,316	9,915	228	10,111	4,587	586
Hale	4,876	4,866	41	4,632	1,905	71
Hall	1,192	527	3	596	636	12
Hamilton	1,731	1,264	9	1,636	1,211	52
Hansford	975	1,506	8	1,677	347	32
Hardeman	1,305	657	4	641	714	12
Hardin	10,621	3,854	64	5,497	3,868	176
Harris	473,429	317,656	6,230	327,411	203,551	11,277
Harrison	11,991	7,175	364	8,688	5,611	254
Hartley	778	939	15	1,115	430	18
Haskell	2,126	738	7	1,216	1,123	22
Hays	15,569	6,922	527	9,081	7,823	588
Hemphill	779	891	9	1,120	376	27
Henderson	12,349	8,270	148	9,711	7,163	312
Hidalgo	59,198	21,030	374	23,882	23,369	1,374
Hill	5,407	3,573	23	4,158	3,330	152
Hockley	3,773	3,531	66	3,412	1,389	114
Hood	5,788	5,737	87	6,169	3,558	238
Hopkins	6,834	2,939	24	4,515	3,381	80
Houston	5,020	2,328	38	3,536	2,305	· 43
Howard	6,375	4,447	75	4,332	2,583	143
Hudspeth	527	215	4	350	183	6
Hunt	12,034	8,849	144	9,814	5,584	344
Hutchinson	4,491	5,994	89	6,014	2,377	197
Irion	563	273	2	436	152	13
Jack	1,949	1,012	8	1,188	847	38
Jackson	2,791	2,076	26	2,496	1,203	36
Jasper	8,559	2,916	74	3,915	3,362	117
Jeff Davis	479	321	19	449	179	15
Jefferson	68,487	21,819	741	32,018	30,431	895
Jim Hogg	1,807	230	4	567	1,081	16
Jim Wells	10,110	2,635	54	3,455	4,372	64
Johnson	16,846	13,045	226	14,388	8,909	662
Jones	3,746	1,914	31	2,546	1,583	45
Karnes	3,119	1,621	15	1,958	1,136	63
Kaufman	9,697	6,177	161	6,992	4,861	361

Table 25: Senatorial Races

	General Elections, 1988-1990					
Year	1988			1990		
County	Lloyd Bentsen (D)	Beau Boulter (R)	Jeff Daiell (LT)	Phil Gramm (R)	Hugh Parmer (D)	Gary Johnsn (LT)
Kendall	2,321	3,736	88	3,617	1,043	183
Kenedy	148	32	0	84	59	5
Kent	467	178	3	319	243	13
Kerr	5,433	9,130	142	7,477	2,791	447
Kimble	800	707	7	1,115	370	33
King	89	84	0	121	59	2
Kinney	823	465	8	631	392	25
Kleberg	6,422	2,839	164	3,257	2,800	93
Knox	1,229	520	4	680	733	14
La Salle	1,760	422	11	513	969	16
Lamar	10,486	4,693	37	6,110	4,490	72
Lamb	2,841	2,330	17	2,313	1,136	45
Lampasas	2,752	1,875	25	2,129	1,535	52
Lavaca	4,742	2,805	39	3,128	2,017	76
Lee	3,270	1,424	32	2,446	1,648	44
Leon	3,125	1,803	18	2,411	1,503	40
Liberty	10,883	5,802	117	6,873	4,613	193
Limestone	4,162	2,478	18	2,505	2,502	55
Lipscomb	549	929	10	885	307	26
Live Oak	2,187	1,541	32	1,724	830	59
Llano	3,564	2,709	29	3,271	2,215	89
Loving	38	34	0	62	19	1
Lubbock	32,163	42,901	440	38,147	12,526	877
Lynn	1,467	856	6	1,049	612	20
Madison	2,450	1,141	8	293	290	4
Marion	2,749	1,186	20	1,730	1,348	54
Martin	950	609	3	838	333	11
Mason	916	666	6	840	422	22
Matagorda	7,815	4,497	93	5,310	3,547	151
Maverick	4,716	914	24	2,147	2,486	112
McCulloch	2,116	1,026	20	1,610	912	21
McLennan	35,136	30,683	373	28,094	22,121	631
McMullen	166	202	3	249	74	3
Medina	5,645	3,956	72	4,358	2,317	205
Menard	743	364	3	593	319	10
Midland	14,252	24,556	277	24,496	5,379	776
Milam	5,888	2,305	27	2,907	3,787	83
Mills	1,082	737	5	858	686	35
Mitchell	2,245	910	29	1,490	896	19
Montague	4,585	2,469	18	2,799	2,032	88
Montgomery	28,521	29,828	477	31,806	12,266	942
Moore	2,451	2,823	44	3,167	1,191	84
Morris	4,304	1,108	11	1,704	2,107	38
Motley	304	361	3	403	192	8
Nacogdoches	10,865	7,390	387	8,365	4,056	268
Navarro	8,169	4,769	32	5,826	4,508	196
Newton	4,209	853	19	1,246	1,862	37
Nolan	3,763	1,802	35	2,561	1,583	87
Nueces	60,920	29,594	668	36,102	23,711	1,199
Ochiltree	1,048	2,392	17	2,386	399	53
Oldham	508	475	4	512	224	15
Orange	22,374	7,016	263	9,954	9,628	379
Palo Pinto	5,012	3,383	46	3,705	2,715	142
Panola	5,850	2,754	29	3,417	2,566	79
Parker	12,254	10,200	172	11,245	6,224	553
Parmer	1,286	1,490	14	1,417	678	38
Pecos	2,882	1,688	29	2,471	1,416	82
Polk	7,443	4,046	208	4,869	3,839	182
Potter	12,491	13,356	266	12,991	6,493	549
Presidio	1,314	361	11	649	933	20
Rains	1,734	882	9	1,097	926	31
Randall	13,987	22,658	229	22,460	6,156	518
Reagan	736	568	4	864	173	3
Real	621	553	11	785	299	27
Red River	4,041	1,361	14	1,948	1,888	44

Table 25: Senatorial Races

General Elections, 1988-1990					
Year	**1988**			**1990**	
County	Lloyd Bentsen (D)	Beau Boulter (R)	Jeff Daiell (LT)	Phil Gramm (R)	Hugh Parmer (D)	Gary Johnsn (LT)
Reeves	3,375	1,200	29	1,536	1,360	45
Refugio	2,415	1,155	12	1,670	1,073	40
Roberts	226	345	4	393	123	8
Robertson	4,212	1,491	14	2,001	2,601	43
Rockwall	4,546	5,322	88	5,660	1,851	226
Runnels	2,585	1,397	13	2,132	946	44
Rusk	7,898	5,970	143	7,413	3,361	182
Sabine	2,602	1,115	18	1,555	1,414	44
San Augustine	2,741	997	29	1,500	1,291	54
San Jacinto	3,592	1,888	28	2,239	1,708	74
San Patricio	11,678	6,038	381	6,492	4,525	229
San Saba	1,462	683	17	801	729	15
Schleicher	702	398	10	620	240	7
Scurry	3,355	2,754	35	3,000	1,059	63
Shackelford	983	605	7	776	334	15
Shelby	6,033	1,886	33	3,090	2,334	153
Sherman	607	840	13	749	281	57
Smith	27,769	25,954	423	27,984	12,025	786
Somervell	1,326	814	17	1,107	666	59
Starr	7,128	729	20	988	3,144	54
Stephens	2,185	1,538	18	1,967	826	35
Sterling	336	275	2	396	80	5
Stonewall	848	358	6	386	437	11
Sutton	915	562	8	764	259	6
Swisher	2,301	851	11	1,027	1,244	27
Tarrant	210,852	178,721	2,868	175,629	104,985	8,147
Taylor	21,273	19,557	532	21,220	7,603	485
Terrell	443	174	2	242	213	5
Terry	2,471	1,960	14	2,268	1,087	53
Throckmorton	665	323	1	424	327	13
Titus	6,140	2,177	14	3,215	2,460	58
Tom Green	19,573	13,700	444	16,730	6,321	434
Travis	170,403	60,029	2,789	87,145	98,983	5,833
Trinity	3,431	1,412	32	2,008	1,567	41
Tyler	5,230	1,633	44	2,480	2,139	59
Upshur	7,074	3,709	42	4,755	3,391	152
Upton	954	679	16	1,010	261	25
Uvalde	4,710	2,727	54	3,384	1,923	99
Val Verde	6,412	3,376	42	3,394	3,125	125
Van Zandt	8,025	5,140	51	6,221	4,014	165
Victoria	12,226	10,610	296	12,750	5,001	256
Walker	8,491	5,373	96	6,810	3,452	177
Waller	5,068	2,470	67	3,271	3,012	73
Ward	2,827	1,853	34	2,185	996	65
Washington	4,588	4,241	41	6,069	2,490	108
Webb	19,312	3,782	199	6,982	7,026	285
Wharton	8,398	4,496	88	5,629	3,250	114
Wheeler	1,371	1,361	7	1,458	689	29
Wichita	22,869	18,174	371	18,038	12,002	588
Wilbarger	3,004	1,846	9	1,974	1,441	29
Willacy	3,513	1,200	25	1,719	1,814	56
Williamson	30,211	16,288	419	23,068	15,033	1,033
Wilson	5,069	2,921	46	3,746	2,664	162
Winkler	1,462	1,231	12	1,247	494	28
Wise	6,722	4,265	47	4,957	3,993	276
Wood	6,217	4,290	40	5,425	2,869	183
Yoakum	1,171	1,429	18	1,172	436	34
Young	4,105	2,896	30	3,862	1,918	76
Zapata	2,340	598	14	767	889	12
Zavala	3,377	394	7	531	1,777	20
Official Totals	3,149,806	2,129,228	43,989	2,302,357	1,429,986	89,089
Unofficial Totals	**3,149,806**	**2,129,228**	**43,989**	**2,302,357**	**1,429,986**	**89,089**

Senatorial Candidates in Texas

Two hundred and thirteen men and women have run for the U.S. Senate in Texas since the office became elective in 1916. Democrats had required candidates to stand for election in primaries before 1916. Charles A. Culberson was the first senator to be directly elected. Morris Sheppard gained office after winning the 1912 primary. The candidates are:

Adams, Elmer; 1957 sp; none; m.
Alford, James F.; 1948 dp; dem; m.
Allen, G.H.; 1961 sp; none; m.
Allred, James V.; 1942 dp; dem; m.
Amaya, Flores; 1972 gen; raza; m.
Amos, Jim W.; 1961 sp; none; m.
Anderson, Darryl; 1982 gen; w-i; m.
Antoine Sr., H.J.; 1957 sp; none; m.
Atcheson, Alex W.; 1916 gen; rep; m.
*Bailey, Joseph W.; 1906, 1934 dp; dem; m.
Baker, Dale; 1961 sp; none; m.
Banks, M.T.; 1957 sp; none; m.
Barraco, Mali J.R.; 1961 sp; none; f.
Barton, Tom E.; 1961 sp; none; m.
Becker, R.G.; 1961 sp; none; m.
Beckworth, Lindley; 1952 dp; dem; m.
Belcher, A.P.; 1940 dp; dem; m .
*Bentsen, Lloyd; 1970, 1976, 1982, 1988 dp; gen;
   dem; m.
Bergolofsky, Jacob; 1957 sp, 1961 sp; none; m.
Berry, W.A.; 1930 gen; com; m.
Bisland, Ted; 1961 sp; none; m.
Blakley, William A.; 1958 dp, 1961 sp; dem; m.
Blanton, Thomas L.; 1928 dp; dem; m.
Blewett, G. E.; 1961 sp; none; m .
Bosworth Jr., Lawrence S.; 1961 sp; none; m.
Boulter, Beau; 1988 rp, gen; rep; m.
Bracewell, Searcy; 1957 sp; none; m.
Bradshaw, Joyce J; 1961 sp; none; f.
Brooks, Chester D.; 1961 sp; none; m.
Brooks, Homer; 1940 gen; const; m.
Brooks, S.P.; 1916 dp; dem; m.
Burlison, W. L.; 1961 sp; none; m.
Burns Sr., John C.; 1957 sp; none; m.
Bush, George; 1964, 1970 rp, gen; rep; m.
Bush, Richard C.; 1936 dp; dem; m.
Byers, Ronald J.; 1961 sp; none; m.
Campbell, Tom M.; 1916 dp; dem; m.
Carr, Waggoner; 1966 dp, gen; dem; m.
Carswell, Jack; 1964 gen; const; m.
Carter, Joseph M.; 1961 sp; none; m.
Cartlidge, Thomas M.; 1972 dp; dem; m.
Christie, Joe; 1978 dp; dem; m.
Clark, F.B.; 1948 dp; dem; m.
Collier, Roscoe H.; 1948 dp; dem; m.
Collins, Jim; 1982 rp, gen; rep; m.
Colquitt, O.B.; 1916 dp; dem; m.
Conibear, E.H.; 1916 gen; proh; m.
Connally, H. Frank Jr.; 1957sp; none; m.
*Connally, Tom; 1928, 1934, 1940, 1946 dp, gen;
   dem; m.
Cortez, Frank G.; 1948 dp, 1957 sp; dem; m.
Courtney, J. Cal; 1957;sp; none; m.

Cox, Jack; 1964 rp; rep; m.
*Culberson, Charles A.; 1910 dp, gen, 1916 dp,
   gen, 1922 dp; dem; m.
Cunningham, Minnie F.; 1928 dp; dem; f.
Curran, David; 1928 gen; soc; m.
Currin, R. W.; 1957 sp; none; m.
*Daniel, Price; 1952 dp, rp, gen; dem; m.
Davis, Cyclone; 1946, 1948 dp; dem; m.
Davis, Fred W.; 1924 dp; dem; m.
Davis, John; 1916 dp; dem; m.
Davis, Milton V.; 1964 rp; rep; m.
Davisson, George A.; 1961 sp; none; m.
Derrick, Winnie K.; 1961 sp; none; f.
Diaz de Leon, Luis A.; 1978 gen; raza; m.
Diehl, Harry R.; 1961 sp; none; m.
Dies, Martin; 1941, 1957 sp; dem; m.
Doggett, Lloyd; 1984 dp; dem; m.
Dougherty, Dudley T.; 1954 dp; dem; m.
Dugi, Leon; 1976 dp; dem; m.
Eagle, Joe H.; 1936 dp; dem; m.
Eaton, Harvill O.; 1961 sp; none; m.
Eckman, Jonnie Mae; 1961 sp; none; f.
Eix, Paul F.; 1961 sp; none; m.
Faber, Ben H.; 1961 sp; none; m.
Fanning, H.E.; 1961 sp; none; m.
Ferguson, James E.; 1922 dp; dem; m.
Fisher, Guy B.; 1934, 1936, 1940 dp; dem; m.
Flanagan, J. Webster; 1918 gen; rep; m.
Foerster Jr., Charles O.; 1957, 1961 sp; none; m.
Ford, Curtis; 1957 sp; none; m.
Ford, John E.; 1982 gen; lib; m.
Fox, Milton E.; 1988 rp; rep; m.
Franklin, Harold; 1961 sp; none; m.
Gallagher Jr., George N.; 1961 sp; none; m.
Gallion, Marjorie; 1976 gen; am; f.
Gay, Richard J.; 1961 sp; none; m.
George, Van T., Jr.; 1961 sp; none; m.
Gilbreath, Wes; 1988 rp; rep; m.
Glenn, J. Edward; 1936 dp; dem; m.
Glover, Arthur; 1961 sp; none; m.
Goen, U.S.; 1934 gen; rep; m.
Gonzalez, Henry B.; 1961 sp; none; m.
*Gramm, Phil; 1976 dp; 1984, rp, gen; dem, rep;
   m.
Grandstaff, Delbert E.; 1961 sp; none; m.
Grover, Henry; 1984 rp; rep; m.
Haesly, Doran John; 1930 rp, rep; m.
Haines, Harve H; 1930 rp; rep; m.
Hammonds, Ralph W.; 1957 sp; none; m.
Hance, Kent; 1984 dp; dem; m.
Harris, C.O.; 1930 rp; rep; m.
Hart, James P.; 1957 sp; none; m.
Henry, Robert L.; 1916, 1922, 1930 dp; dem; m.

Hickey, T.A.; 1916 gen; soc; m.
Hill, Charles W.; 1957 sp; none; m.
Hill, Curtis E.; 1961 sp; none; m.
Holland, J. Barker; 1966 gen; const; m.
Holland, Willard Park; 1961 sp; none; m.
Hopkins, John N.; 1961 sp; none; m.
Houston, Mary Hazel; 1961 sp; none; f.
Hutcheson, Thad; 1957 sp; none; m.
Johnson, Ben M.; 1961 sp; none; m.
Johnson, Gary; 1990 gen; lib; m.
Johnson, Guy; 1961 sp; none; m.
*Johnson, Lyndon B.; 1941 sp, 1948, 1954, 1960 dp, gen; dem; m.
Johnson, Morgan H.; 1961 sp; none; m.
Keel, L.C.; 1934 gen; com; m.
Kennedy, C.B.; 1961 sp; none; m.
Kennerly, T.M.; 1924, 1928 gen; rep; m.
Knoblauch, H. Springer; 1961 sp; none; m.
Krueger, Robert; 1978 dp, gen; 1984 dp; dem; m.
Lawson, Dudley; 1942 gen; rep; m.
Lea, Hugh O.; 1961 sp; none; m.
Leman, Louis; 1976 rp; rep; m.
Leonard, Tom; 1972 gen; soc; m.
Logan, Bard A.; 1958, 1960 gen; const; m.
Logan, V.C.; 1961 sp; none; m.
Lorette, Lineaus H.; 1982 gen; const; m.
Maddox, John F.; 1924 dp; dem; m.
Mann, Gerald C.; 1941 sp; dem; m.
Matera, Frank A.; 1961 sp; none; m.
Maverick Jr., Maury; 1961 sp; none; m.
*Mayfield, Earle B.; 1922 dp, gen, 1928 dp; dem; m.
McCallum, Brown; 1961 sp; none; m.
McKee, James E.; 1961 sp; none; m.
McLemore, Jeff; 1928 dp; dem; m.
McLendon, Gordon; 1964 dp; dem; m.
McNutt, Walter S.; 1957 sp; none; m.
Mengden Jr., Walter; 1982 rp; rep; m.
Mitchner, C.A.; 1930 dp; dem; m.
Moody, Dan; 1942 dp; dem; m.
Morris, Robert; 1964, 1970 rp; rep; m.
Morris, Sam; 1948 gen; proh; m.
Mosbacher, Robert; 1984 rp; rep; m.
Myers, Otis C.; 1948 dp; dem; m.
Napier, E.W.; 1952 dp; dem; m.
Nemecek, Steve; 1961 sp; none; m.
Noyes, George E.; 1961 sp; none; m.
*O'Daniel, W. Lee; 1941 sp, 1942 dp, gen; dem; m.
Orms, Clyde R.; 1957 sp; none; m.
Ousley, Clarence; 1922 dp; dem; m.
Owsley, Alvin; 1928 dp; dem; m.
Parmer, Hugh; 1990 dp, gen; dem; m.
Paul, Ron; 1984 rp; rep; m.
Payne, Floyd; 1961 sp; none; m.
Peddy, George E.B.; 1922 gen, 1948 dp; rep, dem; m.
Pendas, Miguel; 1978 gen; socwor; m.
Perkins, Cecil D.; 1961 sp; none; m.
Porter, Jack; 1948 gen; rep; m.
Posey, W.H.; 1961 sp; none; m.
Price, Joseph H.; 1936 dp; dem; m.
Randall, Choice B.; 1912 dp; dem; m.

Red, George; 1961 sp; none; m.
Richardson, Don L.; 1982 rp; rep; m.
Riddle, G.W.; 1916 dp; dem; m.
Roberts, Wesley; 1961 sp; none; m.
Rust, John; 1928 gen; com; m.
Ryan, Floyd E.; 1942, 1946 dp; dem; m.
Sampson, D.T.; 1961 sp; none; m.
Sams, Eristus; 1961 sp; none; m.
Sanders, Barefoot; 1972 dp, gen; dem; m.
Saunders, Jesse C.; 1948 dp; dem; m.
Savage, A. Dale; 1961 sp; none; m.
Schlanger, Harley; 1984, 1990dp; dem; m.
Schrade, Carl A.; 1961 sp; none; m.
Sells, Murray C.; 1946 gen; rep; m.
Shannon, George; 1940 gen; rep; m.
*Sheppard, Morris; 1912 dp, 1918, 1924, 1930, 1936 dp, gen; dem; m.
Sledge, Terrell; 1946, 1948 dp; dem; m.
Smith, Albert Roy; 1961 sp; none; m.
Smith, Guy L.; 1930 gen; soc; m.
Smith, M.A.; 1918 gen; soc; m .
Snead, Ned; 1988 rp; rep; m.
Somerville, Charles; 1942 gen; pup; m.
Sommerville, Laverne; 1946 dp; dem; f.
Spangler, Fred T.; 1954 gen; const; m.
Stalarow, Homer Hyrim; 1961 sp; none; m.
Stanford, Frank; 1961 sp; none; m.
Starr, W.B.; 1934, 1936 gen; soc; m.
Steelman, Alan; 1976 rp, gen; rep; m.
Stevenson, Coke; 1948 dp; dem; m.
Strong, Sterling P.; 1922 dp; dem; m.
Sullivan, Joe; 1982, 1988 dp; dem; m.
Sullivan, Robert; 1984 dp; dem; m.
Sweeney, Hugh; 1976 rp; rep; m.
Sypert, John B.; 1961 sp; none; m.
Thomas, Cullen F.; 1922 dp; dem; m.
*Tower, John G.; 1961 sp, 1966, 1972, 1978 rp, gen; rep; m.
Tredway, Martha; 1961 sp; none; f.
Vasques, Pedro; 1976 gen; socwor; m.
Vela, S.S.; 1961 sp; none; m.
Veloz, Alfonso; 1972 dp; dem; m.
Watson, Carlos G.; 1936, 1954 gen; rep; m.
White, John C.; 1957 sp; none; m.
Whitten, Bill; 1961 sp; none; m.
Whittenburg, Roy; 1958 gen; rep; m.
Willoughby, John R.; 1966 dp; dem; m.
Wills, J. Perrin; 1957 sp; none; m.
Wilson, Gertrude; 1936 gen; union; f.
Wilson, Hoyt G.; 1961 sp; none; m.
Wilson, Hugh; 1957, 1961 sp, 1972, 1976 dp; dem; m.
Wilson, Will; 1961 sp; none; m.
Wolters, Jacob F.; 1912 dp; dem; m.
Wright, Jim; 1961 sp; none; m.
*Yarborough, Ralph W.; 1957 sp, 1958, 1964, dp, gen; 1970, 1972 dp; dem; m.
Young, David; 1984 dp; dem; m.
Zertuche, Marcos; 1961 sp; none; m.
Zollner, Matthew; 1912 dp; dem; m.

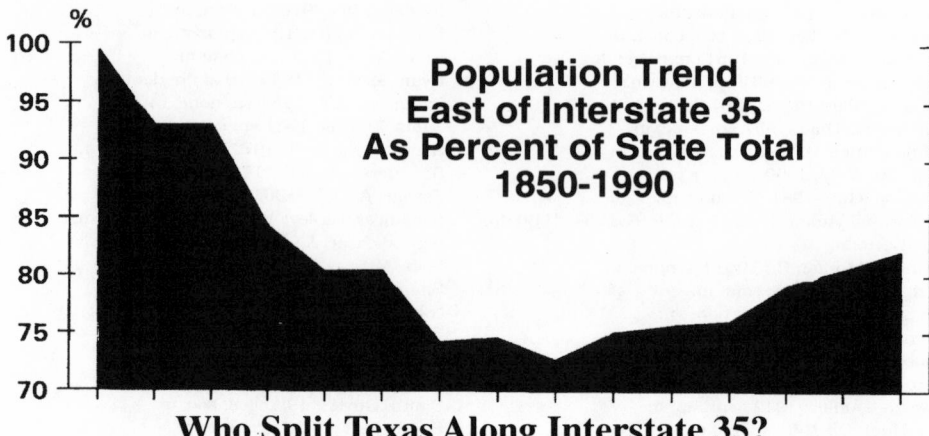

Population Trend
East of Interstate 35
As Percent of State Total
1850-1990

Who Split Texas Along Interstate 35?

There is a definite division in Texas. It is along Interstate Highway 35 that enters the state from Oklahoma just north of Denton and ends at Laredo after pushing through several population centers. Dallas and Fort Worth both claim parts of I-35. Waco, Austin and San Antonio all host the route and Laredo is one of the key border cities in Texas.

West Texans sometimes talk as if there was a conspiracy afoot in the state to deny them their proper role in running the state and in sharing in the state's programs. Fact is, that most of the people in Texas are east of I-35, as is the money, business activity, and, probably most important, the water. The area west of I-35 produces more oil.

Some demographics on the facing page show the dramatic division of "the action" in the state in several categories. The population chart above reveals the population trend in which Texas east of I-35 is gaining population faster than the other section of the state. The population imbalance has not been so great in a century.

But who split the state? As popular as the idea might be, it was not a conspiracy. Most of the highway runs along the route of the Republic of Texas' Central Road that ran from Preston (now under the waters of Lake Texoma) through Dallas to Waco and then southward to Austin and San Antonio. The southern leg from San Antonio to Laredo generally follows another well-used route of the 19th century.

The Central Road was a frontier route in the 1840s when the Republic planned it. As with many projects, funding was not available to do the whole job, but a beginning was made. The route was used by many settler as a springboard to moving into western Texas.

Western Texas gave the state its frontier image. But even in the best of times, the eastern part of the state has been the most populous. After that, everything else falls into place — along I-35, the state's main street.

Table 1:

Interstate 35 Split Demographics

General Demographics

Category	West of I-35	Pct.	East of I-35	Pct
No. Counties	135	53.1	119	46.9
Population	3,038,519	17.9	13,957,991	82.1
Area (mi. sq.)	158,607	59.0	109,991	41.0
Water Area (mi. sq.)	624	9.3	6,050	90.7
Population Density	19	12.4	134	87.6
Retail Sales (1990)	$19,818,055,684	14.9	$112,952,511,464	85.1
Civilian Labor Force	1,381,425	16.4	7,061,646	83.6
Registered Voters	1,637,647	20.5	6,334,152	79.5
Total Income (1989)	$42,199,000,000	16.0	$221,346,000,000	84.0
Per Capita Income	$13,934	46.8	$15,858	53.2
Total Wages	$17,660,528,505	11.6	$134,002,512,821	88.4
Weekly Wage	$245.85	40.2	$364.93	59.8
Housing(Units)	1,238,459	17.7	5,747,871	82.3
Banks	348	29.4	835	70.6
Bank Deposits	$21,421,793,000	14.9	$122,268,371,000	85.1
Bank Assets	$24,058,019,000	14.2	$144,864,371,000	85.8
Jobless Rate (%)	6.6	52.0	6.1	48.0
Gross Sales	$45,905,859,857	11.8	$343,655,294,021	88.2
Vehicles	2,639,749	18.9	11,325,415	81.1
Highway Lane Miles	79,995	44.0	101,670	56.0
Tax Values	$136,717,278,710	19.1	$579,385,251,502	80.9
Federal Spending	$9,665,829,000	17.3	$46,286,226,000	82.7
Defense Spending	$21,421,793	0.2	$13,172,030,000	99.8

Ethnicity

	West of I-35	Pct.	East of I-35	Pct
Total Population	3,038,519	17.9	13,957,991	82.1
White	2,479,911	19.4	10,294,851	80.6
Black	130,121	6.4	1,891,511	93.6
American Indian	14,388	21.8	51,489	78.2
Asian	24,378	7.6	295,081	92.4
Other	379,721	21.0	1,425,059	79.0
Hispanics	961,058	22.1	3,378,847	77.9

Vital Statistics (1989)

	West of I-35	Pct.	East of I-35	Pct
Births	54,076	17.6	253,464	82.4
Deaths	25,368	20.4	99,195	79.6
Marriages	32,834	19.2	138,103	80.8
Divorces	16,234	17.4	77,200	82.6

Voting Age Population History

	West of I-35	Pct.	East of I-35	Pct
1900	144,669	19.6	593,099	80.4
1910	258,513	25.8	744,844	74.2
1920	615,604	25.3	1,815,111	74.7
1930	847,320	26.1	2,401,967	73.9
1940	958,270	24.5	2,951,236	75.5
1950	1,133,399	23.9	3,603,826	76.1
1960	1,320,215	23.9	4,214,062	76.1
1970	1,504,568	20.9	5,692,326	79.1
1980	1,918,667	19.3	8,004,418	80.7
1990	2,142,029	17.6	10,008,642	82.4

10

Women Not Political Newcomers

With Ann Richards' election as governor in 1990, a new era for women in Texas politics began. The day after her victory, she vowed she would open doors to women and minorities in an administration that would represent a "sociological change, not just government change."

After a 50-year suffrage movement, Texas became the ninth state and the first in the South to ratify the 19th Amendment giving women the right to vote in 1919. Since then women have made sporadic progress in breaking into the male-dominated world of Texas politics.

After the 1990 elections, Texas had a woman governor and a woman state treasurer. Females filled 23 of the 181 legislative seats, including a record four in the 31-member State Senate. The 100-year-old, three-member Texas Railroad Commission had its first woman commissioner, Lena Guerrero. And at one point in 1991, there were women mayors in 11 major cities, a 1,000 percent increase from 1981 when only one major city had a female mayor.

The progress of women in the macho state prompted the National Women's Political Caucus to call Gov. Richards' New Texas "a role model state for women candidates." But it was a long time coming.

Annie Webb Blanton, who was the first woman ever elected president of the Texas State Teachers Association, broke the gender barrier in Texas for a statewide office in 1918. She was elected to the statewide post of State Superintendent of Public Instruction with the help of women who had been granted the right to vote in Democratic Party primaries only days before the election.

Miriam "Ma" Ferguson became the first female governor of the state when she was elected to the Governor's office in Texas in 1924. She was subsequently elected to another term in 1932. However, "Ma" Ferguson was not elected in her own right. Her husband, Jim "Pa" Ferguson, had served as governor before being impeached and convicted.

He managed both of his wife's campaigns. And she campaigned on the theme of "two governors for the price of one." Ironically, her husband was one of the most ardent opponents of the suffrage movement.

Ann Richards became the first woman elected to the coveted governor's office on her own right with her victory over Republican Clayton Williams in 1990. With women rallying behind her and Williams branded a sexist because of some of his comments about women, Ms. Richards was able to overcome an early 20-point deficit in the public opinion polls for a victory. Ms. Richards, a longtime supporter of women's rights, had twice been elected state treasurer in 1982 and 1986 before she ran for governor. Prior to her election, she gained national fame with her folksy keynote speech at the Democratic National Convention in 1988.

One of Ms. Richards' mentors, Barbara Jordan, was the first black woman to give a keynote speech to the Democratic National Convention in 1976. It was one of many political firsts for Ms. Jordan. In 1966, she was elected to the State Senate, becoming the first black woman to serve in that body. In 1972, she became the first black congresswoman from the Deep South. Her booming oratory during the 1974 Watergate impeachment hearings and during her national convention keynote speech gave her national prominence.

Ms. Jordan was not the first woman to deliver a keynote speech to a national convention. That honor went to longtime Republican activist Anne Armstrong of Texas. Mrs. Armstrong was the keynoter at the Republican National Convention in Miami in 1972.

Texas women were also trailblazers at other national conventions. Dallas Democrat Sarah T. Hughes, who was the state's first female state district and federal judge, was the first woman nominated for vice president in 1952. But "Sissy" Farenthold became the first woman nominated and voted on at the Democratic National Convention in 1972.

Kay Bailey Hutchison of Dallas twice made her mark on Republican politics. While a Houston resident, she was the first GOP woman elected to the Texas House in 1972. And then in 1990, she became the first Republican woman elected to a statewide office when she succeeded Ms. Richards as State Treasurer.

The gender barrier was broken in the Texas Legislature two years after women were granted the right to vote in 1920. Edith Wilmans of Dallas was elected to the Texas House in 1922. The first woman to serve in the Texas Senate was Margie Neal of Carthage, who won election in 1926. Irma Rangel of Kingsville became the first Hispanic woman to serve in the Legislature with her election in 1972.

Only two women have served as members of Congress from Texas. Lera Thomas of Houston was the first in 1966 when she won a special election to fill the vacancy left by the death of her husband, Albert. Ms Jordan is the only other woman from Texas to serve in Congress.

Barbara Jordan, left, was the first African-American to serve in the U.S. Congress from Texas since Reconstruction when she was elected from a district in Houston after redistricting in the 1960s. Lena Guerrero was a state representative when Gov. Ann Richards selected her to fill a vacancy on the Texas Railroad Commission. The body had been exclusively a man's domain since it was created a century ago to regulate railroads. Dallas News Photos.

In her book *Texas Women A Pictorial History*, Ruthe Winegarten notes that even before women earned the right to vote, they were serving in political office. Ms. Winegarten wrote that the first woman officeholder in Texas was Mrs. L.P. Carlisle, who was appointed as county clerk of Hunt County to succeed her husband in 1902.

This article was written by Sam Attlesey, political writer for The Dallas Morning News.

11

Scandals, Scams and Scamps

Texas' tradition for down and dirty politics can be traced to scandals, scams and scamps.

Ballot Box 13, Sharpstown, Brilab. The Duke of Duval and Don Yarbrough, Mike Martin and Rocky Mountain. The Dirty 30, the Killer Bees and the beer-drinking presidential petition forgery parties. Bad turkey sandwiches and cattle rustling. They have all played their part in checkering and coloring the Lone Star State's rich political lore.

Ballot Box 13 is the most infamous event in a long list of political schemes and scams in Texas. The ballad of Ballot Box 13 can begin or conclude with a story that has many versions and that reportedly was repeatedly told by Lyndon B. Johnson.

This is the version related by historian and political consultant Frank A. Driskill: In a small South Texas town, a Mexican-American boy sat on a curb and cried. A merchant walked by and asked the lad named Carlos why he was crying. Carlos said he was sad because his grandfather came to town the day before and did not come by to visit him. The merchant said the boy was mixed up because his grandfather had been dead for five years. But Carlos insisted his grandfather had been in town. He must have been in town. He had voted for Lyndon Johnson.

"Landslide Lyndon" became a U.S. Senator in 1948 with an 87-vote-margin victory in a Democratic primary runoff because of Ballot Box 13 in the small town of Alice in Jim Wells County.

Several days after the runoff election between Johnson and Coke Stevenson, an amended vote tally from Box 13 showed Johnson had received an extra 202 votes and Stevenson had picked up only one more vote. The votes for Johnson were cast in alphabetical order. The signatures on the ballots were in the same handwriting and with the same pen. And many of the people shown as casting votes either had

House Speaker Gus Mutscher was toppled from leadership and later faced criminal charges for his role in the Sharpstown scandal that rocked Texas politics in the early 1970s. Mutscher later served as a county judge. Billy Clayton, also a speaker of the Texas House, also faced criminal charges during his record tenure in the 1980s, but he was acquitted. Dallas Morning News Photos.

not paid their poll taxes or were dead.

Despite court challenges and investigations by the Texas Rangers, the election results were upheld. Ballot Box 13 propelled Johnson to a Senate career that would ultimately result in his becoming president of the United States. The contested final results gave Stevenson 494,104 votes and Johnson 494,191, thanks to the late reporting of 202 votes from Ballot Box 13.

Johnson's margin of victory became widely known as "the 87 votes that changed history." But Johnson biographer Robert Caro in his book *Means of Ascent* documents that thousands of votes across the state were stolen for Johnson in the Aug. 28, 1948, runoff.

In defense of LBJ, many of his modern-day supporters say that Johnson believed the 1941 special Senate election was stolen from him, and he vowed that it would not happen again.

Ballot Box 13 was the most notorious legacy of the legendary Duke of Duval, George B. Parr, whose political machine controlled at least 13 and as many as 30 counties in South Texas.

Historians say Parr, the longtime county judge in Duval County, would give away money, food and medical services to mostly poor and illiterate Hispanics in exchange for votes for his hand-picked lieutenants on election day.

His political operatives would teach voters unable to read English how to cast ballots for Parr-backed candidates. One method was string voting, in which a voter would be given a string with knots in it. The string would be placed over the paper ballot, and voters were told to cast their ballots for the candidates where the knots appeared. Another technique was line voting. If a Parr-backed contender appeared on the third line of the ballot, voters were told to count down three lines and cast their vote for that candidate.

Allegations and suspicions of voter fraud, vote stealing and Election Day mischief have been common throughout Texas' political history. "Walking around money" and "vote early, vote often" have become part of the state's political lexicon.

For example, Richard M. Nixon and state Republicans have long suspected he lost Texas by 46,233 votes in the 1960 presidential contest because of voter theft. Some of his aides wanted him to ask for a recount, but he declined.

Election fraud became an issue in the 1988 presidential race when massive forgeries were discovered on the presidential nominating petitions of three Republican candidates, Pete du Pont, Bob Dole and Alexander Haig.

Forgeries also were found on the petitions used by Democratic candidate Jesse Jackson to qualify for a place on the ballot.

The Republican petitions contained signatures of dead people, of Texans who were nowhere near the state when they allegedly signed the documents and of Democrats who said they would never sign a GOP petition or who said they had never heard of du Pont, Dole or Haig. The petition scam ignited a grand jury investigation, forced du Pont to withdraw from the Texas primary and created widespread embarrassment for the state Republican Party.

Southern Political Consulting of Houston and the firm's vice president, Rocky Mountain, were convicted on 38 counts each of misdemeanor forgery involving the petitions for du Pont.

Testimony in the June 1988 trial in San Marcos indicated that the firm and Mountain arranged a forgery party in December 1987. Teenagers were hired, given free beer and told to fake names on the nominating petitions.

In sentencing the firm and Mountain, Harris County Court-at-law Judge Sherman Ross said, "At the grass-roots level, the most important level of politics, we have to maintain the integrity of the system. We can't corrupt the system at the grass-roots," the judge said. "I hope this message rolls like thunder across the country."

It wasn't rolling thunder but rather the famous flight of the killer bees that grabbed national attention in another scheme involving presidential politics in May 1979. In an effort to break a quorum in the State

Senate, a dozen Democratic senators eluded the Texas Rangers, state troopers and the press for nearly five days.

The liberal legislators' successful game of hide-and-seek effectively killed a proposed bill that would have benefited presidential hopefuls John Connally and Ronald Reagan. The legislation would have created a separate presidential primary for the state in the 1980 race for the White House. Under the proposal, conservative Democrats would have been able to crossover to the GOP primary to vote for Connally or Reagan and then return to a separate regular Democratic primary to vote for local and legislative candidates.

The killer bee senators realized the only way they could kill the bill in the final days of the session was to break a quorum. So they buzzed away for four and one-half days. Nine stowed away in a cramped West Austin apartment. One hid in Houston, one in Mexico and another in South Texas.

The killer bees included Chet Brooks, Ron Clower, Lloyd Doggett, Glenn Kothmann, Raul Longoria, Gene Jones, Oscar Mauzy, Carl Parker, Bill Patman, Babe Schwartz, Carlos Truan and Bob Vale.

They had earned their nickname from the presiding officer of the Senate, Lt. Gov. Bill Hobby, who said of the senators, "You never know where they're going to hit next." The senators who stayed in session and repeatedly blasted the killer bees dubbed themselves the "worker bees." Law enforcement officers, who failed to capture any of the killer bees and even mistakenly arrested the brother of Gene Jones, were branded the "bumble bees."

The dozen liberal senators, who finally returned to the Senate chamber as conquering heroes after killing the split primary bill, had pulled off one of the most successful schemes in Texas political history.

The Sharpstown Bank stock scandal of 1971 changed the course of Texas politics forever. It destroyed or blunted the aspirations of some of the state's most prominent politicians, and it sparked significant legislative change thanks to a group of reform-minded lawmakers called the Dirty 30.

Several top state officials were suspected of receiving favors from Houston banker Frank Sharp in return for having legislation he favored considered in a 1969 special legislative session.

An investigation by the Securities and Exchange Commission, grand jury probes, indictments, convictions and suspicions took a monumental toll on state leaders. House Speaker Gus Mutscher, his aide Rush McGinty and state Rep. Tommy Shannon were found guilty of conspiring to accept a bribe from Sharp, who pleaded guilty to two minor charges in exchange for immunity.

Attorney General Waggoner Carr was also named in the scandal. Even though he was acquitted of all charges, his political career was destroyed. Gov. Preston Smith and Lt. Gov. Ben Barnes were never directly linked to the scandal, but the Sharpstown affair also damaged their political ambitions. In the 1972 Democratic gubernatorial primary, Smith finished fourth and Barnes ran third. Voters also reacted to the scandal by turning 76 veteran legislators out of office.

Meanwhile, in the Texas House an unlikely coalition of liberal Democrats and conservative Republicans was forming to fight the Mutscher machine. The Dirty 30 legislators were led by Corpus Christi Democrat Frances "Sissy" Farenthold, who ran for governor in 1972 and finished ahead of both Barnes and Smith before ultimately losing to Dolph Briscoe in a runoff. The Dirty 30 successfully fought to limit the power of the speaker and ultimately the coalition was responsible for passage of laws governing financial disclosure for public officials, open records and lobby registration.

In addition to Ms. Farenthold, the Dirty 30 lawmakers included Fred Agnich, Dave Allred, Maurice Angly, Bill Bass, Tom Bass, John Bigham, Bill Blythe, Rex Braun, Neil Caldwell, Tom Craddick, Lane Denton, Jim Earthman, Bob Gammage, Ben Grant, Curtis Graves, John Hannah, Ed Harris, Fred Head, Zan Holmes, Edmond "Sonny" Jones, Walter Mengden, Tom Moore, Paul Moreno, Roy Nichols, Charles Patterson, Dick Reed, Lindsey Rodriguez, Carlos Truan and Bob Vale.

Despite efforts by the Dirty 30 to clean up government, scandal rocked the state again in 1980 when Texas House Speaker Billy Clayton was embroiled in a federal sting operation called Brilab. Clayton, a legislator from West Texas, ran into legal problems after allegedly taking a $5,000 contribution from a group wanting his aid in obtaining a $76 million insurance contract for state workers. A federal grand jury indicted the speaker on six counts of racketeering and conspiracy. However, Clayton was acquitted, and he was re-elected speaker in 1981. He did not seek re-election in 1982, and he was succeeded as speaker by Rep. Gib Lewis in 1983.

The Fort Worth Democrat quickly found himself in legal difficulties of his own. In his first term as speaker, Lewis pleaded no contest and paid an $800 fine for failing to disclose his holdings in dozens of firms in the financial statements he filed with the state. In 1990, he was indicted on two misdemeanor charges of illegally accepting a gift and of failing to report it. In early1991, Lewis announced that he would not seek re-election. In a plea bargain agreement with prosecutors, those two charges were dropped, and he pleaded no-contest to two new minor ethics charges. He was fined $1,000 on each count but did not have to serve any time in jail.

Over the years, state officials and legislators have been indicted for bribery, perjury, promotion of prostitution, pornography, using state employees for campaign purposes, cocaine delivery and cattle rustling.

Frances "Sissy" Farenthold was one of the maverick Dirty 30 in the Texas House that launched a rebellion against House Speaker Gus Mutscher in the early 1970s. She took her image into a primary campaign against Gov. Dolph Briscoe, losing in a runoff. Lyndon B. Johnson, one of Texas' great politicians, was plagued throughout his career with allegations that he stole the 1948 gubernatorial runoff in the Democratic primary for the U. S. Senate. Dallas Morning News Photos

Many of the legal and political problems encountered by state officials have been either zany or bizarre or both.

There was the strange saga of Republican Rep. Mike Martin. He was indicted for perjury after a grand jury investigation into an incident in which he was wounded by shotgun blasts. Law enforcement officials became convinced Martin arranged the shooting to win sympathy votes for a planned race for the State Senate. Martin's cousin testified that Martin offered him a $30,000-a-year state job in exchange for doing the shooting. Martin pleaded guilty to a misdemeanor charge in 1981 and agreed not to seek re-election. But not before bumper stickers started appearing on cars in his hometown of Longview that asked: "Who Shot Mike? Cult, Satan, Cuz, Politician, Other."

There was Texas Supreme Court Justice Donald Yarbrough, who said God told him to run for the high court. He also was convicted of lying to a grand jury that was investigating allegations that he planned to have a South Texas banker killed to prevent him from testifying against him in a civil case. Before his conviction, Yarbrough was forced to resign from the Supreme Court in 1977 in the face of impeachment proceedings by the Legislature.

There was Agriculture Commissioner Reagan Brown losing a re-election bid in 1982 after he made a racial slur. He blamed it on a slip of the tongue and finally attributed it to food poisoning from a "bad turkey sandwich in Laredo." Craig Washington, a black legislator, said Brown must have been eating a "big redneck sandwich."

There was State Treasurer Warren G. Harding dropping out of a Democratic primary race for re-election in 1982. He was indicted on charges of misusing state employees for campaign purposes, but after a plea bargain, he pleaded guilty to a misdemeanor after he withdrew from the race.

There was Stanley Edward Adams of Austin filing for the Democratic nomination for governor in 1990 and listing as his occupation: "alleged white collar racketeer."

There was poultry magnate Lonnie "Bo" Pilgrim openly handing out $10,000 checks to nine state senators viewed as "swing votes" in the high-stakes legislative fight over workers' compensation in 1989. Pilgrim, who distributed some of the checks on the Senate floor, said they were meant to be legal campaign contributions and not bribes. An investigation was launched, but no action was taken against Pilgrim. Prosecutors said there were flaws in the state's bribery laws. But that incident sparked the most significant crusade for ethics reform since the Sharpstown affair. The Pilgrim episode shocked even the most seasoned political veterans. "It was not unusual," longtime Lt. Gov. Hobby said. "It was unique."

This article was written by Sam Attlesey, political writer for The Dallas Morning News.

12

The Voting Rights Struggle

The determined, courageous struggle of black Texans to regain their voting rights in the 20th century is one of the most heroic stories in the state's political history. In the early years of freedom in the 19th century, there was little question that the former slaves would be full citizens. With the freedom came full rights in the political system, going beyond simple voting to office-holding.

Because of the number of black males in the population, the voting strength of the freedmen was substantial. In many coastal counties and in the counties of the southern river basins, blacks were the majority race. In East Texas, many counties had 30 to 40 percent black populations, which mirrored the voting strength.

Only in the West Texas counties of Menard, Presidio and Terrell, where Buffalo Soldiers formed the majority of the population, were there black majorities that did not cause undue alarm among whites. The military of the national government could not vote in Texas at the time.

Through the Reconstruction years, black voters participated fully in the political system. Often with federal officials looking over the shoulders of white election officials. Black officeholders were not unusual in local government or in Austin. White attitudes toward the former slaves were uncompromising, however. Blacks represented a necessary evil that had to be tolerated.

One of the major drives of the state in the early post-Civil War years was to attract immigrants, both from other states and from foreign countries. Texas was a large, under-populated territory. And labor was scarce — when the employers were unwilling to hire black farm hands. Immigration was needed to bring more white settlers into regions where the former slaves held political supremacy.

Blacks formed the backbone of the early Republican Party, an allegiance that hampered their integration into the state's political system.

Through Reconstruction, Republican leadership remained in the hands of white politicians, like former governor E.J. Davis and U.S. Senator Morgan Hamilton, who controlled the party's patronage strings in the state.

With the death of Davis in 1883, Norris Wright Cuney, an educated black man, assumed control of the party and of the related patronage. He was named national committeeman in 1886 and became the most powerful black and Republican politician in the state. White elements in the party began agitation for greater control of Republican affairs, although blacks made up about 90 percent of the party's voting strength.

Racial prejudice among whites made black politicians' job much more difficult. Black support of a candidate could easily be his death knell. It was not until Jim Hogg sought black support in 1890 did Democratic politicians begin making serious efforts to attract black votes, and he got about 50 percent of the vote two years later.

But Jim Crow was afoot, and even progressive officials like Hogg supported a reduction of black rights. Under Hogg, for example, railroads were required to supply separate-but-equal accommodations for black customers in a separate passenger coach. The Jim Crow movement also accelerated the infringement on black voter rights that eventually resulted in at best a second-class citizenship for a large portion of the state's population.

The White Primary

Texas' major contribution to the development of this racist state of affairs was the "white primary," which excluded black voters from the most important elective decisions. The first of these primaries was held in Panola County in 1874. Particulars differed from county to county. But in essence the practice was to hold a closed primary before the general election. Party officials systematically excluded black voters. White voters were pledged to vote for the winners of the white primary in the general election months later.

Panola County had only about 35 to 40 percent black voters. That was enough to raise fears of coalitions between blacks and other groups. In neighboring Harrison County, blacks represented 68 percent of the electorate. In 1878, whites took control of the courthouse by force after blacks won many local offices.

Even the white primary was not consistent in its discrimination. In Gonzales County, for example, neither blacks nor Mexican-Texans could vote. But in the Lower Rio Grande Valley, Mexican-Texans were considered white and were encouraged to vote — or even paid to do so.

Through the latter part of the 19th century, Texas did not enact restrictive laws to exclude blacks. Intimidation — even deadly violence

— was widely used, however. It is estimated that between 300 to 500 blacks were lynched in Texas in the last years of the century. When whites were charged with intimidation, penalties usually were light. After an 1880 election, 65 people were charged with use of intimidation, fraud and violence against blacks. Forty-five pleaded guilty and were fined $1 and court costs.

In Washington County, three blacks were lynched in 1886 after killing the son of a candidate who stole a ballot box. A black constable and five other blacks died in violence in Matagorda County in 1887 after two whites refused to work with blacks on a county road gang.

Black rule in Robertson County ended when a district judge shot a black attorney to death after the lawyer made an alleged "insolent remark" while defending a client.

Other methods of discouraging black participation in political life were more subtle. Aspiring black officeholders found it difficult to find sponsors to underwrite the high bonds required for office. When these tactics discouraged voting or office-seeking, more aggressive steps were taken to keep blacks "in their place," which meant away from the polls.

Coming of the Poll Tax

Five attempts to impose a poll tax as a voting qualification before the Populist uprising in the 1890s. Third parties, like the Greenbackers, openly courted the black vote, and Democratic officials feared the black vote could swing tight elections even in counties in which blacks were not in the majority. At the height of the movement in 1896, black voters split about equally between the Populist and Democratic parties. Democrats became concerned about the challenge to their power by the poor farmers, both black and white. But black support of the Populist cause was used against the party, much as it had been used against Republicans after the Civil War.

The pleadings of A.W. Terrell, later a state senator, became more attractive. Terrell made no secret of his white supremacist attitude stating on one occasions that "the foremost man of all the world is the Anglo-Saxon American white man." Terrell also noted that the 15th Amendment to the U.S. Constitution, which assured black voting rights, was "the political blunder of the century." After the politically chaotic period, the Democrat-controlled Legislature approved a constitutional amendment levying the poll tax, and voters ratified it in 1902. Terrell sponsored a series of election reforms in 1905 that became known as the Terrell Election Law. It severely restricted voter participation.

In the election reform, state Sen. Tom Love of Dallas amended the new law to allow county executive committees to levy more qualifications to vote than required by state law. In 1904, the State Democratic Executive Committee approved use of the white primary. Courts initially approved the use of the primary because it was conducted by a private agency, a political party.

Texas blacks were particularly economically disadvantaged, even when compared to other states of the Old South. In 1900, 68 percent of the adult males and females were engaged in agriculture. Texas had the smallest number of black wage earners to black population of any state. Blacks in the state had not been trained as artisans as in other states, even in the South. Both working arrangements meant financial dependence on white employers or white merchants, and through this dependence, political activity could be controlled.

Voter participation among all groups dropped dramatically after the passage of the Terrell law. Black participation declined from an estimated 100,000 in the 1890s to about 5,000 in 1906. Houston levied a $2.50 city poll tax, and an estimated 7,500 "irresponsible voters" were removed from the voting rolls.

Some political leaders would have gone even further, although it is difficult to see how that could have been done. They wanted "disenfranchisement of the negro (sic), not because he owns no property, not because he has not paid a poll tax; but because he is a negro (sic); inferior in intellect, in morals and in aspirations to the white man, and therefore unfit to have a voice in the government of his superiors."

Political Limbo

As the 20th century opened, Texas blacks had been excluded from the white primary by a racist party policy and, for all practical purposes, had been stripped of their vote in the fall general election by the poll tax. Between 1904 and 1944, black participation in elections went into an eclipse, although black leaders did not stop trying to find a niche in the system. Black Texans were unusually assertive in their efforts to participate in the Democratic primary. It was apparent to them that without the right to vote in the meaningful Democratic primary that other issues such as education could not be addressed. Although blacks could vote in the general election, it was a meaningless exercise since the most important decisions, such as selection of candidates, already had been addressed in the primary.

From 1876 to 1893, the U.S. Supreme Court overturned the enabling legislation that supported the amendments to the constitution that conferred full civil rights to blacks. The most bizarre of the decisions, according to historian Darlene Clark Hine, was one that held that individuals can interfere with another's civil rights while the state cannot. Otherwise the Democratic primary stayed closed to black voters because the party was not a government institution.

Texas was among the last of the state to adopt the formal primary system in the South. Other states used the poll tax, literacy tests, and understanding and good character clauses to keep blacks from voting. Texas' primary law was enacted in 1903 as an election reform to standardize procedures statewide, and local party officials were given great latitude in setting the rules. The unspoken understanding that black voters would be barred, although the state did not directly mandate the exclusion.

Success of the woman's suffrage movement expanded the electorate to reinforce the support of the white primary. After 1905, most legislative sessions saw some change in the voting law. With the rise of the Ku Klux Klan in the 1920s, Texas blacks stepped up their efforts to regain a voice in the primary, which was the major election in the state at the time. Improving economic conditions for blacks made the poll tax less of a barrier, and blacks voted in nonpartisan elections in the major cities throughout the period. In 1923, the legislature passed a law limiting participation in the Democratic primary to white voters. The door was opened for a challenge of the law then because election judges became agents of the state.

Blacks in Houston tested laws in court. A middle class of blacks had developed in the city. Many were independent of the white economy and were invulnerable to economic pressures. They could afford to finance court tests of the law.

In 1915, an Oklahoma law exempting persons who had been eligible to vote in 1866 and their descendants from literacy tests. A Texas attorney, James W. Bailey, argued Oklahoma's case. But the U.S. Supreme Court overturned the law, the first time in 45 years the high court had looked at local laws that were only shams to disenfranchise blacks.

The National Association for the Advancement of Colored People began looking for test cases to challenge the white primary after the 1915 decision signaled a new attitude by the Supreme Court. One was found in Texas.

Dr. Lawrence A. Nixon, a physician in El Paso, tried to vote in the Democratic primary on July 26, 1924, and was denied the right. The election judge signed a statement to the effect that Dr. Nixon was denied the right to vote solely on the basis of his race. The case was taken to federal court.

Challenging the Primary

A year and a half later, the U.S. Supreme Court ruled in Nixon's favor. The state's role in prohibiting him from voting was a violation of the 15th amendment to the constitution. Texas had withheld equal protection under the law. The Nixon vs. Herndon decision left the door open for the party, as a private institution, to bar black voters.

With the victory, the NAACP began a membership drive in Texas seeking 10,000 to 20,000 new members. But it continued to face funding problems, and philosophical differences arose with Texas blacks who wanted a more assertive campaign against discrimination. Texas

Thurgood Marshall, left, later a Supreme Court justice, was one of the attorneys who filed the decisive case in Texas that finally brought down the white primary in 1944. Dr. Lawrence Nixon of El Paso repeatedly challenged the white primary system. Photos courtesy Associated Press and Corpus Christi Caller-Times.

blacks also complained about the organization's use of white attorneys.

White primaries were challenged in other states. Virginia preferred to allow blacks to vote than fund primaries. The Florida supreme court overturned that state's white primary on findings based on the Nixon case in Texas.

Critics openly questioned why blacks were so adamant about voting in the Democratic primary when the party was so white supremacist. But in the South, the Democratic primary was "the" election, since Democrats were seldom seriously challenged in the general election.

The Texas Legislature repealed the 1923 law and returned the responsibility for defining membership back to the party, where black voters could be excluded again.

Dr. Nixon tried again to vote in the 1928 Democratic primary, and again he was denied the right. Election judge James Condon signed a statement that Nixon was not given a ballot because he was black and the primary was only open to whites.

Again, the Supreme Court overturned the law, ruling that the State Democratic Executive Committee was discharging state powers and in doing so ran afoul of the 14th amendment. But still the polls were not opened to black voters.

In 1932, most blacks voted Republican. But the black community was particularly hard hit by the Depression. President Franklin D.

Roosevelt did not give attention to black issues or appointments as governor of New York nor did he court their vote in 1932. Blacks benefited psychologically from the New Deal. For the first time since Reconstruction, they gained participation in the federal government.

Support for the black cause got mild support in the white community. The conservative *Dallas Morning News*, while supporting the party's right to bar blacks, commented in 1930, "The number of negroes (sic) who would actually enter a Texas primary would not be large enough to imperil anything. The kind of negro who would affiliate genuinely with the Democratic Party in Texas would be of the better, substantial sort. His vote would do no harm, and his presence would cause no more disturbance than it does in the general election, where he has as good a legal right as anybody else."

White supremacists held, however, that all blacks must be barred from participation in the party to assure white supremacy. This was not a secret attitude held while officials spouted higher aims but an overt policy that received a large degree of public approval. Indeed, officeholders often were expected to be vocal in their stand for white supremacy.

Texas lawmakers tried to shift the responsibility for barring black voters from the primary to the state Democratic convention. Again Dr. Nixon challenged the law, and a federal district court upheld the physician. The effect was limited since the case was not appealed. But some county officials began to allow blacks to participate in the Democratic primary. In 1934, the Bexar County chairman allow blacks to vote, and several smaller counties followed.

In a case out of Houston, the U. S. Supreme Court upheld the white primary in 1935, noting again that the party was a private organization. The NAACP was not involved in the case.

Throughout these challenges of the Texas law, the national NAACP and Texas blacks were often at odds. Texans wanted a more aggressive challenge and more attention given to local desires. In 1939, the Houston chapter was reorganized. In 1940, NAACP chapters from Texas met in Corpus Christi and set a 10-year agenda. A top priority was to challenge the white primary followed by improved educational opportunities and a broad attack on Jim Crow laws.

Victory At Last

The white primary finally fell in 1944 after Thurgood Marshall, later a justice on the Supreme Court, and W. J. Durham, a Sherman attorney, filed Smith vs. Allwright. The state prevailed in district and appellate courts, but the Supreme Court finally recognized that the primary was an integral part of the election process. By an 8-1 vote, the court overturned the white primary, ending a 20-year battle by Texas blacks.

In 1946, an estimated 75,000 blacks voted in the Democratic primary, a 50 percent increase over previous particpation. Most voted for

Homer Rainey, a liberal and former president of the University of Texas at Austin, as the party nominee for governor. Beauford Jester won the election, but he, too, with other Democratic candidates, courted the black vote. Candidates appeared before black audiences and placed advertising in black newspapers. For the first time in more than half a century, black Texans were a force in the state's primaries.

It was another 20 years before the poll tax also was thrown out as a voting requisite and other impediments were removed.

Blacks made the destruction of the white primary a basic goal because it was an impediment to voting that transcended economic bounds. No matter if the potential voter were a pauper or a millionaire, if the skin were black, there was no right to vote in the most meaningful of elections in Texas at the time, the Democratic primary.

Still a factor in opening the election to participation by all citizens, black, white, rich and poor, was the poll tax. Actions against it continued until 1966, when the U. S. Supreme Court declared it unconstitutional. Texas' white politicans were noting if not resourceful. They instituted a system of annual voter registration, again designed to make voting difficult, if not impossible. The high court eventually struck down this law.

Also in 1966, the Supreme Court mandated one-man, one-vote redistricting that opened the doors of officeholding to minority candidates. Barbara Jordan of Houston became the first black state senator in a century after winning an election based on the new redistricting. Several black and Hispanic legislators were sent to Austin, too.

Even with most barriers lowered, some local officials still tried to discourage minority voting by making it as difficult as possible. Voting precinct lines were drawn so that minority precincts often had the largest populations, causing long lines on election days. In some cases, inadequate election materials were provided for minority precincts.

But after all the effort, bloodshed and tragedy expended by generations of blacks to regain full voting rights, the black community in Texas still exhibits an apathy on election day. The next step in the drive toward full equality must come from within the black community itself by encouraging — even demanding — that every qualified voter go the to polls on election day. The perseverance displayed by black Texans throughout the 20th century to regain full voting rights is one of Texas' most heroic episodes.

This article was written by Mike Kingston, editor of the Texas Almanac.

Why All This Fuss?

From W. Lee O'Daniel's "pass the biscuits pappy" crusade, to Ma Ferguson's pledge to give voters two governors for the price of one, to the record-shattering $50 million 1990 race, gubernatorial campaigns in Texas have provided another wild and wacky chapter in the state's political history.

Although the office is a weak one, it is, nevertheless, the most coveted and glamorous position in state government. Because the Governor's Mansion is located on Colorado Avenue in Austin, political watchers note that Texans itching to reside in one of the country's oldest structures have contracted a severe case of Colorado Fever.

How coveted is the office of governor? Well, the state's first Republican governor, Edmund Davis, barricaded himself in the office and refused to leave. One U.S. Senator, Price Daniel, was willing to give up his Washington, D.C. seat in order to return to Texas to run for governor. And the 1990 GOP nominee, Clayton Williams, was willing to spend more than $8 million of his own money to try and add the governor of Texas to a list of his titles that already included big game hunter, rancher, oilman and banker.

For the most part, Texans have elected conservative, white, male Democrats to serve as their chief executives. No ethnic minority has ever been elected. Only two women and two Republicans have served as governor.

After being nearly hanged by Confederates during the Civil War, Davis was elected the first GOP governor in Reconstruction Texas in 1869. He won by less than 1,000 votes over A.J. Hamilton. His administration was marked by corruption, and he even disbanded the Texas Rangers to form his own state militia. After being overwhelmingly defeated by Democrat Richard Coke in 1873, Davis temporarily refused to leave office. Only after President U.S. Grant refused to help his cause did Davis finally give up his office.

More than a century would pass before Texans elected another

Republican governor. In a stunning upset victory in 1978, bulldozer-blunt Bill Clements of Dallas became the second GOP governor with a win over Democrat John Hill. Clements, the world's largest oil drilling contractor, sought re-election in 1982, but he and other Republicans fell victim to a nose-diving economy in Texas. He was upset by Attorney General Mark White. Four years later, driven by what many political observers said was revenge, Clements ran against White again in a nasty rematch. White, weakened by his support of large tax increases and education reforms that included the controversial no-pass, no-play rule, was defeated in 1986 by the Dallas Republican. Clements' last term in office was marred by his role in the Southern Methodist University football pay-for-play scandal. As an official of the Dallas college, Clements and other members of the school's board of governors had authorized the continued payments to athletes. The continued "phasing out" of payments were part of the board of governors' efforts to clean up the program, Clements insisted. Clements did not seek another term in 1990, and he vowed never to run for public office again. But his election in 1978 had been another giant step in making Texas a two-party state. The only benchmark with more significance in the development of the Republican Party in Texas was John Tower's victory in the 1961 special U.S. Senate election.

Clements' role in the SMU sports scandal spawned calls for impeachment from a handful of legislators, but those efforts never got anywhere mainly because no taxpayer money was involved and Clements had not been governor of Texas when the authorization of payments to athletes took place. Only one governor, James E. Ferguson, has been impeached, convicted by the Senate and forced to resign.

The impeachment of "Farmer Jim" in 1917 was instrumental in Texas electing its first woman governor. Campaigning on the theme "two governors for the price of one," Miriam A. "Ma" Ferguson became the first female chief executive with her victory on Nov. 4, 1924. But she had to share the title of being the first woman governor in the United States with Nellie Taylor Ross of Wyoming, who was also elected on that same day. Campaigning in a sunbonnet and running mainly to vindicate her husband, who had been banned from seeking public office, "Ma" Ferguson was twice elected to the office. But it was "Pa" Ferguson who handled many of the daily chores of being governor of Texas.

It was not until 1990 that a woman was elected governor of Texas on her own right. Democrat Ann Richards, viewed by some as a "good ole girl" and by others as a feminist, overcame a 20-point deficit in the polls to win a stunning victory over Republican nominee Clayton Williams. When she was inaugurated in January 1991, Ms. Richards, who had served as a county commissioner and state treasurer before running for governor, promised a "New Texas" that would open the door to all Texans, especially women and minorities.

Even though she was elected on her own right, most political observers credit her victory to a series of costly and embarrassing mistakes by her Republican opponent.

Williams, a colorful cowboy known to friend and foe as "Claytie," suffered from a severe case of boot-in-mouth disease that became known as Claytie's Gaffes. They included everything from telling a joke in which he compared bad weather to rape, saying, "If it's inevitable just relax and enjoy it." At one point he refused to shake hands with Ms. Richards and called her a liar. The day after Ms. Richards celebrated her 10th anniversary of sobriety, Williams said, "I hope she didn't go back to drinking again." He acknowledged he sought the services of prostitutes in Mexico as a youth because it was the only way to get "serviced." And four days before the election, for some reason Williams acknowledged that he had not paid any federal income taxes in 1986.

While digging a hole for himself with his ill-timed comments, Williams also set a record for digging into his own pocketbook for campaign cash in the governor's race. He spent more than $8 million of his own money in the race. Campaign finance reports show the Williams camp spent a total of $21,978,529. The finance reports show Ms. Richards' campaign spent $14,488,402. Counting what the two nominees kicked in and what the five major losing candidates in the Democratic and Republican primaries doled out, more than $50 million was spent in the 1990 governor's race. That was easily a record for campaign spending in a Texas governor's race.

Campaign spending has grown dramatically in recent years because of the reliance by candidates to get their names known and messages delivered through costly television commercials. Also, Texas has no limits on how much a candidate can collect or spend.

According to Common Cause of Texas, all candidates for governor in 1978 spent a total of $15 million. In the 1982 campaign, the total spending grew to $28 million and it climbed to $34 million in the 1986 contest. Clements was involved in all three of the races, and his campaign spent a total of more than $31 million to win two and lose one.

Natural population growth and increased visibility of the candidates and their campaigns have combined to increase turnouts in the gubernatorial contests through the years.

In the 1990 governor's race, 3,892,746 Texans, who were either turned off by Williams or turned on by Ms. Richards, turned out to elect the first woman on her own right.

In the state's first gubernatorial election in 1845, only 9,578 Texans voted in the race that made J. Pinckney Henderson the first governor. Henderson was a southern aristocrat who had helped with Texas' annexation discussions with the United States in 1844. He was a lawyer and a native of North Carolina.

It was 1890 before a native Texan was elected governor. James

Hogg of Rusk holds the honor of being the first born and bred Texan to serve in the Governor's Mansion.

Hogg had served as attorney general before running for governor. And the office of attorney general has been one of the most popular steppingstones for seeking the top state office.

Of the forty men and two women who have served as governor, eight had been attorneys general before reaching the highest office. In fact, 32 of the 42 people who have served as governor were lawyers. Eighteen served in the State Legislature and five served in Congress before becoming governor. Ten of the governors served as lieutenant governor before moving up. Three governors served as secretary of state. Eight former governors had held no elective office before becoming chief executive, and five had no government experience at all.

Despite the stereotype of Texans as cattle barons and "J.R." wheelers and dealers, only seven former governors were ranchers or in the oil business.

But only one, Pappy Lee O'Daniel, was a hillbilly flour salesman. Only one, Sam Houston, was a former president of the Republic of Texas. And only one, Hardin Runnels, can claim to have defeated Sam Houston at the polls in Texas when Runnels was elected governor in 1857.

The Houston-Runnels race in 1857 and a rematch won by Houston in 1859 showed how fickle Texas voters can be. Houston, the hero of Texas' victory at San Jacinto in 1836, lost because he opposed secession. Runnels campaigned in favor of the state leaving the Union. Even though he was elected governor in 1859, Houston was removed from office because he would not swear allegiance to the Confederacy.

Most Texas governors last at least one term. But two have not. Edward Clark, the lieutenant governor who succeeded Sam Houston in 1861, served only seven and one-half months. Clark was beaten by 124 votes, the closest margin ever for the office, by Francis R. Lubbock. James W. Throckmorton served one day short of a year before federal Reconstruction officials ousted him from office on August 8, 1867.

Pendleton Murrah, the last Civil War governor, fled to Mexico before he completed his term. Fletcher S. Stockton, Murrah's lieutenant governor, often is listed as a former governor, but technically Andrew J. Hamilton, appointed provisional governor by President Abraham Lincoln, succeeded Murrah.

Today governors have four-year terms. Until voters adopted a constitutional amendment in 1972, the term was two years. But beginning with the 1974 campaign, the term of office was four years.

George Christian, a veteran political consultant from Austin, explained the significance of the term change in a column in *The Dallas Morning News* several years ago.

"Thanks to former Lt. Gov. Ben Barnes, state officeholders with four-year terms will never have to run in a presidential election year.

"When a constitutional amendment was devised in 1971 to lengthen terms from two years to four years, Barnes wanted the new system to become effective in the 'off' year of 1974.

"For the Democrats, Ben gets the gold cup for foresight," Christian wrote.

It was fortunate foresight for Democrats because their candidates for governor and most other statewide offices do not have to run in presidential election years. In recent presidential elections where Republicans have popular nominees and Democrats do not, down-ballot Democratic contenders have lost or barely escaped defeat because of the presidential landslide at the top of the ticket.

The powers are weak, the cost immense and the mansion is old, but being governor is the most coveted political office in Texas. It is the prestige of the position more than its power that drives men and women to risk life, limb, reputation and sanity to run for the office.

This article was written by Sam Attlesey, political writer for The Dallas Morning News.

Texas Governors Fall Often

This article was published in the 1988-89 Texas Almanac.

When Gov. Mark White lost the 1986 general election to former Gov. William P. Clements Jr., he became the fifth of the last six Texas governors to be ousted from office by the state's voters. Only John Connally, who served as governor from 1963-1969, escaped embarrassment by the electorate. Texas, in fact, has been hard on governors, sending to defeat 11 (27 percent) of 41 persons who served as chief executive.

The trend began early. George T. Wood, the state's second governor, was defeated in 1849 by Peter Hansbrough Bell, who served two terms.

The Civil War and Reconstruction periods were the most volatile and turbulent in the state's history. Between 1859 and 1873, five governors were ousted from office, one by Reconstruction officials, one by political pressure and three by voters. Another was defeated at the polls and still served almost a full term.

Sam Houston opened the period by defeating incumbent Gov. Hardin R. Runnels in the 1859 general election. Two years earlier, Runnels had dealt Houston his only defeat at the polls in Texas in the gubernatorial race. A failure to solve the intractable problems on the frontier and the general unrest that developed prior to the war made Runnels unpopular, however, and led to his defeat. Houston, in turn, was forced from office in 1861 when he refused to pledge an oath of allegiance to the Confederacy.

Lt. Gov. Edward Clark served the remaining months of Houston's term but was defeated in his 1861 election bid for a full term by 124 votes by Francis R. Lubbock. The margin of defeat was the narrowest in a Texas gubernatorial race.

Then there was the unusual case of Elisha M. Pease. Twice he was elected governor of Texas, serving from 1853 to 1857. However, in

1866, James W. Throckmorton defeated Pease in the general election. But the military authorities who ran Reconstruction Texas removed Throckmorton from office in 1867 and appointed Pease, who served until 1869. Pease served although defeated by voters.

Reconstruction ended when Democrat Richard Coke defeated the unpopular incumbent Republican Edmund J. Davis in 1873. Davis was the state's only Republican governor until Clements won the office in 1978 and the only governor to serve a four-year term before Dolph Briscoe did a century later.

For more than 50 years, Texas governors generally served a pair of two-year terms and retired peacefully. Then came the Ferguson era. James E. Ferguson was twice elected governor, but in 1917, he was impeached, convicted and removed from office. He lost a bid to regain the office from William P. Hobby the following year. Ferguson remained active in politics, and in 1924, his wife, Miriam A. "Ma" Ferguson, defeated a Ku Klux Klan-backed opponent to become Texas' first and only woman chief executive. Two years later, she was defeated by the state's attractive young attorney general, Dan Moody.

Four years later, Mrs. Ferguson in a comeback defeated incumbent Ross S. Sterling. In 1932, the Depression was at its height in Texas, and voters wanted a change, any change. Mrs. Ferguson did not seek re-election in 1934, but she was the first Texas governor to be voted out of office and then to regain the post.

For the next 30 years, incumbent governors managed to retain office. But Democrat Price Daniel in 1962 challenged history by attempting to become the first governor to be elected to a fourth two-year term. He failed even to make the Democratic primary run-off that eventually pitted John Connally and Don Yarborough. Connally won and was elected governor in November of 1962.

Preston Smith succeeded Connally in 1969 and served two terms. The Sharpstown scandal struck state government, and though Smith was not involved in influence peddling, voters turned him out in the Democratic primary in 1972, in which he became the second governor not to make the primary runoff. Dolph Briscoe was elected governor in November.

After serving a two-year term, Briscoe was re-elected in 1974 and became the first Texas governor in a century to serve a four-year term after the state constitution was amended in 1972. But Briscoe lost a re-election bid without a runoff in the Democratic primary in 1978 to Attorney General John Hill. But Hill became the first Democrat gubernatorial candidate in more than a century to lose to a Republican when Clements defeated him in the general election.

In 1982, Clements' bid for a second term was thwarted by Democratic Attorney General Mark W. White Jr., who surprised pollsters and political pundits alike in defeating the incumbent.

White was forced to approve tax hikes shortly before the election and had led an unpopular drive for improved public education that made him vulnerable to Clements' comeback bid in the 1986 general election. Thus a new tradition of turning out the incumbent governor was continued.

Table 27: Gubernatorial Races

	Democratic Primaries, 1908-1912								
Year	1908		1910					1912	
County	T. M. Campbell	R. R. Williams	William Poindexter	R. V. Davidson	O. B. Colquitt	Cone Johnson	J. M. Jones	O. B. Colquitt	W. F. Ramsey
Anderson	1,932	327	483	120	885	809	11	1,289	1,503
Andrews	0	0	42	38	55	48	0	56	99
Angelina	1,493	483	355	276	869	647	18	1,045	894
Aransas	139	74	28	39	167	56	0	193	113
Archer	248	228	177	56	288	79	2	434	350
Armstrong	152	125	249	27	114	90	1	203	236
Atascosa	422	263	182	254	283	43	20	735	482
Austin	1,541	386	57	346	1,379	31	3	1,773	161
Bailey	0	0	0	0	0	0	0	0	0
Bandera	169	194	79	12	73	30	0	143	117
Bastrop	1,208	546	317	241	981	372	5	1,240	889
Baylor	512	286	332	102	429	147	2	544	498
Bee	514	170	252	221	331	86	12	528	491
Bell	3,385	2,218	584	1,166	2,201	1,749	21	2,968	3,018
Bexar	3,244	2,608	202	386	4,301	259	8	9,703	1,843
Blanco	274	105	85	55	204	47	0	341	180
Borden	103	112	57	50	54	45	2	105	116
Bosque	1,348	1,081	634	698	878	506	16	1,382	1,256
Bowie	1,924	594	470	245	800	889	10	1,415	1,416
Brazoria	312	90	112	90	335	67	1	513	447
Brazos	689	607	271	321	577	208	15	897	749
Brewster	128	161	70	50	163	69	8	171	89
Briscoe	91	120	74	57	118	41	3	191	165
Brooks	0	0	0	0	0	0	0	250	51
Brown	1,867	511	471	483	935	871	5	1,504	1,425
Burleson	866	643	264	344	741	175	13	1,101	623
Burnet	1,073	336	394	442	490	160	7	701	783
Caldwell	1,391	363	387	384	707	383	3	970	1,080
Calhoun	182	123	49	44	204	47	6	390	236
Callahan	486	1,107	396	130	838	377	6	975	674
Cameron	818	35	27	83	1,081	28	3	1,436	285
Camp	613	328	159	61	375	269	2	434	513
Carson	93	80	86	96	82	38	3	187	163
Cass	1,509	442	634	196	919	537	7	1,139	1,213
Castro	72	71	126	18	58	38	3	138	147
Chambers	66	4	61	172	197	40	2	302	179
Cherokee	1,756	567	214	191	1,189	1,002	51	1,447	1,398
Childress	526	336	330	240	343	253	1	428	698
Clay	858	388	646	191	613	305	16	778	892
Cochran	0	0	0	0	0	0	0	0	0
Coke	310	412	146	219	159	173	8	282	399
Coleman	1,319	601	675	442	792	564	15	1,107	1,357
Collin	2,944	2,090	2,078	631	1,322	1,155	12	2,247	3,154
Collingsworth	233	359	347	70	105	117	0	299	561
Colorado	791	633	93	239	985	161	1	1,190	368
Comal	738	166	7	41	1,159	6	1	1,339	19
Comanche	2,003	969	666	603	946	577	4	1,586	1,585
Concho	315	96	239	128	168	145	0	388	315
Cooke	2,258	983	1,273	80	994	475	5	1,407	1,363
Coryell	1,771	1,089	544	930	1,164	554	5	1,587	1,346
Cottle	104	209	150	52	237	90	3	274	217
Crane	0	0	0	0	0	0	0	0	0
Crockett	96	30	42	19	35	6	1	98	79
Crosby	66	130	65	65	57	59	1	181	196
Culberson	0	0	0	0	0	0	0	131	45
Dallam	82	32	95	66	191	101	4	207	198
Dallas	4,021	6,376	1,849	2,077	5,056	3,038	29	7,131	6,392
Dawson	140	197	70	77	66	77	1	116	166
DeWitt	1,320	313	94	139	1,439	138	0	2,086	306
Deaf Smith	301	90	306	49	95	58	0	96	236
Delta	808	771	530	104	606	494	0	973	939
Denton	2,220	1,175	1,326	199	1,227	554	14	1,891	1,890
Dickens	135	71	118	48	113	64	2	215	266
Dimmit	16	29	21	31	27	6	0	50	102

Table 27: Gubernatorial Races

Democratic Primaries, 1908-1912									
Year	1908		1910					1912	
County	T. M. Campbell	R. R. Williams	William Poindexter	R. V. Davidson	O. B. Colquitt	Cone Johnson	J. M. Jones	O. B. Colquitt	W. F. Ramsey
Donley	459	215	260	90	162	52	4	397	442
Duval	4	614	0	0	773	0	0	684	14
Eastland	1,751	901	827	346	735	685	8	1,187	1,416
Ector	105	104	45	66	70	50	1	116	71
Edwards	12	5	0	0	0	0	0	0	0
El Paso	1,940	431	150	351	1,823	409	44	3,722	1,232
Ellis	3,496	2,173	2,007	791	1,952	1,522	21	2,981	3,396
Erath	2,377	1,187	980	480	989	922	15	1,583	1,950
Falls	1,494	1,354	915	632	1,225	498	7	1,997	1,581
Fannin	3,072	1,739	1,643	563	1,478	1,446	26	2,367	2,459
Fayette	2,139	625	217	254	2,424	105	3	3,146	352
Fisher	778	490	405	204	355	321	7	425	689
Floyd	207	237	266	102	103	200	2	284	487
Foard	303	151	203	46	282	114	1	326	295
Fort Bend	325	256	34	90	455	93	0	679	395
Franklin	823	469	293	81	563	301	15	865	592
Freestone	1,357	381	306	379	681	527	8	1,065	1,020
Frio	300	151	240	121	175	64	8	274	422
Gaines	131	60	53	55	50	40	6	62	102
Galveston	2,132	1,046	86	2,214	916	138	1	3,388	1,363
Garza	70	34	89	30	66	27	5	124	167
Gillespie	105	86	19	47	240	6	0	794	80
Glasscock	51	60	27	23	57	19	0	69	92
Goliad	0	0	52	12	54	69	1	401	122
Gonzales	1,838	525	525	426	1,051	392	13	1,374	1,219
Gray	0	0	64	46	25	29	1	143	251
Grayson	4,111	1,849	1,791	479	2,750	1,178	36	3,662	3,344
Gregg	531	270	193	80	230	394	3	410	698
Grimes	724	169	328	115	633	147	1	847	719
Guadalupe	849	325	105	107	1,172	166	0	1,356	349
Hale	355	106	318	132	223	305	4	380	669
Hall	578	278	338	137	232	252	5	507	636
Hamilton	966	968	590	535	647	395	3	1,115	965
Hansford	0	0	0	0	0	0	0	0	0
Hardeman	605	279	388	206	393	232	1	470	777
Hardin	815	250	218	146	534	318	9	744	697
Harris	5,199	2,667	402	1,741	5,629	1,078	14	8,580	3,403
Harrison	1,182	674	378	191	763	698	13	1,104	1,113
Hartley	153	79	30	26	89	26	0	101	65
Haskell	1,167	602	674	195	628	295	8	769	868
Hays	1,042	301	509	257	431	188	5	663	850
Hemphill	37	11	18	9	38	9	0	80	142
Henderson	1,205	901	184	467	613	792	15	1,117	1,402
Hidalgo	586	2	11	37	664	19	2	813	99
Hill	3,287	1,697	1,926	617	1,640	1,333	8	2,552	3,043
Hockley	0	0	0	0	0	0	0	0	0
Hood	939	503	384	162	382	451	6	586	792
Hopkins	1,441	2,310	1,052	384	1,133	1,253	15	1,668	2,105
Houston	1,473	606	532	470	941	495	8	1,463	1,095
Howard	520	317	205	163	352	172	8	426	427
Hudspeth	0	0	0	0	0	0	0	0	0
Hunt	2,330	2,724	2,208	495	1,425	1,432	8	2,371	3,182
Hutchinson	0	0	5	6	19	6	0	25	11
Irion	139	71	69	61	75	22	4	151	121
Jack	754	343	362	114	266	145	3	602	621
Jackson	252	52	57	97	116	104	0	246	320
Jasper	610	258	219	563	499	185	16	579	422
Jeff Davis	26	13	0	0	0	0	0	7	17
Jefferson	1,589	1,307	305	903	1,380	450	8	1,986	1,205
Jim Hogg	0	0	0	0	0	0	0	0	0
Jim Wells	0	0	0	0	0	0	0	207	136
Johnson	2,832	1,583	1,939	270	873	775	6	1,701	2,722
Jones	1,750	758	1,015	272	704	505	4	1,029	1,390
Karnes	809	319	177	285	695	261	15	1,039	555
Kaufman	1,896	1,278	737	274	1,584	1,077	2	1,951	1,823

Table 27: Gubernatorial Races

County	Democratic Primaries, 1908-1912								
Year	**1908**		**1910**					**1912**	
	T. M. Campbell	R. R. Williams	William Poindexter	R. V. Davidson	O. B. Colquitt	Cone Johnson	J. M. Jones	O. B. Colquitt	W. F. Ramsey
Kendall	85	115	6	29	267	17	1	355	34
Kenedy	0	0	0	0	0	0	0	0	0
Kent	112	153	93	77	129	27	5	213	137
Kerr	151	47	62	46	142	56	0	342	244
Kimble	150	137	117	71	136	98	2	326	187
King	40	47	33	20	36	17	3	65	34
Kinney	51	69	23	10	62	0	0	38	18
Kleberg	0	0	0	0	0	0	0	0	0
Knox	734	356	350	176	369	171	6	517	531
La Salle	115	32	9	31	214	28	0	290	129
Lamar	2,782	1,995	1,211	453	1,904	1,397	25	2,724	2,408
Lamb	0	0	0	0	0	0	0	0	0
Lampasas	762	453	143	225	413	273	4	584	589
Lavaca	1,852	551	241	304	2,061	147	17	2,502	406
Lee	913	239	146	166	882	76	9	1,002	312
Leon	1,131	188	267	340	425	281	2	776	881
Liberty	602	184	287	88	468	134	4	686	500
Limestone	1,766	1,500	923	735	1,177	727	12	1,630	1,559
Lipscomb	0	0	0	0	0	0	0	46	53
Live Oak	55	9	50	25	39	12	0	46	45
Llano	593	233	136	345	395	136	7	636	428
Loving	0	0	0	0	0	0	0	0	0
Lubbock	124	172	204	78	168	126	7	299	375
Lynn	174	71	70	76	46	64	0	118	159
Madison	845	216	274	134	398	251	1	616	730
Marion	229	269	98	28	156	190	3	235	271
Martin	193	134	106	20	60	51	0	112	115
Mason	171	29	53	68	142	64	0	356	183
Matagorda	332	125	136	93	395	107	0	612	523
Maverick	132	30	6	13	78	17	0	54	40
McCulloch	645	283	424	151	513	237	7	544	614
McLennan	3,800	3,262	1,141	1,197	2,848	1,696	11	4,051	4,002
McMullen	68	50	21	50	59	7	1	87	52
Medina	182	44	206	24	507	17	0	559	249
Menard	240	94	84	44	155	18	4	291	106
Midland	315	141	136	60	117	101	0	153	209
Milam	2,549	933	519	849	1,567	814	7	1,955	1,853
Mills	723	408	242	260	415	288	4	510	565
Mitchell	551	510	244	155	278	384	2	453	567
Montague	1,893	1,025	978	146	894	526	5	1,393	1,351
Montgomery	862	327	228	330	531	144	7	693	629
Moore	0	0	74	16	27	11	1	75	52
Morris	688	281	313	88	335	329	4	605	518
Motley	177	122	44	11	130	76	4	168	216
Nacogdoches	1,987	621	587	248	1,147	816	37	1,271	1,380
Navarro	2,563	2,034	1,002	1,142	1,582	1,076	15	2,404	2,743
Newton	322	191	192	117	237	152	117	331	366
Nolan	654	366	358	129	347	332	5	677	608
Nueces	621	187	126	298	668	160	9	862	477
Ochiltree	48	63	22	44	50	49	1	45	135
Oldham	0	0	25	9	13	3	0	47	14
Oran ge	514	290	198	85	431	80	1	576	439
PaloPinto	1,400	1,067	510	285	836	487	6	1,103	1,035
Panola	941	627	275	246	726	591	12	948	1,004
Parker	2,054	1,196	911	236	931	909	11	1,486	1,705
Parmer	85	28	83	11	42	17	2	85	86
Pecos	34	63	0	0	0	0	0	117	78
Polk	905	210	297	227	538	254	4	634	825
Potter	838	268	367	241	609	180	8	737	868
Presidio	123	186	17	28	93	17	0	177	17
Rains	302	344	224	78	225	201	3	374	350
Randall	162	106	151	16	127	89	5	173	216
Reagan	13	89	0	0	0	0	0	36	37
Real	0	0	0	0	0	0	0	0	0
Red River	1,163	1,621	941	334	920	816	25	1,882	1,538

Table 27: Gubernatorial Races

Democratic Primaries, 1908-1912											
Year	1908		1910						1912		
County	T. M. Campbell	R. R. Williams	William Poindexter	R. V. Davidson	O. B. Colquitt	Cone Johnson	J. M. Jones		O. B. Colquitt	W. F. Ramsey	
Reeves	259	134	101	80	157	175	0		178	421	
Refugio	53	16	6	4	185	6	0		131	48	
Roberts	17	20	22	9	26	29	0		39	96	
Robertson	1,167	586	361	362	795	311	17		1,087	1,046	
Rockwall	608	461	351	118	241	367	0		474	731	
Runnels	1,377	659	751	441	749	464	7		1,071	1,039	
Rusk	1,505	673	491	122	1,189	676	11		1,275	1,405	
Sabine	439	341	158	126	339	235	15		636	461	
San Augustine	539	218	123	148	420	440	16		619	437	
San Jacinto	393	164	121	54	331	115	4		264	391	
San Patricio	27	74	45	22	198	32	1		231	98	
San Saba	934	385	350	171	499	104	8		814	685	
Schleicher	200	58	125	80	74	7	0		120	158	
Scurry	693	499	463	236	302	291	9		577	825	
Shackelford	221	216	202	85	201	56	1		276	214	
Shelby	2,237	653	680	391	1,181	683	26		1,568	1,539	
Sherman	0	0	27	25	57	59	5		60	112	
Smith	1,521	1,267	138	216	723	2,320	8		1,359	1,921	
Somervell	218	314	150	87	199	104	5		270	212	
Starr	350	0	19	32	581	10	1		535	2	
Stephens	625	400	269	369	295	176	2		494	466	
Sterling	145	91	79	60	33	32	3		118	149	
Stonewall	335	230	124	52	257	151	12		329	285	
Sutton	216	24	66	62	69	32	11		139	135	
Swisher	211	114	187	37	127	164	1		209	318	
Tarrant	5,589	3,584	2,608	482	5,229	2,087	30		6,941	5,141	
Taylor	1,656	657	1,195	200	984	522	10		1,180	1,490	
Terrell	43	42	4	16	39	9	0		35	10	
Terry	130	171	49	91	30	95	3		101	144	
Throckmorton	253	213	233	51	210	105	1		250	343	
Titus	1,004	684	300	192	662	706	6		997	1,008	
Tom Green	1,228	437	411	327	646	477	11		926	938	
Travis	2,790	1,548	240	1,094	2,520	951	12		3,332	2,364	
Trinity	693	341	193	193	694	220	114		736	518	
Tyler	920	193	346	100	585	105	4		595	530	
Upshur	1,033	856	368	199	974	672	16		1,167	1,259	
Upton	0	0	12	20	42	14	0		56	26	
Uvalde	280	246	287	192	169	198	8		512	503	
Val Verde	173	103	11	69	49	20	0		64	104	
Van Zandt	1,726	1,246	264	351	851	1,259	7		1,012	1,632	
Victoria	923	220	76	74	914	129	5		1,370	339	
Walker	524	249	223	89	608	66	2		547	618	
Waller	772	223	233	197	456	82	3		538	438	
Ward	159	111	65	56	75	78	0		138	139	
Washington	864	1,149	86	443	1,048	24	3		2,047	238	
Webb	85	25	9	83	196	7	0		383	43	
Wharton	644	172	91	191	467	181	2		810	576	
Wheeler	193	168	172	109	159	120	2		275	386	
Wichita	451	312	347	200	580	315	9		889	814	
Wilbarger	739	369	462	149	512	273	6		849	741	
Willacy	0	0	0	0	0	0	0		73	1	
Williamson	2,456	1,238	664	610	1,996	966	7		2,659	1,988	
Wilson	1,002	360	284	254	1,097	297	32		1,373	650	
Winkler	0	0	27	5	24	10	0		38	34	
Wise	1,960	1,145	1,483	213	955	738	6		1,537	2,095	
Wood	1,134	709	279	371	1,160	843	16		1,521	1,161	
Yoakum	50	12	27	43	32	15	1		49	70	
Young	742	510	633	367	332	351	10		563	944	
Zapata	0	0	0	0	0	0	0		0	0	
Zavala	0	0	0	0	0	0	0		0	0	
Official Totals	206,038	119,378	80,060	53,367	146,871	76,268	1,719		219,808	179,857	
Unofficial Totals	**206,038**	**119,378**	**80,538**	**52,905**	**147,740**	**76,958**	**1,734**		**219,808**	**180,237**	

Table 28: Gubernatorial Races

	Democratic Primary, 1924										
Year	1924									Runoff	
County	Felix D. Robertson	George W. Dixon	W. E. Pope	Joe Burkett	Miriam A. Ferguson	Lynch Davidson	V. A. Collins	T. W. (Whit) Davidson	Thomas D. Barton	Felix D. Robertson	Miriam A. Ferguson
Anderson	1,714	27	60	57	1,295	711	254	827	123	2,849	2,881
Andrews	21	2	0	70	21	19	2	11	17	65	87
Angelina	820	9	46	48	2,308	499	435	888	99	1,406	4,048
Aransas	128	2	6	3	20	69	10	66	8	238	170
Archer	188	11	34	0	275	292	46	177	83	465	948
Armstrong	112	4	49	24	35	308	28	43	182	540	270
Atascosa	560	17	35	26	139	126	13	717	117	775	763
Austin	451	8	17	30	1,305	459	19	808	32	568	3,520
Bailey	13	8	5	37	41	101	6	69	66	161	233
Bandera	200	4	6	38	42	32	1	143	14	363	338
Bastrop	1,095	11	36	23	647	525	60	540	75	1,708	2,379
Baylor	308	36	15	127	410	563	67	183	37	555	1,201
Bee	915	1	5	5	8	10	8	14	44	1,106	61
Bell	3,024	129	87	164	3,560	835	144	724	319	5,259	5,959
Bexar	8,262	46	155	120	1,173	2,629	332	11,666	1,385	8,916	13,194
Blanco	61	3	3	29	450	121	1	116	21	209	873
Borden	66	1	9	22	36	19	8	20	9	0	0
Bosque	757	14	51	170	1,585	675	70	595	125	1,298	3,407
Bowie	1,300	44	55	80	827	1,290	385	1,066	80	2,438	3,061
Brazoria	781	7	13	7	248	245	52	171	31	1,494	1,162
Brazos	902	10	25	27	268	551	186	279	265	1,763	1,286
Brewster	103	0	8	13	39	165	3	130	17	198	256
Briscoe	78	27	27	184	131	49	6	112	89	286	554
Brooks	86	1	2	1	6	47	5	94	17	92	92
Brown	747	14	89	174	1,436	1,385	45	265	117	1,701	2,969
Burleson	412	6	45	18	405	266	106	1,540	107	763	2,399
Burnet	304	5	14	99	949	537	10	194	73	926	1,665
Caldwell	980	4	32	32	779	312	52	426	123	1,616	1,737
Calhoun	328	3	15	1	132	114	12	415	29	411	693
Callahan	287	19	32	375	787	305	62	144	81	808	1,774
Cameron	859	20	119	50	274	1,057	69	557	165	1,521	1,526
Camp	581	4	5	11	474	184	37	505	17	729	1,165
Carson	252	4	26	11	150	194	16	71	293	642	626
Cass	833	21	50	119	626	329	81	1,006	37	1,725	2,049
Castro	12	3	4	16	34	118	13	73	70	58	261
Chambers	204	5	6	6	108	150	31	109	12	294	388
Cherokee	1,455	19	66	32	1,453	705	156	1,239	207	2,642	3,680
Childress	527	4	45	90	378	656	38	293	97	983	1,389
Clay	370	19	56	264	633	830	105	489	97	1,267	1,972
Cochran	0	1	1	2	18	12	1	7	0	22	76
Coke	160	3	105	247	286	216	14	123	30	427	590
Coleman	774	9	61	129	1,577	892	25	424	88	1,465	2,903
Collin	3,712	14	148	101	1,486	931	166	3,563	94	4,673	6,714
Collingsworth	497	11	136	98	237	371	25	399	77	902	1,091
Colorado	642	16	22	14	469	296	28	1,291	148	1,008	2,495
Comal	18	2	0	5	689	60	4	258	12	48	2,111
Comanche	726	17	218	246	1,558	1,042	43	215	257	1,789	3,039
Concho	173	6	21	51	501	408	18	46	42	374	871
Cooke	1,657	19	80	183	467	879	160	1,235	101	2,468	2,532
Coryell	775	11	32	85	1,797	947	84	478	51	1,780	3,503
Cottle	121	9	101	55	464	286	110	183	70	482	978
Crane	0	0	0	0	0	0	0	0	0	0	0
Crockett	32	1	4	28	30	186	8	16	3	42	137
Crosby	385	18	24	197	396	458	29	106	91	482	0
Culberson	13	0	0	9	0	112	0	2	2	43	87
Dallam	198	15	72	23	91	435	30	216	125	405	312
Dallas	15,533	72	258	123	1,966	6,137	2,500	4,917	263	23,328	15,755
Dawson	369	21	42	213	229	171	34	251	119	813	1,072
DeWitt	1,007	21	38	14	1,151	572	24	1,063	248	1,368	3,483
Deaf Smith	63	3	129	9	30	294	12	25	283	346	202
Delta	899	7	43	149	388	329	36	720	33	1,573	1,894
Denton	1,157	10	51	91	1,144	1,051	264	1,461	365	3,247	3,788
Dickens	168	11	108	179	320	444	48	116	68	717	1,070
Dimmit	56	1	3	2	41	113	2	54	32	125	227

Table 28: Gubernatorial Races

	Democratic Primary, 1924									Runoff	
Year	1924									Runoff	
County	Felix D. Robertson	George W. Dixon	W. E. Pope	Joe Burkett	Miriam A. Ferguson	Lynch Davidson	V. A. Collins	T. W. (Whit) Davidson	Thomas D. Barton	Felix D. Robertson	Miriam A. Ferguson
Donley	307	12	48	95	62	260	43	377	106	845	508
Duval	8	0	2	0	3	1,234	0	10	0	5	1,260
Eastland	1,342	16	146	2,380	1,054	682	96	262	634	3,143	4,242
Ector	30	0	35	15	17	155	2	16	11	66	208
Edwards	50	0	12	3	15	74	0	42	4	98	157
El Paso	2,333	18	65	75	187	3,901	46	538	48	3,074	3,114
Ellis	2,928	8	84	68	2,108	1,896	168	656	163	4,560	5,888
Erath	510	9	259	194	1,491	967	70	667	79	1,378	3,145
Falls	707	10	49	32	1,489	1,346	129	224	231	1,686	2,924
Fannin	2,387	13	150	161	1,434	928	143	1,568	254	4,327	4,535
Fayette	266	7	15	25	1,245	761	22	1,142	41	482	5,413
Fisher	472	3	36	232	444	447	24	380	70	1,140	1,942
Floyd	293	23	45	110	355	402	107	253	334	874	973
Foard	70	7	26	44	311	347	33	57	141	266	571
Fort Bend	278	1	36	4	421	440	36	168	97	619	1,857
Franklin	249	5	23	110	402	264	46	762	58	673	1,310
Freestone	896	8	93	37	1,237	773	87	332	186	1,871	2,215
Frio	298	96	43	25	106	95	106	243	40	728	596
Gaines	105	3	38	57	67	84	6	50	38	180	104
Galveston	2,023	34	45	22	2,260	2,142	96	1,104	127	2,561	4,411
Garza	742	6	2	110	276	118	11	69	57	858	519
Gillespie	43	5	8	101	271	93	4	328	19	188	2,413
Glasscock	20	2	1	53	25	63	1	21	6	66	101
Goliad	333	3	16	5	138	53	3	251	43	332	622
Gonzales	1,070	53	38	69	752	286	75	606	636	1,763	2,171
Gray	331	7	12	51	99	231	52	116	187	433	388
Grayson	3,678	174	483	138	1,357	2,387	303	1,476	118	6,463	5,518
Gregg	722	5	24	18	229	234	75	611	134	1,053	1,077
Grimes	647	2	50	5	389	239	44	131	95	1,289	1,471
Guadalupe	201	1	13	11	514	111	9	224	26	429	2,127
Hale	538	10	138	73	171	763	86	362	300	1,075	1,163
Hall	647	41	114	46	297	374	88	322	187	1,305	891
Hamilton	203	5	204	93	1,378	803	57	131	93	968	2,490
Hansford	130	6	17	40	14	59	6	53	160	285	241
Hardeman	389	11	43	107	279	739	104	264	80	974	1,266
Hardin	835	3	12	7	576	213	562	200	30	1,304	1,502
Harris	10,463	460	182	96	2,077	12,613	1,759	5,740	317	14,962	14,201
Harrison	1,117	4	15	3	469	157	50	2,622	55	1,654	2,612
Hartley	33	1	0	25	26	127	7	41	141	172	159
Haskell	837	15	90	253	1,058	693	62	340	130	1,528	2,451
Hays	1,029	13	11	15	413	363	57	380	104	1,554	1,039
Hemphill	59	21	37	20	23	307	18	34	91	171	103
Henderson	1,314	32	60	56	1,628	508	79	1,046	151	2,077	3,652
Hidalgo	685	18	1,376	39	105	1,151	81	225	77	1,423	747
Hill	2,306	15	95	55	2,263	1,297	191	751	545	4,718	4,379
Hockley	98	5	14	10	39	97	2	30	6	0	0
Hood	104	2	616	34	454	398	12	217	28	623	1,346
Hopkins	1,886	21	83	160	788	633	63	1,986	119	3,217	3,156
Houston	697	11	123	44	1,499	673	177	546	224	1,554	2,596
Howard	670	6	12	65	203	282	57	443	20	1,090	961
Hudspeth	64	0	2	38	9	69	13	8	1	94	37
Hunt	4,373	20	184	172	1,860	806	548	1,788	261	6,653	4,776
Hutchinson	7	0	0	15	0	1	0	0	2	0	0
Irion	71	0	0	147	102	99	2	22	17	173	135
Jack	563	10	59	32	253	340	84	337	129	981	1,044
Jackson	651	3	8	20	133	335	22	217	40	746	718
Jasper	228	6	96	25	774	333	394	56	51	800	1,332
Jeff Davis	73	1	0	3	8	85	1	50	4	107	57
Jefferson	3,462	28	45	20	754	1,662	2,005	1,043	61	6,118	4,314
Jim Hogg	6	0	3	0	4	81	0	56	0	116	17
Jim Wells	353	0	45	6	155	127	10	426	31	380	640
Johnson	1,631	12	148	207	1,850	1,245	117	396	446	3,642	3,505
Jones	1,195	17	87	247	886	730	80	682	167	2,049	2,960
Karnes	1,017	0	18	17	900	255	33	482	63	1,157	1,877
Kaufman	2,055	6	90	128	1,912	800	275	737	196	3,303	4,359

Table 28: Gubernatorial Races

	Democratic Primary, 1924										
Year	**1924**									**Runoff**	
County	Felix D. Robertson	George W. Dixon	W. E. Pope	Joe Burkett	Miriam A. Ferguson	Lynch Davidson	V. A. Collins	T. W. (Whit) Davidson	Thomas D. Barton	Felix D. Robertson	Miriam A. Ferguson
Kendall	59	1	0	2	51	62	1	77	3	141	510
Kenedy	2	0	0	0	0	104	0	0	0	4	88
Kent	209	8	54	91	145	136	11	81	37	0	0
Kerr	439	4	8	40	59	132	25	174	19	654	691
Kimble	181	10	15	67	193	431	30	120	22	433	682
King	20	2	1	20	40	25	23	16	5	59	94
Kinney	12	0	1	1	4	74	1	43	4	19	88
Kleberg	690	3	24	14	109	325	19	151	34	751	467
Knox	1,176	13	56	127	685	199	28	370	22	1,338	1,382
La Salle	67	8	2	15	33	284	4	23	18	175	355
Lamar	3,602	40	101	93	1,542	1,415	254	1,018	231	4,961	3,814
Lamb	157	10	71	88	55	133	41	84	54	470	390
Lampasas	326	4	22	220	819	526	52	203	80	938	1,485
Lavaca	854	5	21	50	1,593	1,073	33	1,516	37	1,182	5,120
Lee	181	1	40	23	574	484	57	714	75	496	2,123
Leon	486	24	465	67	814	220	91	421	43	989	1,663
Liberty	795	14	26	12	613	297	344	138	22	1,454	1,549
Limestone	1,527	35	96	71	2,299	1,636	73	224	123	2,769	4,269
Lipscomb	31	0	3	47	37	60	2	13	113	58	74
Live Oak	365	0	8	5	108	36	10	60	13	0	0
Llano	62	8	19	643	503	216	34	97	68	540	1,191
Loving	0	0	0	0	0	0	0	0	0	0	0
Lubbock	875	27	81	266	355	1,193	51	837	347	2,064	1,802
Lynn	675	15	49	160	493	202	23	222	98	1,033	1,217
Madison	472	2	321	51	941	190	12	79	65	869	1,412
Marion	179	1	4	2	42	37	2	365	3	472	589
Martin	229	3	3	16	49	64	3	46	3	351	271
Mason	106	7	47	139	254	333	18	177	49	459	1,136
Matagorda	520	14	5	6	90	236	11	180	51	1,127	1,002
Maverick	15	0	3	0	9	183	2	24	2	68	127
McCulloch	900	4	61	45	503	775	23	103	87	1,227	1,628
McLennan	4,176	84	97	63	1,809	2,624	118	482	343	7,324	5,588
McMullen	62	1	7	3	26	30	2	92	6	40	73
Medina	504	2	10	30	253	78	9	551	35	729	1,389
Menard	107	4	15	129	208	321	8	66	44	340	590
Midland	89	4	14	22	96	368	3	70	12	249	571
Milam	1,599	13	51	35	2,687	588	118	1,502	94	2,283	4,632
Mills	200	1	21	402	818	458	19	78	41	593	1,486
Mitchell	133	17	32	329	381	613	41	125	172	885	1,234
Montague	316	67	214	340	615	720	100	1,183	268	1,662	2,839
Montgomery	583	3	35	6	165	298	18	212	190	1,004	1,176
Moore	7	3	4	27	17	41	3	8	124	67	32
Morris	193	1	15	189	146	261	15	703	9	565	733
Motley	129	11	85	181	166	138	24	195	47	382	448
Nacogdoches	763	13	37	20	1,709	629	168	1,019	96	1,536	3,126
Navarro	2,232	28	26	46	1,793	1,610	114	1,064	208	4,349	5,221
Newton	203	11	11	17	567	178	202	23	9	417	1,078
Nolan	680	13	46	273	689	727	87	140	123	1,333	1,424
Nueces	1,685	7	992	48	139	344	46	498	248	2,839	2,625
Ochiltree	101	9	19	68	28	42	11	22	318	288	50
Oldham	18	0	5	39	17	120	1	21	22	93	87
Orange	516	7	10	11	423	440	152	224	66	1,222	1,271
Palo Pinto	774	9	144	106	523	607	68	785	130	1,562	1,533
Panola	437	30	99	91	1,224	581	161	448	61	1,194	2,294
Parker	926	20	126	122	530	732	78	1,145	122	2,002	2,026
Parmer	40	8	8	36	31	168	8	47	104	207	119
Pecos	14	1	4	12	16	188	3	4	5	105	158
Polk	499	122	23	44	781	123	831	122	38	1,149	1,473
Potter	272	11	17	26	147	822	25	368	1,550	2,731	1,021
Presidio	50	1	6	1	13	275	5	151	25	113	192
Rains	143	3	61	37	420	239	80	293	67	521	1,143
Randall	97	3	6	32	60	539	40	68	285	509	376
Reagan	17	2	2	56	29	86	2	8	3	64	30
Real	26	0	5	20	16	20	1	25	20	32	40
Red River	1,074	26	104	329	1,149	778	122	724	215	1,701	2,698

Table 28: Gubernatorial Races

Year	1924									Runoff	
County	Felix D. Robertson	George W. Dixon	W. E. Pope	Joe Burkett	Miriam A. Ferguson	Lynch Davidson	V. A. Collins	T. W. (Whit) Davidson	Thomas D. Barton	Felix D. Robertson	Miriam A. Ferguson
Reeves	133	1	3	63	43	346	21	54	12	331	301
Refugio	167	0	25	10	51	57	0	322	7	242	617
Roberts	121	6	21	14	9	49	3	10	159	314	169
Robertson	519	28	39	17	767	701	89	234	143	1,331	2,054
Rockwall	473	2	12	23	360	212	61	613	15	716	1,176
Runnels	1,037	7	51	180	1,119	985	80	269	105	1,759	2,626
Rusk	1,356	12	111	54	1,468	324	158	773	116	2,029	2,375
Sabine	219	6	22	3	1,300	149	206	121	15	593	1,685
San Augustine	187	7	36	20	1,237	108	86	176	36	392	1,742
San Jacinto	237	3	49	4	374	47	91	23	16	400	540
San Patricio	1,184	12	59	2	81	153	20	182	52	1,541	727
San Saba	282	5	65	114	1,048	499	18	145	50	793	1,736
Schleicher	28	3	7	28	109	245	4	42	13	135	307
Scurry	875	10	150	200	347	444	140	140	91	1,539	1,033
Shackelford	735	9	98	245	262	454	17	88	33	373	925
Shelby	528	18	162	33	2,183	593	265	941	154	1,727	3,780
Sherman	33	1	65	12	22	97	8	18	53	138	31
Smith	2,916	17	130	62	665	550	94	1,024	129	4,353	2,453
Somervell	89	3	23	32	345	125	29	58	26	166	621
Starr	0	0	481	0	0	109	0	0	0	5	667
Stephens	520	15	41	358	990	796	42	506	122	1,428	2,181
Sterling	75	1	32	17	123	142	7	24	20	192	250
Stonewall	399	2	41	186	339	210	22	100	20	410	827
Sutton	16	2	54	11	123	222	14	27	12	68	269
Swisher	142	7	23	87	210	254	35	100	175	564	430
Tarrant	7,118	124	634	190	2,113	4,897	777	2,853	1,156	14,832	10,379
Taylor	1,280	63	143	804	808	641	223	260	437	3,139	2,689
Terrell	65	0	0	1	5	16	1	48	0	98	60
Terry	323	8	5	154	156	176	14	375	33	594	847
Throckmorton	532	4	25	146	178	115	5	85	16	686	556
Titus	294	81	105	69	587	570	78	829	143	1,086	1,971
Tom Green	975	9	39	144	721	1,246	128	327	98	1,545	2,104
Travis	2,112	10	39	36	1,513	2,456	446	1,834	818	4,764	5,630
Trinity	456	20	88	77	901	161	101	220	91	692	1,587
Tyler	291	7	17	15	679	54	384	32	22	610	910
Upshur	770	0	61	51	1,294	126	35	1,263	52	1,307	2,721
Upton	10	0	6	26	8	30	0	3	1	6	26
Uvalde	740	3	11	14	152	276	25	806	37	897	1,066
Val Verde	319	0	11	6	39	415	15	483	11	420	731
Van Zandt	1,745	12	113	147	1,441	358	315	1,158	194	3,010	3,583
Victoria	494	4	18	11	357	350	54	1,422	25	595	2,135
Walker	441	21	114	18	596	275	165	180	37	882	1,105
Waller	670	6	6	18	134	266	25	316	16	729	839
Ward	40	0	3	54	47	190	2	31	9	143	227
Washington	297	11	32	4	1,744	1,263	26	444	76	402	3,446
Webb	65	6	6	1	10	206	2	507	5	175	852
Wharton	509	1	32	11	401	633	72	294	283	1,320	1,911
Wheeler	210	18	27	101	301	500	17	158	130	670	1,034
Wichita	2,174	257	61	166	1,468	1,776	264	1,739	427	4,354	5,220
Wilbarger	681	19	54	85	551	921	94	261	180	1,380	1,670
Willacy	13	1	6	6	51	116	0	6	10	40	80
Williamson	1,514	33	28	180	2,242	1,712	149	1,178	248	2,885	6,750
Wilson	217	13	161	55	723	691	40	251	219	524	2,087
Winkler	0	0	0	5	2	22	0	0	0	1	13
Wise	1,121	28	51	126	389	846	144	1,388	175	2,545	2,101
Wood	927	9	32	104	1,117	238	182	1,152	116	2,018	3,048
Yoakum	17	1	0	93	47	30	3	23	11	36	94
Young	477	9	485	69	515	545	44	255	124	1,324	1,706
Zapata	0	0	0	0	0	76	2	114	1	13	128
Zavala	208	3	9	23	62	100	13	99	28	283	277
Official Totals	193,508	4,035	17,136	21,720	146,424	141,208	24,864	125,011	29,217	316,019	413,751
Unofficial Totals	195,612	3,960	17,154	21,780	146,570	141,386	24,894	125,097	29,323	345,441	441,632

Table 29: Gubernatorial Races

	Democratic Primaries, 1926-1928											
Year	1926						Runoff		1928			
County	Lynch Davidson	Miriam A. Ferguson	Kate M. Johnston	Dan Moody	Edith E. Wilmans	O.F. Zimmerman	Miriam A. Ferguson	Dan Moody	William E. Hawkins	Dan Moody	Louis J. Wardlaw	Edith E. Wilmans
Anderson	475	1,847	9	3,142	26	43	1,944	3,773	253	3,261	1,051	176
Andrews	19	68	0	91	0	2	39	84	24	59	73	2
Angelina	143	3,397	3	2,343	13	45	3,342	2,537	227	2,734	2,455	113
Aransas	83	96	1	216	3	1	57	251	31	274	77	13
Archer	460	754	3	660	2	5	621	721	181	849	608	60
Armstrong	264	181	0	505	4	6	177	718	25	541	189	20
Atascosa	241	862	10	1,166	4	3	888	1,489	81	1,410	733	50
Austin	293	2,171	17	934	6	4	2,631	1,190	116	1,239	1,964	66
Bailey	148	191	0	305	2	12	202	390	46	369	251	35
Bandera	60	144	0	275	1	0	166	430	0	0	0	0
Bastrop	408	1,552	2	1,797	7	11	1,276	1,836	106	1,987	1,086	114
Baylor	523	691	2	741	19	11	779	1,076	152	1,138	514	55
Bee	164	146	0	889	5	6	250	1,092	66	499	121	9
Bell	1,101	4,020	7	5,076	11	19	4,008	5,941	269	4,795	3,168	145
Bexar	2,792	8,625	18	12,896	26	23	5,386	14,382	857	13,641	9,092	316
Blanco	50	353	0	399	0	1	364	440	18	353	296	3
Borden	51	152	1	166	4	2	91	138	22	111	137	9
Bosque	847	1,506	32	1,647	32	19	1,523	1,981	156	1,992	1,785	99
Bowie	1,186	2,558	15	3,930	22	60	3,125	5,333	455	4,517	1,035	363
Brazoria	180	857	1	1,591	2	21	660	1,817	34	653	278	18
Brazos	295	1,110	1	1,653	3	7	1,075	1,728	60	2,056	724	51
Brewster	140	197	2	448	0	1	98	392	44	567	276	17
Briscoe	163	324	4	546	5	8	334	675	51	529	369	60
Brooks	27	87	0	170	1	2	58	151	3	190	24	3
Brown	1,307	1,629	5	2,276	29	22	1,899	3,411	112	2,308	2,181	76
Burleson	398	1,443	2	1,097	0	9	1,552	1,335	170	1,340	1,196	51
Burnet	354	1,036	0	1,387	3	3	940	1,505	72	1,237	830	19
Caldwell	375	1,209	2	1,793	4	9	996	1,993	307	2,120	1,111	59
Calhoun	145	423	4	525	2	8	267	520	79	706	238	29
Callahan	557	1,109	0	1,145	4	6	1,206	1,559	45	1,130	1,424	40
Cameron	639	1,066	14	2,547	4	11	340	2,704	0	3,767	916	0
Camp	276	776	0	853	4	13	747	1,054	140	1,252	398	37
Carson	198	335	2	545	1	3	279	480	71	900	547	38
Cass	601	1,769	5	1,532	13	128	1,826	2,667	252	2,181	820	147
Castro	261	231	2	244	2	6	309	519	33	467	313	22
Chambers	67	309	1	368	3	1	325	366	44	425	170	30
Cherokee	513	2,362	12	2,810	12	42	2,398	3,322	218	3,504	1,275	218
Childress	562	761	1	1,138	5	6	767	1,661	89	1,549	1,104	90
Clay	883	1,014	2	1,547	11	5	1,227	2,329	127	1,884	866	158
Cochran	56	84	0	153	0	1	99	193	10	115	120	11
Coke	274	410	0	546	3	10	473	838	51	569	344	19
Coleman	1,138	1,679	6	1,945	4	12	1,746	2,678	82	1,883	1,892	85
Collin	1,361	3,558	7	4,061	14	14	3,844	5,600	411	3,763	2,694	247
Collingsworth	429	577	2	1,037	2	11	492	1,169	103	1,244	888	68
Colorado	314	1,719	2	1,316	6	9	1,883	1,549	139	1,065	1,148	69
Comal	112	837	1	318	0	1	1,125	414	31	717	437	4
Comanche	707	1,717	1	2,155	5	8	1,821	2,750	134	1,896	1,904	131
Concho	315	628	3	486	2	5	575	655	25	709	659	21
Cooke	990	1,621	5	2,250	6	31	1,754	3,110	175	2,226	1,505	143
Coryell	627	2,021	3	1,940	2	23	2,224	2,505	92	1,930	1,659	53
Cottle	221	659	4	955	9	6	553	967	68	914	613	87
Crane	0	0	0	0	0	0	0	0	14	126	214	11
Crockett	136	111	0	125	1	0	25	161	6	290	175	9
Crosby	552	710	2	1,118	5	13	705	1,507	98	1,185	887	43
Culberson	50	31	0	18	0	0	16	93	2	118	75	1
Dallam	161	494	14	819	9	10	128	602	32	1,013	212	50
Dallas	7,044	5,709	27	23,188	105	87	4,727	28,431	2,242	20,891	5,816	718
Dawson	400	959	3	1,258	6	11	949	1,567	126	945	1,053	50
DeWitt	777	2,270	3	1,159	0	4	2,371	1,515	91	1,675	1,665	53
Deaf Smith	217	182	3	732	7	14	158	893	50	887	128	34
Delta	578	1,302	0	1,359	7	12	1,342	1,986	23	1,531	1,064	6
Denton	966	2,077	3	3,862	10	15	1,804	4,256	184	3,802	1,914	168
Dickens	375	720	6	921	1	9	703	1,096	85	1,198	623	75
Dimmit	152	203	0	294	0	9	110	393	29	420	201	20

Table 29: Gubernatorial Races

	Democratic Primaries, 1926-1928											
Year	1926						Runoff		1928			
County	Lynch Davidson	Miriam A. Ferguson	Kate M. Johnston	Dan Moody	Edith E. Wilmans	O.F. Zimmerman	Miriam A. Ferguson	Dan Moody	William E. Hawkins	Dan Moody	Louis J. Wardlaw	Edith E. Wilmans
Donley	400	350	2	1,443	4	8	388	1,703	81	1,412	550	53
Duval	8	1,315	0	20	0	0	1,210	25	2	28	1,161	0
Eastland	1,000	2,030	2	3,422	9	9	1,949	4,043	258	3,114	3,060	81
Ector	136	58	0	100	0	0	58	161	11	168	309	14
Edwards	0	0	0	0	0	0	68	147	3	125	155	0
El Paso	945	1,716	31	6,137	10	21	511	5,919	355	7,537	1,390	190
Ellis	2,159	3,221	3	4,396	12	22	3,490	6,066	327	4,743	2,754	169
Erath	925	2,008	1	2,134	6	22	2,066	2,823	157	1,993	2,419	139
Falls	1,102	1,684	3	1,494	10	23	2,067	2,297	62	2,497	1,806	104
Fannin	1,275	3,153	11	3,938	10	36	3,387	5,378	320	3,949	1,785	174
Fayette	467	3,854	24	1,514	4	19	3,976	1,473	132	1,545	3,382	163
Fisher	544	1,245	3	1,408	6	31	1,438	1,710	133	1,415	1,052	42
Floyd	313	686	4	1,625	10	11	711	1,973	81	1,152	709	75
Foard	425	466	5	524	7	0	551	940	86	789	521	100
Fort Bend	239	1,391	6	1,170	1	5	1,470	1,444	130	1,799	734	150
Franklin	180	820	0	967	6	25	971	1,198	157	1,217	402	72
Freestone	741	1,241	5	1,685	21	24	1,338	2,512	155	2,137	737	72
Frio	199	396	0	838	5	1	345	1,156	70	941	235	27
Gaines	79	177	0	368	2	11	161	432	20	403	150	21
Galveston	653	3,555	2	3,933	7	16	2,178	4,107	6	3,843	3,207	0
Garza	211	449	2	879	3	13	477	1,054	40	691	502	19
Gillespie	148	683	3	379	0	3	763	513	10	289	291	4
Glasscock	90	86	0	135	1	1	101	189	3	63	62	2
Goliad	61	212	2	332	0	0	418	437	1	117	158	0
Gonzales	324	1,511	4	2,197	4	3	1,327	2,182	125	2,239	602	72
Gray	0	0	0	0	0	0	180	508	138	1,687	610	110
Grayson	2,279	3,311	4	5,956	30	22	3,277	8,142	314	6,510	2,308	268
Gregg	332	676	1	1,105	1	5	503	1,296	126	1,470	510	47
Grimes	123	873	0	1,359	1	0	716	1,261	67	1,274	361	35
Guadalupe	106	613	2	561	2	1	909	687	17	289	331	3
Hale	593	463	9	1,849	13	9	568	2,462	132	1,963	1,168	76
Hall	406	766	0	1,713	2	13	780	2,118	126	1,556	757	84
Hamilton	518	1,316	9	1,308	7	6	1,427	1,652	55	1,214	1,402	30
Hansford	78	118	2	212	6	1	47	181	30	470	59	41
Hardeman	543	665	7	1,632	9	24	762	2,039	62	1,460	1,335	101
Hardin	141	1,299	12	1,198	4	11	1,143	1,327	215	1,251	564	133
Harris	3,236	8,640	49	22,508	42	57	5,379	22,299	1,080	16,823	5,713	623
Harrison	365	1,216	4	2,487	2	15	1,216	2,694	0	3,410	992	4
Hartley	59	177	6	268	3	1	67	176	24	350	119	25
Haskell	515	1,699	1	1,752	3	8	1,852	2,184	220	2,062	1,768	96
Hays	263	545	4	1,596	3	2	445	1,763	66	1,573	330	22
Hemphill	79	75	0	252	5	1	24	237	21	635	70	18
Henderson	726	2,568	3	1,604	22	24	2,967	2,323	303	2,493	1,554	207
Hidalgo	410	359	2	3,912	2	0	213	3,890	49	4,462	272	19
Hill	1,534	2,444	8	3,968	19	19	2,768	5,229	257	3,903	2,177	110
Hockley	205	326	4	530	5	14	374	730	120	675	390	63
Hood	369	703	30	938	7	5	1,147	661	52	740	582	13
Hopkins	1,197	2,229	6	2,814	9	71	2,074	3,858	246	3,466	932	202
Houston	406	1,816	4	1,960	5	15	1,677	2,108	186	2,181	919	91
Howard	392	767	3	1,170	4	13	789	1,406	97	761	1,060	35
Hudspeth	45	86	0	183	0	0	38	186	14	203	122	4
Hunt	2,046	3,073	7	4,877	34	42	3,315	7,013	382	5,219	2,048	262
Hutchinson	2	95	0	14	1	1	0	0	124	636	358	58
Irion	94	153	3	226	3	3	147	278	4	237	194	13
Jack	401	520	3	895	3	11	494	1,164	73	1,013	633	51
Jackson	191	627	3	872	3	7	470	809	83	826	352	56
Jasper	126	1,203	15	1,034	1	3	1,098	1,122	168	1,426	565	93
Jeff Davis	72	61	0	169	2	1	22	171	13	122	40	1
Jefferson	908	3,954	9	6,963	15	20	3,272	7,211	886	10,271	2,162	565
Jim Hogg	26	95	0	55	0	0	4	129	4	254	12	5
Jim Wells	146	632	19	510	4	2	466	603	2	521	364	0
Johnson	1,251	1,902	10	3,805	12	7	2,340	5,004	152	3,197	2,089	105
Jones	711	1,410	1	2,062	8	3	1,676	2,494	132	2,354	1,784	49
Karnes	374	1,682	3	1,011	4	18	1,526	1,249	97	1,176	1,466	40
Kaufman	1,069	2,498	0	3,078	11	11	2,388	3,817	134	2,917	1,676	74

Table 29: Gubernatorial Races

	Democratic Primaries, 1926-1928											
Year	1926						Runoff		1928			
County	Lynch Davidson	Miriam A. Ferguson	Kate M. Johnston	Dan Moody	Edith E. Wilmans	O.F. Zimmerman	Miriam A. Ferguson	Dan Moody	William E. Hawkins	Dan Moody	Louis J. Wardlaw	Edith E. Wilmans
Kendall	33	122	0	88	0	0	207	184	5	29	55	0
Kenedy	60	35	0	8	0	0	28	22	0	56	35	0
Kent	202	441	0	341	2	7	335	347	45	471	303	24
Kerr	100	528	0	592	1	4	378	856	23	566	139	5
Kimble	262	499	3	588	4	0	428	811	25	626	578	0
King	34	92	0	122	0	2	79	143	10	126	73	9
Kinney	44	43	0	90	0	0	31	124	0	90	44	1
Kleberg	169	342	1	914	1	3	206	874	170	931	379	24
Knox	489	883	4	1,152	8	5	996	1,413	177	1,275	893	73
La Salle	66	352	2	394	2	3	198	417	11	277	283	4
Lamar	1,312	2,318	11	4,582	19	10	2,354	5,377	323	4,854	1,386	274
Lamb	222	509	2	1,175	3	9	451	1,287	125	1,111	594	61
Lampasas	294	878	3	1,313	2	9	833	1,487	92	1,377	897	34
Lavaca	647	4,410	2	1,622	6	6	4,762	1,782	167	1,918	3,168	103
Lee	167	1,462	4	848	2	6	1,646	936	85	1,236	1,158	62
Leon	213	1,204	4	1,222	7	66	1,126	1,371	110	1,475	631	84
Liberty	136	1,067	3	1,452	6	20	1,050	1,555	140	1,532	587	85
Limestone	1,406	2,372	8	2,824	23	24	2,665	3,759	251	3,454	2,233	179
Lipscomb	40	38	1	78	0	0	52	135	16	186	47	7
Live Oak	110	641	0	629	1	19	485	675	110	734	560	39
Llano	252	577	2	886	5	5	572	995	41	975	413	19
Loving	0	0	0	0	0	0	0	0	0	0	0	0
Lubbock	1,255	1,168	11	2,901	7	11	1,423	3,683	140	3,528	1,524	84
Lynn	341	882	1	1,323	6	11	841	1,413	78	1,181	1,307	48
Madison	132	843	0	1,068	1	35	936	1,222	81	1,260	423	138
Marion	93	353	0	331	0	1	371	448	9	302	166	12
Martin	163	370	1	406	3	15	280	442	39	382	390	24
Mason	314	472	2	637	2	4	333	595	31	789	469	8
Matagorda	142	580	0	1,270	1	7	531	1,436	31	471	198	10
Maverick	46	28	0	265	0	0	18	304	0	104	143	0
McCulloch	718	938	1	1,379	2	12	1,158	1,897	79	1,429	1,267	24
McLennan	3,626	3,420	18	5,864	11	59	3,909	8,933	249	8,370	3,829	241
McMullen	45	153	2	151	0	0	146	217	17	180	110	9
Medina	114	921	1	583	0	2	792	684	51	444	613	10
Menard	237	399	1	587	3	3	417	795	15	461	542	10
Midland	294	314	0	340	1	6	260	506	41	384	428	23
Milam	748	3,354	3	2,411	3	3	3,263	3,002	164	3,003	2,886	91
Mills	408	929	5	920	3	16	982	1,208	71	902	731	71
Mitchell	538	676	2	1,388	8	3	720	1,626	93	1,163	826	47
Montague	711	1,283	5	1,803	12	14	1,107	2,173	174	1,941	1,208	170
Montgomery	146	952	47	1,138	2	3	873	1,298	297	1,608	679	144
Moore	27	39	1	87	0	0	0	0	34	153	63	13
Morris	238	724	2	808	8	95	580	1,100	66	1,222	324	60
Motley	219	364	3	784	6	3	373	918	72	751	334	36
Nacogdoches	316	2,248	3	2,396	6	24	2,305	2,574	251	2,999	1,395	157
Navarro	1,805	2,703	4	3,703	14	32	2,901	5,463	515	5,360	2,142	208
Newton	48	1,048	1	509	0	2	958	532	168	932	419	73
Nolan	655	900	5	2,100	4	7	905	2,359	56	1,810	1,154	56
Nueces	647	1,584	6	2,800	3	14	972	2,911	143	3,355	1,426	46
Ochiltree	109	146	4	432	2	6	83	328	56	471	96	26
Oldham	82	122	6	182	3	1	125	279	11	297	77	8
Orange	279	1,346	4	1,201	46	0	987	1,258	181	1,492	644	100
Palo Pinto	540	1,111	5	2,014	5	9	871	2,177	205	1,813	1,199	154
Panola	463	1,699	3	1,377	12	22	1,806	1,806	162	1,538	868	79
Parker	921	1,449	2	2,444	2	12	1,402	3,101	150	2,140	1,718	132
Parmer	155	203	9	376	4	3	101	276	56	454	178	25
Pecos	103	95	0	220	1	1	64	229	4	144	164	5
Polk	134	1,321	3	1,128	6	8	1,180	1,195	224	1,513	770	118
Potter	640	892	2	1,985	32	4	732	2,645	165	4,622	1,097	121
Presidio	116	170	4	346	0	4	29	344	20	438	187	3
Rains	157	854	1	487	17	6	997	700	62	641	381	68
Randall	356	315	2	687	5	7	341	990	56	1,038	345	35
Reagan	41	92	0	114	0	0	69	248	29	342	328	8
Real	20	58	0	53	0	0	32	70	1	39	54	0
Red River	623	2,092	2	2,630	13	16	1,701	2,843	193	2,867	999	231

Table 29: Gubernatorial Races

| | Democratic Primaries, 1926-1928 | | | | | | | | | | | |
| Year | 1926 | | | | | | Runoff | | 1928 | | | |
County	Lynch Davidson	Miriam A. Ferguson	Kate M. Johnston	Dan Moody	Edith E. Wilmans	O.F. Zimmerman	Miriam A. Ferguson	Dan Moody	William E. Hawkins	Dan Moody	Louis J. Wardlaw	Edith E. Wilmans
Reeves	241	211	2	418	2	3	177	516	19	391	319	11
Refugio	41	206	0	205	0	0	219	334	7	157	126	1
Roberts	89	81	0	207	0	0	37	220	19	290	69	9
Robertson	468	1,252	6	1,240	1	4	1,229	1,620	136	1,511	942	106
Rockwall	461	577	3	942	12	2	444	1,182	65	1,047	403	45
Runnels	793	1,591	2	1,896	0	3	1,538	2,381	76	1,663	1,973	23
Rusk	582	1,812	3	2,312	5	18	1,876	3,069	163	2,867	1,265	200
Sabine	149	1,206	2	745	2	12	1,231	911	233	1,253	438	113
San Augustine	85	1,450	4	610	2	10	1,487	696	195	967	896	144
San Jacinto	33	549	1	466	1	2	544	497	70	551	258	32
San Patricio	597	428	2	1,126	1	3	371	1,677	156	1,335	612	45
San Saba	651	1,056	5	1,005	3	8	1,003	1,443	48	1,212	1,077	26
Schleicher	174	179	1	286	0	3	126	356	12	394	182	12
Scurry	393	713	7	1,709	2	6	784	1,983	83	1,403	1,109	55
Shackelford	259	419	6	664	3	5	321	707	38	810	661	22
Shelby	405	2,841	7	1,942	8	40	3,236	2,511	174	2,869	2,075	146
Sherman	17	43	0	158	1	1	22	125	9	230	21	16
Smith	895	1,880	4	3,820	7	32	1,997	4,925	455	4,155	1,382	191
Somervell	155	307	0	254	3	5	373	424	20	363	411	10
Starr	4	848	0	21	0	0	3	1,007	0	896	4	0
Stephens	500	1,234	21	1,871	13	8	1,007	2,100	512	1,431	1,520	40
Sterling	120	105	0	177	0	1	117	238	10	205	125	3
Stonewall	235	826	2	486	10	9	684	515	81	533	835	38
Sutton	240	123	0	198	2	0	78	319	2	258	265	1
Swisher	265	285	4	735	12	7	372	1,166	71	1,034	496	43
Tarrant	5,073	5,914	8	17,237	18	87	4,978	20,801	842	14,482	13,620	201
Taylor	720	1,181	3	3,714	4	4	1,595	4,542	195	4,493	1,402	67
Terrell	19	26	0	70	0	0	0	0	4	29	25	0
Terry	535	483	1	637	0	7	564	963	79	856	529	29
Throckmorton	366	282	3	486	5	14	327	768	88	533	598	20
Titus	397	1,209	1	1,021	5	19	968	1,103	109	1,936	778	172
Tom Green	699	929	8	2,281	3	7	814	1,806	90	2,809	1,483	59
Travis	567	3,401	1	8,649	10	3	2,541	9,046	290	7,695	1,777	104
Trinity	45	1,186	0	948	2	9	1,273	999	139	1,053	625	60
Tyler	94	849	1	720	3	9	827	758	104	853	442	53
Upshur	522	2,156	3	1,477	11	46	1,971	1,901	119	2,165	1,417	63
Upton	15	5	0	20	0	0	5	58	16	227	363	21
Uvalde	673	621	0	686	0	11	590	1,455	153	1,362	533	23
Val Verde	268	314	0	671	1	1	145	772	0	314	403	0
Van Zandt	766	2,609	4	2,661	22	51	2,707	3,418	149	2,580	1,479	141
Victoria	151	1,878	2	1,008	6	11	1,522	1,000	69	991	1,555	31
Walker	123	869	2	1,231	7	7	920	1,356	109	1,376	478	59
Waller	130	695	3	699	1	14	567	969	50	773	493	30
Ward	97	126	0	139	0	2	55	189	19	263	308	13
Washington	472	2,403	1	923	0	3	2,222	976	0	1,014	1,942	0
Webb	100	422	14	492	1	4	120	824	0	720	130	0
Wharton	286	1,477	2	1,675	4	1	1,508	1,737	172	1,687	1,008	82
Wheeler	381	685	2	830	3	16	646	1,049	80	997	839	53
Wichita	2,364	2,600	5	5,562	10	21	2,705	6,681	566	6,633	1,656	410
Wilbarger	733	970	5	1,773	9	6	1,013	2,097	199	2,141	1,315	219
Willacy	127	80	1	185	3	0	40	250	42	681	79	20
Williamson	805	3,344	2	5,418	9	19	3,368	5,700	200	4,182	2,514	70
Wilson	289	2,050	6	1,064	3	11	2,337	1,175	104	1,137	1,494	51
Winkler	14	5	0	9	0	0	4	7	6	104	313	16
Wise	853	1,373	2	2,601	9	14	1,121	2,813	140	1,899	1,351	76
Wood	591	1,821	5	1,659	8	17	2,158	2,360	271	1,550	1,103	106
Yoakum	77	68	1	112	2	3	85	196	12	142	111	17
Young	898	1,001	6	1,421	4	21	976	2,023	161	1,645	1,323	51
Zapata	2	46	0	206	0	0	6	157	0	281	0	0
Zavala	157	186	4	477	0	3	170	676	57	608	135	19
Official Totals	122,449	283,482	1,029	409,732	1,580	2,962	270,595	295,723	32,076	442,080	245,508	18,237
Unofficial Totals	122,446	283,510	1,031	409,655	1,543	2,971	270,658	493,606	32,089	442,570	245,508	18,243

Table 30: Gubernatorial Races

County	Miriam A. Ferguson	Thomas B. Love	Paul Loven	Earle B. Mayfield	Barry Miller	C.C. Moody	Frank Putnam	Clint C. Small	Ross S. Sterling	James Young	C.E. Walker	Ross S. Sterling	Miriam A. Ferguson
Anderson	1,866	438	18	520	128	40	9	68	1,555	1,322	21	3,408	3,137
Andrews	49	12	1	11	2	0	0	110	9	6	2	77	106
Angelina	3,521	250	10	225	175	11	2	44	1,754	244	4	2,504	3,705
Aransas	49	50	0	19	22	6	0	0	212	130	1	245	81
Archer	620	132	13	55	90	24	6	776	161	69	1	752	1,239
Armstrong	71	60	1	11	4	3	1	821	11	5	0	632	263
Atascosa	572	263	23	403	244	26	6	26	559	87	3	1,204	747
Austin	1,337	52	13	38	1,060	5	16	9	883	65	1	1,177	2,218
Bailey	357	163	3	51	6	3	6	448	12	23	2	476	635
Bandera	99	65	1	3	6	2	0	5	30	100	0	260	248
Bastrop	1,221	124	8	498	242	12	8	54	494	277	2	1,358	1,702
Baylor	433	177	5	88	108	10	6	475	276	207	13	799	750
Bee	160	234	2	55	26	10	1	18	361	17	0	855	431
Bell	4,090	773	5	330	81	20	1	155	898	2,918	12	4,537	5,097
Bexar	7,225	2,675	216	3,532	5,866	542	86	343	8,727	1,267	29	15,069	11,843
Blanco	229	47	2	27	31	0	8	45	156	35	1	427	398
Borden	127	26	1	30	6	2	1	147	21	7	0	84	126
Bosque	1,772	274	6	842	103	11	0	522	259	288	5	1,718	2,759
Bowie	1,408	777	27	367	280	60	7	125	1,814	1,015	13	2,702	2,326
Brazoria	598	136	6	17	86	1	4	40	1,086	87	0	1,858	900
Brazos	753	183	5	39	127	14	3	39	1,620	280	10	2,127	1,021
Brewster	140	85	2	31	61	18	2	327	147	68	1	499	228
Briscoe	270	71	4	35	30	4	2	570	21	16	0	515	519
Brooks	6	31	7	6	10	1	0	4	252	7	1	416	26
Brown	1,580	558	8	205	319	31	7	999	912	797	5	3,314	2,426
Burleson	1,007	124	8	160	526	20	20	45	640	256	4	1,060	1,653
Burnet	831	311	11	102	62	14	2	383	334	148	5	1,249	1,251
Caldwell	1,354	723	10	350	237	6	16	149	705	351	7	2,060	1,811
Calhoun	259	122	2	24	83	9	2	7	645	63	2	754	530
Callahan	1,077	243	17	117	164	2	6	974	176	31	0	1,210	1,574
Cameron	418	582	21	140	568	47	34	277	3,283	202	7	4,721	1,413
Camp	678	106	8	88	46	15	0	32	167	642	41	897	971
Carson	237	56	3	29	27	4	0	1,157	28	12	0	751	504
Cass	1,686	359	10	444	86	15	2	58	824	656	6	2,030	2,503
Castro	168	62	2	17	9	18	0	860	21	11	2	677	577
Chambers	381	70	1	1	23	0	0	2	424	34	1	495	503
Cherokee	1,944	488	5	349	136	66	19	194	1,122	973	8	2,913	2,942
Childress	739	231	6	158	17	3	0	1,613	90	28	2	1,509	1,351
Clay	814	286	9	158	63	30	10	1,003	435	220	14	1,713	1,561
Cochran	144	32	1	24	4	2	0	214	4	22	0	233	238
Coke	414	82	6	44	34	16	9	572	214	28	3	791	652
Coleman	1,268	392	10	84	114	18	5	1,204	500	760	3	2,538	1,877
Collin	2,700	904	5	794	323	29	8	249	696	1,278	7	4,108	4,458
Collingsworth	305	276	7	76	6	8	1	2,343	40	29	1	978	1,183
Colorado	875	215	8	52	480	4	27	11	1,122	98	1	1,532	1,751
Comal	255	20	33	30	582	3	19	5	135	3	0	670	1,004
Comanche	1,429	433	4	268	326	20	5	1,031	283	294	2	2,122	2,311
Concho	573	122	9	35	27	13	1	719	100	30	0	801	909
Cooke	1,136	1,131	39	361	168	48	51	568	464	752	12	3,036	2,006
Coryell	1,892	274	8	628	111	19	29	813	372	351	7	2,242	2,638
Cottle	623	79	9	34	22	11	1	1,079	73	46	4	900	1,040
Crane	289	24	2	31	24	10	1	226	61	17	2	268	406
Crockett	75	17	2	19	15	6	0	111	277	21	0	366	103
Crosby	762	332	3	304	20	7	1	988	63	44	13	1,236	1,131
Culberson	41	9	1	6	1	3	0	101	108	6	2	210	102
Dallam	165	151	4	88	17	26	2	913	59	139	2	761	252
Dallas	4,444	7,869	38	2,365	9,043	55	49	2,236	7,151	2,721	99	27,688	11,220
Dawson	1,153	553	8	119	34	14	3	871	50	54	0	1,361	1,608
DeWitt	1,269	121	10	77	311	17	91	126	1,549	122	0	1,739	1,752
Deaf Smith	120	77	1	21	22	8	1	1,144	44	22	4	1,075	295
Delta	1,106	231	4	250	155	16	6	160	304	646	10	1,453	1,577
Denton	1,592	1,051	3	432	338	15	12	896	630	936	23	3,634	2,629
Dickens	907	155	0	125	17	13	6	1,340	27	28	3	945	1,539
Dimmit	177	55	2	39	13	5	2	26	549	14	0	676	172

Table 30: Gubernatorial Races

	Democratic Primary, 1930												
Year	1930											Runoff	
County	Miriam A. Ferguson	Thomas B. Love	Paul Loven	Earle B. Mayfield	Barry Miller	C.C. Moody	Frank Putnam	Clint C. Small	Ross S. Sterling	James Young	C.E. Walker	Ross S. Sterling	Miriam A. Ferguson
Duval	13	9	2	0	1,473	3	4	0	60	6	0	78	1,171
Eastland	1,830	755	9	584	183	20	63	2,267	605	153	3	3,417	3,052
Ector	131	25	0	8	13	0	0	387	45	7	0	374	232
Edwards	29	18	0	6	14	2	1	21	16	115	0	202	126
El Paso	720	891	41	260	350	107	120	2,911	1,260	1,878	10	6,335	1,555
Ellis	2,282	971	10	952	512	20	1	469	1,656	1,187	63	5,197	4,278
Erath	1,939	498	3	291	167	20	3	1,343	255	402	2	2,457	2,840
Falls	1,871	212	18	153	167	14	12	390	659	1,135	2	2,086	2,687
Fannin	2,280	939	6	751	291	54	29	495	1,096	891	13	3,879	3,444
Fayette	1,862	108	21	69	1,854	14	141	15	1,300	152	6	1,680	3,602
Fisher	798	474	2	78	35	9	17	918	258	69	1	1,312	1,248
Floyd	828	463	5	165	84	11	1	1,614	82	48	3	1,941	1,451
Foard	445	75	3	18	21	5	1	850	83	39	2	719	787
Fort Bend	1,162	68	11	28	272	10	13	21	1,629	184	0	1,795	1,768
Franklin	500	93	1	64	40	4	0	45	123	327	0	678	839
Freestone	1,148	410	11	403	146	18	10	241	1,012	256	3	2,183	1,710
Frio	271	248	2	58	66	7	0	39	426	38	7	770	396
Gaines	190	85	0	34	21	6	0	382	7	6	2	345	364
Galveston	2,933	523	12	128	1,589	23	48	181	2,095	908	12	3,470	3,680
Garza	427	266	4	98	24	5	1	514	47	12	0	623	521
Gillespie	151	7	1	10	39	5	30	27	245	9	1	468	520
Glasscock	67	53	2	15	7	1	1	110	17	4	1	82	58
Goliad	116	22	1	4	17	3	1	6	313	9	0	407	240
Gonzales	1,083	564	25	107	357	21	23	108	1,383	411	9	2,078	1,590
Gray	315	115	2	52	21	6	3	2,559	62	28	5	1,656	1,222
Grayson	2,457	1,765	11	700	571	37	18	688	2,994	1,477	15	7,716	4,685
Gregg	669	130	3	593	41	1	4	71	389	714	4	1,332	972
Grimes	599	144	3	47	54	1	0	21	845	144	0	1,575	1,031
Guadalupe	318	124	11	19	216	5	14	17	154	27	2	812	955
Hale	397	613	4	112	20	9	1	1,998	105	76	3	2,131	1,030
Hall	786	231	3	80	18	8	17	1,987	114	35	4	1,793	1,383
Hamilton	1,131	225	15	127	55	10	5	633	222	382	4	1,560	1,951
Hansford	181	45	5	19	25	14	0	576	14	4	6	359	232
Hardeman	745	247	5	71	56	16	2	1,842	169	35	2	1,787	1,620
Hardin	1,551	295	8	87	193	4	1	6	927	43	1	1,123	1,763
Harris	9,235	2,761	26	650	2,216	57	110	246	20,872	2,006	34	28,134	12,395
Harrison	1,118	314	6	230	68	18	15	54	2,361	467	28	3,674	1,649
Hartley	85	25	0	15	1	14	1	407	14	30	0	239	120
Haskell	1,220	439	12	179	119	6	5	1,083	362	207	2	1,682	1,794
Hays	480	553	7	302	279	18	4	137	396	140	1	1,438	647
Hemphill	55	38	2	23	4	7	0	960	11	9	1	536	172
Henderson	2,358	390	14	364	96	17	13	58	370	1,372	5	2,085	3,448
Hidalgo	205	92	10	212	142	13	8	91	1,727	134	3	1,821	732
Hill	2,542	798	6	1,074	302	15	5	653	1,016	567	6	4,110	4,122
Hockley	591	389	9	50	19	13	1	623	31	48	5	799	934
Hood	628	119	5	136	80	15	5	540	55	48	4	752	775
Hopkins	1,777	889	10	802	161	31	15	137	1,125	675	1	3,451	2,594
Houston	1,645	116	10	149	47	6	9	57	1,606	303	1	2,052	1,752
Howard	1,022	276	2	226	128	9	4	840	273	57	6	1,436	1,372
Hudspeth	45	13	0	8	7	2	0	157	131	36	0	239	50
Hunt	2,584	881	12	948	267	23	23	291	925	1,757	5	4,434	3,930
Hutchinson	556	56	8	47	30	25	3	1,190	95	35	3	1,104	1,066
Irion	208	47	1	23	24	2	1	162	71	23	3	263	244
Jack	703	412	11	136	61	14	24	587	137	118	2	1,067	1,127
Jackson	358	179	34	16	89	11	8	11	811	60	2	928	518
Jasper	1,296	117	6	113	77	3	0	12	933	86	6	1,209	1,411
Jeff Davis	11	122	1	7	22	7	0	67	54	15	1	198	44
Jefferson	4,427	2,540	44	422	2,012	94	55	178	5,032	1,009	18	11,057	6,880
Jim Hogg	16	6	0	9	7	3	1	6	291	0	1	261	84
Jim Wells	263	113	18	25	197	9	24	112	404	28	1	574	478
Johnson	2,123	1,174	16	1,039	139	36	18	1,308	673	300	13	3,471	3,305
Jones	1,338	677	2	254	71	10	3	1,387	374	144	1	2,087	2,071
Karnes	736	224	12	88	682	21	24	77	747	160	4	971	1,232
Kaufman	1,534	641	9	153	87	23	1	117	367	2,504	1	2,832	2,927
Kendall	38	14	0	7	9	0	4	4	37	6	0	238	172

Table 30: Gubernatorial Races

| | Democratic Primary, 1930 | | | | | | | | | | | | Runoff | |
| Year | 1930 | | | | | | | | | | | | Runoff | |
County	Miriam A. Ferguson	Thomas B. Love	Paul Loven	Earle B. Mayfield	Barry Miller	C.C. Moody	Frank Putnam	Clint C. Small	Ross S. Sterling	James Young	C.E. Walker	Ross S. Sterling	Miriam A. Ferguson
Kendall	38	14	0	7	9	0	4	4	37	6	0	238	172
Kenedy	2	1	0	4	44	1	1	0	42	7	0	58	37
Kent	397	78	2	39	2	4	0	464	13	5	2	380	623
Kerr	94	164	1	28	40	0	1	17	373	11	1	1,098	464
Kimble	424	117	3	41	90	11	1	401	242	34	5	711	448
King	88	12	0	3	1	0	0	151	7	4	1	135	164
Kinney	35	6	0	0	9	0	0	0	98	10	0	182	83
Kleberg	313	443	12	131	49	6	8	25	701	90	4	1,055	532
Knox	628	232	4	88	65	8	6	1,016	121	237	0	1,061	1,303
La Salle	402	41	1	21	10	1	0	21	220	21	0	324	402
Lamar	2,019	774	39	401	352	121	13	1,440	1,130	789	7	4,505	3,022
Lamb	1,012	595	17	109	36	30	2	1,507	67	70	3	1,657	1,607
Lampasas	913	279	5	124	39	12	1	571	168	369	4	1,185	996
Lavaca	2,634	218	31	94	848	35	61	29	2,062	92	8	1,808	3,703
Lee	946	104	14	46	127	31	83	382	535	114	11	758	1,370
Leon	1,165	173	4	159	23	6	0	64	931	170	2	1,509	1,675
Liberty	1,443	209	6	39	127	17	3	6	1,407	118	1	1,698	1,691
Limestone	2,597	553	16	633	374	18	3	1,130	890	463	7	3,128	3,781
Lipscomb	15	4	0	4	0	2	0	297	3	4	0	266	120
Live Oak	490	291	12	85	106	10	13	19	323	37	5	668	664
Llano	395	212	8	33	71	19	4	221	302	40	2	913	615
Loving	0	0	0	0	0	0	0	0	0	0	0	0	0
Lubbock	1,096	904	6	206	84	10	14	2,791	317	114	3	3,785	2,169
Lynn	1,102	733	7	129	20	9	5	594	73	105	1	1,394	1,447
Madison	910	116	1	26	20	6	0	22	817	180	1	1,163	1,124
Marion	232	18	1	18	18	1	2	8	293	34	0	489	389
Martin	514	137	1	11	2	4	0	406	18	28	2	437	747
Mason	430	4	233	23	29	10	0	472	329	25	15	1,110	631
Matagorda	363	172	3	9	84	7	5	12	941	66	1	1,610	701
Maverick	11	11	0	4	16	1	1	2	249	33	0	359	30
McCulloch	970	397	8	131	41	11	1	1,131	168	136	4	1,471	1,356
McLennan	4,255	1,366	42	1,180	629	58	11	1,129	3,742	2,202	50	8,866	5,961
McMullen	104	21	2	40	20	5	1	5	117	30	0	78	73
Medina	350	153	8	58	61	2	2	8	195	14	0	642	888
Menard	404	96	1	39	32	13	2	506	90	23	2	546	551
Midland	435	102	3	46	75	6	0	827	54	43	1	887	622
Milam	2,388	338	29	163	305	18	16	122	1,004	704	8	2,500	3,443
Mills	785	139	7	387	26	7	1	453	69	147	6	936	1,124
Mitchell	726	267	0	106	31	26	2	1,381	127	71	2	1,435	1,235
Montague	1,104	426	8	208	147	33	4	1,389	207	135	7	1,678	1,996
Montgomery	1,310	163	5	48	60	6	3	9	775	216	3	1,124	1,505
Moore	40	1	0	3	0	1	1	196	3	3	0	136	89
Morris	611	76	2	244	79	3	0	38	317	243	3	791	790
Motley	313	75	2	36	20	2	1	838	55	31	1	759	529
Nacogdoches	1,993	285	12	195	63	17	12	68	1,287	784	10	2,378	2,728
Navarro	2,651	1,055	11	963	260	15	10	459	1,554	1,171	2	5,393	4,039
Newton	1,178	94	3	130	156	4	0	13	306	31	0	546	1,504
Nolan	841	452	11	183	214	16	3	1,380	189	68	1	2,143	1,281
Nueces	1,753	1,063	26	89	434	20	5	368	2,453	275	2	3,297	2,355
Ochiltree	112	195	5	19	6	28	1	817	164	13	4	929	393
Oldham	74	12	1	10	0	6	1	297	4	3	1	207	121
Orange	1,153	328	14	122	394	13	3	29	802	113	5	1,208	1,744
Palo Pinto	1,003	542	3	283	173	20	17	1,339	174	234	6	1,934	1,583
Panola	1,340	201	8	108	31	22	3	33	959	667	2	1,822	2,189
Parker	1,180	661	22	613	84	29	5	1,277	242	152	10	2,587	2,037
Parmer	218	100	6	40	25	6	6	666	17	36	3	754	527
Pecos	276	69	6	44	29	11	4	386	432	53	4	760	388
Polk	1,362	96	1	32	44	5	2	15	994	154	1	1,202	1,414
Potter	754	290	8	160	148	14	4	3,984	220	77	3	4,352	1,661
Presidio	101	59	3	57	44	10	10	207	224	98	6	413	120
Rains	692	76	1	83	240	9	12	48	11	190	10	483	1,089
Randall	269	123	4	60	25	6	2	1,318	55	47	1	1,352	596
Reagan	193	60	3	20	34	3	3	355	127	29	2	432	221
Real	54	3	0	18	2	1	0	34	28	8	3	166	108
Red River	1,705	535	26	183	353	35	9	664	722	618	6	2,188	1,948

Table 30: Gubernatorial Races

County	Democratic Primary, 1930											Runoff	
Year	**1930**											**Runoff**	
County	Miriam A. Ferguson	Thomas B. Love	Paul Loven	Earle B. Mayfield	Barry Miller	C.C. Moody	Frank Putnam	Clint C. Small	Ross S. Sterling	James Young	C.E. Walker	Ross S. Sterling	Miriam A. Ferguson
Refugio	125	20	5	5	20	6	5	11	227	26	8	388	244
Roberts	29	26	3	3	2	2	0	398	50	7	0	374	87
Robertson	1,062	209	2	135	123	4	8	107	631	300	4	1,256	1,338
Rockwall	478	181	2	72	52	8	0	183	134	476	1	953	813
Runnels	1,231	464	26	126	172	21	16	1,343	413	83	7	2,172	2,154
Rusk	1,025	304	304	632	35	5	25	60	525	1,506	31	2,340	2,118
Sabine	1,363	86	2	334	60	32	2	12	337	81	3	686	1,629
San Augustine	1,654	46	6	166	9	6	0	9	306	160	2	603	1,818
San Jacinto	632	17	3	32	5	3	0	1	402	44	0	484	699
San Patricio	455	550	4	222	77	5	2	54	863	135	2	1,629	734
San Saba	793	273	12	174	51	9	1	592	219	119	0	1,146	1,288
Schleicher	149	65	1	23	25	6	0	266	114	31	3	413	255
Scurry	631	435	0	264	35	23	11	1,011	101	33	3	1,426	1,234
Shackelford	547	108	25	29	20	11	1	754	210	71	2	917	782
Shelby	2,571	269	18	571	157	26	6	41	1,033	347	22	2,055	3,398
Sherman	28	10	0	2	2	7	3	271	6	9	0	218	66
Smith	2,180	1,065	24	1,454	95	13	3	182	888	1,698	7	4,618	3,348
Somervell	492	140	6	60	11	6	1	119	33	83	3	304	551
Starr	1	0	0	0	117	0	6	2	400	0	0	496	72
Stephens	1,119	276	5	123	92	19	7	1,374	466	130	5	1,927	1,635
Sterling	64	8	3	11	18	2	0	237	49	5	0	290	95
Stonewall	693	143	1	26	18	7	0	445	47	18	0	409	870
Sutton	134	7	0	12	11	2	1	97	109	202	4	318	162
Swisher	194	113	0	40	15	4	2	1,203	10	25	3	961	502
Tarrant	6,308	3,096	26	5,122	931	262	68	9,268	2,741	1,035	427	18,676	10,687
Taylor	1,708	1,395	16	197	120	27	5	1,656	1,493	110	4	4,800	2,633
Terrell	17	42	2	18	8	0	0	17	47	27	0	157	57
Terry	424	219	8	57	23	5	1	851	32	35	4	725	929
Throckmorton	395	363	43	29	9	4	1	546	32	15	0	716	625
Titus	1,313	255	4	262	151	24	15	144	398	246	1	933	1,467
Tom Green	1,403	589	11	190	324	23	7	1,266	1,458	219	12	3,732	1,854
Travis	2,520	1,382	17	1,808	833	16	37	1,316	2,578	1,217	10	8,182	4,632
Trinity	1,118	71	4	50	33	5	2	6	614	104	2	922	1,339
Tyler	790	87	0	27	27	5	3	4	817	18	2	901	884
Upshur	1,738	160	8	326	96	17	2	77	429	1,017	6	1,742	2,428
Upton	404	51	2	32	27	10	11	339	180	23	3	585	536
Uvalde	414	275	3	234	160	19	3	275	438	237	9	1,357	618
Val Verde	104	69	5	47	72	11	11	204	389	284	9	738	234
Van Zandt	2,268	696	13	154	134	20	4	124	350	1,692	7	2,489	3,518
Victoria	639	82	2	39	85	4	17	103	1,402	46	0	1,402	1,014
Walker	822	107	2	82	47	1	2	8	850	224	4	1,205	1,038
Waller	474	110	3	21	120	10	3	7	552	107	3	669	591
Ward	259	52	2	14	17	4	1	327	57	58	1	367	387
Washington	1,049	10	3	12	979	13	8	9	912	161	2	1,166	1,982
Webb	170	33	0	3	19	3	1	8	1,337	18	0	1,466	400
Wharton	854	231	15	30	452	17	3	20	2,195	163	8	2,574	1,769
Wheeler	489	102	0	39	17	10	5	2,178	21	23	0	1,259	1,490
Wichita	1,709	1,011	13	805	34	67	15	3,781	1,326	330	25	5,937	3,792
Wilbarger	995	415	5	146	41	21	3	1,904	170	300	10	1,751	1,795
Willacy	159	88	8	150	29	14	1	18	572	19	1	792	427
Williamson	2,439	675	19	515	1,110	7	22	429	1,242	1,031	7	3,989	4,596
Wilson	885	85	8	50	398	17	23	7	263	252	1	836	1,652
Winkler	466	48	1	35	23	21	1	217	89	85	4	362	572
Wise	1,274	640	6	770	85	32	3	1,118	293	246	20	2,037	1,757
Wood	1,384	447	7	252	97	19	1	96	260	1,004	17	1,883	2,380
Yoakum	118	32	4	5	7	3	0	187	9	5	0	161	204
Young	873	377	9	82	47	20	4	1,649	201	105	12	1,751	1,945
Zapata	1	5	6	11	6	5	5	5	133	11	7	87	2
Zavala	166	70	6	257	29	8	4	12	403	25	3	690	295
Official Totals	242,959	87,068	2,724	54,459	54,652	4,382	2,365	138,934	170,754	73,385	1,760	473,371	384,402
Unofficial Totals	**242,960**	87,068	**2,724**	54,966	**54,658**	4,346	**2,371**	138,934	**170,744**	73,385	1,760	**473,371**	384,402

Table 31: Gubernatorial Races

Democratic Primary, 1932										
Year				1932					Runoff	
County	Roger Q. Evans	Miriam A. Ferguson	C.A. Frakes	J. Ed Glenn	Tom F. Hunter	Frank Putnam	Ross S. Sterling	M.H. Wolfe	Ross S. Sterling	Miriam A. Ferguson
Anderson	8	3,036	9	6	1,734	6	839	151	2,155	3,696
Andrews	1	137	4	2	39	1	68	8	131	158
Angelina	40	4,079	7	20	1,003	13	1,374	57	2,310	4,136
Aransas	2	154	4	1	74	11	216	11	333	192
Archer	1	696	2	1	1,071	1	347	26	977	1,059
Armstrong	2	229	1	2	251	2	480	38	745	280
Atascosa	100	1,324	2	9	533	10	599	46	999	1,433
Austin	3	2,556	2	5	539	5	603	18	921	2,606
Bailey	6	607	0	6	313	6	195	89	508	844
Bandera	1	190	1	0	89	0	113	11	385	411
Bastrop	6	1,926	7	3	740	9	911	44	1,496	2,287
Baylor	4	511	2	2	801	1	476	16	922	921
Bee	3	528	2	1	362	10	486	83	958	834
Bell	31	4,197	7	5	3,759	14	1,707	104	4,339	5,528
Bexar	636	23,944	14	35	4,926	80	13,704	353	17,745	21,202
Blanco	3	521	0	1	113	1	238	8	420	685
Borden	2	166	0	2	101	0	64	8	134	236
Bosque	5	2,200	1	141	1,163	0	670	117	1,664	2,642
Bowie	22	2,493	6	15	1,519	16	2,030	178	3,393	3,148
Brazoria	7	1,418	3	1	301	5	1,256	22	1,544	1,449
Brazos	11	1,200	3	6	674	7	1,486	107	2,002	1,362
Brewster	7	332	1	1	118	4	756	32	918	496
Briscoe	4	551	0	0	323	4	272	54	522	673
Brooks	0	81	1	1	83	1	353	6	381	148
Brown	15	1,840	0	5	2,062	3	1,209	99	2,754	2,527
Burleson	4	1,996	4	10	550	17	494	41	897	2,203
Burnet	6	1,193	1	1	628	4	597	43	1,159	1,465
Caldwell	14	1,764	8	3	708	25	1,655	57	2,276	2,095
Calhoun	5	575	6	1	175	5	466	34	694	459
Callahan	107	1,103	2	1	928	3	577	51	1,205	1,691
Cameron	14	3,208	5	28	1,176	21	3,559	211	4,753	3,586
Camp	4	1,032	3	11	434	11	291	158	759	1,111
Carson	3	746	0	3	414	3	653	22	932	899
Cass	3	2,024	1	21	578	3	968	277	1,734	2,368
Castro	6	542	3	15	202	6	264	59	539	658
Chambers	3	557	0	1	129	3	463	6	518	630
Cherokee	6	2,263	10	8	1,562	9	1,000	175	2,312	2,764
Childress	4	925	2	2	731	2	886	133	1,449	1,262
Clay	6	1,140	2	2	1,318	1	572	105	1,523	1,792
Cochran	0	239	0	4	113	6	152	33	265	293
Coke	1	610	5	5	498	2	294	38	698	802
Coleman	4	1,339	2	11	1,242	3	1,056	100	1,911	1,850
Collin	11	4,018	5	8	1,125	20	1,853	809	3,709	5,061
Collingsworth	6	1,061	6	6	772	5	469	219	1,117	1,457
Colorado	5	1,847	6	6	680	12	754	35	1,320	2,124
Comal	22	1,482	4	3	354	22	747	8	788	1,397
Comanche	5	1,580	12	6	1,859	4	615	71	1,939	2,439
Concho	1	678	0	1	700	4	225	20	651	958
Cooke	7	1,498	4	22	1,791	8	957	342	2,500	2,212
Coryell	10	2,207	3	12	1,353	8	704	169	1,810	2,584
Cottle	4	651	1	6	497	11	371	51	720	840
Crane	2	264	0	2	94	2	226	12	300	328
Crockett	1	157	0	5	126	2	325	0	488	153
Crosby	6	1,010	1	6	414	5	565	186	1,183	1,174
Culberson	2	76	0	3	41	2	255	9	236	98
Dallam	8	634	17	22	616	21	1,281	66	1,558	518
Dallas	42	13,731	40	28	6,258	176	18,575	5,448	29,653	16,679
Dawson	6	1,068	1	5	590	7	515	153	1,002	1,257
DeWitt	6	2,289	5	15	689	21	1,101	34	1,672	2,426
Deaf Smith	6	509	3	5	314	7	967	33	1,310	658
Delta	1	1,131	7	16	799	5	369	301	1,118	1,612
Denton	22	2,403	17	18	1,478	7	2,160	390	3,825	3,338
Dickens	5	967	3	3	677	1	282	35	823	1,146
Dimmit	12	425	3	4	422	1	316	26	656	413

Table 31: Gubernatorial Races

County	Democratic Primary, 1932								Runoff	
Year	1932								Runoff	
	Roger Q. Evans	Miriam A. Ferguson	C.A. Frakes	J. Ed Glenn	Tom F. Hunter	Frank Putnam	Ross S. Sterling	M.H. Wolfe	Ross S. Sterling	Miriam A. Ferguson
Donley	2	691	0	7	520	15	885	144	1,255	936
Duval	0	114	0	0	23	0	1,669	0	1,249	108
Eastland	23	2,034	14	13	2,611	12	1,768	123	3,385	3,049
Ector	3	186	0	1	262	1	328	46	498	262
Edwards	0	269	0	1	255	0	105	9	352	242
El Paso	76	3,789	65	16	1,510	165	8,112	635	8,164	4,888
Ellis	12	2,890	14	7	2,237	16	2,381	363	4,420	4,163
Erath	37	1,772	3	24	1,408	2	1,238	166	2,412	2,344
Falls	166	2,171	3	6	1,245	23	933	72	1,856	2,732
Fannin	27	3,044	15	11	1,126	15	2,154	972	3,652	3,923
Fayette	4	3,855	3	7	1,120	39	808	29	1,429	4,270
Fisher	4	797	10	11	527	6	634	72	1,037	1,010
Floyd	55	1,017	2	13	411	6	813	302	1,543	1,170
Foard	2	448	4	4	415	2	277	25	676	555
Fort Bend	7	1,872	3	1	461	15	1,173	31	1,477	2,077
Franklin	3	1,033	6	16	347	5	309	220	829	1,134
Freestone	9	1,371	10	7	931	3	1,171	122	1,973	1,655
Frio	18	599	0	1	335	4	473	40	671	719
Gaines	2	312	1	7	113	1	268	21	399	328
Galveston	20	5,839	32	9	1,609	85	3,084	85	2,722	4,968
Garza	1	446	1	1	390	3	313	77	639	563
Gillespie	12	1,050	3	2	569	22	367	13	787	1,509
Glasscock	1	116	0	2	116	1	91	8	160	160
Goliad	1	551	1	2	84	8	345	9	451	604
Gonzales	15	1,906	7	6	1,026	19	1,324	93	2,172	2,167
Gray	4	1,380	9	5	1,295	8	1,456	75	2,280	2,153
Grayson	26	4,495	12	41	3,019	44	3,746	699	6,766	5,684
Gregg	21	4,105	8	8	1,197	29	1,849	59	2,380	4,588
Grimes	2	829	3	3	597	2	852	20	1,425	1,187
Guadalupe	26	1,532	3	3	345	16	842	7	1,105	1,570
Hale	162	1,053	3	23	1,150	9	1,093	283	2,357	1,458
Hall	1	956	4	6	572	4	963	74	1,547	1,124
Hamilton	7	1,775	4	26	935	4	649	94	1,363	2,054
Hansford	7	388	4	3	197	4	376	18	605	490
Hardeman	9	880	3	3	1,018	4	786	60	1,543	1,284
Hardin	4	2,315	10	13	541	6	586	25	1,075	2,467
Harris	300	22,027	784	25	8,770	377	24,159	760	28,774	24,637
Harrison	3	1,676	25	4	965	13	2,519	93	3,354	2,148
Hartley	1	271	2	3	146	1	368	9	473	215
Haskell	4	1,277	0	5	1,138	5	775	147	1,669	1,648
Hays	12	761	2	2	720	3	1,032	47	1,507	897
Hemphill	4	388	4	5	63	4	760	24	661	204
Henderson	13	2,742	16	19	1,291	28	722	101	1,781	3,244
Hidalgo	17	1,094	5	1	409	6	3,165	35	2,966	1,457
Hill	10	2,788	6	18	1,202	9	1,814	659	3,189	3,528
Hockley	3	1,137	1	3	630	3	192	76	649	1,407
Hood	6	707	4	17	462	4	560	54	915	852
Hopkins	14	2,672	5	7	1,152	10	930	523	2,547	3,053
Houston	2	1,838	0	5	849	4	1,140	34	1,857	2,030
Howard	6	1,098	1	3	1,365	6	723	23	1,466	1,694
Hudspeth	5	123	0	2	59	3	306	9	318	76
Hunt	42	3,233	12	8	1,718	11	1,923	1,088	4,023	4,509
Hutchinson	14	856	6	16	569	9	1,010	26	1,305	1,305
Irion	2	236	2	2	182	6	168	15	269	238
Jack	4	720	17	9	680	4	584	121	1,149	956
Jackson	3	939	22	12	152	4	794	33	982	836
Jasper	1	1,460	3	0	591	2	596	12	1,041	1,429
Jeff Davis	2	52	2	2	53	2	327	4	281	60
Jefferson	29	9,166	211	16	3,645	60	9,567	190	11,588	10,020
Jim Hogg	3	187	0	0	32	0	275	4	327	255
Jim Wells	9	689	4	1	340	7	707	18	1,056	921
Johnson	30	2,408	13	38	1,699	6	1,938	273	3,261	3,103
Jones	9	1,578	4	9	1,146	10	982	164	1,897	1,970
Karnes	11	1,879	12	1	653	6	561	19	1,162	1,784
Kaufman	15	2,271	4	9	888	6	1,325	259	2,517	2,563

Table 31: Gubernatorial Races

Democratic Primary, 1932									Runoff	
Year	1932								Runoff	
County	Roger Q. Evans	Miriam A. Ferguson	C.A. Frakes	J. Ed Glenn	Tom F. Hunter	Frank Putnam	Ross S. Sterling	M.H. Wolfe	Ross S. Sterling	Miriam A. Ferguson
Kendall	2	167	0	0	19	0	339	4	433	361
Kenedy	0	17	0	0	6	0	99	0	88	18
Kent	1	254	0	0	489	1	111	10	394	459
Kerr	11	378	2	2	153	3	801	15	1,306	675
Kimble	5	561	0	2	454	1	356	13	777	637
King	1	209	0	3	59	1	88	7	153	211
Kinney	7	168	1	0	72	2	189	0	196	121
Kleberg	6	793	1	1	533	9	822	33	966	560
Knox	4	763	5	3	809	2	450	74	975	1,148
La Salle	5	468	0	3	71	2	191	13	300	550
Lamar	234	3,383	140	12	2,031	18	1,732	598	4,330	3,994
Lamb	42	2,102	1	38	1,104	12	612	122	1,668	2,408
Lampasas	5	1,067	0	8	891	3	505	49	1,164	1,226
Lavaca	4	4,155	8	4	1,076	18	808	24	1,661	4,693
Lee	16	1,493	3	7	443	16	431	33	850	1,735
Leon	11	1,716	5	13	555	20	824	78	1,316	1,683
Liberty	1	1,813	7	2	507	9	1,005	34	1,445	1,936
Limestone	10	2,294	8	6	1,503	8	1,730	139	2,737	3,054
Lipscomb	1	64	1	0	16	5	233	9	747	101
Live Oak	13	744	3	6	458	7	343	17	597	718
Llano	1	782	0	5	561	5	462	49	988	920
Loving	0	119	0	0	43	1	70	4	90	153
Lubbock	17	2,412	0	71	2,544	5	1,770	193	3,704	2,999
Lynn	11	1,274	3	10	997	7	435	103	1,155	1,608
Madison	1	884	3	3	368	3	578	20	897	1,008
Marion	4	360	0	1	210	3	344	25	528	486
Martin	0	407	5	4	405	1	125	33	349	615
Mason	5	563	0	6	699	6	367	13	859	778
Matagorda	4	808	3	2	393	2	855	23	1,428	932
Maverick	5	85	0	0	79	0	413	4	488	89
McCulloch	4	940	0	3	1,380	3	560	17	1,391	1,382
McLennan	11	5,565	4	4	5,649	19	4,354	378	8,356	6,989
McMullen	7	180	0	4	44	0	68	2	74	131
Medina	16	731	2	1	238	6	227	16	582	1,288
Menard	10	635	2	8	401	1	337	11	579	726
Midland	5	613	1	2	327	7	795	54	883	625
Milam	63	3,076	8	9	1,575	6	1,146	68	2,161	3,563
Mills	3	985	0	6	867	9	238	45	826	1,378
Mitchell	1	592	2	7	758	3	702	56	1,178	881
Montague	10	1,413	4	12	1,451	19	916	98	2,035	2,123
Montgomery	11	1,639	8	3	371	14	552	75	902	1,883
Moore	1	245	4	2	87	1	416	8	396	172
Morris	6	701	3	7	343	8	422	73	618	618
Motley	1	411	0	7	284	9	392	44	686	518
Nacogdoches	8	2,379	7	15	1,184	4	990	145	1,843	2,748
Navarro	13	3,047	16	15	2,303	15	2,710	331	4,505	3,906
Newton	1	1,556	5	1	331	8	197	19	509	1,624
Nolan	40	1,032	1	5	1,056	10	905	57	1,627	1,517
Nueces	12	3,439	8	10	2,241	30	2,410	367	4,014	4,317
Ochiltree	5	367	1	2	109	2	747	62	1,084	386
Oldham	1	185	0	2	53	2	315	9	334	126
Orange	2	2,384	17	3	598	3	483	14	987	2,447
Palo Pinto	21	1,504	1	19	855	16	1,234	92	2,012	2,030
Panola	11	1,840	1	10	658	8	711	166	1,438	2,159
Parker	8	1,588	13	17	712	31	1,620	295	2,333	1,872
Parmer	2	698	3	6	207	4	420	142	695	890
Pecos	5	610	2	5	280	8	880	49	1,189	757
Polk	4	1,657	7	4	474	5	701	41	1,158	1,755
Potter	6	2,333	14	6	1,315	0	4,021	73	5,218	2,867
Presidio	5	328	0	0	117	5	595	19	603	289
Rains	0	872	1	2	136	3	133	67	364	975
Randall	12	679	6	6	277	3	964	30	1,313	757
Reagan	2	341	1	3	187	5	434	15	738	316
Real	4	354	2	9	112	1	167	4	340	417

Table 31: Gubernatorial Races

Democratic Primary, 1932									
Year			1932					Runoff	
County	Roger Q. Evans	Miriam A. Ferguson	C.A. Frakes	J. Ed Glenn	Tom F. Hunter	Frank Putnam	Ross S. Sterling	M.H. Wolfe	Ross S. Sterling	Miriam A. Ferguson
Reeves	1	308	3	3	211	7	835	22	882	391
Refugio	1	315	0	2	76	2	251	16	536	396
Roberts	4	153	1	3	114	2	336	12	427	154
Robertson	6	1,375	4	6	734	6	747	111	1,434	1,732
Rockwall	1	793	1	4	508	0	375	80	715	888
Runnels	16	1,402	4	7	1,332	10	971	119	1,983	2,134
Rusk	32	3,493	3	36	1,386	17	1,863	224	2,874	3,961
Sabine	1	1,542	2	2	420	4	250	32	541	1,801
San Augustine	7	1,791	5	3	275	0	217	25	470	1,960
San Jacinto	3	699	1	3	90	4	257	3	389	732
San Patricio	5	866	6	3	994	10	787	31	1,706	1,163
SanSaba	1	1,051	2	7	839	3	525	66	1,154	1,311
Schleicher	4	212	1	7	258	1	235	11	462	284
Scurry	7	766	3	21	839	2	563	150	1,328	961
Shackelford	11	610	3	2	751	4	408	22	840	834
Shelby	10	2,756	5	18	627	22	750	242	1,540	3,169
Sherman	2	159	18	1	12	7	430	51	444	212
Smith	10	3,632	7	5	3,385	18	2,046	261	4,310	4,790
Somervell	2	479	1	16	200	2	173	20	366	591
Starr	1	93	0	1	1	0	476	0	381	175
Stephens	8	1,254	4	8	924	4	922	74	1,678	1,696
Sterling	1	98	1	4	143	0	253	1	379	102
Stonewall	0	712	0	4	319	1	297	46	554	857
Sutton	3	202	0	0	123	1	302	2	420	252
Swisher	11	783	2	2	565	6	582	119	1,083	907
Tarrant	81	12,426	38	108	7,612	119	15,522	1,593	20,776	14,727
Taylor	12	1,548	4	4	2,304	9	2,773	135	4,559	2,386
Terrell	4	111	2	1	87	1	230	9	255	98
Terry	6	861	4	7	676	3	403	82	904	1,094
Throckmorton	0	467	2	6	578	2	230	143	786	651
Titus	3	2,227	2	7	635	15	462	104	1,217	2,353
Tom Green	21	1,647	21	16	2,551	14	2,181	121	4,010	2,486
Travis	22	5,078	6	27	3,196	27	6,346	153	8,050	6,473
Trinity	4	1,185	4	1	504	3	264	17	670	1,309
Tyler	3	1,060	11	2	283	3	559	19	793	1,069
Upshur	13	2,421	3	15	750	5	653	148	1,412	2,618
Upton	3	502	1	2	274	7	481	25	697	585
Uvalde	5	974	3	5	884	0	778	20	1,361	1,030
Val Verde	12	375	3	0	1,053	3	438	34	1,030	723
Van Zandt	12	3,140	10	13	783	12	1,133	463	2,068	3,744
Victoria	12	1,936	3	12	450	25	969	30	1,372	2,001
Walker	8	1,032	3	4	469	7	789	33	1,096	1,216
Waller	6	830	1	2	267	15	416	32	540	745
Ward	1	400	3	6	164	9	267	18	378	470
Washington	1	2,480	0	7	322	7	1,167	11	1,229	2,419
Webb	5	722	1	3	175	3	1,893	7	1,877	830
Wharton	10	2,032	9	8	1,101	16	1,230	33	2,029	2,477
Wheeler	6	1,372	3	30	511	8	883	88	1,134	1,304
Wichita	4	1,527	8	6	7,269	3	1,694	46	6,222	3,912
Wilbarger	14	1,350	10	5	1,721	6	1,103	93	2,216	2,050
Willacy	12	701	4	6	240	103	509	64	678	891
Williamson	8	3,751	41	16	2,184	16	2,001	77	3,285	4,643
Wilson	22	2,233	2	3	434	11	631	26	1,189	1,544
Winkler	7	319	1	0	167	2	287	15	416	511
Wise	4	1,418	5	5	654	2	1,215	150	2,233	1,877
Wood	3	2,051	1	0	1,037	11	649	187	1,730	2,536
Yoakum	10	195	2	4	95	1	71	27	157	240
Young	87	1,158	6	3	1,753	2	1,067	113	2,148	1,793
Zapata	0	27	0	0	5	0	121	0	134	36
Zavala	13	336	2	2	479	5	264	5	590	558
Official Totals	3,974	402,238	2,338	2,089	220,391	2,962	296,383	32,241	473,846	477,644
Unofficial Totals	3,974	402,238	2,339	2,088	220,391	2,952	296,385	32,241	473,846	477,644

Table 32: Gubernatorial Races

	Democratic Primaries, 1934-1936													
Year	1934							Runoff		1936				
County	James V. Allred	Tom F. Hunter	C.C. McDonald	Clint C. Small	Edgar E. Witt	Maury Hughes	Edward K. Russell	James V. Allred	Tom F. Hunter	James V. Allred	P.Pierce Brooks	F.W. Fischer	Tom F. Hunter	Roy Sanderford
Anderson	1,955	1,671	1,131	708	421	519	65	3,833	3,150	3,215	145	1,235	1,476	502
Andrews	31	66	61	73	10	6	3	80	164	150	23	9	116	26
Angelina	1,733	1,986	1,876	475	293	183	23	2,622	3,316	2,886	252	944	1,546	1,073
Aransas	124	152	75	16	24	17	4	154	110	141	87	80	110	45
Archer	763	1,034	453	129	35	23	1	1,104	1,279	1,269	45	274	660	45
Armstrong	202	198	50	602	11	13	3	785	394	738	30	162	168	18
Atascosa	617	867	685	74	71	429	14	768	1,064	1,704	187	162	681	84
Austin	771	724	902	107	435	433	7	1,574	1,704	1,901	20	373	744	320
Bailey	273	309	172	495	41	18	3	752	633	579	87	125	380	62
Bandera	154	93	106	32	2	6	1	354	249	176	26	31	91	47
Bastrop	1,002	1,329	1,039	250	100	170	11	1,261	1,359	2,146	97	462	991	513
Baylor	747	673	446	230	92	53	11	1,241	1,068	992	59	404	824	79
Bee	749	507	555	105	361	101	8	1,474	1,109	1,623	358	231	557	226
Bell	3,100	2,818	2,670	421	950	227	0	5,559	4,959	4,279	237	815	1,488	3,837
Bexar	8,801	11,917	8,409	1,734	2,071	2,746	274	16,470	21,431	27,174	1,130	2,209	11,761	1,479
Blanco	141	180	177	16	14	13	0	273	401	354	62	43	288	120
Borden	89	184	64	77	14	11	1	148	194	155	19	39	197	35
Bosque	1,066	1,423	1,095	433	530	198	20	1,928	2,213	2,188	96	1,027	1,002	686
Bowie	2,520	1,399	1,577	790	731	240	141	3,365	3,112	3,208	324	2,659	1,386	96
Brazoria	582	433	562	134	62	46	4	1,226	1,026	1,189	42	171	450	282
Brazos	1,630	782	517	151	535	263	9	1,866	1,556	2,881	69	154	701	165
Brewster	342	160	301	449	44	18	44	821	485	890	177	50	210	52
Briscoe	207	293	319	358	145	10	4	562	712	672	46	98	491	148
Brooks	188	57	572	61	9	11	2	250	594	438	40	8	39	9
Brown	1,926	1,474	1,317	697	509	290	7	2,830	3,251	2,952	503	601	1,518	925
Burleson	693	792	599	73	263	721	16	1,639	1,464	1,812	53	123	593	719
Burnet	787	628	882	123	162	22	4	1,127	1,135	1,135	139	131	724	462
Caldwell	1,172	1,356	1,275	368	283	77	8	1,747	2,144	2,541	154	161	948	567
Calhoun	260	333	326	57	50	80	6	483	459	567	64	180	439	81
Callahan	641	1,148	554	360	189	63	6	1,224	1,403	1,249	85	224	815	294
Cameron	2,732	2,602	1,383	381	364	637	32	5,108	3,941	5,103	280	315	3,108	310
Camp	856	506	468	143	63	132	33	1,182	1,061	785	35	521	609	72
Carson	635	288	182	782	83	5	0	1,119	668	1,222	41	252	458	28
Cass	1,919	980	623	237	117	133	42	2,325	1,806	1,915	42	672	1,181	124
Castro	378	193	148	600	41	14	3	871	521	686	37	109	283	53
Chambers	473	359	309	44	44	24	0	693	464	866	14	82	370	126
Cherokee	2,097	1,599	1,334	409	174	224	25	3,227	2,960	2,528	254	1,287	1,600	803
Childress	1,049	652	600	835	84	52	12	1,632	1,474	1,541	199	492	714	198
Clay	1,391	1,005	633	218	153	58	5	2,032	1,611	1,751	46	728	714	121
Cochran	188	154	152	197	16	19	2	401	370	430	43	94	332	55
Coke	462	317	320	211	131	28	9	791	513	793	146	152	242	168
Coleman	1,138	784	1,168	1,031	262	283	2	2,601	2,015	2,488	215	599	929	465
Collin	3,427	1,559	1,512	369	234	579	44	4,747	3,212	4,215	146	2,642	1,089	427
Collingsworth	1,172	391	278	1,502	38	6	8	1,996	1,040	1,626	79	602	633	49
Colorado	938	796	692	159	184	248	10	1,441	1,134	1,898	63	345	464	293
Comal	215	911	955	47	55	156	2	793	1,427	1,708	34	158	675	94
Comanche	906	1,581	1,139	305	254	227	13	2,212	2,566	1,807	132	840	942	920
Concho	275	574	401	379	79	33	4	662	1,081	879	79	109	386	200
Cooke	1,972	975	829	425	259	720	41	3,354	2,028	3,071	178	1,292	1,084	115
Coryell	1,682	617	1,489	289	368	219	5	2,474	1,931	2,151	98	361	626	1,223
Cottle	402	687	404	333	43	31	3	747	1,041	865	57	406	597	39
Crane	140	167	140	135	21	15	4	249	381	411	63	54	171	19
Crockett	115	62	63	94	17	12	0	142	97	358	60	25	108	74
Crosby	896	501	365	651	350	50	7	1,628	1,104	1,431	107	302	651	142
Culberson	53	15	93	210	23	8	1	213	211	257	12	18	98	31
Dallam	531	271	114	900	58	11	5	858	399	1,172	42	597	241	13
Dallas	10,953	10,176	3,012	3,451	2,313	9,260	161	20,770	18,213	25,096	1,416	7,480	8,012	1,682
Dawson	1,074	539	566	473	138	40	20	1,647	1,059	1,663	229	253	774	250
DeWitt	735	694	1,418	238	166	286	4	1,156	1,367	1,977	88	577	694	519
Deaf Smith	432	148	107	952	47	39	4	1,246	521	1,035	56	218	110	27
Delta	935	1,041	322	94	112	443	61	1,728	1,352	1,269	58	682	820	85
Denton	2,550	2,102	855	743	300	343	12	3,930	3,304	3,390	169	1,570	1,836	317
Dickens	749	611	322	361	65	141	0	1,364	1,095	1,389	58	180	717	43
Dimmit	614	412	217	59	85	32	5	831	591	778	241	159	211	27
Donley	1,350	490	99	488	44	9	0	1,612	722	1,358	116	378	451	29

Table 32: Gubernatorial Races

Democratic Primaries, 1934-1936														
Year	1934							Runoff		1936				
County	James V. Allred	Tom F. Hunter	C.C. McDonald	Clint C. Small	Edgar E. Witt	Maury Hughes	Edward K. Russell	James V. Allred	Tom F. Hunter	James V. Allred	P.Pierce Brooks	F.W. Fischer	Tom F. Hunter	Roy Sanderford
Duval	33	28	2,261	509	306	1	0	107	3,253	2,579	29	12	34	13
Eastland	1,247	1,950	1,193	1,118	268	628	11	2,464	3,867	3,039	333	610	2,567	719
Ector	119	243	209	260	29	35	2	254	660	626	72	26	215	61
Edwards	351	134	103	60	36	11	0	505	303	453	165	63	75	44
El Paso	3,386	1,485	3,350	3,519	413	460	26	4,768	4,338	7,656	403	232	2,929	259
Ellis	2,596	2,217	779	656	519	1,023	19	4,157	3,689	4,033	82	1,566	1,372	500
Erath	1,427	1,538	1,085	769	259	220	17	2,904	2,708	2,237	162	824	1,185	755
Falls	1,405	1,070	1,411	270	1,096	207	11	2,689	2,514	2,610	77	1,300	739	376
Fannin	3,274	823	2,571	460	415	258	91	4,879	2,977	4,018	191	1,442	2,427	266
Fayette	818	1,447	1,501	153	994	1,157	13	2,720	3,319	3,186	97	1,546	1,026	418
Fisher	1,064	820	574	384	216	232	13	1,624	1,590	1,488	94	436	949	171
Floyd	992	308	265	750	81	37	64	1,926	723	1,634	104	286	823	127
Foard	308	372	220	260	103	25	3	540	516	810	25	170	466	56
Fort Bend	968	800	1,057	139	330	354	36	2,044	1,552	1,928	29	193	628	241
Franklin	705	716	263	69	31	79	15	1,112	883	759	49	440	994	135
Freestone	1,519	534	784	414	255	236	12	2,420	1,650	2,070	81	852	1,017	171
Frio	498	481	303	95	68	90	45	805	625	904	206	213	280	33
Gaines	258	184	187	175	71	19	0	451	463	562	74	82	189	51
Galveston	3,029	1,871	2,738	506	721	401	21	4,317	2,845	5,059	90	485	4,274	803
Garza	563	235	311	336	50	57	6	898	633	698	72	193	385	86
Gillespie	147	295	311	24	34	77	10	213	788	452	47	272	380	92
Glasscock	100	135	70	70	28	5	3	117	120	229	33	18	67	17
Goliad	52	27	35	32	30	18	0	181	113	146	10	16	59	13
Gonzales	1,383	1,430	580	584	187	235	4	2,651	2,094	2,621	170	292	1,325	266
Gray	553	1,210	436	1,807	92	76	7	1,355	2,464	3,018	81	448	1,509	75
Grayson	4,673	2,378	2,105	990	579	819		6,665	4,453	6,413	260	3,799	2,096	408
Gregg	2,566	2,134	1,003	1,492	268	380	41	2,515	3,808	5,457	177	1,712	2,496	518
Grimes	1,115	606	617	172	130	198	1	1,748	1,254	1,665	23	179	408	109
Guadalupe	547	797	993	107	90	106	1	593	1,258	1,544	49	147	682	219
Hale	1,264	687	413	1,583	215	102	0	2,437	1,458	2,201	68	581	793	165
Hall	860	579	498	1,004	139	28	6	1,532	1,385	1,346	353	489	922	114
Hamilton	1,014	596	764	223	255	48	0	1,538	1,525	1,815	67	342	614	677
Hansford	150	107	57	573	8	8	2	696	259	696	11	240	72	13
Hardeman	894	773	511	819	355	26	0	1,696	1,484	1,600	232	596	656	48
Hardin	809	875	1,289	349	81	15	1	1,771	1,664	1,653	154	292	1,224	398
Harris	13,908	10,014	12,446	4,920	3,035	3,139	60	23,331	19,619	34,661	763	5,090	14,833	8,938
Harrison	2,412	1,748	677	585	134	162	30	3,506	2,199	3,364	155	775	1,202	234
Hartley	166	79	137	514	12	3	3	502	345	505	15	106	82	11
Haskell	1,607	999	923	598	154	83	17	2,458	1,799	2,241	175	497	1,186	277
Hays	1,062	826	586	197	182	96	11	1,325	1,344	1,550	118	335	813	242
Hemphill	153	75	80	1,094	10	4	1	344	175	829	28	376	173	8
Henderson	1,664	1,877	1,045	262	209	496	31	2,993	2,534	2,614	98	1,568	1,060	328
Hidalgo	4,580	3,264	1,040	655	557	894	53	6,234	4,778	5,184	430	346	3,245	382
Hill	1,789	2,703	1,018	683	718	508	22	3,894	3,806	3,758	164	1,836	1,380	702
Hockley	781	426	421	341	316	55	20	1,359	907	1,431	95	187	626	182
Hood	768	299	461	341	72	51	10	1,148	760	1,181	27	225	457	111
Hopkins	1,970	1,690	795	179	158	282	39	3,083	1,982	2,203	127	1,267	1,321	441
Houston	1,292	1,189	733	225	112	758	7	2,054	2,387	2,386	107	446	1,391	220
Howard	1,063	1,041	798	710	169	110	7	1,825	1,932	2,439	211	358	896	282
Hudspeth	81	26	54	253	3	5	0	166	60	389	26	16	171	14
Hunt	2,934	2,019	1,210	375	243	816	40	3,527	3,194	4,091	190	3,128	1,401	272
Hutchinson	589	455	351	1,376	41	25	2	1,445	1,321	1,908	42	472	565	40
Irion	197	160	146	175	132	19	4	450	338	412	63	39	162	62
Jack	631	859	295	264	90	75	9	1,303	1,182	1,175	56	244	802	104
Jackson	497	544	431	82	62	211	32	1,179	893	930	67	166	431	212
Jasper	539	717	876	490	200	32	10	1,102	1,627	1,450	80	136	789	459
Jeff Davis	95	56	190	157	6	5	2	206	142	271	23	85	71	16
Jefferson	5,598	6,088	3,477	4,822	1,332	718	59	11,687	9,057	11,086	563	997	5,362	1,524
Jim Hogg	191	128	130	16	4	14	1	357	407	408	25	26	187	9
Jim Wells	556	611	452	89	46	207	8	911	1,239	1,113	129	136	435	90
Johnson	2,410	1,466	1,168	693	242	172	90	3,554	2,877	3,168	177	1,473	1,292	627
Jones	1,919	819	1,076	1,001	301	129	12	2,485	2,279	2,419	181	401	1,151	234
Karnes	863	754	711	100	286	229	18	1,063	1,270	2,019	159	409	878	225
Kaufman	1,937	1,153	1,988	381	153	252	11	3,167	2,720	3,139	188	873	928	531
Kendall	100	97	112	5	12	15	0	176	252	116	3	34	42	15
Kenedy	14	14	18	36	52	3	0	57	91	73	1	11	9	3

Table 32: Gubernatorial Races

Democratic Primaries, 1934-1936													
Year	1934							Runoff		1936				
County	James V. Allred	Tom F. Hunter	C.C. McDonald	Clint C. Small	Edgar E. Witt	Maury Hughes	Edward K. Russell	James V. Allred	Tom F. Hunter	James V. Allred	P. Pierce Brooks	F.W. Fischer	Tom F. Hunter	Roy Sanderford
Kent	200	733	113	69	17	10	5	329	649	456	26	76	449	33
Kerr	300	312	159	122	147	40	4	625	765	439	35	58	142	31
Kimble	409	435	294	128	69	23	5	717	678	731	101	273	281	151
King	44	155	99	78	6	9	0	61	152	157	7	46	169	10
Kinney	193	24	91	27	13	3	1	294	87	111	23	3	19	2
Kleberg	828	445	369	354	87	98	22	881	775	1,384	158	56	348	187
Knox	1,116	502	699	488	84	29	8	1,801	1,148	1,674	54	272	580	248
La Salle	246	48	306	11	13	10	2	425	415	520	25	10	45	7
Lamar	2,590	2,317	1,809	810	515	309	93	3,889	3,959	3,974	211	2,793	1,740	512
Lamb	925	688	620	1,245	162	131	0	1,987	1,426	1,743	169	327	955	162
Lampasas	807	966	744	259	104	45	7	1,408	1,618	1,394	136	164	434	651
Lavaca	974	790	1,452	167	378	1,577	34	2,264	1,726	2,264	264	364	773	416
Lee	576	449	776	142	126	339	6	1,013	1,115	1,387	40	440	426	248
Leon	1,354	406	1,109	280	270	150	20	2,196	1,459	2,096	40	298	633	343
Liberty	968	1,011	782	362	205	235	19	1,731	1,591	2,280	115	243	1,095	542
Limestone	2,151	1,434	1,298	470	820	341	5	3,316	3,300	3,022	161	2,182	1,118	390
Lipscomb	25	15	18	463	6	1	6	195	106	306	12	135	75	14
Live Oak	405	730	390	54	78	79	10	738	852	852	232	156	529	250
Llano	650	618	521	122	88	22	1	750	777	930	102	108	710	259
Loving	26	70	59	58	5	5	1	54	133	60	21	7	55	7
Lubbock	2,312	1,362	1,307	2,264	366	336	22	4,454	3,012	5,116	213	1,019	1,631	404
Lynn	1,206	688	738	495	125	128	0	1,706	1,385	1,476	192	218	782	306
Madison	1,003	558	412	98	125	44	4	1,463	967	1,488	26	187	560	165
Marion	311	152	62	46	21	33	5	398	258	333	55	133	175	15
Martin	221	415	320	170	54	41	176	432	728	534	181	180	317	79
Mason	492	615	379	174	83	22	0	1,012	764	1,032	63	133	359	199
Matagorda	444	349	365	90	275	68	2	958	682	998	37	128	342	122
Maverick	341	179	120	48	41	49	0	220	170	712	246	23	110	21
McCulloch	725	1,069	863	436	209	66	7	1,419	1,954	1,571	143	200	598	593
McLennan	3,935	3,914	2,688	294	6,190	274	34	7,672	7,438	8,437	450	4,149	3,483	1,053
McMullen	143	104	176	14	12	9	2	170	141	245	69	25	69	114
Medina	486	253	515	25	22	43	6	819	814	1,006	132	76	264	83
Menard	377	246	354	189	70	75	3	641	486	844	159	163	225	188
Midland	194	523	310	231	51	60	31	374	774	1,272	96	107	505	38
Milam	1,665	1,440	2,245	209	636	411	25	3,063	3,315	3,139	261	961	1,500	1,025
Mills	633	501	456	219	180	99	11	1,029	966	796	137	250	461	236
Mitchell	966	779	485	671	272	497	7	1,616	1,625	1,468	144	172	862	231
Montague	2,131	942	820	257	125	72	6	2,540	1,620	2,568	43	896	940	77
Montgomery	1,093	851	1,402	165	240	243	8	2,196	1,806	2,148	169	281	1,471	425
Moore	101	28	168	430	6	1	3	421	339	544	9	43	92	6
Morris	571	499	363	163	67	188	12	1,023	959	842	20	258	540	22
Motley	334	384	217	364	122	52	0	658	747	709	52	94	506	51
Nacogdoches	1,788	1,380	1,554	421	212	316	49	3,034	2,617	2,556	217	1,132	1,244	720
Navarro	2,478	2,488	1,265	905	948	851	54	4,530	4,648	4,942	270	1,545	2,210	796
Newton	491	685	636	199	81	38	19	850	1,141	864	91	208	633	420
Nolan	1,102	1,007	915	772	366	170	22	2,034	2,152	2,056	180	453	1,237	402
Nueces	1,773	2,453	1,703	1,629	395	421	22	4,009	4,533	4,210	533	302	2,047	1,599
Ochiltree	136	235	149	931	14	7	0	471	306	500	24	313	155	25
Oldham	65	72	129	331	4	5	1	200	164	202	3	53	133	70
Orange	849	1,062	1,267	191	116	50	11	1,601	1,763	1,455	173	290	962	750
Palo Pinto	1,239	1,459	716	727	191	149	26	2,107	2,288	1,933	201	659	1,259	212
Panola	1,320	756	913	957	286	170	32	2,111	2,398	2,088	72	687	1,137	504
Parker	1,913	1,418	780	579	194	240	8	2,763	2,323	2,334	107	644	1,436	176
Parmer	234	189	269	817	19	19	2	506	289	711	62	190	365	96
Pecos	248	459	447	615	68	39	10	741	1,026	1,298	271	76	352	113
Polk	886	634	845	449	254	90	20	1,667	1,476	1,426	163	385	869	407
Potter	1,634	840	1,203	4,211	87	38	7	4,524	2,934	4,311	113	1,699	1,283	239
Presidio	387	143	219	295	52	26	3	709	420	755	67	146	156	37
Rains	438	430	289	62	30	170	14	716	790	540	14	693	249	124
Randall	494	185	265	1,108	27	2	13	1,265	674	1,289	16	319	303	100
Reagan	225	202	200	179	82	20	1	236	358	513	38	33	114	33
Real	162	124	111	129	53	10	3	348	302	331	97	41	94	40
Red River	2,375	1,122	891	294	151	135	156	2,930	1,934	2,209	271	1,333	1,082	271
Reeves	208	352	247	574	46	86	1	599	851	873	107	61	508	59
Refugio	76	122	153	31	43	31	1	298	190	303	27	21	85	223

Table 32: Gubernatorial Races

	Democratic Primaries, 1934-1936													
Year	1934							Runoff		1936				
County	James V. Allred	Tom F. Hunter	C.C. McDonald	Clint C. Small	Edgar E. Witt	Maury Hughes	Edward K. Russell	James V. Allred	Tom F. Hunter	James V. Allred	P.Pierce Brooks	F.W. Fischer	Tom F. Hunter	Roy Sanderford
Roberts	68	68	60	383	10	1	5	236	212	370	6	24	139	3
Robertson	1,518	523	885	135	728	147	12	1,898	1,204	2,244	174	554	922	377
Rockwall	688	585	254	99	32	184	5	836	862	1,018	32	329	300	144
Runnels	1,273	867	711	756	327	238	45	2,098	2,388	2,466	201	391	891	382
Rusk	2,015	2,401	1,499	1,139	349	454	48	3,467	4,496	3,752	325	3,009	1,870	470
Sabine	638	601	851	75	50	73	13	1,221	1,119	1,251	58	258	655	250
San Augustine	404	693	983	85	45	271	21	1,181	1,388	720	120	281	381	681
San Jacinto	264	237	468	58	52	68	11	463	500	661	36	172	258	107
San Patricio	690	896	501	224	119	83	5	976	864	1,520	343	160	643	333
San Saba	909	588	740	326	73	23	2	1,351	1,222	1,098	111	214	679	651
Schleicher	293	345	83	84	29	7	3	385	361	508	77	31	134	49
Scurry	1,041	769	403	428	194	99	3	1,460	1,427	1,256	141	509	954	166
Shackelford	330	550	204	356	87	62	1	679	1,065	781	95	78	688	83
Shelby	1,581	888	2,400	131	675	218	53	3,030	3,471	2,505	55	2,344	1,027	218
Sherman	108	49	22	529	0	5	3	525	228	477	6	67	69	2
Smith	2,907	3,245	1,554	1,321	364	777	51	5,104	5,039	3,873	60	5,092	1,058	471
Somervell	319	206	218	54	28	29	0	443	422	385	34	151	244	66
Starr	142	17	1,249	4	4	14	4	384	1,223	2,552	6	6	38	5
Stephens	811	755	813	1,101	106	171	18	1,319	2,102	1,925	111	197	1,265	248
Sterling	334	89	39	77	19	8	0	290	100	368	22	16	40	25
Stonewall	436	552	523	171	70	40	18	651	837	895	68	151	622	70
Sutton	192	199	189	71	24	20	3	217	229	512	57	21	68	15
Swisher	840	263	267	718	40	11	1	1,397	588	1,064	44	312	464	152
Tarrant	11,439	8,209	6,167	5,362	2,048	1,749	203	17,828	17,563	19,743	953	6,136	9,562	1,358
Taylor	2,241	2,428	1,215	1,987	337	93	0	3,686	4,296	4,809	186	807	1,978	723
Terrell	296	73	83	74	43	12	1	195	100	358	87	17	46	9
Terry	583	711	466	324	76	30	10	996	1,116	1,412	145	151	504	146
Throckmorton	329	584	247	256	35	24	14	718	830	821	33	147	665	29
Titus	972	502	1,461	113	299	62	21	1,985	1,571	1,475	59	735	950	413
Tom Green	2,389	1,317	1,323	946	1,067	293	19	3,745	3,030	4,287	373	628	1,179	836
Travis	6,743	3,260	3,424	1,195	1,219	634	29	9,018	6,464	9,386	245	1,122	3,474	1,977
Trinity	585	647	634	97	190	137	8	1,110	1,316	1,141	82	293	558	266
Tyler	804	576	710	129	41	46	9	1,079	1,139	735	62	128	396	645
Upshur	1,345	1,067	730	785	160	311	43	2,521	2,265	1,586	127	1,139	1,562	744
Upton	365	278	226	368	45	43	5	593	578	900	130	65	154	36
Uvalde	1,718	673	593	282	547	32	1	1,143	994	1,568	237	87	539	109
Val Verde	1,116	267	612	91	34	31	6	1,210	644	1,352	255	41	222	27
Van Zandt	2,795	1,261	1,231	252	140	732	64	4,438	2,125	2,582	109	2,230	1,040	245
Victoria	667	349	1,501	197	111	92	13	1,523	1,298	2,324	89	169	424	316
Walker	1,289	471	727	238	103	59	3	1,919	1,030	1,633	36	529	627	100
Waller	567	459	529	59	62	50	11	664	502	1,011	47	102	443	212
Ward	141	413	220	218	24	51	2	303	712	681	96	35	563	54
Washington	825	507	1,230	102	899	212	14	1,193	1,031	1,535	49	528	575	492
Webb	1,805	473	728	92	82	23	3	2,401	1,509	2,479	68	13	209	62
Wharton	1,140	1,095	905	170	224	386	10	2,271	1,655	3,188	43	479	773	269
Wheeler	878	489	544	1,345	27	27	25	2,072	1,366	1,769	50	610	976	58
Wichita	3,762	5,013	1,933	492	173	59	29	4,883	5,886	6,954	93	1,221	3,389	304
Wilbarger	1,457	1,580	1,099	454	109	36	9	2,167	2,424	2,552	182	666	1,099	373
Willacy	204	472	299	154	156	77	9	717	812	1,144	178	58	507	70
Williamson	2,492	1,692	1,345	467	505	1,060	0	3,668	3,515	4,399	427	505	1,669	692
Wilson	816	653	1,453	138	108	476	29	2,123	1,618	2,445	75	376	817	277
Winkler	208	268	256	166	17	46	7	358	559	563	87	41	371	33
Wise	1,925	910	706	587	258	121	13	1,805	3,086	2,326	76	886	1,499	164
Wood	1,612	1,047	615	335	68	625	43	2,004	2,544	1,720	34	1,901	716	201
Yoakum	65	148	91	90	32	4	0	175	226	191	20	11	146	48
Young	1,241	1,645	695	478	119	40	8	2,024	2,514	2,120	67	435	1,319	191
Zapata	85	51	168	0	5	4	1	527	98	337	0	0	5	0
Zavala	298	599	301	46	45	36	8	695	594	715	218	41	272	51
Official	298,903		207,200		62,476		4,454	459,106		33,391		239,460		
Totals		243,254		125,324		58,815		499,343		553,219		145,877		81,170
Unofficial	299,743		207,193		62,074		4,454	459,784		33,391		239,460		
Totals		243,215		125,274		58,829		500,060		553,220		145,877		81,180

Table 33: Gubernatorial Races

Democratic Primary, 1938													
Year	1938												
County	W. Lee O'Daniel	Ernest O. Thompson	William McCraw	Tom F. Hunter	S.T. Brogdon	Joseph King	Clarence E. Farmer	P.D. Renfro	Karl A. Crowley	Clarence R. Miller	James A. Ferguson	Thomas Self	Marvin P. McCoy
Anderson	3,484	829	985	1,258	9	57	9	28	206	6	92	9	16
Andrews	352	114	29	41	0	0	2	0	10	0	3	0	2
Angelina	4,074	625	1,353	443	13	1	6	691	261	7	66	4	15
Aransas	363	169	79	21	0	1	0	0	0	1	0	1	0
Archer	1,469	494	89	356	0	0	3	3	35	0	2	1	0
Armstrong	529	439	54	51	1	0	4	0	7	1	0	0	2
Atascosa	2,265	843	299	116	5	1	1	3	58	1	5	5	4
Austin	1,563	854	415	357	1	4	2	0	56	2	24	1	4
Bailey	794	196	118	108	2	1	0	1	33	1	9	0	1
Bandera	391	112	34	64	0	0	0	1	44	0	2	1	2
Bastrop	1,971	885	617	126	3	1	5	2	81	2	9	0	5
Baylor	1,372	469	144	232	7	0	4	3	32	0	5	0	4
Bee	2,121	799	296	139	0	0	1	1	22	0	14	2	2
Bell	4,944	1,994	1,043	899	3	2	21	23	98	0	138	4	0
Bexar	24,161	10,541	7,731	4,246	45	77	50	176	569	28	202	38	78
Blanco	743	187	116	64	3	0	6	0	5	0	2	2	0
Borden	276	109	15	32	2	0	1	0	7	0	1	2	1
Bosque	3,218	952	358	409	6	1	4	2	134	0	9	3	5
Bowie	5,200	1,228	1,344	387	14	2	15	117	215	7	34	19	9
Brazoria	1,639	731	562	520	3	3	3	13	3	0	5	0	4
Brazos	2,030	961	550	485	7	1	3	225	64	4	8	8	5
Brewster	399	576	238	90	3	0	4	6	80	0	6	5	3
Briscoe	959	190	83	169	1	1	9	1	33	1	7	0	2
Brooks	423	225	124	24	2	5	8	1	6	0	16	26	0
Brown	3,623	1,280	543	660	2	1	42	8	145	5	10	3	4
Burleson	1,565	1,060	590	202	5	1	4	7	30	1	11	2	7
Burnet	1,831	480	216	104	0	0	1	2	21	0	6	1	1
Caldwell	2,761	1,087	432	236	2	1	1	2	40	0	6	8	2
Calhoun	796	225	118	81	1	2	0	2	22	3	5	1	1
Callahan	1,751	519	217	370	1	1	8	2	43	0	9	0	1
Cameron	4,843	2,104	790	1,003	11	9	9	25	127	9	14	2	20
Camp	1,418	159	197	345	1	5	3	0	24	0	4	1	2
Carson	978	758	236	145	0	0	4	1	19	1	2	1	0
Cass	2,973	556	718	509	2	2	8	20	670	6	25	1	8
Castro	796	428	67	73	0	0	3	1	25	0	3	0	1
Chambers	902	398	152	183	0	1	1	61	21	3	5	3	2
Cherokee	3,491	529	650	1,236	2	7	6	63	442	2	21	13	1
Childress	1,955	826	423	193	0	3	7	2	29	4	7	2	0
Clay	2,130	726	216	472	4	0	5	9	86	1	6	2	4
Cochran	642	118	60	97	6	0	0	1	127	1	3	1	5
Coke	977	406	62	48	4	0	4	0	30	0	3	3	0
Coleman	2,599	1,156	203	275	3	2	21	9	34	0	9	1	2
Collin	5,538	965	1,093	1,116	1	2	3	24	161	4	10	6	4
Collingsworth	1,894	540	253	132	1	0	2	0	20	0	5	4	3
Colorado	1,739	726	425	359	2	5	2	15	62	4	18	2	1
Comal	1,601	595	213	451	1	0	10	6	27	2	4	2	3
Comanche	3,023	616	381	416	5	2	43	4	102	0	23	2	4
Concho	961	329	75	121	1	0	2	2	19	1	2	1	1
Cooke	3,790	1,289	658	694	5	3	26	4	72	6	29	0	9
Coryell	2,501	890	396	254	3	3	9	7	47	1	14	3	6
Cottle	1,865	183	103	181	1	9	2	3	61	3	5	1	2
Crane	313	355	102	88	0	0	2	4	7	0	2	2	1
Crockett	172	139	30	13	0	0	0	0	2	0	2	0	0
Crosby	1,608	459	186	210	1	0	2	1	58	1	10	1	2
Culberson	105	127	101	23	1	1	1	0	39	1	0	0	1
Dallam	502	822	589	99	1	0	3	0	16	0	11	3	3
Dallas	19,186	5,610	11,632	6,136	38	52	359	157	591	54	25	26	73
Dawson	2,282	736	186	129	3	2	3	0	325	0	9	3	14
DeWitt	1,788	1,575	370	332	4	2	3	2	32	1	17	11	17
Deaf Smith	629	773	111	119	3	0	1	0	20	1	2	0	2
Delta	1,865	407	203	660	1	2	1	3	28	0	6	0	1
Denton	3,678	1,298	1,007	900	4	0	16	16	153	9	8	4	2
Dickens	1,810	382	191	152	3	0	3	0	61	0	15	0	1
Dimmit	933	405	129	46	0	0	2	0	8	0	2	0	0

Table 33: Gubernatorial Races

	Democratic Primary, 1938												
Year	1938												
County	W. Lee O'Daniel	Ernest O. Thompson	William McCraw	Tom F. Hunter	S.T. Brogdon	Joseph King	Clarence E. Farmer	P.D. Renfro	Karl A. Crowley	Clarence R. Miller	James A. Ferguson	Thomas Self	Marvin P. McCoy
Donley	1,284	653	128	157	1	6	0	0	16	0	0	0	0
Duval	340	198	2,921	12	0	0	1	0	5	0	0	0	1
Eastland	4,225	1,052	711	787	1	1	97	4	199	5	15	8	3
Ector	1,133	820	325	268	1	0	18	14	34	3	20	2	0
Edwards	408	160	103	15	0	0	0	3	10	0	1	0	0
El Paso	919	4,528	4,173	775	25	13	16	39	739	9	37	8	31
Ellis	4,168	1,423	850	1,839	1	4	19	18	138	2	12	3	6
Erath	3,305	792	977	427	40	0	24	5	123	2	11	3	3
Falls	3,018	949	514	544	1	1	10	1	50	3	6	11	7
Fannin	5,415	1,325	1,189	727	4	3	10	7	162	3	21	1	184
Fayette	3,623	1,498	582	556	2	2	7	10	132	4	23	4	7
Fisher	2,012	614	210	236	1	0	3	1	74	0	7	1	6
Floyd	1,921	622	144	186	0	0	0	0	31	0	3	0	0
Foard	931	452	69	65	1	0	1	0	18	1	2	2	1
Fort Bend	1,864	816	714	261	3	3	3	13	36	12	7	0	3
Franklin	1,962	329	85	203	1	0	8	2	38	0	4	4	3
Freestone	2,140	557	968	493	2	2	15	20	127	14	16	1	10
Frio	1,040	373	266	98	1	1	1	2	31	1	5	2	1
Gaines	751	250	101	58	1	4	1	0	85	0	5	0	1
Galveston	3,496	2,147	3,304	1,063	5	6	9	116	105	6	33	8	15
Garza	1,141	358	88	115	1	0	5	1	18	0	8	2	1
Gillespie	1,090	543	308	169	4	3	0	4	73	0	11	0	5
Glasscock	179	97	20	22	0	0	0	0	4	0	0	0	0
Goliad	329	226	64	31	0	0	0	2	11	0	2	0	0
Gonzales	2,591	1,465	668	233	1	3	0	10	45	3	9	5	0
Gray	2,537	1,538	223	462	0	3	2	4	25	1	8	3	1
Grayson	7,098	4,050	1,232	924	8	4	25	11	236	4	18	3	14
Gregg	6,075	875	1,189	1,597	21	7	4	50	139	0	7	3	7
Grimes	1,175	715	591	236	0	0	2	29	49	1	0	2	0
Guadalupe	1,960	619	182	168	0	1	1	9	20	0	2	0	1
Hale	2,691	1,219	322	261	3	1	7	0	27	1	5	1	2
Hall	1,970	540	184	239	0	0	2	1	29	1	7	7	0
Hamilton	1,897	667	363	175	1	0	15	2	31	10	6	1	3
Hansford	356	308	123	12	0	0	1	1	15	0	0	0	0
Hardeman	1,662	683	198	241	1	2	7	4	25	3	16	13	3
Hardin	2,600	645	412	344	5	1	4	150	44	1	25	9	15
Harris	22,341	12,670	15,653	7,916	25	93	77	613	619	12	177	42	173
Harrison	2,769	1,677	1,145	548	8	5	9	35	46	1	66	4	7
Hartley	153	398	85	17	4	0	0	2	5	0	1	1	1
Haskell	2,899	909	165	282	6	2	22	1	80	0	22	3	2
Hays	1,874	815	423	80	0	0	1	0	18	1	2	0	2
Hemphill	823	486	134	29	2	0	7	3	7	0	5	2	5
Henderson	3,737	425	549	1,270	6	0	32	41	373	1	53	4	28
Hidalgo	5,139	1,732	1,088	2,156	9	17	3	25	80	8	18	47	13
Hill	4,211	1,449	631	1,274	3	2	27	9	91	12	25	7	9
Hockley	1,675	439	253	219	1	1	5	3	31	4	9	5	3
Hood	911	355	192	213	1	0	58	2	48	0	7	0	0
Hopkins	4,183	897	586	517	3	0	2	4	312	1	20	1	4
Houston	3,317	552	451	345	3	1	4	19	163	1	16	467	3
Howard	2,444	1,544	754	159	2	2	15	6	96	1	33	3	9
Hudspeth	105	110	158	44	0	1	2	0	0	0	1	0	2
Hunt	5,049	1,805	1,250	1,052	15	4	26	16	474	3	20	13	31
Hutchinson	1,641	1,321	355	235	1	1	1	2	18	0	6	5	1
Irion	472	203	38	26	0	0	0	0	10	0	2	0	0
Jack	1,767	412	205	316	28	0	22	1	27	0	5	1	1
Jackson	1,172	560	131	186	1	0	12	2	44	1	10	2	1
Jasper	1,141	529	666	493	4	1	4	132	37	0	24	2	4
Jeff Davis	47	230	98	40	0	0	0	1	10	0	1	0	1
Jefferson	10,234	3,183	3,907	1,739	12	9	7	2,361	185	8	63	10	16
Jim Hogg	156	401	166	56	2	1	0	3	8	1	1	2	0
Jim Wells	1,440	923	313	114	1	0	1	4	17	3	6	1	11
Johnson	2,931	1,292	685	1,122	4	3	29	14	49	1	5	4	4
Jones	2,701	917	350	341	0	3	13	2	47	0	9	0	2
Karnes	2,522	791	269	207	4	2	1	15	74	1	23	17	4
Kaufman	3,950	598	813	1,082	1	1	7	9	244	2	7	2	1

Table 33: Gubernatorial Races

Democratic Primary, 1938													
Year	1938												
County	W. Lee O'Daniel	Ernest O. Thompson	William McCraw	Tom F. Hunter	S.T. Brogdon	Joseph King	Clarence E. Farmer	P.D. Renfro	Karl A. Crowley	Clarence R. Miller	James A. Ferguson	Thomas Self	Marvin P. McCoy
Kendall	326	191	72	42	0	0	1	0	14	0	0	0	4
Kenedy	12	87	0	7	0	2	0	1	0	0	0	0	3
Kent	726	216	37	206	2	0	0	0	31	0	4	1	1
Kerr	1,384	913	394	123	0	1	2	6	34	2	6	7	5
Kimble	896	384	194	69	2	1	0	10	13	2	5	2	2
King	307	59	11	25	0	0	0	1	7	0	2	0	0
Kinney	94	73	32	4	0	0	0	0	4	1	2	0	0
Kleberg	806	640	489	92	1	14	2	10	15	0	13	3	2
Knox	1,631	733	123	104	1	0	5	0	55	1	5	1	1
La Salle	414	451	45	12	11	0	0	1	4	0	2	1	2
Lamar	5,656	1,544	832	1,565	3	1	9	6	73	0	53	2	15
Lamb	2,740	729	409	267	0	1	3	1	63	1	10	6	4
Lampasas	1,845	486	226	151	1	2	3	4	31	0	12	5	2
Lavaca	3,490	1,872	528	286	2	5	6	22	57	5	31	5	11
Lee	1,648	578	248	144	8	1	3	5	52	0	27	0	3
Leon	1,985	436	610	279	1	3	3	4	205	2	7	9	2
Liberty	2,203	1,277	397	551	2	4	3	138	117	10	28	6	7
Limestone	3,848	996	592	1,286	1	1	3	10	79	3	26	8	2
Lipscomb	411	394	87	31	1	2	1	2	23	5	3	2	3
Live Oak	1,253	430	117	113	0	1	0	0	22	0	4	0	0
Llano	1,244	422	147	123	1	0	4	4	28	0	11	0	2
Loving	72	39	11	25	0	0	0	0	3	0	0	0	0
Lubbock	3,405	2,412	1,169	695	1	1	17	2	128	8	16	2	8
Lynn	2,303	684	230	172	0	1	4	1	22	3	10	3	2
Madison	1,262	385	317	393	5	3	2	3	82	0	21	3	1
Marion	602	193	346	96	1	1	2	11	31	0	7	0	1
Martin	662	265	54	39	0	0	0	1	61	0	5	1	0
Mason	1,039	387	140	103	0	0	2	0	86	0	4	0	1
Matagorda	1,272	750	206	248	0	1	3	6	38	0	4	5	1
Maverick	741	263	160	44	1	3	2	5	41	2	8	3	0
McCulloch	1,374	573	218	117	1	5	3	3	36	0	6	3	3
McLennan	8,111	4,057	2,480	1,626	3	11	21	13	134	4	18	66	6
McMullen	349	164	65	29	1	0	1	2	8	0	0	0	0
Medina	1,103	279	198	87	1	3	1	1	29	0	1	3	0
Menard	730	186	180	51	0	1	0	0	42	0	1	0	2
Midland	1,124	1,069	186	183	1	0	36	14	26	4	16	6	6
Milam	4,108	1,283	629	449	3	3	12	5	105	0	12	2	4
Mills	1,145	3	165	179	3	2	3	2	55	1	5	1	2
Mitchell	1,675	749	194	193	4	1	2	13	44	1	6	1	3
Montague	3,161	751	300	414	10	1	3	1	116	4	20	1	7
Montgomery	2,666	862	444	476	27	4	13	65	76	4	30	3	13
Moore	367	528	104	29	0	0	0	0	5	1	1	0	1
Morris	1,390	275	233	182	0	0	0	1	35	3	6	0	2
Motley	965	167	111	98	1	0	0	0	18	2	2	0	1
Nacogdoches	3,508	788	581	855	6	8	25	83	188	1	54	6	15
Navarro	5,334	1,216	699	1,877	14	7	14	24	134	15	88	9	4
Newton	904	400	452	379	6	5	1	187	34	10	65	4	5
Nolan	2,262	947	633	534	0	2	13	2	73	1	3	1	1
Nueces	6,041	3,606	1,430	398	56	13	23	17	40	4	21	3	15
Ochiltree	601	453	36	41	0	0	2	1	8	2	18	1	0
Oldham	169	308	37	25	0	0	0	0	7	0	3	1	0
Orange	2,309	328	479	720	1	2	1	101	33	3	14	3	4
Palo Pinto	3,106	623	580	681	2	0	49	5	43	0	7	3	2
Panola	2,171	618	1,053	722	3	3	7	66	101	8	42	6	20
Parker	2,580	698	363	1,193	4	7	131	1	56	7	22	2	2
Parmer	1,040	309	157	143	1	1	0	0	32	1	8	0	7
Pecos	922	750	136	148	0	1	13	5	63	2	8	0	6
Polk	2,340	444	231	361	3	2	8	116	76	2	27	1	4
Potter	1,768	4,456	707	308	2	3	13	3	15	1	5	0	3
Presidio	187	430	218	49	2	6	3	4	56	9	2	5	8
Rains	1,233	119	187	216	0	1	0	3	54	0	20	8	3
Randall	517	1,149	258	114	0	1	2	0	11	0	2	0	4
Reagan	159	264	28	21	1	0	0	0	5	0	0	0	0
Real	560	102	65	4	0	0	1	2	5	0	1	0	1
Red River	4,226	654	648	575	0	4	8	2	20	3	25	1	6

Table 33: Gubernatorial Races

	Democratic Primary, 1938												
Year	1938												
County	W. Lee O'Daniel	Ernest O. Thompson	William McCraw	Tom F. Hunter	S.T. Brogdon	Joseph King	Clarence E. Farmer	P.D. Renfro	Karl A. Crowley	Clarence R. Miller	James A. Ferguson	Thomas Self	Marvin P. McCoy
Reeves	488	665	263	178	1	1	0	4	26	1	3	2	2
Refugio	661	523	108	42	0	0	0	0	7	0	1	2	0
Roberts	258	216	17	21	0	0	0	0	12	0	1	1	1
Robertson	2,384	572	595	373	4	4	27	13	113	0	39	6	6
Rockwall	1,038	224	246	455	1	1	1	3	21	2	1	1	1
Runnels	2,657	1,349	270	207	8	4	12	6	28	2	10	1	1
Rusk	5,838	704	1,324	2,025	18	14	18	167	157	21	114	29	11
Sabine	955	397	363	454	3	1	8	73	25	2	62	6	1
San Augustine	1,218	399	203	577	4	4	7	186	218	0	58	6	12
San Jacinto	768	114	90	199	1	2	0	38	41	0	18	3	0
San Patricio	2,134	1,148	537	104	8	2	2	21	11	1	2	1	1
San Saba	1,385	444	327	118	0	1	15	0	14	0	4	2	0
Schleicher	288	152	99	35	0	0	1	0	5	0	1	2	3
Scurry	1,736	661	272	222	1	0	7	1	50	0	17	2	6
Shackelford	1,356	331	89	233	0	1	0	0	10	2	4	0	1
Shelby	3,163	527	697	1,077	4	8	21	278	270	0	83	6	11
Sherman	173	413	40	16	1	0	0	0	1	2	2	0	0
Smith	6,751	1,031	994	2,273	2	5	10	137	206	8	21	8	6
Somervell	597	142	65	79	1	3	10	1	8	0	2	0	3
Starr	26	1,750	16	29	0	0	0	1	0	0	0	0	0
Stephens	2,517	381	193	595	2	1	19	3	19	0	6	0	3
Sterling	148	214	33	6	0	0	2	0	3	0	0	0	0
Stonewall	1,241	397	65	165	0	0	1	1	14	0	4	0	2
Sutton	264	196	67	18	0	0	1	4	2	0	3	0	0
Swisher	1,141	545	267	148	1	0	2	0	30	0	1	2	0
Tarrant	10,835	8,546	7,713	6,689	20	22	1,463	100	690	11	62	25	20
Taylor	4,097	2,614	824	515	3	1	17	6	53	0	3	1	4
Terrell	117	161	176	51	0	1	1	3	9	1	0	1	0
Terry	1,517	506	168	180	0	1	8	2	145	1	5	9	2
Throckmorton	1,121	148	115	128	0	0	0	0	19	2	4	1	0
Titus	3,140	633	490	657	1	2	5	14	90	5	22	3	5
Tom Green	4,064	2,181	724	369	1	2	2	11	107	85	17	7	7
Travis	9,553	4,756	4,248	613	1	6	10	80	121	4	11	4	5
Trinity	1,422	209	344	370	3	1	6	22	40	2	19	9	1
Tyler	1,129	398	349	327	4	2	2	67	67	0	26	2	6
Upshur	4,530	202	686	732	5	7	14	22	61	4	18	5	1
Upton	722	546	142	121	1	0	3	1	10	0	3	1	4
Uvalde	1,754	677	311	158	0	0	1	9	38	2	5	1	2
Val Verde	816	704	499	83	1	4	4	7	83	2	4	2	2
Van Zandt	4,832	436	626	1,348	10	2	26	11	241	0	45	6	4
Victoria	1,542	942	735	223	0	0	1	8	46	0	5	0	3
Walker	1,766	475	472	319	0	0	4	80	27	0	7	3	2
Waller	793	272	215	160	1	0	16	17	21	0	15	0	1
Ward	1,047	598	206	334	0	1	6	4	38	2	13	2	3
Washington	2,122	733	443	328	1	1	2	10	22	1	23	1	8
Webb	582	2,452	426	17	1	0	17	1	9	0	0	1	1
Wharton	2,539	1,679	588	418	2	2	1	9	23	2	26	1	6
Wheeler	2,077	671	237	359	1	0	2	3	18	3	6	0	3
Wichita	4,830	3,205	532	3,292	2	14	27	12	81	3	4	6	10
Wilbarger	2,896	935	344	667	10	0	8	5	40	0	12	0	0
Willacy	1,263	140	145	240	1	1	13	10	39	3	6	3	1
Williamson	5,050	2,020	1,119	301	1	0	5	20	57	2	6	6	8
Wilson	2,299	1,303	249	215	9	3	4	10	31	5	10	1	3
Winkler	776	572	210	344	3	1	1	1	27	2	13	0	2
Wise	3,085	817	661	528	5	2	44	5	74	1	9	5	9
Wood	3,529	450	649	746	5	1	4	8	223	3	25	1	3
Yoakum	291	113	20	86	0	0	0	0	22	2	2	1	0
Young	2,723	1,044	271	639	4	2	9	16	13	3	7	2	1
Zapata	95	269	273	4	0	0	0	1	1	0	1	0	0
Zavala	881	244	106	75	0	0	2	1	12	0	8	1	1
Official	573,166		152,278		892		3,869		19,153		3,800		
Totals		231,630		117,634		773		8,127		667		1,405	1,491
Unofficial	**573,166**		**152,278**		**892**		**3,869**		**19,153**		**3,800**		
Totals		**231,630**		**117, 634**		**773**		**8,127**		**667**		**1,405**	**1,491**

Table 34: Gubernatorial Elections

| County | Democratic Primaries, 1940-1942 | | | | | | | | | | | | | |
| | 1940 | | | | | | | | 1942 | | | | | |
	W. Lee O'Daniel	Harry Hines	Jerry Sadler	Miriam A. Ferguson	R.P. Condron	Derden	Ernest O. Thompson	Cyclone Davis Jr.	Hal H. Collins	Alex M. Ferguson	Gene S. Porter	Charles L. Somervile	Coke R. Stevensn	Hope Wheeler
Anderson	3,965	709	973	566	12	0	803	20	2,736	57	24	28	4,074	18
Andrews	439	39	8	25	1	0	40	1	115	3	1	0	294	4
Angelina	5,853	449	423	801	9	0	1,257	0	2,934	81	22	15	4,108	22
Aransas	633	18	34	59	2	0	193	5	233	15	11	4	569	17
Archer	1,649	348	99	147	3	0	146	5	903	15	1	8	1,428	17
Armstrong	786	136	45	35	1	0	180	0	176	2	7	4	522	48
Atascosa	2,306	177	128	197	0	3	507	8	922	20	13	6	1,725	5
Austin	1,758	213	182	279	5	0	823	19	649	39	16	5	2,452	5
Bailey	1,317	192	73	64	0	0	201	2	309	3	2	20	723	6
Bandera	1,075	35	91	185	3	0	197	3	295	9	10	4	934	28
Bastrop	2,065	335	139	353	0	0	928	11	814	22	14	3	2,032	15
Baylor	1,403	367	155	80	2	0	349	8	831	11	11	3	1,195	8
Bee	2,142	131	75	322	6	0	622	8	787	14	8	4	1,672	7
Bell	4,760	1,054	235	882	35	0	2,742	27	2,086	45	252	11	4,903	40
Bexar	23,526	1,890	3,366	9,868	81	0	11,086	149	3,662	684	99	255	15,858	835
Blanco	569	24	38	72	1	0	205	1	283	5	0	2	665	5
Borden	261	120	15	24	0	0	58	2	157	0	7	1	265	3
Bosque	2,830	434	213	191	7	0	881	4	1,395	30	15	42	2,644	25
Bowie	5,749	475	536	459	25	0	1,731	29	2,652	37	38	24	3,597	114
Brazoria	2,350	202	197	382	0	0	899	8	1,110	36	4	9	2,781	39
Brazos	2,387	411	225	321	8	11	1,432	9	1,062	34	13	9	3,364	11
Brewster	539	140	101	154	3	0	572	9	83	6	5	5	909	19
Briscoe	1,008	192	79	89	1	0	148	6	328	13	4	4	802	14
Brooks	565	84	38	121	3	0	134	2	85	28	9	8	574	9
Brown	4,339	602	283	319	4	0	1,535	16	1,331	29	39	9	3,743	86
Burleson	1,758	120	348	255	4	0	1,021	7	751	27	13	9	2,025	16
Burnet	1,776	147	101	293	2	0	631	7	740	6	3	3	1,470	14
Caldwell	2,983	382	162	387	3	0	860	7	1,023	11	15	3	2,656	7
Calhoun	1,056	63	126	112	0	0	249	4	478	13	11	2	883	4
Callahan	2,063	497	86	107	6	0	450	23	893	24	6	14	1,864	25
Cameron	4,816	1,092	365	542	76	0	1,288	18	1,327	237	62	62	4,560	414
Camp	1,345	141	103	71	2	0	259	56	822	11	10	4	780	10
Carson	1,335	300	86	105	2	0	352	3	253	21	6	2	1,456	15
Cass	2,892	582	354	371	1	0	710	24	1,707	58	12	12	2,552	77
Castro	1,039	155	85	50	3	0	172	5	285	12	8	5	949	13
Chambers	1,132	172	63	173	1	0	371	5	416	8	3	7	1,060	4
Cherokee	4,694	704	446	580	4	0	1,180	9	2,255	33	7	12	3,329	106
Childress	2,112	695	157	171	2	0	507	5	1,346	24	6	12	1,989	31
Clay	1,899	651	123	184	3	0	301	9	1,459	14	20	9	2,026	20
Cochran	942	61	21	84	0	0	177	9	296	10	12	3	826	15
Coke	713	174	54	57	1	0	256	6	393	2	1	0	624	7
Coleman	2,981	452	159	190	12	0	762	14	1,686	20	20	12	2,803	52
Collin	5,783	758	376	676	10	0	1,666	31	2,915	22	20	84	2,827	44
Collingsworth	2,192	238	112	99	1	0	339	9	1,228	11	8	6	1,252	3
Colorado	1,721	177	280	347	2	4	828	4	695	34	15	4	2,175	15
Comal	1,651	171	216	171	3	0	580	7	294	84	18	9	2,276	24
Comanche	3,398	359	211	238	5	0	711	41	1,702	11	5	25	2,562	30
Concho	1,122	107	78	67	2	0	425	4	387	4	3	0	959	6
Cooke	3,803	760	473	399	15	0	1,190	14	2,108	50	17	12	3,461	79
Coryell	3,066	380	224	194	2	0	1,062	5	1,477	17	30	5	2,251	36
Cottle	1,692	344	98	146	3	0	231	4	854	13	9	7	905	9
Crane	540	151	17	95	1	0	167	5	98	12	1	3	731	2
Crockett	150	60	12	10	1	0	113	0	80	3	3	1	527	1
Crosby	1,806	308	48	115	34	0	452	3	710	8	17	8	1,419	18
Culberson	142	49	23	37	0	0	155	3	13	0	2	0	165	2
Dallam	1,347	156	186	62	2	0	518	2	150	25	15	15	1,111	170
Dallas	18,815	9,227	3,123	4,386	114	0	13,021	211	7,531	327	383	772	27,975	252
Dawson	2,371	627	102	160	5	1	456	2	1,200	18	14	3	1,958	14
DeWitt	2,528	422	281	379	4	1	1,242	12	774	17	16	3	2,704	15
Deaf Smith	1,087	304	78	42	3	0	267	0	266	10	6	10	1,185	7
Delta	2,054	219	274	131	10	0	465	2	1,211	12	7	7	1,283	7
Denton	4,060	1,011	600	276	21	0	1,953	26	2,293	25	22	21	4,400	23
Dickens	1,830	276	94	93	3	0	325	44	845	10	9	0	1,353	15
Dimmit	898	41	71	42	0	0	297	4	205	4	4	2	534	62

Table 34: Gubernatorial Elections

County	Democratic Primaries, 1940-1942													
Year	**1940**								**1942**					
	W. Lee O'Daniel	Harry Hines	Jerry Sadler	Miriam A. Ferguson	R.P. Condron	Derden	Ernest O. Thompson	Cyclone Davis Jr.	Hal H. Collins	Alex M. Fergusn	Gene S. Porter	Charles L. Somervlle	Coke R. Stevensn	Hope Wheeler
Donley	1,407	280	71	60	0	0	443	4	612	5	1	2	1,124	12
Duval	3,728	29	11	35	1	1	100	3	72	0	5	0	2,836	0
Eastland	4,527	810	326	417	8	0	1,291	31	2,213	46	14	21	4,043	37
Ector	2,076	442	50	287	6	0	581	12	313	10	14	7	2,218	11
Edwards	555	122	71	35	1	0	170	5	170	1	2	3	683	16
El Paso	1,954	537	706	1,600	32	0	6,368	55	319	156	97	83	9,093	129
Ellis	4,569	1,164	522	522	10	0	2,185	30	2,331	32	18	14	5,466	16
Erath	3,493	827	450	286	8	0	790	10	2,219	35	22	10	3,365	44
Falls	3,069	727	168	249	12	0	1,423	7	1,497	30	19	56	2,902	16
Fannin	7,385	783	380	393	8	0	1,528	21	4,627	67	14	12	4,192	47
Fayette	2,891	345	551	666	13	0	1,549	20	1,272	85	27	16	4,533	24
Fisher	1,973	360	113	103	4	0	608	16	940	6	9	4	1,595	20
Floyd	2,138	411	87	52	6	0	435	5	894	14	9	18	1,754	18
Foard	935	173	50	35	0	0	291	3	540	7	8	16	786	19
Fort Bend	1,919	226	163	403	16	0	1,017	12	728	26	4	3	2,173	3
Franklin	1,836	198	125	97	1	0	347	9	1,329	30	3	4	1,007	6
Freestone	2,240	614	305	397	4	0	1,063	8	1,276	28	16	11	2,218	11
Frio	1,184	67	93	69	2	0	387	13	370	14	4	3	704	2
Gaines	1,135	429	44	158	1	0	181	4	387	12	6	3	994	9
Galveston	4,069	423	934	3,645	16	0	3,234	23	1,314	100	80	98	8,000	128
Garza	1,091	161	20	53	2	0	244	4	483	12	3	1	955	11
Gillespie	677	45	70	51	2	0	233	1	245	6	0	1	1,287	33
Glasscock	225	59	15	13	2	0	61	1	47	2	1	0	210	0
Goliad	335	35	34	17	0	0	140	0	159	5	0	2	421	3
Gonzales	2,344	221	313	379	11	0	1,453	6	1,611	12	14	5	2,666	9
Gray	3,741	929	218	279	10	0	563	25	900	42	48	10	3,254	107
Grayson	8,207	798	422	669	12	0	4,201	11	4,519	176	51	11	8,455	80
Gregg	6,805	1,792	620	1,157	23	0	1,131	35	2,526	89	89	26	5,871	71
Grimes	1,703	178	284	155	1	0	688	6	644	13	26	1	1,344	5
Guadalupe	1,147	77	96	156	2	3	292	10	442	13	8	14	1,604	6
Hale	2,695	803	86	107	1	0	965	6	994	14	23	4	2,635	129
Hall	2,073	462	73	99	3	0	379	7	1,187	21	6	10	1,441	126
Hamilton	2,216	372	152	144	2	0	580	9	1,136	18	8	3	1,967	6
Hansford	537	75	48	26	13	0	161	1	73	3	4	1	514	6
Hardeman	1,803	320	126	85	3	0	487	10	740	10	9	4	1,390	6
Hardin	2,183	95	100	434	2	0	585	6	1,194	47	10	3	1,598	3
Harris	30,998	4,921	4,558	13,337	84	0	20,639	144	9,134	221	206	132	51,591	405
Harrison	3,198	568	365	473	6	0	1,695	16	1,010	47	14	21	3,538	80
Hartley	468	46	57	32	1	0	181	1	77	22	8	1	428	9
Haskell	2,641	579	431	157	4	0	615	9	1,588	20	18	5	2,544	16
Hays	3,206	156	102	188	3	0	927	4	617	14	8	7	1,937	2
Hemphill	824	87	61	22	4	0	263	3	388	8	6	0	801	25
Henderson	3,834	653	475	520	9	0	888	27	2,152	58	28	12	2,501	19
Hidalgo	7,007	1,062	249	512	41	0	1,260	40	2,171	64	40	31	6,209	201
Hill	4,073	1,200	211	439	6	0	1,770	12	2,449	39	15	11	3,798	127
Hockley	2,382	308	87	141	4	0	496	5	907	20	21	6	2,477	24
Hood	1,440	264	121	100	2	0	376	2	521	6	17	2	811	8
Hopkins	4,338	885	336	360	9	0	1,225	19	3,024	38	20	12	2,931	34
Houston	3,239	404	584	374	6	0	871	20	2,105	24	9	5	2,907	7
Howard	2,684	726	288	489	4	0	1,184	12	1,029	28	15	9	3,002	27
Hudspeth	177	40	51	54	5	0	239	4	25	11	10	0	409	8
Hunt	5,316	1,365	645	572	22	0	2,625	16	3,177	57	13	10	5,148	21
Hutchinson	2,252	831	120	242	3	0	381	4	228	28	18	12	2,146	26
Irion	508	34	22	44	1	0	183	0	238	3	5	3	403	10
Jack	1,811	290	89	136	4	0	519	11	931	11	15	9	1,496	13
Jackson	1,540	184	100	226	2	0	584	5	930	19	6	7	1,493	23
Jasper	1,789	78	241	208	2	4	858	5	1,070	63	44	5	1,520	22
Jeff Davis	114	75	44	72	0	0	144	7	22	7	2	5	294	1
Jefferson	10,333	1,934	1,631	2,442	36	0	6,458	30	2,986	142	91	64	13,662	199
Jim Hogg	598	29	32	52	2	0	191	2	31	12	2	37	481	0
Jim Wells	1,670	159	109	209	12	0	516	57	696	54	16	10	2,166	13
Johnson	3,471	567	338	494	8	0	1,889	20	1,702	25	16	9	4,098	31
Jones	2,998	764	152	172	7	0	854	11	1,315	11	12	3	2,861	51
Karnes	2,214	230	298	280	7	44	609	79	910	38	9	11	1,998	43
Kaufman	3,206	1,103	354	411	9	0	797	7	2,235	44	5	12	3,215	25

Table 34: Gubernatorial Elections

	Democratic Primaries, 1940-1942													
Year	1940								1942					
County	W. Lee O'Daniel	Harry Hines	Jerry Sadler	Miriam A. Ferguson	R.P. Condron	Derden	Ernest O. Thompson	Cyclone Davis Jr.	Hal H. Collins	Alex M. Fergusn	Gene S. Porter	Charles L. Somerville	Coke R. Stevensn	Hope Wheeler
Kendall	227	11	23	31	0	0	73	0	99	1	0	0	359	0
Kenedy	45	7	0	40	0	0	18	1	2	3	6	3	89	2
Kent	737	107	55	90	0	0	144	4	421	9	62	5	624	4
Kerr	1,300	98	216	135	3	0	693	4	549	5	3	1	1,436	7
Kimble	1,047	122	72	103	12	0	378	24	363	8	12	7	1,248	2
King	247	43	8	10	0	0	28	0	155	2	3	2	182	0
Kinney	64	25	29	17	0	0	40	0	16	3	0	6	175	0
Kleberg	716	138	51	190	3	0	389	10	237	4	7	3	973	16
Knox	1,637	383	126	82	3	0	362	2	960	12	14	2	1,527	8
La Salle	414	26	17	165	0	0	171	0	119	2	3	1	527	0
Lamar	7,390	734	629	460	0	0	2,413	31	4,070	35	111	15	4,080	80
Lamb	2,866	635	129	116	5	0	577	9	1,094	42	29	2	2,644	44
Lampasas	1,692	247	167	138	5	0	571	6	821	17	16	13	1,626	19
Lavaca	3,063	330	640	543	10	0	1,301	9	1,241	66	18	31	3,876	95
Lee	1,630	120	136	161	3	0	466	4	716	20	32	5	1,441	8
Leon	1,888	409	405	364	4	0	585	8	771	13	8	4	1,591	35
Liberty	2,866	204	200	493	6	0	1,353	4	1,491	31	15	10	2,548	14
Limestone	3,312	1,208	194	590	9	0	1,058	11	1,794	22	23	7	3,623	24
Lipscomb	533	78	40	5	2	0	143	1	175	1	7	1	327	25
Live Oak	1,447	137	119	114	8	1	297	11	528	15	7	0	893	10
Llano	1,164	132	91	148	1	0	535	3	377	6	3	27	1,116	17
Loving	46	21	4	21	0	0	23	0	8	0	0	1	77	1
Lubbock	4,330	1,972	253	353	9	8	2,869	13	991	33	29	3	6,667	86
Lynn	2,329	350	89	190	8	0	625	9	836	19	6	4	1,858	25
Madison	1,156	147	180	246	3	0	667	2	795	12	10	4	1,327	6
Marion	602	102	77	125	3	0	250	5	248	14	4	3	595	4
Martin	1,024	80	53	75	2	0	237	4	464	3	2	1	590	10
Mason	1,354	178	68	87	2	0	300	4	521	12	17	5	1,169	7
Matagorda	1,558	111	278	162	3	0	585	4	731	17	11	4	1,746	37
Maverick	569	179	42	53	1	0	180	2	96	1	0	1	341	0
McCulloch	2,216	300	114	152	1	0	813	10	1,030	5	9	2	1,950	14
McLennan	8,928	1,589	656	874	14	0	6,924	42	3,562	41	66	252	9,784	68
McMullen	278	67	14	22	1	0	59	2	132	0	3	0	272	2
Medina	1,544	102	160	375	3	0	352	9	496	5	5	1	930	22
Menard	1,092	97	121	136	6	0	347	6	516	23	8	4	1,058	14
Midland	1,418	542	26	111	2	0	390	12	466	12	47	1	1,625	12
Milam	3,789	469	314	507	9	0	1,948	11	2,337	26	37	19	3,466	66
Mills	1,669	208	111	223	8	0	437	15	832	24	6	7	1,338	7
Mitchell	1,906	500	161	147	1	0	391	11	1,040	12	6	6	1,746	32
Montague	3,306	485	208	262	6	0	863	14	1,954	34	17	12	2,622	27
Montgomery	3,087	249	241	652	10	0	896	12	1,682	33	32	14	2,379	27
Moore	759	194	80	56	0	0	245	0	106	8	9	1	685	11
Morris	1,295	270	183	72	0	0	248	4	801	9	13	4	842	6
Motley	1,009	180	69	56	1	0	161	2	417	8	1	4	681	8
Nacogdoches	4,086	451	805	737	16	0	1,120	17	2,054	102	23	5	3,490	57
Navarro	5,177	1,438	461	902	15	0	1,359	19	2,634	50	29	19	4,975	46
Newton	1,408	78	206	306	78	0	514	1	725	55	23	12	907	10
Nolan	2,392	502	442	287	31	0	825	12	1,116	13	64	6	2,579	29
Nueces	6,793	1,144	446	1,013	21	0	3,080	29	2,016	143	51	22	8,115	66
Ochiltree	1,163	98	101	32	2	0	267	1	198	2	4	4	507	45
Oldham	448	38	20	21	2	0	92	1	78	3	3	1	347	4
Orange	2,534	161	204	658	6	0	736	3	1,172	86	39	13	2,622	57
Palo Pinto	2,715	790	279	330	7	0	764	12	1,418	21	14	12	3,187	48
Panola	2,454	504	640	503	0	0	642	22	1,376	153	78	35	2,138	41
Parker	3,067	300	242	234	5	0	1,057	7	1,961	18	3	21	3,039	58
Parmer	1,313	162	89	54	1	0	169	3	321	9	10	5	725	27
Pecos	1,235	259	73	143	16	0	498	52	284	29	13	13	1,745	10
Polk	2,584	288	190	378	3	0	551	8	1,401	28	5	3	1,606	5
Potter	4,045	646	250	246	6	5	3,300	13	743	35	31	121	4,207	104
Presidio	194	117	67	11	5	0	432	10	42	8	5	7	744	12
Rains	1,215	152	168	133	3	0	203	3	982	21	3	7	696	0
Randall	1,133	351	144	60	4	0	602	4	260	19	3	8	1,302	7
Reagan	342	182	12	27	0	0	132	0	67	1	2	1	486	5
Real	507	26	36	50	0	0	158	1	297	7	4	1	450	13
Red River	3,923	273	291	375	7	0	1,123	75	2,383	20	9	7	2,267	18

Table 34: Gubernatorial Elections

Democratic Primaries, 1940-1942

County	1940 W. Lee O'Daniel	Harry Hines	Jerry Sadler	Miriam A. Ferguson	R.P. Condron	Derden	Ernest O. Thompson	Cyclone Davis Jr.	1942 Hal H. Collins	Alex M. Ferguson	Gene S. Porter	Charles L. Somerville	Coke R. Stevensn	Hope Wheeler
Reeves	646	346	115	148	6	0	511	9	69	9	7	5	852	5
Refugio	774	83	36	92	0	0	387	0	241	8	2	0	678	3
Roberts	304	112	19	11	0	0	93	0	80	2	3	1	348	3
Robertson	2,129	271	296	476	16	0	918	6	1,253	53	37	11	2,019	17
Rockwall	1,068	335	120	181	2	0	374	4	704	16	2	11	1,207	24
Runnels	2,736	275	198	178	5	0	1,245	8	1,250	21	13	18	2,438	50
Rusk	6,394	1,971	355	1,047	12	0	985	34	3,011	191	44	41	5,573	53
Sabine	1,502	73	287	331	3	0	558	4	750	64	17	6	1,158	43
San Augustine	1,808	195	309	284	6	0	334	13	1,232	75	12	17	1,161	28
San Jacinto	942	48	96	195	5	0	145	3	524	21	13	3	540	5
San Patricio	2,484	468	146	267	26	0	894	19	854	26	21	7	2,660	41
San Saba	1,926	139	178	123	3	0	553	12	982	7	8	3	1,787	3
Schleicher	520	76	34	45	0	0	214	0	180	3	3	8	614	8
Scurry	1,991	613	83	107	3	0	315	5	879	4	11	2	2,089	7
Shackelford	1,516	307	59	80	7	0	205	8	539	12	9	3	1,104	6
Shelby	3,788	352	689	779	15	0	758	13	2,334	142	32	29	3,078	89
Sherman	388	94	22	17	0	0	163	2	55	8	3	3	404	2
Smith	7,356	1,920	367	827	26	0	1,464	63	3,374	63	30	48	5,933	60
Somervell	655	69	19	44	0	0	199	0	417	5	1	2	403	4
Starr	104	819	3	6	0	0	16	0	10	3	1	0	987	2
Stephens	2,520	484	126	296	4	0	414	9	960	18	12	12	2,074	28
Sterling	192	47	11	8	0	0	214	1	61	1	1	2	300	2
Stonewall	1,252	123	81	61	1	0	210	14	547	19	16	1	906	7
Sutton	299	103	27	63	0	0	206	2	98	3	2	6	591	6
Swisher	1,326	231	49	27	3	0	244	3	404	9	13	5	1,178	10
Tarrant	13,182	3,635	1,090	4,730	65	0	14,621	333	4,892	429	151	77	24,379	531
Taylor	5,124	1,145	387	322	9	0	2,486	59	1,814	26	34	15	6,144	154
Terrell	120	21	60	35	0	0	143	3	31	1	2	1	237	2
Terry	1,814	523	44	118	4	0	349	1	614	14	8	3	1,796	31
Throckmorton	1,326	179	56	69	3	0	83	2	672	10	4	3	772	5
Titus	3,052	484	207	337	3	0	787	11	1,836	26	24	10	2,208	17
Tom Green	3,700	718	287	401	15	0	2,334	9	1,510	24	20	50	4,995	45
Travis	8,676	2,492	591	1,941	34	0	8,146	17	2,325	41	61	295	14,270	57
Trinity	1,834	117	197	400	20	0	434	4	934	26	11	5	1,152	9
Tyler	1,576	151	73	332	2	0	397	1	1,047	35	7	4	1,046	3
Upshur	4,249	558	349	318	11	0	518	16	2,002	51	8	239	2,269	91
Upton	675	305	20	66	1	0	254	2	154	6	9	3	948	9
Uvalde	1,687	125	196	145	5	0	692	11	477	25	5	3	1,632	29
Val Verde	766	651	203	233	12	0	444	21	197	28	13	1	1,167	6
Van Zandt	4,665	935	501	555	9	0	705	45	2,922	27	18	221	2,475	35
Victoria	1,825	145	331	459	4	0	1,066	5	706	6	6	4	1,834	6
Walker	1,765	306	287	237	4	0	564	1	861	31	9	4	1,836	11
Waller	1,017	121	112	203	6	0	460	2	559	14	8	22	997	5
Ward	1,171	366	65	327	1	0	526	8	183	18	17	6	1,273	9
Washington	3,094	116	130	364	1	0	959	4	845	10	5	13	2,218	10
Webb	2,977	138	56	189	10	1	244	7	116	2	2	0	2,940	2
Wharton	2,346	338	491	442	10	0	1,822	0	1,041	106	11	13	3,330	22
Wheeler	2,703	393	151	158	6	0	432	12	1,360	14	10	8	1,671	82
Wichita	7,859	3,133	665	752	33	0	1,183	70	3,260	34	77	76	7,748	87
Wilbarger	2,642	923	133	144	2	0	656	8	1,371	20	7	9	2,561	52
Willacy	1,632	362	38	161	11	0	123	7	688	21	23	24	1,004	83
Williamson	4,508	626	267	366	18	0	2,964	31	1,497	113	17	4	3,900	22
Wilson	2,993	100	156	411	7	0	858	13	1,100	45	20	183	2,269	83
Winkler	941	174	29	185	4	0	437	6	157	19	16	5	1,159	20
Wise	3,151	773	212	220	28	0	919	7	1,740	11	21	20	2,476	20
Wood	3,523	705	393	416	1	0	637	19	2,141	25	20	11	3,332	10
Yoakum	687	102	19	101	1	0	159	10	181	6	0	2	670	6
Young	3,152	825	149	237	5	1	572	9	1,432	14	7	37	2,640	25
Zapata	431	45	17	11	0	0	4	0	10	2	0	0	438	0
Zavala	826	50	70	65	4	0	228	6	303	9	11	0	702	11
Official	645,646		61,396		2,003		256,923		272,469		4,933		651,218	
Totals		119,121		100,578		88		3,623		8,370		4,853		9,373
Unofficial	645,646		61,396		2,003		256,923		272,469		4,933		651,218	
Totals		119,121		100,578		88		3,623		8,370		5,018		9,363

Table 35: Gubernatorial Races

County	Democratic Primary, 1944								
Year	1944								
	Coke R. Stevensn	Martin Jones	W.J. Minton	Alex M. Fergusn	Minnie F. Cunnghm	Gene S. Porter	Edward L. Carey	William F. Grimes	Herbert E. Mills
Anderson	5,110	238	28	86	419	58	38	185	47
Andrews	387	6	1	7	10	8	2	5	3
Angelina	4,275	402	119	169	228	40	16	63	58
Aransas	561	15	8	12	73	8	4	9	9
Archer	1,570	74	32	30	115	10	8	24	10
Armstrong	367	20	7	7	5	6	2	9	1
Atascosa	858	22	2	33	38	17	4	6	4
Austin	1,950	25	10	31	49	11	7	22	10
Bailey	1,174	124	11	15	20	8	4	7	6
Bandera	771	18	8	7	30	14	3	9	4
Bastrop	2,450	34	5	41	156	20	5	39	18
Baylor	1,631	52	14	22	48	17	13	11	2
Bee	2,195	50	25	27	102	12	13	12	31
Bell	7,076	76	54	65	402	532	38	110	98
Bexar	16,144	514	147	928	1,049	463	74	113	165
Blanco	397	17	1	5	74	2	2	0	0
Borden	217	8	8	1	3	5	1	2	1
Bosque	2,893	118	18	34	158	232	9	35	14
Bowie	6,089	247	106	131	166	75	53	68	21
Brazoria	1,795	32	12	13	163	22	6	15	6
Brazos	2,844	67	20	27	260	51	2	33	14
Brewster	964	36	2	31	23	8	1	2	5
Briscoe	857	24	7	15	18	14	4	5	2
Brooks	317	6	1	2	4	2	0	1	0
Brown	3,602	103	42	86	276	73	18	28	27
Burleson	2,066	45	12	68	86	12	6	26	11
Burnet	1,357	30	5	24	108	10	4	6	5
Caldwell	2,831	64	11	21	257	43	4	29	5
Calhoun	511	5	2	14	28	1	0	3	1
Callahan	1,892	50	29	68	100	58	12	24	14
Cameron	5,102	142	95	83	236	135	41	350	101
Camp	1,331	45	19	16	69	15	10	10	6
Carson	1,193	31	7	11	42	6	3	7	10
Cass	3,121	95	41	127	174	29	45	195	15
Castro	945	30	4	9	13	3	2	9	6
Chambers	1,288	30	11	6	46	1	11	10	18
Cherokee	4,146	259	40	109	429	41	41	40	90
Childress	1,938	61	32	26	91	20	5	27	8
Clay	2,494	57	27	27	162	15	25	10	10
Cochran	1,089	19	7	11	15	18	7	11	4
Coke	704	10	2	3	30	7	2	12	1
Coleman	2,625	86	20	25	312	39	5	12	21
Collin	5,779	248	257	242	439	100	50	33	35
Collingsworth	1,598	62	31	23	73	47	10	15	11
Colorado	2,017	23	7	32	77	9	5	14	6
Comal	1,953	19	6	31	37	29	6	6	6
Comanche	2,547	139	29	71	247	106	18	47	29
Concho	949	23	8	4	24	10	1	12	8
Cooke	2,941	120	104	68	189	30	7	27	8
Coryell	2,074	22	46	44	223	209	22	22	5
Cottle	1,191	30	64	27	121	106	8	12	16
Crane	629	10	4	5	19	4	1	6	3
Crockett	365	6	0	1	11	9	1	3	7
Crosby	1,885	52	23	21	57	17	3	20	4
Culberson	146	1	1	2	13	0	0	1	0
Dallam	385	18	8	6	27	33	3	3	3
Dallas	42,750	391	245	517	3,564	396	210	995	928
Dawson	2,084	74	28	30	52	26	6	25	4
DeWitt	2,805	41	5	29	69	5	6	19	7
Deaf Smith	1,260	35	21	10	29	11	2	2	7
Delta	1,797	42	32	37	230	41	17	24	12
Denton	4,698	131	93	76	449	86	24	92	41
Dickens	1,733	65	15	34	119	39	5	26	7
Dimmit	776	23	9	9	50	36	8	13	6

Table 35: Gubernatorial Races

Democratic Primary, 1944									
Year	1944								
County	Coke R. Stevensn	Martin Jones	W.J. Minton	Alex M. Fergusn	Minnie F. Cunnnghm	Gene S. Porter	Edward L. Carey	William F. Grimes	Herbert E. Mills
Donley	1,135	43	19	19	25	18	3	13	4
Duval	3,310	1	1	0	6	8	0	1	0
Eastland	4,098	264	88	169	322	74	22	86	34
Ector	2,430	65	24	36	20	7	19	0	0
Edwards	423	10	2	3	36	2	0	8	5
El Paso	5,568	113	29	50	159	34	15	37	19
Ellis	5,111	125	37	42	315	45	4	40	18
Erath	3,669	136	56	77	174	136	14	68	21
Falls	2,865	55	63	32	281	254	13	26	14
Fannin	5,833	260	237	190	545	41	23	26	81
Fayette	4,809	114	19	116	196	23	27	57	37
Fisher	1,382	13	43	28	181	34	2	15	12
Floyd	1,633	20	20	52	180	150	1	27	2
Foard	870	33	15	22	43	11	9	1	18
Fort Bend	1,759	20	8	28	98	6	5	16	6
Franklin	1,586	111	20	48	133	10	3	18	8
Freestone	2,718	112	14	55	212	119	11	23	37
Frio	582	13	7	10	44	6	1	8	11
Gaines	1,466	29	13	19	29	14	2	24	8
Galveston	6,560	63	26	52	570	53	32	39	395
Garza	1,110	37	18	22	60	16	8	17	1
Gillespie	238	3	2	3	13	0	0	0	0
Glasscock	173	2	2	0	2	1	0	2	0
Goliad	131	3	0	0	16	0	0	0	0
Gonzales	2,262	40	8	48	101	24	14	16	15
Gray	3,274	113	36	38	118	38	15	17	8
Grayson	8,729	319	820	382	561	87	34	64	48
Gregg	6,836	158	24	182	327	42	123	46	29
Grimes	1,067	16	8	11	115	13	3	25	4
Guadalupe	769	11	8	8	53	3	0	2	4
Hale	2,916	97	45	38	129	125	4	25	9
Hall	1,065	38	28	28	65	67	35	13	21
Hamilton	1,656	36	8	32	70	90	3	14	8
Hansford	635	15	5	5	10	6	4	9	3
Hardeman	1,654	107	48	22	107	22	10	56	8
Hardin	1,467	73	15	51	71	8	7	32	6
Harris	45,711	373	244	304	4,739	405	622	1,014	197
Harrison	3,205	129	29	45	126	33	33	23	43
Hartley	356	11	0	0	5	8	1	2	3
Haskell	2,123	38	101	58	156	53	13	32	34
Hays	1,511	17	15	8	150	7	12	8	3
Hemphill	809	33	42	11	31	23	7	12	9
Henderson	3,735	233	56	115	286	132	53	63	143
Hidalgo	6,313	189	82	82	232	69	18	72	21
Hill	4,596	138	52	63	266	332	13	11	35
Hockley	3,113	90	39	58	59	39	21	34	13
Hood	1,370	60	23	41	57	26	8	4	22
Hopkins	4,879	142	71	109	311	49	27	41	104
Houston	3,156	162	8	62	172	32	15	33	61
Howard	2,848	81	13	34	107	34	9	10	39
Hudspeth	256	4	0	3	6	2	0	0	1
Hunt	7,304	266	137	124	399	45	16	82	21
Hutchinson	1,962	68	35	20	170	16	7	14	22
Irion	585	6	10	9	14	7	4	8	5
Jack	1,563	73	35	22	73	17	3	26	3
Jackson	1,738	26	15	18	75	8	7	16	9
Jasper	1,500	136	14	36	76	24	15	17	16
Jeff Davis	124	4	1	0	3	1	0	0	0
Jefferson	16,779	412	75	154	1,652	167	82	193	134
Jim Hogg	277	1	1	0	10	3	0	2	0
Jim Wells	2,427	31	15	31	77	78	11	21	62
Johnson	3,594	167	65	77	360	86	12	50	19
Jones	2,918	111	30	70	194	94	10	67	9
Karnes	1,948	64	12	33	74	11	3	24	6
Kaufman	4,345	152	43	89	358	135	31	34	45

Table 35: Gubernatorial Races

Year	1944								
County	Coke R. Stevensn	Martin Jones	W.J. Minton	Alex M. Fergusn	Minnie F. Cunnnghm	Gene S. Porter	Edward L. Carey	William F. Grimes	Herbert E. Mills
Kendall	34	0	0	0	3	0	0	0	0
Kenedy	75	0	1	0	0	0	0	1	0
Kent	500	25	0	12	40	29	8	4	3
Kerr	1,005	20	3	3	82	9	1	10	0
Kimble	969	1	2	13	57	11	1	20	8
King	96	4	3	0	5	2	0	0	0
Kinney	35	1	1	1	14	0	0	1	3
Kleberg	1,250	39	9	16	88	15	5	16	3
Knox	1,408	41	21	12	99	30	3	14	2
La Salle	721	10	2	4	26	3	0	2	5
Lamar	7,270	314	119	145	441	64	36	41	122
Lamb	2,214	73	27	17	47	35	3	21	1
Lampasas	1,136	10	5	21	95	22	9	3	25
Lavaca	3,685	95	59	120	200	93	16	25	30
Lee	1,645	66	8	34	56	10	6	14	4
Leon	1,697	39	57	39	189	42	5	16	16
Liberty	3,037	96	14	36	182	13	22	50	7
Limestone	3,471	62	46	58	373	217	19	114	76
Lipscomb	245	8	3	3	14	8	1	1	8
Live Oak	1,164	50	8	20	40	10	7	17	8
Llano	1,120	17	2	15	95	12	9	24	4
Loving	74	2	3	0	3	1	0	1	1
Lubbock	7,346	144	80	80	336	103	18	71	15
Lynn	2,011	52	18	63	68	18	5	22	7
Madison	1,561	54	5	12	204	14	7	20	10
Marion	666	25	10	14	33	3	10	27	3
Martin	828	29	17	15	38	17	5	18	5
Mason	1,341	28	7	32	116	15	4	15	24
Matagorda	790	16	2	15	49	3	2	7	5
Maverick	650	20	13	9	18	11	3	22	6
McCulloch	2,309	79	15	12	129	31	11	24	7
McLennan	9,044	103	22	98	841	3,324	242	60	44
McMullen	445	9	1	2	18	3	2	6	5
Medina	838	39	11	11	53	8	5	5	3
Menard	1,165	36	10	13	58	5	3	19	4
Midland	1,775	31	30	29	40	15	28	17	17
Milam	3,820	130	90	100	332	214	32	49	32
Mills	1,431	37	9	19	63	67	4	5	13
Mitchell	1,843	28	11	20	77	13	6	27	8
Montague	2,815	223	120	78	207	40	26	78	18
Montgomery	3,694	112	22	76	339	24	48	115	20
Moore	963	23	7	7	12	13	3	4	1
Morris	1,516	70	19	27	98	19	9	19	7
Motley	784	19	8	11	23	9	29	4	7
Nacogdoches	3,671	677	24	87	144	14	21	74	15
Navarro	5,451	118	109	105	543	197	44	78	55
Newton	1,195	78	16	29	31	3	6	32	7
Nolan	2,658	83	63	37	226	92	22	43	33
Nueces	10,636	154	106	233	694	132	90	165	292
Ochiltree	851	25	17	5	16	33	7	5	7
Oldham	407	15	4	1	14	3	1	0	0
Orange	4,157	147	32	66	107	38	19	28	21
Palo Pinto	2,250	67	51	83	139	76	24	33	72
Panola	2,397	180	52	83	380	20	55	32	18
Parker	2,298	83	31	60	294	58	57	134	29
Parmer	500	22	5	5	11	7	0	8	0
Pecos	1,664	27	13	9	29	17	4	9	21
Polk	2,049	137	4	52	145	11	8	38	5
Potter	4,052	183	47	51	233	88	20	31	21
Presidio	915	15	3	2	9	0	1	8	6
Rains	929	56	22	35	98	14	6	9	14
Randall	1,159	19	7	7	32	7	3	2	1
Reagan	368	10	0	2	15	6	0	5	1
Real	494	19	0	3	44	6	4	6	2
Red River	3,593	73	52	98	334	33	50	13	35

Table 35: Gubernatorial Races

	Democratic Primary, 1944								
Year	1944								
County	Coke R. Stevensn	Martin Jones	W.J. Minton	Alex M. Fergusn	Minnie F. Cunnnghm	Gene S. Porter	Edward L. Carey	William F. Grimes	Herbert E. Mills
Reeves	1,498	46	17	11	29	18	5	18	0
Refugio	377	12	1	0	15	3	3	2	1
Roberts	394	12	2	3	5	4	0	0	1
Robertson	1,702	99	16	46	380	79	34	26	15
Rockwall	1,482	37	22	31	93	14	6	15	9
Runnels	1,024	24	17	9	50	41	4	33	4
Rusk	6,491	462	22	88	176	41	109	53	31
Sabine	1,390	88	44	27	46	6	15	7	4
San Augustine	1,292	323	36	35	56	9	34	12	41
San Jacinto	737	30	9	26	107	4	4	21	1
San Patricio	3,030	78	16	39	340	42	10	15	52
San Saba	1,866	84	25	33	180	29	2	8	23
Schleicher	614	18	3	6	26	18	1	5	1
Scurry	1,754	82	38	23	68	55	14	9	40
Shackelford	1,166	28	13	24	46	22	8	16	20
Shelby	2,654	586	28	104	157	15	11	36	11
Sherman	362	17	3	1	1	5	0	5	1
Smith	7,114	291	74	109	446	87	40	94	188
Somervell	555	37	7	13	30	15	2	10	1
Starr	1,396	1	0	0	1	0	0	0	0
Stephens	1,643	66	25	64	160	41	14	35	11
Sterling	298	5	3	1	18	8	0	4	5
Stonewall	918	31	14	25	24	12	3	8	6
Sutton	468	15	0	2	25	10	0	2	2
Swisher	1,299	44	7	7	32	11	0	12	2
Tarrant	27,100	903	240	473	1,927	648	176	160	151
Taylor	6,596	114	44	79	360	152	67	69	46
Terrell	320	11	1	1	5	0	0	4	0
Terry	1,913	67	37	43	81	37	19	11	36
Throckmorton	929	17	15	22	34	29	3	16	15
Titus	2,844	221	35	95	173	32	79	71	20
Tom Green	5,908	165	65	61	233	241	28	101	45
Travis	12,474	145	159	111	2,328	107	32	63	108
Trinity	1,270	127	17	31	101	5	3	54	8
Tyler	1,214	61	24	97	60	10	10	18	17
Upshur	3,481	151	43	180	215	60	25	100	47
Upton	876	15	4	6	19	9	2	9	2
Uvalde	1,004	20	5	2	63	15	0	11	4
Val Verde	574	4	2	9	9	10	0	4	6
Van Zandt	3,936	398	81	125	294	125	35	125	38
Victoria	1,638	10	32	8	62	11	21	10	7
Walker	1,598	20	6	15	434	2	9	17	11
Waller	1,220	15	6	7	150	22	27	27	6
Ward	1,701	28	18	22	37	20	1	18	36
Washington	3,230	17	4	25	43	17	2	6	11
Webb	2,003	9	2	0	24	0	2	7	0
Wharton	3,082	45	12	54	259	17	21	106	28
Wheeler	1,609	21	20	21	66	18	21	25	28
Wichita	7,805	317	142	168	608	111	19	40	89
Wilbarger	3,204	98	66	55	123	29	10	26	23
Willacy	1,221	56	55	20	54	42	4	29	7
Williamson	3,861	39	10	43	244	32	18	91	14
Wilson	2,597	43	11	114	96	54	11	26	29
Winkler	869	16	3	19	21	5	6	7	6
Wise	3,303	149	76	81	230	153	31	49	23
Wood	3,387	136	38	49	187	53	10	52	9
Yoakum	787	10	22	18	17	8	16	15	4
Young	1,772	68	49	70	221	88	22	39	24
Zapata	317	0	0	1	0	0	0	0	0
Zavala	916	32	6	9	70	9	9	14	22
Official Totals	696,586	21,379	8,537	12,649	48,039	15,243	4,633	9,433	6,640
Unofficial Totals	696,586	21,379	8,537	12,612	48,029	15,243	4,635	9,443	6,640

Table 36: Gubernatorial Races

County	Floyd Brinkley	William V. Brown	A.J. Burks	Charles B. Hutchison	Beauford Jester	Walter S. McNutt	Caso March	W.J. Minton	Homer P. Rainey	Jerry Sadler	Grover Sellers	C.R. Shaw	John Lee Smith	Reese Turner	Beauford Jester	Homer P. Rainey
					Democratic Primary, 1946										Runoff	
					1946											
Anderson	22	30	20	31	2,905	21	115	13	1,335	981	847	83	403	38	4,679	2,330
Andrews	4	0	37	6	261	0	6	2	153	99	82	12	71	12	348	142
Angelina	32	47	36	19	3,910	25	100	10	2,050	949	682	166	647	48	5,420	3,118
Aransas	4	3	0	3	258	9	1	4	273	96	64	4	117	2	321	224
Archer	3	9	2	5	1,004	6	44	6	502	136	109	11	355	14	1,327	528
Armstrong	0	1	5	7	540	1	5	1	143	41	44	2	135	2	441	94
Atascosa	1	2	2	5	835	22	25	6	1,236	275	167	36	511	12	1,317	636
Austin	15	20	4	12	1,085	10	12	8	658	272	454	18	589	19	2,271	981
Bailey	2	5	4	11	511	3	23	0	266	134	109	24	105	7	470	177
Bandera	1	0	5	6	202	1	5	0	98	69	99	3	165	1	388	86
Bastrop	2	10	0	3	1,445	7	56	2	1,299	194	380	35	285	25	1,719	1,493
Baylor	3	6	4	3	678	8	30	3	479	137	187	22	539	10	1,400	759
Bee	7	4	5	6	1,555	7	18	3	419	386	157	41	379	14	1,457	372
Bell	13	14	10	15	3,712	15	82	7	3,104	1,063	2,150	68	865	39	6,509	3,834
Bexar	591	372	236	419	10,501	376	473	98	10,493	6,683	3,902	447	3,589	323	19,446	11,477
Blanco	1	2	1	1	375	3	11	0	219	68	129	14	102	6	403	243
Borden	2	1	4	2	122	2	16	1	36	45	67	10	49	1	225	37
Bosque	9	8	9	11	1,694	10	85	3	967	331	294	27	284	16	2,658	1,409
Bowie	23	294	12	57	2,584	28	250	24	1,801	689	2,727	118	799	18	4,436	1,981
Brazoria	16	3	4	4	1,858	13	39	5	1,257	409	396	38	546	12	3,402	1,718
Brazos	16	8	5	15	2,159	7	24	8	1,994	334	626	12	383	12	2,892	1,958
Brewster	2	4	8	7	389	0	11	12	310	92	207	4	154	2	522	223
Briscoe	1	2	1	0	572	5	10	0	172	92	103	4	153	2	584	154
Brooks	3	3	1	4	173	4	11	5	287	60	132	8	116	5	259	180
Brown	14	13	53	21	2,705	27	62	24	1,526	512	1,527	29	773	34	4,745	2,057
Burleson	21	8	7	14	898	32	40	7	1,209	409	476	122	548	47	1,639	1,479
Burnet	2	8	4	25	1,036	8	14	5	592	241	310	5	280	13	1,425	685
Caldwell	18	13	4	24	1,741	9	39	6	1,229	310	403	33	471	14	1,864	1,100
Calhoun	7	5	3	7	544	6	31	1	212	238	97	29	347	6	778	222
Callahan	5	1	23	1	1,064	2	91	7	615	184	297	7	631	7	1,654	780
Cameron	36	60	59	47	3,601	25	205	68	2,599	736	692	44	475	66	6,134	4,321
Camp	5	15	7	14	446	11	106	6	389	182	1,026	23	100	11	1,164	627
Carson	6	3	2	4	753	5	7	5	393	80	156	8	121	4	702	262
Cass	11	34	7	17	1,136	51	65	31	700	457	1,564	49	202	16	3,761	1,564
Castro	1	3	2	2	741	1	13	1	187	115	79	2	74	2	619	109
Chambers	17	4	5	10	703	8	32	10	323	224	140	52	168	7	1,208	460
Cherokee	11	10	47	10	2,502	36	71	3	1,287	788	1,867	6	362	64	4,044	1,819
Childress	5	8	4	10	1,102	6	55	2	636	247	355	32	398	12	1,777	706
Clay	5	35	4	5	1,434	10	57	6	613	211	381	11	426	8	2,120	686
Cochran	6	9	13	8	467	40	27	3	331	161	139	22	141	9	771	517
Coke	0	2	6	3	495	4	22	0	358	124	138	4	141	2	611	295
Coleman	11	15	68	19	2,194	30	32	10	782	714	607	61	536	39	3,893	1,163
Collin	6	67	3	22	3,249	10	256	39	1,381	701	1,307	7	566	32	4,823	1,790
Collingsworth	8	8	5	9	739	6	23	6	698	334	388	13	204	10	1,330	928
Colorado	13	6	7	11	1,314	9	17	2	612	306	261	69	470	9	2,019	786
Comal	9	12	37	6	1,376	10	15	3	391	295	235	15	323	27	2,216	527
Comanche	8	21	30	30	1,841	19	113	4	1,033	437	50	45	693	34	3,491	1,649
Concho	4	2	1	2	438	4	6	0	315	117	179	9	89	3	512	312
Cooke	8	14	14	36	1,917	17	115	0	939	675	651	47	932	27	3,522	1,185
Coryell	6	24	11	6	1,348	5	72	5	902	947	588	6	224	8	1,883	1,056
Cottle	10	13	13	7	644	8	85	7	399	211	210	11	300	5	1,225	818
Crane	0	1	23	33	337	3	17	1	328	57	48	9	31	2	487	355
Crockett	2	2	3	4	289	1	3	2	123	34	88	6	37	3	412	120
Crosby	2	3	15	8	1,160	7	33	4	524	163	367	17	234	8	1,613	622
Culberson	0	1	5	2	167	0	5	1	63	27	64	3	54	5	146	30
Dallam	8	4	3	8	1,064	0	19	2	361	174	53	9	62	12	607	204
Dallas	375	128	122	156	28,845	364	1,067	168	16,998	2,978	7,778	151	3,471	303	42,670	18,917
Dawson	9	9	17	9	1,246	5	37	8	816	527	301	25	631	16	2,624	1,138
DeWitt	6	6	5	8	1,694	15	20	1	803	353	221	67	752	8	1,211	291
DeafSmith	2	3	31	8	971	4	15	6	298	217	135	7	144	12	1,872	686
Delta	6	38	5	6	688	6	74	5	272	94	1,278	4	139	0	5,164	2,693
Denton	5	15	14	16	3,093	6	139	28	2,076	939	777	14	707	24	2,071	696
Dickens	4	3	13	16	686	14	32	5	727	160	324	18	318	14	1,470	989
Dimmit	4	2	3	11	733	13	13	3	181	99	113	30	87	6	825	316
Donley	2	0	1	4	803	9	6	2	279	116	237	13	282	9	1,296	352

Table 36: Gubernatorial Races

	Democratic Primary, 1946																
Year	1946															Runoff	
County	Floyd Brinkley	William V. Brown	A.J. Burks	Charles B. Hutchison	Beauford Jester	Walter S. McNutt	Caso March	W.J. Minton	Homer P. Rainey	Jerry Sadler	Grover Sellers	C.R. Shaw	John Lee Smith	Reese Turner	Beauford Jester	Homer P. Rainey
Duval	0	0	0	0	92	0	1	0	60	9	4,401	0	8	1	4,018	60
Eastland	19	19	36	40	2,438	11	419	10	1,531	453	1,217	10	1,211	14	4,799	2,424
Ector	2	9	814	13	936	3	27	6	1,048	276	282	16	249	5	1,513	883
Edwards	1	0	1	3	261	3	3	1	75	90	193	8	44	4	310	43
El Paso	36	25	36	67	2,539	131	228	34	4,783	555	2,768	231	416	75	4,063	3,180
Ellis	13	9	20	41	4,419	15	214	14	2,138	675	1,132	47	475	23	5,848	2,288
Erath	13	25	50	35	2,379	20	164	11	1,024	536	786	39	690	16	3,730	1,715
Falls	13	14	26	16	2,887	14	197	35	1,356	317	837	8	363	17	3,965	2,149
Fannin	17	19	27	34	1,698	53	603	56	1,322	870	1,985	169	427	37	6,028	3,044
Fayette	28	33	14	44	1,852	36	85	28	2,117	922	937	151	1,249	34	5,028	3,137
Fisher	3	7	45	16	1,020	1	73	6	738	327	320	4	407	11	1,798	1,035
Floyd	35	28	7	8	1,298	2	20	5	444	542	245	2	242	7	2,018	726
Foard	15	8	7	9	447	3	18	11	319	120	111	2	298	3	902	392
Fort Bend	14	7	1	9	1,227	3	27	2	778	159	228	17	319	7	1,756	1,102
Franklin	3	9	5	4	595	3	140	3	270	195	1,223	15	76	7	1,770	721
Freestone	4	6	7	5	2,265	11	91	3	776	241	509	35	194	10	3,319	1,453
Frio	3	3	3	16	718	5	10	8	281	113	129	7	159	7	782	241
Gaines	3	4	30	13	767	13	19	2	398	281	220	39	168	7	1,196	584
Galveston	58	33	126	40	7,293	31	35	31	2,972	1,000	2,400	78	511	55	8,797	3,089
Garza	3	5	7	4	411	8	43	5	226	117	148	13	392	8	995	323
Gillespie	10	1	0	18	448	0	4	0	83	21	57	6	81	0	806	142
Glasscock	1	1	3	1	105	0	4	1	49	23	32	0	40	2	112	63
Goliad	5	2	2	4	658	4	2	3	220	134	55	20	201	9	586	167
Gonzales	9	14	5	5	2,051	12	40	8	783	692	486	2	527	45	3,330	1,268
Gray	7	12	6	25	1,962	28	22	8	1,296	283	353	35	438	25	2,144	896
Grayson	27	26	26	34	4,111	3	313	118	4,635	1,084	2,358	87	959	44	8,068	5,639
Gregg	25	51	27	55	4,331	44	103	3	2,372	1,082	1,649	99	676	26	5,522	2,608
Grimes	6	5	0	2	769	3	16	1	362	255	143	9	128	3	1,018	472
Guadalupe	2	9	3	3	799	3	1	1	475	259	258	2	530	0	1,789	603
Hale	3	7	6	7	2,280	10	27	6	1,082	271	388	17	262	7	2,649	1,244
Hall	8	6	6	9	959	4	44	5	704	152	263	32	339	7	1,473	1,043
Hamilton	9	9	4	9	1,258	5	42	2	642	597	351	13	400	8	2,254	930
Hansford	2	0	1	1	268	0	3	0	76	30	86	5	22	4	261	65
Hardeman	8	9	8	9	774	9	69	8	518	245	254	20	209	6	915	465
Hardin	24	14	11	24	1,870	20	52	8	970	594	488	112	337	36	1,479	817
Harris	634	106	74	95	34,010	260	719	51	27,587	4,866	6,146	505	7,160	143	46,107	29,071
Harrison	10	22	1	9	1,916	51	87	8	1,382	454	1,515	43	213	9	3,180	1,131
Hartley	1	2	3	0	318	3	6	0	86	31	21	4	16	3	242	92
Haskell	4	5	56	17	900	24	7	5	808	512	364	1	1,007	4	1,326	1,013
Hays	17	5	14	8	1,378	3	22	1	960	202	295	6	307	17	1,448	1,035
Hemphill	4	1	0	3	518	3	3	0	195	85	46	3	41	5	205	62
Henderson	14	23	27	22	3,388	12	191	10	1,102	881	702	12	274	12	5,503	1,900
Hidalgo	42	30	23	41	4,196	56	80	49	3,498	377	746	282	867	41	7,796	5,285
Hill	11	4	12	24	3,503	0	202	8	1,219	782	603	30	620	28	4,413	1,666
Hockley	7	8	24	12	1,425	14	35	12	926	286	605	32	398	14	2,168	1,074
Hood	7	7	14	9	704	9	32	3	200	158	177	24	662	9	1,435	574
Hopkins	3	23	20	9	796	3	223	3	449	324	4,538	5	131	18	4,635	1,695
Houston	20	17	3	5	1,397	23	29	4	1,352	1,013	447	65	478	19	2,882	2,109
Howard	3	11	40	18	1,594	13	87	7	1,646	406	409	29	327	18	2,196	1,881
Hudspeth	0	2	1	0	128	2	12	1	91	20	114	4	10	0	0	0
Hunt	8	11	12	20	1,995	21	224	8	1,428	355	5,079	27	526	25	7,462	2,326
Hutchinson	19	11	11	23	1,418	18	50	17	2,000	445	514	28	225	25	1,382	1,255
Irion	0	0	11	2	217	0	8	1	146	50	53	1	48	0	317	214
Jack	8	13	6	8	691	4	98	3	422	167	221	19	523	8	1,796	750
Jackson	6	2	2	41	771	6	17	1	525	224	150	38	479	16	1,157	695
Jasper	57	10	11	17	1,109	9	28	8	751	534	434	31	283	21	2,191	1,344
Jeff Davis	1	2	6	1	140	0	4	0	84	28	45	3	72	1	314	143
Jefferson	82	46	51	78	7,707	90	222	51	9,691	3,300	1,927	407	2,369	113	13,399	11,265
Jim Hogg	0	0	2	5	206	2	12	6	85	32	227	57	40	2	439	141
Jim Wells	12	7	12	20	1,104	17	36	5	555	286	526	73	337	16	2,137	725
Johnson	4	10	9	9	2,507	11	160	5	1,083	437	668	28	387	27	4,686	2,200
Jones	7	7	28	18	1,621	13	47	5	1,032	357	384	55	870	12	2,834	1,483
Karnes	8	13	4	14	1,243	19	22	10	533	594	252	89	654	32	944	390
Kaufman	15	12	5	20	2,648	24	83	13	950	461	923	16	309	14	3,928	1,032
Kendall	0	2	0	1	141	0	6	0	46	22	32	4	50	1	300	82

Table 36: Gubernatorial Races

| | Democratic Primary, 1946 | | | | | | | | | | | | | | | Runoff | |
| Year | 1946 | | | | | | | | | | | | | | | | |
County	Floyd Brinkley	William V. Brown	A.J. Burks	Charles B. Hutchison	Beauford Jester	Walter S. McNutt	Caso March	W.J. Minton	Homer P. Rainey	Jerry Sadler	Grover Sellers	C.R. Shaw	John Lee Smith	Reese Turner	Beauford Jester	Homer P. Rainey
Kenedy	0	0	0	0	42	0	0	1	1	0	0	2	27	0	78	4
Kent	2	2	4	6	283	4	12	0	166	67	94	11	110	6	503	286
Kerr	13	1	4	5	1,138	7	12	0	251	128	192	24	304	11	1,328	255
Kimble	8	4	2	4	729	3	17	1	161	160	284	2	214	13	1,151	215
King	0	0	0	4	107	2	8	1	58	21	23	6	49	3	166	85
Kinney	0	0	0	0	126	0	0	0	23	4	10	0	9	0	163	28
Kleberg	1	2	1	9	571	11	11	2	790	86	92	37	109	6	578	641
Knox	6	2	4	6	906	6	23	1	613	130	173	20	436	6	1,450	915
La Salle	2	2	2	3	443	1	4	4	182	57	72	7	43	5	5,096	3,278
Lamar	30	30	20	64	1,953	22	161	14	2,192	758	2,801	127	647	17	2,223	903
Lamb	9	12	14	30	2,081	22	20	0	1,172	502	517	52	398	18	1,772	760
Lampasas	1	9	4	3	1,052	2	10	0	379	136	196	0	212	0	487	212
Lavaca	13	27	14	91	1,593	11	26	15	1,687	543	275	182	750	28	2,580	3,161
Lee	11	14	4	8	960	3	31	5	720	219	458	10	240	18	1,808	1,112
Leon	6	5	2	8	1,348	11	53	1	462	578	242	32	227	11	1,695	754
Liberty	23	16	15	25	1,982	48	93	14	1,048	817	538	101	654	26	3,396	1,447
Limestone	42	12	18	19	3,107	12	243	8	1,372	975	579	20	356	22	3,772	2,043
Lipscomb	0	2	2	9	311	3	18	2	140	29	4	2	27	16	362	212
Live Oak	3	6	7	7	676	5	76	4	196	330	172	22	341	8	1,229	348
Llano	2	2	3	2	505	3	9	3	428	178	375	4	142	3	1,165	715
Loving	0	0	2	0	40	0	1	3	19	3	7	2	2	2	19	28
Lubbock	9	15	18	28	5,583	16	42	11	3,923	537	1,071	47	1,009	46	6,441	3,879
Lynn	11	5	13	8	1,410	17	82	8	674	291	381	6	296	7	2,103	969
Madison	3	2	3	6	766	8	12	3	400	458	166	29	159	7	1,226	676
Marion	1	1	0	1	251	76	3	0	127	41	256	4	31	2	561	176
Martin	6	3	24	3	425	5	29	2	371	174	217	9	139	7	405	280
Mason	3	4	9	6	892	41	5	0	291	115	238	4	140	9	1,483	452
Matagorda	0	4	1	5	1,071	3	65	1	528	184	111	17	318	4	1,565	699
Maverick	4	3	1	8	672	3	18	8	153	81	48	20	49	7	927	205
McCulloch	10	13	21	20	1,580	8	23	10	696	243	457	34	342	100	1,900	695
McLennan	21	24	140	52	7,753	46	894	28	8,223	977	1,400	18	641	27	10,740	9,954
McMullen	1	0	0	0	126	1	0	0	35	14	32	3	56	1	207	42
Medina	3	4	1	1	596	1	14	2	283	195	79	20	166	6	1,136	363
Menard	3	7	3	13	722	13	11	3	209	201	254	19	145	11	818	180
Midland	4	5	53	10	1,502	10	21	5	728	147	161	12	281	6	1,838	742
Milam	9	80	22	18	2,206	8	88	3	1,571	562	771	14	509	205	3,353	1,932
Mills	3	1	9	1	1,250	1	25	3	297	166	177	8	188	5	1,562	633
Mitchell	5	8	23	6	1,187	3	40	10	635	283	421	2	307	21	2,157	949
Montague	12	33	12	32	1,913	13	112	13	924	362	478	35	413	12	3,184	1,336
Montgomery	48	15	9	4	1,855	27	258	16	1,014	604	606	125	515	28	3,627	1,489
Moore	3	9	9	12	686	11	42	3	250	141	111	19	67	11	532	217
Morris	2	15	2	9	484	16	106	3	297	207	834	25	96	8	1,487	736
Motley	2	7	3	3	251	3	7	5	168	45	120	2	513	5	451	182
Nacogdoches	37	28	42	32	2,359	24	269	28	1,262	919	585	138	615	22	4,678	2,088
Navarro	11	20	8	8	7,858	16	159	3	744	335	572	21	204	9	8,618	1,298
Newton	13	22	9	15	565	4	86	2	417	257	258	13	118	19	938	521
Nolan	6	8	36	9	1,460	11	263	10	1,106	628	551	29	380	24	2,815	1,612
Nueces	30	67	17	28	5,517	45	62	15	4,291	1,091	1,462	251	784	45	7,244	5,468
Ochiltree	4	7	0	6	502	6	12	1	206	105	58	16	137	10	298	106
Oldham	1	2	1	7	246	1	8	0	69	40	46	10	46	2	177	83
Orange	78	24	8	44	1,994	19	83	17	1,476	803	1,065	62	377	20	4,012	2,778
Palo Pinto	19	19	41	29	1,764	11	169	7	968	536	423	10	641	34	2,611	1,061
Panola	77	13	102	35	914	13	97	9	456	1,147	1,642	38	190	17	2,456	1,015
Parker	9	15	50	66	2,143	148	115	7	1,052	546	553	89	718	20	3,716	2,041
Parmer	5	6	2	18	600	7	7	2	216	109	111	29	73	12	705	272
Pecos	7	24	34	20	726	5	26	7	466	152	290	6	183	6	673	302
Polk	17	16	11	8	1,304	10	43	11	657	335	356	52	549	15	2,756	1,005
Potter	9	13	4	11	4,127	7	51	14	2,020	410	481	12	339	6	5,596	2,540
Presidio	5	3	8	10	516	8	27	5	203	109	180	32	49	8	754	331
Rains	9	2	6	10	308	6	138	0	127	97	851	13	63	6	1,276	480
Randall	0	2	8	4	1,150	1	15	1	365	131	161	1	99	2	1,380	412
Reagan	0	1	7	0	294	1	3	0	193	33	37	2	37	5	288	180
Real	2	3	3	6	282	1	7	0	116	76	135	6	42	7	550	170
Red River	20	18	13	72	1,107	15	154	14	1,068	509	1,553	14	315	21	2,349	1,413
Reeves	6	4	14	11	795	8	14	6	354	154	203	22	98	9	854	326

Table 36: Gubernatorial Races

	Democratic Primary, 1946															
Year	1946														Runoff	
County	Floyd Brinkley	William V. Brown	A.J. Burks	Charles B. Hutchison	Beauford Jester	Walter S. McNutt	Caso March	W.J. Minton	Homer P. Rainey	Jerry Sadler	Grover Sellers	C.R. Shaw	John Lee Smith	Reese Turner	Beauford Jester	Homer P. Rainey
Refugio	0	1	0	1	310	0	1	0	175	24	29	2	52	0	405	351
Roberts	1	2	1	3	248	4	7	0	41	30	47	3	32	1	278	36
Robertson	15	9	96	33	1,649	10	119	15	955	393	517	16	194	61	1,934	1,038
Rockwall	4	0	3	25	692	9	37	2	252	204	603	15	210	5	1,120	276
Runnels	3	11	40	8	1,622	5	43	15	672	478	582	10	425	50	1,803	641
Rusk	44	80	26	47	4,044	34	116	26	1,599	1,109	2,163	254	594	52	7,892	2,473
Sabine	10	12	14	26	571	29	45	9	553	404	447	18	198	6	1,631	765
San Augustine	36	23	7	20	674	25	36	33	520	109	481	80	124	20	1,849	914
San Jacinto	5	5	4	9	445	1	11	4	151	192	205	29	142	9	725	175
San Patricio	3	6	4	11	1,999	8	31	7	973	280	288	23	396	20	2,572	1,503
San Saba	3	3	6	8	882	8	47	5	608	212	624	14	206	14	1,403	847
Schleicher	0	3	6	7	339	0	11	1	225	47	92	4	73	6	338	126
Scurry	9	2	25	19	778	9	59	16	717	311	471	39	538	10	1,901	952
Shackelford	3	1	2	3	675	5	17	1	295	179	89	0	554	5	1,164	416
Shelby	47	27	25	38	1,925	0	139	19	1,202	1,335	807	258	411	38	3,910	2,295
Sherman	1	0	1	3	191	1	5	1	51	24	16	0	21	1	176	46
Smith	31	20	21	38	5,512	20	158	24	2,758	829	2,128	40	725	50	7,695	4,699
Somervell	2	9	4	8	301	4	34	1	156	53	149	17	76	10	630	778
Starr	5	1	2	1	94	0	17	5	722	8	1,634	3	16	3	2,008	460
Stephens	3	3	12	3	1,055	7	94	6	770	195	286	5	594	10	1,669	986
Sterling	0	0	3	0	275	1	2	1	77	17	85	0	22	0	186	50
Stonewall	4	7	6	6	352	25	10	0	268	129	208	25	222	4	1,008	411
Sutton	2	1	2	0	437	1	2	0	98	33	62	5	130	2	728	163
Swisher	7	3	11	11	1,636	4	10	8	296	119	125	2	144	1	954	254
Tarrant	89	161	101	316	16,734	190	1,775	83	11,514	3,663	6,675	441	4,856	148	29,579	15,046
Taylor	8	13	95	15	3,635	16	58	9	2,538	1,018	965	9	1,194	15	5,890	3,434
Terrell	1	0	3	5	165	2	16	1	138	49	138	5	67	4	123	76
Terry	5	11	31	12	1,153	2	71	23	797	313	406	9	234	8	2,064	1,006
Throckmorton	2	4	2	7	268	0	176	4	233	49	64	6	729	2	907	664
Titus	11	23	6	21	1,399	23	80	9	576	531	1,590	43	262	14	3,721	1,086
Tom Green	8	9	44	17	2,754	64	23	5	2,427	324	945	18	706	18	3,983	2,534
Travis	12	12	37	10	10,443	38	65	13	12,278	1,091	1,724	13	1,105	126	11,335	13,305
Trinity	41	9	8	12	886	4	32	45	486	322	296	19	220	11	978	610
Tyler	23	7	8	30	815	5	43	14	336	378	325	25	360	10	1,480	547
Upshur	30	16	28	17	2,149	24	205	17	844	587	1,443	94	198	21	3,653	1,224
Upton	2	3	22	1	545	5	17	4	323	67	100	10	78	4	764	365
Uvalde	6	5	20	6	1,165	6	66	4	382	192	317	4	247	12	1,061	309
Val Verde	1	1	0	10	785	4	10	1	301	68	178	3	80	2	700	256
Van Zandt	21	19	10	45	2,696	18	391	12	1,167	781	1,145	117	359	15	4,842	2,172
Victoria	12	24	35	14	1,979	10	35	5	1,183	599	260	23	478	10	2,866	1,115
Walker	11	7	5	8	1,037	6	65	6	804	624	5	43	188	17	1,671	813
Waller	12	16	4	8	742	3	13	8	631	259	174	16	330	5	1,204	686
Ward	7	9	71	17	223	8	50	7	423	215	227	6	203	23	936	436
Washington	2	24	5	6	2,728	3	13	2	485	169	133	34	1,240	10	3,232	546
Webb	1	8	2	4	212	3	25	6	338	77	4,340	3	88	1	4,266	614
Wharton	25	17	13	12	2,067	53	17	9	1,287	694	376	37	473	13	2,511	1,686
Wheeler	7	10	4	19	1,172	2	9	4	711	165	165	1	147	8	1,188	557
Wichita	21	29	17	22	5,242	9	179	15	4,485	583	619	19	723	31	5,615	3,887
Wilbarger	7	23	7	22	1,337	6	89	6	1,548	327	711	61	482	20	3,084	1,742
Willacy	8	11	0	9	923	11	11	7	546	90	74	38	215	10	600	1,049
Williamson	9	27	10	20	3,576	10	63	10	2,446	476	800	4	728	37	4,751	3,049
Wilson	14	75	16	27	1,290	9	16	5	753	325	348	20	431	16	1,669	831
Winkler	6	4	28	18	802	16	35	3	328	190	206	16	102	10	1,047	475
Wise	11	31	8	34	2,038	21	69	13	846	468	502	61	696	21	2,981	1,294
Wood	7	5	4	12	1,698	7	229	6	657	318	1,712	42	219	13	3,749	1,206
Yoakum	2	8	13	8	452	6	39	4	214	112	127	15	102	2	710	289
Young	2	8	12	8	1,360	2	452	3	1,313	206	314	7	568	6	1,969	1,702
Zapata	0	0	0	0	23	0	1	0	159	4	224	2	5	1	272	282
Zavala	3	6	3	4	587	7	17	3	179	89	157	28	93	7	1,015	307
Official	4,249		4,881		443,804		20,529		291,282		162,431		102,941		701,018	
Totals		3,902		4,616		4,353		2,398		103,120		9,764		4,914		355,654
Unofficial	4,249		4,881		446,857		20,553		291,305		162,465		103,054		701,018	
Totals		3,904		4,616		4,326		2,396		103,146		9,767		4,916		362,655

Table 37: Gubernatorial Races

County	Democratic Primary, 1948							
Year	1948							
County	Beauford H. Jester	Sumpter W. Stockton	Roger Q. Evans	Charles B. Hutchison	Holmes A. May	Caso March	W.J. Minton	Denver S. Whiteley
Anderson	3,552	101	1,571	121	100	1,202	51	109
Andrews	712	46	157	59	27	127	13	16
Angelina	4,946	287	2,442	178	148	690	107	318
Aransas	603	16	288	21	13	93	15	21
Archer	1,349	80	255	52	18	365	16	31
Armstrong	473	9	97	19	7	73	14	4
Atascosa	2,125	49	618	48	57	257	24	39
Austin	2,174	39	405	36	64	210	16	52
Bailey	696	37	232	40	24	142	18	24
Bandera	741	19	97	30	24	68	11	15
Bastrop	2,132	73	860	72	64	745	36	86
Baylor	1,163	49	375	49	23	215	17	49
Bee	1,909	38	641	49	39	487	20	32
Bell	4,224	152	4,036	134	99	1,814	61	100
Bexar	28,456	2,681	10,208	704	695	4,289	1,163	473
Blanco	544	25	178	16	14	145	3	8
Borden	117	6	23	4	3	21	0	0
Bosque	1,726	72	549	84	34	1,292	21	44
Bowie	5,795	127	1,841	371	148	1,336	105	145
Brazoria	2,863	36	1,891	27	102	276	6	49
Brazos	3,296	69	1,050	136	101	990	72	118
Brewster	1,030	37	217	60	15	259	13	14
Briscoe	541	28	150	30	6	78	6	10
Brooks	576	25	320	22	17	137	21	31
Brown	3,538	132	1,038	143	121	1,529	51	95
Burleson	1,219	46	1,445	66	49	223	31	73
Burnet	1,412	40	461	57	95	380	15	23
Caldwell	2,302	52	642	111	65	544	56	60
Calhoun	472	8	131	7	9	25	3	8
Callahan	1,098	62	702	47	39	516	18	19
Cameron	6,511	58	2,341	221	106	978	628	76
Camp	1,180	34	214	69	57	523	12	49
Carson	799	35	259	22	10	96	13	15
Cass	2,991	56	305	82	72	420	31	72
Castro	615	35	113	33	18	161	10	4
Chambers	1,239	21	413	16	46	131	4	39
Cherokee	3,068	191	1,097	117	73	1,014	42	107
Childress	1,639	25	429	165	46	502	57	56
Clay	1,531	61	407	105	21	594	36	24
Cochran	673	51	481	44	39	166	16	28
Coke	806	27	154	31	15	167	4	17
Coleman	2,061	178	563	113	56	684	34	58
Collin	4,307	27	1,831	189	60	1,412	163	35
Collingsworth	1,410	54	264	62	26	223	29	28
Colorado	2,030	36	781	71	60	203	20	81
Comal	2,154	18	460	59	56	130	39	19
Comanche	1,838	255	523	86	44	1,064	25	54
Concho	729	38	151	43	13	302	14	32
Cooke	2,848	78	1,036	89	32	494	97	35
Coryell	1,174	86	534	51	123	1,161	42	17
Cottle	1,001	91	229	58	22	249	22	23
Crane	505	52	300	52	24	233	12	8
Crockett	402	7	53	45	6	89	5	7
Crosby	884	56	547	63	29	607	27	22
Culberson	231	11	111	15	4	39	3	7
Dallam	1,059	20	378	43	19	107	22	11
Dallas	39,580	596	11,932	756	1,494	13,035	584	1,281
Dawson	1,947	229	682	110	79	604	41	43
DeWitt	2,608	52	775	33	34	284	16	40
Deaf Smith	1,410	38	259	33	10	107	22	15
Delta	1,555	25	386	109	68	674	50	26
Denton	3,286	150	2,050	177	58	1,337	239	27
Dickens	732	114	363	85	32	340	32	26
Dimmit	939	19	138	41	17	123	53	4

Table 37: Gubernatorial Races

County	Democratic Primary, 1948							
Year	1948							
County	Beauford H. Jester	Sumpter W. Stockton	Roger Q. Evans	Charles B. Hutchison	Holmes A. May	Caso March	W.J. Minton	Denver S. Whiteley
Donley	1,224	47	222	56	18	183	21	17
Duval	124	2	39	4	2	3,670	0	1
Eastland	2,646	511	1,208	187	111	1,744	53	78
Ector	3,358	201	838	107	66	629	45	65
Edwards	555	12	119	11	8	70	9	11
El Paso	9,033	134	4,313	506	185	1,783	205	197
Ellis	4,267	36	842	205	51	2,086	143	32
Erath	2,597	200	602	131	56	1,508	40	45
Falls	1,765	41	1,686	56	35	1,085	14	29
Fannin	3,984	78	2,421	469	65	1,688	277	68
Fayette	3,141	107	1,085	132	115	776	33	151
Fisher	1,283	134	593	76	60	541	38	40
Floyd	1,697	91	551	68	67	333	91	29
Foard	539	30	120	54	20	105	7	21
Fort Bend	1,755	12	574	121	108	308	23	72
Franklin	1,057	41	243	107	37	761	24	54
Freestone	2,046	220	577	181	54	992	28	53
Frio	1,177	25	175	35	40	141	31	54
Gaines	1,122	67	473	68	54	284	18	36
Galveston	9,002	93	4,161	207	511	945	122	191
Garza	672	47	474	46	37	155	19	21
Gillespie	964	41	79	15	14	78	4	3
Glasscock	193	7	42	14	7	65	4	4
Goliad	701	40	241	30	26	92	6	25
Gonzales	3,178	107	485	86	84	315	21	77
Gray	3,465	91	607	112	60	335	69	45
Grayson	4,169	60	7,783	54	35	887	185	34
Gregg	5,585	156	1,352	110	605	1,262	66	111
Grimes	1,289	13	370	18	16	164	15	29
Guadalupe	980	11	277	11	12	92	9	8
Hale	2,914	133	1,212	112	88	633	50	55
Hall	1,636	53	439	65	39	333	29	26
Hamilton	1,414	79	340	60	21	907	13	45
Hansford	536	9	155	9	3	25	5	3
Hardeman	1,090	35	252	29	21	279	14	27
Hardin	1,531	32	1,891	42	75	479	23	108
Harris	54,481	230	33,934	687	3,011	5,086	632	1,542
Harrison	4,123	41	1,451	102	75	633	40	108
Hartley	339	8	49	8	1	28	3	3
Haskell	1,609	173	713	115	67	817	65	33
Hays	1,872	60	805	54	27	438	12	27
Hemphill	780	6	126	18	7	69	14	33
Henderson	3,363	120	901	192	96	2,066	183	65
Hidalgo	7,983	242	2,628	175	164	1,757	136	205
Hill	3,070	91	1,033	137	51	2,498	39	55
Hockley	1,407	136	1,334	131	80	428	52	55
Hood	1,172	91	324	86	46	394	36	43
Hopkins	2,777	172	991	274	126	1,729	82	63
Houston	2,995	121	749	112	95	527	39	80
Howard	2,877	219	1,144	108	86	748	39	64
Hudspeth	327	12	69	16	8	133	6	6
Hunt	4,893	66	1,548	195	80	1,019	85	55
Hutchinson	2,113	53	2,370	51	29	377	32	20
Irion	292	8	64	39	7	137	15	2
Jack	1,324	109	297	49	20	503	27	36
Jackson	1,079	13	297	87	38	222	24	30
Jasper	1,738	57	924	54	92	494	63	147
Jeff Davis	264	6	129	5	12	29	9	4
Jefferson	10,312	93	13,126	338	360	1,836	208	304
Jim Hogg	379	4	238	3	5	27	8	17
Jim Wells	1,998	34	642	72	58	1,186	32	69
Johnson	2,507	61	946	173	122	1,183	84	110
Jones	2,529	145	751	90	30	801	35	40
Karnes	1,963	45	833	50	39	380	16	60
Kaufman	3,625	189	567	248	84	1,365	64	65

Table 37: Gubernatorial Races

Democratic Primary, 1948								
Year	1948							
County	Beauford H. Jester	Sumpter W. Stockton	Roger Q. Evans	Charles B. Hutchison	Holmes A. May	Caso March	W.J. Minton	Denver S. Whiteley
Kendall	234	6	55	2	11	41	4	4
Kenedy	62	0	2	0	0	3	1	0
Kent	347	59	67	23	6	84	2	9
Kerr	2,536	47	406	44	91	277	13	48
Kimble	1,028	72	355	31	30	116	8	14
King	154	12	28	12	3	62	5	2
Kinney	169	2	25	11	13	8	4	4
Kleberg	1,642	18	1,207	50	67	321	34	45
Knox	1,335	116	335	72	27	407	33	25
La Salle	705	2	140	27	15	56	8	2
Lamar	5,247	197	1,309	354	132	1,337	97	136
Lamb	1,758	137	922	166	70	490	96	63
Lampasas	1,254	55	430	40	21	401	6	20
Lavaca	2,903	51	964	136	44	632	41	47
Lee	1,213	38	1,012	72	55	250	63	50
Leon	1,251	35	561	46	30	456	8	20
Liberty	3,505	55	815	54	206	432	28	160
Limestone	2,228	78	697	98	57	2,350	40	77
Lipscomb	503	16	39	10	5	34	4	4
Live Oak	1,227	34	301	36	28	251	24	37
Llano	897	64	218	12	30	178	5	7
Loving	54	1	13	2	0	1	3	1
Lubbock	1,863	163	8,261	158	126	1,713	172	74
Lynn	992	36	817	71	66	796	39	27
Madison	1,074	40	443	44	46	257	6	34
Marion	1,280	23	88	49	29	116	18	53
Martin	810	67	186	38	22	163	12	24
Mason	930	29	187	89	40	388	29	21
Matagorda	1,135	11	313	22	28	180	12	19
Maverick	754	24	73	23	7	65	15	19
McCulloch	1,554	76	585	76	87	1,023	38	33
McLennan	5,493	140	4,622	174	182	10,477	75	89
McMullen	171	5	93	14	8	28	6	4
Medina	1,206	16	237	53	48	165	37	18
Menard	797	14	229	50	19	263	21	37
Midland	2,494	83	461	114	51	342	54	34
Milam	2,088	65	2,087	101	38	935	41	60
Mills	865	90	285	27	22	434	7	21
Mitchell	1,657	46	313	55	29	356	78	21
Montague	1,910	105	801	107	97	887	60	59
Montgomery	3,292	39	802	114	339	625	57	218
Moore	1,202	39	597	68	26	116	17	14
Morris	1,159	31	108	49	52	594	21	41
Motley	625	29	116	13	53	112	16	8
Nacogdoches	3,537	57	1,000	206	230	1,572	120	184
Navarro	3,773	43	985	177	65	2,463	61	57
Newton	790	32	564	113	41	288	52	100
Nolan	2,076	157	1,148	114	65	791	54	72
Nueces	7,701	130	5,965	358	207	2,044	126	373
Ochiltree	959	22	208	17	7	81	4	14
Oldham	374	12	71	3	9	31	5	6
Orange	2,308	36	4,801	66	194	296	57	35
Palo Pinto	1,381	242	430	62	32	749	39	31
Panola	3,116	37	613	98	323	561	58	93
Parker	2,122	93	571	136	55	1,076	42	40
Parmer	1,097	35	108	30	18	60	14	16
Pecos	1,422	101	268	80	47	342	27	42
Polk	2,184	36	577	40	74	366	15	108
Potter	6,515	52	3,731	130	78	751	75	42
Presidio	711	6	117	33	23	195	43	6
Rains	682	16	117	47	20	478	53	13
Randall	1,903	38	537	39	21	189	18	28
Reagan	259	12	64	7	1	85	2	5
Real	550	11	56	20	8	63	5	10
Red River	2,508	60	426	294	76	1,103	82	52

Table 37: Gubernatorial Races

	Democratic Primary, 1948							
Year	1948							
County	Beauford H. Jester	Sumpter W. Stockton	Roger Q. Evans	Charles B. Hutchison	Holmes A. May	Caso March	W.J. Minton	Denver S. Whiteley
Reeves	1,203	38	226	63	19	318	8	25
Refugio	382	5	97	4	6	55	2	4
Roberts	386	4	18	7	4	17	2	2
Robertson	1,567	44	1,113	67	53	952	40	91
Rockwall	1,122	40	394	64	20	336	23	26
Runnels	2,607	161	644	106	47	674	36	57
Rusk	6,323	218	1,289	343	231	1,379	98	358
Sabine	965	19	378	98	61	557	222	74
San Augustine	1,211	32	250	90	134	362	87	239
San Jacinto	687	20	214	20	27	71	10	45
San Patricio	2,485	64	1,057	73	48	424	29	52
San Saba	1,199	125	289	49	31	773	26	36
Schleicher	456	114	76	122	8	139	1	6
Scurry	1,539	108	402	71	52	399	47	33
Shackelford	734	55	93	32	14	348	37	8
Shelby	3,182	63	659	173	188	927	103	160
Sherman	502	11	72	8	3	31	6	4
Smith	6,526	108	1,973	221	104	2,477	126	82
Somervell	320	40	134	27	13	223	8	23
Starr	2,247	33	635	2	1	10	4	7
Stephens	1,497	475	397	68	79	636	30	18
Sterling	213	2	15	7	1	38	1	1
Stonewall	548	100	139	53	25	362	14	17
Sutton	413	13	59	10	3	50	0	2
Swisher	1,150	46	434	60	10	125	11	16
Tarrant	23,985	997	14,330	1,160	617	7,915	565	367
Taylor	4,929	104	2,315	219	168	1,749	38	50
Terrell	328	14	101	12	11	144	4	9
Terry	666	32	815	38	16	555	26	15
Throckmorton	540	84	86	28	12	490	32	15
Titus	2,039	83	598	130	60	1,117	39	73
Tom Green	4,558	71	1,856	121	245	1,641	84	64
Travis	12,945	104	9,453	677	152	4,472	95	120
Trinity	1,276	87	418	64	135	213	106	39
Tyler	1,039	29	569	41	13	293	27	109
Upshur	2,453	90	560	92	124	1,429	66	155
Upton	684	37	160	36	20	173	13	15
Uvalde	2,162	14	305	48	53	226	21	28
Val Verde	1,261	18	332	57	22	86	11	20
Van Zandt	2,273	87	626	231	149	1,993	301	79
Victoria	1,115	6	444	17	20	318	6	23
Walker	1,802	18	780	53	57	335	42	183
Waller	1,254	9	381	50	49	137	30	27
Ward	1,417	109	471	163	47	455	24	50
Washington	3,056	24	1,419	34	42	159	16	80
Webb	6,804	3	136	11	12	83	28	9
Wharton	2,884	83	722	76	105	437	19	107
Wheeler	1,587	30	231	79	22	231	35	13
Wichita	8,052	20	2,551	6	2	2,634	15	0
Wilbarger	2,415	68	697	91	24	561	24	29
Willacy	1,657	28	737	68	26	129	28	30
Williamson	4,044	148	1,380	103	75	1,344	39	102
Wilson	2,262	27	613	98	59	388	20	42
Winkler	1,323	70	330	118	34	239	80	31
Wise	1,896	157	494	198	85	1,071	75	18
Wood	2,189	66	577	111	77	1,870	67	40
Yoakum	559	60	267	47	27	180	16	28
Young	1,620	142	370	81	26	1,594	89	13
Zapata	577	0	37	1	1	10	7	1
Zavala	933	26	119	23	8	74	9	32
Official Totals	642,025	21,243	279,602	24,441	20,538	187,658	13,659	16,090
Unofficial Totals	**642,025**	**21,243**	**279,602**	**24,441**	**20,538**	**187,658**	**13,659**	**16,090**

Table 38: Gubernatorial Races

County	1950							1952		
	Allan Shivers	Charles B. Hutchison	Wellington Abbey	Caso March	J.M. Wren	Gene S. Porter	Benita L.M. Lawrence	Allan Shivers	Ralph W. Yarborough	Allene M. Traylor
Anderson	4,591	127	58	1,338	65	73	52	3,951	2,298	109
Andrews	1,000	37	4	121	8	13	16	1,030	519	32
Angelina	6,835	145	34	1,489	346	113	52	5,516	5,300	335
Aransas	702	9	8	178	19	37	5	645	351	36
Archer	1,460	38	4	261	21	15	20	1,307	840	45
Armstrong	472	1	0	21	2	4	0	696	241	18
Atascosa	2,845	14	8	358	117	34	20	2,451	1,120	1,495
Austin	3,045	48	6	187	50	37	68	2,896	738	68
Bailey	1,132	10	6	93	10	16	11	1,324	537	65
Bandera	1,183	24	4	100	5	22	11	1,181	360	50
Bastrop	3,034	68	9	680	26	46	52	2,259	1,748	112
Baylor	1,483	32	7	150	11	12	6	1,411	695	43
Bee	2,404	31	17	351	13	30	24	2,772	1,001	77
Bell	6,666	52	22	1,808	65	258	127	6,577	5,985	275
Bexar	36,901	1,591	445	6,413	1,590	398	701	24,753	12,538	1,908
Blanco	215	1	0	53	2	3	1	250	195	5
Borden	218	2	0	9	0	2	6	228	123	16
Bosque	2,598	45	3	888	13	37	24	1,791	1,659	110
Bowie	4,628	153	46	769	42	78	182	8,409	3,329	366
Brazoria	3,200	9	4	893	65	31	14	8,350	3,925	248
Brazos	4,421	53	50	535	77	63	57	4,658	1,593	91
Brewster	1,126	19	4	137	17	18	23	882	319	23
Briscoe	949	14	5	100	6	6	10	768	233	16
Brooks	839	12	4	428	13	6	22	966	503	51
Brown	4,923	73	65	1,165	42	97	70	4,045	2,831	127
Burleson	3,005	47	25	313	51	24	165	2,390	1,071	150
Burnet	2,005	14	1	235	15	43	12	1,507	988	44
Caldwell	3,506	38	6	308	18	20	17	2,215	1,853	67
Calhoun	1,357	30	6	126	26	20	8	1,646	335	39
Callahan	1,862	41	4	534	17	51	14	891	1,758	57
Cameron	10,271	87	114	903	271	152	0	7,113	2,513	357
Camp	1,442	85	8	475	78	12	29	1,661	671	104
Carson	1,451	26	6	151	14	25	11	1,074	636	34
Cass	3,725	54	24	425	37	66	31	3,978	915	72
Castro	1,286	6	0	85	6	5	4	1,198	515	25
Chambers	1,556	15	10	160	47	28	7	1,563	453	38
Cherokee	3,079	131	27	1,248	55	97	40	3,992	3,287	268
Childress	1,981	580	28	405	22	680	17	2,195	1,173	80
Clay	2,376	55	8	400	11	26	9	1,692	1,259	74
Cochran	1,275	26	2	179	36	30	22	1,295	427	59
Coke	979	28	2	165	0	17	2	909	589	61
Coleman	3,067	52	21	631	45	79	44	2,333	1,796	56
Collin	3,957	248	42	1,113	35	60	35	3,415	3,496	163
Collingsworth	1,921	39	46	183	16	36	30	1,788	746	64
Colorado	2,998	22	10	222	99	52	35	3,734	846	127
Comal	2,616	20	3	167	18	18	8	2,896	876	83
Comanche	2,928	45	8	1,228	39	60	29	2,115	2,287	149
Concho	1,196	16	2	120	6	11	8	840	564	28
Cooke	3,595	71	26	759	47	58	62	3,845	1,875	94
Coryell	2,361	31	0	744	20	43	71	1,674	1,940	115
Cottle	1,518	35	21	223	12	17	28	972	648	39
Crane	913	27	4	242	9	8	6	789	603	29
Crockett	460	10	1	47	1	6	3	705	197	24
Crosby	1,933	34	5	434	15	17	16	1,346	859	70
Culberson	355	4	0	40	1	14	4	411	99	11
Dallam	1,548	32	38	274	13	49	41	1,812	483	70
Dallas	34,212	318	312	8,631	659	719	279	41,582	24,009	1,609
Dawson	2,530	42	26	460	33	39	20	2,881	1,232	87
DeWitt	3,891	45	9	247	15	50	32	3,177	667	79
Deaf Smith	1,715	18	9	126	8	20	11	2,113	711	59
Delta	1,422	53	24	400	29	36	28	1,243	1,012	57
Denton	5,173	168	17	1,073	29	46	43	4,367	4,064	146
Dickens	1,530	69	7	245	17	52	37	1,199	893	70
Dimmit	982	14	0	94	5	9	10	1,029	394	46

Table 38: Gubernatorial Races

Democratic Primaries, 1950-1952

County	1950							1952		
	Allan Shivers	Charles B. Hutchison	Wellington Abbey	Caso March	J.M. Wren	Gene S. Porter	Benita L.M. Lawrence	Allan Shivers	Ralph W. Yarborough	Allene M. Traylor
Donley	1,361	24	15	149	14	15	17	1,228	696	88
Duval	108	1	0	4,239	0	1	1	883	2,061	29
Eastland	3,786	115	24	1,740	158	130	71	3,617	3,394	235
Ector	5,450	86	11	800	62	38	48	5,842	2,522	218
Edwards	693	20	2	49	4	18	8	620	159	33
El Paso	14,277	452	52	3,328	174	178	144	14,376	4,521	359
Ellis	4,001	53	20	1,262	44	26	26	4,231	3,474	98
Erath	3,583	61	35	1,212	69	61	44	2,740	2,689	89
Falls	3,075	30	6	1,078	66	45	57	1,393	1,335	63
Fannin	4,223	187	40	1,681	52	52	59	3,632	3,840	335
Fayette	5,150	136	19	78	53	57	290	3,608	1,261	116
Fisher	1,293	9	5	337	26	18	12	1,189	1,602	96
Floyd	2,317	33	20	404	27	36	28	2,405	810	58
Foard	1,030	8	5	99	23	22	21	860	335	38
Fort Bend	1,679	15	14	321	54	27	19	3,119	1,083	77
Franklin	1,316	69	60	766	17	15	24	971	1,045	61
Freestone	3,016	70	22	1,067	39	32	37	2,622	1,503	112
Frio	1,347	12	2	168	11	11	11	1,192	506	96
Gaines	1,795	58	3	272	19	32	16	1,902	804	121
Galveston	12,760	190	77	2,595	118	256	117	12,298	5,306	694
Garza	1,155	33	6	239	11	18	10	1,106	406	64
Gillespie	359	4	0	24	1	5	1	1,453	159	17
Glasscock	298	10	3	36	3	2	4	298	135	11
Goliad	1,069	19	6	80	8	11	10	437	143	12
Gonzales	3,129	37	9	398	15	15	21	2,083	769	71
Gray	3,849	58	34	439	32	72	26	3,222	973	103
Grayson	8,698	128	55	2,549	45	116	114	6,471	6,136	367
Gregg	7,269	66	44	1,561	58	277	160	6,990	4,181	358
Grimes	1,488	19	0	165	24	10	16	1,129	348	24
Guadalupe	669	7	1	103	4	12	4	1,033	343	24
Hale	3,942	55	14	473	22	73	19	2,939	1,116	68
Hall	2,031	20	6	226	22	16	95	1,579	978	59
Hamilton	2,333	56	10	791	20	32	30	1,643	1,473	112
Hansford	789	10	1	32	6	4	13	744	192	24
Hardeman	1,748	55	31	289	14	23	16	1,757	849	54
Hardin	2,676	65	28	636	133	45	21	1,758	3,252	122
Harris	61,198	279	645	15,889	2,664	1,123	503	75,524	42,087	2,628
Harrison	4,550	59	23	1,097	29	29	26	4,985	1,935	141
Hartley	654	10	0	64	2	5	10	624	122	18
Haskell	2,268	68	17	499	10	19	19	1,443	2,002	89
Hays	2,240	13	7	233	7	43	9	1,266	888	17
Hemphill	902	55	42	64	1	27	3	1,010	154	35
Henderson	3,515	156	20	1,971	44	55	47	1,763	4,846	170
Hidalgo	12,250	104	36	1,240	27	63	100	12,879	2,747	358
Hill	4,740	60	35	1,994	20	30	33	3,833	3,425	229
Hockley	3,167	109	8	515	53	114	28	3,126	1,493	147
Hood	1,229	25	3	567	16	38	16	1,026	991	40
Hopkins	3,167	94	54	1,555	126	57	25	3,518	2,253	161
Houston	3,638	27	20	663	50	76	52	3,009	1,486	178
Howard	4,265	67	47	744	21	50	24	3,040	3,303	109
Hudspeth	453	14	1	91	4	3	5	487	113	15
Hunt	5,541	192	45	1,281	41	73	41	5,280	2,451	116
Hutchinson	3,283	46	29	1,411	15	25	23	3,769	2,330	161
Irion	477	12	0	72	2	15	7	344	240	22
Jack	1,595	36	5	377	25	32	13	1,470	904	54
Jackson	1,878	42	8	182	33	21	17	2,574	713	121
Jasper	3,404	35	64	499	49	52	23	1,892	2,319	72
Jeff Davis	388	13	2	50	10	3	7	372	94	15
Jefferson	14,693	149	611	7,917	337	1,005	80	16,594	14,937	309
Jim Hogg	691	7	1	106	4	6	8	547	160	20
Jim Wells	3,764	60	32	863	69	157	20	4,449	1,724	136
Johnson	3,382	89	19	1,148	38	42	17	2,744	2,471	98
Jones	2,266	56	3	470	47	16	20	2,735	2,197	110
Karnes	3,631	31	9	303	23	30	18	2,908	885	84
Kaufman	2,654	70	14	695	18	21	24	3,750	2,324	102

Table 38: Gubernatorial Races

Democratic Primaries, 1950-1952										
Year	1950							1952		
County	Allan Shivers	Charles B. Hutchison	Wellington Abbey	Caso March	J.M. Wren	Gene S. Porter	Benita L.M. Lawrence	Allan Shivers	Ralph W. Yarborough	Allene M. Traylor
Kendall	192	1	0	25	0	2	0	311	82	1
Kenedy	69	0	0	0	1	1	0	77	3	6
Kent	356	11	4	53	3	10	4	409	401	25
Kerr	2,566	25	4	264	21	90	16	2,891	1,086	63
Kimble	1,170	27	0	159	32	15	10	837	494	38
King	159	5	0	28	1	0	2	81	71	1
Kinney	367	4	8	27	2	1	3	139	42	5
Kleberg	2,822	23	12	845	19	25	23	2,143	1,652	160
Knox	1,788	38	13	275	12	13	14	1,495	942	36
La Salle	998	8	2	60	6	16	0	806	302	25
Lamar	4,431	167	67	1,311	48	125	55	6,377	2,637	247
Lamb	2,909	90	11	512	21	49	19	2,771	1,572	108
Lampasas	1,996	48	9	523	27	36	17	1,513	748	42
Lavaca	4,414	35	22	279	42	45	42	3,092	948	83
Lee	2,111	61	6	212	27	62	22	1,601	855	54
Leon	1,193	31	14	582	27	60	17	1,825	1,061	49
Liberty	3,716	45	76	513	102	65	39	4,806	1,741	174
Limestone	3,672	55	42	1,668	47	60	40	3,560	2,542	116
Lipscomb	874	21	13	51	12	20	13	638	86	13
Live Oak	1,464	14	7	143	35	26	13	1,636	483	47
Llano	1,266	13	7	204	6	13	14	1,052	807	62
Loving	0	0	0	0	0	0	0	57	12	2
Lubbock	7,908	104	21	1,510	66	111	47	11,126	4,687	309
Lynn	1,788	74	11	526	9	35	16	1,870	799	80
Madison	1,707	39	15	350	43	9	12	1,159	765	29
Marion	1,493	133	22	139	60	18	17	1,544	403	81
Martin	990	21	1	126	7	14	7	927	602	42
Mason	1,129	68	7	178	8	17	10	1,039	630	30
Matagorda	3,228	38	26	345	86	44	34	3,723	952	175
Maverick	971	13	2	105	1	6	11	939	241	58
McCulloch	2,202	20	8	554	60	41	27	1,887	1,206	60
McLennan	10,844	60	38	7,068	63	140	199	11,985	9,759	438
McMullen	408	2	0	57	2	8	13	324	62	20
Medina	1,059	18	2	127	15	27	6	684	343	30
Menard	1,059	25	13	156	15	22	12	838	455	44
Midland	3,545	28	18	260	9	49	42	4,513	1,511	116
Milam	4,182	63	15	1,038	86	124	143	2,687	2,033	139
Mills	1,425	34	8	386	24	48	10	973	1,062	50
Mitchell	2,044	29	3	432	13	45	17	1,857	1,298	85
Montague	3,056	58	12	702	110	65	29	2,758	2,350	117
Montgomery	4,721	131	30	628	184	124	59	4,443	1,227	197
Moore	1,840	25	10	481	9	27	39	2,279	826	66
Morris	1,307	49	29	613	14	11	0	1,655	874	72
Motley	814	28	1	110	7	28	12	903	290	38
Nacogdoches	4,431	67	15	910	59	169	72	4,654	1,857	191
Navarro	6,115	130	57	1,996	46	87	82	3,554	3,935	165
Newton	1,102	27	12	277	59	19	14	1,049	1,443	97
Nolan	3,099	91	19	711	20	36	31	3,262	2,191	146
Nueces	11,675	111	62	5,874	77	152	134	12,860	11,801	602
Ochiltree	1,371	13	11	79	5	9	19	1,507	215	36
Oldham	467	2	0	18	3	4	5	373	192	7
Orange	6,298	75	24	1,740	166	89	28	4,955	4,816	268
Palo Pinto	2,716	54	6	690	21	27	21	2,802	1,786	120
Panola	3,971	222	61	822	74	43	38	3,325	2,365	104
Parker	3,847	116	12	966	39	43	31	3,200	2,121	138
Parmer	1,340	29	4	49	2	8	15	990	255	29
Pec os	1,769	23	10	152	14	25	35	1,699	716	95
Polk	2,809	29	53	346	73	30	26	2,348	1,390	131
Potter	6,983	106	22	1,204	103	88	59	4,695	1,864	91
Presidio	953	16	21	88	7	14	28	791	244	52
Rains	667	81	26	450	23	11	13	743	514	43
Randall	2,106	22	7	240	25	21	14	2,868	891	62
Reagan	651	11	2	56	5	4	1	649	256	16
Real	569	14	5	61	9	8	7	541	213	32
Red River	2,975	124	38	969	65	51	27	3,576	1,804	214

Table 38: Gubernatorial Races

County	1950							1952		
	Allan Shivers	Charles B. Hutchison	Wellington Abbey	Caso March	J.M. Wren	Gene S. Porter	Benita L.M. Lawrence	Allan Shivers	Ralph W. Yarborough	Allene M. Traylor
Reeves	1,545	17	6	131	11	7	32	1,908	603	79
Refugio	524	1	2	28	3	3	0	1,458	481	39
Roberts	366	5	0	15	3	9	1	192	31	6
Robertson	2,494	21	17	1,078	52	38	69	1,848	1,262	69
Rockwall	1,318	73	5	277	23	9	13	1,157	686	30
Runnels	1,338	25	2	214	14	28	15	1,419	1,087	36
Rusk	5,493	336	105	1,457	144	289	70	6,892	3,069	408
Sabine	1,591	104	20	518	51	67	16	1,459	1,068	103
San Augustine	1,986	47	33	302	54	33	46	1,550	923	107
San Jacinto	896	10	2	132	43	36	15	706	342	41
San Patricio	2,123	24	19	94	17	68	27	2,777	1,797	122
San Saba	1,985	26	8	549	34	42	50	728	1,167	50
Schleicher	719	24	10	77	6	9	6	792	341	21
Scurry	2,409	26	6	318	33	48	17	3,069	1,614	157
Shackelford	1,236	13	1	297	16	13	13	1,000	860	68
Shelby	5,032	187	59	1,304	113	85	63	3,962	2,940	139
Sherman	694	9	1	26	2	4	4	720	108	19
Smith	5,797	91	57	2,046	63	119	76	8,236	7,288	201
Somervell	529	20	2	208	10	7	8	561	394	29
Starr	2,067	21	4	52	1	3	4	3,378	165	219
Stephens	2,075	45	6	767	9	26	35	2,036	1,366	121
Sterling	304	10	0	23	2	2	0	287	88	8
Stonewall	1,029	35	3	189	8	12	6	664	508	46
Sutton	374	6	0	47	4	6	0	417	77	12
Swisher	1,747	28	3	123	10	10	7	1,559	893	38
Tarrant	25,898	285	195	9,040	247	293	507	36,060	24,942	1,135
Taylor	5,107	60	28	1,044	25	56	35	6,557	6,587	171
Terrell	250	5	1	36	3	7	1	234	74	2
Terry	2,375	52	7	545	24	20	22	2,760	827	90
Throckmorton	846	16	2	639	7	12	5	638	781	34
Titus	2,810	75	22	913	23	41	22	3,032	2,136	162
Tom Green	4,562	99	29	1,043	24	69	36	7,028	3,780	333
Travis	15,344	83	122	2,568	42	72	85	16,576	13,179	340
Trinity	2,004	51	10	256	127	54	33	1,576	682	95
Tyler	2,348	22	19	280	57	29	10	1,560	1,215	94
Upshur	3,956	99	20	1,103	42	56	37	3,028	2,595	245
Upton	862	21	2	99	10	5	9	1,053	463	29
Uvalde	2,230	59	12	249	14	31	17	2,155	784	96
Val Verde	1,355	20	23	187	11	11	10	1,645	490	96
Van Zandt	2,990	252	27	2,151	71	156	63	2,917	3,326	130
Victoria	1,400	10	15	169	20	10	29	3,460	1,209	71
Walker	2,999	43	15	252	120	55	23	2,521	790	93
Waller	1,419	20	15	210	72	70	40	1,886	502	56
Ward	2,362	70	8	448	29	38	23	1,875	1,060	84
Washington	2,895	30	1	180	40	22	64	2,645	455	38
Webb	6,107	1	13	32	16	3	3	6,066	272	18
Wharton	4,030	33	33	375	99	81	103	5,867	1,554	289
Wheeler	2,266	77	21	177	20	19	18	1,737	591	49
Wichita	8,767	113	20	1,583	34	35	34	9,986	5,809	280
Wilbarger	3,854	70	10	587	26	36	22	3,148	1,602	88
Willacy	2,559	18	3	161	13	55	22	2,532	538	64
Williamson	3,778	88	21	572	32	57	38	3,158	2,556	102
Wilson	2,854	31	16	257	14	113	36	2,656	1,034	150
Winkler	1,883	104	6	306	33	43	16	1,456	777	95
Wise	3,581	90	24	1,014	74	100	18	2,441	2,522	141
Wood	3,113	63	23	1,455	76	52	33	2,481	2,152	87
Yoakum	1,042	56	9	207	7	14	10	824	550	42
Young	2,303	27	3	1,554	8	21	18	2,303	1,508	102
Zapata	288	0	0	2	1	1	0	398	29	6
Zavala	1,053	23	3	62	1	8	12	1,122	289	53
Official Totals	829,730	16,048	6,381	195,997	14,138	14,728	9,542	833,861	488,345	34,186
Unofficial Totals	829,820	16,048	6,420	195,937	14,198	14,678	9,542	833,859	488,343	34,186

Table 39: Gubernatorial Races

Democratic Primaries, 1954-1956														
Year	1954				Runoff		1956						Runoff	
County	Cyclone Davis	J.J. Holmes	Allan Shivers	Ralph W. Yarborough	Allan Shivers	Ralph W. Yarborough	Price Daniel	J. Evetts Haley	J.J. Holmes	W. Lee O'Daniel	Reuben Senterfitt	Ralph W. Yarborough	Price Daniel	Ralph W. Yarborough
Anderson	135	299	3,634	3,581	4,146	3,888	2,121	364	51	2,238	334	2,398	2,857	3,250
Andrews	18	22	706	914	710	854	718	216	11	729	69	678	892	1,108
Angelina	115	301	4,124	5,767	4,937	5,946	3,141	305	68	2,705	86	4,644	3,781	5,912
Aransas	11	6	598	340	583	319	483	14	13	241	16	321	513	430
Archer	50	20	698	1,061	700	832	626	105	22	498	114	625	676	827
Armstrong	10	15	403	357	360	225	324	180	0	166	3	163	253	261
Atascosa	32	54	1,868	1,863	1,790	1,935	1,680	61	16	975	32	1,155	2,063	1,935
Austin	52	49	2,186	973	2,203	820	1,622	94	77	1,474	75	608	2,460	1,453
Bailey	20	30	881	940	1,049	917	730	221	7	473	51	443	506	749
Bandera	17	14	943	292	904	188	810	38	7	367	17	171	617	176
Bastrop	34	83	1,550	2,247	1,858	2,303	1,413	93	32	1,586	67	1,389	1,598	2,153
Baylor	37	34	827	957	947	822	726	114	12	701	45	428	584	583
Bee	44	75	2,492	1,670	2,596	1,508	1,634	56	28	1,511	77	1,145	1,435	1,384
Bell	138	183	3,348	7,514	4,135	6,679	3,581	385	86	4,815	713	3,499	4,077	7,126
Bexar	1,202	407	31,196	25,900	38,099	31,174	41,913	799	607	8,472	780	23,465	38,985	27,870
Blanco	2	6	442	338	579	375	282	3	4	181	13	172	319	291
Borden	10	24	198	159	158	182	140	67	1	137	7	78	146	178
Bosque	82	53	1,629	1,934	1,868	1,959	1,204	281	24	1,284	157	725	1,497	1,709
Bowie	168	128	5,235	6,929	5,688	6,591	5,062	514	72	4,803	137	4,032	5,676	5,798
Brazoria	128	100	5,320	4,787	6,012	5,722	4,617	207	40	2,983	250	4,393	4,915	6,571
Brazos	52	99	3,335	3,398	3,739	3,542	2,718	160	32	2,022	200	1,576	2,593	2,976
Brewster	20	14	757	408	769	363	651	114	5	163	15	202	475	285
Briscoe	25	33	604	540	601	570	295	270	5	310	16	234	261	343
Brooks	12	13	737	1,048	755	1,216	551	34	21	488	26	765	568	707
Brown	101	174	2,959	2,991	3,250	2,664	2,393	593	35	1,871	557	1,587	2,333	2,681
Burleson	78	69	1,583	2,064	1,345	1,814	865	78	35	1,548	60	859	1,695	2,058
Burnet	33	37	1,164	1,376	1,144	1,060	763	64	5	882	304	684	818	1,097
Caldwell	45	56	1,696	2,040	2,096	2,200	1,499	44	28	1,158	127	1,192	1,953	2,283
Calhoun	28	30	1,385	730	1,108	598	1,112	44	8	990	69	621	1,292	1,078
Callahan	20	76	1,080	1,434	1,339	1,383	757	175	17	569	82	465	710	892
Cameron	68	113	7,790	4,861	9,099	4,734	7,907	283	127	1,625	553	5,073	7,201	4,333
Camp	50	37	1,020	1,122	910	1,210	691	98	5	1,105	10	559	1,056	1,065
Carson	12	21	802	885	830	783	493	151	2	335	23	472	542	788
Cass	124	50	2,595	2,307	3,011	2,644	2,002	260	13	1,794	34	1,599	1,893	2,069
Castro	14	22	877	821	757	616	579	175	2	284	14	547	631	1,002
Chambers	21	16	1,155	625	1,274	764	1,266	47	10	618	21	729	1,289	909
Cherokee	53	85	2,561	3,711	2,876	3,873	1,991	250	42	2,224	109	2,459	2,643	3,640
Childress	73	72	1,418	1,419	1,390	1,471	1,010	461	27	909	67	810	1,392	1,649
Clay	18	51	1,003	1,874	1,179	1,681	854	198	21	872	67	1,001	1,212	1,678
Cochran	31	32	682	771	641	657	527	141	7	394	227	347	657	859
Coke	12	28	509	542	582	421	303	98	4	495	89	197	349	479
Coleman	49	81	1,969	1,672	2,133	1,770	1,368	346	20	1,300	266	665	1,627	1,422
Collin	66	128	3,036	4,256	3,380	4,417	2,733	432	17	2,687	92	2,634	3,495	4,831
Collingsworth	25	43	992	1,180	1,082	1,169	658	247	7	633	19	645	727	1,076
Colorado	76	79	2,804	1,425	2,662	1,368	1,373	113	19	1,707	57	572	1,785	1,486
Comal	33	49	2,724	958	2,751	930	2,187	43	8	608	42	751	2,020	881
Comanche	55	67	1,694	2,377	1,622	2,127	1,060	431	8	1,538	130	977	1,607	2,476
Concho	8	12	527	503	572	519	386	87	6	492	61	259	355	560
Cooke	56	80	3,145	1,712	3,366	1,819	2,521	429	32	1,570	70	1,193	2,829	1,881
Coryell	48	39	1,446	2,241	1,531	1,889	1,182	137	13	1,830	263	826	1,363	1,983
Cottle	20	15	459	1,149	470	982	443	236	4	443	17	637	275	753
Crane	13	25	481	877	494	772	428	179	9	358	38	504	527	978
Crockett	9	15	768	364	624	398	469	98	3	316	34	320	294	237
Crosby	52	46	800	1,440	840	1,518	738	159	19	682	68	1,096	521	1,739
Culberson	3	2	348	169	318	121	316	46	1	194	19	66	242	110
Dallam	19	26	846	921	860	818	687	115	5	274	11	364	503	585
Dallas	729	286	38,454	29,872	57,737	38,782	54,473	8,371	979	16,509	1,066	32,866	68,409	48,017
Dawson	66	114	1,706	1,377	1,776	1,369	1,528	239	10	1,240	69	719	1,317	1,485
DeWitt	58	84	3,516	1,356	3,620	1,286	2,659	50	33	2,060	74	790	3,158	1,389
Deaf Smith	21	38	1,506	670	1,513	666	1,265	335	6	402	69	389	1,196	784
Delta	29	34	801	1,437	947	1,489	538	74	7	1,003	24	599	946	1,219
Denton	70	114	3,686	4,473	3,611	3,787	3,128	862	34	2,427	86	2,652	3,186	3,368
Dickens	23	11	627	1,109	720	1,121	535	142	12	601	44	712	735	1,283
Dimmit	9	36	878	443	1,013	505	429	5	2	381	30	246	447	353

Table 39: Gubernatorial Races

County	1954				Runoff		1956						Runoff	
	Cyclone Davis	J.J. Holmes	Allan Shivers	Ralph W. Yarborough	Allan Shivers	Ralph W. Yarborough	Price Daniel	J.Evetts Haley	J.J. Holmes	W. Lee O'Daniel	Reuben Senterfitt	Ralph W. Yarborough	Price Daniel	Ralph W. Yarborough
Donley	22	27	929	804	838	657	653	348	1	576	16	274	908	919
Duval	9	50	1,378	3,016	1,220	3,310	3,402	25	12	366	53	466	3,523	1,494
Eastland	85	131	2,941	2,991	3,530	3,032	1,890	480	32	2,172	196	1,131	2,060	2,469
Ector	84	164	4,288	3,505	5,523	3,448	5,173	1,274	160	2,608	530	2,376	5,745	5,120
Edwards	8	5	584	210	556	177	404	77	2	197	40	97	444	128
El Paso	120	129	8,962	6,267	10,304	7,339	10,675	532	193	2,120	163	7,327	8,473	7,058
Ellis	66	40	2,937	3,740	2,980	3,938	2,689	718	34	2,049	68	2,667	3,090	3,649
Erath	60	81	2,283	2,443	2,442	2,619	1,864	359	17	1,655	161	1,251	2,279	2,713
Falls	49	112	1,725	2,540	1,896	2,332	1,213	110	11	1,326	71	1,071	1,422	1,966
Fannin	164	129	2,355	4,489	2,091	4,471	1,547	284	26	2,296	76	2,643	1,484	2,955
Fayette	68	101	3,695	2,116	3,753	1,433	2,633	278	41	3,049	137	829	2,950	1,538
Fisher	24	83	941	1,452	1,062	1,537	604	160	19	870	79	884	461	1,286
Floyd	32	51	1,431	1,395	1,671	1,341	1,480	366	17	637	30	622	994	925
Foard	15	14	484	725	374	526	284	103	4	204	25	271	275	411
Fort Bend	48	41	2,490	1,508	2,931	2,058	1,886	150	20	1,825	157	1,118	2,172	1,900
Franklin	97	44	745	1,343	870	1,414	444	90	11	946	18	540	636	968
Freestone	100	64	2,043	2,446	2,082	2,680	1,441	170	30	1,446	46	1,419	1,438	1,451
Frio	15	29	867	817	899	1,033	642	26	4	313	9	615	562	727
Gaines	46	76	1,357	1,221	1,308	1,260	942	248	81	697	65	564	1,012	1,377
Galveston	250	559	10,990	9,218	14,085	10,974	10,157	677	208	2,764	646	12,524	12,360	16,580
Garza	28	34	737	754	619	685	436	130	8	475	29	287	598	792
Gillespie	3	6	860	167	1,576	166	629	4	3	205	52	65	854	123
Glasscock	6	17	267	150	253	101	133	94	5	92	17	52	143	115
Goliad	11	18	1,037	460	778	274	690	24	5	636	4	163	640	275
Gonzales	20	36	1,446	1,289	1,947	1,539	1,620	45	32	1,126	65	728	1,692	1,299
Gray	82	85	2,751	2,011	3,161	2,024	2,022	641	34	1,599	59	1,036	1,958	2,101
Grayson	168	165	4,391	6,827	4,905	6,912	4,634	570	64	3,070	182	5,588	5,047	7,171
Gregg	208	167	5,500	5,705	7,268	6,597	5,264	609	103	4,342	183	3,372	6,097	4,471
Grimes	9	19	1,151	905	1,321	887	740	263	8	773	20	413	1,065	1,361
Guadalupe	11	17	1,518	751	2,498	1,074	1,456	15	13	761	46	688	1,890	1,037
Hale	34	37	2,418	1,525	2,920	1,584	2,663	405	19	1,183	131	1,228	2,325	2,358
Hall	47	29	1,035	1,316	966	1,272	484	385	6	456	45	539	609	1,201
Hamilton	66	47	1,718	1,487	1,649	1,103	1,074	188	12	1,419	206	427	1,300	1,156
Hansford	20	13	927	371	709	259	490	133	3	159	18	106	419	188
Hardeman	71	35	1,187	1,089	1,249	919	786	190	7	648	26	404	761	665
Hardin	67	66	1,514	3,396	1,798	3,582	1,869	113	13	936	84	2,787	1,736	2,968
Harris	335	1,791	51,888	45,915	75,049	66,187	59,344	4,489	1,122	16,384	3,664	46,149	69,564	71,377
Harrison	89	78	3,725	3,290	4,185	2,981	3,026	591	16	1,339	69	2,286	4,001	2,623
Hartley	7	6	320	320	351	242	391	94	2	97	3	163	272	227
Haskell	45	72	1,260	2,536	1,472	2,467	693	223	17	1,696	102	1,130	829	1,997
Hays	24	51	1,768	1,518	1,744	1,382	1,367	35	19	637	71	919	1,374	1,350
Hemphill	11	12	757	465	523	322	355	139	2	145	11	156	265	161
Henderson	56	98	1,760	5,127	1,969	5,638	1,159	240	20	1,603	167	3,060	1,779	4,648
Hidalgo	138	283	11,640	6,054	12,801	6,925	10,363	268	130	2,219	807	6,395	9,278	5,514
Hill	89	81	2,768	4,337	2,771	3,724	2,431	588	19	2,112	135	2,049	2,984	3,515
Hockley	90	95	1,992	1,937	2,097	1,904	1,926	298	51	1,292	127	1,420	1,837	2,853
Hood	42	47	866	1,301	1,026	1,381	528	275	20	736	31	645	493	904
Hopkins	90	101	2,139	3,143	2,362	3,103	1,606	246	26	2,253	58	1,545	2,339	2,890
Houston	57	94	2,254	2,103	2,146	2,301	1,187	195	11	1,951	53	1,478	1,560	2,272
Howard	74	110	2,538	3,225	2,850	3,418	2,308	544	33	1,292	133	2,070	2,572	4,058
Hudspeth	11	12	463	190	306	140	412	59	8	137	13	108	296	132
Hunt	91	85	4,496	3,773	5,390	3,923	3,648	244	29	2,665	76	2,066	3,758	3,184
Hutchinson	45	55	1,963	3,264	2,629	3,125	1,886	631	54	1,223	72	2,120	2,163	3,240
Irion	18	26	250	254	228	147	193	61	6	181	31	66	214	210
Jack	25	24	1,072	940	1,050	773	711	311	7	777	40	442	904	869
Jackson	32	36	2,203	1,149	1,763	933	1,389	106	18	1,490	65	650	1,210	1,149
Jasper	66	47	1,944	3,016	2,302	3,045	1,974	240	31	773	57	2,304	2,191	2,509
Jeff Davis	2	10	232	137	255	194	140	47	10	50	7	76	108	69
Jefferson	481	548	15,677	16,543	21,205	21,079	20,745	1,112	262	2,131	561	17,854	20,834	20,451
Jim Hogg	13	16	513	541	664	587	374	19	7	265	6	529	293	310
Jim Wells	79	58	4,061	3,280	3,681	3,010	2,827	95	32	1,872	192	1,847	2,932	3,133
Johnson	68	89	2,914	3,653	3,120	3,401	1,548	1,447	20	1,060	46	1,631	2,141	2,872
Jones	35	90	2,008	2,141	2,084	2,049	1,430	269	46	1,314	159	1,221	1,621	2,363
Karnes	66	72	2,140	1,856	2,023	1,474	1,786	71	16	986	41	741	1,587	1,134
Kaufman	41	36	2,399	2,656	2,678	2,818	1,850	311	37	1,847	98	1,768	2,880	2,910

Table 39: Gubernatorial Races

Democratic Primaries, 1954-1956													
Year	1954				Runoff		1956						Runoff	
County	Cyclone Davis	J.J. Holmes	Allan Shivers	Ralph W. Yarborough	Allan Shivers	Ralph W. Yarborough	Price Daniel	J Evetts Haley	J.J. Holmes	W. Lee O'Daniel	Reuben Senterfitt	Ralph W. Yarborough	Price Daniel	Ralph W. Yarborough
Kendall	0	0	449	140	835	163	394	6	0	102	7	85	514	132
Kenedy	1	2	129	3	148	8	92	0	2	11	3	1	96	4
Kent	21	12	308	494	241	350	181	177	5	284	14	217	243	508
Kerr	23	25	2,703	946	3,027	850	1,674	47	14	617	87	325	1,923	604
Kimble	34	27	958	563	900	518	485	217	22	412	90	217	863	609
King	0	1	89	158	91	156	39	62	10	71	2	61	39	114
Kinney	4	4	294	209	301	235	215	18	3	73	9	252	302	296
Kleberg	44	23	1,346	1,770	1,334	1,894	1,333	43	32	582	81	2,131	1,482	2,877
Knox	35	33	1,006	1,250	1,127	1,134	636	184	15	684	34	530	709	859
La Salle	6	7	535	332	541	510	368	6	2	151	62	314	333	428
Lamar	147	120	4,459	4,557	4,568	4,380	3,285	403	65	3,853	223	1,780	4,639	3,941
Lamb	40	65	2,144	2,008	2,260	1,830	1,608	467	14	911	130	1,388	1,217	2,159
Lampasas	35	31	1,180	1,076	1,449	1,283	559	78	37	1,031	639	343	930	991
Lavaca	94	100	2,723	1,755	3,335	1,469	2,402	108	32	2,042	90	792	2,822	1,661
Lee	32	23	1,173	1,208	1,192	1,089	629	244	7	1,049	26	726	1,040	1,386
Leon	65	55	1,416	1,774	1,671	2,038	729	138	12	1,304	106	830	753	1,100
Liberty	101	96	3,040	2,557	3,127	2,421	3,424	92	24	2,045	96	1,459	3,312	2,304
Limestone	123	72	2,368	3,544	2,677	3,872	2,038	160	55	1,463	101	1,918	2,146	2,707
Lipscomb	1	5	478	178	522	183	471	68	1	213	9	203	296	163
Live Oak	26	47	1,339	697	1,246	540	579	30	7	532	63	235	670	421
Llano	13	20	536	712	809	654	463	50	10	610	156	459	683	1,095
Loving	3	1	68	11	51	5	25	38	0	27	1	2	23	17
Lubbock	171	222	7,302	6,348	9,133	6,788	9,445	1,131	98	3,309	600	5,371	7,918	8,585
Lynn	39	60	1,091	1,130	1,011	993	1,023	194	15	727	31	679	864	1,248
Madison	16	30	881	1,106	994	1,096	533	98	11	893	38	454	591	719
Marion	18	41	960	743	829	657	652	137	43	721	12	428	708	512
Martin	33	57	492	702	396	561	215	218	5	293	23	167	196	484
Mason	16	20	920	513	828	399	449	38	2	482	76	326	500	539
Matagorda	62	77	3,592	1,466	3,145	1,347	2,767	100	27	1,784	120	983	2,753	1,715
Maverick	3	6	791	277	913	473	1,001	15	4	230	16	675	748	361
McCulloch	38	74	1,927	1,447	1,998	1,465	665	160	15	1,396	370	353	1,089	1,349
McLennan	195	267	8,979	14,010	11,740	13,531	10,518	767	114	5,399	638	8,507	11,551	12,862
McMullen	5	11	313	170	242	128	277	7	4	151	15	76	210	95
Medina	10	13	948	690	1,544	806	1,320	23	33	552	33	430	1,393	756
Menard	7	24	688	420	703	463	333	113	16	485	66	169	588	564
Midland	68	70	4,316	2,203	5,005	2,018	3,914	1,425	52	914	296	1,209	5,575	2,882
Milam	50	102	2,394	2,884	2,423	2,850	1,367	181	32	2,277	104	1,315	1,620	2,551
Mills	48	72	912	996	951	866	426	115	7	881	500	281	546	630
Mitchell	31	78	1,214	1,648	1,270	1,668	855	192	25	1,077	142	820	1,016	2,136
Montague	84	52	1,782	2,405	1,794	2,115	1,545	482	10	1,692	66	1,237	1,345	1,563
Montgomery	116	120	3,325	3,074	3,073	3,664	2,001	190	27	2,745	112	1,861	2,379	3,170
Moore	25	27	1,027	1,453	858	1,064	890	323	17	845	42	967	1,123	1,642
Morris	53	31	1,218	1,775	1,434	1,888	864	290	9	1,302	23	1,110	1,475	1,908
Motley	17	9	628	447	547	319	310	298	8	281	13	247	448	433
Nacogdoches	81	102	2,677	3,370	3,165	3,704	2,549	180	47	1,368	128	2,926	3,247	4,076
Navarro	67	78	2,520	4,170	2,884	4,245	2,731	424	25	1,933	97	3,121	2,915	3,634
Newton	43	156	893	1,579	794	1,565	884	76	27	497	42	1,268	901	1,358
Nolan	42	90	1,726	2,368	2,044	2,295	1,587	180	39	1,330	181	1,252	1,381	2,010
Nueces	531	255	11,685	13,002	14,352	14,408	12,851	414	302	4,816	592	11,859	15,067	17,344
Ochiltree	11	17	968	335	862	230	881	123	6	425	13	234	434	186
Oldham	11	7	303	288	290	251	281	72	3	138	7	137	191	166
Orange	103	108	3,467	5,925	4,114	6,091	4,027	294	33	953	151	4,287	3,817	4,732
Palo Pinto	79	75	2,298	2,128	2,542	2,009	1,843	439	24	1,408	40	1,148	1,810	1,876
Panola	127	113	2,896	3,261	3,102	3,202	1,411	698	27	2,049	44	1,696	3,046	2,791
Parker	99	98	3,029	3,029	3,295	3,002	1,785	729	17	2,117	127	1,420	2,332	2,730
Parmer	8	46	1,097	474	1,040	397	851	316	10	341	29	247	1,036	627
Pecos	48	82	1,403	1,194	1,368	1,282	953	290	14	484	155	599	695	680
Polk	70	90	1,615	1,675	1,969	1,739	1,098	103	21	1,702	112	824	1,423	1,644
Potter	55	103	5,136	5,913	7,007	6,178	4,750	1,385	51	1,609	136	3,595	5,380	5,959
Presidio	39	27	789	394	479	258	548	47	4	58	24	181	359	208
Rains	32	21	575	686	490	672	552	14	4	472	6	221	630	396
Randall	32	55	2,100	1,655	2,571	1,487	1,881	1,246	9	507	87	1,041	2,535	1,943
Reagan	16	20	623	511	380	278	350	213	7	337	237	84	467	521
Real	5	8	235	144	319	148	276	19	3	244	9	97	194	128
Red River	65	68	2,209	3,286	2,107	3,041	1,581	215	25	2,311	44	1,164	2,159	2,201

Table 39: Gubernatorial Races

Democratic Primaries, 1954-1956														
Year	1954				Runoff		1956						Runoff	
County	Cyclone Davis	J.J. Holmes	Allan Shivers	Ralph W. Yarborough	Allan Shivers	Ralph W. Yarborough	Price Daniel	J.Evetts Haley	J.J. Holmes	W. Lee O'Daniel	Reuben Senterfitt	Ralph W. Yarborough	Price Daniel	Ralph W. Yarborough
Reeves	52	32	1,545	959	1,766	965	1,053	561	29	657	174	535	1,669	1,415
Refugio	10	27	1,145	779	1,164	710	1,117	43	12	839	40	524	1,065	961
Roberts	7	5	331	100	295	70	217	47	0	61	2	29	184	77
Robertson	39	32	1,354	2,507	1,488	2,492	866	88	20	915	61	1,292	964	2,057
Rockwall	21	17	575	689	745	837	746	115	1	660	27	432	623	561
Runnels	50	36	1,879	1,134	1,984	1,040	1,201	259	34	1,291	346	569	1,729	1,396
Rusk	377	253	5,154	5,032	5,973	5,515	3,805	459	216	3,035	150	2,399	4,501	4,141
Sabine	47	66	959	1,505	1,132	1,625	704	89	36	909	46	862	757	1,102
San Augustine	56	70	935	1,550	1,304	1,512	655	86	18	836	39	861	766	1,157
San Jacinto	39	31	546	726	473	883	307	15	16	754	40	389	302	664
San Patricio	51	88	2,680	2,869	2,649	2,412	2,383	90	89	1,615	115	2,359	2,103	2,866
San Saba	22	51	832	1,579	891	1,565	106	39	4	697	1,550	252	406	1,337
Schleicher	17	28	648	376	686	353	321	112	15	333	33	127	511	440
Scurry	45	92	1,600	2,014	1,675	1,570	1,637	635	24	1,745	113	960	1,985	2,728
Shackelford	15	28	808	679	801	622	485	259	7	407	54	261	593	540
Shelby	96	63	2,459	4,486	2,626	4,182	1,672	188	57	1,440	94	3,163	2,282	3,806
Sherman	11	6	647	260	627	226	365	70	1	174	7	88	262	149
Smith	140	257	7,792	7,777	8,348	7,616	7,875	327	58	4,129	256	5,904	10,001	8,338
Somervell	14	11	519	504	459	413	225	102	3	531	10	181	478	623
Starr	73	9	3,188	859	1,328	1,168	3,428	9	2	131	10	561	1,250	453
Stephens	41	59	1,762	1,416	1,939	1,451	1,047	229	37	1,207	101	554	1,045	1,173
Sterling	1	8	244	122	214	92	191	48	7	125	21	68	136	99
Stonewall	19	25	465	787	540	828	327	152	22	610	23	326	530	901
Sutton	9	23	517	269	554	252	265	41	3	134	14	116	286	170
Swisher	29	18	1,025	963	1,029	818	638	332	17	391	152	1,033	811	1,386
Tarrant	562	625	29,588	29,104	34,653	29,310	27,447	15,167	307	10,444	1,304	23,255	37,527	34,266
Taylor	47	157	4,783	4,347	5,833	4,691	6,008	399	126	2,617	1,002	3,695	5,475	5,735
Terrell	3	0	341	239	250	163	277	38	4	78	37	230	142	148
Terry	23	36	1,376	1,287	1,432	1,272	1,373	253	37	879	103	989	1,311	1,871
Throckmorton	19	46	629	727	744	740	297	148	9	644	19	348	304	689
Titus	79	78	1,788	2,676	1,898	2,936	1,171	450	17	2,258	41	1,327	2,032	2,297
Tom Green	133	136	5,930	4,067	6,831	4,097	4,641	713	111	3,981	838	2,150	4,923	5,070
Travis	114	388	15,803	13,136	18,416	13,693	17,267	404	354	6,116	1,818	12,733	17,628	16,232
Trinity	61	61	1,253	1,301	1,059	1,191	448	26	14	930	34	589	693	1,170
Tyler	43	42	2,159	1,054	2,367	1,118	1,591	37	7	696	65	716	1,645	872
Upshur	176	52	2,642	3,528	3,068	3,693	1,535	233	20	2,390	44	1,368	1,806	1,893
Upton	30	51	765	758	628	693	479	274	28	523	94	334	497	590
Uvalde	22	40	1,952	992	1,731	721	1,747	83	14	1,142	50	544	2,159	1,291
Val Verde	24	64	1,489	1,217	1,343	1,095	909	40	14	155	36	496	893	532
Van Zandt	62	103	2,104	3,867	1,750	3,161	1,427	240	22	1,941	71	1,984	1,910	3,207
Victoria	41	76	3,839	2,705	3,724	2,360	3,145	132	54	2,643	150	1,979	2,993	2,789
Walker	27	75	1,912	1,841	2,091	1,727	1,222	107	7	1,185	86	1,142	1,803	1,804
Waller	14	28	1,108	802	1,122	791	894	153	13	954	31	629	1,093	1,129
Ward	50	70	1,641	1,563	1,541	1,311	889	722	32	849	85	603	734	1,105
Washington	32	76	3,252	1,218	3,085	1,005	1,934	122	10	1,778	47	606	1,741	761
Webb	18	19	6,800	630	6,215	854	4,858	60	30	577	89	2,100	4,063	2,336
Wharton	72	94	4,370	2,689	4,352	2,475	3,069	135	33	2,146	254	1,723	2,757	2,704
Wheeler	39	71	1,021	1,440	1,062	1,457	660	369	9	704	24	664	671	1,109
Wichita	65	64	5,457	8,223	7,264	8,627	8,162	506	115	3,104	353	7,724	9,003	10,814
Wilbarger	35	67	2,052	1,962	2,245	1,748	1,637	213	12	958	126	899	1,497	1,252
Willacy	63	90	2,052	992	2,150	1,006	1,375	40	17	715	157	464	1,516	764
Williamson	49	63	2,929	3,573	3,343	3,234	2,176	172	28	2,478	285	1,710	2,491	3,289
Wilson	56	69	1,839	2,059	1,578	1,745	1,400	23	17	1,092	28	1,611	2,091	2,527
Winkler	47	37	1,087	1,262	977	955	761	759	30	714	77	526	1,076	1,215
Wise	99	116	1,755	3,139	1,631	2,457	1,158	481	50	1,374	84	1,302	1,177	2,062
Wood	100	77	2,057	2,794	2,117	2,798	1,553	179	12	1,505	48	1,435	1,778	2,051
Yoakum	36	66	761	869	844	924	509	206	11	454	77	397	418	707
Young	19	43	1,385	1,630	1,724	1,649	1,338	282	13	1,183	80	1,010	1,342	1,575
Zapata	2	1	541	27	414	37	731	1	5	14	2	167	421	128
Zavala	29	25	1,064	515	1,035	603	656	42	2	533	21	336	784	666
Official	16,254		668,913		775,088		628,914		10,165		37,774		698,001	
Totals		19,591		645,994		683,132		88,772		347,757		463,416		694,830
Unofficial	16.254		668,913		775,079		628,817		10,165		37,774		698,001	
Totals		19,591		645,994		683,132		88,777		347,755		463,416		694,830

Table 40: Gubernatorial Races

	Democratic Primaries, 1958-1962														
Year	1958				1960		1962							Runoff	
County	Price Daniel	Henry B. Gonzalez	Joe A. Irwin	W. Lee O'Daniel	Jack Cox	Price Daniel	John Connally	Price Daniel	Marshall Formby	Edwin A. Walker	Will Wilson	Don Yarborough		John Connally	Don Yarborough
Anderson	4,043	745	174	1,675	3,089	4,960	1,374	1,571	400	892	890	1,322		2,063	2,611
Andrews	689	157	62	1,511	1,357	1,736	447	183	877	246	583	854		1,048	1,667
Angelina	5,879	963	282	2,948	5,914	6,892	1,843	2,065	166	1,069	2,034	3,873		3,463	6,142
Aransas	854	200	52	233	642	1,279	406	261	72	58	136	222		391	479
Archer	1,086	192	96	477	1,120	815	821	237	301	67	206	226		649	505
Armstrong	485	37	13	99	286	487	100	108	370	81	71	51		234	163
Atascosa	2,124	1,102	42	475	1,789	2,464	2,424	752	112	171	352	364		2,815	1,085
Austin	1,651	124	32	674	1,250	2,222	553	396	62	245	271	569		917	985
Bailey	1,022	103	62	370	1,045	1,048	157	161	757	199	184	256		321	537
Bandera	1,070	105	23	212	449	948	480	309	32	331	179	78		508	352
Bastrop	2,294	471	59	1,096	1,749	2,337	1,233	505	143	213	268	708		1,264	1,326
Baylor	1,105	68	27	327	786	605	639	166	353	71	201	186		778	500
Bee	1,646	1,279	50	478	2,232	2,251	1,190	670	201	175	551	687		1,129	1,336
Bell	6,293	906	283	2,839	4,312	7,521	4,579	1,579	661	512	829	2,017		4,337	3,779
Bexar	33,939	26,029	1,263	6,495	24,104	50,579	41,800	13,602	1,601	4,347	6,048	11,955		41,915	23,296
Blanco	332	37	13	138	252	295	347	95	18	34	80	90		263	224
Borden	240	18	29	115	207	235	104	50	54	72	33	358		62	171
Bosque	2,021	235	75	768	1,321	1,749	1,048	547	367	280	446	519		1,153	951
Bowie	7,182	1,128	145	1,981	4,055	7,153	2,055	3,260	352	923	2,148	2,009		3,197	3,598
Brazoria	8,146	1,829	349	2,255	6,012	9,920	3,127	2,569	644	1,569	1,481	5,458		4,559	6,574
Brazos	4,616	1,142	121	1,508	3,435	5,435	2,153	1,626	484	384	1,367	1,977		2,891	3,323
Brewster	779	339	36	140	569	727	265	282	206	110	310	136		527	592
Briscoe	655	92	31	262	592	474	106	91	523	41	90	130		283	285
Brooks	569	1,411	18	188	1,191	1,238	683	184	79	37	104	211		424	493
Brown	3,963	502	222	1,898	4,098	2,946	2,156	735	581	1,240	949	619		2,816	2,333
Burleson	1,704	354	62	1,067	1,572	2,080	920	543	72	199	544	952		1,179	1,680
Burnet	1,405	136	101	702	1,129	1,271	922	262	151	123	175	439		1,024	864
Caldwell	2,367	464	66	630	1,497	1,772	1,639	693	145	204	458	423		1,456	897
Calhoun	1,623	570	71	574	1,719	2,095	902	532	100	126	261	983		1,182	1,323
Callahan	1,293	138	72	554	1,495	1,168	567	340	449	466	589	153		1,339	996
Cameron	7,665	5,806	208	752	7,721	9,191	3,894	1,369	1,381	931	871	3,505		4,156	4,116
Camp	1,371	226	61	661	733	1,603	449	370	153	179	234	625		623	754
Carson	860	191	28	269	752	989	288	208	313	123	199	494		409	669
Cass	3,472	373	79	1,102	1,772	3,607	986	1,166	580	795	712	1,191		1,978	1,957
Castro	950	231	64	335	741	894	134	120	789	57	176	281		501	830
Chambers	1,421	219	45	438	1,184	1,675	659	595	105	212	423	770		880	984
Cherokee	3,097	558	111	1,734	3,205	4,724	1,525	1,009	378	395	1,039	1,544		1,977	2,542
Childress	1,334	136	69	410	832	1,551	540	321	655	131	210	271		599	532
Clay	1,712	270	80	549	812	1,031	1,016	302	232	103	422	478		659	548
Cochran	864	67	65	451	749	943	176	149	564	75	148	147		558	610
Coke	856	96	65	405	629	827	308	141	237	207	289	138		305	310
Coleman	1,998	170	59	842	1,843	1,984	609	489	206	705	598	161		1,105	986
Collin	4,493	453	174	1,746	2,993	4,578	1,907	1,000	662	402	790	1,151		2,232	1,891
Collingsworth	1,267	90	48	420	761	1,218	203	193	845	120	198	115		286	328
Colorado	2,618	500	55	1,070	1,637	2,602	880	594	120	434	577	931		1,467	1,746
Comal	1,815	338	35	322	1,425	1,797	2,062	657	151	245	481	312		2,181	1,168
Comanche	1,643	224	118	902	2,257	1,822	1,033	221	303	420	328	424		911	807
Concho	548	127	43	327	548	622	211	80	88	136	201	123		255	289
Cooke	3,383	436	98	1,013	2,034	3,757	1,303	821	589	689	719	777		1,681	1,257
Coryell	2,196	99	84	908	1,528	2,401	1,242	576	199	214	416	621		1,274	1,049
Cottle	784	119	71	379	422	412	508	91	408	63	73	65		405	207
Crane	615	96	47	261	756	949	271	85	219	251	239	337		489	744
Crockett	397	80	15	143	437	605	243	138	71	121	359	151		504	481
Crosby	1,094	180	86	420	937	1,790	213	194	1,395	61	134	248		562	914
Culberson	298	86	10	44	151	235	145	91	86	67	142	70		183	129
Dallam	942	143	39	286	341	893	213	190	351	110	181	262		423	473
Dallas	60,995	18,318	1,947	11,903	29,920	44,937	37,781	16,758	6,303	13,582	14,041	16,463		45,633	27,335
Dawson	1,973	182	87	727	2,032	1,853	540	273	945	130	274	408		1,121	1,015
DeWitt	2,519	532	39	641	1,543	1,987	1,225	737	644	312	571	382		1,854	1,369
Deaf Smith	1,199	189	46	237	1,453	1,323	142	74	1,851	75	187	150		660	486
Delta	1,035	81	33	502	698	1,201	596	299	98	92	389	247		934	660
Denton	4,382	922	140	1,471	2,944	4,287	1,650	1,104	672	427	751	1,602		2,439	2,307
Dickens	1,051	93	58	411	818	966	89	84	1,396	35	40	82		399	518
Dimmit	752	430	12	169	360	929	670	579	145	129	191	132		907	521

Table 40: Gubernatorial Races

Democratic Primaries, 1958-1962														
Year	1958				1960		1962						Runoff	
County	Price Daniel	Henry B. Gonzalez	Joe A. Irwin	W. Lee O'Daniel	Jack Cox	Price Daniel	John Connally	Price Daniel	Marshall Formby	Edwin A. Walker	Will Wilson	Don Yarborough	John Connally	Don Yarborough
Donley	936	71	22	227	741	1,025	261	126	419	144	279	91	511	456
Duval	776	3,327	45	202	1,487	2,338	2,641	217	33	48	179	184	3,081	223
Eastland	3,056	368	140	1,804	4,123	1,995	1,522	681	837	944	1,001	562	2,721	2,443
Ector	3,833	974	200	1,253	7,081	5,502	1,984	951	1,142	2,590	2,220	2,110	2,821	3,555
Edwards	474	33	20	101	209	439	272	89	56	139	132	20	483	180
El Paso	10,661	7,648	561	1,037	4,140	8,164	4,090	4,038	875	711	3,554	4,957	7,713	9,435
Ellis	3,155	454	95	801	2,969	5,247	1,755	997	466	574	871	1,039	2,726	2,110
Erath	2,483	356	132	1,121	1,691	2,048	1,432	778	551	487	484	649	1,600	1,460
Falls	1,976	412	112	877	1,957	2,610	1,300	558	180	158	364	670	1,228	1,215
Fannin	3,318	411	112	1,405	1,809	3,588	2,374	877	200	245	755	780	2,962	1,734
Fayette	2,696	479	52	1,269	1,820	2,980	1,540	880	168	338	849	1,078	2,323	2,248
Fisher	1,357	183	117	601	1,112	1,488	493	233	420	113	437	636	533	894
Floyd	1,706	71	83	490	614	1,074	128	147	1,523	119	144	114	866	728
Foard	727	58	52	202	438	550	316	81	96	44	66	51	237	135
Fort Bend	2,712	657	55	956	2,801	4,462	1,376	1,557	231	904	695	1,850	2,047	2,375
Franklin	1,140	124	48	619	611	1,251	487	286	157	91	373	357	579	582
Freestone	2,317	351	84	946	1,404	2,208	635	430	500	307	586	899	1,109	1,373
Frio	1,094	627	31	240	680	1,151	969	441	80	139	194	171	642	264
Gaines	1,528	157	98	759	1,299	1,669	265	186	687	134	316	298	538	670
Galveston	11,557	5,238	988	2,402	9,884	15,757	4,170	5,160	905	1,510	2,129	10,478	8,758	12,202
Garza	746	56	43	373	777	984	184	154	567	107	95	296	514	869
Gillespie	727	82	12	127	140	389	424	113	24	128	138	32	572	137
Glasscock	221	21	13	117	225	204	80	26	57	60	89	31	105	87
Goliad	749	265	15	201	514	832	280	329	54	134	114	107	500	377
Gonzales	2,481	264	61	541	903	1,552	1,867	724	99	214	439	197	1,810	715
Gray	2,978	397	130	1,201	2,997	3,016	776	499	875	449	693	583	1,454	1,561
Grayson	5,550	900	176	1,556	3,932	7,616	3,569	2,133	755	684	1,730	3,156	3,639	4,175
Gregg	6,750	1,209	539	2,388	4,806	5,759	2,762	1,214	1,209	1,916	1,460	1,381	3,483	2,775
Grimes	1,087	147	59	389	784	1,363	576	450	75	280	325	1,262	749	1,294
Guadalupe	1,631	504	23	250	1,275	1,618	1,903	547	87	175	910	233	2,434	1,060
Hale	3,473	337	129	1,160	2,369	2,875	399	322	4,955	302	444	404	2,152	2,421
Hall	1,331	155	54	365	862	890	334	193	889	143	216	176	587	494
Hamilton	1,282	92	46	686	1,561	1,317	640	321	297	320	414	357	325	791
Hansford	634	67	29	148	441	797	164	243	354	208	242	64	244	152
Hardeman	1,391	102	62	345	1,036	1,454	478	296	398	117	211	149	534	305
Hardin	2,817	783	115	1,315	2,393	4,051	831	785	94	402	649	2,486	827	2,264
Harris	78,635	30,917	3,999	15,743	52,508	98,329	31,985	33,483	3,138	19,315	10,862	56,154	54,252	66,218
Harrison	5,320	800	200	1,028	2,857	6,616	1,678	1,600	406	2,227	1,866	1,218	2,862	2,661
Hartley	436	43	15	101	249	534	140	83	280	39	104	81	288	172
Haskell	1,844	239	118	931	1,725	1,866	715	385	573	188	619	421	1,148	1,161
Hays	1,782	426	56	417	1,669	2,346	1,475	1,032	256	182	425	490	1,734	1,317
Hemphill	705	48	8	168	358	666	72	90	346	60	69	55	103	101
Henderson	3,003	743	159	1,632	2,164	4,103	1,589	1,005	569	342	574	1,640	1,575	2,164
Hidalgo	8,261	8,493	244	1,174	9,410	13,417	5,900	2,406	1,816	2,083	921	4,606	7,245	7,375
Hill	4,218	369	128	2,120	2,292	4,128	1,972	1,531	452	359	624	728	2,296	2,004
Hockley	2,930	282	130	1,199	1,974	2,962	564	463	1,568	152	270	496	1,384	1,367
Hood	1,218	183	74	452	914	1,123	348	158	110	178	177	254	402	464
Hopkins	3,006	350	158	1,623	1,774	2,595	547	562	1,885	178	981	428	1,544	1,501
Houston	1,951	391	86	1,444	2,262	2,691	976	669	195	349	830	1,687	1,601	2,809
Howard	2,904	726	232	1,117	2,241	4,565	1,010	767	887	384	922	2,330	1,433	2,894
Hudspeth	389	107	18	58	218	511	222	101	66	79	77	64	250	199
Hunt	4,536	460	104	1,306	2,883	5,061	1,749	1,347	554	613	905	1,030	2,379	1,798
Hutchinson	3,196	781	173	854	3,038	4,336	1,068	697	1,034	746	638	1,450	1,723	2,283
Irion	306	48	13	172	231	238	102	66	57	5	99	113	135	173
Jack	1,349	155	90	606	1,419	1,026	606	188	547	195	284	287	678	582
Jackson	1,913	500	53	744	1,501	2,356	921	550	128	262	459	783	642	870
Jasper	3,255	405	135	1,017	1,893	2,884	969	800	245	259	587	1,646	1,071	2,348
Jeff Davis	184	105	5	21	103	105	42	42	61	37	52	134	123	316
Jefferson	19,868	6,578	1,025	2,162	10,710	19,511	11,313	6,058	2,353	4,009	3,644	15,360	14,472	21,328
Jim Hogg	285	1,109	6	25	503	833	911	343	41	32	80	134	1,275	510
Jim Wells	2,282	3,418	98	729	3,457	3,349	2,843	1,738	384	333	811	1,022	3,404	3,778
Johnson	2,799	472	176	1,044	2,902	4,238	1,647	670	475	945	532	833	1,831	1,697
Jones	2,307	171	115	744	2,481	2,284	676	413	835	239	809	368	1,326	1,438
Karnes	2,635	906	54	576	1,534	2,057	2,702	885	86	155	433	192	2,028	589
Kaufman	3,371	313	69	1,104	2,226	3,629	1,389	999	417	567	534	608	1,449	1,010

Table 40: Gubernatorial Races

| Democratic Primaries, 1958-1962 | | | | | | | | | | | | | | |
| County | 1958 | | | | 1960 | | 1962 | | | | | | Runoff | |
	Price Daniel	Henry B. Gonzalez	Joe A. Irwin	W. Lee O'Daniel	Jack Cox	Price Daniel	John Connally	Price Daniel	Marshall Formby	Edwin A. Walker	Will Wilson	Don Yarborough	John Connally	Don Yarborough
Kendall	393	42	7	60	103	181	215	78	15	94	52	29	256	111
Kenedy	73	10	1	8	30	109	51	36	2	0	11	10	67	20
Kent	588	35	23	221	355	386	70	82	390	20	90	93	249	509
Kerr	2,333	289	62	638	1,498	2,191	798	507	102	1,292	309	151	942	639
Kimble	311	580	13	60	379	322	390	167	93	269	189	87	317	186
King	139	12	7	55	104	87	41	24	113	13	12	18	77	41
Kinney	287	213	10	80	80	207	101	49	8	10	25	11	80	30
Kleberg	1,555	1,399	71	314	1,853	3,287	980	1,167	246	241	364	941	1,666	1,753
Knox	1,199	77	42	347	784	977	651	308	524	73	230	182	1,034	696
La Salle	632	403	23	80	278	349	639	97	8	17	47	25	364	81
Lamar	4,545	600	147	2,110	3,327	6,307	1,459	1,323	588	390	1,392	911	3,127	2,544
Lamb	2,427	287	101	947	2,031	2,604	414	275	1,839	157	309	527	1,330	1,370
Lampasas	1,423	115	49	532	1,099	1,136	1,080	272	183	249	299	406	745	475
Lavaca	2,529	447	49	814	1,788	2,758	1,114	369	110	213	1,050	606	1,651	963
Lee	1,219	274	37	803	1,020	1,173	763	362	59	176	363	667	851	1,231
Leon	1,962	280	50	859	1,137	1,903	707	668	170	215	328	987	1,353	1,859
Liberty	3,552	520	83	1,073	2,969	4,015	1,095	2,067	119	421	817	1,639	1,367	2,823
Limestone	2,892	537	114	1,137	2,034	3,152	1,149	855	288	362	525	1,384	1,540	2,162
Lipscomb	670	46	11	191	273	733	147	251	244	118	162	104	437	291
Live Oak	1,112	306	38	333	874	888	605	390	426	198	238	219	1,107	1,052
Llano	691	136	57	386	918	825	451	148	67	84	154	380	484	560
Loving	45	9	3	38	48	39	7	10	27	12	8	8	9	15
Lubbock	9,906	1,259	400	2,482	7,297	12,502	2,771	2,015	7,925	1,968	1,192	2,848	6,831	6,944
Lynn	1,409	78	50	489	1,248	1,686	314	239	838	132	135	200	1,061	551
Madison	1,145	134	42	543	721	1,258	485	354	47	183	183	56	807	1,059
Marion	1,218	109	31	353	379	831	272	369	63	288	222	192	402	229
Martin	475	51	21	271	453	496	190	78	185	87	152	108	253	219
Mason	664	93	33	403	818	587	325	144	79	195	376	198	305	322
Matagorda	2,225	577	47	657	2,048	2,695	792	1,204	202	647	617	958	1,236	1,092
Maverick	602	1,000	15	82	301	1,368	701	594	39	123	127	205	669	321
McCulloch	1,354	161	67	791	1,150	1,310	927	269	189	278	544	215	771	609
McLennan	14,911	3,096	556	4,377	9,316	19,327	8,640	5,642	1,748	1,350	2,465	6,128	10,236	10,653
McMullen	325	107	6	84	151	206	153	59	39	43	26	19	124	80
Medina	1,555	474	28	297	668	1,122	1,703	577	41	185	291	190	1,626	694
Menard	510	125	22	351	588	591	161	66	46	155	154	58	230	198
Midland	4,028	806	129	934	5,680	5,479	2,173	675	781	1,529	1,456	790	3,598	2,043
Milam	2,917	451	160	2,207	2,295	2,737	1,284	674	210	255	437	1,564	1,395	2,046
Mills	972	77	47	536	1,181	942	436	170	184	302	222	180	399	360
Mitchell	1,562	216	95	759	1,275	1,978	377	235	702	151	281	550	889	1,039
Montague	2,285	255	80	976	2,025	2,713	1,607	531	571	501	566	545	1,035	872
Montgomery	3,148	440	115	1,891	3,361	4,027	1,321	1,360	121	755	684	1,828	1,690	2,451
Moore	1,531	293	77	544	1,085	1,541	270	238	686	159	257	342	624	717
Morris	1,778	275	86	685	1,013	2,938	656	676	396	519	397	1,302	1,788	1,935
Motley	622	66	40	279	353	496	51	43	498	42	23	47	239	198
Nacogdoches	3,995	448	126	1,347	3,642	4,412	1,605	1,167	569	460	1,069	1,739	1,971	2,563
Navarro	3,656	975	129	1,244	3,078	4,858	1,765	1,200	628	460	778	1,204	2,493	2,265
Newton	1,607	219	52	791	1,064	1,819	451	641	61	223	393	805	723	1,459
Nolan	2,447	317	133	998	2,262	2,608	994	531	803	490	720	1,018	1,607	2,246
Nueces	13,058	8,384	598	2,552	12,454	20,574	10,699	7,721	2,010	1,615	3,290	6,110	13,702	13,768
Ochiltree	1,048	117	20	284	664	875	214	245	722	274	225	107	942	513
Oldham	375	68	7	99	261	371	150	98	238	54	103	75	170	139
Orange	5,973	1,130	200	1,411	4,129	6,319	1,991	1,920	305	804	950	4,819	2,802	6,189
Palo Pinto	2,482	397	94	1,096	2,502	2,378	1,072	542	458	380	460	464	1,341	976
Panola	3,265	201	121	922	3,343	2,518	708	767	278	1,600	508	698	1,661	1,452
Parker	2,579	292	123	1,359	3,227	3,769	1,793	836	464	760	846	737	2,584	1,942
Parmer	1,329	68	29	386	906	948	102	117	892	119	114	274	450	535
Pecos	1,385	514	92	430	1,329	1,735	680	545	350	223	483	349	662	524
Polk	1,944	267	72	1,179	1,544	2,204	624	800	113	403	491	1,070	695	1,189
Potter	5,781	1,452	249	947	6,844	9,605	2,928	1,425	2,401	828	1,023	1,958	4,837	3,737
Presidio	424	464	9	42	486	747	270	244	136	113	235	157	212	169
Rains	585	30	20	300	357	638	189	249	74	58	161	115	450	391
Randall	3,093	491	112	458	3,291	4,182	1,113	571	1,737	530	535	746	2,531	1,546
Reagan	797	85	50	266	571	596	293	90	168	107	210	166	419	364
Real	425	56	26	179	259	392	132	65	19	82	67	19	130	51
Red River	2,494	222	73	1,463	2,005	2,191	1,146	1,102	451	195	720	621	1,823	1,722

Table 40: Gubernatorial Races

Democratic Primaries, 1958-1962													
Year	1958				1960		1962						Runoff	
County	Price Daniel	Henry B. Gonzalez	Joe A. Irwin	W. Lee O'Daniel	Jack Cox	Price Daniel	John Connally	Price Daniel	Marshall Formby	Edwin A. Walker	Will Wilson	Don Yarborough	John Connally	Don Yarborough
Reeves	1,366	356	63	351	1,773	1,472	975	535	202	192	560	515	1,041	571
Refugio	1,052	453	25	238	1,094	1,583	676	412	78	81	179	236	584	525
Roberts	201	28	6	48	141	217	52	54	169	45	61	23	93	68
Robertson	1,860	503	80	858	1,290	2,351	893	525	156	192	282	1,490	887	1,858
Rockwall	1,116	98	31	402	678	1,054	442	262	445	104	182	220	397	279
Runnels	1,791	177	126	773	1,711	1,135	480	271	368	373	740	159	937	837
Rusk	5,335	910	146	2,442	3,774	5,266	1,967	1,329	905	846	1,134	2,096	3,270	4,232
Sabine	1,440	110	61	583	956	1,665	344	396	76	154	353	593	400	1,101
San Augustine	1,306	134	107	645	1,197	1,525	389	447	65	250	373	694	768	1,496
San Jacinto	375	124	14	282	633	838	282	299	23	157	158	585	581	1,164
San Patricio	3,163	1,677	144	825	3,827	3,414	2,281	1,413	648	261	833	1,382	2,686	3,384
San Saba	1,111	141	101	622	645	693	735	248	147	257	315	419	901	1,012
Schleicher	451	46	31	275	263	375	156	91	63	109	112	114	188	231
Scurry	2,537	291	169	1,237	2,249	3,061	616	439	1,333	288	583	1,173	1,305	2,498
Shackelford	834	78	24	422	1,114	413	146	73	254	135	211	63	317	255
Shelby	3,655	442	211	1,711	2,236	4,808	1,388	837	434	873	718	1,065	2,231	2,563
Sherman	525	67	13	73	347	547	106	141	201	156	101	37	190	116
Smith	8,286	1,923	297	2,643	7,038	9,853	3,327	1,947	1,720	758	1,582	2,204	4,866	4,526
Somervell	485	71	65	385	450	518	219	157	76	107	116	144	179	198
Starr	921	2,796	5	35	219	3,419	3,181	58	18	43	161	143	1,716	149
Stephens	1,571	173	49	667	2,658	613	811	251	290	244	514	292	1,055	952
Sterling	285	21	14	81	232	192	65	21	67	25	29	26	77	60
Stonewall	745	65	35	375	672	720	130	117	431	53	158	259	149	426
Sutton	351	155	9	66	422	522	175	229	82	126	106	59	464	207
Swisher	1,241	430	557	108	841	1,454	157	287	826	56	191	579	349	868
Tarrant	36,483	9,896	1,632	7,540	36,189	39,814	28,957	9,239	5,985	8,542	6,050	11,910	31,296	20,221
Taylor	6,870	769	306	2,191	8,186	7,039	3,045	1,789	3,100	1,486	2,588	1,295	4,943	3,640
Terrell	303	75	11	66	228	337	86	73	39	105	185	180	83	176
Terry	1,804	230	119	704	1,851	1,444	469	218	746	125	211	472	989	862
Throckmorton	588	85	47	303	933	438	413	75	126	53	129	133	389	273
Titus	2,551	363	146	1,089	1,862	3,614	790	910	521	412	656	1,609	1,330	1,795
Tom Green	5,358	1,379	171	2,612	3,992	4,587	2,359	1,191	1,061	1,398	2,108	2,229	3,234	3,896
Travis	17,971	7,428	717	4,310	14,881	25,971	13,027	8,615	2,378	1,747	4,778	9,742	17,406	17,729
Trinity	1,164	235	42	952	1,365	1,171	405	427	54	172	463	880	487	1,316
Tyler	2,073	164	42	730	1,209	1,588	534	494	95	245	509	852	977	1,447
Upshur	3,234	434	129	1,806	2,140	4,078	1,233	796	473	617	660	1,522	2,299	2,901
Upton	766	121	61	394	670	874	342	155	212	210	340	241	690	822
Uvalde	2,099	546	76	576	1,063	1,624	1,169	646	154	333	519	226	1,462	791
Val Verde	1,375	904	18	129	870	2,131	1,178	563	74	131	186	239	1,458	842
Van Zandt	2,845	489	142	1,667	1,159	2,013	1,476	986	400	378	738	1,100	1,656	1,940
Victoria	3,410	1,323	114	1,126	3,777	5,992	1,979	1,677	170	438	624	1,108	1,716	1,714
Walker	2,110	520	42	739	1,577	2,150	661	680	69	406	336	818	977	1,353
Waller	1,102	231	21	433	883	1,935	421	643	102	347	259	735	974	1,408
Ward	1,584	265	72	563	2,010	1,689	847	345	240	471	542	596	1,164	1,187
Washington	1,960	185	29	749	1,730	2,899	804	554	60	215	333	688	957	1,169
Webb	2,540	7,670	34	224	3,612	5,983	4,623	816	35	45	247	496	4,624	1,966
Wharton	3,911	1,147	115	1,346	2,077	3,976	1,447	929	153	395	691	1,813	2,079	2,365
Wheeler	1,552	105	42	514	589	1,258	197	253	708	183	217	177	467	452
Wichita	8,902	2,356	355	1,810	9,898	11,151	5,883	2,347	1,267	532	2,118	2,873	6,442	5,277
Wilbarger	3,076	226	112	751	1,173	1,553	733	542	879	430	390	252	1,114	665
Willacy	1,274	584	25	264	1,239	1,891	998	528	302	344	208	458	1,203	881
Williamson	3,511	488	122	1,598	2,463	3,122	2,584	1,231	233	326	681	1,334	2,516	2,512
Wilson	2,014	883	57	655	1,346	2,376	3,631	350	31	103	169	144	3,237	627
Winkler	1,096	161	61	514	1,479	1,395	458	180	631	408	345	516	833	1,200
Wise	2,350	424	149	1,139	1,928	2,314	1,289	514	467	447	491	533	1,895	1,621
Wood	3,220	448	148	1,211	1,548	2,834	964	720	569	231	646	936	1,662	1,923
Yoakum	1,135	92	63	560	1,059	1,359	330	208	618	185	247	487	664	953
Young	2,493	270	91	646	1,492	1,852	1,073	305	356	290	345	488	892	660
Zapata	72	826	0	4	177	346	762	142	5	22	8	27	488	62
Zavala	935	566	25	181	496	781	724	306	70	78	260	145	672	434
Official	799,107	33,643			619,834		431,498		139,094		171,617		565,174	
Totals		245,969		238,767		908,992		248,524		138,387		317,986		538,924
Unofficial	**799,107**	**33,643**			**619,834**		**431,498**		**139,094**		**171,617**		**565,169**	
Totals		**245,969**		**238,797**		**908,992**		**248,524**		**138,387**		**317,986**		**538,924**

Table 41: Gubernatorial Races

| | Democratic Primaries, 1964-1968 | | | | | | | | | | | | | |
| Year | 1964 | | | | 1966 | | | 1968 (Part) | | | | | | |
County	John Connally	Don Yarborough	M.T. Banks	Johnnie M. Hackworthe	John Connally	Stanley C. Woods	Johnnie M. Hackworthe	Preston Smith	Pat O'Daniel	John Hill	Waggoner Carr	Eugene Locke	Dolph Briscoe	Edward L. Whittenbrg
Anderson	6,544	1,933	117	71	3,663	1,073	112	1,541	370	766	1,187	835	775	67
Andrews	2,226	1,101	95	25	2,007	997	77	911	108	165	400	171	238	6
Angelina	7,301	7,049	84	33	7,710	3,453	256	2,325	316	1,254	1,288	764	1,247	99
Aransas	1,248	890	16	4	715	256	35	419	33	232	248	406	412	15
Archer	1,343	552	23	10	1,507	403	49	454	96	385	133	161	400	5
Armstrong	638	143	18	6	570	113	16	95	42	47	144	118	171	13
Atascosa	2,447	620	35	17	2,236	614	59	437	118	106	253	291	2,235	28
Austin	1,710	678	27	29	2,461	343	115	994	115	151	332	196	459	61
Bailey	885	419	44	8	1,066	232	31	566	37	79	451	117	119	202
Bandera	1,157	359	41	20	1,269	327	36	193	20	43	92	180	770	7
Bastrop	2,504	1,423	19	28	2,566	779	86	611	90	297	652	360	828	16
Baylor	961	263	13	4	1,543	284	34	753	101	139	248	187	305	11
Bee	2,510	1,275	22	45	2,958	739	84	472	95	190	264	277	1,225	19
Bell	9,402	4,000	51	53	6,205	1,661	138	2,741	363	1,901	2,326	1,261	1,325	84
Bexar	49,793	31,056	952	1,256	62,603	22,300	3,019	16,103	1,567	3,362	6,525	11,948	18,643	853
Blanco	445	149	7	0	605	156	9	134	17	33	72	69	326	2
Borden	260	115	7	6	313	118	9	134	11	11	51	27	115	2
Bosque	2,279	554	34	35	2,081	496	87	1,009	139	155	576	215	451	38
Bowie	9,146	3,529	348	99	3,848	1,500	144	3,963	751	1,022	1,374	566	752	85
Brazoria	11,027	5,606	138	64	6,770	3,023	141	2,878	379	2,096	2,133	1,437	1,660	304
Brazos	6,400	2,365	67	47	6,919	1,537	163	1,392	153	1,176	2,223	1,952	1,486	139
Brewster	1,338	420	12	19	950	361	16	263	30	63	152	184	501	2
Briscoe	918	283	18	1	428	73	16	194	49	55	194	79	265	19
Brooks	1,687	642	37	8	1,531	252	68	98	16	57	99	193	316	9
Brown	4,017	1,201	58	37	3,094	655	61	1,727	231	915	1,017	604	1,469	55
Burleson	1,918	984	29	33	2,306	480	130	536	60	133	390	138	236	14
Burnet	1,921	902	13	8	1,293	398	38	507	75	349	605	355	1,135	14
Caldwell	2,565	772	20	21	2,323	546	31	695	114	228	539	352	1,499	27
Calhoun	2,194	1,286	16	17	2,656	733	104	877	67	475	410	599	455	43
Callahan	1,711	712	32	10	1,820	551	73	664	203	225	220	282	561	28
Cameron	8,881	6,090	165	421	7,406	2,820	852	2,099	232	684	1,115	3,565	1,560	186
Camp	1,443	619	52	11	1,456	483	53	627	91	112	246	130	124	85
Carson	1,202	490	28	10	1,029	322	19	158	58	147	256	214	176	20
Cass	3,228	1,052	71	36	3,273	907	142	1,139	83	177	314	214	142	16
Castro	897	482	18	3	946	363	44	476	70	123	443	168	392	27
Chambers	1,863	1,231	48	14	1,204	450	59	658	109	424	347	150	269	35
Cherokee	5,532	2,777	100	34	2,683	1,205	173	1,826	192	1,104	785	585	1,002	61
Childress	1,622	976	24	10	1,360	483	57	814	181	117	191	144	217	16
Clay	1,864	722	32	12	1,793	607	47	526	141	320	244	201	341	6
Cochran	1,089	378	38	9	1,053	227	40	664	51	47	352	69	138	129
Coke	551	132	18	6	934	191	21	288	44	70	141	86	307	7
Coleman	2,383	995	75	11	2,310	721	81	699	242	248	354	370	244	24
Collin	6,645	1,311	61	37	5,475	967	200	2,824	750	756	2,992	2,040	725	133
Collingsworth	1,291	373	18	13	1,257	185	25	470	104	127	312	117	253	23
Colorado	3,480	1,322	43	31	2,621	506	102	899	136	767	420	453	916	91
Comal	2,475	841	14	7	2,273	534	42	894	32	70	279	253	599	10
Comanche	2,494	679	40	17	1,795	485	63	964	177	220	732	540	473	47
Concho	951	193	16	10	577	126	24	173	43	63	95	63	427	11
Cooke	4,980	997	69	26	4,513	874	76	1,125	262	651	842	565	370	44
Coryell	2,151	733	18	12	2,924	720	66	1,178	129	335	754	240	1,201	34
Cottle	1,071	251	14	6	935	157	9	431	60	49	149	87	166	4
Crane	937	390	34	6	665	249	23	292	63	67	162	129	208	4
Crockett	831	178	20	9	1,000	163	33	91	18	47	110	55	633	4
Crosby	1,693	631	22	6	1,689	322	31	1,209	39	40	539	119	207	22
Culberson	539	193	12	7	540	134	11	214	11	99	80	38	195	4
Dallam	811	298	19	10	999	260	33	142	37	264	282	145	128	27
Dallas	99,086	21,551	2,164	744	61,751	12,877	1,123	24,894	3,461	7,850	33,853	42,679	6,250	2,210
Dawson	2,929	897	58	12	1,851	459	56	1,666	77	72	643	106	205	6
DeWitt	3,857	901	46	19	2,330	526	47	787	77	206	581	196	816	19
Deaf Smith	1,909	557	140	10	1,961	374	50	841	66	244	451	536	586	36
Delta	1,373	277	29	8	1,246	221	29	477	109	253	434	131	243	14
Denton	6,534	1,912	44	16	2,459	621	96	2,187	368	953	2,001	2,313	1,037	107
Dickens	1,057	474	25	7	585	181	14	606	79	29	343	107	122	14
Dimmit	1,268	255	12	4	1,481	367	44	34	6	14	5	51	614	3

Table 41: Gubernatorial Races

| | Democratic Primaries, 1964-1968 | | | | | | | | | | | | | |
| Year | 1964 | | | | 1966 | | | 1968 (Part) | | | | | | |
County	John Connally	Don Yarborough	M.T. Banks	Johnnie M. Hackworthe	John Connally	Stanley C. Woods	Johnnie M. Hackworthe	Preston Smith	Pat O'Daniel	John Hill	Waggoner Carr	Eugene Locke	Dolph Briscoe	Edward L. Whittenbrg
Donley	1,319	483	30	13	1,056	228	33	346	79	119	289	184	258	23
Duval	3,985	232	1	11	3,789	38	36	818	8	19	41	2,609	226	0
Eastland	3,935	1,686	79	49	3,347	949	114	1,572	289	538	641	379	551	81
Ector	6,517	2,784	105	103	5,222	1,966	360	2,893	592	885	2,156	1,324	858	57
Edwards	626	69	11	4	559	95	20	71	12	7	38	10	416	1
El Paso	4,986	1,109	37	12	15,025	6,830	1,936	7,152	389	3,196	3,391	3,060	2,104	576
Ellis	18,584	7,872	394	534	4,210	793	123	1,895	283	280	1,730	714	680	74
Erath	3,546	740	68	26	3,101	624	81	1,464	277	507	933	333	522	77
Falls	3,111	1,060	32	27	2,270	497	65	1,022	223	260	834	779	996	72
Fannin	5,162	1,352	57	23	3,021	681	88	1,202	369	307	1,855	512	343	89
Fayette	2,878	1,234	37	51	2,460	550	205	1,105	144	496	716	474	780	33
Fisher	1,714	683	18	2	1,611	373	46	713	115	116	168	220	406	22
Floyd	1,812	574	32	17	585	136	12	861	75	51	608	131	235	16
Foard	379	120	6	3	539	103	14	381	37	43	107	96	180	3
Fort Bend	5,670	2,322	86	42	5,426	1,378	211	1,993	219	459	697	552	1,790	131
Franklin	1,411	384	33	12	1,336	293	43	578	120	157	350	163	190	4
Freestone	2,807	890	39	39	2,750	556	79	791	183	431	749	282	387	39
Frio	1,677	455	21	13	1,509	268	27	85	23	33	97	63	1,585	10
Gaines	1,750	648	59	32	1,000	317	39	1,535	99	76	563	133	198	12
Galveston	13,872	9,422	529	363	15,284	6,489	524	5,005	522	2,449	3,344	3,264	1,208	567
Garza	1,163	547	27	19	1,078	310	36	682	91	25	331	114	177	24
Gillespie	671	96	2	0	772	125	17	276	8	26	87	65	275	6
Glasscock	179	40	4	8	118	35	4	76	6	7	63	57	98	2
Goliad	673	356	13	4	535	161	11	188	27	56	191	153	247	5
Gonzales	2,543	469	35	8	1,490	278	12	835	105	223	254	182	2,079	16
Gray	2,151	992	42	22	2,995	1,157	139	634	175	630	1,043	678	575	137
Grayson	8,603	2,644	97	53	6,852	2,159	235	3,019	597	824	2,807	1,780	617	44
Gregg	8,630	3,167	451	216	8,530	2,236	364	3,049	346	2,739	695	1,083	563	163
Grimes	2,236	1,021	17	21	2,474	527	86	650	120	177	400	239	596	41
Guadalupe	2,142	737	24	6	2,597	594	79	866	111	223	512	507	1,352	26
Hale	4,360	1,644	82	116	2,682	661	61	2,193	157	408	1,761	469	549	61
Hall	1,659	524	24	15	956	165	19	454	100	105	375	216	248	10
Hamilton	2,355	574	22	29	1,816	440	103	718	13	180	574	191	493	31
Hansford	384	94	5	4	798	120	17	183	22	142	257	97	139	23
Hardeman	1,948	503	36	10	1,336	260	25	1,011	106	94	197	188	218	11
Hardin	3,079	4,132	91	23	3,944	2,588	177	1,312	209	586	1,387	507	581	24
Harris	104,101	61,698	1,344	580	96,663	44,788	2,263	52,220	3,063	20,958	19,736	22,181	8,804	5,559
Harrison	5,791	1,321	202	73	6,342	1,292	131	3,013	355	668	1,107	1,372	452	32
Hartley	413	96	5	1	655	117	12	99	14	120	164	120	120	9
Haskell	2,270	1,115	27	8	2,053	648	87	1,057	206	209	381	358	445	21
Hays	3,210	1,264	32	11	3,061	657	58	863	60	382	371	390	1,068	19
Hemphill	845	228	12	5	679	108	27	122	31	115	182	94	151	12
Henderson	4,742	1,876	67	51	4,389	1,903	171	973	236	317	1,272	426	653	64
Hidalgo	12,564	8,588	779	230	14,761	4,656	224	6,218	444	624	1,500	4,184	4,368	403
Hill	5,057	1,099	34	20	3,048	362	32	1,447	225	312	885	425	519	37
Hockley	3,190	1,005	49	19	2,450	621	114	1,679	105	142	1,066	247	340	577
Hood	1,252	314	20	7	1,342	368	36	369	59	145	323	115	229	14
Hopkins	4,096	1,037	67	29	3,475	740	84	1,415	268	686	1,294	597	306	60
Houston	2,783	2,443	47	17	3,200	950	80	924	198	1,104	668	336	540	130
Howard	4,665	2,600	91	75	3,638	1,658	100	1,134	121	203	1,635	663	656	26
Hudspeth	446	214	23	4	455	95	19	156	11	135	70	69	113	6
Hunt	7,257	1,392	118	47	4,252	1,190	180	2,039	421	1,169	3,030	959	646	81
Hutchinson	3,403	2,216	89	33	2,624	1,763	72	730	147	357	668	502	327	59
Irion	412	63	12	10	391	126	12	43	23	37	55	18	222	3
Jack	1,526	538	33	11	1,571	336	40	611	116	218	264	163	437	14
Jackson	2,498	880	47	20	2,890	647	124	666	147	424	519	303	1,033	46
Jasper	2,911	2,599	66	15	3,265	1,680	108	1,106	103	321	907	251	536	26
Jeff Davis	149	79	3	0	356	83	10	67	0	34	16	32	90	5
Jefferson	29,232	24,381	3,019	341	17,469	10,319	483	6,894	530	2,729	4,504	2,674	2,751	228
Jim Hogg	1,037	591	4	13	829	125	19	215	5	48	62	131	382	7
Jim Wells	5,853	2,606	66	53	5,809	1,269	163	889	87	354	686	720	1,874	37
Johnson	6,275	1,402	83	42	2,698	798	65	2,044	370	585	2,284	1,023	713	90
Jones	3,306	1,026	30	17	2,375	439	53	1,377	291	327	358	451	885	26
Karnes	2,944	670	26	6	2,095	641	55	633	117	134	388	353	1,515	13
Kaufman	5,074	948	43	24	5,014	910	145	1,642	359	596	1,553	801	492	60

Table 41: Gubernatorial Races

	Democratic Primaries, 1964-1968													
Year	1964				1966			1968 (Part)						
County	John Connally	Don Yarborough	M.T. Banks	Johnnie M. Hackworthe	John Connally	Stanley C. Woods	Johnnie M. Hackworthe	Preston Smith	Pat O'Daniel	John Hill	Waggoner Carr	Eugene Locke	Dolph Briscoe	Edward L. Whittenbrg
Kendall	317	45	2	2	251	35	1	78	7	7	47	65	253	0
Kenedy	100	8	0	0	98	8	7	17	0	3	5	40	65	0
Kent	480	242	7	6	581	167	25	259	37	19	98	58	154	5
Kerr	1,895	415	33	29	1,826	362	56	714	107	234	446	391	1,234	19
Kimble	1,009	170	15	5	811	166	27	335	48	31	66	48	637	5
King	183	41	3	1	173	34	3	109	28	2	26	26	41	1
Kinney	369	100	8	6	438	96	20	32	19	9	27	60	388	3
Kleberg	3,258	1,896	21	32	3,739	1,047	137	800	34	396	374	389	1,013	20
Knox	1,141	300	14	6	1,192	253	28	774	66	105	207	95	272	13
La Salle	896	158	4	7	760	183	27	56	4	32	40	30	499	4
Lamar	6,247	1,564	176	65	4,960	1,182	189	1,726	624	374	2,854	472	329	55
Lamb	2,709	1,056	47	17	2,314	587	96	1,866	103	76	1,326	341	569	124
Lampasas	1,495	608	28	15	1,136	299	34	567	104	172	500	187	766	26
Lavaca	3,949	773	34	28	2,639	655	102	1,285	81	268	501	266	799	23
Lee	1,192	857	12	11	1,358	497	81	333	37	109	214	74	337	11
Leon	1,851	916	22	15	949	198	207	517	98	162	410	202	590	23
Liberty	4,174	2,467	88	33	3,164	1,395	99	2,173	383	755	825	413	644	98
Limestone	3,311	1,377	41	24	2,733	652	93	841	136	176	884	264	870	27
Lipscomb	737	189	23	6	707	118	9	99	39	49	207	51	95	26
Live Oak	1,662	542	18	11	1,405	424	59	337	110	83	231	181	1,161	10
Llano	1,204	662	31	8	961	355	22	410	45	189	357	196	763	9
Loving	39	28	4	2	46	15	2	18	1	3	9	5	29	0
Lubbock	15,447	5,031	245	42	9,129	2,581	172	14,935	464	868	7,055	2,116	1,357	303
Lynn	2,021	433	24	24	1,680	294	81	1,501	39	52	574	136	182	11
Madison	1,370	487	40	18	1,326	321	38	363	105	194	360	134	533	32
Marion	1,223	284	59	27	1,388	304	36	529	78	85	164	145	52	6
Martin	619	158	8	3	409	109	21	229	24	14	121	45	126	1
Mason	813	310	18	8	668	165	13	222	46	57	149	73	919	3
Matagorda	3,559	1,429	47	22	3,371	716	84	1,408	212	867	898	390	817	103
Maverick	1,958	506	21	14	2,154	334	60	143	24	28	106	635	931	5
McCulloch	1,657	579	34	11	1,477	346	34	635	71	87	257	162	1,017	13
McLennan	19,501	8,219	145	96	9,919	3,733	213	5,659	686	2,277	5,924	3,681	3,196	320
McMullen	223	79	4	4	243	101	15	46	24	14	57	25	259	3
Medina	1,853	462	17	5	1,821	314	44	320	40	28	114	154	1,722	19
Menard	320	91	9	2	601	130	24	119	11	35	73	26	244	0
Midland	6,562	2,170	83	54	4,562	1,231	87	1,856	441	604	2,205	1,694	1,497	127
Milam	2,870	1,861	22	18	2,678	907	106	1,030	174	397	914	309	953	26
Mills	1,368	499	25	16	744	213	40	311	87	80	326	112	647	16
Mitchell	1,475	483	17	1	1,779	480	32	711	89	51	333	339	495	14
Montague	2,919	1,143	42	85	2,461	557	125	1,307	327	311	665	460	691	19
Montgomery	5,122	2,278	186	45	6,050	1,808	316	2,468	683	1,520	1,048	745	784	153
Moore	2,042	1,059	61	15	2,100	711	88	559	123	517	821	410	357	97
Morris	2,547	771	101	28	2,272	534	61	1,037	182	226	367	319	195	18
Motley	735	232	8	10	718	168	17	432	36	38	229	59	94	10
Nacogdoches	5,300	2,977	79	31	5,122	1,288	222	1,375	313	1,182	691	397	1,778	66
Navarro	4,620	1,443	42	18	4,595	1,114	132	1,281	511	642	2,128	1,035	805	114
Newton	1,403	1,346	41	13	2,103	808	96	709	77	181	565	159	344	10
Nolan	3,705	1,049	33	19	2,780	981	60	1,009	190	478	438	575	849	21
Nueces	21,894	13,329	142	136	20,715	5,431	1,876	5,007	406	5,118	2,252	5,002	7,546	563
Ochiltree	725	181	21	7	706	138	18	367	45	103	218	121	122	27
Oldham	352	107	6	5	441	69	3	67	19	54	107	112	166	20
Orange	6,405	5,245	173	91	5,297	3,391	206	3,515	224	652	3,279	1,065	714	73
Palo Pinto	3,670	790	51	32	2,921	640	66	1,407	299	934	1,264	549	607	67
Panola	3,153	903	51	101	2,395	728	117	1,249	204	238	525	186	1,227	20
Parker	4,654	1,201	85	20	3,197	920	96	1,383	338	1,352	1,228	470	493	75
Parmer	1,001	451	36	11	1,059	229	31	701	65	89	389	102	129	71
Pecos	1,725	564	55	26	994	275	22	505	79	113	320	216	885	14
Polk	2,472	1,605	46	46	2,538	769	130	1,169	169	522	648	258	309	33
Potter	8,145	3,998	154	32	4,004	1,177	60	1,097	347	1,335	2,332	2,584	1,093	280
Presidio	1,017	368	21	14	995	176	34	254	15	57	134	167	274	41
Rains	870	184	18	5	718	257	33	147	51	155	179	69	38	12
Randall	4,069	1,281	60	21	2,093	526	25	1,065	199	960	1,616	1,778	1,013	213
Reagan	766	242	23	10	536	154	16	195	23	116	228	81	286	7
Real	391	50	5	2	167	28	3	56	9	9	23	27	448	0
Red River	3,537	937	73	39	2,605	519	75	1,346	321	309	1,045	224	303	24

Table 41: Gubernatorial Races

| | Democratic Primaries, 1964-1968 | | | | | | | | | | | | | |
| County | 1964 | | | | 1966 | | | 1968 (Part) | | | | | | |
	John Connally	Don Yarborough	M.T. Banks	Johnnie M. Hackworthe	John Connally	Stanley C. Woods	Johnnie M. Hackworthe	Preston Smith	Pat O'Daniel	John Hill	Waggoner Carr	Eugene Locke	Dolph Briscoe	Edward L. Whittenbrg
Reeves	2,218	600	49	32	1,948	355	37	730	63	115	398	242	828	26
Refugio	1,450	520	18	10	1,207	338	36	481	52	270	310	303	819	10
Roberts	161	39	4	1	347	48	7	53	5	32	116	61	44	6
Robertson	1,746	1,215	21	8	2,069	624	75	720	145	261	565	338	600	27
Rockwall	1,359	212	17	3	1,139	170	24	379	56	754	311	101	66	9
Runnels	2,439	712	68	25	1,270	247	42	1,121	113	160	279	240	921	10
Rusk	6,203	2,052	164	402	5,155	2,011	242	1,337	233	2,338	680	453	1,382	59
Sabine	1,207	1,153	68	21	1,426	448	88	987	93	102	433	89	309	9
San Augustine	1,188	1,038	32	33	1,670	492	99	726	101	191	235	97	383	39
San Jacinto	1,134	975	30	40	893	459	71	386	132	236	246	127	102	18
San Patricio	4,725	2,951	61	35	3,981	1,236	120	850	153	894	662	491	2,256	32
San Saba	1,531	718	19	8	1,071	255	33	381	55	89	401	163	780	31
Schleicher	509	124	10	2	683	179	34	83	14	49	157	39	419	1
Scurry	3,250	1,440	79	28	2,974	943	117	1,325	118	91	526	651	617	26
Shackelford	1,031	432	19	7	1,164	248	35	332	70	525	86	92	175	7
Shelby	4,440	1,959	219	122	4,105	1,177	209	1,925	365	963	655	285	625	21
Sherman	447	163	21	7	598	88	16	102	24	92	223	82	121	39
Smith	11,153	4,201	310	85	8,539	3,063	264	2,217	386	2,249	3,171	1,570	1,859	191
Somervell	769	197	10	9	541	120	20	136	50	28	219	100	130	11
Starr	3,581	537	44	5	2,985	130	42	261	13	24	66	1,105	654	18
Stephens	2,187	617	36	11	1,803	347	34	833	174	430	394	294	506	14
Sterling	140	34	0	0	106	20	3	49	12	5	41	30	180	0
Stonewall	847	499	13	8	897	217	26	449	62	28	88	88	234	4
Sutton	454	54	11	1	310	54	3	159	8	31	76	45	235	5
Swisher	1,553	863	25	8	915	229	32	813	97	162	466	214	293	25
Tarrant	62,265	14,697	538	231	36,924	12,814	678	15,776	1,609	11,780	15,995	13,545	6,910	986
Taylor	12,086	3,151	125	34	8,827	1,707	101	5,713	1,186	1,365	2,273	2,929	2,104	235
Terrell	269	104	7	1	271	76	3	46	12	12	41	21	233	6
Terry	3,031	827	39	11	2,207	523	74	1,561	108	104	1,019	422	289	68
Throckmorton	911	353	13	3	869	199	26	298	55	154	113	108	291	5
Titus	2,731	787	52	30	1,814	388	50	1,422	326	248	675	412	351	37
Tom Green	8,905	1,712	117	39	7,196	1,705	237	2,163	302	1,154	2,293	1,384	3,895	125
Travis	29,899	14,633	211	85	23,794	7,885	362	9,816	539	7,939	6,502	7,055	8,379	435
Trinity	1,278	1,311	38	18	2,014	587	82	647	113	285	264	154	173	34
Tyler	1,589	1,203	51	27	1,433	867	59	737	168	272	687	213	411	21
Upshur	3,836	1,766	145	126	2,565	1,155	104	876	194	658	322	279	539	33
Upton	793	334	31	8	726	265	40	310	57	87	194	187	404	10
Uvalde	3,019	600	62	27	1,802	639	67	97	43	18	50	89	4,106	5
Val Verde	2,616	877	15	19	2,699	622	66	342	44	92	277	422	1,655	22
Van Zandt	3,861	994	60	39	2,987	1,508	87	842	337	349	1,583	429	458	62
Victoria	5,454	2,043	63	34	5,655	1,471	147	1,702	162	1,367	1,255	1,095	1,526	55
Walker	2,698	1,095	49	18	2,274	535	59	1,474	106	709	450	308	277	43
Waller	1,448	642	38	35	2,315	353	52	556	90	183	258	138	314	71
Ward	1,884	786	49	17	1,777	743	57	1,143	90	152	611	264	435	19
Washington	1,288	382	11	14	2,007	282	54	867	36	356	188	124	346	17
Webb	5,813	1,646	62	16	8,082	446	55	277	16	92	120	416	4,488	31
Wharton	5,263	2,006	61	33	4,738	896	225	1,239	85	932	615	467	855	55
Wheeler	1,093	339	40	7	1,571	300	37	324	113	175	552	209	271	44
Wichita	12,007	5,693	118	57	7,325	2,418	175	4,365	574	2,550	1,633	1,994	1,578	148
Wilbarger	3,047	1,099	51	24	2,561	398	39	1,403	131	185	510	532	481	22
Willacy	2,110	723	28	20	2,531	520	61	493	49	66	253	530	967	28
Williamson	4,786	2,041	36	43	4,646	1,224	165	2,320	122	477	1,023	440	1,865	35
Wilson	3,029	938	12	15	3,025	969	120	417	189	290	213	919	1,590	20
Winkler	2,093	1,091	77	39	1,320	505	50	918	92	416	393	265	267	25
Wise	3,057	701	61	16	978	323	37	1,085	247	605	790	334	562	40
Wood	3,430	1,066	78	32	2,467	843	62	925	193	864	1,022	579	396	48
Yoakum	1,464	614	38	14	1,488	597	46	1,041	107	60	534	86	100	43
Young	2,710	929	57	16	2,402	416	47	763	103	1,371	316	256	307	12
Zapata	1,103	108	9	2	957	37	1	597	0	4	9	16	52	0
Zavala	1,769	1,199	15	14	1,514	725	89	84	12	29	49	48	1,216	6
Official	1,125,884		22,047		932,641		31,105	47,912		257,543			225,686	
Totals		471,411		10,955		291,651			386,875		154,908	218,118		22,957
Unofficial	**1,125,884**		**22,047**		**932,641**		**31,105**	**47,912**		**257,543**			**225,686**	
Totals		**471,411**		**10,955**		**291,651**			**386,875**		**154,908**	**218,118**		**22,957**

Table 42: Gubernatorial Races

| | Democratic Primaries, 1968-1972 | | | | | | | | | | | | | |
| County | 1968 (Cont.) | | | Runoff | | 1972 | | | | | | | Runoff | |
	Don Yarborough	Alfonso Veloz	Johnnie M. Hackworthe	Preston Smith	Don Yarborough	Ben Barnes	Dolph Briscoe	Frances Farenthold	Robert E. Looney	William H. Posey	Preston Smith	Gordon F. Wills	Dolph Briscoe	Frances Farenthold
Anderson	1,403	14	18	2,777	2,620	1,550	4,628	900	22	29	987	42	5,638	1,997
Andrews	619	3	1	1,002	459	373	1,305	534	6	14	384	10	1,149	679
Angelina	4,085	15	29	3,209	3,682	2,329	5,773	5,606	148	50	1,615	67	7,703	6,897
Aransas	726	7	4	862	840	301	1,235	838	6	13	233	12	1,134	752
Archer	194	2	2	965	546	239	1,237	272	5	7	210	7	1,019	519
Armstrong	86	0	2	254	153	153	539	97	1	2	84	2	436	117
Atascosa	806	81	13	1,732	848	712	3,067	678	20	18	353	12	3,529	1,474
Austin	511	7	20	1,144	493	565	2,051	645	10	19	379	15	2,066	1,207
Bailey	198	3	1	1,048	327	357	780	117	2	0	207	2	994	300
Bandera	64	1	2	676	141	154	1,447	275	11	44	167	4	1,586	553
Bastrop	659	3	8	1,185	887	578	2,448	656	12	9	447	13	2,567	1,070
Baylor	176	1	3	1,007	308	206	1,227	289	6	14	269	7	1,185	549
Bee	1,141	23	5	1,589	1,835	550	2,394	1,597	22	16	419	29	2,407	1,345
Bell	2,179	26	44	5,575	4,666	2,765	9,305	3,854	56	135	1,324	167	10,217	6,468
Bexar	26,604	2,047	293	39,292	36,288	23,962	53,599	31,501	1,110	2,101	2,608	1,711	72,207	57,218
Blanco	45	0	3	373	109	68	573	105	1	4	43	1	641	166
Borden	55	0	1	260	73	49	256	50	0	1	52	3	267	93
Bosque	359	4	6	1,339	703	653	2,409	449	8	22	259	14	2,288	817
Bowie	2,715	19	31	5,450	3,119	2,836	5,686	2,217	89	75	4,019	79	6,891	5,098
Brazoria	4,629	32	56	5,376	6,547	2,960	8,408	9,873	82	124	1,556	110	9,340	12,336
Brazos	2,848	20	20	4,331	4,378	1,684	6,486	4,209	18	29	630	19	6,634	5,471
Brewster	315	70	5	567	277	203	822	262	3	10	283	7	729	368
Briscoe	190	4	4	459	288	204	534	72	2	7	162	3	470	150
Brooks	474	44	3	422	960	661	781	1,363	22	17	234	20	1,081	2,213
Brown	1,268	15	41	3,973	1,866	3,502	3,350	601	4	6	453	9	3,972	1,133
Burleson	536	5	133	745	747	692	1,571	853	11	19	548	12	1,992	1,731
Burnet	258	8	3	1,504	711	504	2,620	659	16	9	231	5	2,349	924
Caldwell	563	18	8	1,798	985	559	2,748	726	8	11	380	11	2,780	989
Calhoun	1,753	18	9	2,190	2,530	690	2,213	2,291	10	20	307	12	2,536	2,751
Callahan	350	0	1	1,553	796	424	1,688	290	2	7	310	9	1,775	590
Cameron	4,366	365	286	5,957	5,502	5,532	9,937	4,692	142	117	2,834	107	11,369	10,617
Camp	739	2	5	991	964	513	1,237	398	32	9	494	7	1,608	873
Carson	307	3	0	426	420	375	813	245	0	7	214	2	857	489
Cass	699	2	6	1,331	746	1,282	3,119	853	30	26	1,513	27	2,681	1,479
Castro	524	20	7	572	591	487	1,177	203	3	3	178	6	1,104	439
Chambers	496	4	3	1,209	1,045	390	1,391	864	8	17	425	13	1,605	1,317
Cherokee	1,247	8	14	2,247	2,051	1,095	4,200	1,472	27	29	1,522	28	4,237	2,592
Childress	224	2	0	958	306	176	1,190	154	4	7	314	2	1,026	263
Clay	312	4	4	671	417	276	1,567	417	5	16	284	4	1,538	851
Cochran	104	14	2	1,055	185	356	824	197	10	5	215	11	984	423
Coke	97	2	2	452	105	191	711	112	0	3	91	1	691	196
Coleman	428	10	0	1,530	667	755	1,916	221	2	10	223	6	1,830	492
Collin	1,844	13	25	6,740	3,779	3,674	6,199	1,919	41	48	835	29	6,203	3,147
Collingsworth	149	0	0	646	244	226	1,027	121	0	5	346	3	1,170	301
Colorado	763	14	16	2,055	1,310	666	2,830	957	7	20	401	18	3,083	1,958
Comal	410	7	2	1,327	581	775	2,896	926	2	13	271	13	2,498	1,050
Comanche	325	2	2	1,679	704	2,031	2,031	280	7	9	186	5	2,864	1,066
Concho	69	6	1	655	249	132	772	83	1	4	89	2	771	229
Cooke	799	3	15	2,184	863	883	3,559	1,330	32	17	342	14	3,616	1,501
Coryell	488	0	6	2,291	1,103	741	3,432	702	10	10	474	14	2,869	999
Cottle	170	13	0	445	215	232	474	99	7	6	410	4	531	196
Crane	229	6	3	469	306	209	1,108	210	4	3	360	8	839	326
Crockett	179	53	0	719	387	128	782	251	2	6	163	1	761	337
Crosby	283	6	0	1,456	501	362	1,148	316	5	7	668	5	1,206	434
Culberson	98	39	1	343	193	145	435	68	10	11	243	3	341	106
Dallam	148	4	1	402	224	189	364	96	20	2	81	2	373	220
Dallas	31,539	502	802	80,141	47,540	41,910	66,069	52,485	1,078	1,382	8,801	612	90,489	80,153
Dawson	241	7	3	2,109	328	255	1,855	419	5	9	547	11	1,953	605
DeWitt	303	8	6	1,798	641	711	2,686	714	9	13	243	11	2,375	996
Deaf Smith	389	46	2	1,180	544	600	1,489	186	6	8	382	6	1,714	500
Delta	209	0	5	1,097	612	574	732	330	10	6	262	9	1,040	433
Denton	2,364	17	16	5,137	3,583	3,285	6,993	5,714	56	59	964	43	9,249	7,360
Dickens	229	5	3	1,016	368	317	745	174	2	14	206	5	584	297
Dimmit	340	61	2	562	340	354	1,386	221	10	10	133	7	1,226	686

Table 42: Gubernatorial Races

County	Democratic Primaries, 1968-1972													
	1968 (Cont.)			Runoff		1972							Runoff	
	Don Yarborough	Alfonso Veloz	Johnnie M. Hackworthe	Preston Smith	Don Yarborough	Ben Barnes	Dolph Briscoe	Frances Farenthold	Robert E. Looney	William H. Posey	Preston Smith	Gordon F. Wills	Dolph Briscoe	Frances Farenthold
Donley	137	1	3	445	261	279	816	141	3	6	233	2	764	323
Duval	165	4	6	3,265	400	3,739	322	286	3	2	144	3	3,424	889
Eastland	746	4	13	1,808	1,017	1,006	2,984	745	21	16	599	13	3,053	1,340
Ector	2,441	44	11	4,362	2,482	1,504	6,157	1,879	37	62	3,330	71	7,450	3,374
Edwards	8	2	0	347	30	27	530	21	0	0	32	0	452	37
El Paso	10,369	903	96	12,545	14,667	8,928	11,499	18,010	267	685	5,932	768	18,099	28,518
Ellis	1,057	7	9	3,342	1,663	2,270	5,172	1,509	32	29	837	0	4,183	2,086
Erath	439	3	4	1,937	899	2,031	3,033	640	14	11	455	24	3,885	1,533
Falls	958	13	17	2,030	1,554	889	2,852	718	12	15	41	13	2,423	1,363
Fannin	1,319	16	18	2,380	1,983	1,542	3,684	991	26	34	593	37	3,477	1,557
Fayette	453	7	6	1,961	895	735	2,963	1,012	14	32	414	8	2,723	1,752
Fisher	476	8	1	1,070	759	345	1,359	273	8	7	256	4	1,079	440
Floyd	216	5	3	1,250	300	701	1,387	302	8	18	419	6	1,730	567
Foard	103	7	0	299	106	41	357	54	0	3	111	3	303	75
Fort Bend	1,783	33	14	4,272	3,018	1,124	4,149	2,888	13	24	490	26	4,220	3,900
Franklin	315	2	4	1,101	807	341	919	213	10	8	223	11	764	244
Freestone	669	2	11	1,490	1,245	938	1,745	409	17	34	325	17	2,365	1,019
Frio	669	117	5	1,118	874	171	2,122	330	7	6	106	7	1,763	512
Gaines	258	15	2	1,308	270	342	1,194	322	5	9	554	2	1,484	805
Galveston	11,672	148	178	8,415	14,577	5,022	8,551	18,203	258	141	2,573	131	10,848	22,014
Garza	211	4	0	608	207	175	721	283	2	4	206	0	702	517
Gillespie	48	0	0	634	83	89	1,134	138	2	3	49	2	1,119	294
Glasscock	32	0	1	104	30	52	268	26	0	2	27	2	199	44
Goliad	326	9	4	405	294	224	682	197	2	2	89	4	645	347
Gonzales	263	9	3	1,559	438	387	2,370	364	3	6	218	8	2,168	598
Gray	803	1	2	1,357	936	786	2,501	526	14	20	603	19	2,185	988
Grayson	2,857	15	15	4,908	4,519	3,564	7,688	3,626	46	60	1,177	49	7,701	4,335
Gregg	1,265	24	124	5,855	2,247	1,978	10,205	1,761	178	148	1,712	128	9,702	2,598
Grimes	575	4	23	1,304	1,008	789	1,882	462	7	16	362	17	2,138	1,205
Guadalupe	505	13	8	1,846	890	1,033	3,945	1,312	14	31	477	24	3,608	1,970
Hale	636	17	5	3,175	746	1,083	3,199	843	17	32	1,102	17	3,845	1,378
Hall	271	0	5	820	359	327	971	125	3	6	347	5	1,124	355
Hamilton	230	2	6	971	314	411	1,538	201	3	4	113	7	1,370	436
Hansford	68	1	0	286	105	300	728	117	2	3	183	7	824	247
Hardeman	281	3	4	996	487	171	771	176	5	4	282	5	676	320
Hardin	2,923	7	6	1,765	2,937	1,464	2,910	3,249	24	38	1,420	32	4,454	4,343
Harris	75,780	641	333	81,400	95,616	49,378	92,555	125,066	755	2,425	16,119	972	111,678	176,244
Harrison	1,491	7	22	4,370	2,561	2,105	3,895	1,152	271	40	2,599	89	4,858	2,566
Hartley	77	3	1	319	121	101	373	46	1	3	132	2	396	173
Haskell	616	4	5	1,484	902	538	1,897	279	6	8	309	7	1,518	432
Hays	716	11	7	1,756	1,338	746	3,367	2,237	8	38	350	14	3,292	2,203
Hemphill	86	0	1	169	104	170	455	122	2	0	82	0	293	196
Henderson	1,489	1	6	1,696	2,020	2,262	4,178	1,789	86	63	944	59	4,953	2,947
Hidalgo	9,569	266	61	13,619	15,717	6,603	13,297	8,543	673	733	2,642	128	16,907	15,002
Hill	519	9	23	2,423	1,103	1,022	4,103	569	16	31	660	11	4,691	1,436
Hockley	438	50	5	2,409	551	671	2,367	775	16	20	705	21	3,076	1,391
Hood	222	0	1	553	320	732	1,445	329	7	7	209	12	1,634	668
Hopkins	886	3	9	3,065	1,695	1,280	2,969	871	21	18	571	24	3,583	1,378
Houston	1,416	4	11	2,217	2,573	708	2,643	1,721	27	36	584	35	2,556	1,740
Howard	1,915	43	10	2,311	2,755	734	2,614	1,576	15	24	510	18	2,865	1,867
Hudspeth	105	26	3	413	294	129	295	75	5	6	141	2	300	152
Hunt	1,446	5	21	3,905	2,312	2,385	3,951	3,063	67	19	711	29	4,233	3,128
Hutchinson	1,226	4	3	1,240	1,335	1,155	2,286	659	14	17	568	25	1,944	1,292
Irion	41	5	1	272	114	58	348	73	0	5	34	5	309	119
Jack	259	0	7	765	330	554	1,314	478	10	16	301	17	1,773	777
Jackson	758	22	6	1,826	1,219	453	2,105	1,079	12	18	309	9	2,052	1,321
Jasper	1,026	5	20	1,783	1,788	1,230	2,532	2,337	25	31	1,228	43	3,665	3,613
Jeff Davis	62	6	0	133	97	41	271	69	4	2	141	2	204	109
Jefferson	10,783	104	249	11,637	21,629	6,715	18,668	18,881	147	468	4,388	617	20,063	23,758
Jim Hogg	500	31	9	351	684	518	383	826	12	5	203	9	542	1,142
Jim Wells	3,638	93	31	2,888	6,075	2,204	3,079	4,058	28	45	558	40	3,555	4,931
Johnson	1,833	3	15	3,172	2,212	2,007	5,075	1,826	40	39	620	60	6,082	2,829
Jones	571	13	8	2,237	984	511	2,533	360	8	15	421	8	2,465	880
Karnes	430	18	5	2,269	1,379	614	2,512	639	18	20	298	7	2,544	1,152
Kaufman	1,185	7	19	2,357	1,048	1,439	3,064	873	27	11	575	20	2,808	1,283

Table 42: Gubernatorial Races

County	Democratic Primaries, 1968-1972														
Year	1968 (Cont.)			Runoff		1972								Runoff	
	Don Yarborough	Alfonso Veloz	Johnnie M. Hackworthe	Preston Smith	Don Yarborough	Ben Barnes	Dolph Briscoe	Frances Farenthold	Robert E. Looney	William H. Posey	Preston Smith	Gordon F. Wills		Dolph Briscoe	Frances Farenthold
Kendall	38	1	0	307	68	75	608	113	2	1	37	3		660	206
Kenedy	19	3	0	77	51	28	105	39	0	3	11	2		111	64
Kent	121	6	1	268	102	134	418	62	1	2	114	2		538	146
Kerr	299	5	3	1,492	392	433	3,164	638	8	18	333	10		2,518	817
Kimble	46	6	1	548	103	57	1,031	112	1	3	59	2		1,015	189
King	8	1	0	57	7	41	112	15	2	1	24	3		95	21
Kinney	96	26	0	301	247	116	348	30	2	2	61	1		335	150
Kleberg	2,273	93	8	1,703	3,061	610	2,916	3,417	8	31	545	14		3,093	3,658
Knox	146	1	2	721	200	219	963	170	2	6	450	4		1,080	370
La Salle	157	13	0	308	236	167	966	110	5	0	82	3		887	221
Lamar	1,955	3	12	3,066	2,124	3,042	4,643	1,080	26	44	1,129	52		6,647	2,917
Lamb	654	28	7	2,723	646	437	1,856	271	8	6	366	11		1,913	652
Lampasas	273	4	5	1,643	767	298	2,126	290	5	10	166	4		1,686	486
Lavaca	436	4	6	1,685	648	480	2,580	1,271	5	17	299	16		2,272	1,200
Lee	214	5	3	671	446	427	1,499	572	8	15	235	13		1,414	755
Leon	401	1	5	783	619	395	1,556	415	13	21	377	9		1,243	628
Liberty	2,041	22	10	3,571	3,464	1,325	3,831	2,457	17	36	753	45		4,241	4,374
Limestone	998	1	4	1,651	1,257	897	2,755	499	15	24	558	13		3,064	1,145
Lipscomb	71	1	0	207	138	226	348	58	3	4	116	3		259	153
Live Oak	388	30	4	1,675	1,164	332	1,692	448	10	26	223	16		1,651	502
Llano	178	3	3	1,091	433	228	1,632	322	1	0	112	7		1,488	549
Loving	10	0	0	23	10	18	45	9	0	0	8	0		39	3
Lubbock	5,145	46	39	20,564	6,238	3,556	11,358	8,036	42	45	8,870	64		16,509	11,623
Lynn	181	15	3	2,122	345	265	1,325	360	8	6	565	5		1,484	488
Madison	423	3	12	708	498	654	1,337	360	7	11	242	84		1,973	440
Marion	285	6	8	623	383	436	1,003	341	21	18	639	14		21,532	13,996
Martin	42	1	1	370	90	142	534	122	3	4	131	3		275	52
Mason	98	2	0	1,176	452	135	972	138	0	6	66	2		1,195	617
Matagorda	1,315	15	12	3,500	2,702	914	2,719	1,555	18	14	476	10		1,325	822
Maverick	533	68	8	620	627	1,360	1,177	476	16	9	378	15		490	177
McCulloch	185	9	6	999	330	506	1,985	209	6	5	287	6		899	227
McLennan	8,300	23	63	13,046	12,313	4,726	20,509	9,240	53	107	2,577	66		2,565	2,150
McMullen	59	4	3	169	64	79	308	30	3	4	34	1		1,386	1,790
Medina	423	7	3	1,184	671	461	3,782	681	12	16	241	16		2,929	941
Menard	76	2	0	313	122	114	708	119	4	7	106	6		508	175
Midland	1,582	86	15	4,564	2,178	1,884	5,741	2,075	69	95	1,095	35		5,739	3,172
Milam	1,257	7	16	1,872	2,109	669	2,905	1,759	7	21	447	9		2,991	2,239
Mills	140	0	4	480	153	303	1,222	177	2	4	80	6		995	238
Mitchell	385	11	2	1,004	613	351	1,761	362	12	3	197	6		1,104	464
Montague	651	1	5	2,363	1,293	656	2,347	471	7	8	343	17		1,906	721
Montgomery	1,978	17	54	3,259	2,306	3,023	5,750	4,266	44	97	1,268	50		6,430	5,675
Moore	783	5	4	886	916	605	1,116	367	6	11	320	8		1,170	724
Morris	928	9	16	1,042	698	458	1,904	746	22	14	678	14		2,454	1,507
Motley	99	3	1	474	100	182	472	96	7	7	164	1		439	143
Nacogdoches	1,855	4	20	3,115	2,509	1,156	4,575	3,500	26	37	805	49		4,949	3,658
Navarro	1,879	8	20	3,850	3,492	2,093	4,356	1,248	36	41	1,017	43		5,377	2,580
Newton	745	3	15	974	1,312	729	1,060	1,107	11	24	810	12		1,877	2,155
Nolan	676	39	5	2,394	1,355	639	2,777	512	3	3	363	12		2,630	963
Nueces	16,566	357	73	16,001	25,459	5,918	19,497	24,292	579	219	3,243	156		24,001	27,321
Ochiltree	71	1	2	491	139	430	1,088	191	9	8	209	3		924	202
Oldham	81	0	0	151	84	110	320	55	8	5	71	2		294	112
Orange	5,377	11	23	5,753	9,468	3,132	6,648	7,395	53	78	1,719	113		7,988	9,195
Palo Pinto	934	5	5	2,686	1,832	1,507	3,160	909	19	27	634	28		3,343	1,501
Panola	776	12	26	2,853	1,531	804	3,565	364	18	42	996	36		3,498	969
Parker	1,359	6	7	3,274	2,548	1,586	4,480	1,783	45	39	731	24		5,642	2,492
Parmer	138	0	3	854	246	226	978	143	3	8	206	3		988	256
Pecos	504	60	3	1,252	883	363	1,744	363	6	33	620	9		1,394	727
Polk	1,102	4	8	1,912	1,812	938	2,124	1,261	42	17	836	23		2,566	2,035
Potter	3,228	19	16	3,580	5,286	3,811	5,544	2,290	30	34	1,189	59		5,550	4,995
Presidio	364	135	5	713	699	223	686	100	7	6	264	12		469	151
Rains	126	1	3	282	207	394	759	176	3	4	194	5		579	285
Randall	1,457	12	19	2,886	2,527	2,166	4,526	1,557	16	43	880	18		2,798	4,736
Reagan	90	11	1	292	75	134	564	127	0	8	84	7		413	168
Real	12	0	0	332	23	46	575	16	0	0	29	0		506	39
Red River	319	19	11	2,594	1,198	882	3,078	408	11	19	596	34		2,976	1,125

Table 42: Gubernatorial Races

	Democratic Primaries, 1968-1972														
Year	1968 (Cont.)			Runoff		1972								Runoff	
County	Don Yarborough	Alfonso Veloz	Johnnie M. Hackworthe	Preston Smith	Don Yarborough	Ben Barnes	Dolph Briscoe	Frances Farenthold	Robert E. Looney	William H. Posey	Preston Smith	Gordon F. Wills	Dolph Briscoe	Frances Farenthold
Reeves	446	188	6	1,166	504	491	1,866	523	12	20	814	25	1,327	612
Refugio	780	28	5	1,191	763	390	1,405	992	12	6	324	5	1,845	1,414
Roberts	35	1	0	111	57	77	136	26	3	2	23	1	196	53
Robertson	1,352	6	17	1,513	2,191	584	2,175	1,167	11	11	512	17	1,802	1,757
Rockwall	164	1	3	698	223	735	1,199	345	6	3	250	3	1,042	408
Runnels	257	6	0	1,966	505	428	2,142	245	4	3	262	4	1,918	452
Rusk	1,240	55	78	3,793	3,268	1,732	5,017	1,151	245	46	1,126	110	5,740	2,043
Sabine	536	4	23	461	440	512	969	542	12	16	691	28	884	743
San Augustine	473	6	13	548	408	427	1,241	515	9	18	481	20	1,400	975
San Jacinto	659	0	16	526	710	506	885	564	23	18	477	30	746	753
San Patricio	2,893	61	11	3,174	4,145	1,412	4,936	4,554	29	58	709	20	5,440	5,158
San Saba	189	2	16	1,440	688	310	1,469	165	1	6	151	3	1,216	310
Schleicher	80	5	3	498	198	116	648	112	3	1	69	1	647	162
Scurry	530	9	4	1,647	1,003	520	3,061	479	21	14	452	9	2,864	977
Shackelford	183	0	6	926	519	261	973	152	3	3	129	2	728	243
Shelby	1,491	4	18	2,781	2,811	1,284	3,163	940	18	32	1,760	60	4,118	2,341
Sherman	108	2	0	371	208	160	329	62	1	2	52	2	298	116
Smith	3,453	11	22	6,760	6,011	2,714	11,378	3,716	141	120	1,684	72	13,157	6,206
Somervell	149	1	1	272	194	226	684	118	4	7	89	7	640	227
Starr	1,607	20	11	1,337	2,854	1,176	1,612	521	9	12	823	9	3,297	1,852
Stephens	470	2	4	1,706	983	689	2,044	412	8	13	253	9	2,248	1,039
Sterling	43	1	0	159	43	19	205	23	0	1	19	1	184	48
Stonewall	197	3	0	463	299	162	561	69	3	3	98	1	540	185
Sutton	65	21	0	328	86	61	461	59	2	2	45	0	398	116
Swisher	895	16	5	970	962	763	797	345	2	8	445	0	1,128	737
Tarrant	17,468	347	812	34,552	25,012	25,313	46,375	34,852	762	566	5,804	1,001	57,097	46,027
Taylor	2,424	16	9	8,431	3,791	2,661	10,743	2,775	71	95	1,434	43	10,292	4,420
Terrell	63	6	0	185	102	50	345	71	3	3	106	4	286	83
Terry	510	24	7	1,866	461	499	1,545	459	4	11	458	12	1,748	589
Throckmorton	153	1	2	676	368	221	722	129	2	4	130	4	460	183
Titus	1,640	5	5	2,457	1,961	743	2,291	651	19	16	896	23	2,353	923
Tom Green	1,611	33	11	5,020	2,310	1,665	7,903	3,026	19	29	1,070	29	7,581	3,940
Travis	11,217	87	76	24,841	18,625	8,261	34,234	39,828	126	126	6,263	127	44,408	41,915
Trinity	632	2	13	573	612	406	1,394	611	11	18	410	21	1,092	1,026
Tyler	801	8	5	1,551	1,624	776	1,679	1,030	7	11	675	25	2,116	1,707
Upshur	1,240	5	5	1,497	1,770	1,063	3,608	802	35	44	1,047	38	3,077	1,101
Upton	170	35	2	731	369	216	662	153	3	17	312	10	596	303
Uvalde	549	62	5	2,216	779	207	4,445	229	4	5	84	5	4,376	354
Val Verde	1,537	157	8	1,017	872	1,160	2,264	577	22	22	485	6	2,210	1,723
Van Zandt	885	1	6	1,534	1,350	1,183	3,580	760	22	18	454	36	3,324	1,390
Victoria	1,847	30	10	4,346	3,355	2,308	6,843	3,530	11	40	739	22	5,964	4,430
Walker	1,196	11	17	1,699	1,288	1,032	2,493	2,152	28	38	780	13	2,771	2,733
Waller	729	3	7	733	647	920	1,736	713	11	12	517	15	1,645	1,186
Ward	541	128	5	1,707	1,228	421	1,399	324	12	16	596	17	1,153	457
Washington	282	4	8	1,263	373	417	2,794	526	9	14	610	10	3,519	1,287
Webb	2,057	38	10	4,124	3,838	5,191	3,588	2,439	40	58	486	39	7,208	4,519
Wharton	925	11	9	2,573	1,420	1,319	2,680	2,047	10	18	352	21	3,158	3,145
Wheeler	241	1	2	761	483	248	836	112	2	3	213	3	787	261
Wichita	3,662	28	11	7,084	5,509	2,709	10,795	5,567	29	46	2,354	58	8,447	7,153
Wilbarger	355	5	4	1,764	438	431	1,706	304	93	7	414	11	1,945	541
Willacy	732	66	6	1,466	1,072	817	1,916	533	23	15	624	12	2,034	1,455
Williamson	776	7	5	4,155	1,589	691	5,129	1,990	18	29	878	7	5,355	2,244
Wilson	796	40	7	2,659	2,025	885	2,966	704	20	28	439	20	3,123	1,318
Winkler	430	11	6	1,954	1,057	641	1,660	415	16	24	683	29	1,952	975
Wise	584	0	9	1,661	809	915	3,212	740	17	16	309	23	2,849	905
Wood	799	5	6	2,370	2,212	891	2,652	601	36	15	532	29	3,065	1,097
Yoakum	249	10	1	1,019	213	296	1,210	346	5	12	417	7	1,336	528
Young	449	2	6	1,915	826	652	2,520	647	9	18	626	16	2,080	991
Zapata	55	1	0	506	125	401	514	329	7	3	132	33	366	412
Zavala	818	43	5	801	492	62	1,233	70	3	5	71	2	1,059	86
Official	421,607		5,484	621,226		963,397			10,225		190,709		1,095,168	
Totals		9,562		767,490		392,356		612,051		13,727		10,438		884,594
Unofficial	421,617		5,484	621,226		963,417			10,225		190,709		1,100,599	
Totals		9,562		767,544		392,358		612,051		13,731		10,739		889,544

Table 43: Gubernatorial Races

	Democratic Primaries, 1974-1982									
Year	1974				1978			1982		
County	Dolph Briscoe	Frances Farenthold	W.H. Posey	Steve S. Alexander	Dolph Briscoe	John Hill	Preston Smith	Bob Armstrong	Mark White	Buddy Temple
Anderson	4,314	781	53	63	3,443	3,332	405	1,021	2,317	1,924
Andrews	1,841	519	85	87	1,132	727	172	326	1,421	467
Angelina	6,098	1,832	145	99	2,808	5,825	564	1,441	3,561	7,362
Aransas	1,139	446	39	48	1,024	1,156	79	330	941	342
Archer	1,450	317	27	30	736	874	84	231	744	281
Armstrong	424	104	11	18	323	400	63	117	270	83
Atascosa	2,886	846	132	91	2,645	3,052	152	792	1,671	2,129
Austin	2,183	608	60	67	1,447	1,592	180	167	650	418
Bailey	850	131	25	15	295	618	123	199	603	244
Bandera	1,616	353	59	64	1,272	1,016	105	234	630	580
Bastrop	2,832	983	89	41	1,993	2,803	278	1,539	2,382	1,180
Baylor	1,150	227	13	16	751	680	85	182	402	186
Bee	2,786	993	84	90	2,118	1,674	111	498	658	456
Bell	8,000	3,420	281	260	7,913	8,590	944	2,837	4,500	1,707
Bexar	56,612	37,364	2,045	1,271	42,259	66,175	2,455	8,130	33,087	31,306
Blanco	525	85	11	7	313	361	39	101	130	63
Borden	359	45	13	8	182	164	33	61	210	87
Bosque	2,125	428	34	98	1,529	1,405	185	621	1,784	893
Bowie	8,191	2,639	238	313	6,687	7,215	855	1,864	2,683	9,785
Brazoria	9,590	5,189	313	325	9,302	9,509	659	2,027	7,059	2,143
Brazos	5,363	2,542	127	93	4,897	8,298	409	2,879	5,447	2,217
Brewster	1,090	453	39	27	891	700	120	388	772	227
Briscoe	555	90	19	9	183	570	73	168	381	109
Brooks	1,493	1,509	36	55	1,227	1,777	100	489	1,532	1,139
Brown	3,200	420	48	637	2,901	2,902	362	1,541	2,584	754
Burleson	1,652	685	49	47	863	1,782	176	419	833	719
Burnet	2,446	646	66	43	1,749	3,084	304	1,388	1,598	645
Caldwell	2,754	732	86	65	1,669	1,925	216	765	1,309	821
Calhoun	2,096	965	40	28	1,639	2,362	175	476	1,451	1,273
Callahan	1,636	228	31	41	1,601	1,457	161	529	658	302
Cameron	10,556	5,899	306	403	8,590	13,027	1,141	4,064	12,374	8,727
Camp	1,354	412	34	44	1,097	1,184	101	252	972	1,070
Carson	994	293	29	26	780	996	221	257	917	218
Cass	3,920	1,006	71	73	2,172	2,800	455	656	1,128	4,648
Castro	1,364	355	24	30	426	1,356	247	430	1,076	293
Chambers	1,998	732	67	42	1,617	1,808	231	505	1,945	1,041
Cherokee	4,260	1,327	114	124	2,457	3,767	328	854	2,531	2,240
Childress	1,429	183	37	27	881	671	151	152	501	97
Clay	1,617	437	42	40	1,121	1,072	106	721	1,507	674
Cochran	756	136	40	23	377	764	191	150	705	277
Coke	779	119	16	19	610	363	72	452	474	238
Coleman	2,609	361	56	66	1,182	895	126	465	476	237
Collin	5,713	1,715	162	124	4,228	5,506	429	1,493	3,158	1,041
Collingsworth	868	153	15	14	524	783	128	240	788	136
Colorado	2,539	736	59	56	1,131	1,194	110	246	1,201	563
Comal	2,770	722	57	54	2,171	2,180	198	405	797	615
Comanche	2,286	403	67	42	1,259	1,544	165	809	1,718	674
Concho	683	92	8	6	751	400	41	261	539	173
Cooke	3,968	1,073	69	117	2,419	2,689	343	706	1,450	947
Coryell	2,818	545	74	63	2,066	1,914	314	581	2,349	821
Cottle	626	124	13	7	294	605	234	216	254	171
Crane	949	196	35	36	666	561	116	124	703	196
Crockett	607	138	12	10	495	233	20	170	319	117
Crosby	1,166	206	19	15	639	1,110	236	373	686	219
Culberson	529	98	11	19	289	311	31	84	291	153
Dallam	443	119	21	17	432	540	129	141	613	174
Dallas	69,709	37,933	3,130	1,805	54,108	64,123	7,541	15,759	24,517	16,135
Dawson	2,131	476	87	45	1,183	1,003	285	416	1,918	580
DeWitt	2,491	599	70	70	1,205	1,113	87	357	1,242	692
Deaf Smith	2,147	467	82	53	1,269	2,389	432	480	1,374	527
Delta	1,370	205	35	41	473	945	102	226	795	259
Denton	7,547	4,197	203	233	4,544	7,195	510	1,859	2,762	1,124
Dickens	868	129	28	32	332	759	106	232	651	262
Dimmit	1,791	718	28	49	1,401	1,886	98	466	981	1,590

Table 43: Gubernatorial Races

County	Democratic Primaries, 1974-1982									
Year	1974				1978			1982		
	Dolph Briscoe	Frances Farenthold	W.H. Posey	Steve S. Alexander	Dolph Briscoe	John Hill	Preston Smith	Bob Armstrong	Mark White	Buddy Temple
Donley	678	182	23	28	428	849	151	178	668	174
Duval	3,399	592	29	13	2,776	2,162	117	610	2,264	2,211
Eastland	3,457	669	88	127	1,887	1,782	164	996	1,469	676
Ector	5,109	1,373	170	226	3,896	3,457	670	900	4,291	1,268
Edwards	489	37	7	7	412	140	26	73	171	155
El Paso	14,296	9,749	441	531	14,848	26,946	1,355	6,648	12,612	11,307
Ellis	6,027	1,389	118	104	3,870	3,698	448	1,411	3,095	1,580
Erath	3,957	711	115	66	2,252	2,206	260	859	2,268	755
Falls	2,482	692	61	48	2,409	1,884	214	461	1,620	797
Fannin	4,435	1,656	99	139	2,179	2,474	238	1,193	2,997	1,054
Fayette	3,163	1,184	252	77	1,555	2,206	153	660	2,391	1,021
Fisher	1,553	257	45	27	828	1,036	111	665	870	405
Floyd	1,788	257	51	46	962	1,198	189	253	576	184
Foard	638	88	18	14	455	407	72	129	291	157
Fort Bend	6,040	2,534	161	117	5,279	6,141	570	834	2,065	1,246
Franklin	883	157	17	24	551	839	84	148	307	455
Freestone	2,323	399	42	57	1,445	1,568	138	309	1,090	784
Frio	2,156	293	40	28	1,883	2,025	70	315	1,099	1,496
Gaines	1,877	377	80	61	1,175	1,332	390	274	938	265
Galveston	14,888	9,945	636	241	11,118	13,303	790	3,955	8,561	3,948
Garza	699	282	23	12	439	703	100	135	501	209
Gillespie	858	137	8	13	596	565	56	192	162	100
Glasscock	265	24	5	7	240	82	31	88	165	84
Goliad	925	297	27	31	850	474	36	164	348	321
Gonzales	2,766	679	65	67	1,633	1,429	104	535	1,233	818
Gray	2,386	605	116	95	1,821	1,883	413	436	1,399	376
Grayson	7,874	2,247	175	184	6,106	7,035	470	1,603	2,573	1,001
Gregg	9,220	1,641	254	118	5,124	6,564	483	1,557	3,772	4,008
Grimes	2,121	597	49	32	1,355	1,346	138	420	1,413	816
Guadalupe	2,747	984	75	53	3,359	3,413	311	751	2,263	1,659
Hale	3,199	686	88	46	2,499	3,108	608	829	1,312	443
Hall	1,068	199	31	19	328	694	143	293	786	190
Hamilton	1,624	290	29	32	890	856	111	295	1,038	551
Hansford	912	198	41	29	461	595	168	127	485	154
Hardeman	1,244	252	45	18	761	866	162	210	731	368
Hardin	4,276	1,961	115	105	3,067	3,858	340	773	3,994	3,142
Harris	95,344	65,494	2,474	1,958	76,546	89,890	9,774	15,197	43,334	23,004
Harrison	5,753	1,746	289	104	4,127	5,027	397	1,218	2,265	5,118
Hartley	561	92	27	25	459	463	117	105	486	118
Haskell	2,383	331	52	42	1,260	1,480	173	572	671	370
Hays	3,700	2,144	74	60	1,922	4,561	250	1,691	1,903	892
Hemphill	645	236	19	13	419	456	94	133	334	100
Henderson	5,195	1,410	139	202	2,609	3,920	321	1,423	3,327	2,191
Hidalgo	14,311	7,245	945	969	12,748	13,758	704	2,828	10,696	11,317
Hill	3,586	488	53	32	2,951	2,136	331	843	2,710	1,131
Hockley	3,931	825	133	137	1,470	2,751	343	535	1,736	1,021
Hood	1,652	295	31	31	1,125	1,120	102	795	1,914	1,468
Hopkins	3,312	556	66	94	2,460	2,704	482	616	2,062	1,072
Houston	2,667	808	84	63	1,748	2,732	259	468	1,952	1,806
Howard	3,607	1,127	84	59	3,326	2,621	443	1,118	2,022	803
Hudspeth	438	90	9	13	347	301	16	104	276	193
Hunt	5,895	1,611	85	89	3,627	4,601	482	1,297	3,471	1,567
Hutchinson	2,817	805	137	134	2,083	1,943	455	454	2,090	483
Irion	307	96	10	14	253	147	17	81	119	37
Jack	1,271	254	33	36	871	525	65	202	597	418
Jackson	1,164	268	25	13	1,333	1,185	108	389	991	877
Jas per	3,222	1,366	65	94	2,202	3,136	264	532	3,333	2,557
JeffDavis	247	54	4	4	285	235	35	71	105	43
Jefferson	18,780	10,118	341	256	13,801	17,093	923	3,964	22,739	12,787
Jim Hogg	952	963	17	26	870	1,284	69	367	1,114	707
Jim Wells	5,245	3,171	114	127	4,348	4,064	380	1,370	3,155	3,852
Johnson	4,973	1,079	101	66	4,080	4,006	272	1,193	3,626	1,163
Jones	2,581	356	57	59	2,239	1,947	271	907	1,228	514
Karnes	2,778	761	80	60	1,964	1,199	92	303	901	916
Kaufman	3,681	730	93	75	2,460	3,399	403	1,253	2,571	1,610

Texas Political History

Table 43: Gubernatorial Races

	Democratic Primaries, 1974-1982									
Year	1974				1978			1982		
County	Dolph Briscoe	Frances Farenthold	W.H. Posey	Steve S. Alexander	Dolph Briscoe	John Hill	Preston Smith	Bob Armstrong	Mark White	Buddy Temple
Kendall	536	99	16	6	551	546	11	62	137	117
Kenedy	133	29	4	0	106	54	6	38	86	67
Kent	445	59	12	9	242	351	78	139	248	115
Kerr	2,376	515	51	25	1,528	1,349	137	265	643	450
Kimble	854	113	11	20	602	265	33	169	364	109
King	100	12	7	5	36	84	12	42	81	53
Kinney	618	166	27	22	474	389	36	107	310	302
Kleberg	2,357	2,043	47	44	2,013	2,592	172	1,281	1,953	1,575
Knox	1,021	142	17	21	546	626	129	296	598	213
La Salle	1,099	238	28	12	704	515	34	176	655	641
Lamar	5,461	1,073	165	122	3,470	4,770	664	2,334	1,636	1,564
Lamb	2,875	563	65	88	1,164	2,208	282	700	1,745	647
Lampasas	1,635	281	33	29	1,421	1,289	119	547	1,142	471
Lavaca	2,545	725	77	55	1,585	1,626	131	429	1,380	1,070
Lee	1,675	511	93	68	576	1,074	126	386	1,030	630
Leon	2,036	390	34	30	1,324	1,428	138	225	1,056	620
Liberty	5,034	2,131	214	107	3,028	4,116	351	789	3,275	2,275
Limestone	1,682	280	18	27	1,748	1,982	373	844	1,912	1,198
Lipscomb	339	135	11	15	381	628	145	161	606	193
Live Oak	1,964	420	64	51	1,391	999	89	342	761	592
Llano	1,755	478	38	42	1,024	1,584	129	733	1,188	414
Loving	39	6	5	0	22	25	3	6	42	8
Lubbock	15,170	6,201	664	391	8,393	14,015	4,514	5,361	8,830	3,037
Lynn	1,056	121	24	18	700	1,183	322	322	1,282	323
Madison	1,812	417	34	34	978	1,249	158	255	990	688
Marion	1,322	387	48	63	947	922	94	231	303	1,149
Martin	466	72	8	7	723	370	99	193	531	167
Mason	972	138	29	33	254	212	27	96	262	95
Matagorda	3,298	1,242	78	44	2,289	2,255	249	504	1,618	1,265
Maverick	1,977	1,392	77	106	1,118	2,528	45	268	1,056	2,903
McCulloch	1,606	219	29	24	1,217	910	216	446	1,123	349
McLennan	13,822	4,366	210	307	16,944	14,341	1,499	4,076	13,056	6,401
McMullen	366	51	10	8	171	96	11	36	66	57
Medina	3,185	527	72	38	2,998	1,704	132	533	1,314	1,627
Menard	489	94	14	3	355	252	26	188	359	127
Midland	3,880	1,128	91	134	2,688	2,091	411	625	1,114	322
Milam	2,059	749	57	56	1,910	2,863	242	999	2,757	1,227
Mills	1,151	162	30	28	791	692	112	239	560	224
Mitchell	1,551	302	38	20	986	839	88	515	1,108	572
Montague	2,561	490	51	59	1,682	1,299	208	660	1,617	1,003
Montgomery	6,713	2,701	243	192	5,796	8,134	841	1,104	4,406	3,236
Moore	1,480	458	63	49	1,376	2,038	428	466	1,717	525
Morris	2,480	691	51	76	1,184	1,644	182	294	925	2,036
Motley	502	105	11	11	302	397	71	110	290	131
Nacogdoches	4,035	1,653	78	73	2,328	3,732	266	999	2,539	2,911
Navarro	4,166	790	65	48	3,534	4,764	356	1,419	3,255	1,797
Newton	1,608	850	58	41	709	1,285	98	203	1,154	1,485
Nolan	2,963	436	36	64	1,786	1,879	159	978	1,411	696
Nueces	22,382	14,072	1,006	1,211	14,951	21,905	1,517	7,077	12,551	14,166
Ochiltree	1,368	305	73	51	736	622	184	164	700	246
Oldham	483	119	20	17	316	425	91	88	287	66
Oran ge	7,952	3,457	186	175	4,894	7,313	380	2,364	6,912	4,979
PaloPinto	2,377	594	39	89	2,548	2,113	277	753	1,823	750
Panola	3,695	860	131	167	2,685	2,303	206	358	724	2,768
Parker	4,942	1,080	262	201	3,250	3,835	334	956	2,458	1,343
Parmer	1,490	273	58	40	467	1,007	317	265	782	215
Pecos	2,258	648	96	86	2,149	1,477	391	707	1,563	596
Polk	3,142	1,205	104	118	1,734	3,624	283	444	2,803	1,843
Potter	5,915	2,842	281	227	4,117	5,815	1,020	1,614	4,804	1,633
Presidio	870	249	31	35	633	553	67	213	510	182
Rains	1,094	254	24	33	511	765	90	254	698	309
Randall	4,772	1,897	302	87	2,815	4,133	688	1,299	3,636	849
Reagan	933	244	44	43	558	490	64	191	495	164
Real	359	24	5	2	746	349	34	132	375	306
Red River	2,971	719	94	100	1,683	1,952	360	824	848	2,023

Table 43: Gubernatorial Races

Democratic Primaries, 1974-1982

Year	1974				1978			1982		
County	Dolph Briscoe	Frances Farenthold	W.H. Posey	Steve S. Alexander	Dolph Briscoe	John Hill	Preston Smith	Bob Armstrong	Mark White	Buddy Temple
Reeves	1,680	439	58	51	1,678	1,093	362	497	1,740	504
Refugio	1,506	539	57	37	1,229	1,064	92	349	1,014	926
Roberts	261	48	18	8	122	140	20	57	113	35
Robertson	2,725	981	75	88	1,398	1,978	266	478	1,875	1,051
Rockwall	1,735	382	22	47	1,323	1,600	209	421	1,028	495
Runnels	1,718	233	35	29	1,334	707	92	656	1,049	540
Rusk	6,588	1,345	217	317	2,992	4,493	451	750	2,938	2,778
Sabine	1,802	682	87	67	980	1,756	138	216	793	1,957
San Augustine	1,412	406	59	65	704	1,355	113	197	746	1,683
San Jacinto	1,842	785	69	53	1,209	1,757	148	401	1,450	1,147
San Patricio	5,124	2,286	211	76	5,108	4,516	535	1,663	2,475	3,062
San Saba	971	117	16	20	617	565	63	336	655	258
Schleicher	649	83	14	15	596	196	29	182	312	130
Scurry	3,274	407	71	56	2,324	1,632	328	521	1,156	460
Shackelford	551	110	10	19	590	589	62	222	324	201
Shelby	3,379	1,019	60	133	2,155	2,732	300	350	658	3,362
Sherman	496	116	33	18	322	472	89	117	502	120
Smith	11,193	3,250	306	397	7,575	9,202	793	1,557	5,112	3,009
Somervell	754	244	38	27	666	597	106	203	574	240
Starr	2,983	1,052	25	44	1,695	2,773	74	27	2,563	1,258
Stephens	1,549	266	22	22	1,330	983	111	489	1,230	425
Sterling	182	23	1	4	245	109	20	74	185	64
Stonewall	736	114	35	13	506	492	66	216	246	141
Sutton	420	74	2	8	519	274	34	181	329	146
Swisher	1,207	430	42	34	561	1,661	254	842	1,217	368
Tarrant	41,840	20,640	1,573	1,200	34,354	43,543	2,854	10,541	18,988	12,565
Taylor	9,367	1,975	188	142	9,914	7,570	652	3,343	3,897	1,775
Terrell	548	149	28	12	277	163	16	90	287	122
Terry	2,089	397	52	46	881	1,707	232	343	1,007	409
Throckmorton	764	146	22	10	385	402	59	155	282	159
Titus	2,992	759	54	60	1,724	2,428	469	469	1,415	2,849
Tom Green	6,550	2,489	173	154	5,506	4,175	405	2,562	3,075	1,154
Travis	35,175	31,153	822	649	20,315	44,183	3,474	31,018	15,711	5,930
Trinity	2,257	669	101	58	1,041	1,547	88	457	1,928	1,703
Tyler	2,302	899	91	45	1,150	1,929	242	394	1,785	1,623
Upshur	4,730	1,135	236	188	2,132	2,973	224	681	1,872	2,414
Upton	939	219	59	50	572	387	76	158	441	143
Uvalde	3,455	293	33	13	4,505	759	58	513	1,655	1,536
Val Verde	2,786	790	46	82	2,261	1,456	163	635	2,056	1,604
Van Zandt	4,008	832	154	123	2,678	3,772	337	1,080	3,036	1,586
Victoria	4,317	1,277	199	93	4,596	4,905	369	1,135	3,842	2,663
Walker	3,899	1,662	98	93	2,114	4,105	370	699	2,831	1,268
Waller	1,793	688	51	29	1,795	1,424	314	445	1,345	789
Ward	1,806	411	41	37	1,313	1,241	251	400	2,107	659
Washington	2,821	735	109	49	1,233	2,470	285	392	1,871	700
Webb	4,522	2,035	71	105	5,445	10,245	429	822	4,349	4,609
Wharton	4,597	1,881	120	150	2,562	3,182	303	900	2,080	1,369
Wheeler	1,435	340	33	33	711	1,152	276	186	724	181
Wichita	11,087	3,761	187	243	7,071	6,897	699	2,225	3,040	1,239
Wilbarger	2,105	309	27	55	1,888	2,149	271	261	1,486	624
Willacy	2,077	615	73	46	1,133	1,434	100	474	1,652	1,324
Williamson	4,584	1,326	125	67	3,624	5,258	708	2,844	3,468	1,326
Wilson	2,658	941	96	60	2,366	2,318	214	508	1,595	1,824
Winkler	1,461	360	63	76	965	954	155	131	698	209
Wise	3,446	668	69	77	1,589	1,841	140	767	1,836	632
Wood	2,714	617	97	66	2,054	2,850	203	751	2,393	1,518
Yoakum	1,468	313	85	81	788	1,066	260	352	1,121	476
Young	2,408	514	38	41	1,523	1,661	127	373	993	411
Zapata	871	572	13	10	900	801	29	183	929	568
Zavala	1,021	70	27	13	627	268	24	276	593	1,173
Official Totals	1,025,632	437,287	31,498	26,889	753,309	932,345	92,202	262,189	592,658	402,693
Unofficial Totals	1,025,632	438,087	31,498	26,889	753,309	932,345	92,204	262,129	592,658	402,693

Table 44: Gubernatorial Races

Democratic Primaries, 1986-1990															
Year	1986						1990							Runoff	
County	Sheila Bilyeu	Andrew C. Briscoe III	A. Don Crowder	Bobby Locke	Ron Slover	Mark White	Stanley Adams	Theresa Hearn-Hyns	Earl Holmes	Jim Mattox	Ray Rachal	Ann W. Richards	Mark White	Jim Mattox	Ann W. Richards
Anderson	190	1,914	901	526	135	2,559	87	89	281	2,962	145	2,271	1,502	2,940	2,965
Andrews	73	424	349	124	55	303	56	45	56	1,070	35	452	311	795	495
Angelina	354	2,677	1,180	669	351	2,816	204	136	237	4,960	121	4,473	1,721	4,342	5,631
Aransas	23	177	79	15	7	346	20	17	24	736	5	613	268	374	535
Archer	74	447	140	52	386	490	18	18	21	1,277	5	464	166	874	557
Armstrong	25	138	53	23	214	170	10	3	16	266	2	98	59	125	98
Atascosa	187	1,472	397	643	67	2,184	157	120	72	1,827	52	1,574	869	1,398	1,541
Austin	65	425	229	134	55	897	37	26	43	1,329	6	746	714	1,210	682
Bailey	18	112	49	20	81	236	21	18	17	872	13	213	235	541	223
Bandera	86	355	93	118	23	481	16	15	11	354	5	328	93	213	280
Bastrop	246	1,274	716	390	113	3,308	82	95	90	2,756	34	2,852	1,052	2,720	3,078
Baylor	53	517	171	41	156	412	29	13	13	804	4	314	146	450	357
Bee	153	1,104	278	215	173	1,806	59	55	60	1,676	20	1,060	836	1,378	1,044
Bell	204	1,675	788	657	234	3,672	81	165	66	3,078	132	3,865	2,145	2,571	4,559
Bexar	3,783	7,712	1,639	3,631	1,214	35,503	1,403	2,271	624	21,957	308	38,880	10,237	15,968	35,495
Blanco	8	70	19	9	11	171	4	5	6	146	2	229	90	126	246
Borden	15	94	57	20	4	45	5	2	10	170	1	70	39	78	52
Bosque	66	1,068	171	99	30	723	75	40	80	1,451	37	1,210	572	1,295	1,384
Bowie	311	2,872	1,534	1,083	200	5,759	95	64	108	4,611	75	2,479	1,417	4,120	2,845
Brazoria	283	1,976	905	629	194	5,434	100	201	131	4,687	63	4,858	3,518	5,405	5,917
Brazos	168	1,568	403	454	77	3,596	94	44	36	1,281	24	3,174	1,630	1,295	3,616
Brewster	42	375	153	49	41	573	18	31	9	439	6	364	337	189	268
Briscoe	18	155	223	25	185	233	5	5	11	448	4	134	100	382	224
Brooks	145	755	405	204	98	1,902	40	52	35	1,814	58	1,142	599	1,565	1,396
Brown	89	1,230	793	156	78	1,433	50	51	71	1,769	19	1,302	732	1,110	1,271
Burleson	56	504	154	159	41	743	48	76	37	1,499	28	1,064	745	1,779	1,450
Burnet	61	506	278	156	65	1,312	70	80	116	2,086	23	1,955	803	2,349	2,233
Caldwell	155	883	242	398	72	2,006	53	82	81	1,679	45	1,833	824	1,715	2,332
Calhoun	164	1,002	544	276	72	1,959	77	71	76	1,334	20	1,490	893	1,779	1,787
Callahan	78	853	307	116	74	656	43	73	84	1,468	17	618	339	1,165	851
Cameron	865	5,102	2,278	1,051	355	11,393	250	323	171	9,286	289	5,133	5,050	10,320	9,167
Camp	113	653	198	117	49	973	26	14	90	935	14	776	444	1,054	990
Carson	45	161	64	42	305	297	26	21	26	899	10	356	171	655	421
Cass	170	1,360	1,008	217	70	2,134	49	25	67	2,640	27	1,437	742	2,841	1,940
Castro	27	136	111	28	202	388	23	33	29	866	8	244	308	333	242
Chambers	146	905	427	201	95	1,641	100	38	59	1,463	31	805	875	850	649
Cherokee	189	2,131	694	237	200	1,557	120	68	160	2,370	27	1,898	979	2,029	2,095
Childress	36	300	111	63	373	326	17	3	12	356	3	210	120	197	229
Clay	48	532	188	79	306	686	34	33	29	1,533	4	713	298	1,272	1,112
Cochran	28	257	137	74	37	284	18	10	12	583	8	137	186	574	223
Coke	49	338	135	45	29	307	74	16	32	371	13	272	188	417	478
Coleman	45	378	158	40	58	384	54	42	67	1,364	23	668	368	1,076	803
Collin	70	368	621	86	38	1,858	52	61	36	1,940	38	5,458	2,142	1,922	5,723
Collingsworth	36	327	134	67	389	420	12	9	15	466	5	169	81	275	146
Colorado	110	886	492	178	136	1,500	60	64	76	2,170	77	1,051	1,146	1,962	1,027
Comal	70	201	62	92	30	925	37	20	23	573	5	1,129	348	385	1,105
Comanche	75	623	508	146	48	805	52	44	71	1,012	18	1,045	406	608	747
Concho	22	117	44	32	14	189	7	26	22	290	11	218	169	372	384
Cooke	102	430	784	110	80	880	42	48	122	1,415	42	1,286	593	965	1,096
Coryell	120	655	1,198	122	103	1,167	82	36	56	1,848	13	1,274	695	1,595	1,495
Cottle	33	127	92	61	219	350	11	15	18	524	3	226	142	313	213
Crane	78	446	234	91	53	305	20	34	40	702	10	270	204	983	508
Crockett	44	296	253	72	21	349	37	22	18	433	17	312	265	671	520
Crosby	42	307	139	58	115	801	11	13	8	605	5	220	204	378	266
Culberson	32	140	89	56	23	337	10	14	7	309	7	88	251	309	164
Dallam	71	140	67	38	271	262	13	8	21	471	9	162	145	199	141
Dallas	912	4,678	3,819	894	491	38,152	275	1,071	301	30,731	212	53,995	18,659	30,538	59,677
Dawson	99	593	326	103	122	845	38	34	75	1,510	19	378	520	585	252
DeWitt	79	661	218	175	30	828	19	18	45	866	7	579	378	798	696
Deaf Smith	128	491	387	115	814	1,062	54	51	67	1,237	22	494	457	491	300
Delta	54	251	252	78	49	628	21	14	37	573	25	492	344	646	590
Denton	134	568	508	142	62	2,598	55	76	40	2,019	30	5,693	1,839	1,818	6,320
Dickens	39	204	140	59	69	447	6	4	6	396	3	112	105	252	128
Dimmit	204	606	204	59	69	231	53	1,792	31	930	31	893	872	954	965

Table 44: Gubernatorial Races

	Democratic Primaries, 1986-1990														
Year	1986						1990							Runoff	
County	Sheila Bilyeu	Andrew C. Briscoe III	A. Don Crowder	Bobby Locke	Ron Slover	Mark White	Stanley Adams	Theresa Hearn-Hyns	Earl Holmes	Jim Mattox	Ray Rachal	Ann W. Richards	Mark White	Jim Mattox	Ann W. Richards
Donley	30	180	88	30	243	219	10	7	6	429	11	183	84	182	132
Duval	155	1,049	263	568	83	2,252	207	37	39	1,464	64	1,922	854	1,424	1,907
Eastland	177	1,374	638	128	143	1,023	88	70	194	2,055	63	1,110	475	1,201	1,196
Ector	177	1,676	527	359	105	2,262	51	105	63	2,220	52	1,908	1,294	1,559	2,107
Edwards	19	128	32	36	19	106	5	6	7	113	1	44	41	33	32
El Paso	1,098	3,667	1,358	1,087	613	18,269	273	678	426	20,544	260	14,488	9,467	13,177	13,951
Ellis	218	1,238	758	452	258	3,229	51	56	54	2,089	31	2,559	1,125	1,580	2,293
Erath	124	978	462	238	56	1,294	85	63	79	1,288	31	1,952	620	1,189	1,789
Falls	105	758	163	217	127	1,299	81	27	47	1,158	14	857	588	572	686
Fannin	122	938	956	244	71	1,533	25	33	54	1,014	14	1,267	702	928	1,359
Fayette	103	961	582	274	94	1,356	56	53	95	2,087	27	1,070	796	1,864	1,019
Fisher	46	302	277	68	22	502	20	28	19	813	4	430	194	734	656
Floyd	65	419	192	131	148	532	16	21	29	965	7	321	325	357	283
Foard	15	1,514	51	9	142	168	7	5	4	371	1	136	70	285	225
Fort Bend	164	1,830	174	207	77	3,749	59	177	48	2,811	35	3,925	2,614	3,738	5,160
Franklin	94	484	292	171	52	888	10	15	26	632	15	403	276	613	494
Freestone	70	619	354	133	128	1,202	40	32	77	1,178	23	1,087	457	529	757
Frio	142	946	155	258	45	1,930	56	105	52	1,277	32	1,105	645	844	1,086
Gaines	77	739	304	128	71	613	24	43	39	963	22	316	281	915	432
Galveston	573	3,340	1,407	782	157	9,824	219	235	154	8,941	81	10,176	6,090	8,692	9,827
Garza	26	203	159	59	27	269	32	13	28	906	10	143	169	724	280
Gillespie	6	31	21	8	4	226	0	3	8	137	4	308	86	117	330
Glasscock	17	145	72	20	8	83	9	5	11	139	5	55	44	77	36
Goliad	102	523	123	107	39	701	15	24	25	593	16	348	253	644	450
Gonzales	124	1,134	376	246	71	1,042	62	73	67	1,496	21	1,115	488	980	979
Gray	31	238	155	93	412	580	23	23	35	990	7	421	245	466	439
Grayson	179	1,229	1,020	228	120	2,474	149	100	121	3,074	53	4,354	1,986	3,460	5,255
Gregg	174	3,168	819	174	309	2,563	51	104	129	2,895	173	3,276	1,629	2,882	3,938
Grimes	79	747	276	247	42	1,185	25	17	42	1,034	4	649	587	1,362	830
Guadalupe	69	498	93	285	27	1,302	21	52	42	1,140	20	1,544	410	615	1,265
Hale	85	414	359	139	90	850	42	28	89	1,159	37	493	483	541	532
Hall	26	161	77	24	192	305	19	18	11	738	8	344	152	491	351
Hamilton	58	495	241	77	42	632	33	28	54	693	8	742	293	785	917
Hansford	23	152	51	22	215	153	18	13	23	616	9	191	121	592	264
Hardeman	47	290	113	26	245	432	26	11	24	869	4	303	153	608	410
Hardin	296	1,357	2,050	361	174	2,576	84	79	106	4,869	42	2,164	1,334	4,092	2,570
Harris	1,225	8,826	2,324	1,179	384	53,984	523	13,003	605	30,318	446	60,184	35,413	37,434	66,199
Harrison	184	1,234	1,149	222	172	3,227	224	97	116	3,450	99	2,053	1,905	3,725	2,721
Hartley	19	91	53	19	193	205	24	12	20	457	4	159	136	395	206
Haskell	36	535	274	31	48	312	16	11	31	514	6	477	174	313	570
Hays	204	954	487	308	139	3,296	72	106	117	2,605	33	4,003	1,460	2,377	4,207
Hemphill	42	179	82	32	288	172	3	4	9	178	1	152	49	60	131
Henderson	236	1,855	527	268	256	3,032	75	72	128	3,226	68	3,384	1,270	2,812	3,438
Hidalgo	1,307	8,886	1,697	757	780	19,917	198	389	188	14,390	344	8,161	7,855	14,427	15,308
Hill	131	967	448	183	90	1,447	64	38	85	1,670	16	1,465	719	1,237	1,408
Hockley	108	844	367	183	88	973	63	40	58	1,996	28	572	776	1,190	627
Hood	76	384	499	206	41	1,020	21	34	37	1,046	8	1,639	462	851	1,765
Hopkins	101	893	582	213	62	1,525	50	36	99	1,431	15	1,565	931	1,719	1,904
Houston	136	1,688	814	317	132	1,974	103	36	51	1,850	18	1,428	866	1,447	1,185
Howard	224	1,061	774	196	83	1,658	91	27	69	1,457	16	1,149	791	1,244	1,227
Hudspeth	23	146	35	33	24	321	4	8	3	208	7	124	122	83	89
Hunt	208	1,389	1,030	362	197	3,213	73	69	77	1,881	38	2,297	1,445	2,096	2,626
Hutchinson	63	316	150	78	499	746	45	41	56	1,506	5	561	350	731	606
Irion	45	194	82	43	18	144	15	22	18	223	7	180	124	138	158
Jack	35	265	88	96	40	327	30	25	50	780	13	653	234	369	421
Jackson	109	824	251	327	85	1,093	87	37	38	1,304	23	752	662	1,085	662
Jasper	224	1,520	867	534	326	2,214	59	62	123	3,503	27	1,630	1,075	3,672	2,270
Jeff Davis	8	74	16	5	5	75	9	17	7	186	2	123	91	283	208
Jefferson	906	4,652	7,195	839	981	14,536	163	268	150	14,762	245	11,185	5,412	12,993	12,136
Jim Hogg	80	387	123	282	48	1,439	17	25	27	968	21	503	767	576	445
Jim Wells	384	1,584	888	618	307	4,490	66	77	64	2,489	78	2,103	1,171	2,988	3,201
Johnson	95	986	560	159	85	1,899	106	74	98	2,855	63	3,974	1,462	2,605	4,290
Jones	124	734	395	213	147	697	46	28	48	1,421	12	790	258	1,080	1,050
Karnes	80	663	108	156	39	761	62	77	134	1,494	44	744	596	1,453	1,104
Kaufman	290	1,457	1,001	308	172	3,221	78	79	81	2,031	42	2,137	1,296	2,441	2,438

Table 44: Gubernatorial Races

| | Democratic Primaries, 1986-1990 | | | | | | | | | | | | | | |
| Year | 1986 | | | | | | 1990 | | | | | | | Runoff | |
County	Sheila Bilyeu	Andrew C. Briscoe III	A. Don Crowder	Bobby Locke	Ron Slover	Mark White	Stanley Adams	Theresa Hearn-Hyns	Earl Holmes	Jim Mattox	Ray Rachal	Ann W. Richards	Mark White	Jim Mattox	Ann W. Richards
Kendall	8	28	12	5	2	198	30	3	2	96	1	294	96	97	298
Kenedy	0	24	11	15	7	111	1	4	1	83	1	42	51	52	41
Kent	28	172	100	54	46	180	7	5	8	347	2	102	79	309	150
Kerr	25	88	47	24	6	653	5	32	17	321	2	540	152	211	560
Kimble	13	130	23	15	6	147	13	12	21	213	5	161	153	169	152
King	7	73	34	27	45	36	4	3	2	101	1	48	24	77	62
Kinney	46	264	55	35	19	427	30	20	16	442	16	274	212	261	216
Kleberg	105	818	382	120	113	1,437	65	66	44	2,503	118	1,071	638	1,435	980
Knox	37	186	111	37	82	182	7	8	18	405	1	231	107	290	353
La Salle	45	357	94	130	15	1,124	21	29	10	618	20	318	638	971	707
Lamar	226	1,220	2,439	512	189	2,686	142	111	152	2,216	51	2,663	1,630	2,027	2,596
Lamb	26	182	302	24	47	398	23	32	35	1,227	16	413	287	1,126	705
Lampasas	89	583	282	79	165	933	39	39	32	758	11	699	301	501	614
Lavaca	120	1,389	474	156	100	1,245	51	27	57	1,243	14	695	415	1,009	737
Lee	94	636	336	159	118	1,005	34	42	82	1,120	15	705	411	1,239	790
Leon	44	311	774	70	75	713	34	21	58	1,215	14	750	471	558	567
Liberty	240	1,657	672	430	458	3,968	79	114	122	3,458	73	2,452	2,452	2,604	1,808
Limestone	118	1,023	279	209	223	1,506	51	48	48	1,469	33	1,421	607	939	1,333
Lipscomb	23	89	45	30	243	203	11	11	18	378	5	185	110	325	254
Live Oak	135	957	280	246	98	859	36	35	33	801	12	455	227	390	331
Llano	48	340	129	91	20	882	22	6	38	819	8	887	302	764	980
Loving	3	18	8	3	2	13	2	0	3	16	1	11	7	4	14
Lubbock	216	828	679	319	123	4,824	107	100	84	4,919	59	3,492	1,870	2,961	4,537
Lynn	31	261	115	37	29	376	19	19	22	858	5	173	242	279	174
Madison	64	763	236	101	103	794	34	8	23	763	9	538	320	514	408
Marion	64	284	462	101	42	1,078	49	23	60	1,684	23	1,069	497	2,048	1,319
Martin	13	149	75	29	15	179	14	8	14	259	7	161	114	266	188
Mason	6	65	19	9	6	165	12	4	12	231	7	185	99	153	182
Matagorda	192	1,759	475	424	176	2,753	106	102	73	2,442	35	1,815	1,473	1,823	1,633
Maverick	261	680	443	383	95	2,765	67	150	52	1,149	46	1,569	923	448	919
McCulloch	33	272	290	37	16	495	27	35	50	547	23	643	348	359	586
McLennan	672	5,792	1,251	882	544	10,422	177	205	163	6,772	107	9,060	3,898	6,314	11,318
McMullen	5	50	34	13	1	41	6	10	12	110	2	68	77	85	73
Medina	145	1,666	320	356	73	1,866	77	90	58	1,895	36	1,495	697	1,166	1,092
Menard	38	173	43	43	10	216	9	17	29	256	6	211	166	106	165
Midland	55	301	257	111	82	1,071	30	40	17	925	9	1,115	603	469	1,156
Milam	109	901	484	199	115	1,798	53	66	59	2,131	31	1,515	932	2,140	1,839
Mills	35	337	205	36	38	302	21	14	16	293	4	245	142	229	255
Mitchell	66	391	319	70	35	519	57	35	38	1,318	19	570	365	1,175	883
Montague	103	1,112	432	147	253	1,076	54	53	87	2,424	19	1,275	562	2,041	1,539
Montgomery	211	1,557	551	388	141	3,907	58	66	86	2,821	52	3,450	1,955	3,024	3,692
Moore	78	311	193	88	678	466	54	57	72	1,570	22	527	338	476	372
Morris	160	884	307	149	108	1,348	51	28	50	1,603	16	993	553	1,321	955
Motley	4	65	22	23	63	80	7	7	11	348	6	81	63	226	92
Nacogdoches	264	2,058	873	397	198	1,821	82	46	131	2,649	139	2,633	1,481	2,395	3,136
Navarro	210	1,244	759	205	248	3,019	100	86	114	2,274	51	2,301	1,627	2,543	2,934
Newton	107	819	442	121	135	1,358	43	58	23	1,971	21	909	633	1,852	1,268
Nolan	91	642	492	123	64	785	67	26	45	1,076	13	693	357	782	832
Nueces	718	4,456	2,161	2,185	258	14,014	277	726	1,011	12,195	396	8,964	4,520	10,114	10,617
Ochiltree	88	325	209	71	881	422	39	15	150	811	12	281	172	918	537
Oldham	25	113	64	23	214	196	24	23	19	396	0	121	84	223	138
Orange	393	1,895	3,206	547	297	5,164	161	140	121	7,746	51	3,871	2,097	7,134	5,080
Palo Pinto	162	953	518	269	97	1,480	88	65	69	1,311	27	1,833	666	988	1,627
Panola	162	1,672	682	358	78	1,685	118	40	79	2,831	17	1,417	718	2,780	1,844
Parker	132	982	659	221	69	1,764	54	67	108	1,812	29	2,730	945	1,439	2,579
Parmer	31	224	103	34	254	277	46	18	29	797	18	241	267	847	456
Pecos	100	754	324	181	70	884	62	75	54	999	31	671	733	999	671
Polk	286	1,918	525	359	235	2,324	116	129	88	3,076	69	1,958	1,421	3,458	2,683
Potter	216	805	484	214	1,751	2,880	70	117	62	2,986	37	1,817	1,001	1,771	2,257
Presidio	32	482	59	66	22	505	32	42	45	612	17	262	310	864	485
Rains	42	353	188	96	188	727	25	29	49	932	9	557	414	1,159	700
Randall	92	600	439	59	664	1,712	26	30	33	1,856	27	1,674	684	918	1,676
Reagan	50	404	177	42	12	220	13	6	11	194	2	63	78	111	50
Real	54	278	31	56	36	295	28	19	17	388	8	244	110	107	127
Red River	116	759	726	151	89	1,314	66	43	96	2,238	41	841	746	917	537

Table 44: Gubernatorial Races

	Democratic Primaries, 1986-1990														
Year	1986						1990							Runoff	
County	Sheila Bilyeu	Andrew C. Briscoe III	A. Don Crowder	Bobby Locke	Ron Slover	Mark White	Stanley Adams	Theresa Hearn-Hyns	Earl Holmes	Jim Mattox	Ray Rachal	Ann W. Richards	Mark White	Jim Mattox	Ann W. Richards
Reeves	170	1,060	412	249	116	1,836	52	126	59	1,593	38	709	868	744	454
Refugio	152	736	317	188	57	1,196	41	54	39	1,169	22	632	367	797	687
Roberts	7	72	46	18	175	94	5	2	8	120	6	56	24	61	29
Robertson	132	1,104	295	184	179	1,761	52	40	47	1,751	26	1,305	951	1,533	1,474
Rockwall	10	169	74	27	22	431	18	14	47	476	27	720	373	595	822
Runnels	63	399	239	82	28	383	39	26	79	951	23	508	279	885	822
Rusk	193	2,136	1,003	418	191	1,700	93	73	267	3,148	43	1,906	1,385	3,082	2,538
Sabine	80	346	264	146	42	496	25	27	68	1,541	19	842	499	1,418	1,035
San Augustine	105	684	280	144	190	1,013	54	25	36	1,485	16	712	638	1,754	1,438
San Jacinto	144	709	211	271	93	1,508	40	49	48	1,490	92	916	734	1,197	825
San Patricio	303	1,819	847	447	121	3,497	262	98	159	3,658	58	1,972	1,299	1,924	1,689
San Saba	43	414	153	163	60	685	6	8	27	281	6	273	189	343	371
Schleicher	12	123	52	39	9	145	30	24	17	237	10	207	183	269	294
Scurry	98	701	910	172	64	843	96	57	61	1,423	23	643	412	896	591
Shackelford	39	432	186	37	31	242	19	20	19	334	4	225	97	216	172
Shelby	147	1,504	645	263	100	1,766	91	23	56	2,825	36	1,648	1,083	1,801	1,649
Sherman	14	100	46	17	231	153	12	9	23	327	13	98	87	232	139
Smith	111	2,494	543	127	104	2,791	61	55	125	3,034	43	4,470	1,643	2,331	4,508
Somervell	48	325	163	163	55	482	38	39	36	699	15	651	323	829	871
Starr	163	1,846	126	161	111	2,373	22	57	36	1,763	21	594	1,593	651	408
Stephens	92	661	321	189	52	474	47	54	86	1,194	16	575	311	741	589
Sterling	34	134	72	35	13	112	2	4	5	114	6	69	40	36	49
Stonewall	48	333	180	52	59	283	6	14	14	525	9	225	83	281	228
Sutton	35	273	210	49	11	215	12	16	11	237	13	157	105	61	64
Swisher	37	204	285	39	311	797	15	10	25	849	7	475	477	400	513
Tarrant	943	4,110	1,704	979	486	20,323	266	574	324	17,578	167	39,370	12,682	16,159	40,912
Taylor	286	2,032	1,018	347	192	3,140	72	47	52	2,774	36	2,900	1,017	1,694	3,247
Terrell	21	128	54	29	13	256	18	12	12	143	5	149	189	65	60
Terry	64	542	418	55	67	786	46	49	43	1,725	27	462	537	1,569	848
Throckmorton	34	302	97	54	64	150	10	8	16	386	4	168	80	115	152
Titus	134	993	697	207	134	2,271	98	45	91	1,943	43	1,395	913	1,791	1,449
Tom Green	120	898	366	235	66	2,000	69	60	64	1,297	42	2,266	1,274	1,003	2,667
Travis	1,185	6,770	3,548	708	503	33,943	313	714	252	14,945	132	47,578	10,569	16,708	53,722
Trinity	95	1,828	336	2,518	94	1,149	54	31	66	1,853	26	950	695	1,058	793
Tyler	135	800	872	291	126	1,342	71	37	38	2,581	23	1,218	727	1,625	1,091
Upshur	211	1,785	758	298	262	2,045	111	42	262	3,203	27	2,177	798	3,170	2,564
Upton	98	554	291	124	45	273	13	27	17	525	17	166	163	604	324
Uvalde	144	1,190	312	396	82	2,096	99	71	108	1,781	85	1,681	851	1,446	1,367
Val Verde	79	633	138	105	24	1,169	42	103	58	1,437	43	1,714	698	1,660	2,090
VanZandt	113	1,832	440	271	192	1,906	66	79	147	2,237	69	2,085	1,007	1,915	2,059
Victoria	419	2,018	667	332	162	2,944	133	121	95	2,013	105	2,238	1,402	1,313	1,519
Walker	136	887	404	285	114	1,897	64	66	96	2,096	34	1,771	1,559	1,217	1,255
Waller	52	645	148	148	58	1,244	68	88	55	1,536	29	1,527	1,007	1,730	1,936
Ward	132	907	481	174	136	587	97	64	64	1,349	56	623	428	1,400	1,003
Washington	38	483	463	126	37	1,102	26	18	41	1,079	15	794	960	752	583
Webb	706	2,075	1,132	708	100	12,183	72	248	83	5,138	92	4,799	4,027	8,159	8,173
Wharton	64	920	403	230	107	1,662	56	64	58	2,089	32	1,461	1,518	1,860	1,310
Wheeler	49	262	146	85	518	363	43	22	24	925	12	221	171	621	305
Wichita	223	1,405	572	221	648	2,932	79	130	80	4,508	46	3,456	1,114	2,793	4,070
Wilbarger	59	356	127	47	362	586	33	29	26	1,373	3	444	281	433	369
Willacy	147	1,276	226	171	87	1,839	39	102	40	1,644	39	541	664	1,992	1,224
Williamson	109	732	569	176	63	2,724	49	74	87	3,169	34	5,765	1,910	3,140	6,250
Wilson	98	875	157	462	31	1,765	81	69	64	2,025	71	1,593	776	1,258	1,233
Winkler	50	398	221	110	69	432	28	42	50	698	26	320	218	223	173
Wise	148	1,100	641	319	298	1,755	85	103	124	1,905	49	2,415	858	2,144	2,766
Wood	86	1,431	373	121	106	1,196	34	39	237	1,675	28	1,580	804	1,084	1,306
Yoakum	106	609	270	193	66	430	31	12	22	715	12	228	200	535	307
Young	71	393	231	88	106	473	52	36	80	1,978	39	999	475	1,536	1,244
Zapata	97	553	221	123	71	1,253	10	41	25	961	12	598	440	224	217
Zavala	99	253	162	232	47	2,405	41	53	21	827	24	1,029	446	802	1,228
Official Totals	39,370		120,999		38,861		16,118		17,904			580,191		481,739	
		248,850		58,936		589,536		31,395		546,103	9,388		286,161		640,995
Unofficial Totals	39,370		120,999		38,861		16,118		17,904			580,191		481,739	
		248,850		58,936		590,329		31,395		546,103	9,388		286,161		640,995

Texas Political History

Table 45: Gubernatorial Races

County	General Elections, 1900-1904													
Year	1900				1902				1904					
	J. D. Sayers (D)	R. E. Hanny (R)	T. J. McMn (PE)	G. H. Royall (SL)	S. W. T. Lanham (D)	George W. Burkett (R)	J. M. Mallett (PE)	G. W. Carroll (P)	S. W. T. Lanham (D)	J. G. Lowden (R)	W. D. Jackson (P)	Frank Leitner (SL)	Pat B. Clark (PE)	W. H. Mills (SD)
Anderson	2,698	1,388	0	0	1,944	845	1	16	1,729	894	27	1	28	19
Andrews	0	0	0	0	0	0	0	0	0	0	0	0	0	0
Angelina	1,414	441	201	0	1,255	306	3	11	979	211	17	1	38	1
Aransas	214	114	9	0	274	109	3	2	56	46	6	0	9	0
Archer	468	81	14	0	418	75	0	0	326	79	20	0	9	0
Armstrong	196	34	24	0	260	6	1	6	223	17	19	0	8	0
Atascosa	941	134	54	0	1,222	90	42	46	709	101	14	2	38	4
Austin	2,056	932	1	4	1,859	1,022	0	1	1,512	622	4	0	0	15
Bailey	0	0	0	0	0	0	0	0	0	0	0	0	0	0
Bandera	550	350	46	0	696	183	5	7	541	125	8	1	20	18
Bastrop	2,617	1,425	121	0	2,101	1,206	9	7	1,061	44	6	0	8	0
Baylor	534	69	0	0	515	38	1	47	449	31	24	0	5	4
Bee	1,080	287	13	0	866	216	1	17	660	147	11	0	5	9
Bell	4,690	1,212	298	1	3,984	173	43	57	2,534	284	28	1	108	12
Bexar	5,787	3,318	56	71	5,455	2,090	35	94	3,735	1,362	25	43	12	90
Blanco	557	356	101	0	656	143	52	18	595	207	14	1	20	19
Borden	138	28	20	0	246	0	17	9	188	5	9	0	12	3
Bosque	1,836	407	343	0	1,577	170	56	23	1,116	343	34	1	51	3
Bowie	2,068	1,791	69	0	3,058	867	12	69	1,555	1,008	36	0	48	8
Brazoria	1,244	374	15	0	824	154	2	75	487	275	61	1	9	1
Brazos	2,348	1,048	0	0	1,922	730	4	14	1,103	178	11	0	9	1
Brewster	268	199	0	0	285	102	0	0	253	63	0	0	0	2
Briscoe	230	17	18	0	261	6	5	0	250	10	6	0	1	4
Brooks	0	0	0	0	0	0	0	0	0	0	0	0	0	0
Brown	1,996	544	176	0	1,450	191	10	67	1,320	256	17	0	59	15
Burleson	2,282	657	35	0	1,856	297	8	49	919	450	6	2	5	8
Burnet	1,651	29	172	0	1,661	54	25	46	962	127	40	0	122	11
Caldwell	2,301	827	231	0	1,844	293	8	200	1,092	110	24	0	24	12
Calhoun	323	67	0	0	174	94	5	1	313	85	4	0	3	2
Callahan	869	118	5	0	771	99	39	62	575	108	17	0	67	1
Cameron	1,600	1,526	0	0	1,715	1,013	0	2	1,080	74	0	0	0	2
Camp	698	693	83	0	873	335	23	9	574	300	2	0	16	3
Carson	105	21	2	0	142	9	1	3	137	18	11	0	5	0
Cass	1,421	1,655	451	0	1,449	316	99	22	1,180	919	38	3	126	2
Castro	124	22	0	0	197	0	0	0	178	14	0	0	4	2
Chambers	325	0	0	0	303	172	0	3	284	124	6	0	0	0
Cherokee	2,023	1,160	608	0	1,759	466	75	48	1,605	423	24	6	354	6
Childress	401	38	24	0	542	10	34	13	395	30	15	1	8	5
Clay	1,219	254	68	0	1,074	0	0	169	606	118	87	0	15	21
Cochran	0	0	0	0	0	0	0	0	0	0	0	0	0	0
Coke	374	121	100	0	477	76	63	29	399	54	8	1	159	3
Coleman	1,525	201	53	0	948	30	23	10	796	60	8	1	26	5
Collin	5,178	1,530	187	0	3,386	356	12	41	3,447	947	88	1	77	37
Collingsworth	212	21	24	0	269	7	2	7	253	13	6	0	15	7
Colorado	2,072	1,367	50	0	1,263	539	0	208	1,108	341	7	2	36	13
Comal	803	479	1	0	849	477	2	0	883	238	2	1	3	4
Comanche	2,210	346	1,518	0	2,017	292	1,490	212	1,638	274	39	2	1,108	7
Concho	220	66	21	0	274	38	39	4	286	56	6	0	34	0
Cooke	3,338	550	18	0	2,071	113	5	17	1,964	411	12	8	18	38
Coryell	2,262	416	327	0	1,903	145	162	0	1,273	168	12	3	72	17
Cottle	156	27	12	0	184	52	0	2	135	13	1	1	1	1
Crane	0	0	0	0	0	0	0	0	0	0	0	0	0	0
Crockett	175	172	0	0	251	72	0	41	142	60	4	1	0	0
Crosby	174	5	0	0	186	2	4	0	157	7	3	0	16	2
Culberson	0	0	0	0	0	0	0	0	0	0	0	0	0	0
Dallam	35	0	0	0	222	20	0	1	170	33	3	3	5	28
Dallas	9,035	2,732	145	23	5,355	744	83	370	5,989	1,243	137	14	47	86
Dawson	0	0	0	0	0	0	0	0	0	0	0	0	0	0
DeWitt	1,701	1,241	87	0	1,422	1,079	37	68	1,450	776	25	3	17	11
Deaf Smith	198	39	0	0	356	8	3	14	298	28	11	0	1	0
Delta	1,537	559	723	0	1,637	121	498	6	977	167	21	0	201	16
Denton	3,417	890	35	0	2,196	392	3	50	2,429	528	41	2	17	6
Dickens	195	6	26	0	219	0	17	7	198	20	7	1	20	0
Dimmit	145	124	19	0	217	63	5	7	135	79	4	12	13	9

Table 45: Gubernatorial Races

County	1900				1902				1904					
	J. D. Sayers (D)	R. E. Hanny (R)	T. J. McMn (PE)	G. H. Royall (SL)	S. W.T. Lanham (D)	George W. Burkett (R)	J. M. Mallett (PE)	G. W. Carroll (P)	S. W. T. Lanham (D)	J. G. Lowden (R)	W. D. Jackson (P)	Frank Leitner (SL)	Pat B. Clark (PE)	W. H. Mills (SD)
Donley	391	68	43	0	357	35	22	75	393	57	0	1	19	12
Duval	468	438	0	0	727	462	0	0	462	673	0	0	0	0
Eastland	1,987	441	718	0	2,275	243	467	49	1,599	212	37	4	555	30
Ector	85	30	0	0	115	3	0	3	165	5	4	0	1	0
Edwards	294	238	26	0	371	1	0	197	253	170	4	4	5	23
El Paso	2,682	819	0	0	2,702	138	0	0	1,772	732	10	3	11	29
Ellis	5,735	903	333	0	4,832	429	60	68	3,598	376	66	6	43	14
Erath	3,075	730	696	0	2,560	188	316	363	1,784	379	105	7	177	46
Falls	3,456	1,559	89	0	2,608	392	0	34	1,683	460	15	2	11	10
Fannin	5,848	1,638	279	0	4,928	1,180	10	30	3,234	785	1	0	0	105
Fayette	3,792	2,103	188	0	3,551	1,873	75	20	2,781	1,235	11	2	56	11
Fisher	446	91	181	0	484	74	197	2	411	42	36	0	115	1
Floyd	275	47	43	0	355	34	55	9	326	49	31	0	34	7
Foard	242	57	46	0	300	31	56	31	262	22	5	2	23	8
Fort Bend	1,362	35	23	0	728	132	8	26	1,237	16	10	1	11	1
Franklin	1,106	206	185	0	859	0	0	7	626	78	18	1	22	1
Freestone	1,489	1,171	209	0	1,468	636	93	12	948	355	9	2	36	0
Frio	541	200	34	0	529	209	5	9	457	146	5	0	21	9
Gaines	0	0	0	0	0	0	0	0	0	0	0	0	0	0
Galveston	3,771	1,576	1	0	4,324	1,355	0	75	2,174	592	34	3	3	29
Garza	0	0	0	0	0	0	0	0	0	0	0	0	0	0
Gillespie	478	1,117	0	0	598	924	0	10	328	978	4	0	4	0
Glasscock	19	5	0	0	95	0	5	0	99	15	0	0	13	4
Goliad	754	672	39	0	759	894	1	3	599	435	7	2	28	10
Gonzales	2,515	1,249	587	0	2,704	1,239	205	29	1,525	588	17	2	58	11
Gray	0	0	0	0	119	0	0	0	138	12	6	1	6	6
Grayson	6,763	2,211	73	0	4,358	871	14	114	3,557	1,095	69	8	39	164
Gregg	817	888	22	0	906	520	0	28	600	419	24	3	20	4
Grimes	1,605	71	255	0	1,067	44	1	26	922	117	7	1	32	3
Guadalupe	1,756	1,740	0	0	1,722	1,789	0	38	1,105	1,447	7	1	6	2
Hale	281	43	33	0	350	3	12	107	384	31	19	0	20	0
Hall	316	26	9	0	356	28	24	7	172	13	8	0	1	0
Hamilton	1,192	364	534	0	1,475	156	525	43	1,074	359	26	0	136	2
Hansford	29	21	0	0	78	13	8	0	100	10	0	0	0	0
Hardeman	571	62	22	0	626	27	5	33	529	45	17	0	10	5
Hardin	603	335	3	0	596	319	22	20	786	236	27	0	10	0
Harris	5,837	2,310	20	0	5,193	1,808	5	105	4,269	0	0	0	0	0
Harrison	1,408	822	21	0	2,834	182	0	45	707	173	8	0	3	0
Hartley	119	1	0	0	225	0	0	3	183	23	7	0	3	3
Haskell	460	39	55	0	752	702	20	8	597	65	3	0	59	3
Hays	1,462	429	35	0	1,507	336	6	60	1,167	196	29	0	16	0
Hemphill	157	52	0	0	168	29	21	196	143	41	8	0	1	0
Henderson	1,670	853	289	0	1,793	366	249	25	1,400	390	15	3	78	9
Hidalgo	1,397	426	0	0	950	70	0	0	475	37	0	0	0	0
Hill	4,811	762	602	0	3,541	332	69	29	2,875	348	40	1	137	2
Hockley	0	0	0	0	0	0	0	0	0	0	0	0	0	0
Hood	1,171	240	261	0	705	0	200	114	574	95	17	0	55	0
Hopkins	2,569	1,046	341	0	2,442	324	6	0	1,778	253	86	4	30	17
Houston	2,195	1,009	78	0	1,799	471	3	4	1,259	439	13	0	45	3
Howard	339	95	9	0	558	69	5	6	370	21	4	0	13	26
Hudspeth	0	0	0	0	0	0	0	0	0	0	0	0	0	0
Hunt	4,754	1,036	430	0	3,669	334	24	143	3,520	591	89	4	67	61
Hutchinson	0	0	0	0	130	2	0	0	130	7	1	0	2	2
Irion	159	49	0	0	182	0	7	0	172	26	5	1	10	3
Jack	1,037	305	480	0	912	151	529	31	0	0	0	0	0	0
Jackson	471	357	41	0	534	483	41	3	265	160	3	0	26	2
Jasper	530	460	64	0	381	141	0	48	618	308	24	2	34	3
Jeff Davis	109	139	0	0	139	155	0	0	119	61	2	0	0	0
Jefferson	1,755	275	0	0	2,041	523	6	502	1,649	853	72	16	8	42
Jim Hogg	0	0	0	0	0	0	0	0	0	0	0	0	0	0
Jim Wells	0	0	0	0	0	0	0	0	0	0	0	0	0	0
Johnson	3,705	871	465	0	2,144	30	404	86	2,227	294	40	15	139	151
Jones	755	130	299	0	942	67	96	24	732	76	18	1	44	22
Karnes	1,009	232	158	0	1,122	336	123	43	1,005	145	28	1	31	1
Kaufman	3,553	648	77	0	3,666	496	44	60	2,279	318	22	2	66	23

Table 45: Gubernatorial Races

Year	1900				1902				1904					
County	J. D. Sayers (D)	R. E. Hanny (R)	T. J. McMn (PE)	G. H. Royall (SL)	S. W.T. Lanham (D)	George W. Burkett (R)	J. M. Mallett (PE)	G. W. Carroll (P)	S. W. T. Lanham (D)	J. G. Lowden (R)	W. D. Jackson (P)	Frank Leitner (SL)	Pat B. Clark (PE)	W. H. Mills (SD)
Kendall	294	461	17	0	322	458	0	0	153	534	1	5	0	8
Kenedy	0	0	0	0	0	0	0	0	0	0	0	0	0	0
Kent	175	27	16	0	192	13	21	0	188	8	4	0	7	0
Kerr	576	344	13	0	652	245	0	0	580	228	4	3	7	22
Kimble	306	115	5	0	479	22	0	1	351	124	32	0	10	2
King	129	5	0	0	122	0	0	0	102	0	0	0	0	0
Kinney	186	194	1	0	278	155	0	0	219	200	2	1	0	1
Kleberg	0	0	0	0	0	0	0	0	0	0	0	0	0	0
Knox	424	23	41	0	597	41	57	11	447	70	6	1	22	2
La Salle	185	323	0	0	404	50	0	0	300	79	4	0	4	0
Lamar	4,257	1,527	184	0	3,251	333	6	69	2,562	739	41	7	99	29
Lamb	0	0	0	0	0	0	0	0	0	0	0	0	0	0
Lampasas	972	0	136	0	869	168	90	258	751	202	126	5	88	12
Lavaca	0	0	0	0	2,377	802	291	50	1,819	517	19	1	57	38
Lee	1,418	877	39	0	1,326	944	39	25	982	392	3	0	4	0
Leon	1,736	1,074	95	0	1,117	588	26	40	1,117	336	4	2	30	14
Liberty	824	307	45	0	780	532	27	17	685	310	11	2	11	2
Limestone	3,330	935	238	0	2,357	252	8	11	1,654	197	25	3	52	35
Lipscomb	135	60	0	0	143	50	0	0	116	46	1	0	0	0
Live Oak	414	51	5	0	404	47	0	19	279	29	4	0	25	0
Llano	860	238	165	0	990	62	99	34	849	118	38	0	63	0
Loving	0	0	0	0	0	0	0	0	0	0	0	0	0	0
Lubbock	197	0	6	0	298	13	25	6	244	13	4	2	5	2
Lynn	0	0	0	0	0	0	0	0	131	8	17	1	13	3
Madison	1,000	466	234	0	1,052	333	244	7	541	178	6	0	40	5
Marion	1,752	124	114	0	315	114	0	18	274	483	6	0	10	0
Martin	87	9	0	0	164	0	0	2	170	24	2	0	1	0
Mason	627	350	77	0	667	257	50	53	603	236	22	3	20	1
Matagorda	352	252	6	0	515	1	0	12	338	83	17	3	3	1
Maverick	415	411	0	0	436	285	0	3	295	205	1	0	1	4
McCulloch	552	203	47	0	762	95	0	15	604	104	10	5	26	4
McLennan	5,372	1,726	60	0	4,138	393	27	82	3,727	640	103	3	23	53
McMullen	158	64	1	0	136	38	2	1	87	27	0	0	2	0
Medina	920	501	21	0	739	634	7	14	595	438	14	0	2	4
Menard	334	147	18	0	419	8	2	8	357	57	14	0	18	1
Midland	278	71	0	0	347	37	0	11	134	18	1	0	0	0
Milam	3,470	1,107	575	0	2,834	479	222	32	2,120	353	17	0	151	17
Mills	845	288	286	0	647	31	252	27	463	118	18	3	45	13
Mitchell	460	133	21	0	501	66	16	46	471	71	29	0	9	0
Montague	3,081	310	93	0	1,965	99	31	46	1,623	218	59	4	28	27
Montgomery	1,455	877	128	0	1,367	1,036	34	4	865	380	3	1	23	7
Moore	59	7	0	0	122	1	0	1	99	2	0	0	0	1
Morris	738	586	119	0	1,004	213	19	23	569	233	15	0	36	0
Motley	261	6	0	0	259	9	0	71	240	10	14	0	0	0
Nacogdoches	1,870	1,005	1,096	0	1,813	761	665	169	1,593	220	19	1	874	3
Navarro	4,577	1,222	662	0	3,619	489	153	159	2,406	398	40	2	73	23
Newton	824	342	40	0	684	357	0	99	470	317	71	3	10	2
Nolan	404	125	41	0	600	88	45	3	531	79	12	1	46	2
Nueces	1,167	440	1	0	1,225	593	0	7	581	144	7	0	6	26
Ochiltree	23	10	0	0	120	0	0	0	81	18	39	0	1	0
Oldham	86	16	675	0	75	9	0	1	63	13	1	0	0	0
Orange	675	387	23	0	846	405	5	95	607	196	6	3	0	14
Palo Pinto	1,516	83	438	0	1,528	32	59	124	974	151	64	12	64	33
Panola	1,780	667	17	0	1,370	0	0	0	1,182	339	8	0	45	1
Parker	2,789	396	798	0	2,342	223	503	182	1,826	478	74	4	142	60
Parmer	0	0	0	0	0	0	0	0	0	0	0	0	0	0
Pecos	295	184	0	0	348	92	0	0	228	68	0	0	0	2
Polk	1,156	860	332	0	744	232	30	12	520	152	8	0	37	1
Potter	349	84	2	0	475	59	1	47	579	81	12	4	3	16
Presidio	409	286	0	0	453	118	0	0	278	96	0	0	0	0
Rains	556	444	124	0	676	236	163	44	495	137	8	4	12	166
Randall	229	37	11	0	276	19	7	31	291	34	15	0	4	0
Reagan	0	0	0	0	0	0	0	0	73	3	0	0	0	0
Real	0	0	0	0	0	0	0	0	0	0	0	0	0	0
Red River	2,641	834	472	0	2,492	831	74	12	1,587	614	28	4	109	2

Table 45: Gubernatorial Races

	General Elections, 1900-1904													
Year	1900				1902				1904					
County	J. D. Sayers (D)	R. E. Hanny (R)	T. J. McMn (PE)	G. H. Royall (SL)	S. W.T. Lanham (D)	George W. Burkett (R)	J. M. Mallett (PE)	G. W. Carroll (P)	S. W. T. Lanham (D)	J. G. Lowden (R)	W. D. Jackson (P)	Frank Leitner (SL)	Pat B. Clark (PE)	W. H. Mills (SD)
Reeves	578	24	15	0	314	4	0	0	320	20	1	0	0	0
Refugio	216	57	0	0	219	135	0	1	148	87	1	0	2	0
Roberts	220	71	21	0	142	8	0	2	100	19	12	1	7	0
Robertson	2,111	598	6	0	3,173	163	0	11	1,448	100	6	0	12	1
Rockwall	1,145	120	49	0	757	32	6	31	641	48	28	0	16	10
Runnels	654	118	6	0	677	48	23	30	800	63	18	19	17	4
Rusk	2,271	1,611	184	0	1,760	920	67	7	1,972	1,113	3	0	85	0
Sabine	621	0	0	0	0	0	0	0	652	223	40	1	48	5
San Augustine	699	357	314	0	1,026	179	94	0	423	155	7	1	23	0
San Jacinto	663	993	26	0	714	1,005	0	3	470	542	7	4	7	0
San Patricio	473	40	0	0	477	56	1	4	185	35	3	0	0	0
San Saba	1,225	0	295	0	1,070	108	74	10	878	131	26	2	42	2
Schleicher	0	0	0	0	187	21	22	0	214	23	0	0	8	1
Scurry	398	100	298	0	484	71	301	99	462	107	35	1	216	15
Shackelford	269	60	0	0	204	8	0	0	162	23	1	0	5	0
Shelby	1,779	367	60	0	1,170	131	8	13	1,534	186	19	3	42	7
Sherman	24	8	0	0	144	3	0	0	112	24	7	0	1	5
Smith	2,802	2,324	145	0	2,154	904	52	72	2,409	1,183	82	12	58	75
Somervell	437	23	252	0	402	1	243	5	377	38	8	1	84	1
Starr	1,248	856	0	0	1,190	589	0	0	905	323	0	0	0	0
Stephens	867	34	211	0	540	11	3	1	385	13	8	0	20	26
Sterling	149	47	57	0	173	33	40	3	131	14	4	1	19	1
Stonewall	400	25	5	0	410	13	11	1	333	25	4	0	10	1
Sutton	182	162	0	0	214	94	1	0	239	27	1	0	2	0
Swisher	166	40	8	0	222	30	18	5	230	17	9	0	5	0
Tarrant	5,766	1,228	201	0	5,102	989	98	303	4,060	766	129	31	109	106
Taylor	1,298	323	230	0	1,005	48	35	55	1,038	161	26	2	79	6
Terrell	0	0	0	0	0	0	0	0	0	0	0	0	0	0
Terry	0	0	0	0	0	0	0	0	124	6	4	0	3	0
Throckmorton	256	59	46	0	220	28	32	22	141	20	14	0	24	1
Titus	1,018	406	189	0	934	171	139	4	734	129	5	2	0	0
Tom Green	620	219	3	0	725	155	3	6	740	122	17	1	7	0
Travis	4,975	1,924	116	0	3,817	1,379	15	52	2,523	670	34	7	13	25
Trinity	1,156	479	45	0	1,128	295	2	1	608	169	3	0	35	0
Tyler	1,256	482	55	0	876	274	9	52	660	110	13	0	19	5
Upshur	1,444	866	211	0	1,062	145	1	20	816	336	21	15	39	1
Upton	0	0	0	0	0	0	0	0	0	0	0	0	0	0
Uvalde	595	250	0	0	657	235	0	2	454	70	1	2	0	5
Val Verde	654	145	0	0	770	40	0	0	471	118	4	0	1	22
Van Zandt	2,291	0	0	0	2,687	84	149	29	1,555	238	29	11	36	205
Victoria	1,271	957	0	0	1,243	1,144	1	3	861	351	5	0	3	1
Walker	1,364	1,086	103	0	1,065	336	42	3	710	593	3	0	20	0
Waller	958	794	6	0	739	776	48	52	807	529	8	0	45	5
Ward	226	134	0	0	313	15	1	23	158	20	19	0	1	0
Washington	2,348	1,030	2	0	2,973	658	0	2	1,336	622	5	0	3	2
Webb	1,230	1,655	0	0	2,212	869	0	0	526	1,004	0	0	0	0
Wharton	797	523	5	0	463	619	2	47	607	463	24	0	3	34
Wheeler	120	22	2	0	168	0	2	1	200	9	5	0	8	2
Wichita	922	205	18	0	781	149	16	51	661	113	16	3	5	9
Wilbarger	685	76	11	0	822	78	15	62	410	52	25	2	9	31
Willacy	0	0	0	0	0	0	0	0	0	0	0	0	0	0
Williamson	4,580	762	512	0	3,217	548	123	109	2,403	559	90	2	139	9
Wilson	1,839	433	70	0	2,273	601	0	52	993	272	10	1	75	9
Winkler	0	0	0	0	0	0	0	0	0	0	0	0	0	0
Wise	3,033	642	336	0	2,492	189	137	145	1,664	339	97	1	96	13
Wood	1,654	671	532	0	1,803	288	60	29	1,341	441	33	1	35	78
Yoakum	0	0	0	0	0	0	0	0	0	0	0	0	0	0
Young	917	148	74	0	970	61	6	74	903	87	43	1	53	12
Zapata	159	413	0	0	159	279	0	0	52	257	0	0	0	0
Zavala	139	28	7	0	153	16	0	0	152	6	1	0	2	0
Official	303,556		26,579		271,578		12,393		206,167		4,509		9,301	
Totals		112,864		155		66,930		8,711		56,865		552		2,847
Unofficial	303,558		27,264		273,086		12,311		205,311		4,407		9,477	
Totals		111,864		99		66,639		8,880		56,565		447		2,907

Table 46: Gubernatorial Races

General Elections, 1906-1910

County	T. M. Campbll (D)	C. A. Gray (R)	J. W. Pearson (P)	G. C. Edwards (S)	A. S. Dowlr (SL)	A. W. Atchsn (RE)	T. M. Campbll (D)	J. N. Simpsn (R)	E. C. Heath (P)	J. C. Rhodes (S)	W. B. Cook (SL)	O.B. Colquitt (D)	J.O. Terrell (R)	A. J. Houston (P)	Redding Andrws (S)	Carl Schmdt (SL)
	1906						1908					1910				
Anderson	1,383	177	1	6	0	96	1,634	639	0	25	3	1,429	198	28	64	3
Andrews	0	0	0	0	0	0	0	0	0	0	0	97	3	0	1	0
Angelina	567	13	13	7	0	0	1,110	248	0	0	0	1,182	92	29	98	2
Aransas	105	6	0	0	0	3	186	35	0	0	0	133	16	3	3	0
Archer	186	27	5	0	0	1	331	57	0	0	0	303	23	11	29	2
Armstrong	130	10	5	0	0	0	235	32	9	1	0	186	9	13	5	0
Atascosa	341	53	2	8	0	0	631	139	0	10	0	576	79	18	23	2
Austin	1,655	493	1	18	0	22	1,294	657	0	8	0	1,186	169	2	9	1
Bailey	0	0	0	0	0	0	0	0	0	0	0	0	0	0	0	0
Bandera	372	164	12	10	4	0	471	281	0	20	3	409	231	22	23	4
Bastrop	733	91	10	1	3	59	1,203	539	0	8	1	826	204	25	32	0
Baylor	178	7	2	2	0	0	601	50	0	34	0	557	13	9	48	0
Bee	348	61	7	1	0	0	532	146	0	24	1	342	52	35	23	0
Bell	1,948	87	23	18	5	27	3,007	48	0	0	1	1,603	78	50	49	0
Bexar	3,513	713	15	37	20	89	2,957	4,577	0	69	7	5,478	1,128	113	58	14
Blanco	512	164	14	17	2	16	432	265	0	0	3	522	147	13	11	2
Borden	185	7	13	6	2	1	134	5	0	11	0	114	2	7	6	0
Bosque	808	77	12	4	1	0	1,420	251	0	25	0	962	73	17	35	0
Bowie	928	118	14	2	0	40	1,680	685	0	104	9	1,322	144	49	305	3
Brazoria	305	139	20	9	2	67	557	418	1	25	1	410	173	101	25	0
Brazos	456	31	1	3	0	127	852	141	0	0	0	744	79	23	0	0
Brewster	240	53	4	6	0	2	291	24	0	2	0	151	11	7	12	0
Briscoe	76	1	1	1	1	0	118	7	0	90	0	164	2	2	7	0
Brooks	0	0	0	0	0	0	0	0	0	0	0	0	0	0	0	0
Brown	1,096	126	14	12	1	2	1,672	358	1	90	0	1,159	114	37	85	2
Burleson	822	93	1	5	0	158	1,186	377	0	20	4	711	101	6	6	0
Burnet	555	41	29	2	1	5	858	275	1	8	0	606	78	58	24	1
Caldwell	879	45	6	2	0	40	1,173	272	0	14	0	846	141	11	13	0
Calhoun	274	81	3	10	2	2	226	75	0	14	0	197	19	13	7	0
Callahan	457	15	3	12	1	1	868	100	0	71	1	686	24	15	92	3
Cameron	786	170	0	0	0	0	1,210	973	0	2	0	1,765	1,146	22	5	0
Camp	403	121	0	2	0	17	583	305	0	5	1	458	224	6	9	0
Carson	115	17	4	2	0	1	164	39	0	3	0	187	39	6	7	0
Cass	883	155	9	7	0	0	1,660	942	0	39	0	870	469	29	96	3
Castro	122	10	5	2	0	0	66	9	0	2	0	111	19	14	15	0
Chambers	176	104	3	7	0	0	333	270	0	20	0	168	68	0	7	11
Cherokee	1,233	90	7	24	1	9	1,513	211	2	84	3	1,231	51	20	96	0
Childress	166	12	2	0	0	0	613	80	0	0	0	414	38	7	24	1
Clay	495	35	52	12	2	2	1,076	277	1	37	0	975	141	50	71	0
Cochran	0	0	0	0	0	0	0	0	0	0	0	0	0	0	0	0
Coke	280	34	8	5	1	0	355	54	0	27	0	269	19	8	17	1
Coleman	585	21	6	15	0	0	1,180	124	0	0	1	852	71	19	106	2
Collin	2,367	298	31	46	0	17	3,837	790	0	128	1	2,173	292	58	126	2
Collingsworth	153	8	6	0	0	0	397	30	0	14	0	286	8	22	38	0
Colorado	808	251	3	22	2	68	867	748	7	0	0	765	129	30	30	1
Comal	737	233	0	0	0	0	509	627	19	0	0	924	64	0	1	1
Comanche	1,243	161	39	25	1	3	2,427	228	0	136	6	1,456	145	59	367	3
Concho	148	7	1	1	0	0	239	26	2	31	0	298	16	2	32	1
Cooke	1,415	156	9	40	2	31	2,075	708	0	95	0	1,403	163	21	96	5
Coryell	1,078	46	3	15	1	3	1,686	175	0	28	1	1,212	60	13	48	0
Cottle	79	4	0	0	0	0	162	11	0	10	0	144	3	2	4	1
Crane	0	0	0	0	0	0	7	0	0	2	0	0	0	0	0	0
Crockett	58	8	0	1	0	0	65	13	0	3	0	31	1	0	5	0
Crosby	153	11	2	8	1	0	139	11	0	11	0	124	7	5	11	0
Culberson	0	0	0	0	0	0	0	0	0	0	0	0	0	0	0	0
Dallam	169	32	5	29	7	2	311	92	2	41	0	196	25	18	24	1
Dallas	3,332	264	77	52	0	136	7,028	2,498	2	120	6	4,800	347	397	85	4
Dawson	39	0	0	0	0	0	158	5	0	0	1	95	8	9	13	1
DeWitt	725	268	8	7	0	39	792	1,022	0	0	0	1,164	160	17	10	1
Deaf Smith	122	4	3	0	0	0	275	47	0	2	1	245	16	13	2	0
Delta	619	5	7	7	0	1	966	120	0	23	0	674	35	16	93	5
Denton	1,345	162	25	20	0	2	2,731	512	0	0	81	1,572	137	23	77	0
Dickens	81	18	2	1	0	0	201	33	0	0	1	198	14	10	36	1
Dimmit	147	93	1	2	2	0	149	104	0	1	0	232	217	13	6	2

Table 46: Gubernatorial Races

	General Elections, 1906-1910															
Year	1906						1908					1910				
County	T. M. Campbll (D)	C. A. Gray (R)	J. W. Pearson (P)	G. C. Edwards (S)	A. S. Dowlr (SL)	A. W. Atchsn (RE)	T. M. Campbll (D)	J. N. Simpsn (R)	E. C. Heath (P)	J. C. Rhodes (S)	W. B. Cook (SL)	O.B. Colquitt (D)	J.O. Terrell (R)	A. J. Houston (P)	Redding Andrws (S)	Carl Schmdt (SL)
Donley	362	43	1	11	1	26	409	36	0	0	12	226	11	20	10	0
Duval	370	266	0	0	0	0	700	602	0	0	0	528	18	0	2	0
Eastland	1,375	71	0	71	1	1	0	0	0	0	0	1,369	107	94	270	0
Ector	100	3	3	0	0	0	137	5	0	2	0	85	4	6	1	0
Edwards	243	127	9	83	3	0	217	223	0	0	0	180	141	21	70	0
El Paso	1,244	197	6	17	2	7	2,095	1,116	0	80	0	2,078	328	52	20	1
Ellis	2,753	137	44	5	0	24	4,457	638	0	22	22	2,372	122	89	38	0
Erath	1,072	92	29	22	1	4	2,114	458	1	249	5	1,529	190	67	233	3
Falls	1,288	294	10	22	0	38	1,766	524	0	0	0	1,358	342	22	97	11
Fannin	2,852	450	12	37	3	5	3,177	604	0	0	4	1,729	177	50	60	0
Fayette	2,175	782	4	10	2	26	1,961	1,524	0	0	1	2,044	497	15	31	2
Fisher	373	23	16	3	0	7	808	46	0	43	0	608	31	37	143	0
Floyd	152	10	6	4	1	0	293	17	0	14	0	232	12	24	32	0
Foard	248	24	6	9	0	4	303	37	0	15	4	401	46	3	92	0
Fort Bend	345	176	8	4	1	106	543	359	7	0	0	463	157	21	15	0
Franklin	495	21	3	3	0	2	658	654	0	16	0	495	15	10	13	0
Freestone	689	64	2	0	0	152	1,194	231	0	9	0	982	272	4	14	3
Frio	470	132	3	16	0	1	392	118	0	10	0	331	54	5	2	0
Gaines	40	3	1	0	0	0	96	3	0	3	0	66	2	0	4	1
Galveston	1,775	202	21	18	1	77	2,020	1,070	0	0	4	1,471	272	102	38	7
Garza	0	0	0	0	0	0	72	6	0	1	0	88	2	3	3	0
Gillespie	316	924	8	1	2	6	241	1,390	0	3	0	791	688	6	6	2
Glasscock	48	2	0	0	0	0	73	16	0	0	0	66	3	0	0	0
Goliad	461	432	4	10	0	11	389	659	0	60	0	517	562	54	56	2
Gonzales	1,163	241	12	41	0	114	1,364	678	0	43	0	1,030	199	17	38	0
Gray	199	13	16	21	3	1	341	78	0	41	2	317	55	51	34	1
Grayson	3,582	640	62	75	8	261	4,415	1,505	0	178	11	2,750	469	70	124	5
Gregg	432	43	3	1	0	63	578	264	0	1	25	393	57	17	6	1
Grimes	597	27	3	1	0	7	996	86	0	8	0	727	15	10	3	1
Guadalupe	1,060	1,289	9	1	0	9	897	1,811	0	1	0	1,772	1,009	33	8	0
Hale	158	6	2	2	0	0	408	40	0	3	0	378	15	19	25	0
Hall	171	5	3	0	1	0	526	45	4	17	0	343	14	9	37	0
Hamilton	983	121	17	0	0	0	1,140	213	0	6	0	851	62	7	8	1
Hansford	73	6	0	0	1	0	96	28	0	8	0	114	14	13	7	0
Hardeman	246	5	12	0	1	0	680	97	0	31	2	483	70	19	40	1
Hardin	597	46	7	11	0	3	898	226	0	26	0	746	112	55	136	4
Harris	2,442	313	21	72	17	79	4,788	2,004	1	128	12	6,265	449	282	146	16
Harrison	810	32	4	3	1	210	1,260	127	0	7	0	781	66	38	5	0
Hartley	65	0	0	0	0	0	157	0	0	0	0	93	3	3	0	0
Haskell	451	39	5	3	0	0	1,250	147	0	97	3	1,008	64	21	225	0
Hays	575	17	1	6	3	11	871	131	0	0	0	565	31	12	3	0
Hemphill	0	0	0	0	0	0	188	89	0	12	0	261	92	25	9	2
Henderson	1,061	73	4	18	1	97	1,155	255	0	102	0	982	120	22	173	0
Hidalgo	601	14	0	0	0	0	561	28	0	1	0	892	64	8	18	0
Hill	1,935	75	17	2	0	80	3,304	410	0	15	1	1,879	92	54	22	2
Hockley	0	0	0	0	0	0	0	0	0	0	0	0	0	0	0	0
Hood	408	47	18	3	0	3	985	142	0	29	0	617	85	21	37	1
Hopkins	1,725	106	39	53	1	13	2,204	289	0	131	3	1,855	131	70	134	31
Houston	768	83	1	0	0	0	1,337	477	0	23	0	974	96	25	50	0
Howard	272	6	2	12	0	0	509	49	0	41	0	454	14	22	75	1
Hudspeth	0	0	0	0	0	0	0	0	0	0	0	0	0	0	0	0
Hunt	2,093	217	53	43	2	98	3,788	525	0	155	2	2,440	220	50	230	1
Hutchinson	118	11	3	0	0	0	122	37	0	2	0	118	30	6	5	0
Irion	72	2	0	5	0	0	103	5	0	2	0	108	0	1	2	0
Jack	715	177	39	17	2	4	792	263	11	61	1	554	154	29	106	0
Jackson	126	32	4	1	0	0	300	147	0	6	0	166	52	23	9	1
Jasper	457	54	0	1	1	38	726	166	0	80	0	604	93	4	119	4
Jeff Davis	106	64	1	2	0	1	128	82	0	6	0	92	90	4	1	0
Jefferson	1,148	160	14	28	2	25	2,026	879	2	111	5	1,040	141	65	78	2
Jim Hogg	0	0	0	0	0	0	0	0	0	0	0	0	0	0	0	0
Jim Wells	0	0	0	0	0	0	0	0	0	0	0	1,483	113	29	122	2
Johnson	1,247	78	20	80	4	10	2,737	388	0	129	3	1,040	83	27	146	1
Jones	624	40	27	45	0	0	1,764	196	0	151	2	1,040	83	27	146	1
Karnes	508	37	4	1	0	4	608	249	0	7	0	460	64	25	0	0
Kaufman	1,464	161	11	12	0	42	2,165	411	0	81	1	1,594	149	24	74	1

Table 46: Gubernatorial Races

	General Elections, 1906-1910																
Year	1906						1908					1910				
County	T. M. Campbll (D)	C. A. Gray (R)	J. W. Pearson (P)	G. C. Edwards (S)	A. S. Dowlr (SL)	A. W. Atchsn (RE)	T. M. Campbll (D)	J. N. Simpsn (R)	E. C. Heath (P)	J. C. Rhodes (S)	W. B. Cook (SL)	O.B. Colquitt (D)	J.O. Terrell (R)	A. J. Houston (P)	Redding Andrws (S)	Carl Schmdt (SL)
Kendall	155	295	1	23	1	1	123	537	0	17	0	414	178	4	12	1
Kenedy	0	0	0	0	0	0	0	0	0	0	0	0	0	0	0	0
Kent	80	3	0	0	0	0	208	10	0	2	0	129	1	5	14	0
Kerr	366	245	12	15	2	8	477	356	0	21	0	543	214	34	29	2
Kimble	271	68	31	20	4	0	189	56	0	16	0	159	13	12	20	0
King	91	0	0	0	0	0	69	1	0	0	0	42	0	0	0	0
Kinney	144	235	0	7	2	2	165	280	0	3	0	130	250	1	13	2
Kleberg	0	0	0	0	0	0	0	0	0	0	0	0	0	0	0	0
Knox	327	15	3	2	1	0	772	131	0	16	0	522	32	11	73	0
La Salle	237	61	2	0	0	0	325	237	0	1	1	231	37	2	1	0
Lamar	1,654	109	10	11	0	86	2,872	479	0	37	0	1,775	120	26	39	0
Lamb	0	0	0	0	0	0	16	3	0	0	0	27	16	25	0	1
Lampasas	1,059	156	100	14	1	17	753	299	0	9	1	481	87	65	28	2
Lavaca	1,522	463	5	96	5	15	1,368	1,189	0	198	1	1,690	197	50	192	3
Lee	571	116	4	0	0	84	820	508	0	13	0	720	123	17	24	0
Leon	682	81	1	8	2	72	871	346	0	17	3	531	163	13	70	0
Liberty	519	109	3	2	0	123	549	246	0	10	0	835	235	7	15	36
Limestone	1,272	55	16	11	1	35	1,809	223	0	41	2	1,163	56	36	108	2
Lipscomb	126	16	4	0	0	0	172	62	0	17	0	211	91	18	40	0
Live Oak	285	46	8	1	1	2	316	82	0	1	0	266	82	17	6	0
Llano	346	18	11	0	0	1	491	118	0	7	0	391	24	9	11	0
Loving	0	0	0	0	0	0	0	0	0	0	0	0	0	0	0	0
Lubbock	193	13	3	0	0	3	231	24	0	1	0	213	12	30	8	0
Lynn	104	7	6	6	0	3	269	6	0	9	0	109	4	4	9	0
Madison	308	8	2	0	1	54	548	122	0	5	0	362	80	12	10	0
Marion	195	87	14	3	1	2	416	340	0	4	3	190	18	32	3	0
Martin	54	0	0	0	0	0	246	18	0	2	1	86	2	4	8	0
Mason	237	102	7	5	0	0	454	335	0	93	0	462	238	22	61	4
Matagorda	260	13	25	2	0	0	584	177	0	0	4	391	58	74	28	2
Maverick	267	211	0	7	0	3	245	293	0	7	0	214	227	3	4	0
McCulloch	605	81	6	1	7	0	669	186	0	14	8	488	32	18	106	12
McLennan	1,696	165	44	35	2	195	3,795	751	0	96	1	2,087	135	109	44	1
McMullen	58	12	0	0	0	0	84	35	0	1	0	50	1	0	0	0
Medina	500	445	22	2	5	0	476	812	0	6	1	899	317	33	12	2
Menard	106	10	2	0	0	0	159	35	0	6	0	81	8	1	13	0
Midland	89	11	2	1	0	0	305	28	0	7	0	168	20	0	3	0
Milam	1,225	79	13	46	9	18	2,057	505	0	149	1	1,898	102	29	289	1
Mills	264	39	2	19	1	0	549	210	0	58	0	687	133	19	66	1
Mitchell	224	9	3	0	0	2	638	81	0	42	0	500	42	11	74	0
Montague	1,244	155	37	33	4	2	2,008	370	0	90	3	1,258	164	52	240	3
Montgomery	746	133	3	13	7	51	783	270	1	17	0	471	33	15	9	0
Moore	87	2	3	1	2	0	95	24	0	2	1	44	3	2	0	0
Morris	509	43	1	2	0	11	656	133	1	3	1	568	42	8	0	0
Motley	189	6	0	1	0	0	129	15	0	12	1	89	3	3	12	0
Nacogdoches	1,060	14	12	14	1	10	1,498	177	0	34	0	1,004	87	26	79	0
Navarro	1,752	117	15	17	0	59	2,866	604	0	24	0	1,830	63	40	52	0
Newton	279	40	17	1	0	37	388	90	0	6	0	366	53	4	17	0
Nolan	210	16	6	0	0	0	765	96	0	31	1	568	47	25	39	1
Nueces	711	170	6	17	2	12	824	268	0	0	0	805	120	32	95	1
Ochiltree	129	0	2	3	0	21	151	43	0	2	0	114	3	5	2	0
Oldham	54	5	1	0	0	0	41	13	0	1	0	95	37	16	0	0
Orange	502	23	12	15	0	70	515	126	0	13	0	384	11	7	10	1
Palo Pinto	737	30	36	48	3	3	1,524	235	0	91	0	982	57	73	210	1
Panola	959	41	1	7	0	3	1,247	247	0	63	0	859	61	12	78	0
Parker	1,318	86	31	151	2	6	2,098	295	0	308	2	1,661	107	92	346	0
Parmer	0	0	0	0	0	0	103	28	0	2	0	140	32	8	1	0
Pecos	135	54	0	1	0	0	162	97	0	0	0	86	51	14	1	2
Polk	364	42	1	0	0	8	656	216	0	0	0	421	14	3	5	1
Potter	451	28	24	26	2	0	825	158	0	46	1	718	58	50	52	1
Presidio	369	28	2	0	0	0	235	143	0	1	0	284	33	5	2	1
Rains	417	28	12	61	0	39	433	56	0	87	1	353	36	4	140	3
Randall	191	18	4	2	0	0	229	47	0	1	0	195	12	13	1	0
Reagan	35	0	0	0	0	0	47	3	0	2	0	38	1	0	0	0
Real	0	0	0	0	0	0	0	0	0	0	0	0	0	0	0	0
Red River	1,191	109	7	17	1	36	1,831	577	0	31	0	1,124	98	19	34	1

Table 46: Gubernatorial Races

General Elections, 1906-1910

County	1906						1908					1910				
	T.M. Campbll (D)	C.A. Gray (R)	J.W. Pearson (P)	G.C. Edwards (S)	A.S. Dowlr (SL)	A.W. Atchsn (RE)	T.M. Campbll (D)	J.N. Simpsn (R)	E.C. Heath (P)	J.C. Rhodes (S)	W.B. Cook (SL)	O.B. Colquitt (D)	J.O. Terrell (R)	A.J. Houston (P)	Redding Andrws (S)	Carl Schmdt (SL)
Reeves	197	7	3	1	0	0	295	29	0	0	0	181	11	16	5	1
Refugio	125	105	0	0	0	1	127	190	0	0	0	159	63	10	33	4
Roberts	82	15	9	2	0	1	129	27	4	1	1	119	23	8	1	0
Robertson	687	51	1	1	0	73	1,225	403	0	12	2	911	54	16	32	1
Rockwall	373	13	13	4	0	1	721	38	0	16	0	409	8	10	0	0
Runnels	519	43	11	16	1	1	990	70	3	41	1	776	47	27	64	0
Rusk	1,313	110	6	0	13	289	1,602	876	0	25	0	1,227	499	9	36	0
Sabine	267	10	5	1	0	0	463	49	0	9	0	374	5	6	16	0
San Augustine	242	14	0	1	0	0	433	74	0	12	0	408	24	8	33	0
San Jacinto	389	0	0	2	0	222	380	271	0	0	0	356	154	0	0	0
San Patricio	222	49	3	2	1	1	322	83	0	10	0	326	129	78	38	4
San Saba	435	38	10	9	0	2	744	121	1	0	2	427	32	7	88	2
Schleicher	108	9	1	0	0	0	126	3	0	0	0	93	12	0	0	0
Scurry	559	70	57	48	9	0	772	96	0	144	0	697	39	52	131	0
Shackelford	78	2	1	1	0	12	263	34	0	11	1	215	9	3	33	0
Shelby	1,046	29	1	9	0	2	1,749	168	0	83	0	1,262	46	6	117	6
Sherman	112	15	2	3	0	0	162	34	0	6	0	86	15	12	1	0
Smith	1,526	247	7	108	1	0	2,121	814	25	166	2	1,444	530	54	200	0
Somervell	169	22	3	1	0	0	252	33	0	11	0	220	9	5	19	1
Starr	747	588	0	0	0	0	910	414	0	0	0	823	121	11	2	0
Stephens	259	10	3	26	1	1	708	22	1	90	0	541	9	5	77	0
Sterling	100	6	2	0	0	0	148	4	0	0	0	112	2	1	0	0
Stonewall	113	3	0	9	0	0	331	14	0	48	0	394	18	3	147	0
Sutton	56	6	1	2	0	0	83	8	0	0	0	73	3	0	0	0
Swisher	94	5	2	0	0	0	246	21	0	0	1	309	46	28	0	0
Tarrant	3,916	306	57	105	5	51	6,309	1,568	0	176	4	3,182	231	162	194	2
Taylor	794	20	11	14	1	0	1,726	168	0	119	4	1,028	74	27	75	0
Terrell	74	42	3	1	2	0	108	68	0	14	0	122	30	0	6	1
Terry	139	0	4	2	0	1	172	5	0	2	0	88	3	2	3	0
Throckmorton	142	8	3	2	0	0	237	25	0	10	0	260	14	5	27	0
Titus	505	35	5	1	0	0	939	178	0	6	0	750	39	22	8	0
Tom Green	573	42	5	7	1	3	924	106	0	23	0	578	24	10	48	0
Travis	1,998	201	18	38	2	95	2,305	1,364	1	68	3	2,088	292	73	66	2
Trinity	813	101	0	4	0	2	647	134	0	4	0	502	44	3	17	5
Tyler	440	33	4	3	0	2	671	117	0	14	0	448	12	6	38	1
Upshur	648	65	4	1	7	0	914	278	0	14	0	846	84	66	23	0
Upton	0	0	0	0	0	0	707	401	0	54	2	30	0	0	0	0
Uvalde	621	285	11	5	2	2	0	0	0	0	0	985	138	25	46	1
Val Verde	518	82	5	17	0	13	259	298	9	14	0	359	214	22	25	4
Van Zandt	1,199	75	8	162	1	2	1,596	195	9	351	1	1,386	55	47	436	3
Victoria	772	108	0	1	0	77	492	410	0	6	0	488	35	10	5	2
Walker	535	74	1	4	0	234	634	421	0	2	0	583	170	12	11	1
Waller	859	206	7	7	0	279	675	371	0	2	0	485	62	17	3	0
Ward	144	14	9	1	0	0	230	30	0	4	1	146	11	11	1	0
Washington	843	306	1	0	1	137	1,394	907	0	1	0	1,101	242	12	8	2
Webb	450	338	0	1	0	0	214	1,130	0	1	0	484	542	3	1	0
Wharton	0	0	0	0	0	0	738	477	0	64	1	387	41	74	75	0
Wheeler	251	17	2	12	0	2	345	45	8	8	2	353	69	11	10	4
Wichita	483	94	23	14	0	0	816	270	0	23	0	963	176	40	25	0
Wilbarger	289	14	9	20	0	0	791	105	0	33	1	572	17	9	49	2
Willacy	0	0	0	0	0	0	0	0	0	0	0	0	0	0	0	0
Williamson	1,497	125	26	7	4	16	2,413	729	1	217	3	1,579	91	61	43	1
Wilson	694	107	5	13	2	7	848	277	0	12	0	756	87	39	16	1
Winkler	0	0	0	0	0	0	0	0	0	0	0	26	0	2	0	0
Wise	1,600	136	65	22	2	0	2,245	346	33	91	3	1,577	156	55	74	7
Wood	829	42	5	25	0	9	1,315	355	0	111	0	1,097	52	23	86	1
Yoakum	0	0	0	0	0	0	39	1	0	0	0	49	0	0	0	0
Young	546	44	10	4	0	0	820	84	0	21	0	687	45	20	38	1
Zapata	4	358	0	0	0	0	0	428	0	0	0	0	462	0	0	0
Zavala	134	17	0	1	2	0	125	33	0	12	1	123	38	11	23	1
Official Totals	149,105	23,711	2,215	2,958	260	5,395	218,956	73,305	148	8,100	234	173,993	26,107	11,638	6,179	347
Unofficial Totals	149,253	23,778	2,231	2,965	259	5,401	220,263	73,360	156	7,673	350	174,083	26,207	11,566	6,077	346

Table 47: Gubernatorial Races

County	General Elections, 1912-1918																
Year	1912						1914				1916				1918		
County	O. B. Colquitt (D)	Ed C. Lasatr (PR)	C. W. Johnson (R)	A. J. Houston (P)	Redding Andrs (S)	K. E. Chote (SL)	J. E. Fergusn (D)	F. M. Ethrdg (PR)	John W. Philp (R)	E. R. Meitzen (S)	J. E. Fergusn (D)	R. B. Creager (R)	H. W. Lewis (P)	E. R. Meitzen (S)	W. P. Hobby (D)	Charles A. Boyntn (R)	William D. Simpsn (S)
Anderson	1,821	56	425	8	301	2	1,927	7	231	331	1,962	484	11	188	1,222	261	13
Andrews	94	4	1	0	1	0	54	0	1	2	73	0	0	1	39	0	0
Angelina	1,120	10	22	10	378	0	1,099	4	11	518	1,352	49	7	341	675	37	10
Aransas	194	25	3	4	7	0	148	2	4	6	173	22	5	6	150	6	0
Archer	474	24	19	6	77	1	395	2	6	50	501	52	8	39	299	8	0
Armstrong	298	22	22	5	8	0	162	0	2	3	337	34	21	8	169	10	1
Atascosa	647	20	16	5	81	1	476	2	6	56	647	70	12	56	305	17	0
Austin	1,279	53	175	3	10	2	1,183	4	86	7	1,427	242	2	9	649	384	25
Bailey	0	0	0	0	0	0	0	0	0	0	0	0	0	0	0	0	0
Bandera	458	91	136	16	75	4	504	10	107	44	534	159	9	45	357	58	11
Bastrop	1,155	70	168	15	53	0	904	1	85	61	1,456	392	15	22	754	211	0
Baylor	579	25	11	6	97	0	360	1	4	66	684	25	22	80	366	16	5
Bee	503	53	27	10	42	0	328	4	8	39	627	105	18	19	563	74	4
Bell	3,079	3	10	0	222	0	1,988	4	33	16	3,667	222	71	182	2,065	250	15
Bexar	7,072	481	957	38	211	20	5,355	75	157	76	9,144	3,290	80	150	2,885	1,793	28
Blanco	504	49	103	3	13	0	696	6	58	13	695	164	7	18	474	121	3
Borden	132	0	2	1	5	0	63	0	0	1	103	0	0	1	30	0	0
Bosque	1,260	58	54	3	97	0	1,002	4	25	132	1,573	141	8	73	864	291	3
Bowie	1,626	167	160	21	487	5	952	20	57	391	1,963	350	32	295	1,178	54	7
Brazoria	825	258	229	39	76	3	743	30	137	58	1,001	526	118	73	466	313	14
Brazos	772	35	131	11	7	0	544	2	31	6	1,082	228	6	4	882	262	1
Brewster	367	24	20	5	16	2	199	1	9	9	207	42	2	8	111	3	0
Briscoe	147	3	2	0	7	0	100	0	2	6	243	4	14	22	114	1	1
Brooks	373	197	19	5	0	1	105	0	2	0	99	62	5	1	68	5	0
Brown	1,600	76	98	18	176	0	892	7	33	126	1,966	56	11	105	848	57	8
Burleson	1,028	67	194	1	18	1	727	1	83	26	1,158	248	2	21	550	135	0
Burnet	648	38	58	9	32	0	448	2	37	20	831	92	25	24	470	84	3
Caldwell	1,110	65	61	2	19	0	847	7	22	21	1,286	171	5	19	568	83	1
Calhoun	376	36	33	10	61	1	319	9	4	51	391	66	14	64	242	25	2
Callahan	820	22	29	10	120	1	515	28	20	62	963	44	9	83	547	19	3
Cameron	2,160	110	134	13	18	4	1,937	37	69	39	880	793	16	38	791	41	0
Camp	487	56	149	2	25	0	641	4	190	32	728	198	1	34	365	89	2
Carson	223	31	15	12	20	0	121	1	6	2	337	54	7	5	151	7	0
Cass	1,351	178	325	9	222	2	1,174	6	137	234	1,537	658	0	138	1,065	220	9
Castro	188	14	10	0	8	0	126	5	6	4	181	45	4	5	133	19	1
Chambers	242	30	74	0	25	0	292	3	46	39	243	95	3	43	122	32	0
Cherokee	1,707	42	129	24	282	2	1,515	1	65	410	2,011	229	23	237	1,415	165	23
Childress	724	24	27	9	79	1	281	4	14	43	932	28	9	75	377	14	1
Clay	946	108	47	12	86	0	633	2	12	63	1,327	156	6	53	792	11	8
Cochran	0	0	0	0	0	0	0	0	0	0	0	0	0	0	0	0	0
Coke	307	12	7	3	45	0	283	0	10	36	478	24	7	42	176	5	2
Coleman	1,270	44	41	5	208	4	916	3	26	212	1,676	78	7	199	799	44	10
Collin	3,301	189	329	16	331	7	2,067	20	120	282	4,053	582	49	162	2,186	308	21
Collingsworth	426	13	11	1	52	0	418	3	14	83	689	24	0	61	290	17	4
Colorado	1,053	118	99	14	42	3	676	14	38	52	1,185	205	10	68	553	246	25
Comal	864	50	40	1	37	1	672	2	9	9	838	337	0	30	344	302	22
Comanche	1,720	86	44	31	539	2	1,082	15	45	454	1,463	103	27	306	828	262	25
Concho	359	11	11	3	86	0	305	1	1	87	425	27	2	53	200	22	1
Cooke	1,826	120	195	15	188	1	1,150	15	63	92	2,376	270	13	105	1,281	127	3
Coryell	1,351	42	33	5	68	2	1,004	6	22	86	1,842	113	12	74	929	93	8
Cottle	317	12	3	0	109	1	337	1	2	122	459	10	5	69	168	1	0
Crane	0	0	0	0	0	0	0	0	0	0	0	0	0	0	0	0	0
Crockett	55	1	2	0	7	0	37	0	1	1	56	11	9	5	29	1	2
Crosby	278	8	2	4	61	0	299	2	4	58	465	21	3	44	303	8	4
Culberson	144	1	0	0	0	0	39	0	0	0	117	1	0	1	43	1	0
Dallam	278	45	13	9	52	1	165	6	12	25	376	65	8	40	146	31	4
Dallas	8,440	834	489	151	371	16	4,268	79	280	179	13,224	2,179	280	204	4,007	443	17
Dawson	94	2	7	3	21	0	68	0	2	9	275	8	16	10	149	4	3
DeWitt	1,268	74	124	4	25	2	957	2	35	21	1,747	384	7	21	518	90	3
Deaf Smith	221	24	21	7	5	0	148	2	4	3	318	84	10	15	172	28	0
Delta	928	21	40	9	179	3	999	6	26	255	1,230	77	24	114	583	28	1
Denton	2,268	104	191	21	182	1	1,363	5	94	203	2,834	379	28	156	1,631	274	12
Dickens	281	14	8	5	111	0	145	1	2	88	380	10	2	40	228	19	2
Dimmit	295	44	127	8	14	1	166	9	27	4	198	68	10	6	102	17	0

Table 47: Gubernatorial Races

General Elections, 1912-1918																			
Year	1912						1914				1916				1918				
County	O. B. Colquitt (D)	Ed C. Lasatr (PR)	C. W. Johnson (R)	A. J. Houston (P)	Redding Andrs (S)	K. E. Chote (SL)	J. E. Fergusn (D)	F. M. Ethrdg (PR)	John W. Philp (R)	E. R. Meitzen (S)	J. E. Fergusn (D)	R. B. Creager (R)	H. W. Lewis (P)	E. R. Meitzen (S)	W. P. Hobby (D)	Charles A. Boyntn (R)	William D. Simpsn (S)		
Donley	378	34	11	3	40	2	363	5	3	69	601	35	25	55	301	11	0		
Duval	940	37	41	0	2	0	683	0	3	0	604	28	0	3	277	4	0		
Eastland	1,489	45	62	13	392	2	1,072	11	51	292	1,391	131	50	300	816	55	22		
Ector	94	2	2	0	0	0	78	0	0	0	121	1	0	0	69	0	0		
Edwards	163	61	95	11	55	.2	138	6	37	8	307	68	3	5	246	20	2		
El Paso	3,327	434	134	36	114	8	1,668	17	15	19	4,186	1,201	37	98	680	44	2		
Ellis	3,528	107	268	15	112	4	2,867	12	50	135	4,694	390	26	92	2,104	403	9		
Erath	1,616	106	107	28	391	5	1,212	11	40	366	1,930	137	41	340	1,015	150	14		
Falls	1,731	124	299	26	169	2	1,348	25	123	346	2,305	489	27	243	2,017	261	9		
Fannin	2,641	186	219	27	276	3	1,872	22	100	365	3,414	460	23	232	1,902	201	16		
Fayette	2,186	147	372	3	96	1	1,724	9	166	46	2,462	683	17	51	1,081	721	21		
Fisher	574	12	10	6	124	4	368	0	3	194	932	31	11	235	370	9	6		
Floyd	391	27	12	12	88	0	308	1	10	68	597	42	11	77	434	13	11		
Foard	428	36	17	12	121	1	232	2	21	77	479	41	5	89	308	23	5		
Fort Bend	726	107	264	11	33	0	589	7	48	27	902	214	10	12	383	107	0		
Franklin	583	3	15	1	12	0	355	3	23	60	657	63	3	42	430	51	2		
Freestone	1,331	23	487	2	178	1	1,143	4	374	217	1,561	635	4	93	927	555	11		
Frio	445	19	16	3	8	1	255	0	0	0	415	36	4	4	192	6	0		
Gaines	69	2	0	0	3	0	37	0	0	2	73	0	0	3	73	1	0		
Galveston	2,751	241	269	0	0	10	1,311	21	61	47	3,787	1,009	79	62	1,115	466	8		
Garza	154	3	4	0	7	0	97	0	0	0	334	11	0	14	138	5	0		
Gillespie	746	653	143	3	4	1	1,136	31	285	2	603	1,276	2	10	289	717	96		
Glasscock	68	0	0	0	8	0	53	0	0	3	100	4	0	4	53	0	1		
Goliad	508	40	345	9	70	1	630	3	344	64	668	493	5	60	202	15	4		
Gonzales	1,409	69	291	1	80	4	1,002	4	79	100	1,776	533	18	51	1,025	185	4		
Gray	294	29	8	9	54	0	252	4	4	45	492	36	23	34	216	22	2		
Grayson	4,013	351	460	44	361	2	2,666	53	210	419	5,088	941	41	234	2,682	536	16		
Gregg	609	18	103	1	33	1	391	0	23	33	826	152	2	25	378	51	3		
Grimes	976	27	23	5	22	2	1,135	5	12	72	1,131	68	4	29	587	30	3		
Guadalupe	1,599	171	741	13	14	3	1,877	34	673	5	1,318	1,323	9	5	712	1,171	15		
Hale	575	43	16	9	43	1	320	2	2	35	886	69	23	44	373	29	1		
Hall	769	31	20	4	27	2	359	5	4	95	906	41	12	92	547	7	6		
Hamilton	938	69	59	5	52	0	615	11	12	36	1,320	146	2	29	633	89	1		
Hansford	96	28	11	6	8	0	131	10	19	11	163	26	4	15	67	7	1		
Hardeman	863	35	30	13	118	1	460	4	14	127	916	76	20	123	416	33	8		
Hardin	1,077	61	74	7	192	2	749	42	17	107	1,359	135	7	98	359	53	4		
Harris	7,103	599	510	101	713	57	3,856	53	233	312	11,109	1,815	103	418	5,346	1,462	97		
Harrison	1,176	18	29	6	42	1	650	2	5	46	1,301	70	24	52	563	45	3		
Hartley	131	17	12	2	1	0	86	1	0	2	155	21	3	3	25	1	0		
Haskell	1,054	29	33	6	359	1	752	3	20	353	1,225	75	4	369	630	26	27		
Hays	953	35	48	6	8	0	555	5	10	8	1,008	98	7	8	499	14	0		
Hemphill	327	105	61	10	32	3	337	25	53	25	493	126	24	25	207	32	2		
Henderson	1,384	84	135	8	435	7	1,512	4	179	650	1,791	261	3	361	1,224	224	30		
Hidalgo	1,205	75	41	12	43	1	1,211	16	14	33	1,316	288	13	32	1,009	112	6		
Hill	2,712	76	104	26	115	1	1,579	9	65	88	3,930	283	34	73	2,107	290	5		
Hockley	0	0	0	0	0	0	0	0	0	0	0	0	0	0	0	0	0		
Hood	676	40	32	5	59	1	559	5	29	93	681	59	4	82	432	29	0		
Hopkins	2,007	56	120	35	275	1	1,685	2	215	324	2,495	219	12	224	1,754	132	13		
Houston	1,598	45	313	1	264	1	1,229	4	111	282	1,757	373	0	162	1,076	256	9		
Howard	551	9	12	10	115	0	378	0	5	99	736	30	6	103	335	3	8		
Hudspeth	0	0	0	0	0	0	0	0	0	0	0	0	0	0	58	0	0		
Hunt	3,452	200	227	47	376	2	2,492	28	113	302	4,217	422	24	155	2,591	196	13		
Hutchinson	139	10	11	2	1	0	128	4	10	7	156	25	3	6	78	13	4		
Irion	136	4	0	0	11	0	88	0	0	10	150	3	1	11	93	0	2		
Jack	770	63	80	35	178	0	559	2	54	164	857	107	9	113	441	59	16		
Jackson	340	65	36	7	81	0	243	9	19	116	390	114	13	67	249	30	11		
Jasper	602	30	35	6	200	0	745	3	23	138	917	66	3	39	388	25	2		
Jeff Davis	133	11	79	1	7	0	112	2	19	2	233	66	2	1	78	0	0		
Jefferson	1,845	214	154	17	166	2	792	16	22	125	312	359	35	146	1,646	105	19		
Jim Hogg	0	0	0	0	0	0	357	2	2	32	187	10	0	0	41	3	0		
Jim Wells	245	35	21	7	42	1	224	0	0	0	395	39	4	36	232	8	3		
Johnson	2,506	72	98	7	361	3	1,317	6	53	254	3,037	241	17	170	1,551	177	18		
Jones	1,304	42	51	11	195	2	694	7	15	179	1,775	98	13	216	822	60	7		
Karnes	761	28	31	2	3	1	806	5	3	3	988	148	7	8	331	38	0		
Kaufman	2,070	73	226	7	260	2	1,603	14	87	236	2,771	410	2	173	1,474	261	6		

Table 47: Gubernatorial Races

General Elections, 1912-1918

County	O. B. Colquitt (D)	Ed C. Lasatr (PR)	C. W. Johnson (R)	A. J. Houston (P)	Redding Andrs (S)	K. E. Chote (SL)	J. E. Fergusn (D)	F. M. Ethrdg (PR)	John W. Philp (R)	E. R. Meitzen (S)	J. E. Fergusn (D)	R. B. Creager (R)	H. W. Lewis (P)	E. R. Meitzen (S)	W. P. Hobby (D)	Charles A. Boyntn (R)	William D. Simpsn (S)
	1912						1914				1916				1918		
Kendall	453	77	95	1	9	2	445	3	55	6	410	418	1	5	197	480	4
Kenedy	0	0	0	0	0	0	0	0	0	0	0	0	0	0	0	0	0
Kent	153	6	2	1	20	0	151	2	0	14	215	2	5	26	94	0	0
Kerr	665	60	102	5	36	3	714	9	79	14	683	238	9	29	223	55	3
Kimble	145	12	14	0	20	0	144	21	0	0	246	14	0	12	136	2	1
King	79	0	2	0	2	0	23	0	2	0	47	3	0	0	13	0	0
Kinney	81	87	96	1	14	1	174	13	141	8	233	200	1	8	126	78	0
Kleberg	0	0	0	0	0	0	428	6	9	77	455	83	10	50	270	21	3
Knox	672	24	29	4	127	0	386	3	9	105	911	35	6	99	427	23	4
La Salle	349	25	13	4	16	0	273	1	5	6	343	37	2	3	168	5	0
Lamar	2,407	86	137	8	136	0	1,465	9	35	123	3,437	294	6	99	1,348	71	6
Lamb	45	20	8	10	0	0	74	9	6	1	143	10	16	3	85	7	0
Lampasas	543	32	59	10	61	2	422	4	55	36	792	103	7	29	414	91	2
Lavaca	1,715	82	155	15	184	8	1,490	11	54	476	2,196	473	16	267	709	517	13
Lee	734	37	105	3	98	1	641	1	69	107	1,088	288	7	81	870	289	13
Leon	886	45	154	23	270	1	846	6	78	363	984	315	1	173	634	265	7
Liberty	599	90	81	5	72	5	568	8	149	120	715	210	7	79	342	136	3
Limestone	1,718	49	121	10	214	2	1,655	7	55	222	2,204	207	8	107	1,427	256	7
Lipscomb	258	97	40	14	50	4	254	31	62	41	336	112	25	38	297	96	19
Live Oak	288	42	50	0	19	2	415	1	5	30	416	90	12	48	255	8	6
Llano	478	18	14	5	28	0	353	1	5	17	747	29	6	22	325	19	0
Loving	0	0	0	0	0	0	0	0	0	0	0	0	0	0	0	0	0
Lubbock	377	11	14	10	13	0	208	3	8	13	614	27	16	27	436	13	1
Lynn	125	2	4	2	11	0	87	0	1	1	322	11	5	9	176	4	0
Madison	391	19	35	4	45	0	511	1	41	92	710	113	12	44	566	127	2
Marion	354	61	77	0	0	0	219	3	12	5	439	162	2	1	222	46	0
Martin	123	2	1	1	5	0	66	0	1	10	121	13	3	22	59	1	0
Mason	557	122	107	10	81	3	206	0	10	20	471	84	3	33	210	17	5
Matagorda	759	135	85	35	86	0	514	22	71	116	761	230	24	80	423	86	4
Maverick	191	70	137	1	6	1	214	13	53	2	205	236	1	2	112	43	0
McCulloch	637	41	31	9	137	6	536	2	11	142	850	48	2	120	430	22	3
McLennan	3,854	176	219	25	169	1	1,679	4	43	102	5,045	656	21	118	1,705	337	8
McMullen	61	1	1	0	0	0	99	0	3	1	115	19	0	0	65	4	0
Medina	877	88	123	6	27	1	1,185	20	168	18	850	543	11	26	539	413	16
Menard	143	13	7	0	35	0	73	0	3	28	288	23	3	34	70	0	0
Midland	215	6	11	1	8	0	255	2	3	1	330	19	3	7	133	9	1
Milam	1,916	40	217	14	480	43	1,604	11	28	432	2,395	351	20	237	1,236	134	41
Mills	608	43	65	5	175	0	477	2	23	137	0	0	0	0	463	48	7
Mitchell	556	27	14	5	79	1	228	2	5	56	777	35	1	80	291	12	2
Montague	1,541	89	125	11	336	1	1,063	4	55	287	1,855	231	18	244	1,074	52	26
Montgomery	643	74	122	3	100	2	727	38	88	177	873	177	5	141	538	103	3
Moore	63	3	6	0	0	0	36	0	0	0	101	2	4	0	44	0	0
Morris	640	30	57	3	9	0	467	1	16	32	578	80	0	3	498	39	1
Motley	203	5	4	3	28	1	110	0	2	21	395	7	1	28	162	0	0
Nacogdoches	1,640	24	71	9	332	4	1,382	4	25	271	1,765	84	4	157	1,018	60	8
Navarro	2,617	93	157	14	170	0	1,840	23	67	240	3,494	283	12	102	2,551	420	14
Newton	284	12	8	1	43	0	407	1	10	27	498	18	1	42	246	8	0
Nolan	665	13	55	9	68	2	476	1	22	65	1,054	69	10	78	368	21	0
Nueces	942	94	64	20	164	0	1,856	20	54	188	1,724	379	40	144	738	90	10
Ochiltree	94	15	3	0	3	0	115	0	3	0	241	32	5	6	241	6	1
Oldham	90	18	23	8	3	0	93	3	21	1	133	40	4	0	92	22	0
Orange	577	31	18	1	46	0	435	10	7	42	775	66	7	41	375	20	4
Palo Pinto	1,214	39	49	29	364	3	983	9	35	371	1,375	92	43	292	754	64	18
Panola	1,213	49	85	1	181	0	890	3	82	153	1,205	118	0	74	957	119	4
Parker	1,776	62	96	31	417	1	1,188	5	74	391	1,791	142	26	242	1,125	58	31
Parmer	114	46	6	8	0	0	103	10	12	4	186	57	12	11	119	11	0
Pecos	246	64	67	5	10	0	349	7	42	5	397	93	16	1	174	14	1
Polk	634	31	37	8	71	1	475	0	3	52	947	87	1	113	527	27	4
Potter	807	79	35	33	83	0	320	10	18	27	1,238	128	32	85	449	36	5
Presidio	280	17	45	0	5	0	309	6	3	0	259	12	3	0	229	8	0
Rains	496	17	42	11	238	0	508	2	36	327	538	65	1	294	393	29	15
Randall	287	11	14	7	4	0	136	1	2	1	358	51	14	6	183	9	0
Reagan	34	0	0	0	0	0	165	4	22	19	54	1	3	0	40	0	0
Real	0	0	0	0	0	0	73	0	0	0	238	15	1	25	147	12	7
Red River	1,559	162	213	20	139	0	1,425	11	95	159	1,998	331	17	143	1,317	73	7

Table 47: Gubernatorial Races

General Elections, 1912-1918																	
Year	**1912**						**1914**				**1916**				**1918**		
County	O. B. Colquitt (D)	Ed C. Lasatr (PR)	C. W. Johnson (R)	A. J. Houston (P)	Redding Andrs (S)	K.E. Chote (SL)	J. E. Fergusn (D)	F. M. Ethrdg (PR)	John W. Philp (R)	E. R. Meitzen (S)	J. E. Fergusn (D)	R. B. Creager (R)	H. W. Lewis (P)	E. R. Meitzen (S)	W. P. Hobby (D)	Charles A. Boyntn (R)	William D. Simpsn (S)
Reeves	289	25	8	5	4	3	188	2	3	0	344	31	12	5	0	0	0
Refugio	234	23	110	9	35	2	364	9	136	63	414	221	11	50	186	60	10
Roberts	195	20	12	1	5	1	79	3	0	0	214	18	1	3	86	10	1
Robertson	1,149	17	89	1	62	0	855	1	13	114	1,325	181	1	45	583	51	1
Rockwall	650	16	17	5	23	0	512	7	7	20	821	26	2	16	445	14	4
Runnels	1,170	31	35	12	204	0	613	4	17	135	1,494	129	29	139	662	68	9
Rusk	1,484	77	465	2	210	0	1,354	7	165	285	1,887	447	6	204	1,141	502	2
Sabine	457	2	9	2	43	0	424	0	1	66	756	19	15	56	332	7	1
San Augustine	352	9	7	2	78	1	554	3	12	72	692	12	5	52	202	35	3
San Jacinto	382	34	186	0	20	0	420	0	87	12	467	238	1	10	189	39	1
San Patricio	567	60	151	33	69	0	410	9	30	52	580	111	27	69	529	47	7
San Saba	707	23	30	6	164	0	513	2	25	137	908	49	19	101	456	127	1
Schleicher	131	7	3	0	3	0	93	0	3	0	164	7	0	1	92	3	0
Scurry	677	18	20	10	89	1	426	1	9	82	988	28	16	77	294	4	5
Shackelford	264	13	7	9	50	0	229	1	0	52	377	43	3	38	145	18	3
Shelby	1,493	19	78	4	288	2	1,395	1	22	330	1,771	128	5	206	1,313	93	5
Sherman	109	15	18	2	9	0	93	4	3	3	151	32	11	9	106	5	0
Smith	2,017	353	462	31	386	4	2,346	8	411	826	2,421	747	26	280	1,893	354	25
Somervell	275	6	5	13	95	1	268	3	3	138	292	17	1	84	142	0	0
Starr	677	3	248	0	0	0	645	1	1	0	481	150	0	0	340	7	0
Stephens	466	2	9	1	92	0	281	2	3	90	571	10	0	103	213	14	1
Sterling	170	2	3	1	1	0	156	1	1	0	202	6	4	0	104	16	0
Stonewall	360	7	10	1	70	0	273	0	3	100	516	10	10	113	182	6	5
Sutton	73	11	6	0	1	0	79	1	2	1	131	5	0	0	136	2	0
Swisher	290	24	16	9	2	0	160	1	2	1	382	49	8	11	154	15	0
Tarrant	7,917	654	386	84	494	0	5,961	44	131	394	10,328	1,179	142	330	4,532	398	41
Taylor	1,562	46	49	14	189	1	848	2	11	94	2,122	96	15	120	682	27	5
Terrell	123	33	36	1	3	1	143	2	16	2	179	58	1	2	108	16	0
Terry	102	1	2	1	0	0	79	0	0	0	140	0	1	0	84	2	1
Throckmorton	249	8	2	1	60	0	285	2	6	105	348	9	2	63	232	4	0
Titus	985	41	56	4	150	0	1,081	9	62	148	1,176	0	30	80	619	71	2
Tom Green	951	43	32	8	62	1	469	1	3	47	1,189	72	32	62	454	77	6
Travis	3,126	151	298	23	168	2	1,925	7	135	72	3,976	629	42	73	1,681	218	11
Trinity	703	25	88	5	118	2	610	0	67	127	943	131	4	94	453	39	12
Tyler	537	3	31	1	81	2	471	1	7	49	641	33	0	31	408	18	2
Upshur	970	30	137	11	71	1	791	4	45	150	1,342	187	19	119	838	61	13
Upton	31	1	1	0	1	0	59	0	0	0	49	1	0	1	0	0	0
Uvalde	627	41	43	4	43	0	354	5	12	37	724	77	2	24	339	18	0
Val Verde	327	89	141	3	25	0	554	10	43	15	469	109	4	5	186	19	1
Van Zandt	1,852	62	69	21	840	4	1,788	21	120	1,021	2,061	186	23	649	1,474	87	37
Victoria	770	82	99	9	52	0	905	62	40	58	1,087	269	14	34	327	118	2
Walker	684	22	284	1	54	3	649	2	191	58	764	305	2	24	493	184	14
Waller	680	54	86	3	20	1	414	10	54	9	677	139	2	4	347	98	0
Ward	165	12	3	1	5	0	115	1	4	7	170	13	15	9	102	9	1
Washington	1,471	25	295	1	4	0	972	0	190	3	1,989	419	0	3	550	282	1
Webb	697	25	840	0	4	0	772	4	8	3	723	420	0	0	457	52	0
Wharton	808	162	96	20	133	1	506	15	61	176	959	325	66	89	490	200	14
Wheeler	415	34	31	9	66	0	276	2	13	54	547	56	12	79	316	43	3
Wichita	1,157	104	93	10	111	2	578	4	25	0	2,137	303	24	135	804	65	9
Wilbarger	1,072	39	25	7	189	2	567	4	6	143	1,228	58	6	113	563	13	8
Willacy	102	0	1	0	0	0	90	0	0	0	112	8	0	0	42	0	0
Williamson	2,223	99	147	27	102	2	1,532	6	27	91	3,419	332	25	81	1,344	349	10
Wilson	954	25	70	11	37	1	572	3	16	31	955	229	22	21	430	76	2
Winkler	26	0	0	0	0	0	24	0	0	0	21	0	0	0	7	0	0
Wise	1,840	111	134	19	148	2	1,291	9	47	167	2,232	216	22	153	1,183	110	9
Wood	1,480	52	119	30	399	0	1,455	4	88	535	1,677	229	18	411	1,258	215	45
Yoakum	42	0	0	0	0	0	44	0	0	0	83	1	0	0	22	0	0
Young	911	32	38	6	181	2	725	2	11	169	1,124	52	17	121	713	22	8
Zapata	176	0	23	0	0	0	266	0	0	0	24	215	0	0	77	12	0
Zavala	248	47	44	5	66	1	303	4	28	37	238	33	4	17	156	8	4
Official	234,352	23,089		25,268			176,599	11,411			296,667	3,200			148,982		
Totals		15,794		2,356		400		1,794		24,977		49,118		14,580		26,713	1,660
Unofficial	234,290	23,089		25,270			175,372	11,381			293,461	3,386			149,066		
Totals		15,704		2,356		399		1,786		24,931		49,198		19,271		26,650	1,658

Table 48: Gubernatorial Races

General Elections, 1920-1928													
Year	1920					1922		1924		1926			1928	
County	Pat M. Neff (D)	J. G. Culbrsn (R)	L. L. Rhodes (S)	T. H. McGregr (A)	H. Capers (BT)	Pat M. Neff (D)	W. H. Atwell (R)	Miriam A. Fergsn (D)	George C. Butte (R)	Dan Moody (D)	H. H. Haines (R)	M. A. Smith (S)	Dan Moody (D)	W. H. Holmes (R)
Anderson	2,527	220	68	616	868	2,251	305	2,769	1,896	1,447	82	5	3,274	292
Andrews	74	9	0	0	0	49	3	45	27	0	0	0	87	12
Angelina	1,697	126	87	666	127	2,954	199	3,785	1,152	1,271	207	2	3,277	282
Aransas	158	36	0	2	0	234	31	131	161	0	0	0	247	66
Archer	457	110	9	61	0	710	109	859	349	416	37	0	1,347	235
Armstrong	414	68	2	0	1	383	32	218	353	236	8	0	602	80
Atascosa	570	169	12	55	7	682	77	786	813	635	68	0	1,451	259
Austin	495	325	8	1,989	78	1,552	817	3,183	594	819	337	3	2,379	230
Bailey	129	33	0	2	0	96	8	138	103	239	12	2	478	140
Bandera	337	185	13	82	0	527	279	558	607	669	181	9	592	572
Bastrop	1,077	321	5	542	180	1,514	494	2,433	1,274	773	65	1	2,146	249
Baylor	626	99	23	98	0	685	57	893	401	424	15	6	1,190	105
Bee	567	225	10	208	0	1,041	331	1,439	1,354	1,281	1,025	14	1,659	466
Bell	3,568	301	66	2,121	175	3,709	304	5,224	4,211	2,220	97	6	5,905	621
Bexar	7,057	6,976	107	2,323	593	11,464	6,188	15,689	13,006	10,386	2,531	38	25,800	9,267
Blanco	422	205	3	455	12	585	470	852	278	596	368	2	769	403
Borden	93	0	1	11	0	59	7	77	46	53	0	0	157	14
Bosque	1,549	392	24	570	26	1,790	346	2,414	773	839	110	1	2,265	475
Bowie	2,507	855	126	41	244	1,713	198	2,806	1,474	1,288	179	11	4,499	698
Brazoria	1,249	1,120	46	150	24	1,308	378	1,373	1,857	784	310	3	1,629	870
Brazos	1,293	233	5	127	490	1,272	80	1,209	1,298	777	27	2	2,079	138
Brewster	221	94	1	16	0	259	23	271	255	389	35	0	584	90
Briscoe	255	28	7	27	0	263	3	337	140	187	8	3	548	74
Brooks	136	26	0	0	0	118	20	154	134	111	6	0	443	49
Brown	1,563	258	23	526	16	1,793	190	2,837	1,280	1,044	80	4	3,472	459
Burleson	986	114	2	429	439	1,234	234	2,358	422	618	38	0	1,813	115
Burnet	801	138	4	324	2	793	157	1,457	720	534	59	0	1,141	234
Caldwell	1,235	152	4	467	165	1,445	225	1,721	1,191	877	31	0	2,195	192
Calhoun	365	55	27	52	35	522	197	672	330	310	29	1	592	105
Callahan	737	103	27	310	1	783	127	1,612	511	506	40	3	1,690	236
Cameron	1,134	752	12	4	1	1,296	324	1,425	2,321	1,632	268	0	5,101	1,585
Camp	673	107	4	97	440	669	80	1,038	380	485	31	0	992	152
Carson	477	194	7	24	0	502	87	529	499	213	52	0	1,041	444
Cass	1,619	1,340	53	199	187	1,173	311	1,846	1,424	789	72	1	2,377	637
Castro	175	98	3	4	0	218	18	216	128	0	0	0	625	81
Chambers	0	0	0	0	0	226	59	383	264	158	22	0	402	135
Cherokee	2,227	339	72	629	267	2,350	178	3,666	1,706	1,551	129	4	3,500	380
Childress	1,198	102	38	68	1	1,041	166	920	480	463	24	4	1,849	270
Clay	1,300	379	13	87	2	1,474	184	1,392	780	787	121	3	2,176	354
Cochran	0	0	0	0	0	0	0	85	18	288	8	1	273	34
Coke	446	39	19	59	1	541	47	586	279	252	29	3	0	0
Coleman	1,429	226	66	451	5	1,814	165	2,580	1,014	1,065	64	14	2,760	319
Collin	3,911	1,209	82	409	28	5,505	776	6,017	3,550	3,400	757	9	5,446	1,415
Collingsworth	654	287	48	12	1	965	77	693	506	353	108	0	1,411	290
Colorado	786	291	64	980	325	1,482	636	2,316	1,045	519	199	1	2,236	423
Comal	145	415	14	1,221	31	663	945	2,208	285	820	667	11	2,073	274
Comanche	1,586	811	82	330	4	746	258	2,371	1,084	1,105	174	5	2,535	366
Concho	452	91	12	145	1	416	71	744	160	362	28	0	777	81
Cooke	2,052	1,042	61	99	89	2,980	337	2,363	1,908	1,963	239	4	3,472	683
Coryell	1,502	189	12	1,009	4	1,722	238	2,841	853	967	73	0	2,174	245
Cottle	512	118	36	43	3	564	75	491	211	270	15	0	842	67
Crane	0	0	0	0	0	0	0	0	0	0	0	0	269	13
Crockett	135	35	1	1	0	72	13	0	0	75	1	0	277	47
Crosby	615	94	28	48	4	769	53	866	549	450	11	2	1,556	186
Culberson	120	14	0	0	0	86	7	95	40	78	2	0	148	8
Dallam	498	163	37	45	0	570	101	550	576	302	33	4	940	222
Dallas	14,193	4,601	116	473	1,677	17,025	3,670	16,005	24,187	25,659	1,523	52	33,964	10,343
Dawson	317	41	16	434	0	233	45	969	607	508	37	1	1,406	418
DeWitt	1,033	731	12	1,153	384	1,968	1,689	2,879	1,170	706	427	1	2,363	351
Deaf Smith	517	151	0	32	0	304	51	226	576	574	127	0	784	200
Delta	1,078	288	21	56	51	1,311	103	1,664	996	814	30	0	1,525	179
Denton	2,523	873	57	445	97	2,846	420	3,485	2,498	2,446	121	6	4,348	652
Dickens	456	66	27	17	3	512	52	660	468	0	0	0	1,029	116
Dimmit	238	93	2	17	0	145	35	224	315	131	26	0	614	251

Table 48: Gubernatorial Races

General Elections, 1920-1928														
Year	1920					1922		1924		1926			1928	
County	Pat M. Neff (D)	J. G. Culbrsn (R)	L. L. Rhodes (S)	T. H. McGregr (A)	H. Capers (BT)	Pat M. Neff (D)	W. H. Atwell (R)	Miriam A. Fergsn (D)	George C. Butte (R)	Dan Moody (D)	H. H. Haines (R)	M. A. Smith (S)	Dan Moody (D)	W. H. Holmes (R)
Donley	800	163	24	6	0	998	45	531	790	499	23	3	1,200	239
Duval	389	80	3	3	0	547	232	960	111	906	18	0	1,251	440
Eastland	2,982	797	66	183	0	3,261	418	3,506	2,519	1,594	191	3	4,639	1,064
Ector	96	22	0	3	0	99	7	122	32	76	3	0	285	32
Edwards	298	257	15	31	0	311	138	275	391	418	88	4	427	164
El Paso	4,036	4,078	27	30	14	6,009	2,450	4,665	5,949	4,476	623	15	9,893	2,053
Ellis	3,967	660	15	796	321	4,341	448	5,686	3,673	2,409	115	3	6,953	971
Erath	1,874	244	64	410	19	1,847	243	2,852	1,227	1,260	226	98	2,768	524
Falls	1,877	383	39	723	639	1,185	179	2,802	880	1,051	65	0	0	0
Fannin	3,412	1,049	112	224	307	3,689	316	4,166	2,414	2,344	176	3	3,995	633
Fayette	775	469	8	2,895	338	1,876	3,893	5,548	1,414	1,645	652	2	3,932	414
Fisher	766	97	63	61	4	908	76	1,468	692	586	24	7	1,781	284
Floyd	985	121	35	25	1	726	98	782	734	460	24	1	1,604	214
Foard	498	99	33	7	0	499	55	499	197	334	25	2	766	113
Fort Bend	752	533	20	599	387	1,019	320	1,827	610	458	57	1	2,172	202
Franklin	579	155	10	149	23	538	74	1,094	304	383	56	1	1,018	118
Freestone	1,405	352	24	341	629	1,906	451	2,192	1,068	0	0	0	2,202	359
Frio	447	69	4	7	1	810	38	391	507	625	17	3	800	136
Gaines	131	7	0	1	0	158	13	173	172	194	12	3	386	65
Galveston	2,463	867	30	1,699	75	3,061	926	5,029	3,207	1,933	259	6	8,095	2,092
Garza	398	50	7	61	0	377	48	479	632	411	77	4	918	162
Gillespie	146	671	7	1,270	0	351	1,849	2,003	758	718	1,334	10	1,590	985
Glasscock	101	21	6	8	0	96	7	102	30	74	3	0	130	10
Goliad	463	431	17	197	66	656	892	1,105	694	509	421	5	750	286
Gonzales	1,333	578	12	363	171	1,505	366	2,183	1,380	982	210	1	2,124	269
Gray	557	197	22	15	0	592	44	0	0	235	39	0	2,023	806
Grayson	5,080	2,054	115	228	357	4,955	1,274	5,333	5,857	3,579	677	15	8,499	2,269
Gregg	1,058	230	5	41	177	921	40	943	694	543	39	1	1,488	141
Grimes	1,037	158	3	224	4	1,101	150	1,402	1,051	715	41	0	1,787	125
Guadalupe	573	1,359	7	1,425	95	1,132	2,394	2,734	1,559	1,334	1,838	29	2,099	1,231
Hale	1,289	291	17	40	0	1,274	125	958	1,152	569	76	1	2,627	552
Hall	949	144	43	59	1	1,120	56	697	435	587	35	2	1,648	233
Hamilton	1,035	301	14	257	2	1,082	248	1,917	555	676	96	0	1,628	317
Hansford	130	45	6	0	0	234	18	173	204	87	6	0	611	118
Hardeman	955	174	26	115	0	1,074	78	838	574	715	45	0	2,003	229
Hardin	1,010	129	21	166	63	1,064	101	1,315	1,033	502	35	0	1,675	285
Harris	14,255	6,391	259	2,404	5,205	16,508	3,547	15,774	19,715	6,776	906	20	39,058	9,730
Harrison	1,962	253	8	75	411	1,270	366	2,479	720	872	30	0	3,466	340
Hartley	163	58	6	3	0	133	9	134	126	108	9	0	300	58
Haskell	1,116	198	115	166	1	1,262	110	1,918	913	871	54	5	2,693	251
Hays	1,097	86	0	475	17	1,090	58	986	1,267	882	31	0	1,513	207
Hemphill	458	214	12	0	0	377	40	280	358	133	29	0	667	122
Henderson	1,692	448	140	465	120	1,774	360	3,250	1,104	1,276	170	7	2,448	304
Hidalgo	2,429	927	31	14	0	2,613	780	2,957	2,038	4,298	1,747	9	5,061	3,146
Hill	3,121	558	29	1,352	24	3,753	402	4,379	2,866	2,192	99	1	4,342	502
Hockley	0	0	0	0	0	67	5	136	50	255	13	3	721	271
Hood	695	127	13	180	24	605	118	970	357	434	46	0	931	207
Hopkins	2,161	789	107	116	90	3,365	164	2,999	1,856	1,514	115	6	3,256	423
Houston	1,497	315	58	652	439	1,636	181	3,019	922	1,056	68	2	2,036	272
Howard	672	88	42	80	0	846	30	932	648	463	9	4	1,272	200
Hudspeth	92	41	0	1	0	102	9	75	79	198	1	1	208	27
Hunt	4,314	802	71	305	195	5,743	242	4,953	3,919	3,448	142	8	5,661	847
Hutchinson	123	71	0	12	0	187	43	121	125	293	27	0	1,173	657
Irion	158	36	6	22	0	155	16	188	131	108	7	1	339	34
Jack	810	225	48	26	0	962	197	929	737	522	76	2	1,166	305
Jackson	581	323	17	132	5	724	336	668	692	272	48	1	797	240
Jasper	816	58	11	286	26	1,004	53	1,192	589	637	36	0	1,397	115
Jeff Davis	98	31	0	4	0	156	5	77	125	102	8	0	244	16
Jefferson	4,460	1,129	105	434	768	3,697	682	4,945	6,460	1,541	140	1	12,358	4,036
Jim Hogg	76	8	0	0	0	59	8	119	39	88	6	0	354	16
Jim Wells	308	79	11	105	0	476	29	667	387	272	27	0	1,003	175
Johnson	2,932	498	41	679	44	2,830	309	3,186	2,902	1,806	109	3	4,173	959
Jones	1,765	204	62	221	1	1,578	129	2,582	1,386	937	64	4	3,129	420
Karnes	648	285	1	578	48	1,677	318	1,788	1,026	802	129	4	1,788	312
Kaufman	2,787	435	27	359	537	2,790	298	4,203	2,522	1,844	163	0	3,960	436

Table 48: Gubernatorial Races

	General Elections, 1920-1928															
Year	1920					1922		1924		1926			1928		
County	Pat M. Neff (D)	J. G. Culbrsn (R)	L. L. Rhodes (S)	T. H. McGregr (A)	H. Capers (BT)	Pat M. Neff (D)	W. H. Atwell (R)	Miriam A. Fergsn (D)	George C. Butte (R)	Dan Moody (D)	H. H. Haines (R)	M. A. Smith (S)	Dan Moody (D)	W. H. Holmes (R)
Kendall	141	631	2	380	2	237	916	731	567	164	293	3	487	530
Kenedy	0	0	0	0	0	48	4	66	9	67	1	0	127	3
Kent	231	45	20	2	1	193	7	349	151	93	1	0	283	30
Kerr	637	315	20	149	0	542	171	840	1,079	1,262	233	3	1,379	745
Kimble	355	88	13	38	0	428	38	504	305	240	16	0	635	162
King	42	0	2	2	0	172	5	71	20	37	0	0	112	8
Kinney	108	133	1	18	0	197	132	166	216	180	45	1	284	92
Kleberg	446	154	13	43	10	840	45	510	725	302	15	0	1,265	205
Knox	773	113	22	115	0	999	48	1,185	883	708	33	1	1,457	247
La Salle	254	35	0	11	0	190	7	321	211	284	6	0	723	84
Lamar	3,699	579	59	105	457	3,525	181	3,404	2,606	1,841	60	1	4,550	488
Lamb	298	77	5	44	0	257	12	249	297	311	20	6	1,221	426
Lampasas	803	138	9	406	2	777	149	1,237	719	592	53	0	1,311	133
Lavaca	1,152	410	27	2,366	130	1,259	1,840	4,870	684	1,030	0	0	3,480	390
Lee	734	82	25	1,093	316	1,157	1,311	1,964	491	810	231	4	1,459	162
Leon	1,116	154	26	796	66	947	166	1,484	635	752	50	8	1,242	208
Liberty	808	368	47	178	5	977	158	1,311	1,130	597	70	1	1,632	262
Limestone	2,146	306	38	481	400	2,218	162	3,777	1,501	1,533	66	1	2,945	371
Lipscomb	365	409	44	0	0	493	279	361	584	524	232	9	618	486
Live Oak	239	63	38	97	0	500	130	532	630	392	23	3	753	97
Llano	671	59	4	419	3	508	96	770	368	799	38	1	866	74
Loving	0	0	0	0	0	0	0	13	3	0	0	0	13	2
Lubbock	1,207	155	25	55	5	1,112	83	1,600	1,530	1,060	61	3	4,380	648
Lynn	554	44	21	61	0	484	26	975	625	518	65	3	1,712	284
Madison	657	49	4	311	126	619	63	1,341	574	0	0	0	788	64
Marion	452	361	0	6	309	536	111	662	390	208	33	0	745	288
Martin	138	32	0	7	0	164	19	288	220	219	14	0	474	67
Mason	349	173	10	166	1	275	81	502	284	298	38	0	863	149
Matagorda	1,041	826	38	180	68	1,338	396	1,082	1,495	610	95	4	1,496	535
Maverick	186	284	3	8	1	245	131	179	378	308	58	0	315	184
McCulloch	789	143	24	110	2	867	70	1,335	821	684	26	2	1,682	318
McLennan	5,029	1,193	59	0	178	5,472	893	5,620	5,634	2,545	237	5	9,570	1,512
McMullen	81	24	0	1	0	107	5	133	102	203	3	0	180	8
Medina	525	608	4	561	3	752	1,225	1,565	916	765	404	0	1,898	672
Menard	208	177	21	91	0	249	43	348	256	196	28	0	686	125
Midland	280	53	0	6	0	194	18	315	137	164	3	0	575	94
Milam	2,601	148	86	1,672	422	2,666	558	4,732	1,761	1,390	117	8	3,821	290
Mills	664	128	18	402	0	780	185	1,152	444	457	58	0	1,006	203
Mitchell	682	86	27	51	0	734	63	1,027	550	697	47	0	1,660	232
Montague	1,694	458	143	73	0	1,769	161	1,946	898	779	94	6	2,475	393
Montgomery	0	0	0	0	0	801	48	1,167	637	673	41	1	1,397	103
Moore	93	3	0	1	0	37	0	56	42	0	0	0	183	27
Morris	644	182	0	24	71	538	63	723	325	517	12	0	1,014	71
Motley	360	25	7	3	0	295	18	298	171	219	13	5	690	60
Nacogdoches	1,883	193	69	368	257	1,718	0	2,876	881	1,134	99	9	2,551	135
Navarro	3,214	560	22	1,080	231	3,685	564	4,984	2,872	2,608	158	2	6,148	837
Newton	429	47	9	166	32	354	20	833	243	312	15	0	855	101
Nolan	0	0	0	0	0	1,037	90	1,211	843	750	88	0	2,180	370
Nueces	1,254	330	30	111	51	2,274	574	2,410	2,306	1,413	161	2	4,411	1,051
Ochiltree	297	129	0	0	0	251	23	154	410	164	10	0	610	198
Oldham	152	37	0	0	0	171	7	138	140	102	5	0	251	62
Orange	1,012	98	5	301	59	1,019	62	1,239	884	720	17	0	1,967	251
Palo Pinto	1,651	253	74	156	16	1,980	191	1,451	1,402	1,070	51	5	2,524	557
Panola	1,084	249	22	205	97	1,011	57	1,768	463	541	117	0	1,680	63
Parker	1,789	453	92	26	7	1,810	156	1,783	1,561	1,229	89	12	2,700	521
Parmer	229	99	11	4	0	439	48	161	179	0	0	0	739	178
Pecos	410	339	2	52	1	478	51	394	365	557	38	3	0	0
Polk	806	230	23	164	57	842	50	1,447	675	566	71	0	11,402	117
Potter	1,549	293	26	43	1	1,602	142	1,226	2,737	505	86	2	4,493	1,692
Presidio	248	108	0	1	0	200	58	185	188	271	9	0	486	46
Rains	472	158	121	40	26	781	116	897	178	400	63	3	681	77
Randall	373	115	2	31	0	432	36	426	476	364	24	0	1,171	197
Reagan	52	6	0	0	0	259	116	113	57	266	9	0	517	87
Real	216	143	13	12	1	91	3	216	339	265	65	3	238	328
Red River	2,333	722	45	55	381	2,113	174	2,479	1,145	1,319	60	0	2,530	358

Table 48: Gubernatorial Races

General Elections, 1920-1928														
Year	1920					1922		1924		1926			1928	
County	Pat M. Neff (D)	J.G. Culbrsn (R)	L.L. Rhodes (S)	T.H. McGregr (A)	H. Capers (BT)	Pat M. Neff (D)	W.H. Atwell (R)	Miriam A. Fergsn (D)	George C. Butte (R)	Dan Moody (D)	H.H. Haines (R)	M.A. Smith (S)	Dan Moody (D)	W.H. Holmes (R)
Reeves	452	86	2	2	0	358	23	260	297	272	30	0	665	74
Refugio	236	325	15	77	1	392	301	762	391	339	187	10	847	230
Roberts	182	51	1	5	0	203	10	129	239	84	11	0	265	77
Robertson	1,394	159	0	595	133	1,124	114	1,774	806	805	36	0	2,038	212
Rockwall	865	97	3	12	3	882	41	1,101	428	591	6	0	1,074	79
Runnels	1,217	217	31	418	4	1,541	376	2,210	1,132	1,275	84	3	2,825	333
Rusk	1,531	651	37	337	278	1,799	161	2,509	1,450	1,182	101	0	2,484	352
Sabine	413	84	6	431	28	644	0	1,205	261	436	17	5	1,162	44
San Augustine	630	82	8	691	7	700	98	1,602	213	358	129	8	1,233	70
San Jacinto	326	60	5	217	173	276	36	587	173	0	0	0	749	67
San Patricio	651	263	12	32	4	1,129	261	806	1,567	648	93	1	1,450	514
San Saba	842	65	16	545	2	844	84	1,617	504	609	48	0	1,312	74
Schleicher	207	55	0	23	0	182	22	253	146	124	8	0	309	42
Scurry	815	126	19	35	0	929	49	908	894	566	20	1	1,748	279
Shackelford	330	99	34	50	2	699	35	670	247	229	41	0	950	111
Shelby	1,706	108	92	262	175	2,642	191	3,168	730	1,268	63	1	2,487	159
Sherman	195	50	3	1	0	140	15	84	240	91	12	0	287	92
Smith	2,939	574	79	444	0	2,977	467	2,909	3,286	2,299	289	1	4,859	840
Somervell	180	47	14	122	563	224	37	432	82	295	25	0	345	35
Starr	444	66	0	0	12	357	30	745	38	0	0	0	770	34
Stephens	611	117	25	47	0	1,074	91	1,695	982	771	86	7	2,373	563
Sterling	155	8	0	25	0	212	7	189	108	150	4	0	279	13
Stonewall	362	73	18	91	0	384	33	939	364	271	12	3	818	116
Sutton	213	74	0	22	0	219	19	169	145	105	4	0	340	33
Swisher	495	108	7	6	1	469	41	362	510	509	47	0	957	293
Tarrant	12,924	3,192	142	414	800	12,006	1,675	9,851	13,420	5,115	342	6	22,742	6,571
Taylor	1,887	230	49	198	9	2,043	171	2,491	1,896	1,562	78	2	5,050	906
Terrell	159	76	5	25	1	193	48	107	191	212	56	1	257	184
Terry	281	27	4	35	0	254	17	682	360	303	27	0	841	205
Throckmorton	403	38	16	17	0	0	0	371	458	309	3	1	817	145
Titus	1,242	0	0	0	0	877	91	1,373	0	581	75	2	1,540	126
Tom Green	1,210	181	20	133	17	1,450	158	1,747	1,289	1,204	50	4	3,599	492
Travis	3,506	717	48	1,278	366	4,150	609	5,767	5,366	4,008	226	6	8,298	1,167
Trinity	644	93	29	293	50	711	76	1,366	433	400	50	3	1,159	100
Tyler	1,057	108	15	178	67	1,107	7	860	312	377	11	0	915	36
Upshur	1,163	465	29	532	96	1,215	230	2,293	721	1,003	274	3	2,054	195
Upton	46	24	0	0	0	32	2	40	8	83	1	0	0	0
Uvalde	763	188	13	43	0	703	39	1,052	835	740	47	0	1,628	327
Val Verde	469	239	1	14	1	323	77	515	551	344	70	0	1,016	452
Van Zandt	2,034	583	264	254	14	2,287	240	2,961	0	1,648	314	15	2,873	394
Victoria	623	579	14	573	59	794	474	1,828	691	853	209	1	2,123	251
Walker	771	344	5	446	125	643	97	1,529	608	643	20	0	1,141	96
Waller	689	117	4	237	207	850	77	840	607	377	26	0	818	76
Ward	198	60	6	1	0	174	36	145	135	113	12	1	399	77
Washington	915	402	6	1,413	145	2,088	817	3,814	474	883	127	0	2,659	120
Webb	691	381	0	21	0	1,012	133	1,187	673	628	148	0	1,943	417
Wharton	0	0	0	0	0	1,539	441	1,735	1,472	650	155	3	2,128	549
Wheeler	535	178	32	2	1	735	96	679	497	412	60	0	1,449	310
Wichita	3,662	1,540	77	57	20	3,121	308	4,606	4,728	2,047	268	8	9,123	2,893
Wilbarger	1,056	359	50	60	2	1,402	51	1,148	733	574	16	1	2,659	383
Willacy	48	9	0	3	0	191	64	319	193	523	66	7	654	124
Williamson	2,655	558	19	1,767	77	3,363	824	5,974	2,052	2,206	143	3	5,098	472
Wilson	806	544	8	410	5	948	694	1,991	659	915	463	4	1,866	245
Winkler	10	1	0	7	0	17	3	15	1	13	1	0	423	40
Wise	2,022	504	46	100	0	2,764	182	1,906	1,853	1,251	71	1	2,344	885
Wood	1,636	512	87	766	136	1,944	251	2,712	1,206	1,230	107	5	2,295	301
Yoakum	89	3	0	0	0	103	2	107	21	95	2	0	129	21
Young	1,220	192	36	24	1	1,692	92	1,479	926	528	37	0	0	0
Zapata	99	49	0	0	0	254	196	317	212	213	8	0	302	13
Zavala	284	59	15	22	0	0	0	228	304	317	14	0	538	260
Official Totals	289,188	90,217	6,796	69,380	26,091	334,199	73,327	422,558	294,970	233,002	34,819	786	582,968	123,337
Unofficial Totals	288,986	90,237	6,803	70,229	26,257	333,157	74,388	422,563	294,911	231,933	32,444	774	583,852	123,325

Table 49: Gubernatorial Races

General Elections, 1930-1936																
Year	1930				1932						1934				1936	
County	Ross S. Sterling (D)	William E. Talbot (R)	L. L. Rhodes (S)	J. Stedhm (C)	Miriam A. Fergsn (D)	Orville Bullngtn (R)	George C. Edwrds (S)	Philip L. Howe (C)	George W. Amstrng(J)	Otho L. Hiett (L)	James V. Allred (D)	D.E. Waggnr (R)	George C. Edwrds (S)	Enoch Hrdwy (CM)	James V. Allred (D)	C.O. Harris (R)
Anderson	1,852	281	5	3	3,664	1,165	11	0	1	0	2,617	35	6	0	3,917	118
Andrews	74	4	1	0	132	60	0	0	0	0	188	2	1	0	295	10
Angelina	1,998	0	0	0	3,590	1,416	3	0	1	0	2,086	15	15	0	4,147	129
Aransas	154	19	0	0	174	145	2	0	1	0	138	2	4	0	228	41
Archer	526	167	2	0	1,054	635	1	0	0	0	906	12	5	0	1,736	83
Armstrong	344	46	1	0	366	430	0	0	2	0	514	6	0	0	916	20
Atascosa	831	130	5	0	1,637	641	5	0	1	2	1,140	16	6	1	2,182	165
Austin	790	384	2	1	2,529	536	0	0	1	0	1,493	35	1	0	1,818	132
Bailey	480	85	5	0	615	345	1	0	1	0	485	16	5	1	870	99
Bandera	575	331	3	2	658	637	4	0	0	1	1,030	118	10	2	806	343
Bastrop	864	158	5	0	2,470	758	1	0	0	0	1,419	31	5	1	2,514	81
Baylor	366	55	4	0	931	497	1	0	3	0	773	10	1	0	1,621	60
Bee	1,152	409	20	28	1,514	1,170	9	0	4	0	1,181	45	5	1	1,864	216
Bell	2,085	349	5	1	5,395	2,874	8	0	2	0	6,520	34	10	0	6,141	202
Bexar	19,137	5,098	58	42	30,731	15,935	103	9	10	4	17,530	1,027	101	20	42,012	6,798
Blanco	707	444	1	3	995	390	2	0	5	1	1,094	130	7	1	1,190	220
Borden	84	11	0	0	200	40	0	0	0	0	123	1	0	0	229	13
Bosque	891	392	1	1	2,518	902	0	0	0	0	1,655	50	2	1	2,438	191
Bowie	1,623	263	11	1	3,827	1,709	8	0	6	1	3,766	49	15	0	5,288	267
Brazoria	1,108	353	4	1	2,309	1,359	3	0	0	0	915	64	2	1	2,443	244
Brazos	976	32	1	0	1,656	1,036	3	0	2	0	1,343	15	1	0	2,698	46
Brewster	339	22	0	1	526	457	1	0	0	0	654	5	0	5	938	66
Briscoe	0	0	0	0	675	318	1	0	2	0	412	0	0	0	873	31
Brooks	1,314	5	0	0	514	196	0	0	2	0	628	2	0	0	431	62
Brown	1,290	276	2	3	2,698	1,504	7	0	4	1	1,770	32	8	3	4,221	247
Burleson	930	78	0	0	2,331	313	49	0	0	0	1,070	20	0	0	1,675	63
Burnet	605	134	0	0	1,280	748	0	0	2	1	956	23	0	0	1,658	62
Caldwell	1,089	219	0	0	2,387	1,176	0	0	0	0	1,429	11	0	1	3,176	93
Calhoun	788	45	6	1	586	335	0	0	0	0	901	9	5	0	725	49
Callahan	695	166	0	0	1,635	593	0	0	3	0	0	0	0	0	1,840	140
Cameron	3,049	779	2	0	4,545	4,241	21	1	9	2	3,237	198	2	1	6,770	1,336
Camp	307	61	0	0	1,013	392	1	0	0	0	758	9	0	0	909	30
Carson	313	137	0	0	0	0	0	0	0	0	1,243	28	6	1	1,629	88
Cass	1,003	394	3	0	2,557	658	0	0	0	0	1,584	41	5	1	2,518	115
Castro	277	70	1	0	638	377	3	0	0	0	493	9	1	0	986	38
Chambers	431	108	1	0	638	315	3	0	1	0	337	8	1	0	1,078	67
Cherokee	1,651	377	4	0	2,863	1,424	4	0	3	0	2,629	44	11	0	4,066	122
Childress	645	113	0	0	1,307	886	9	0	5	0	1,046	27	12	1	2,201	111
Clay	737	167	3	0	1,568	895	4	0	3	0	1,235	16	5	0	2,262	88
Cochran	292	7	0	1	247	154	7	0	0	0	428	5	6	0	700	31
Coke	425	56	4	0	666	364	6	0	1	0	607	11	12	0	883	42
Coleman	1,161	264	5	0	1,949	1,119	6	0	2	0	2,436	27	16	0	3,065	164
Collin	2,224	821	6	1	5,040	1,910	22	1	7	0	3,135	101	13	0	5,852	373
Collingsworth	410	14	0	0	1,167	669	6	0	9	0	891	21	2	0	2,067	99
Colorado	684	223	8	0	2,150	922	7	0	1	1	1,301	61	4	0	1,596	194
Comal	1,409	892	6	2	1,795	534	3	0	1	0	1,028	88	2	0	1,997	177
Comanche	1,000	344	4	0	2,058	1,203	7	0	4	0	1,548	42	8	3	2,677	0
Concho	393	70	0	0	841	333	3	1	0	0	550	9	0	0	1,110	58
Cooke	1,501	558	3	1	2,336	1,894	10	0	1	0	2,624	79	8	0	4,048	356
Coryell	917	288	3	0	2,523	1,016	2	0	1	0	1,652	28	2	0	2,147	93
Cottle	344	32	4	1	844	356	0	0	2	0	646	9	6	0	1,272	55
Crane	198	47	1	0	257	199	0	0	0	0	420	8	0	0	638	8
Crockett	192	7	1	0	147	348	0	1	1	0	138	1	0	0	270	31
Crosby	540	74	0	0	1,029	637	0	0	0	0	1,013	4	0	0	1,786	79
Culberson	152	7	0	0	193	115	0	0	0	1	108	1	0	0	260	12
Dallam	1,011	81	10	0	895	1,418	9	2	2	0	799	15	10	1	1,524	109
Dallas	8,063	2,359	31	2	21,132	25,836	193	9	103	5	27,041	969	187	11	44,192	5,176
Dawson	405	169	3	0	1,119	699	0	0	1	0	770	7	7	0	1,891	88
DeWitt	1,109	666	2	0	2,346	1,161	2	0	2	0	1,216	42	1	0	2,356	183
Deaf Smith	313	78	0	0	547	1,038	0	0	0	0	571	28	3	0	1,310	80
Delta	802	43	1	0	1,541	461	1	0	2	0	1,547	18	1	0	1,498	45
Denton	1,603	270	13	0	3,358	2,307	13	1	3	3	0	0	0	0	5,284	271
Dickens	419	76	1	0	1,103	421	5	1	0	1	0	0	0	0	1,551	64
Dimmit	217	64	1	0	509	574	0	0	0	0	566	35	0	0	852	160

Table 49: Gubernatorial Races

General Elections, 1930-1936

County	1930				1932						1934				1936	
	Ross S. Sterling (D)	William E. Talbot (R)	L. L. Rhodes (S)	J. Stedhm (C)	Miriam A. Fergsn (D)	Orville Bullngtn (R)	George C. Edwrds (S)	Philip L. Howe (C)	George W. Amstrng(J)	Otho L. Hiett (L)	James V. Allred (D)	D.E. Waggnr (R)	George C. Edwrds (S)	Enoch Hrdwy (CM)	James V. Allred (D)	C.O. Harris (R)
Donley	531	75	2	0	891	912	1	1	1	0	847	9	2	1	1,581	84
Duval	1,743	119	0	0	1,495	97	0	0	0	0	3,007	2	0	0	2,926	129
Eastland	0	0	0	0	3,209	2,272	26	0	3	0	2,251	77	37	2	4,985	409
Ector	160	20	0	0	267	297	0	0	0	20	205	2	0	0	879	28
Edwards	460	162	2	0	406	395	1	0	0	1	616	7	3	0	444	79
El Paso	4,328	568	10	2	7,514	6,558	101	1	4	0	5,049	125	15	1	12,510	972
Ellis	2,058	257	9	1	4,708	2,634	19	0	11	0	2,884	44	4	0	5,753	210
Erath	1,061	455	6	2	0	0	0	0	0	0	1,722	39	14	2	2,838	159
Falls	1,307	448	0	0	3,218	939	12	0	0	0	0	0	0	0	3,526	82
Fannin	1,842	284	0	0	3,872	1,791	8	0	0	0	2,713	91	8	1	5,304	236
Fayette	1,598	747	5	2	4,383	878	1	1	0	1	3,263	115	5	1	3,232	264
Fisher	540	104	2	0	1,028	489	0	0	2	0	1,070	10	3	3	2,136	66
Floyd	581	190	3	0	1,125	987	1	0	2	1	1,083	20	2	0	1,970	119
Foard	279	64	0	0	577	344	7	0	10	0	509	11	5	0	950	54
Fort Bend	1,054	89	4	0	2,491	750	4	0	1	0	1,447	18	2	0	2,718	78
Franklin	271	126	2	0	1,035	279	0	0	2	0	627	30	2	0	947	52
Freestone	1,100	265	2	0	1,692	901	5	0	0	0	1,458	29	4	0	1,987	82
Frio	493	41	0	0	705	494	0	0	0	0	617	8	2	0	1,123	82
Gaines	189	26	2	0	293	270	6	0	1	0	266	2	0	0	701	18
Galveston	2,277	1,071	7	9	9,001	3,244	20	4	7	3	4,251	161	6	3	10,141	919
Garza	224	134	1	0	510	383	4	0	0	0	456	6	3	0	857	75
Gillespie	1,007	1,691	6	0	2,038	1,303	6	0	2	1	1,700	1,087	22	8	1,332	1,151
Glasscock	66	33	1	0	0	0	0	0	0	0	122	1	2	0	269	22
Goliad	727	528	5	1	1,227	520	1	1	0	3	1,147	197	6	5	1,249	274
Gonzales	2,042	243	1	0	2,381	1,312	0	0	4	0	1,454	26	2	2	2,920	131
Gray	1,968	351	2	2	2,130	1,763	9	1	6	1	1,858	39	24	5	4,507	309
Grayson	4,190	1,138	12	0	5,856	5,154	23	0	7	0	5,176	153	10	1	10,986	578
Gregg	889	139	0	0	4,101	1,467	10	0	0	0	2,222	35	6	1	6,697	334
Grimes	763	47	1	0	1,312	888	2	0	1	0	1,231	8	3	0	1,965	47
Guadalupe	1,400	2,472	9	4	2,995	1,445	3	0	4	1	3,031	1,127	5	2	3,431	912
Hale	797	279	2	0	1,608	1,832	4	0	10	0	0	0	0	0	3,234	257
Hall	643	113	2	0	1,141	993	4	0	15	0	941	14	2	0	2,219	69
Hamilton	736	216	1	0	0	0	0	0	0	0	1,043	44	3	0	2,074	90
Hansford	721	90	1	1	500	369	17	0	0	0	388	6	9	0	861	47
Hardeman	644	87	0	0	1,310	755	1	0	0	0	1,041	13	1	0	2,076	123
Hardin	593	33	1	0	2,370	340	0	0	0	0	988	6	0	0	2,387	0
Harris	9,556	1,449	43	7	32,717	22,382	200	39	20	6	40,418	541	132	26	63,019	3,982
Harrison	1,098	33	0	2	2,148	2,344	13	0	1	0	1,493	0	0	0	3,568	108
Hartley	0	0	0	0	329	335	0	0	0	0	559	9	0	0	582	37
Haskell	774	92	6	1	1,666	831	3	0	3	0	1,373	25	8	1	2,786	85
Hays	864	73	1	0	1,207	963	0	0	0	1	1,279	11	1	0	2,161	98
Hemphill	701	79	1	1	355	699	1	1	1	0	799	18	1	0	1,055	76
Henderson	1,157	657	7	1	2,999	856	5	0	1	0	2,114	33	8	0	3,401	128
Hidalgo	5,384	3,604	19	12	7,798	5,962	39	4	42	10	8,285	528	28	7	8,170	1,882
Hill	2,046	423	5	0	3,632	1,878	1	0	5	0	2,727	41	2	0	4,843	153
Hockley	407	60	3	0	1,175	412	25	4	1	1	821	6	28	0	1,760	58
Hood	375	93	0	0	784	435	3	0	1	1	653	15	7	0	1,042	61
Hopkins	1,623	0	0	0	2,700	1,311	4	0	0	0	2,210	43	6	0	2,865	156
Houston	1,123	213	5	0	2,166	1,029	3	0	0	0	2,278	75	4	0	2,470	66
Howard	977	168	3	1	1,748	1,112	1	0	1	0	1,270	5	1	0	3,141	101
Hudspeth	183	7	1	0	198	178	0	0	0	0	216	3	2	0	384	9
Hunt	2,231	327	13	1	0	0	0	0	0	0	2,775	71	3	0	5,931	230
Hutchinson	1,190	110	0	0	1,341	1,181	15	2	5	0	1,830	42	16	1	2,645	248
Irion	159	23	2	0	239	213	7	0	0	0	208	7	6	1	517	18
Jack	499	2	1	0	882	760	4	0	3	1	981	27	4	0	1,286	102
Jackson	437	67	3	1	838	658	4	0	0	0	603	15	2	1	1,013	103
Jasper	687	28	0	0	1,489	579	0	0	4	0	1,003	11	1	1	1,539	62
Jeff Davis	186	9	1	0	115	182	2	0	0	0	135	1	1	0	327	6
Jefferson	2,586	451	11	1	12,515	8,936	52	7	6	2	4,478	311	34	5	19,506	1,342
Jim Hogg	365	85	0	0	302	170	0	0	0	0	225	13	0	0	736	24
Jim Wells	919	95	1	1	1,096	519	1	2	1	0	770	16	0	0	1,953	139
Johnson	1,380	493	1	1	2,962	2,312	8	0	8	0	1,840	41	3	0	4,390	169
Jones	999	251	7	2	1,968	1,108	12	3	9	0	1,809	23	9	4	3,621	182
Karnes	1,048	258	0	1	1,958	706	0	0	1	1	1,493	32	1	1	2,379	149
Kaufman	1,604	396	1	0	2,940	1,324	0	0	3	0	2,184	42	2	1	4,028	144

Table 49: Gubernatorial Races

| | General Elections, 1930-1936 | | | | | | | | | | | | | | | | |
| Year | 1930 | | | | 1932 | | | | | | 1934 | | | | 1936 | |
County	Ross S. Sterling (D)	William E. Talbot (R)	L. L. Rhodes (S)	J. Stedhm (C)	Miriam A. Fergsn (D)	Orville Bullngtn (R)	George C. Edwrds (S)	Philip L. Howe (C)	George W. Amstrng(J)	Otho L. Hiett (L)	James V. Allred (D)	D.E. Waggnr (R)	George C. Edwrds (S)	Enoch Hrdwy (CM)	James V. Allred (D)	C.O. Harris (R)
Kendall	421	720	2	5	845	778	2	0	0	3	803	344	10	9	572	574
Kenedy	83	3	0	0	117	12	0	0	0	0	126	3	0	0	119	7
Kent	174	21	0	0	451	131	3	0	0	0	336	2	3	0	554	9
Kerr	1,422	449	15	2	1,412	1,425	9	0	8	1	2,216	281	18	5	1,981	632
Kimble	235	28	0	0	591	449	2	0	0	0	352	11	0	0	760	61
King	67	0	0	0	190	38	0	0	0	0	123	0	0	0	211	13
Kinney	323	86	1	7	562	227	0	0	1	0	608	31	1	0	446	124
Kleberg	520	46	0	0	1,201	698	7	0	3	0	1,343	2	3	0	1,623	74
Knox	532	59	5	0	1,106	543	3	0	3	0	905	16	9	0	1,892	93
La Salle	383	10	3	0	680	214	1	0	0	0	585	5	0	1	751	45
Lamar	1,775	207	3	0	4,166	1,933	12	1	7	2	3,839	121	12	1	5,746	195
Lamb	384	130	0	0	2,049	1,128	10	1	0	0	1,043	16	13	0	2,403	194
Lampasas	539	206	1	0	1,097	885	0	0	0	0	907	18	0	0	1,501	52
Lavaca	1,317	561	2	6	4,041	860	2	0	4	0	2,117	53	9	0	2,480	183
Lee	611	495	1	2	1,571	477	0	0	0	0	1,019	57	2	0	1,349	106
Leon	727	175	12	0	1,512	600	2	0	0	0	1,183	21	5	0	1,771	63
Liberty	667	81	11	3	1,935	818	7	0	0	0	997	15	11	0	2,902	151
Limestone	1,894	211	3	0	3,179	1,324	3	0	7	1	2,027	15	1	0	3,949	96
Lipscomb	581	352	6	0	342	877	7	0	0	0	836	152	11	0	1,036	230
Live Oak	521	123	6	1	899	369	4	0	1	1	573	16	9	0	1,062	133
Llano	612	61	1	0	938	473	1	0	1	0	1,019	19	0	0	1,342	63
Loving	0	0	0	0	142	61	0	0	1	0	130	0	0	0	133	4
Lubbock	1,126	243	4	0	3,171	2,744	14	2	1	0	2,425	44	18	9	6,679	918
Lynn	484	158	0	0	1,325	745	8	0	0	0	926	12	4	0	2,084	94
Madison	579	125	0	0	958	350	1	0	8	0	1,088	7	0	0	1,107	23
Marion	277	66	0	0	714	205	1	0	3	0	366	13	0	0	953	98
Martin	205	82	0	0	541	203	1	0	4	5	407	5	4	0	812	42
Mason	323	46	0	0	581	596	3	0	0	0	866	42	3	0	1,000	138
Matagorda	646	177	5	0	1,319	1,095	6	2	4	0	888	44	4	0	1,863	300
Maverick	231	33	1	0	634	411	3	0	1	1	480	18	0	0	965	99
McCulloch	595	210	4	2	1,395	889	1	0	0	0	985	13	3	1	1,985	145
McLennan	4,274	746	15	0	7,635	6,075	52	2	9	1	5,935	92	53	15	13,058	569
McMullen	143	8	0	0	215	48	0	0	0	0	213	4	0	0	285	18
Medina	1,182	842	0	4	2,118	938	1	0	2	1	2,606	380	8	7	2,398	676
Menard	239	46	2	0	597	431	1	0	0	0	400	14	2	0	817	81
Midland	396	53	0	0	640	763	2	1	0	11	384	11	0	0	1,352	85
Milam	1,388	416	4	1	3,705	1,207	5	0	2	0	2,906	31	5	0	3,537	125
Mills	388	161	2	0	1,038	525	0	0	0	0	669	29	5	0	1,017	93
Mitchell	643	112	0	2	1,019	752	0	0	0	0	1,038	18	1	0	2,089	139
Montague	789	308	8	1	2,090	1,219	13	0	5	2	1,576	37	10	0	0	0
Montgomery	1,357	214	1	1	1,655	474	0	0	0	0	1,316	16	6	0	2,563	61
Moore	129	15	0	0	213	401	0	0	0	1	294	4	2	0	604	31
Morris	438	41	0	0	0	0	0	0	0	0	0	0	0	0	1,229	34
Motley	246	34	0	0	524	384	0	0	0	1	414	4	3	0	895	37
Nacogdoches	1,184	127	3	0	2,811	859	1	0	2	0	1,810	23	3	0	4,200	87
Navarro	2,970	400	5	0	4,273	2,624	3	0	1	0	4,239	72	0	0	6,017	169
Newton	383	24	0	0	1,403	225	1	0	1	0	676	7	3	0	1,159	63
Nolan	785	124	1	0	1,550	1,055	3	0	1	1	1,247	27	1	0	3,038	154
Nueces	2,759	397	2	2	4,471	3,045	11	2	3	0	4,093	107	9	4	7,266	529
Ochiltree	310	55	2	0	486	804	2	0	2	0	912	12	9	0	1,163	65
Oldham	161	14	0	0	230	255	0	0	0	0	335	3	0	0	541	14
Orange	873	32	3	1	2,410	647	1	0	0	0	1,135	7	0	0	2,389	90
Palo Pinto	862	200	7	1	1,753	1,274	4	0	1	0	1,395	37	12	0	2,896	189
Panola	856	48	0	0	2,108	500	6	0	4	0	1,473	7	11	0	2,425	95
Parker	1,038	256	11	0	1,850	1,539	19	1	4	0	0	0	0	0	2,662	189
Parmer	0	0	0	0	766	540	8	0	0	0	604	26	4	0	1,088	95
Pecos	480	53	1	0	902	638	3	0	1	0	873	16	1	1	1,416	93
Polk	639	82	4	0	1,581	545	0	0	1	0	1,321	18	6	1	1,703	62
Potter	1,185	291	7	2	3,413	4,142	10	2	1	0	3,477	127	12	3	6,922	607
Presidio	220	18	1	0	624	332	1	0	0	0	540	7	0	0	1,024	32
Rains	360	139	22	0	882	96	3	0	0	0	493	16	4	0	712	39
Randall	431	72	0	0	779	941	1	1	2	0	782	13	1	0	1,760	55
Reagan	398	42	0	0	316	494	1	0	0	0	387	7	0	0	510	29
Real	336	73	1	4	291	181	0	0	1	0	287	6	1	1	220	37
Red River	1,172	174	1	0	2,358	874	3	0	4	0	1,685	27	3	0	2,789	87

Table 49: Gubernatorial Races

County	General Elections, 1930-1936 1930 Ross S. Sterling (D)	William E. Talbot (R)	L.L. Rhodes (S)	J. Stedhm (C)	1932 Miriam A. Fergsn (D)	Orville Bullngtn (R)	George C. Edwrds (S)	Philip L. Howe (C)	George W. Amstrng(J)	Otho L. Hiett (L)	1934 James V. Allred (D)	D.E. Waggnr (R)	George C. Edwrds (S)	Enoch Hrdwy (CM)	1936 James V. Allred (D)	C.O. Harris (R)
Reeves	316	42	0	0	586	613	0	0	0	0	319	9	1	1	1,196	50
Refugio	668	182	9	12	907	474	2	1	8	4	1,204	76	3	8	1,187	177
Roberts	136	20	1	0	177	323	0	0	0	0	195	8	1	0	433	25
Robertson	797	140	5	1	0	0	0	0	0	0	1,272	2	0	0	2,683	51
Rockwall	648	41	0	0	956	356	0	0	1	0	551	7	0	0	1,179	14
Runnels	924	285	2	0	2,039	1,137	10	0	5	0	1,514	23	6	0	3,153	161
Rusk	1,042	145	3	0	4,047	1,314	4	0	1	0	2,353	29	7	0	5,740	243
Sabine	706	47	5	1	1,617	221	4	0	0	0	1,048	16	8	2	1,272	45
San Augustine	631	272	1	0	1,672	151	0	0	1	0	900	0	0	0	1,081	27
San Jacinto	283	52	3	0	699	132	0	0	0	0	426	0	0	0	606	19
San Patricio	794	185	0	2	1,290	1,311	5	0	10	0	1,058	23	9	1	2,511	192
San S aba	634	152	0	0	0	0	0	0	0	0	1,323	17	2	0	1,573	71
Schleicher	0	0	0	0	314	268	0	0	0	0	242	5	1	0	522	41
Scurry	0	0	0	0	954	715	1	0	3	0	998	12	1	0	1,857	73
Shackelford	370	130	3	4	833	569	2	0	4	0	580	19	2	0	1,229	61
Shelby	1,234	111	3	0	3,097	563	18	0	0	0	2,094	19	55	0	3,238	71
Sherman	160	30	0	0	244	358	3	0	0	0	276	10	0	0	579	25
Smith	2,034	631	7	1	5,053	2,917	11	1	6	0	3,064	59	14	2	7,438	393
Somervell	0	0	0	0	417	195	3	0	3	0	237	4	3	0	341	40
Starr	792	8	0	0	712	67	0	0	0	0	657	1	0	0	2,323	289
Stephens	771	233	4	5	1,710	1,270	5	3	1	0	1,711	42	7	23	2,234	155
Sterling	164	7	0	0	163	188	0	0	0	0	200	2	0	0	398	12
Stonewall	193	47	1	0	808	213	2	0	0	0	526	8	1	0	1,028	33
Sutton	99	18	0	0	221	286	0	0	0	0	114	5	1	0	423	39
Swisher	342	124	2	1	820	820	4	0	11	0	810	15	8	0	1,504	84
Tarrant	4,543	1,097	16	0	16,580	16,125	115	5	116	2	20,299	354	101	8	31,400	2,322
Taylor	2,403	319	3	0	2,946	2,790	5	1	2	0	2,275	30	7	0	6,543	313
Terrell	316	96	1	0	318	295	2	0	0	0	174	4	0	0	380	37
Terry	283	100	2	0	1,014	501	10	9	9	1	720	4	6	0	1,644	54
Throckmorton	329	24	1	0	550	423	1	0	3	0	635	17	2	0	1,023	45
Titus	578	155	1	0	2,523	75	3	1	0	0	981	15	0	0	1,901	38
Tom Green	1,781	191	3	0	2,652	3,091	3	1	3	0	1,934	41	63	1	4,928	530
Travis	3,936	442	17	0	8,109	5,227	18	1	3	1	6,233	85	24	3	12,766	492
Trinity	383	74	0	0	1,230	369	0	0	0	0	845	22	0	0	1,307	46
Tyler	583	9	1	0	1,079	380	1	0	0	0	1,005	12	2	0	1,150	50
Upshur	970	340	4	2	2,346	667	4	0	5	5	1,326	30	6	0	0	0
Upton	357	27	2	1	658	478	3	0	3	1	0	0	0	0	795	50
Uvalde	637	69	0	0	1,310	848	0	0	0	0	1,053	24	4	1	1,903	201
Val Verde	839	154	3	0	916	914	1	0	0	0	824	62	0	0	1,515	251
Van Zandt	0	0	0	0	3,396	869	18	0	6	1	2,177	38	33	0	3,357	159
Victoria	606	167	1	1	2,192	748	4	0	2	1	1,830	48	2	1	2,264	166
Walker	625	86	1	0	1,391	508	1	0	0	1	1,095	5	1	0	1,716	22
Waller	394	58	1	0	958	316	1	0	0	0	0	0	0	0	952	46
Ward	0	0	0	0	515	236	1	0	2	0	333	8	1	0	1,131	83
Washington	851	145	0	0	3,085	412	2	0	0	0	1,316	17	3	0	2,110	72
Webb	1,304	178	0	0	3,697	1,209	1	0	2	1	2,476	73	2	5	3,998	376
Wharton	2,616	210	8	2	2,284	1,444	7	1	6	1	1,645	38	19	0	3,215	173
Wheeler	612	265	1	0	1,514	894	8	1	1	0	1,031	38	16	0	2,530	179
Wichita	2,286	665	10	1	4,487	5,787	11	0	2	1	3,116	79	21	0	9,817	726
Wilbarger	797	97	1	0	2,213	1,272	5	0	11	0	1,431	15	4	0	3,432	141
Willacy	396	58	0	0	837	489	0	0	2	0	605	62	0	0	1,174	212
Williamson	1,823	415	3	1	0	0	0	0	0	0	3,154	32	1	1	5,252	188
Wilson	1,124	512	2	1	2,018	585	2	0	0	0	1,370	32	1	0	2,728	141
Winkler	376	57	2	0	473	271	4	0	1	1	424	13	1	0	940	51
Wise	971	338	1	0	1,713	1,201	11	0	2	0	1,448	44	2	0	2,837	229
Wood	1,044	327	10	0	2,724	737	13	1	1	0	1,773	42	10	0	2,842	135
Yoakum	0	0	0	0	0	0	0	0	0	0	147	0	1	0	233	14
Young	616	0	0	0	1,984	1,467	1	0	2	1	1,485	25	3	0	3,173	175
Zapata	209	16	0	0	265	35	0	0	0	0	411	4	0	0	298	20
Zavala	434	57	0	0	538	455	2	0	0	0	558	7	0	1	917	105
Official	252,738	829			522,395		1,873		768		428,734	1,862			782,083	
Totals		62,224		231		317,590		138		134		13,703		260		58,842
Unofficial	253,732	832			522,395		1,873		763		425,872	1,863			779,650	
Totals		62,344		237		317,590		138		132		13,701		260		58,644

Table 50: Gubernatorial Races

County	1938 W. Lee O'Daniel (D)	Alexander Boyntn (R)	Earl E. Miller (S)	Homer Brks(CM)	1940 W. Lee O'Danil (D)	George C. Hopkns (R)	Ben H. Laudrdl(CM)	1942 Coke R. Stevnsn (D)	C.K. McDowll (R)	1944 Coke R. Stevnsn (D)	B.J. Peasley (R)	1946 Beauford H. Jester (D)	Eugene Nite Jr. (R)	1948 Beauford H. Jester (D)	Alvin H. Lane (R)	Gerald Ovrhlt (P)	Herman Wright (PR)
Anderson	1,839	29	1	0	5,899	155	0	1,617	12	5,308	157	1,606	49	4,497	604	20	1
Andrews	421	9	1	1	463	7	0	264	1	386	7	272	0	766	66	2	1
Angelina	0	0	0	0	0	127	1	1,048	12	5,163	490	1,287	60	5,604	555	26	9
Aransas	182	2	1	5	664	20	0	138	2	547	82	197	27	530	133	6	4
Archer	919	16	0	1	2,109	62	0	491	6	1,956	81	577	21	1,721	107	5	0
Armstrong	312	6	0	0	961	17	0	234	4	734	55	277	10	744	56	0	11
Atascosa	871	17	0	1	2,290	79	2	635	14	2,438	290	1,044	84	2,401	0	7	3
Austin	842	32	0	0	2,697	107	0	903	27	2,915	221	1,036	87	2,247	601	5	1
Bailey	242	20	0	1	1,310	56	0	186	8	1,245	169	315	63	1,226	160	11	2
Bandera	1,144	111	1	2	1,214	102	0	1,048	55	961	294	0	0	748	372	3	1
Bastrop	1,057	16	0	2	2,943	65	0	737	16	3,081	187	991	45	3,236	192	4	2
Baylor	748	8	0	0	1,779	30	0	391	0	1,706	49	1,055	8	1,609	52	3	0
Bee	1,352	38	3	1	2,717	56	2	555	13	2,388	167	1,058	77	2,027	356	10	3
Bell	2,335	32	2	0	8,097	165	1	1,723	16	8,416	334	2,362	102	8,414	604	23	17
Bexar	15,618	884	20	28	47,050	9,209	36	9,611	1,023	39,736	18,096	10,778	3,861	42,961	15,159	234	430
Blanco	1,212	86	2	5	1,447	161	3	984	58	1,247	272	1,040	156	1,249	309	3	57
Borden	116	0	0	0	416	5	0	96	0	290	15	98	1	220	7	4	0
Bosque	1,258	54	0	0	3,564	116	0	934	26	2,991	263	1,102	0	2,628	325	3	4
Bowie	2,258	27	0	1	7,703	299	0	1,426	11	8,086	436	2,233	96	8,324	1,216	23	26
Brazoria	929	41	0	0	4,365	216	0	768	19	6,595	522	1,678	118	6,686	1,070	22	123
Brazos	951	10	0	0	4,663	119	0	839	12	4,102	182	1,365	36	4,723	682	9	5
Brewster	318	6	0	0	1,220	45	0	274	9	1,094	80	414	35	1,108	136	4	2
Briscoe	376	8	0	0	1,051	23	0	247	0	802	33	215	13	747	49	3	1
Brooks	1,151	6	1	1	891	23	0	215	3	596	49	236	7	1,205	92	2	4
Brown	1,553	30	2	1	5,020	131	2	1,063	17	5,274	242	1,688	84	5,830	534	21	9
Burleson	958	6	0	0	2,273	68	0	681	7	2,255	76	695	13	2,277	110	4	2
Burnet	769	16	1	0	2,382	58	0	589	13	2,006	135	651	51	2,159	159	3	1
Caldwell	1,268	17	0	0	4,105	75	0	2,450	17	3,635	164	1,248	89	3,298	293	23	6
Calhoun	411	10	0	0	1,065	27	0	298	2	999	83	458	26	840	114	6	0
Callahan	1,171	43	0	0	0	64	0	786	22	2,297	45	829	42	2,034	135	8	2
Cameron	4,363	191	3	10	8,780	749	4	2,717	124	7,967	1,685	2,656	426	9,402	2,329	22	15
Camp	735	6	0	0	1,494	47	0	531	4	1,237	78	1,288	31	1,285	160	0	0
Carson	837	41	0	0	1,929	94	0	376	9	1,520	218	725	69	1,495	270	2	2
Cass	1,367	27	0	0	4,040	191	0	1,002	14	3,316	315	1,106	64	3,048	412	21	1
Castro	418	6	0	0	1,189	33	0	257	6	1,073	90	553	36	1,256	92	3	0
Chambers	438	25	0	0	1,453	62	0	298	6	1,276	138	322	12	1,166	156	1	0
Cherokee	2,224	25	0	1	5,995	139	2	1,375	21	4,734	271	1,734	52	3,957	635	23	3
Childress	989	18	2	0	2,991	68	0	555	11	2,591	151	831	61	2,630	142	19	3
Clay	1,230	16	0	0	2,689	91	0	811	10	2,647	161	739	34	2,321	204	7	0
Cochran	390	9	3	0	862	24	0	192	3	907	41	290	22	1,034	124	2	1
Coke	492	3	2	0	1,054	18	1	308	3	921	24	296	5	998	0	2	3
Coleman	1,596	16	1	0	3,070	110	0	1,149	18	3,340	253	1,165	55	3,091	300	11	1
Collin	2,801	99	0	0	8,011	393	1	2,045	54	7,350	689	2,232	152	6,255	832	21	9
Collingsworth	798	12	0	0	2,296	74	0	532	13	2,051	107	694	58	1,938	115	5	5
Colorado	682	40	1	0	2,644	206	0	597	42	2,646	331	826	110	2,265	727	8	1
Comal	890	37	2	1	2,454	184	0	734	47	2,651	351	1,079	189	2,367	760	0	2
Comanche	1,609	29	0	0	3,785	72	0	1,163	19	3,465	169	1,682	41	3,281	266	12	2
Concho	655	7	0	0	1,455	40	0	360	13	1,311	61	464	26	1,273	73	5	3
Cooke	1,999	115	5	1	5,502	345	0	1,416	36	4,559	477	1,387	119	4,070	692	13	7
Coryell	1,286	23	0	0	3,543	80	0	795	28	2,817	190	830	24	2,545	164	7	1
Cottle	1,541	29	0	1	1,688	70	0	268	13	1,359	71	607	34	1,367	68	1	0
Crane	479	11	0	0	867	25	0	302	1	632	9	171	6	887	40	1	0
Crockett	69	13	1	0	513	31	0	135	2	444	32	106	6	478	53	0	0
Crosby	745	20	1	0	1,947	40	1	458	1	1,971	64	742	16	1,877	150	8	1
Culberson	132	3	0	0	343	14	0	85	0	243	5	188	5	276	17	1	0
Dallam	613	20	1	1	1,895	111	2	337	20	1,481	142	428	62	1,704	228	6	2
Dallas	10,025	794	32	11	56,432	8,679	34	10,818	651	71,433	13,612	12,942	3,629	60,172	27,216	301	699
Dawson	935	13	0	0	3,101	63	0	595	8	2,617	261	824	58	2,865	237	10	0
DeWitt	1,065	34	0	0	0	0	0	878	20	3,621	543	1,291	244	2,852	791	6	6
Deaf Smith	310	15	0	0	1,595	106	0	375	12	1,568	179	709	109	1,736	296	13	1
Delta	928	13	0	0	0	0	0	537	8	1,871	59	0	0	1,786	83	25	3
Denton	2,122	45	0	0	6,925	312	0	1,429	28	6,561	413	2,336	102	5,945	851	11	9
Dickens	699	21	0	1	1,949	40	0	461	3	1,777	55	600	20	1,565	77	10	1
Dimmit	320	15	0	0	1,010	67	0	282	5	870	108	392	39	1,101	170	6	1

Table 50: Gubernatorial Races

General Elections, 1938-1948

County	1938				1940			1942		1944		1946		1948			
	W. Lee O'Daniel (D)	Alexander Boyntn (R)	Earl E. Miller (S)	Homer Brks(CM)	W. Lee O'Danil (D)	George C. Hopkns (R)	Ben H. Laudrll(CM)	Coke R. Stevnsn (D)	C.K. McDowll (R)	Coke R. Stevnsn (D)	B.J. Peasley (R)	Beauford H. Jester (D)	Eugene Nite Jr. (R)	Beauford H. Jester (D)	Alvin H. Lane (R)	Gerald Ovrhlt (P)	Herman Wright (PR)
Donley	555	0	0	0	1,821	40	0	378	10	1,409	132	692	64	1,527	138	6	0
Duval	2,015	1	0	0	3,366	38	0	2,125	1	3,468	29	4,150	7	3,617	53	2	0
Eastland	2,308	75	3	0	6,644	257	1	1,873	39	5,558	358	1,901	140	5,945	698	27	5
Ector	563	49	2	1	3,110	119	0	573	5	2,847	221	682	73	4,965	630	9	8
Edwards	226	14	0	0	714	32	0	192	0	519	58	195	19	435	93	0	1
El Paso	2,993	92	7	1	14,466	1,416	4	2,120	167	13,873	1,417	2,982	430	17,877	3,056	23	131
Ellis	2,542	32	0	0	8,376	181	0	1,799	28	7,809	340	2,261	59	6,814	693	22	10
Erath	1,749	56	0	0	4,312	158	0	1,167	24	3,844	209	1,499	102	3,508	332	19	4
Falls	2,008	23	0	0	0	0	0	1,303	18	3,995	143	1,603	52	3,832	306	9	3
Fannin	2,731	50	0	0	7,931	284	0	1,804	50	6,419	464	1,910	85	6,539	404	8	8
Fayette	1,797	54	1	0	4,822	272	0	1,520	63	5,316	647	1,929	168	4,291	942	5	7
Fisher	922	6	0	0	2,431	36	0	1,210	7	2,186	74	694	12	2,122	119	4	1
Floyd	779	17	0	0	2,314	70	0	578	7	2,235	156	718	28	2,400	217	10	0
Foard	442	18	0	0	1,103	41	0	312	3	1,010	53	332	8	811	66	3	0
Fort Bend	1,510	22	0	0	3,751	115	0	974	14	3,676	212	1,196	71	3,155	439	3	11
Franklin	636	16	0	0	1,740	62	0	773	8	1,463	75	689	17	1,405	94	7	0
Freestone	1,517	18	0	0	3,865	136	1	1,177	18	2,786	144	1,132	26	2,757	376	8	7
Frio	414	5	0	0	1,211	42	0	321	10	1,208	138	453	29	1,158	166	7	1
Gaines	355	11	0	0	1,645	60	0	433	7	1,362	80	403	13	1,620	130	5	2
Galveston	2,295	70	1	1	12,835	822	9	3,484	167	13,644	836	3,353	391	15,959	2,142	30	126
Garza	453	15	0	0	1,276	19	0	269	11	1,057	232	366	14	956	188	6	2
Gillespie	1,969	420	2	2	2,446	1,112	4	2,053	531	1,753	1,789	1,450	1,194	1,390	2,026	1	0
Glasscock	81	12	0	0	317	4	0	68	1	254	9	87	7	246	26	4	0
Goliad	1,322	108	0	3	1,240	208	0	802	61	1,053	346	358	73	653	360	4	0
Gonzales	1,128	9	0	0	3,637	88	0	931	15	3,641	314	1,273	55	3,262	267	7	6
Gray	1,157	62	2	1	5,125	384	1	1,684	59	4,241	630	1,947	328	4,738	871	17	0
Grayson	3,867	97	5	2	13,486	619	2	3,198	96	12,773	885	3,750	233	12,411	1,416	14	7
Gregg	3,270	4	0	0	10,021	927	2	1,283	81	7,450	946	1,867	277	6,683	2,201	33	55
Grimes	791	9	0	0	2,456	45	0	569	2	1,980	70	655	16	1,506	198	6	3
Guadalupe	3,944	608	5	10	3,988	883	3	2,778	541	3,182	1,271	3,391	1,321	3,255	1,726	6	14
Hale	1,211	30	2	1	3,988	188	0	1,013	19	3,418	0	1,174	85	4,534	596	14	4
Hall	959	10	0	0	2,393	53	0	537	6	1,946	99	969	75	2,235	114	1	1
Hamilton	1,053	25	0	0	2,809	107	0	753	24	2,205	207	941	53	2,026	0	2	3
Hansford	455	12	2	0	842	38	0	181	7	799	48	296	21	1,032	86	2	5
Hardeman	1,006	17	1	0	2,268	62	0	418	7	2,016	132	591	27	1,836	117	4	2
Hardin	0	0	0	0	3,181	55	0	616	7	2,864	0	739	0	2,767	140	14	5
Harris	36,775	744	45	27	89,053	4,910	22	31,365	525	90,483	7,380	43,417	4,702	95,751	21,039	252	633
Harrison	1,236	22	0	0	5,010	154	1	629	3	4,517	219	0	0	4,319	663	25	7
Hartley	124	3	0	0	625	37	0	175	0	597	32	193	15	528	35	2	1
Haskell	1,196	20	1	2	3,273	92	0	1,012	11	2,866	142	874	24	2,852	115	1	0
Hays	962	14	0	0	2,787	63	0	889	13	2,284	170	799	38	2,728	202	9	4
Hemphill	542	10	0	0	0	0	0	191	6	1,015	114	0	0	1,012	101	12	2
Henderson	3,651	101	6	3	4,785	163	0	1,441	24	3,887	209	0	0	4,143	362	3	0
Hidalgo	4,496	243	2	6	11,468	904	0	2,886	161	10,655	1,861	4,552	606	12,040	3,412	57	20
Hill	2,668	42	0	1	6,461	121	0	1,732	24	5,494	243	1,761	57	4,923	423	13	4
Hockley	663	18	3	0	2,617	60	0	521	5	3,140	142	867	50	2,266	267	8	2
Hood	0	0	0	0	1,453	56	0	367	12	1,369	83	464	31	1,358	115	5	0
Hopkins	2,016	30	1	0	5,343	150	0	1,428	45	4,447	277	1,521	66	4,309	319	14	5
Houston	1,473	9	0	0	3,893	130	0	1,008	11	2,888	97	1,071	18	2,767	271	11	3
Howard	982	39	1	0	11,690	95	1	715	5	4,019	230	1,057	38	4,762	276	16	2
Hudspeth	249	0	0	0	476	11	0	65	0	383	7	109	2	464	21	2	3
Hunt	3,859	67	0	0	8,655	383	64	2,370	30	7,308	400	2,004	109	5,872	758	15	3
Hutchinson	1,396	67	0	1	3,836	296	0	534	30	3,216	484	1,549	220	5,114	835	7	11
Irion	428	4	1	1	615	7	4	212	0	436	25	0	0	402	24	0	3
Jack	888	29	0	0	2,240	90	0	563	11	1,839	140	585	43	1,516	173	22	0
Jackson	541	13	3	0	1,755	65	1	456	8	2,026	178	611	42	1,680	260	7	8
Jasper	657	10	0	0	2,406	57	0	484	6	2,152	157	732	13	2,230	183	7	4
Jeff Davis	0	0	0	0	0	0	0	211	0	381	13	113	0	139	25	1	0
Jefferson	4,012	110	4	7	23,712	1,115	4	2,596	104	27,110	1,701	9,172	474	29,038	3,727	83	86
Jim Hogg	281	18	0	0	904	32	0	267	18	699	14	544	0	752	27	1	1
Jim Wells	804	21	20	0	2,996	60	0	607	16	3,213	215	3,897	0	4,853	441	10	6
Johnson	1,532	0	0	0	5,892	164	0	1,259	29	5,320	279	1,456	102	4,557	502	19	6
Jones	1,407	32	1	0	4,010	66	1	1,312	12	3,833	198	1,466	32	3,818	233	15	1
Karnes	1,113	24	1	2	2,577	59	0	970	16	2,623	247	1,365	46	2,704	242	1	1
Kaufman	2,276	37	1	0	5,553	169	0	1,610	32	4,787	223	1,625	66	4,349	489	7	6

Table 50: Gubernatorial Races

General Elections, 1938-1948

County	W. Lee O'Daniel (D)	Alexander Boyntn (R)	Earl E. Miller (S)	Homer Brks(CM)	W. Lee O'Danil (D)	George C. Hopkns (R)	Ben H. Laudrdl(CM)	Coke R. Stevnsn (D)	C.K. McDowll (R)	Coke R. Stevnsn (D)	B.J. Peasley (R)	Beauford H. Jester (D)	Eugene Nlte Jr. (R)	Beauford H. Jester (D)	Alvin H. Lane (R)	Gerald Ovrhlt (P)	Herman Wright (PR)
	1938				**1940**			**1942**		**1944**		**1946**		**1948**			
Kendall	974	258	2	2	1,251	463	2	1,044	294	885	902	640	556	903	917	4	2
Kenedy	78	0	0	0	0	0	0	96	0	74	16	58	5	59	23	0	0
Kent	222	3	0	0	791	10	0	274	1	623	9	209	5	493	27	0	0
Kerr	915	89	0	1	2,432	277	0	544	72	2,440	479	684	219	2,351	812	6	5
Kimble	449	12	0	0	1,294	48	0	347	3	1,151	69	454	23	1,102	129	1	1
King	122	0	0	0	286	3	0	84	0	251	5	117	1	240	2	0	0
Kinney	428	41	0	1	526	64	1	160	22	594	100	394	58	456	105	0	0
Kleberg	589	7	0	0	2,017	48	0	355	3	1,799	135	498	46	2,497	315	12	10
Knox	714	15	2	1	1,898	53	0	508	5	2,003	69	689	14	1,922	86	7	0
La Salle	433	1	0	0	784	12	0	295	1	829	25	0	0	858	52	2	0
Lamar	3,467	45	2	1	8,315	162	1	1,606	16	6,989	405	1,691	70	7,619	544	15	8
Lamb	1,199	34	1	1	3,607	161	0	537	12	3,021	304	1,252	62	3,436	313	5	3
Lampasas	732	13	0	0	2,203	57	1	507	14	1,921	116	511	27	1,680	125	0	0
Lavaca	1,861	43	3	3	3,736	165	0	1,281	32	4,553	430	1,634	126	3,944	523	12	11
Lee	695	13	0	0	1,996	150	0	684	26	1,879	299	656	37	1,907	220	5	1
Leon	1,016	11	0	0	0	0	0	617	9	1,745	83	808	10	1,499	140	3	1
Liberty	1,000	10	0	0	3,820	154	0	1,971	12	3,263	176	931	40	3,123	457	42	8
Limestone	2,696	24	0	0	5,260	53	1	1,550	7	3,934	72	1,547	47	3,808	510	13	5
Lipscomb	528	55	0	0	1,062	148	0	333	42	890	220	425	86	786	249	7	0
Live Oak	548	10	0	0	1,355	52	0	337	4	1,211	187	518	54	1,249	263	9	4
Llano	665	15	0	0	1,694	37	1	948	12	1,444	77	757	42	1,558	126	1	2
Loving	83	3	1	0	117	2	0	43	4	81	4	80	4	80	5	0	0
Lubbock	1,492	59	1	3	9,116	286	4	1,422	40	9,871	577	2,818	263	12,139	2,599	58	20
Lynn	949	13	0	0	2,836	61	0	460	4	2,304	115	857	30	2,298	186	8	1
Madison	661	3	0	0	1,612	35	0	421	3	1,239	76	374	8	1,006	106	11	1
Marion	395	18	0	0	1,194	93	0	276	14	1,203	0	347	31	1,099	198	3	1
Martin	341	8	0	0	1,158	32	0	223	2	951	40	331	23	1,012	48	6	0
Mason	561	7	0	0	1,478	103	3	278	14	1,251	214	530	79	1,049	298	9	2
Matagorda	791	28	1	0	2,650	140	0	664	21	2,811	266	778	78	2,645	531	9	3
Maverick	542	14	3	0	1,104	48	1	219	8	993	74	245	16	890	114	2	5
McCulloch	1,557	43	2	0	2,744	79	0	570	8	2,568	205	785	50	2,407	220	4	0
McLennan	7,557	143	9	5	17,595	521	7	3,058	82	17,075	911	3,216	237	18,046	1,702	72	76
McMullen	274	0	0	0	0	0	0	231	1	364	56	168	4	262	35	1	0
Medina	2,173	207	1	5	0	0	0	1,725	191	2,236	823	1,424	517	2,440	1,098	7	7
Menard	1,168	19	0	0	1,362	46	0	331	3	1,030	81	362	29	870	148	6	1
Midland	999	41	0	2	2,479	118	0	1,484	18	2,605	172	623	98	3,290	508	4	5
Milam	2,143	25	6	2	5,130	114	3	1,499	22	4,539	275	1,312	0	3,872	337	21	12
Mills	605	30	0	0	1,884	42	0	481	5	1,592	104	466	19	1,261	120	2	2
Mitchell	844	17	0	0	2,654	58	0	797	10	2,364	120	797	28	2,342	118	8	1
Montague	1,457	41	2	0	3,829	127	0	1,127	20	3,353	255	2,915	136	3,140	301	8	1
Montgomery	1,617	14	1	0	3,680	82	0	1,201	15	3,421	108	1,052	21	2,774	356	32	6
Moore	224	7	0	0	1,169	44	1	187	2	1,277	105	525	33	1,891	177	3	1
Morris	674	17	0	0	0	0	0	389	6	1,345	77	563	13	1,370	117	0	1
Motley	448	4	0	0	1,042	24	0	238	0	882	34	292	9	847	42	2	2
Nacogdoches	2,004	13	0	0	5,249	120	1	1,117	10	3,863	175	1,313	0	3,979	425	32	3
Navarro	3,259	34	1	2	8,155	220	0	2,387	23	6,993	215	2,366	57	5,802	716	38	6
Newton	661	6	0	0	1,926	41	0	488	6	1,146	106	343	17	1,135	108	14	12
Nolan	1,281	33	2	0	3,723	131	0	1,146	18	3,506	134	956	73	3,761	295	0	2
Nueces	2,225	83	4	0	12,286	582	12	2,207	44	14,215	1,262	5,614	437	17,789	3,410	151	74
Ochiltree	938	14	0	0	1,446	73	1	281	15	1,175	117	512	44	1,210	181	4	0
Oldham	178	3	0	0	492	5	0	152	7	393	37	179	19	403	51	0	0
Orange	1,171	4	0	2	3,344	64	1	672	5	5,472	389	3,995	89	5,900	743	5	9
Palo Pinto	1,434	68	3	0	3,955	118	0	999	17	3,935	239	1,138	90	4,307	619	25	10
Panola	1,165	15	4	0	3,072	37	0	753	3	2,309	0	748	11	2,527	203	7	2
Parker	1,717	44	10	2	4,030	113	2	1,243	30	4,083	334	1,363	81	3,569	425	17	5
Parmer	451	23	1	1	0	0	0	269	47	1,177	202	0	0	1,212	195	4	0
Pecos	507	21	0	0	1,912	38	1	438	11	1,571	102	377	30	1,622	158	2	1
Polk	789	6	0	0	0	0	0	616	4	2,097	82	1,168	13	2,074	168	13	8
Potter	1,445	84	2	0	8,802	0	0	1,296	98	8,668	1,202	3,913	551	11,691	2,346	29	31
Presidio	203	11	2	0	1,065	43	3	291	8	947	49	311	20	1,022	105	2	5
Rains	568	7	0	0	1,158	70	0	355	2	761	91	381	5	815	100	1	0
Randall	523	5	0	0	2,073	79	1	393	12	1,932	149	931	75	2,428	341	4	8
Reagan	191	8	0	0	589	15	0	239	2	498	20	159	13	518	26	0	0
Real	211	14	0	0	542	40	0	170	8	495	65	185	16	521	73	1	0
Red River	1,819	10	0	0	4,286	174	0	1,170	11	3,503	198	967	17	3,557	211	6	3

Table 50: Gubernatorial Races

General Elections, 1938-1948

Year / County	1938 W. Lee O'Daniel (D)	1938 Alexander Boyntn (R)	1938 Earl E. Miller (S)	1938 Homer Brks(CM)	1940 W. Lee O'Danil (D)	1940 George C. Hopkns (R)	1940 Ben H. Laudrdl(CM)	1942 Coke R. Stevnsn (D)	1942 C.K. McDowll (R)	1944 Coke R. Stevnsn (D)	1944 B.J. Peasley (R)	1946 Beauford H. Jester (D)	1946 Eugene Nite Jr. (R)	1948 Beauford H. Jester (D)	1948 Alvin H. Lane (R)	1948 Gerald Ovrhlt (P)	1948 Herman Wright (PR)
Reeves	399	18	0	0	1,514	47	0	252	8	1,405	83	474	37	1,579	146	1	1
Refugio	1,432	63	2	9	1,960	129	4	603	16	1,396	158	977	85	1,920	269	4	3
Roberts	0	0	0	0	457	14	0	95	8	390	22	159	17	380	32	1	0
Robertson	1,139	9	0	1	3,350	46	0	783	5	2,966	64	750	11	2,602	253	8	1
Rockwall	521	4	1	0	1,594	13	0	587	6	1,283	34	501	8	1,086	85	28	2
Runnels	1,448	40	2	0	3,816	105	0	821	17	3,318	317	861	67	3,338	249	25	9
Rusk	2,727	18	1	1	8,434	248	0	2,138	32	6,342	287	2,157	70	6,038	948	28	15
Sabine	1,992	5	0	0	1,661	37	0	438	3	1,333	88	598	7	1,294	95	9	2
San Augustine	965	3	0	0	0	0	0	648	9	1,176	102	520	9	1,044	94	16	1
San Jacinto	286	4	0	0	858	30	0	248	4	689	20	907	3	650	86	4	4
San Patricio	940	34	4	0	3,883	133	2	833	23	3,563	258	1,007	82	3,258	508	18	8
San Saba	955	19	1	0	2,525	27	0	679	10	2,231	103	746	17	2,213	77	4	0
Schleicher	282	11	0	1	0	0	0	181	3	621	43	161	14	568	75	0	0
Scurry	816	17	0	0	0	0	0	935	4	2,020	95	885	29	2,162	103	10	2
Shackelford	580	14	0	0	1,721	35	0	437	8	1,240	78	409	19	1,052	102	0	0
Shelby	1,603	15	2	1	4,983	89	0	1,024	22	3,470	180	1,292	35	3,823	240	7	5
Sherman	124	9	0	0	628	30	0	108	2	551	32	78	3	533	45	4	1
Smith	3,505	78	2	0	10,619	341	0	2,789	47	8,804	492	2,641	213	9,039	2,051	44	18
Somervell	596	4	0	0	662	20	0	524	6	521	53	231	22	502	67	2	0
Starr	1,300	3	0	0	1,253	16	0	617	2	1,353	24	1,971	15	2,091	79	0	1
Stephens	1,284	38	2	0	3,146	93	2	1,029	12	2,623	114	825	45	2,581	276	12	4
Sterling	212	3	0	0	436	9	0	128	1	342	10	135	5	261	9	0	0
Stonewall	498	4	0	0	1,308	38	0	332	1	1,040	29	500	17	1,010	40	2	1
Sutton	94	6	0	0	632	28	0	158	4	605	34	518	11	549	59	0	0
Swisher	547	44	0	0	1,654	65	0	364	15	1,629	149	586	37	1,842	176	4	2
Tarrant	8,624	601	10	1	41,552	1,974	6	22,725	494	47,422	2,512	12,361	1,515	47,237	9,789	163	134
Taylor	1,907	41	0	0	8,597	192	0	2,064	25	9,091	317	2,436	93	9,471	733	41	10
Terrell	137	2	0	0	494	47	0	86	8	455	93	99	27	216	43	1	1
Terry	559	13	0	2	2,227	41	2	401	4	2,284	144	624	47	2,409	218	11	3
Throckmorton	1,010	4	0	0	1,121	17	0	360	6	1,150	29	617	4	1,081	37	0	0
Titus	1,013	15	0	0	3,814	77	0	719	2	2,831	106	3,107	73	2,753	246	3	3
Tom Green	1,819	82	4	0	7,174	345	0	1,394	43	7,593	467	1,910	166	8,003	1,023	24	17
Travis	3,687	75	9	2	19,957	679	2	3,716	62	16,831	1,119	7,030	393	24,426	2,252	47	202
Trinity	720	8	1	0	2,030	53	0	995	8	1,401	74	442	9	1,255	128	10	3
Tyler	596	6	1	0	1,825	26	0	430	1	1,246	109	541	24	1,311	168	9	1
Upshur	1,764	39	2	0	3,998	144	0	1,004	51	3,014	210	1,044	38	2,615	432	9	2
Upton	611	17	0	2	0	0	0	323	1	861	50	254	9	909	95	1	1
Uvalde	700	21	0	0	2,353	102	2	476	10	2,010	312	0	0	2,064	417	14	0
Val Verde	599	76	0	0	2,002	248	0	330	54	1,723	279	578	107	1,636	334	1	0
Van Zandt	2,167	58	3	1	5,249	168	0	1,492	38	3,765	279	1,379	68	3,776	475	31	10
Victoria	938	32	0	1	3,299	287	0	660	25	3,134	553	915	131	3,365	607	8	3
Walker	810	2	0	0	2,352	23	1	576	4	1,638	145	602	22	2,122	246	14	0
Waller	500	5	0	0	1,398	54	0	289	1	1,337	48	473	18	1,338	200	5	9
Ward	401	29	1	2	2,131	80	3	331	8	1,716	120	503	46	2,392	222	3	5
Washington	1,013	11	1	0	3,264	79	0	764	15	3,739	191	1,382	54	2,578	1,245	0	0
Webb	2,376	23	2	2	4,767	222	1	998	15	5,461	103	2,454	73	5,160	420	7	32
Wharton	1,136	33	3	0	4,573	164	0	843	26	4,625	261	1,148	60	3,990	630	8	13
Wheeler	801	72	0	0	2,977	174	1	630	29	2,264	261	921	86	2,183	204	14	1
Wichita	3,082	145	1	0	13,109	691	0	2,034	62	13,061	968	3,143	270	13,808	1,425	21	20
Wilbarger	1,696	24	0	0	3,854	127	0	865	5	4,127	241	892	50	3,463	299	7	4
Willacy	807	18	0	0	0	0	0	512	35	1,311	410	484	69	1,528	362	5	5
Williamson	2,464	36	1	0	7,476	258	1	1,870	42	5,729	695	2,127	116	6,390	601	8	12
Wilson	1,298	24	1	0	3,284	78	2	755	24	3,249	229	1,391	83	2,726	288	1	4
Winkler	359	27	1	0	1,473	59	0	253	3	1,141	48	277	29	1,792	168	10	3
Wise	1,558	43	2	1	4,119	125	0	1,118	30	3,588	245	1,179	89	3,358	307	10	1
Wood	1,800	25	0	0	0	0	0	1,221	17	3,647	261	1,404	76	3,224	519	12	9
Yoakum	152	6	0	0	0	0	0	169	1	768	37	278	6	917	90	7	3
Young	1,458	47	1	0	4,059	114	1	949	13	3,766	209	1,116	52	3,544	309	15	3
Zapata	575	41	0	0	705	487	0	716	347	525	20	309	5	640	406	0	0
Zavala	322	14	0	0	984	54	0	284	13	949	112	474	35	834	152	1	2
Official	358,943		207		59,885			280,735		1,007,826		345,513		1,024,160		3,554	
Totals		11,309		282	1,019,338		266		9,204		100,287		33,231		177,399		3,747
Unofficial	358,949		213		59,653			280,737		1,005,272		345,509		1,034,156		3,574	
Totals		11,309		339	1,024,470		296		9,254		100,927		33,277		177,399		3,749

Table 51: Gubernatorial Races

General Elections, 1950-1960												
Year	**1950**		**1952**		**1954**		**1956**			**1958**		**1960**	
County	Allan Shivers (D)	Ralph W. Currie (R)	Allan Shivers (D)	Allan Shivers (R)	Allan Shivers (D)	Tod R. Adams (R)	Price Daniel (D)	William R. Bryant (R)	W. Lee O'Daniel(WI)	Price Daniel (D)	Edwin S. Mayer (R)	Price Daniel (D)	William M. Steger (R)
Anderson	1,383	50	7,340	519	2,492	111	0	0	0	2,366	92	5,745	1,519
Andrews	230	10	1,200	196	747	30	1,699	158	220	924	58	2,829	568
Angelina	4,021	159	8,500	1,446	2,910	124	0	0	0	4,088	149	9,397	2,363
Aransas	364	23	974	256	280	27	0	0	0	346	31	1,429	513
Archer	645	30	1,640	177	617	44	1,613	116	158	1,143	39	1,744	307
Armstrong	635	24	758	134	393	20	670	49	62	335	14	676	152
Atascosa	894	42	3,556	586	1,136	72	3,109	293	239	1,033	62	3,144	878
Austin	920	65	3,731	589	1,034	82	2,866	305	389	1,013	88	2,918	865
Bailey	313	44	1,461	407	460	50	0	0	0	818	74	1,761	749
Bandera	377	66	1,235	452	508	77	1,076	223	94	396	74	1,024	560
Bastrop	947	27	3,755	358	1,319	57	3,241	186	0	1,549	63	3,963	602
Baylor	516	16	1,591	136	572	29	1,503	76	126	558	17	1,600	288
Bee	836	117	4,181	0	2,116	90	3,601	353	262	1,004	92	3,667	1,336
Bell	2,097	82	10,359	1,362	3,512	126	11,450	607	1,351	4,695	160	13,392	2,092
Bexar	9,105	2,818	56,572	46,919	24,360	4,503	71,673	26,227	816	24,163	6,213	85,701	45,445
Blanco	1,150	168	959	513	862	127	1,033	236	128	863	130	1,032	481
Borden	111	0	273	43	159	3	287	16	56	173	7	298	70
Bosque	996	69	3,095	380	1,150	87	2,685	279	304	1,425	96	2,420	814
Bowie	2,882	157	14,256	1,334	3,680	163	11,807	760	1,807	3,742	150	13,277	2,239
Brazoria	3,474	224	11,716	4,088	3,932	813	0	0	0	6,092	868	13,886	6,134
Brazos	1,297	78	7,312	1,152	2,219	118	6,850	708	604	4,511	285	8,642	2,004
Brewster	723	36	1,223	349	668	56	1,090	155	38	500	67	1,282	295
Briscoe	611	23	795	168	385	17	846	44	71	345	10	892	192
Brooks	1,199	29	2,067	279	1,067	39	1,708	146	68	881	39	2,490	312
Brown	0	0	5,541	1,224	2,204	159	5,024	461	1,181	2,442	183	5,752	1,796
Burleson	710	8	3,191	179	947	31	2,421	168	298	961	18	2,921	357
Burnet	685	23	1,883	382	913	52	2,100	182	239	982	87	2,387	687
Caldwell	1,102	60	3,783	362	1,577	54	3,668	277	257	1,524	56	3,572	735
Calhoun	313	25	1,581	452	688	56	2,219	209	264	901	63	3,046	749
Callahan	677	34	2,167	366	768	53	1,749	153	374	804	42	2,183	650
Cameron	2,563	437	14,453	6,123	3,752	615	16,975	2,588	493	5,124	723	17,076	6,976
Camp	427	23	1,956	212	776	8	1,483	57	341	771	21	1,960	501
Carson	1,305	129	1,709	597	849	119	1,590	209	211	699	82	1,782	668
Cass	1,373	41	4,643	588	1,678	81	4,093	416	817	2,057	56	4,392	1,080
Castro	1,108	49	1,726	0	656	41	1,652	92	164	847	32	2,090	323
Chambers	345	30	2,128	339	635	32	1,871	187	109	691	37	2,377	602
Cherokee	1,407	78	6,576	792	2,957	179	5,157	385	1,316	3,455	104	6,871	1,031
Childress	1,788	102	2,660	380	1,116	64	0	0	0	942	55	2,246	573
Clay	1,430	54	2,301	271	970	62	2,396	188	132	971	59	2,319	455
Cochran	427	29	1,429	133	553	24	1,251	91	89	595	28	1,508	279
Coke	296	3	1,132	94	441	6	916	63	158	604	45	1,152	225
Coleman	1,243	60	3,272	727	2,230	85	2,898	224	603	1,447	81	3,079	891
Collin	1,879	180	6,676	1,795	2,675	205	7,185	702	734	2,850	157	7,427	1,968
Collingsworth	1,504	78	1,805	483	854	62	1,695	120	102	711	25	1,461	436
Colorado	978	94	4,326	756	1,662	123	3,407	475	417	1,290	132	3,673	1,157
Comal	1,081	107	3,508	1,084	1,447	151	3,668	706	108	1,621	315	3,233	1,945
Comanche	1,126	84	3,322	504	1,431	117	3,016	264	367	1,265	82	2,946	896
Concho	994	12	1,148	151	446	21	809	51	263	351	52	1,009	248
Cooke	1,256	141	5,208	1,143	1,784	218	0	0	0	2,093	167	5,312	1,581
Coryell	791	42	3,040	284	1,140	38	3,084	228	418	1,942	80	3,563	621
Cottle	968	27	949	135	701	40	1,202	67	160	548	26	1,210	148
Crane	982	36	1,009	155	755	32	1,054	114	115	577	53	1,317	215
Crockett	147	1	738	144	286	32	766	77	116	279	66	930	260
Crosby	616	27	1,771	284	652	36	2,046	106	191	853	32	2,398	326
Culberson	258	6	446	80	262	9	446	43	48	231	15	560	144
Dallam	1,149	135	1,848	506	937	113	1,570	215	226	641	84	1,498	432
Dallas	23,632	7,233	84,515	85,440	40,504	10,650	119,604	44,864	6,049	88,008	23,950	126,004	94,690
Dawson	0	0	3,399	613	1,578	63	2,756	253	508	1,104	65	355	941
DeWitt	971	181	4,884	778	1,713	148	3,856	472	370	1,294	147	3,498	1,414
Deaf Smith	1,650	163	2,459	781	1,157	93	2,451	320	203	852	94	2,670	729
Delta	508	6	1,774	178	712	18	1,424	72	345	627	12	1,659	181
Denton	1,681	151	8,139	962	2,430	283	8,042	822	1,112	3,340	261	6,714	2,276
Dickens	479	37	1,594	131	766	36	1,402	92	127	658	20	1,444	224
Dimmit	333	25	1,146	247	567	32	976	98	25	439	27	1,366	327

Table 51: Gubernatorial Races

General Elections, 1950-1960

County	1950 Allan Shivers (D)	1950 Ralph W. Currie (R)	1952 Allan Shivers (D)	1952 Allan Shivers (R)	1954 Allan Shivers (D)	1954 Tod R. Adams (R)	1956 Price Daniel (D)	1956 William R. Bryant (R)	1956 W. Lee O'Daniel(WI)	1958 Price Daniel (D)	1958 Edwin S. Mayer (R)	1960 Price Daniel (D)	1960 William M. Steger (R)
Donley	1,143	112	1,581	314	694	44	1,494	107	79	555	39	1,356	311
Duval	4,794	3	3,871	148	2,690	122	4,605	101	89	3,680	74	4,333	486
Eastland	1,579	156	5,699	1,065	2,346	196	4,482	503	1,005	2,252	189	4,901	1,838
Ector	863	102	9,563	2,716	2,494	355	9,913	2,423	413	3,224	745	12,634	5,252
Edwards	274	20	611	159	324	22	557	73	21	297	77	363	379
El Paso	0	0	25,524	6,636	10,171	1,168	24,831	7,024	206	12,743	1,458	30,995	14,606
Ellis	1,825	104	7,306	1,237	2,414	165	7,226	544	831	4,001	127	8,237	1,498
Erath	1,130	108	4,200	844	1,623	166	4,165	422	504	1,794	153	3,794	1,815
Falls	1,225	37	4,038	470	1,470	75	3,560	183	651	1,640	90	4,330	666
Fannin	2,299	89	5,501	717	2,358	155	5,321	413	599	2,241	8	5,383	866
Fayette	1,680	123	5,744	1,047	2,194	123	4,648	451	589	1,984	125	4,787	1,103
Fisher	560	0	1,702	173	904	25	1,834	67	298	1,640	31	2,590	550
Floyd	849	61	2,737	464	1,285	73	2,574	146	317	1,042	43	2,589	575
Foard	340	15	896	111	344	13	787	45	47	365	21	879	135
Fort Bend	1,204	95	5,946	907	1,880	111	5,082	653	382	2,178	139	6,128	1,854
Franklin	359	17	1,286	145	587	20	1,284	60	264	636	16	1,559	289
Freestone	1,325	45	3,586	372	1,288	54	2,757	243	282	1,327	62	2,989	825
Frio	413	30	1,631	234	598	28	1,482	153	79	591	49	1,448	386
Gaines	445	15	2,033	290	682	27	2,186	145	314	1,875	45	2,494	612
Galveston	5,127	600	21,321	9,661	7,476	1,615	23,359	6,278	298	10,159	1,646	25,867	9,342
Garza	251	25	1,199	194	403	27	1,115	80	149	431	27	1,344	300
Gillespie	1,592	1,370	1,243	2,882	1,835	508	1,882	926	535	1,142	696	1,675	2,111
Glasscock	113	19	326	74	188	5	313	45	31	179	16	315	77
Goliad	302	65	1,234	389	403	56	963	156	138	286	40	1,071	537
Gonzales	1,048	40	4,098	475	2,740	127	3,567	254	263	1,358	30	3,599	619
Gray	4,299	553	5,611	2,651	3,330	345	5,730	1,130	940	2,651	368	5,844	3,428
Grayson	3,333	258	11,737	2,510	3,997	344	12,588	1,730	1,391	5,029	286	14,203	3,347
Gregg	2,164	445	10,107	5,709	3,322	646	8,980	2,368	461	3,707	574	10,153	6,557
Grimes	0	0	2,428	365	696	37	2,139	100	174	863	35	2,359	460
Guadalupe	3,217	758	4,148	2,582	3,454	510	4,826	1,271	0	3,062	701	4,869	2,426
Hale	1,329	118	5,689	1,664	1,689	102	6,098	531	756	1,976	121	6,626	2,117
Hall	1,760	60	2,218	240	1,051	47	1,919	101	85	796	22	1,781	328
Hamilton	745	69	2,660	417	967	82	2,223	207	366	1,029	86	1,981	773
Hansford	956	58	1,114	474	667	48	1,205	153	47	514	56	1,325	574
Hardeman	674	47	2,132	371	739	38	2,018	110	200	750	32	2,054	493
Hardin	979	15	4,060	554	1,186	79	3,244	281	708	1,674	74	5,569	977
Harris	20,662	4,048	165,667	71,280	80,934	14,319	165,872	60,824	1,847	88,628	16,981	199,280	96,353
Harrison	1,168	117	7,528	1,403	2,357	78	6,654	486	434	2,238	232	7,037	1,885
Hartley	529	19	651	128	347	15	641	42	97	282	20	728	134
Haskell	916	32	2,855	283	1,037	55	2,909	152	311	1,283	33	3,249	392
Hays	849	27	3,086	465	1,091	57	3,124	257	247	1,244	69	3,708	837
Hemphill	764	73	1,013	324	646	48	0	0	0	667	47	707	506
Henderson	1,583	63	4,655	656	2,291	116	3,698	260	1,516	2,231	77	4,692	1,281
Hidalgo	4,017	733	16,467	7,303	9,581	1,067	18,866	3,137	1,026	8,746	1,744	21,471	10,378
Hill	1,723	66	5,633	587	2,545	117	5,303	279	918	2,332	48	6,852	893
Hockley	928	59	3,946	744	1,109	55	4,160	314	404	1,624	100	4,624	993
Hood	449	23	1,435	205	683	16	1,429	118	233	626	35	1,418	334
Hopkins	1,664	62	4,637	538	1,870	78	4,365	233	577	1,883	68	4,226	1,039
Houston	2,549	334	4,226	469	1,149	162	3,166	226	396	1,506	56	3,758	663
Howard	3,159	103	5,779	811	1,965	118	6,587	305	0	2,376	172	6,997	1,464
Hudspeth	131	2	399	144	380	10	554	44	34	246	11	638	117
Hunt	2,257	130	8,389	1,360	2,823	142	6,957	555	946	2,781	112	7,789	1,893
Hutchinson	4,249	416	6,269	2,639	2,343	520	6,533	1,040	1,325	2,654	512	7,070	2,988
Irion	208	7	423	83	180	7	298	31	82	209	60	352	148
Jack	612	52	2,167	242	798	82	1,721	208	300	788	70	1,737	645
Jackson	604	49	2,970	533	894	40	2,647	274	408	1,002	61	3,247	819
Jas per	890	36	3,845	447	1,179	77	3,365	213	601	1,966	54	4,194	1,072
JeffDavis	0	0	395	68	230	12	0	0	0	133	21	340	92
Jefferson	5,264	502	32,781	17,325	10,981	1,991	39,462	8,843	984	35,973	4,539	47,142	16,795
Jim Hogg	733	6	1,248	68	593	7	874	61	17	605	3	1,418	117
Jim Wells	2,965	80	6,562	713	4,253	147	5,259	555	0	1,760	63	6,649	1,424
Johnson	1,298	120	5,495	1,088	2,253	234	5,240	658	1,056	2,369	211	6,322	2,304
Jones	1,108	42	3,963	656	1,454	65	3,633	248	649	1,579	55	4,288	883
Karnes	1,040	54	3,847	270	1,648	59	3,054	193	166	1,318	39	3,040	464
Kaufman	1,352	91	5,306	882	1,974	93	4,662	405	489	1,998	115	4,338	1,190

Table 51: Gubernatorial Races

Year	1950		1952		1954		1956			1958		1960	
General Elections, 1950-1960													
County	Allan Shivers (D)	Ralph W. Currie (R)	Allan Shivers (D)	Allan Shivers (R)	Allan Shivers (D)	Tod R. Adams (R)	Price Daniel (D)	William R. Bryant (R)	W. Lee O'Daniel(WI)	Price Daniel (D)	Edwin S. Mayer (R)	Price Daniel (D)	William M. Steger (R)
Kendall	654	384	728	1,424	1,224	341	1,230	518	168	942	388	648	570
Kenedy	61	5	96	25	100	0	105	27	3	93	5	105	44
Kent	239	8	597	45	441	10	628	18	84	461	1	595	89
Kerr	1,337	269	3,182	1,578	2,129	188	3,309	708	438	1,950	420	2,913	2,088
Kimble	371	18	1,056	391	495	29	1,083	102	70	420	117	943	346
King	0	0	138	13	126	1	164	8	46	128	3	169	11
Kinney	269	16	596	92	195	19	0	0	0	167	24	486	133
Kleberg	871	37	3,854	596	1,001	106	3,761	393	81	1,292	119	5,175	895
Knox	655	21	1,978	202	777	50	1,773	90	146	722	18	1,903	269
La Salle	431	13	1,150	145	400	12	956	38	7	474	15	962	160
Lamar	1,667	75	7,985	929	2,553	100	6,346	305	1,548	2,464	101	7,758	1,269
Lamb	967	67	3,983	807	1,126	76	4,204	284	365	1,586	66	4,616	1,198
Lampasas	0	0	1,995	288	748	56	1,901	172	321	699	62	2,198	459
Lavaca	1,508	110	5,368	811	2,075	117	4,097	340	373	1,764	112	4,776	873
Lee	788	23	2,188	285	790	40	1,689	140	350	720	33	1,974	528
Leon	0	0	2,499	238	777	23	1,839	175	214	2,329	38	2,170	392
Liberty	1,094	72	6,087	989	1,620	121	4,804	608	660	2,586	138	5,869	1,857
Limestone	1,485	64	4,017	1,863	1,962	82	4,225	249	634	2,898	50	4,640	785
Lipscomb	806	152	976	475	617	76	872	185	33	430	78	771	452
Live Oak	1,385	63	1,700	297	717	22	1,276	154	164	438	34	1,302	710
Llano	478	20	1,273	201	602	34	1,344	98	199	579	30	1,488	345
Loving	59	3	65	16	61	3	61	13	20	0	0	62	27
Lubbock	2,768	434	18,815	5,972	5,336	508	21,191	2,344	1,172	6,915	663	25,687	9,686
Lynn	616	33	2,182	358	829	31	2,259	125	199	886	25	2,566	357
Madison	541	19	1,478	178	566	22	1,225	75	166	627	17	1,305	231
Marion	430	25	1,189	552	601	19	1,471	202	118	628	31	1,357	391
Martin	320	5	1,031	50	677	19	991	52	124	599	20	1,126	140
Mason	373	55	1,199	355	542	65	1,022	178	148	403	115	836	579
Matagorda	847	118	5,257	888	1,406	123	4,307	423	525	1,719	144	4,567	1,652
Maverick	309	20	1,365	348	468	25	1,392	140	22	749	35	1,865	371
McCulloch	868	49	2,536	464	1,076	54	1,959	160	371	890	71	2,340	543
McLennan	4,167	317	21,508	4,857	7,706	466	24,289	2,477	3,685	9,417	598	30,501	5,636
McMullen	341	6	371	57	233	11	359	25	28	151	3	236	152
Medina	2,445	506	3,005	1,767	1,363	238	3,186	765	275	1,875	356	2,814	1,237
Menard	303	30	902	233	366	30	0	0	0	342	102	792	339
Midland	648	162	5,812	4,802	2,703	428	7,786	3,021	246	3,468	1,230	10,227	6,321
Milam	1,354	53	4,797	457	1,876	108	4,411	348	654	2,220	91	4,854	904
Mills	730	41	421	269	545	58	1,357	129	209	575	47	1,476	410
Mitchell	924	32	2,336	324	980	48	2,391	180	268	1,090	50	2,855	478
Montague	1,140	78	3,690	619	1,322	133	3,502	345	327	1,423	70	3,727	992
Montgomery	1,496	42	5,363	746	1,847	115	4,744	490	427	2,643	130	5,431	1,745
Moore	1,814	139	2,695	747	1,264	139	3,107	395	343	1,035	152	3,188	1,033
Morris	559	40	2,174	150	794	34	0	0	0	1,116	53	3,051	677
Motley	561	30	833	172	395	12	742	27	127	427	6	822	146
Nacogdoches	2,471	0	5,364	635	1,831	84	0	0	0	2,527	66	5,540	1,230
Navarro	2,194	94	6,818	549	2,556	88	0	0	0	2,790	129	7,697	1,321
Newton	532	13	2,100	162	743	31	1,551	108	219	1,189	15	2,181	415
Nolan	930	67	4,746	673	1,345	71	3,492	276	884	1,827	110	4,668	1,062
Nueces	4,757	594	26,308	9,490	7,133	1,158	29,471	6,326	363	12,192	1,449	34,187	10,637
Ochiltree	1,024	129	1,382	727	1,198	80	1,420	169	82	869	79	1,516	931
Oldham	365	37	404	127	305	23	467	50	27	329	31	545	113
Orange	1,456	67	8,047	1,869	2,245	168	0	0	0	4,114	191	12,628	2,484
Palo Pinto	1,046	135	4,199	903	1,630	168	4,108	395	576	1,048	127	4,365	979
Panola	1,148	27	4,361	355	1,599	36	3,921	213	445	1,568	43	3,981	815
Parker	1,199	112	4,504	1,112	1,906	215	4,651	588	911	1,906	148	5,496	1,866
Parmer	1,064	130	1,646	383	631	78	1,986	166	122	903	44	2,028	722
Pecos	643	32	2,368	0	847	53	0	0	0	949	19	2,427	531
Polk	678	18	3,207	290	1,037	50	2,451	182	306	1,545	41	2,858	518
Potter	8,334	991	12,515	8,330	6,974	1,001	15,487	2,847	1,126	7,263	1,479	16,097	6,862
Presidio	429	24	959	408	480	16	912	73	9	441	32	1,208	197
Rains	406	12	812	96	374	30	745	70	122	350	17	895	277
Randall	2,094	168	3,870	1,935	2,239	205	0	0	0	2,870	507	7,188	3,237
Reagan	251	18	707	141	329	23	818	108	89	428	38	998	187
Real	190	20	573	131	245	16	408	99	8	201	33	450	258
Red River	1,151	34	4,642	348	1,577	53	3,562	132	757	1,750	51	3,626	603

Table 51: Gubernatorial Races

General Elections, 1950-1960													
Year	1950		1952		1954		1956			1958		1960	
County	Allan Shivers (D)	Ralph W. Currie (R)	Allan Shivers (D)	Allan Shivers (R)	Allan Shivers (D)	Tod R. Adams (R)	Price Daniel (D)	William R. Bryant (R)	W. Lee O'Daniel(WI)	Price Daniel (D)	Edwin S. Mayer (R)	Price Daniel (D)	William M. Steger (R)
Reeves	936	50	2,092	331	862	28	2,335	285	129	806	90	2,926	787
Refugio	1,589	88	2,322	416	519	33	2,025	207	150	1,074	72	2,573	544
Roberts	383	23	290	142	272	15	333	38	9	157	26	284	182
Robertson	956	20	3,899	288	1,027	42	2,833	213	320	1,508	55	3,389	379
Rockwall	440	8	1,262	198	538	17	1,306	89	129	517	20	1,366	243
Runnels	738	37	3,439	554	1,120	53	2,764	184	824	1,157	144	3,386	772
Rusk	1,988	177	7,741	2,589	4,238	235	6,010	1,441	569	3,034	194	5,539	3,020
Sabine	790	10	1,934	207	675	58	1,478	93	123	669	9	1,579	276
San Augustine	544	8	1,849	183	788	10	1,674	95	141	699	14	1,618	287
San Jacinto	288	7	1,291	157	457	33	992	107	138	403	19	1,156	212
San Patricio	936	72	4,718	1,593	1,426	143	5,776	682	323	2,033	132	7,552	1,514
San Saba	716	16	1,930	195	977	30	1,779	81	268	911	37	1,595	276
Schleicher	0	0	811	102	444	29	596	51	173	280	86	666	216
Scurry	755	25	3,940	542	1,155	90	3,490	350	880	1,357	101	4,312	1,005
Shackelford	360	26	1,401	211	381	19	989	110	278	573	43	1,127	336
Shelby	1,700	35	5,341	234	1,981	51	4,663	257	355	1,988	47	4,093	688
Sherman	414	33	672	229	386	12	742	75	16	353	32	726	267
Smith	2,268	234	14,969	3,604	5,486	338	13,753	1,483	2,884	5,699	499	12,506	9,070
Somervell	170	19	750	131	274	26	519	72	157	462	36	617	216
Starr	1,821	0	3,696	136	2,349	31	3,207	607	14	2,272	6	4,051	284
Stephens	694	51	2,675	446	1,553	82	2,019	237	617	994	111	2,262	780
Sterling	109	3	331	69	136	12	0	0	0	168	18	320	64
Stonewall	290	6	833	93	298	9	902	45	155	392	10	1,062	112
Sutton	140	19	578	285	250	22	643	72	37	307	219	741	241
Swisher	1,489	89	1,978	675	882	74	2,186	194	178	1,005	87	0	0
Tarrant	10,901	2,528	69,201	22,276	28,651	3,694	85,989	12,842	8,537	34,815	4,434	95,741	35,811
Taylor	2,493	135	12,330	3,362	3,217	240	12,443	1,154	2,286	4,798	573	16,986	6,495
Terrell	103	19	491	163	285	20	456	62	22	324	45	519	146
Terry	786	45	2,747	374	886	36	0	0	0	1,401	50	3,275	864
Throckmorton	476	8	1,039	100	457	19	928	64	122	362	8	939	178
Titus	2,328	62	3,898	488	1,149	70	0	0	0	1,304	50	4,035	918
Tom Green	2,051	190	11,442	2,901	3,457	334	9,302	1,108	3,066	4,313	1,378	11,113	4,357
Travis	5,319	285	26,811	8,441	11,834	769	33,775	4,396	3,305	15,391	1,533	40,110	10,910
Trinity	628	19	2,344	195	498	39	1,404	136	0	674	25	1,790	395
Tyler	0	0	2,345	272	958	32	2,066	121	281	1,013	44	1,973	760
Upshur	1,087	45	4,326	616	1,785	64	0	0	0	2,317	88	4,297	1,167
Upton	293	13	1,401	333	1,129	53	1,422	184	174	726	68	1,470	342
Uvalde	558	0	2,411	1,353	931	78	2,694	312	223	972	146	2,456	1,344
Val Verde	481	61	2,371	688	711	62	2,862	338	27	755	137	2,835	931
Van Zandt	1,717	88	4,352	504	1,773	110	3,800	289	782	1,954	77	3,846	1,143
Victoria	527	105	5,638	1,122	1,479	155	6,206	835	1,136	2,031	277	8,466	2,678
Walker	776	29	3,497	339	1,562	47	2,653	251	341	1,027	43	3,229	308
Waller	403	37	2,148	413	695	52	1,833	252	159	793	64	1,768	489
Ward	984	69	2,444	738	976	54	2,465	270	348	962	67	2,035	498
Washington	749	60	4,343	556	1,068	63	3,136	261	570	1,206	53	3,543	1,090
Webb	4,235	58	8,543	523	5,441	67	7,966	699	0	3,649	211	10,973	1,303
Wharton	1,558	111	7,113	1,653	2,406	180	6,727	777	394	3,130	194	6,831	1,483
Wheeler	1,756	160	2,320	488	1,063	118	1,965	213	175	1,288	85	1,820	618
Wichita	3,652	351	16,245	3,393	9,319	718	20,615	2,197	1,082	6,347	562	21,579	5,253
Wilbarger	1,232	58	4,584	340	1,158	55	4,040	238	272	1,662	74	3,929	868
Willacy	378	49	3,030	520	623	47	2,454	290	124	890	65	2,910	858
Williamson	1,946	89	6,325	953	2,543	107	5,975	396	828	2,514	132	7,008	1,186
Wilson	1,262	66	3,504	516	1,579	79	3,169	252	204	1,161	88	3,454	759
Winkler	1,022	48	2,126	444	784	50	2,063	247	355	905	75	2,657	816
Wise	1,302	67	3,603	586	1,362	116	0	0	0	1,978	112	3,812	1,206
Wood	1,213	95	4,465	759	1,552	99	3,674	341	565	1,824	93	3,681	1,354
Yoakum	0	0	1,247	199	654	49	1,462	114	235	702	36	1,907	480
Young	1,126	62	3,219	892	1,314	75	3,355	300	352	1,577	90	3,729	979
Zapata	338	37	764	522	890	600	928	589	2	393	34	720	240
Zavala	0	0	1,335	276	488	21	1,134	129	86	505	37	1,188	402
Official	355,010		1,375,547		569,533		1,350,736		110,234			1,627,698	
Totals		39,737		468,319		66,154		261,283		695,779	94,086		609,808
Unofficial	355,010		1,385,547		568,630		1,353,492		110,742			1,625,699	
Totals		39,767		468,320		66,154		261,539		694,952	94,086		610,295

Table 52: Gubernatorial Races

General Elections, 1962-1966									
Year	**1962**			**1964**			**1966**			
County	John Connlly (D)	Jack Cox (R)	Jack Carswll (CO)	John Connlly (D)	Jack Crichtn (R)	John C. Willims (CO)	John Connlly (D)	T. E. Knnrly (R)	Tommye Gillspe (CO)	Bard Logan (C)
Anderson	2,592	2,296	17	6,095	2,007	7	2,885	625	7	9
Andrews	1,413	1,252	20	2,642	894	9	1,265	445	9	12
Angelina	4,541	2,785	61	10,910	2,235	31	5,053	1,329	51	50
Aransas	776	463	7	1,627	429	5	756	221	10	7
Archer	1,034	335	4	1,874	317	3	1,201	199	1	4
Armstrong	377	294	3	667	213	1	400	89	1	3
Atascosa	1,743	1,000	8	3,628	828	4	1,461	384	6	8
Austin	1,125	1,081	5	2,751	1,135	0	1,483	554	3	7
Bailey	712	936	3	1,897	619	2	942	368	3	15
Bandera	471	670	5	1,095	529	4	703	224	7	10
Bastrop	2,294	870	10	4,247	718	9	2,053	387	16	17
Baylor	856	310	10	1,539	247	0	909	169	0	0
Bee	1,735	1,306	2	3,694	1,142	6	1,700	478	10	14
Bell	7,562	2,285	29	15,472	1,833	18	5,836	1,450	51	35
Bexar	60,719	41,831	441	110,427	41,891	459	64,709	24,454	1,642	2,372
Blanco	588	389	5	1,216	264	2	622	150	2	7
Borden	167	137	5	318	92	0	193	68	0	5
Bosque	1,446	926	7	3,027	681	4	1,615	387	4	5
Bowie	4,526	3,493	31	12,314	4,756	28	5,689	1,896	32	47
Brazoria	7,725	6,703	139	17,618	5,846	84	9,489	3,971	196	105
Brazos	4,029	2,738	13	9,395	2,259	11	5,744	1,015	17	45
Brewster	730	532	2	1,505	357	2	669	192	12	5
Briscoe	554	280	0	1,125	177	3	616	93	1	3
Brooks	1,270	378	1	2,454	281	5	1,322	167	8	12
Brown	2,877	1,964	16	5,980	1,239	10	2,823	591	18	33
Burleson	1,483	441	3	2,720	380	4	1,137	203	5	7
Burnet	1,304	767	8	2,794	561	3	1,276	337	3	10
Caldwell	1,900	812	7	3,850	711	7	2,010	360	6	16
Calhoun	1,316	794	6	3,689	566	10	1,580	399	18	11
Callahan	1,296	800	11	2,364	616	2	1,348	303	8	16
Cameron	9,861	8,216	89	17,032	7,897	73	8,775	4,184	84	70
Camp	852	419	2	2,042	488	9	990	151	6	1
Carson	1,184	864	11	1,847	763	2	1,348	379	2	9
Cass	1,863	1,410	7	4,287	1,769	5	2,273	766	9	24
Castro	1,094	510	4	2,081	355	4	1,210	287	2	7
Chambers	885	568	11	2,233	662	9	851	360	10	11
Cherokee	2,782	1,776	29	6,566	1,821	24	3,065	802	20	38
Childress	1,158	576	6	2,343	542	2	1,165	373	4	9
Clay	1,260	504	4	2,534	438	0	1,485	271	3	5
Cochran	545	452	2	1,466	292	0	896	166	5	15
Coke	538	363	13	997	246	1	530	103	0	2
Coleman	1,607	1,226	7	3,038	1,024	2	1,766	454	7	7
Collin	3,840	2,101	32	8,768	1,949	14	4,927	901	13	26
Collingsworth	787	620	15	1,365	496	3	919	235	0	6
Colorado	1,568	1,307	11	4,232	1,284	8	1,795	685	4	14
Comal	1,461	1,910	12	4,284	1,514	6	2,046	813	27	21
Comanche	1,442	970	9	3,150	648	6	1,677	246	9	14
Concho	555	315	2	1,158	175	2	479	85	4	6
Cooke	1,967	2,354	9	5,163	1,859	5	2,741	771	7	11
Coryell	1,760	789	13	3,940	539	3	2,819	379	6	18
Cottle	842	180	2	1,213	129	1	706	94	0	3
Crane	590	532	13	1,145	392	6	546	176	8	10
Crockett	377	479	6	960	221	4	500	112	3	4
Crosby	1,218	561	8	2,583	285	0	1,354	221	8	10
Culberson	210	212	1	591	195	2	434	77	0	5
Dallam	762	643	8	1,226	515	1	803	237	2	15
Dallas	70,479	95,988	907	191,704	95,244	454	113,155	46,622	1,396	1,088
Dawson	1,503	1,404	10	3,777	1,055	4	1,621	542	4	7
DeWitt	1,443	1,929	3	4,109	1,352	13	1,696	605	5	15
Deaf Smith	1,149	1,172	5	2,751	1,067	12	2,204	549	3	16
Delta	859	175	3	1,741	187	2	717	66	2	1
Denton	3,761	3,131	16	10,222	2,896	7	5,120	1,496	7	19
Dickens	778	208	7	1,446	194	0	747	104	2	6
Dimmit	793	475	3	1,431	269	1	886	123	8	9

Table 52: Gubernatorial Races

General Elections, 1962-1966									
Year	1962			1964			1966			
County	John Connlly (D)	Jack Cox (R)	Jack Carswll (CO)	John Connlly (D)	Jack Crichtn (R)	John C. Willims (CO)	John Connlly (D)	T. E. Knnrly (R)	Tommye Gillspe (CO)	Bard Logan (C)
Donley	625	497	4	1,339	435	2	791	177	1	9
Duval	3,209	836	9	4,504	310	5	3,339	97	2	5
Eastland	2,683	2,108	28	5,227	1,452	3	2,230	738	13	23
Ector	5,720	9,017	295	12,994	8,271	84	6,854	4,643	106	117
Edwards	257	314	1	456	246	2	277	105	2	3
El Paso	17,170	15,913	122	35,114	17,244	271	19,443	12,461	308	178
Ellis	3,416	1,674	24	8,359	1,581	9	4,172	642	3	30
Erath	2,005	1,704	10	4,247	1,174	2	2,191	526	3	12
Falls	2,177	836	9	4,283	773	3	2,284	392	9	8
Fannin	3,066	747	8	6,283	862	3	2,640	287	2	5
Fayette	2,319	1,521	13	4,393	1,289	6	2,272	601	15	8
Fisher	1,312	385	5	2,269	276	6	1,005	134	5	6
Floyd	1,105	1,030	10	2,820	745	3	1,357	445	16	24
Foard	422	102	2	870	103	0	456	62	1	1
Fort Bend	2,777	2,191	17	7,533	2,074	22	4,972	1,090	27	41
Franklin	953	251	3	1,682	247	2	850	121	27	41
Freestone	1,427	832	6	3,239	644	2	1,522	277	3	7
Frio	1,210	525	3	1,699	431	2	928	181	1	19
Gaines	921	783	5	2,458	695	2	1,184	466	7	5
Galveston	16,322	9,893	238	33,060	8,842	128	14,916	4,583	495	248
Garza	471	440	9	1,472	320	5	790	150	7	7
Gillespie	619	1,830	6	2,407	1,547	3	970	848	3	12
Glasscock	123	163	3	247	125	0	171	59	1	4
Goliad	569	433	0	1,150	375	2	282	155	4	4
Gonzales	1,836	862	8	3,850	702	6	1,549	292	4	7
Gray	2,392	4,085	12	5,010	4,057	5	3,856	2,350	7	30
Grayson	7,324	4,028	26	15,834	3,312	12	8,164	1,573	22	34
Gregg	4,515	7,042	84	11,097	8,230	97	6,792	3,137	140	102
Grimes	1,056	716	4	2,661	491	5	1,374	270	1	3
Guadalupe	2,320	2,428	18	5,394	1,777	7	3,708	1,032	21	17
Hale	2,739	2,865	1	7,206	2,220	13	3,473	1,175	5	30
Hall	1,130	472	0	2,022	378	1	1,002	204	3	7
Hamilton	890	979	4	2,313	723	2	1,035	320	3	11
Hansford	454	775	2	1,270	774	2	967	375	1	3
Hardeman	845	685	0	2,041	482	0	1,228	197	5	5
Hardin	1,741	961	18	5,847	1,251	14	2,386	898	31	23
Harris	107,677	110,619	1,275	253,992	114,072	931	161,551	71,909	2,204	945
Harrison	3,800	3,831	23	7,802	4,080	19	5,928	1,597	29	44
Hartley	466	344	2	690	294	4	483	171	0	3
Haskell	1,834	418	8	3,118	315	3	1,405	178	2	4
Hays	1,941	1,211	2	4,113	886	7	2,329	589	12	29
Hemphill	381	416	2	820	362	1	803	180	0	2
Henderson	2,568	1,470	21	5,488	1,106	15	2,410	534	10	20
Hidalgo	13,702	10,321	192	23,490	8,462	68	11,723	5,261	105	69
Hill	2,618	1,166	12	5,762	894	6	2,505	281	11	9
Hockley	2,278	1,484	11	4,751	918	4	2,143	613	13	7
Hood	735	409	3	1,660	289	4	703	134	1	11
Hopkins	2,147	1,080	3	4,707	834	7	2,155	399	4	8
Houston	1,821	933	13	4,201	1,002	8	2,317	353	4	13
Howard	2,981	2,239	15	7,243	1,994	6	3,681	1,220	14	26
Hudspeth	250	179	1	502	140	6	303	48	0	2
Hunt	3,240	2,138	8	7,706	2,032	7	3,595	882	8	9
Hutchinson	2,836	4,396	31	6,078	3,698	14	4,830	2,254	29	38
Irion	281	215	5	406	133	0	404	78	1	4
Jack	904	833	12	1,790	635	5	1,316	322	3	4
Jackson	1,600	1,028	9	3,218	719	7	1,323	401	5	5
Jasper	1,886	1,080	4	4,330	1,134	19	1,818	719	14	15
Jeff Davis	241	158	2	347	124	1	315	40	0	1
Jefferson	24,965	19,063	247	51,599	19,020	379	23,310	13,010	465	279
Jim Hogg	1,418	178	3	1,419	106	2	691	83	4	15
Jim Wells	3,859	2,036	21	7,216	1,563	2	3,629	933	19	65
Johnson	2,794	2,479	15	7,261	2,135	7	3,157	1,009	15	20
Jones	2,016	928	10	4,088	783	3	1,833	335	7	10
Karnes	1,919	810	5	3,576	583	0	1,742	280	5	4
Kaufman	2,251	1,226	9	5,572	1,089	7	2,707	409	9	11
Kendall	409	1,036	2	1,143	972	5	660	533	8	8

Table 52: Gubernatorial Races

General Elections, 1962-1966										
Year	1962			1964			1966			
County	John Connlly (D)	Jack Cox (R)	Jack Carswll (CO)	John Connlly (D)	Jack Crichtn (R)	John C. Willims (CO)	John Connlly (D)	T. E. Knnrly (R)	Tommye Gillspe (CO)	Bard Logan (C)
Kenedy	85	37	1	138	13	0	108	12	0	4
Kent	348	102	1	600	72	0	381	41	2	2
Kerr	1,180	2,239	5	3,402	2,105	3	2,099	1,045	14	57
Kimble	493	532	3	1,032	336	0	514	148	1	6
King	120	28	1	197	19	0	131	14	0	0
Kinney	288	136	0	488	103	0	547	56	3	20
Kleberg	2,253	1,293	13	5,053	1,093	5	2,480	615	13	35
Knox	996	375	7	1,917	292	2	1,110	135	4	5
La Salle	440	158	2	1,071	116	2	514	45	1	3
Lamar	3,332	1,510	13	7,369	1,353	11	3,777	611	15	14
Lamb	2,513	1,718	18	5,060	1,209	5	2,396	813	9	8
Lampasas	957	648	7	2,349	431	3	1,093	231	3	9
Lavaca	2,294	967	2	4,487	1,015	6	1,871	485	10	14
Lee	917	770	9	2,129	631	1	1,164	313	11	8
Leon	1,055	423	9	2,571	364	3	1,076	135	2	5
Liberty	2,758	2,079	34	5,990	2,026	19	2,791	884	14	17
Limestone	1,977	1,021	3	4,247	902	5	2,122	365	8	5
Lipscomb	383	549	2	798	541	3	856	244	2	6
Live Oak	818	700	7	1,660	558	6	812	258	2	3
Llano	754	560	1	1,863	689	2	830	280	5	11
Loving	32	40	0	53	25	0	46	10	2	1
Lubbock	10,453	11,959	86	28,877	9,733	27	17,181	5,975	165	93
Lynn	1,124	592	15	2,663	343	3	1,199	248	0	6
Madison	581	343	2	1,579	330	7	725	140	2	5
Marion	583	482	8	1,478	744	2	718	290	3	6
Martin	476	318	3	1,026	266	0	541	115	2	4
Mason	408	593	1	1,029	492	1	560	227	2	3
Matagorda	1,962	1,952	14	5,084	1,467	13	2,431	876	18	11
Maverick	1,525	367	6	2,309	334	7	1,621	194	12	33
McCulloch	1,118	731	5	2,272	343	3	1,052	223	2	5
McLennan	14,646	8,977	67	32,075	6,729	37	16,348	3,370	44	77
McMullen	156	164	1	304	142	1	232	51	1	1
Medina	2,104	1,420	19	3,865	1,093	3	1,492	547	7	12
Menard	284	324	6	718	266	1	386	156	3	6
Midland	4,578	9,066	96	11,030	8,934	55	8,568	5,037	131	105
Milam	2,507	1,083	11	4,817	854	11	2,199	519	6	10
Mills	488	481	8	1,367	336	5	617	153	5	7
Mitchell	1,513	657	7	2,666	447	2	1,146	218	5	9
Montague	1,854	1,037	17	3,965	774	6	1,991	401	2	3
Montgomery	2,396	1,892	18	5,941	2,002	26	3,795	1,384	20	21
Moore	1,463	1,466	11	2,916	1,188	11	2,241	761	25	16
Morris	1,448	844	8	2,799	741	13	1,541	299	9	25
Motley	363	275	3	801	191	2	587	71	0	7
Nacogdoches	2,626	1,771	17	5,676	1,459	15	2,986	664	33	21
Navarro	3,586	1,689	12	7,359	1,444	1	3,806	529	9	5
Newton	1,200	339	11	2,439	445	7	988	246	8	10
Nolan	2,539	1,409	16	4,581	1,084	8	2,020	436	10	13
Nueces	19,125	12,269	97	41,375	10,596	104	24,005	6,857	527	409
Ochiltree	572	1,307	8	1,569	1,132	3	1,068	514	2	5
Oldham	251	283	1	507	151	3	376	77	0	0
Orange	4,722	3,184	37	11,121	4,208	34	5,197	2,390	45	81
Palo Pinto	1,498	1,501	17	4,307	1,200	4	2,105	545	17	14
Panola	1,408	1,673	7	3,390	1,899	13	1,957	651	10	16
Parker	2,989	2,095	12	5,853	1,546	4	3,183	841	6	18
Parmer	919	1,008	5	2,003	734	8	1,170	426	5	5
Pecos	1,492	1,238	19	2,532	923	6	1,125	493	3	11
Polk	1,154	716	14	2,880	612	7	1,309	273	9	7
Potter	7,489	7,775	50	16,134	7,465	109	9,737	4,331	57	88
Presidio	578	364	4	1,303	273	1	478	117	1	3
Rains	537	206	0	961	183	1	459	60	0	3
Randall	3,536	5,061	20	8,247	5,067	36	6,270	3,044	23	31
Reagan	362	346	3	777	224	1	400	117	0	4
Real	196	222	16	544	198	1	337	101	0	3
Red River	1,878	638	7	3,967	607	4	1,839	382	3	3
Reeves	1,313	1,161	12	2,791	729	12	1,540	314	20	14

Table 52: Gubernatorial Races

General Elections, 1962-1966											
Year	1962			1964			1966				
County	John Connlly (D)	Jack Cox (R)	Jack Carswll (CO)	John Connlly (D)	Jack Crichtn (R)	John C. Willims (CO)	John Connlly (D)	T. E. Knnrly (R)	Tommye Gillspe (CO)	Bard Logan (C)	
Refugio	1,181	692	3	2,543	543	2	978	319	6	1	
Roberts	145	259	4	285	204	0	291	130	0	0	
Robertson	1,622	603	8	3,594	509	2	1,913	240	9	7	
Rockwall	617	261	2	1,464	243	2	725	99	1	3	
Runnels	1,266	1,282	6	3,096	949	4	1,477	416	3	9	
Rusk	3,426	2,861	21	7,633	3,674	31	3,702	1,530	42	35	
Sabine	691	243	2	1,885	337	2	690	179	2	4	
San Augustine	706	444	6	1,313	558	10	732	229	7	10	
San Jacinto	751	247	2	1,762	233	1	738	114	6	2	
San Patricio	3,332	1,888	18	7,684	1,602	11	3,150	935	25	35	
San Saba	1,099	423	1	2,012	248	0	933	145	1	4	
Schleicher	339	374	1	639	254	0	416	125	0	3	
Scurry	1,684	1,453	16	3,975	1,070	4	1,771	432	7	13	
Shackelford	534	455	4	1,071	342	1	575	128	4	6	
Shelby	1,681	1,273	10	4,016	1,632	8	1,834	427	14	0	
Sherman	302	526	0	704	364	1	627	209	0	13	
Smith	6,431	8,455	34	16,326	8,445	68	9,901	4,029	44	75	
Somervell	263	202	1	695	144	2	275	62	1	1	
Starr	3,320	2,252	8	3,970	679	14	2,835	498	7	7	
Stephens	1,000	1,437	11	2,060	776	1	1,192	276	2	1	
Sterling	135	138	2	299	81	0	143	40	0	2	
Stonewall	496	134	0	1,062	141	3	413	51	3	0	
Sutton	342	328	0	812	227	3	393	153	2	2	
Swisher	1,432	579	4	2,759	425	6	1,520	274	4	6	
Tarrant	42,337	41,792	265	106,790	41,425	371	51,970	22,966	359	200	
Taylor	7,511	8,252	58	15,844	5,809	28	9,410	2,670	21	70	
Terrell	200	247	0	444	210	0	277	96	0	8	
Terry	1,482	1,277	10	3,741	829	5	1,896	495	11	26	
Throckmorton	529	209	2	939	178	0	516	72	0	4	
Titus	1,628	999	6	4,044	1,086	6	1,710	413	5	19	
Tom Green	5,171	5,481	64	11,649	4,302	26	6,483	2,467	37	45	
Travis	23,434	17,289	144	50,989	11,842	91	29,575	8,311	133	174	
Trinity	835	448	8	1,873	490	10	795	192	9	9	
Tyler	1,070	863	12	2,159	773	9	1,040	405	7	12	
Upshur	2,153	1,228	11	4,650	1,531	6	2,234	544	10	36	
Upton	648	681	19	1,215	383	8	695	245	6	13	
Uvalde	1,216	1,471	6	2,961	1,328	5	1,259	545	3	9	
Val Verde	1,701	972	4	3,936	926	2	1,514	463	8	9	
Van Zandt	2,197	1,138	10	4,563	1,038	6	2,184	457	7	11	
Victoria	4,067	3,433	27	9,368	2,746	24	5,318	1,771	25	38	
Walker	1,530	1,085	6	3,577	912	4	1,866	479	7	6	
Waller	1,236	725	12	2,458	599	6	1,871	319	4	11	
Ward	1,440	1,456	17	2,663	1,234	4	1,989	642	7	18	
Washington	1,802	1,489	3	3,671	1,157	0	1,803	520	0	3	
Webb	6,442	1,292	15	9,854	742	6	6,444	663	13	7	
Wharton	3,359	2,244	18	7,030	1,843	9	3,425	1,032	15	17	
Wheeler	921	853	4	1,705	792	3	1,349	393	0	3	
Wichita	10,776	6,930	60	21,558	5,910	16	15,082	4,212	31	58	
Wilbarger	1,528	1,321	9	3,717	992	5	2,190	402	5	23	
Willacy	1,306	960	12	2,590	783	7	1,305	295	12	12	
Williamson	4,050	1,672	23	8,052	1,064	10	4,380	689	10	28	
Wilson	2,815	511	4	3,786	466	2	1,590	290	4	2	
Winkler	1,074	1,200	12	2,536	1,074	5	1,446	476	15	29	
Wise	1,973	1,402	7	4,313	880	6	1,796	487	6	4	
Wood	2,093	1,418	9	4,266	1,301	14	2,072	496	7	24	
Yoakum	711	706	8	1,776	467	2	957	373	8	12	
Young	1,763	1,404	14	3,802	1,135	1	2,624	710	1	0	
Zapata	1,098	251	1	1,073	88	1	848	51	0	6	
Zavala	830	548	9	2,074	307	0	1,101	180	9	21	
Official Totals	847,036	715,025	7,120	1,877,793	661,675	5,257	1,037,517	368,025	10,454	9,810	
Unofficial Totals	846,586	714,025	7,120	1,878,793	661,560	5,267	1,037,416	368,025	10,480	9,849	

Table 53: Gubernatorial Races

	General Elections, 1968-1972							
Year	1968		1970		1972			
County	Preston Smith (D)	Paul Eggers (R)	Preston Smith (D)	Paul Eggers (R)	Dolph Briscoe (D)	Henry C. Grover (R)	Ramsey Muniz (RZ)	Deborah Leonard (S)
Anderson	5,881	2,874	3,553	2,537	4,769	3,154	39	5
Andrews	2,016	1,498	1,419	1,030	1,686	1,618	43	10
Angelina	9,594	4,715	6,596	3,776	10,086	6,213	69	12
Aransas	1,553	1,036	904	799	1,424	1,287	126	11
Archer	1,397	893	1,284	569	1,585	555	4	2
Armstrong	418	502	448	308	517	433	1	1
Atascosa	3,348	1,255	2,385	1,087	3,331	1,268	525	6
Austin	2,332	1,815	1,856	1,464	2,159	1,917	4	7
Bailey	1,555	940	1,028	735	1,178	1,097	63	2
Bandera	1,045	691	1,017	720	1,439	776	22	3
Bastrop	3,440	1,349	2,405	1,224	3,434	1,459	152	6
Baylor	1,392	702	1,249	514	1,392	502	3	2
Bee	3,452	1,912	2,283	1,964	2,876	1,659	1,362	54
Bell	14,276	5,530	9,091	4,846	12,391	10,500	212	54
Bexar	103,345	71,449	80,786	57,927	105,503	83,337	32,121	2,556
Blanco	879	516	646	448	1,127	528	19	5
Borden	292	86	217	103	296	136	14	1
Bosque	2,555	1,192	1,960	1,082	2,408	1,524	20	1
Bowie	12,823	5,167	7,532	4,289	11,857	7,358	178	85
Brazoria	14,872	12,954	12,250	11,014	15,944	15,233	651	163
Brazos	7,597	7,360	5,373	5,938	9,529	9,002	1,081	189
Brewster	1,307	704	1,102	649	1,081	692	697	8
Briscoe	735	381	580	222	906	305	4	0
Brooks	2,013	580	1,768	695	975	333	1,369	2
Brown	5,862	2,420	3,464	1,966	5,002	2,940	216	9
Burleson	2,139	798	1,876	581	2,083	919	34	4
Burnet	2,434	1,448	1,997	1,428	2,714	1,738	31	6
Caldwell	3,718	1,241	2,412	1,085	3,172	1,230	738	12
Calhoun	3,542	1,577	2,075	1,371	3,031	1,933	576	8
Callahan	2,148	807	1,552	638	1,894	1,012	1	1
Cameron	16,823	11,271	12,415	9,610	14,354	13,126	4,774	484
Camp	2,025	522	1,434	581	1,903	688	4	6
Carson	1,192	1,459	1,224	929	1,259	1,200	11	3
Cass	5,002	1,467	3,747	1,447	4,540	2,529	9	11
Castro	1,689	1,070	1,401	608	1,503	897	113	3
Chambers	2,035	1,255	1,491	957	2,125	1,449	26	17
Cherokee	5,813	3,193	3,963	2,126	4,803	3,817	15	29
Childress	1,735	960	1,482	730	1,452	979	3	3
Clay	1,876	1,181	1,722	805	2,122	810	12	4
Cochran	1,235	330	763	284	919	547	51	3
Coke	849	278	710	212	792	315	22	1
Coleman	2,499	1,316	1,739	843	2,023	1,013	48	1
Collin	9,961	5,794	6,829	5,962	9,033	12,730	332	221
Collingsworth	170	122	937	439	1,082	654	1	1
Colorado	3,071	2,045	1,986	1,666	2,833	2,036	38	7
Comal	3,598	3,039	2,444	2,860	3,863	4,061	484	22
Comanche	2,829	938	2,147	955	2,416	1,276	35	3
Concho	761	309	551	242	787	195	36	0
Cooke	4,724	2,941	3,017	2,537	4,065	3,841	77	6
Coryell	4,419	1,237	3,303	1,301	3,934	2,447	89	9
Cottle	925	300	932	214	934	197	4	1
Crane	992	656	693	427	780	646	28	8
Crockett	864	460	510	312	657	293	207	4
Crosby	2,272	470	1,669	353	1,675	627	306	4
Culberson	465	263	396	282	407	241	50	3
Dallam	902	1,060	716	675	815	755	7	4
Dallas	167,656	179,386	111,000	150,830	160,980	245,178	18,637	3,228
Dawson	3,180	1,185	2,166	1,115	2,190	1,681	182	5
DeWitt	3,183	1,832	2,051	1,719	3,016	1,835	131	9
Deaf Smith	2,294	2,422	1,882	1,380	2,316	2,269	315	5
Delta	1,497	258	1,087	261	1,109	425	7	1
Denton	10,302	8,105	6,854	7,332	11,761	13,283	2,631	275
Dickens	1,182	275	984	221	886	343	19	0
Dimmit	1,102	469	1,149	527	1,406	239	731	2

Table 53: Gubernatorial Races

	General Elections, 1968-1972							
Year	1968		1970		1972			
County	Preston Smith (D)	Paul Eggers (R)	Preston Smith (D)	Paul Eggers (R)	Dolph Briscoe (D)	Henry C. Grover (R)	Ramsey Muniz (RZ)	Deborah Leonard (S)
Donley	800	771	823	554	857	684	4	0
Duval	4,097	372	3,434	272	3,811	259	308	1
Eastland	4,177	1,893	3,084	1,701	3,276	2,395	36	11
Ector	10,130	12,966	8,966	7,210	10,399	15,381	1,366	175
Edwards	402	217	308	148	514	91	6	0
El Paso	34,966	30,521	27,315	22,547	34,977	31,837	12,763	444
Ellis	8,309	3,245	5,239	3,092	6,984	5,243	181	24
Erath	4,018	1,899	2,811	1,709	3,560	2,705	113	11
Falls	4,025	1,260	2,314	1,018	3,121	1,481	136	4
Fannin	5,479	1,321	4,020	1,283	4,335	1,910	36	4
Fayette	3,551	2,093	2,615	2,001	3,099	2,136	17	9
Fisher	1,924	388	1,303	314	1,630	433	18	0
Floyd	2,340	1,118	1,838	774	1,835	1,051	134	2
Foard	727	207	554	154	547	143	2	1
Fort Bend	6,692	4,338	4,723	4,049	6,963	7,384	474	63
Franklin	1,474	412	1,157	304	1,040	525	4	3
Freestone	2,967	748	1,911	804	2,387	1,219	17	5
Frio	1,719	593	1,136	532	2,273	353	801	5
Gaines	2,638	806	1,615	633	1,549	1,222	60	4
Galveston	27,717	19,927	19,517	16,641	25,183	24,597	2,032	570
Garza	1,189	374	877	451	903	585	51	3
Gillespie	2,001	2,022	1,201	1,724	2,018	1,941	30	4
Glasscock	276	155	193	114	261	115	1	0
Goliad	944	536	700	510	792	477	163	2
Gonzales	3,022	1,166	2,143	897	2,798	943	77	3
Gray	3,448	7,145	3,349	4,559	3,293	5,977	40	14
Grayson	14,794	7,317	9,885	6,172	13,614	9,364	108	47
Gregg	10,877	9,269	6,149	9,518	12,154	11,837	129	183
Grimes	2,153	1,103	1,541	973	2,111	1,157	18	4
Guadalupe	4,688	4,044	3,792	3,628	6,108	4,445	1,034	43
Hale	6,535	3,481	4,389	2,656	4,903	3,847	354	37
Hall	1,384	719	1,215	466	1,272	613	6	0
Hamilton	1,809	898	1,264	775	1,654	911	12	2
Hansford	752	1,389	660	854	920	1,245	5	3
Hardeman	1,630	830	1,305	587	1,372	587	8	2
Hardin	4,771	3,576	3,810	2,119	4,646	3,021	29	18
Harris	209,453	231,617	152,772	205,574	240,458	307,101	17,752	6,932
Harrison	9,596	3,597	5,800	4,303	6,998	5,709	71	85
Hartley	551	597	474	425	633	634	1	2
Haskell	2,463	581	1,954	400	2,091	604	13	0
Hays	4,026	1,948	2,614	2,065	4,165	2,560	2,473	67
Hemphill	542	715	529	527	495	636	8	1
Henderson	5,129	2,265	3,558	2,157	5,256	3,621	55	16
Hidalgo	21,374	12,634	17,154	12,588	16,414	11,712	11,656	834
Hill	4,851	1,624	3,379	1,473	4,055	2,202	39	5
Hockley	4,367	1,590	3,015	1,304	3,283	2,154	284	10
Hood	1,510	581	1,141	485	1,720	919	24	5
Hopkins	4,647	1,460	3,291	1,374	3,549	2,046	14	11
Houston	4,216	1,160	3,169	1,208	3,509	1,465	11	11
Howard	6,213	3,901	4,196	2,928	5,073	4,501	402	13
Hudspeth	470	200	438	156	469	166	47	2
Hunt	7,654	4,522	5,653	3,827	6,569	6,074	280	63
Hutchinson	3,715	6,237	3,120	3,837	3,394	5,617	28	6
Irion	309	165	210	137	293	161	26	1
Jack	1,502	996	1,283	778	1,613	847	6	4
Jackson	2,628	1,371	1,997	1,250	2,237	1,558	48	8
Jasper	4,164	2,497	2,613	1,644	4,624	2,503	12	8
Jeff Davis	295	145	245	137	290	151	106	0
Jefferson	34,683	37,777	27,504	25,377	39,451	32,960	656	481
Jim Hogg	1,294	223	1,003	411	620	201	707	1
Jim Wells	7,216	2,636	4,254	2,518	4,539	2,057	2,534	12
Johnson	7,361	4,229	5,034	3,902	7,733	5,862	96	24
Jones	3,620	1,165	2,472	854	2,988	1,376	37	6
Karnes	3,199	912	2,109	887	2,907	1,039	383	8
Kaufman	5,637	2,056	3,722	1,935	4,821	3,023	93	6

Table 53: Gubernatorial Races

	General Elections, 1968-1972							
Year	1968		1970		1972			
County	Preston Smith (D)	Paul Eggers (R)	Preston Smith (D)	Paul Eggers (R)	Dolph Briscoe (D)	Henry C. Grover (R)	Ramsey Muniz (RZ)	Deborah Leonard (S)
Kendall	964	1,461	745	1,244	1,570	1,503	58	0
Kenedy	149	32	120	36	145	26	33	1
Kent	498	108	410	93	544	130	5	0
Kerr	3,438	3,078	2,489	2,859	4,197	3,402	94	20
Kimble	1,006	320	741	306	912	312	29	5
King	170	42	134	37	178	50	1	0
Kinney	411	114	466	133	0	0	0	0
Kleberg	4,689	3,140	3,217	2,505	4,144	2,770	2,747	29
Knox	1,602	462	1,432	327	1,366	415	4	1
La Salle	837	195	902	256	1,148	133	738	1
Lamar	7,630	2,337	5,081	2,461	6,746	4,055	21	17
Lamb	4,367	1,721	2,609	1,489	3,170	1,916	233	10
Lampasas	2,044	643	1,347	639	1,863	1,059	27	4
Lavaca	3,416	1,175	2,390	1,315	3,051	1,595	8	7
Lee	1,918	1,000	1,292	750	1,805	947	15	4
Leon	2,170	526	1,647	511	1,668	775	2	2
Liberty	6,054	2,851	3,762	2,320	5,493	3,776	29	21
Limestone	4,125	1,246	2,802	1,174	2,821	1,336	2	0
Lipscomb	594	884	631	734	518	827	4	1
Live Oak	1,462	821	1,276	668	1,507	631	154	3
Llano	1,745	1,010	1,284	1,044	1,659	1,287	10	1
Loving	44	31	43	23	38	22	0	0
Lubbock	34,660	14,262	23,615	11,217	24,925	28,033	4,923	270
Lynn	2,327	481	1,448	486	1,560	738	143	0
Madison	1,450	629	1,040	595	1,355	790	7	3
Marion	1,884	503	1,139	633	1,694	863	4	1
Martin	832	352	694	259	695	503	38	0
Mason	886	572	597	566	887	537	38	2
Matagorda	5,187	2,876	3,403	2,381	4,024	3,083	216	22
Maverick	1,776	591	1,339	475	1,332	606	1,156	11
McCulloch	1,871	698	1,444	607	1,750	692	75	3
McLennan	29,880	15,147	20,528	12,599	27,166	18,909	2,971	90
McMullen	271	129	229	132	282	94	7	2
Medina	3,446	1,611	2,183	1,399	3,656	1,355	687	4
Menard	566	364	541	295	608	266	29	1
Midland	8,834	13,136	6,892	9,584	8,295	14,199	440	140
Milam	4,638	1,418	3,149	1,313	3,823	1,777	111	6
Mills	1,091	501	775	389	1,018	417	18	1
Mitchell	2,193	662	1,514	546	1,706	746	49	2
Montague	3,345	1,739	2,575	1,269	2,880	1,575	22	7
Montgomery	7,530	5,158	5,629	5,316	8,290	10,939	64	51
Moore	2,148	2,730	1,835	1,675	2,152	2,321	27	8
Morris	2,963	746	2,020	815	2,550	1,222	13	4
Motley	800	255	500	241	547	332	10	0
Nacogdoches	5,774	2,936	3,994	2,436	6,165	5,410	350	117
Navarro	7,433	2,448	4,884	2,283	5,973	3,184	103	19
Newton	2,218	923	1,681	635	2,461	962	5	8
Nolan	4,220	1,519	2,756	1,134	3,401	1,538	72	5
Nueces	39,053	25,678	22,140	18,395	35,245	24,593	13,813	1,089
Ochiltree	1,071	1,976	1,050	1,284	1,228	1,895	12	8
Oldham	374	387	383	249	498	370	3	1
Orange	10,997	9,120	7,613	6,159	11,795	8,326	50	30
Palo Pinto	4,516	2,639	3,804	2,111	4,150	2,919	91	17
Panola	3,934	1,323	2,565	1,377	3,427	2,282	7	10
Parker	5,813	3,164	4,492	3,168	5,848	4,245	139	10
Parmer	1,667	1,375	1,381	796	1,490	1,326	0	82
Pecos	2,348	1,543	1,869	1,090	1,677	1,253	280	4
Polk	3,169	853	2,150	850	3,043	1,629	13	4
Potter	9,454	16,182	8,610	9,615	9,828	14,177	626	121
Presidio	1,178	349	1,127	323	882	305	265	0
Rains	756	342	691	268	828	417	9	1
Randall	5,380	12,958	6,072	8,006	7,708	14,602	331	74
Reagan	687	398	539	290	570	359	23	1
Real	440	236	323	169	524	98	19	1
Red River	3,807	924	2,953	853	2,936	1,137	9	3

Table 53: Gubernatorial Races

General Elections, 1968-1972							
Year	1968		1970		1972			
County	Preston Smith (D)	Paul Eggers (R)	Preston Smith (D)	Paul Eggers (R)	Dolph Briscoe (D)	Henry C. Grover (R)	Ramsey Muniz (RZ)	Deborah Leonard (S)
Reeves	2,325	1,051	1,627	797	1,887	1,295	605	10
Refugio	2,175	1,028	1,308	785	1,839	838	239	1
Roberts	175	333	219	258	274	269	0	0
Robertson	3,572	850	2,582	860	2,824	979	60	0
Rockwall	1,420	451	1,218	642	1,301	1,176	28	5
Runnels	2,629	1,069	1,719	1,023	2,356	1,033	141	1
Rusk	6,310	4,250	4,180	3,601	5,891	4,366	28	30
Sabine	1,743	458	1,375	462	1,490	691	2	6
San Augustine	1,402	460	1,042	371	1,459	773	7	7
San Jacinto	1,592	405	992	406	1,400	857	2	4
San Patricio	7,948	4,234	4,979	3,028	7,132	3,807	1,388	69
San Saba	1,578	474	1,085	390	1,256	414	15	0
Schleicher	560	365	426	281	620	232	26	1
Scurry	3,140	1,376	2,486	1,152	3,012	1,914	106	3
Shackelford	1,001	434	688	381	811	401	8	1
Shelby	4,632	920	3,099	938	3,786	2,125	7	1
Sherman	515	839	368	452	608	548	2	0
Smith	14,311	14,736	9,726	12,507	14,738	15,949	209	57
Somervell	622	240	449	188	625	313	13	0
Starr	3,001	1,651	3,310	2,184	3,457	1,042	992	8
Stephens	1,971	965	1,349	840	1,827	1,091	11	2
Sterling	260	104	223	93	274	101	6	1
Stonewall	907	152	758	146	836	211	8	4
Sutton	611	275	377	216	645	195	115	1
Swisher	2,264	1,205	1,879	604	2,088	995	47	0
Tarrant	91,516	91,144	62,117	72,706	91,353	114,643	10,591	1,157
Taylor	15,308	9,538	10,278	7,235	13,696	13,728	743	62
Terrell	360	225	246	162	323	196	74	0
Terry	3,035	1,248	2,029	931	2,161	1,738	239	2
Throckmorton	741	288	646	226	685	229	6	0
Titus	4,096	1,216	2,922	1,053	3,661	1,689	6	10
Tom Green	10,505	8,586	7,652	6,266	10,409	9,341	2,060	25
Travis	44,634	36,469	34,933	34,244	60,033	39,810	21,964	1,866
Trinity	1,885	563	1,179	595	1,484	730	4	2
Tyler	2,100	1,335	1,798	1,193	2,576	1,590	7	7
Upshur	4,064	2,002	3,238	1,856	3,971	2,463	6	9
Upton	921	662	718	544	624	772	38	4
Uvalde	2,847	1,713	1,985	1,377	4,339	420	751	3
Val Verde	3,888	1,577	2,819	1,274	3,216	1,287	1,464	10
Van Zandt	4,490	1,860	3,080	1,657	4,035	2,725	21	4
Victoria	8,755	5,467	6,061	4,912	8,024	6,107	1,221	82
Walker	3,281	2,123	2,426	1,661	4,701	3,490	193	127
Waller	2,169	1,067	1,579	800	2,249	1,372	32	4
Ward	2,412	1,732	1,971	1,158	1,820	1,469	235	5
Washington	2,726	2,565	2,410	1,794	295	2,187	12	12
Webb	8,930	2,551	6,942	2,275	8,251	1,827	3,855	24
Wharton	5,978	3,552	3,938	2,989	5,374	3,942	219	13
Wheeler	1,102	1,340	1,060	816	1,153	1,023	3	3
Wichita	16,326	16,389	16,264	11,231	20,942	14,739	570	90
Wilbarger	3,125	1,867	2,764	1,251	2,872	1,613	34	5
Willacy	2,501	945	1,964	981	1,647	957	1,021	5
Williamson	7,177	2,588	4,954	2,228	6,818	3,060	872	23
Wilson	2,959	1,011	2,135	843	3,246	1,139	492	8
Winkler	2,043	1,450	1,716	1,190	1,368	1,614	51	4
Wise	3,688	1,799	2,842	1,622	3,467	2,329	35	5
Wood	3,730	2,108	2,761	1,869	3,806	2,644	26	9
Yoakum	1,749	630	1,123	579	1,276	1,081	45	3
Young	3,383	1,861	2,714	1,428	3,108	1,740	14	3
Zapata	1,011	226	745	392	774	186	387	1
Zavala	1,528	501	1,123	472	1,703	147	2,035	15
Official Totals	1,662,019	1,254,333	1,232,506	1,073,831	1,633,493	1,533,986	214,118	24,103
Unofficial Totals	1,662,019	1,254,333	1,197,943	1,037,577	1,631,246	1,534,486	213,118	24,105

Table 54: Gubernatorial Races

	General Elections, 1974-1978									
Year	1974						1978			
County	Dolph Briscoe (D)	Jim Granbry (R)	Ramsey Muniz (RZ)	Sherry Smith (SW)	Sam W. McDonnll (A)	Other (WI)	John Hill (D)	William P. Cimnts Jr. (R)	Mario C. Compen (RZ)	Sara Jean Johnstn (SW)
Anderson	3,118	754	7	6	10	1	3,777	3,180	1	7
Andrews	957	459	7	4	91	0	753	1,588	3	0
Angelina	5,412	1,706	59	12	71	3	5,384	3,499	0	0
Aransas	901	479	37	3	12	0	939	672	0	7
Archer	1,219	158	2	0	13	0	353	354	0	0
Armstrong	467	214	3	0	1	0	353	354	0	0
Atascosa	1,828	622	93	4	25	0	2,210	2,030	12	6
Austin	1,412	606	9	5	30	1	1,665	1,845	3	1
Bailey	717	486	61	0	2	0	715	819	18	0
Bandera	955	405	7	2	25	0	1,028	1,580	1	5
Bastrop	2,113	728	34	11	19	0	2,651	1,820	14	6
Baylor	1,035	150	3	0	2	1	814	494	0	0
Bee	2,608	766	527	26	18	0	1,423	2,076	78	8
Bell	5,845	2,060	560	27	225	0	10,378	8,779	141	41
Bexar	65,209	37,145	13,280	971	1,204	0	87,709	79,832	2,148	530
Blanco	705	272	6	1	17	0	708	766	0	2
Borden	284	78	1	0	1	0	149	162	0	0
Bosque	1,785	427	8	0	24	0	1,948	1,698	5	3
Bowie	7,241	1,640	52	41	136	0	5,889	5,718	27	13
Brazoria	9,914	4,910	374	54	338	0	13,190	12,299	81	33
Brazos	4,812	1,950	412	99	92	0	7,623	7,298	110	51
Brewster	610	260	132	3	25	2	595	881	8	2
Briscoe	683	159	1	0	3	2	548	226	1	0
Brooks	1,214	109	776	3	2	0	1,220	435	22	3
Brown	2,888	751	17	1	42	1	3,548	2,935	3	3
Burleson	1,313	163	23	3	11	0	1,712	703	6	0
Burnet	2,100	1,076	36	9	17	0	2,669	2,207	5	2
Caldwell	1,909	616	196	7	8	0	2,315	1,727	24	9
Calhoun	1,664	459	133	9	17	2	2,006	1,641	16	4
Callahan	1,334	318	2	31	0	0	1,476	1,288	1	3
Cameron	9,396	4,711	2,423	65	159	1	13,224	10,601	273	108
Camp	1,001	192	3	1	3	0	998	695	1	0
Carson	1,180	592	10	2	19	0	975	872	2	1
Cass	2,938	693	3	5	14	0	3,563	2,521	1	4
Castro	1,110	436	52	2	1	0	1,651	866	51	2
Chambers	1,783	440	11	7	96	0	1,636	1,060	2	9
Cherokee	3,105	929	13	3	13	1	3,679	2,351	1	1
Childress	1,264	430	1	2	6	0	885	722	1	0
Clay	1,672	252	3	2	9	0	1,458	940	0	1
Cochran	547	262	21	1	0	0	725	521	5	0
Coke	803	107	3	0	16	0	692	536	0	0
Coleman	1,550	276	1	1	10	0	1,217	1,079	1	0
Collin	9,483	4,837	207	33	222	4	8,232	13,779	34	33
Collingsworth	935	286	0	1	2	0	783	474	0	2
Colorado	1,976	634	34	7	26	0	1,699	1,494	4	2
Comal	3,507	2,096	134	16	25	5	3,017	5,035	22	3
Comanche	1,783	266	11	2	5	0	1,784	935	2	3
Concho	672	96	1	1	5	0	498	446	1	1
Cooke	2,293	823	21	1	8	0	2,442	3,000	2	7
Coryell	1,942	592	25	6	42	3	2,493	2,475	8	2
Cottle	758	84	4	1	1	0	579	263	1	0
Crane	801	164	14	2	270	0	322	685	2	2
Crockett	510	101	123	0	12	0	349	541	11	1
Crosby	924	360	69	1	2	0	1,473	668	28	5
Culberson	401	108	32	4	3	0	333	392	8	0
Dallam	672	389	2	1	5	0	517	651	1	1
Dallas	100,647	77,273	7,726	1,266	3,410	0	108,617	154,901	1,518	744
Dawson	1,477	836	91	1	7	0	1,770	2,155	55	1
DeWitt	1,401	697	85	4	14	14	1,471	1,889	11	1
Deaf Smith	1,321	859	75	1	54	0	1,680	1,787	58	1
Delta	1,149	172	3	3	1	0	809	292	0	1
Denton	7,294	3,941	786	88	137	0	9,870	11,630	68	50
Dickens	756	162	0	0	2	0	794	266	5	0
Dimmit	1,747	211	722	2	1	1	1,327	925	33	9

Table 54: Gubernatorial Races

General Elections, 1974-1978										
Year	1974						1978			
County	Dolph Briscoe (D)	Jim Granbry (R)	Ramsey Muniz (RZ)	Sherry Smith (SW)	Sam W. McDonnll (A)	Other (WI)	John Hill (D)	William P. Clmnts Jr. (R)	Mario C. Compen (RZ)	Sara Jean Johnstn (SW)
Donley	709	303	7	0	1	0	725	502	3	0
Duval	3,014	74	180	0	1	0	2,188	692	44	1
Eastland	2,650	603	16	4	18	0	2,230	1,834	5	3
Ector	5,174	3,406	248	39	1,035	0	5,174	13,491	226	31
Edwards	311	73	0	1	0	0	189	351	1	1
El Paso	24,217	14,041	4,991	359	1,059	10	31,809	23,490	0	0
Ellis	4,590	955	77	3	39	0	4,758	4,256	7	6
Erath	2,824	852	40	9	13	1	2,413	2,273	5	1
Falls	1,842	285	36	1	35	1	2,634	1,543	7	7
Fannin	3,107	437	14	3	13	0	4,207	2,171	3	4
Fayette	1,905	687	13	6	26	0	2,150	1,726	2	4
Fisher	1,094	111	9	1	7	0	1,178	560	4	1
Floyd	1,168	607	59	3	7	0	1,255	997	11	1
Foard	551	51	0	0	4	0	669	178	1	0
Fort Bend	5,202	3,082	270	14	99	6	7,750	11,298	98	30
Franklin	810	96	1	2	4	0	719	379	0	0
Freestone	1,494	257	4	0	35	0	1,493	1,229	1	2
Frio	2,180	243	776	6	7	0	1,520	1,436	210	7
Gaines	986	504	9	2	6	0	1,238	1,356	15	0
Galveston	13,864	5,998	953	159	416	2	17,396	13,120	162	100
Garza	499	249	9	1	1	0	547	439	4	1
Gillespie	1,532	1,390	13	3	20	2	944	2,595	1	3
Glasscock	304	50	0	0	2	0	94	326	1	0
Goliad	514	155	52	3	6	0	564	579	2	0
Gonzales	1,598	343	91	4	21	0	1,634	1,292	5	1
Gray	3,077	2,710	21	7	50	1	2,658	3,792	1	2
Grayson	7,569	2,373	113	21	32	0	7,534	6,835	30	13
Gregg	7,002	4,188	109	44	84	1	7,230	9,763	29	13
Grimes	1,280	307	5	0	9	0	2,076	1,388	3	4
Guadalupe	2,655	2,000	135	21	37	0	3,550	5,081	31	6
Hale	2,707	2,073	385	0	10	0	3,207	3,356	98	11
Hall	1,201	360	13	0	0	0	817	513	0	2
Hamilton	1,234	268	8	0	15	0	1,051	1,025	1	1
Hansford	805	601	1	0	12	0	582	897	0	0
Hardeman	1,148	231	5	0	11	0	1,198	668	2	0
Hardin	2,224	627	10	10	29	0	5,331	3,127	3	2
Harris	130,622	96,237	10,301	1,720	3,693	0	167,814	190,728	1,025	849
Harrison	4,225	1,571	66	17	32	0	4,611	4,008	28	17
Hartley	649	251	0	1	4	0	573	645	2	0
Haskell	1,764	141	4	0	0	0	1,554	854	3	0
Hays	3,121	1,532	575	50	40	0	3,819	2,657	46	12
Hemphill	469	349	9	1	3	0	435	511	0	1
Henderson	3,704	1,125	23	7	43	0	4,304	3,819	7	3
Hidalgo	8,787	4,593	3,948	64	286	0	17,697	13,557	448	128
Hill	2,830	494	14	3	39	0	2,453	2,199	5	2
Hockley	2,334	889	187	13	13	0	2,680	1,821	22	3
Hood	1,499	297	4	0	11	0	1,716	1,580	2	1
Hopkins	2,580	479	13	5	19	0	2,684	1,704	2	0
Houston	1,748	383	2	2	22	0	2,419	1,280	3	0
Howard	4,829	1,468	162	11	52	4	2,676	3,595	68	8
Hudspeth	696	132	31	2	8	0	221	247	4	3
Hunt	3,752	1,124	88	11	48	3	4,404	3,613	2	6
Hutchinson	3,218	2,583	26	1	221	0	2,884	3,670	3	7
Irion	228	76	5	0	4	0	152	219	1	0
Jack	857	174	0	1	5	0	869	677	0	0
Jackson	1,497	420	14	3	7	0	1,549	1,400	4	1
Jasper	1,986	517	4	3	23	2	2,969	1,692	1	2
Jeff Davis	231	84	31	0	16	0	189	278	1	0
Jefferson	23,074	9,273	362	243	303	0	24,693	16,034	54	90
Jim Hogg	1,210	287	440	2	1	0	1,359	311	15	0
Jim Wells	3,133	696	1,033	4	18	0	3,102	2,339	58	5
Johnson	4,901	1,273	40	5	74	5	5,684	4,658	6	8
Jones	2,963	470	3	0	7	0	2,367	1,784	6	0
Karnes	1,392	338	67	2	6	1	1,413	1,394	9	2
Kaufman	2,806	668	17	2	21	0	3,342	2,456	2	2

Table 54: Gubernatorial Races

General Elections, 1974-1978										
Year	1974						1978			
County	Dolph Briscoe (D)	Jim Granbry (R)	Ramsey Muniz (RZ)	Sherry Smith (SW)	Sam W. McDonnll (A)	Other (WI)	John Hill (D)	William P. Clmnts Jr. (R)	Mario C. Compen (RZ)	Sara Jean Johnstn (SW)
Kendall	1,007	941	17	8	21	0	994	2,284	0	3
Kenedy	137	11	5	0	0	0	62	63	2	0
Kent	347	69	5	0	0	0	330	194	0	0
Kerr	2,856	1,971	43	6	241	2	2,391	5,283	7	2
Kimble	828	169	11	0	8	0	461	702	4	1
King	117	21	0	0	0	0	67	79	0	0
Kinney	465	44	35	1	1	0	235	332	0	1
Kleberg	2,840	759	1,150	14	11	0	2,512	2,176	140	8
Knox	1,024	114	3	0	2	0	918	390	0	0
La Salle	1,207	114	851	3	5	0	1,004	805	237	5
Lamar	5,321	1,356	30	0	37	0	4,735	2,909	5	11
Lamb	1,788	854	42	2	6	3	2,261	1,851	36	5
Lampasas	1,106	307	13	0	13	0	1,178	1,337	1	1
Lavaca	1,829	387	6	1	15	0	2,096	1,483	3	2
Lee	1,175	338	7	0	7	0	1,030	781	1	0
Leon	1,182	165	4	0	2	2	1,189	812	3	0
Liberty	3,082	853	22	8	53	2	3,720	2,476	0	2
Limestone	1,884	302	8	3	20	0	2,541	1,690	0	0
Lipscomb	501	452	4	1	1	0	378	553	0	0
Live Oak	969	278	39	0	3	0	725	1,111	3	0
Llano	1,332	801	4	0	7	0	1,577	1,632	3	0
Loving	34	11	0	0	0	0	19	38	0	0
Lubbock	10,213	13,613	1,581	67	121	0	16,963	21,094	528	76
Lynn	971	376	22	0	1	0	1,203	807	11	0
Madison	905	126	2	0	6	2	930	600	1	1
Marion	1,169	251	0	0	8	0	1,091	727	1	1
Martin	638	125	5	0	11	1	366	666	1	2
Mason	581	276	11	0	12	0	527	803	1	0
Matagorda	2,340	691	52	3	24	0	2,478	2,356	8	3
Maverick	926	152	363	6	10	0	1,627	606	36	0
McCulloch	1,133	175	10	0	4	0	936	1,198	0	0
McLennan	15,227	4,906	742	49	735	29	17,405	16,642	100	15
McMullen	205	51	1	0	3	0	102	224	2	1
Medina	2,632	620	151	5	39	0	1,872	2,852	26	2
Menard	509	123	14	0	1	1	375	398	0	0
Midland	4,952	4,776	201	27	535	1	4,632	13,808	80	30
Milam	2,066	445	21	3	45	4	2,935	1,674	5	1
Mills	705	127	2	0	10	0	639	584	0	1
Mitchell	1,386	251	12	0	6	0	947	866	2	1
Montague	2,050	354	6	2	14	0	1,901	1,568	1	2
Montgomery	7,066	3,213	101	19	254	4	7,159	8,998	23	14
Moore	1,648	1,089	5	2	5	0	1,325	1,599	3	1
Morris	1,552	283	1	2	3	0	1,622	1,101	0	2
Motley	421	163	4	9	3	0	295	381	0	0
Nacogdoches	4,180	1,388	114	38	13	5	3,728	3,026	6	15
Navarro	3,242	729	24	5	15	2	3,992	2,681	6	1
Newton	1,105	190	14	3	3	0	1,454	503	2	2
Nolan	2,071	558	19	0	5	0	1,859	1,790	2	3
Nueces	20,345	7,854	7,316	189	526	2	25,702	21,472	634	131
Ochiltree	910	1,210	6	2	22	0	478	1,328	0	0
Oldham	426	223	1	1	8	0	361	319	0	0
Orange	8,429	1,681	45	25	147	0	7,492	4,572	4	10
Palo Pinto	2,526	522	35	4	32	0	2,487	2,011	3	3
Panola	2,167	551	2	4	13	0	2,044	1,743	1	2
Parker	4,313	1,136	47	7	25	0	4,328	3,517	2	5
Parmer	1,217	783	9	1	12	0	1,164	1,212	7	0
Pecos	1,163	385	65	0	133	0	1,172	1,705	20	6
Polk	1,805	430	14	3	26	0	2,305	1,418	1	1
Potter	7,133	5,311	256	52	195	0	7,188	7,491	73	36
Presidio	846	136	125	5	25	1	521	447	8	4
Rains	637	89	6	0	2	0	675	309	0	0
Randall	5,712	6,742	200	26	247	9	6,235	9,854	22	10
Reagan	424	100	2	0	3	0	299	514	0	0
Real	376	49	7	1	11	0	347	569	12	1
Red River	2,617	479	6	5	8	0	1,652	1,086	2	1

Table 54: Gubernatorial Races

	General Elections, 1974-1978									
Year	1974						1978			
County	Dolph Briscoe (D)	Jim Granbry (R)	Ramsey Muniz (RZ)	Sherry Smith (SW)	Sam W. McDonnll (A)	Other (WI)	John Hill (D)	William P. Clmnts Jr. (R)	Mario C. Compen (RZ)	Sara Jean Johnstn (SW)
Reeves	949	310	64	3	40	1	1,627	1,660	261	12
Refugio	955	234	65	2	2	0	1,725	1,202	17	2
Roberts	272	167	6	0	6	0	134	253	0	0
Robertson	1,948	195	18	3	24	0	2,042	788	1	4
Rockwall	1,173	484	10	2	21	3	1,128	1,676	4	1
Runnels	1,899	438	15	3	12	0	1,142	1,671	6	3
Rusk	3,259	1,556	20	10	29	0	3,217	3,346	13	10
Sabine	1,410	198	3	5	10	0	1,104	469	1	2
San Augustine	735	147	4	0	5	0	1,136	584	1	2
San Jacinto	759	215	9	0	11	0	1,093	699	2	1
San Patricio	3,068	1,077	527	15	48	0	4,232	4,250	88	23
San Saba	457	99	5	2	7	1	927	606	3	2
Schleicher	492	115	5	1	2	0	290	489	0	0
Scurry	2,150	674	39	4	9	0	1,410	2,183	22	4
Shackelford	489	140	1	0	2	0	532	505	0	0
Shelby	2,078	395	10	10	3	0	2,229	1,514	1	1
Sherman	500	316	2	0	5	1	437	524	1	1
Smith	6,821	7,094	74	17	66	0	10,232	14,133	23	16
Somervell	518	77	4	1	4	0	700	365	1	0
Starr	3,201	94	430	10	2	0	3,591	466	32	3
Stephens	1,028	286	4	0	0	0	944	1,012	2	1
Sterling	202	53	2	0	2	0	121	230	0	0
Stonewall	535	64	0	0	1	1	448	237	0	0
Sutton	411	126	32	1	9	0	366	612	6	0
Swisher	1,645	498	23	3	5	4	2,123	620	8	2
Tarrant	60,009	28,731	3,341	505	1,212	0	63,662	70,709	327	290
Taylor	9,282	4,173	236	24	158	7	9,526	12,576	46	38
Terrell	372	86	55	10	14	0	151	265	6	0
Terry	1,534	806	60	2	7	1	1,612	1,502	17	1
Throckmorton	513	67	1	0	1	0	400	230	1	0
Titus	2,314	506	2	0	0	0	2,108	1,505	1	0
Tom Green	6,412	3,181	601	28	99	2	6,674	7,773	46	22
Travis	34,209	27,229	11,221	958	411	30	48,382	38,856	811	456
Trinity	1,607	212	4	2	15	0	1,340	676	4	1
Tyler	1,984	466	5	14	20	0	1,653	1,107	3	1
Upshur	2,492	720	0	3	11	0	2,509	1,923	2	0
Upton	743	224	18	1	31	0	357	653	1	1
Uvalde	3,188	282	409	2	13	0	1,306	3,158	47	0
Val Verde	2,683	429	399	5	14	0	2,607	2,038	15	4
Van Zandt	3,053	816	9	2	36	0	3,550	2,732	5	3
Victoria	3,461	1,455	208	10	48	0	5,211	6,291	94	24
Walker	3,046	934	94	20	32	0	3,059	2,504	1	3
Waller	1,253	348	15	2	26	1	1,595	1,509	1	4
Ward	940	409	29	5	122	0	847	1,532	9	1
Washington	1,200	776	17	4	9	0	1,825	2,073	1	3
Webb	4,174	530	2,229	13	1	3	5,433	3,019	255	38
Wharton	2,841	809	63	7	18	0	3,619	3,086	9	8
Wheeler	1,171	594	7	2	11	0	906	769	0	2
Wichita	13,480	3,920	192	38	163	3	11,312	10,348	33	27
Wilbarger	2,648	531	12	5	117	0	1,688	1,259	0	0
Willacy	1,067	320	345	9	21	0	1,473	1,100	18	6
Williamson	4,169	1,602	220	16	36	14	6,089	5,943	22	15
Wilson	1,588	403	100	1	13	0	1,790	1,555	12	2
Winkler	712	268	10	0	71	0	997	1,413	8	1
Wise	2,733	485	18	2	17	0	2,545	1,888	3	2
Wood	2,293	956	8	3	74	0	2,427	2,080	1	5
Yoakum	904	514	22	0	14	0	759	889	7	1
Young	2,133	444	19	5	21	0	1,999	1,713	1	1
Zapata	855	80	292	1	3	0	765	416	5	2
Zavala	1,623	114	2,034	7	5	0	1,204	741	2,036	5
Official Totals	1,016,334	514,725	93,295	8,171	22,208	251	1,166,919	1,183,828	14,213	4,624
Unofficial Totals	1,016,806	514,268	93,295	8,173	22,227	223	1,166,919	1,183,828	14,213	4,624

Table 55: Gubernatorial Races

	General Elections, 1982-1990											
Year	**1982**					**1986**				**1990**		
County	Mark White (D)	Wm P. Clmnts(R)	David Hutzlmn (I)	Bob Poteet (CI)	Other (WI)	Mark White (D)	William P. Clmnts(R)	Theresa Doyle (LT)	Other (WI)	Ann W. Richards (D)	Clayton Willms (R)	Jeff Daiell (LT)
Anderson	5,048	3,705	9	5	0	3,929	5,216	104	0	4,796	5,133	111
Andrews	1,143	1,556	13	2	0	727	2,625	68	0	787	2,272	62
Angelina	9,412	5,286	177	17	0	6,422	7,639	238	17	8,665	7,385	505
Aransas	1,826	1,932	28	9	0	1,641	2,606	90	6	2,079	2,405	206
Archer	1,421	1,003	6	3	0	1,050	1,664	28	0	1,509	1,419	121
Armstrong	423	454	4	4	0	270	614	6	2	271	433	30
Atascosa	3,258	2,553	15	9	0	2,869	3,659	79	3	3,185	3,420	246
Austin	2,322	2,149	9	2	0	2,069	3,270	35	5	2,093	3,465	138
Bailey	1,011	1,016	3	1	0	660	1,097	21	0	696	996	46
Bandera	962	1,689	15	3	1	871	2,223	61	2	1,152	2,266	200
Bastrop	4,466	2,336	38	23	0	4,800	4,403	126	3	6,101	4,135	235
Baylor	1,042	625	4	2	0	697	1,004	14	0	895	538	23
Bee	3,084	2,238	2	9	0	3,367	3,184	90	0	3,556	3,026	181
Bell	11,437	10,777	203	46	0	11,692	16,400	368	0	15,621	15,903	841
Bexar	99,890	96,441	890	560	1	98,962	97,390	3,414	12	120,468	99,478	8,914
Blanco	892	954	10	3	0	849	1,278	19	2	895	1,392	84
Borden	162	175	0	0	0	105	283	4	0	140	250	5
Bosque	2,419	1,832	15	3	0	1,875	2,848	30	0	2,409	2,592	132
Bowie	9,647	7,201	210	22	0	7,639	7,451	194	0	9,640	8,180	680
Brazoria	19,704	15,054	169	0	0	17,784	20,680	535	3	19,850	23,579	2,158
Brazos	9,641	9,388	355	59	0	11,280	13,368	416	0	14,357	17,225	1,304
Brewster	1,150	923	16	9	0	1,120	1,244	54	1	940	1,321	48
Briscoe	648	304	4	1	0	356	402	7	0	484	319	25
Brooks	2,499	435	8	1	0	3,188	870	53	0	1,685	420	23
Brown	5,205	3,015	11	4	0	3,007	5,068	124	0	4,017	4,762	231
Burleson	2,467	936	9	2	0	1,764	1,757	29	0	2,174	2,012	63
Burnet	3,241	2,462	17	5	0	2,961	4,162	71	3	3,561	4,088	170
Caldwell	3,525	1,887	17	14	0	3,296	3,212	97	0	3,659	1,906	121
Calhoun	3,319	2,006	28	7	4	2,719	2,794	132	0	2,771	2,634	201
Callahan	1,795	1,395	5	6	0	1,123	2,268	50	1	1,607	2,333	91
Cameron	20,095	13,796	160	70	0	19,363	16,548	327	8	20,704	14,989	820
Camp	1,760	994	2	0	0	1,498	1,176	12	0	1,646	1,245	61
Carson	1,324	1,112	11	4	0	764	1,660	44	1	1,136	1,296	117
Cass	5,336	2,651	10	1	0	3,930	3,374	42	1	4,244	3,141	107
Castro	1,524	1,005	7	5	0	1,046	1,108	29	2	1,008	1,046	59
Chambers	3,018	1,487	24	7	0	2,419	2,347	72	0	2,284	2,554	201
Cherokee	5,035	2,845	10	8	0	3,655	5,149	77	0	4,141	4,808	270
Childress	1,107	761	3	0	0	656	1,060	13	0	881	751	12
Clay	2,298	1,179	4	3	0	1,420	1,543	29	0	1,836	1,331	102
Cochran	804	660	3	4	0	613	690	37	1	468	529	44
Coke	730	467	5	1	0	499	742	24	0	522	678	26
Coleman	1,744	1,284	0	1	0	1,094	2,050	25	0	1,307	1,676	50
Collin	14,331	24,851	256	74	1	15,493	31,410	497	3	27,435	40,427	3,711
Collingsworth	888	471	3	1	0	695	875	11	0	638	476	41
Colorado	2,435	1,885	19	2	0	2,174	2,776	33	2	2,222	2,934	111
Comal	3,773	6,428	109	24	0	3,657	8,793	227	1	5,369	8,763	720
Comanche	2,698	1,081	4	3	1	1,639	2,084	50	0	1,978	1,542	100
Concho	714	362	1	0	0	449	535	24	1	450	521	14
Cooke	3,701	3,885	23	9	0	2,737	5,436	110	7	3,097	4,770	409
Coryell	3,262	2,800	10	4	0	2,828	4,286	109	4	3,753	4,055	300
Cottle	753	231	6	2	0	482	331	8	0	528	224	22
Crane	843	736	6	4	0	424	1,275	28	0	464	1,208	53
Crockett	448	450	1	0	0	392	684	8	0	340	679	15
Crosby	1,302	654	7	6	0	1,027	639	15	0	869	844	40
Culberson	571	344	4	2	0	470	359	16	0	322	373	14
Dallam	673	690	7	7	0	402	821	19	2	535	762	79
Dallas	155,337	187,656	2,153	707	30	159,151	204,932	4,001	15	211,728	192,105	17,125
Dawson	2,055	1,792	9	5	0	1,469	2,364	34	0	1,168	2,534	83
DeWitt	2,038	2,287	7	6	0	1,476	3,206	31	3	1,689	2,728	94
Deaf Smith	2,077	2,382	18	11	1	1,359	2,668	40	9	1,435	2,491	148
Delta	1,208	315	2	2	0	758	567	6	0	901	550	19
Denton	15,113	18,143	333	103	0	16,575	26,267	568	4	26,560	30,971	3,355
Dickens	859	260	0	1	0	601	339	16	0	448	402	20
Dimmit	2,182	745	2	1	0	2,117	839	20	2	2,205	1,194	25

Table 55: Gubernatorial Races

	General Elections, 1982-1990											
Year	1982					1986				1990		
County	Mark White (D)	Wm P. Clmnts(R)	David Hutzimn (I)	Bob Poteet (CI)	Other (WI)	Mark White (D)	William P. Clmnts(R)	Theresa Doyle (LT)	Other (WI)	Ann W. Richards (D)	Clayton Willms (R)	Jeff Daiell (LT)
Donley	751	532	7	4	0	431	901	13	0	574	692	42
Duval	3,434	530	24	8	0	3,183	851	29	0	3,174	881	146
Eastland	3,295	2,164	14	5	0	1,803	3,557	59	4	2,493	3,008	153
Ector	9,957	13,511	149	55	1	7,008	17,848	362	0	8,347	16,458	678
Edwards	235	334	0	3	0	101	405	5	0	272	527	12
El Paso	37,725	31,892	716	207	2	37,507	26,884	1,165	27	41,624	32,740	2,389
Ellis	7,987	5,304	30	15	0	7,123	10,087	249	0	9,746	11,210	924
Erath	3,975	2,624	16	6	0	2,709	3,667	63	0	3,286	3,515	198
Falls	2,950	1,344	11	1	0	1,967	2,044	26	0	2,576	1,792	62
Fannin	5,518	1,807	11	6	0	2,901	3,022	63	0	3,822	2,272	204
Fayette	3,030	2,454	5	3	0	2,081	4,173	48	0	2,811	4,224	166
Fisher	1,477	425	5	2	0	868	672	15	0	1,123	582	44
Floyd	1,142	1,009	6	5	0	880	1,357	10	0	958	1,405	44
Foard	594	206	1	1	0	359	264	3	0	454	182	7
Fort Bend	12,407	15,401	139	34	0	18,068	21,039	328	0	21,333	25,040	1,279
Franklin	1,234	611	5	1	0	971	979	16	0	1,061	1,088	58
Freestone	2,374	1,419	6	3	0	2,106	2,550	32	6	2,153	2,364	104
Frio	2,156	1,217	9	3	0	2,133	1,554	26	0	1,458	1,130	34
Gaines	1,089	1,053	12	4	0	818	1,702	57	0	905	1,820	92
Galveston	28,741	14,966	739	242	1	27,702	18,653	652	11	29,303	21,006	1,545
Garza	576	474	2	2	0	322	788	4	0	494	788	35
Gillespie	1,388	3,121	13	4	0	1,169	4,294	49	0	1,619	3,895	233
Glasscock	176	264	2	0	2	93	344	6	0	101	421	11
Goliad	936	840	12	0	1	890	1,514	24	2	872	1,079	44
Gonzales	2,033	1,594	7	4	0	1,415	2,689	40	2	1,783	2,234	75
Gray	3,240	4,423	32	13	0	1,882	6,083	160	11	2,679	4,845	490
Grayson	12,827	8,286	331	36	0	9,228	12,670	292	0	11,597	10,410	1,013
Gregg	10,365	13,353	152	38	0	8,716	16,913	332	0	12,053	15,344	909
Grimes	2,169	1,211	7	3	0	2,345	2,313	30	1	1,873	2,020	105
Guadalupe	5,190	6,905	36	15	0	4,311	8,751	237	8	5,756	8,586	754
Hale	3,597	3,948	27	5	1	2,319	4,196	47	0	2,363	3,971	149
Hall	1,113	549	6	1	0	688	710	4	0	753	514	15
Hamilton	1,500	1,001	4	0	0	1,027	1,566	28	2	1,363	1,535	67
Hansford	595	1,122	0	0	0	398	1,566	11	0	476	1,495	76
Hardeman	1,086	521	3	0	0	690	708	6	0	827	518	28
Hardin	7,222	2,924	22	8	0	4,321	4,242	175	0	5,151	3,931	368
Harris	240,279	231,045	2,808	915	3	267,685	238,119	4,221	117	280,159	259,821	15,545
Harrison	6,581	5,215	120	18	0	6,386	6,042	103	0	7,186	7,104	331
Hartley	643	703	5	1	0	429	827	14	0	569	891	54
Haskell	1,656	670	4	3	0	912	1,222	24	0	1,366	922	42
Hays	5,503	3,862	81	77	0	7,032	6,749	259	14	10,044	7,157	515
Hemphill	629	696	4	0	0	427	1,106	22	3	595	862	66
Henderson	7,549	4,497	17	6	0	6,566	9,041	137	0	8,472	8,032	562
Hidalgo	31,292	17,771	157	73	2	29,532	19,663	408	0	33,167	18,942	946
Hill	4,077	2,411	17	3	0	2,626	3,812	51	0	3,816	3,519	253
Hockley	2,460	2,088	19	13	0	2,080	2,845	97	0	1,994	2,761	193
Hood	3,401	2,587	3	1	0	2,609	4,146	122	2	4,257	5,053	449
Hopkins	4,217	2,059	6	1	0	3,246	3,415	42	0	4,219	3,714	239
Houston	3,724	1,555	6	3	0	2,540	2,822	46	0	3,037	2,728	125
Howard	4,695	3,624	48	9	0	3,525	4,889	132	0	3,270	4,512	224
Hudspeth	320	256	0	0	0	286	311	11	0	234	335	9
Hunt	7,612	4,999	46	10	0	5,975	7,262	159	1	7,030	7,978	565
Hutchinson	3,195	4,284	40	12	0	2,137	5,613	161	0	3,118	4,645	568
Irion	265	268	4	0	0	238	526	23	0	245	352	15
Jack	1,201	874	3	1	0	740	1,254	23	0	999	1,053	68
Jackson	2,300	1,758	8	4	1	1,695	2,655	26	1	1,591	2,080	88
Jasper	5,028	2,122	14	4	0	3,046	3,411	154	4	4,176	2,881	333
Jeff Davis	262	281	2	0	0	221	333	9	1	257	416	16
Jefferson	40,030	18,707	272	60	0	34,847	22,500	1,162	9	40,288	21,718	1,901
Jim Hogg	1,526	251	0	1	0	1,498	475	9	0	1,318	381	5
Jim Wells	6,320	2,642	26	10	0	5,203	3,335	42	2	5,464	2,624	120
Johnson	10,262	6,504	53	16	1	7,883	11,063	179	0	10,945	11,491	1,102
Jones	2,775	1,622	12	5	0	1,615	2,516	42	4	2,057	2,080	91
Karnes	1,971	1,512	6	3	0	1,496	2,131	32	0	1,267	1,902	65
Kaufman	6,246	3,459	14	2	0	4,756	5,770	123	0	5,987	5,885	467

Table 55: Gubernatorial Races

General Elections, 1982-1990											
Year	1982					1986				1990		
County	Mark White (D)	Wm P. Clmnts(R)	David Hutzlmn (I)	Bob Poteet (CI)	Other (WI)	Mark White (D)	William P. Clmnts(R)	Theresa Doyle (LT)	Other (WI)	Ann W. Richards (D)	Clayton Willms (R)	Jeff Daiell (LT)
Kendall	1,007	2,739	13	3	0	967	3,194	53	1	1,359	3,177	238
Kenedy	153	42	0	0	0	141	56	1	0	82	65	4
Kent	438	172	0	0	0	176	227	9	1	98	99	5
Kerr	2,944	6,158	36	5	0	2,792	7,774	128	4	3,301	6,761	520
Kimble	539	599	4	3	0	475	899	11	0	529	976	53
King	115	83	1	0	0	67	146	3	0	76	109	2
Kinney	590	414	6	2	0	405	519	11	0	487	590	33
Kleberg	4,146	2,246	68	20	0	3,411	2,433	66	1	3,743	2,500	153
Knox	989	441	5	2	0	618	686	16	0	876	519	32
La Salle	1,636	718	3	0	0	1,576	645	11	0	1,059	481	10
Lamar	6,994	2,992	12	8	1	4,731	5,098	79	7	5,826	4,517	276
Lamb	2,024	1,787	9	9	0	1,502	2,439	46	0	1,364	2,017	82
Lampasas	2,148	1,312	7	1	0	1,511	2,326	39	2	1,622	2,023	73
Lavaca	2,865	1,972	7	2	0	2,159	3,617	46	0	2,510	2,675	135
Lee	1,792	1,025	7	2	0	1,473	2,083	23	0	1,642	2,537	65
Leon	1,826	923	4	4	0	1,530	2,231	20	3	1,821	2,040	93
Liberty	6,933	3,478	30	10	1	5,729	5,999	83	2	5,389	5,961	329
Limestone	3,268	1,643	7	7	0	2,329	2,542	32	0	2,788	2,141	111
Lipscomb	491	665	2	0	1	462	1,053	23	2	428	676	58
Live Oak	1,185	1,219	3	2	0	1,248	2,200	32	0	1,060	1,465	100
Llano	2,347	2,020	3	1	2	1,813	3,243	35	1	2,223	3,205	102
Loving	20	37	0	0	0	28	60	2	1	31	65	0
Lubbock	20,915	25,222	309	121	0	18,641	27,241	710	20	20,643	29,100	1,480
Lynn	1,147	900	3	3	0	1,057	1,196	32	0	663	998	33
Madison	1,414	730	6	1	0	1,167	1,464	13	0	1,417	1,392	10
Marion	1,756	1,058	6	3	0	1,354	1,089	18	0	2,015	1,385	104
Martin	585	519	4	3	2	354	791	12	0	330	876	18
Mason	556	650	0	0	0	469	929	5	0	485	787	28
Matagorda	3,858	2,788	26	11	0	4,103	4,517	125	0	4,146	4,574	286
Maverick	2,820	678	18	11	0	3,168	1,223	40	1	3,553	1,439	67
McCulloch	1,770	966	3	0	0	1,016	1,366	27	0	1,204	1,323	43
McLennan	22,712	18,601	141	48	0	19,266	24,951	534	34	27,414	21,671	1,112
McMullen	135	188	0	0	0	105	244	1	0	89	217	17
Medina	2,909	2,905	15	6	0	2,675	3,937	70	0	2,727	3,953	266
Menard	479	345	1	0	0	422	614	19	0	458	465	26
Midland	6,011	15,762	197	37	0	6,382	17,878	344	7	6,672	23,184	707
Milam	4,136	1,714	11	4	0	3,021	2,935	48	0	4,069	2,758	105
Mills	924	549	4	2	0	529	977	17	0	709	832	28
Mitchell	1,385	918	4	0	0	964	1,308	26	3	1,259	1,216	33
Montague	3,024	1,764	15	2	0	2,051	2,878	40	0	2,510	2,280	281
Montgomery	14,223	14,865	128	40	4	14,096	22,013	483	18	16,454	27,499	1,425
Moore	1,669	2,017	18	3	1	986	2,970	75	0	1,542	2,513	240
Morris	2,883	1,280	7	3	0	2,233	1,379	30	1	2,528	1,353	67
Motley	362	318	2	1	0	250	422	6	0	223	362	32
Nacogdoches	4,969	4,357	96	23	0	4,242	6,115	129	1	5,958	6,298	324
Navarro	5,520	2,901	19	10	0	4,689	4,516	50	0	5,343	4,763	344
Newton	3,084	516	24	1	0	2,011	1,236	86	18	2,274	909	77
Nolan	2,547	1,677	12	4	0	1,507	2,166	71	0	2,080	2,058	131
Nueces	38,455	25,357	331	167	0	34,141	27,282	751	1	37,019	24,317	1,963
Ochiltree	917	1,837	9	5	0	503	2,421	18	1	636	2,042	94
Oldham	366	325	7	1	0	236	476	10	0	274	422	64
Orange	15,283	5,537	88	14	0	10,081	6,656	482	10	12,366	6,727	651
Palo Pinto	4,099	2,481	13	8	0	2,679	3,752	70	5	3,197	3,128	233
Panola	3,064	2,191	10	4	0	2,839	3,024	53	0	3,166	2,908	99
Parker	6,976	5,033	40	22	0	5,530	8,808	222	0	7,344	9,380	869
Parmer	997	1,432	1	0	0	680	1,482	27	0	685	1,288	58
Pecos	1,563	1,472	14	7	0	1,730	2,572	60	0	1,441	3,256	64
Polk	4,172	1,804	82	6	0	3,439	4,223	151	0	4,321	4,265	331
Potter	9,044	9,312	300	48	0	6,168	11,475	392	15	9,233	9,855	873
Presidio	904	428	7	1	0	470	442	15	0	1,062	635	19
Rains	1,351	560	8	3	0	887	1,014	18	0	1,041	1,016	53
Randall	7,899	14,463	87	46	0	6,383	17,790	345	26	10,842	17,924	1,273
Reagan	510	505	4	2	1	253	732	20	0	242	807	13
Real	717	639	5	6	0	370	868	15	4	418	671	43
Red River	2,927	1,141	0	4	0	1,842	1,500	14	0	2,179	1,711	119

Table 55: Gubernatorial Races

General Elections, 1982-1990											
Year	1982					1986				1990		
County	Mark White (D)	Wm P. Clmnts(R)	David Hutzlmn (I)	Bob Poteet (CI)	Other (WI)	Mark White (D)	William P. Clmnts(R)	Theresa Doyle (LT)	Other (WI)	Ann W. Richards (D)	Clayton Wilms (R)	Jeff Daiell (LT)
Reeves	2,503	1,191	16	9	0	2,402	1,986	81	11	1,600	1,686	43
Refugio	1,456	974	7	6	0	1,401	1,647	47	4	1,553	1,246	65
Roberts	180	263	6	1	0	135	479	7	0	165	331	22
Robertson	2,890	923	8	4	0	2,334	1,844	42	0	2,883	1,676	75
Rockwall	2,101	2,971	13	4	0	2,012	4,448	78	1	2,752	4,625	440
Runnels	1,584	1,406	5	4	0	1,018	2,152	51	2	1,200	1,894	80
Rusk	4,563	4,931	25	16	0	3,333	6,431	71	0	4,699	6,197	378
Sabine	1,654	795	3	1	0	1,247	1,463	52	1	1,728	1,336	72
San Augustine	1,461	723	2	1	0	1,075	1,057	16	1	1,753	1,290	83
San Jacinto	2,481	870	14	2	0	1,590	1,937	28	0	2,009	2,023	109
San Patricio	7,047	4,704	197	33	0	5,777	6,218	166	0	6,202	5,088	473
San Saba	1,164	539	0	1	0	750	940	21	0	692	847	20
Schleicher	431	389	0	0	0	281	542	23	0	321	535	19
Scurry	1,774	2,146	18	7	0	1,498	3,385	55	0	1,614	3,107	165
Shackelford	604	542	2	2	0	328	882	11	1	406	719	25
Shelby	2,981	1,812	4	2	0	2,985	2,573	35	2	3,247	2,264	113
Sherman	425	598	5	1	0	313	814	15	5	311	627	56
Smith	14,878	17,336	127	31	3	12,717	24,698	450	2	15,874	23,493	1,454
Somervell	927	419	5	3	0	554	760	15	3	819	951	98
Starr	4,750	842	9	5	0	3,750	1,053	17	0	3,582	653	24
Stephens	1,396	1,364	6	2	0	789	2,036	23	3	1,033	1,707	94
Sterling	233	240	1	0	0	156	436	33	1	146	357	6
Stonewall	717	331	23	1	0	424	607	17	2	519	308	13
Sutton	512	629	2	3	0	277	847	20	0	383	639	20
Swisher	2,131	801	11	6	0	1,449	898	35	2	1,440	799	48
Tarrant	107,971	103,501	1,034	418	0	104,196	128,263	2,999	15	139,788	131,234	12,849
Taylor	12,221	15,108	102	50	0	9,275	18,355	462	3	11,976	16,705	754
Terrell	322	264	3	0	0	264	235	15	1	250	242	6
Terry	1,877	1,577	10	2	0	1,384	1,910	31	1	1,354	1,897	91
Throckmorton	449	255	0	0	0	315	462	4	0	374	367	34
Titus	3,934	2,166	8	4	0	3,290	2,688	36	3	3,138	2,503	118
Tom Green	9,766	10,072	81	29	0	7,864	12,944	467	5	9,607	13,040	779
Travis	72,149	50,410	2,106	2,409	5	86,152	64,649	2,489	14	128,120	63,376	4,135
Trinity	2,322	798	8	1	0	1,673	1,863	36	0	1,919	1,712	109
Tyler	2,980	1,268	4	2	0	2,077	2,235	91	2	2,763	1,840	164
Upshur	4,401	2,638	15	0	0	3,393	4,046	60	11	4,159	3,851	269
Upton	558	490	1	3	0	229	1,074	16	0	313	1,005	33
Uvalde	2,776	2,715	10	6	0	2,332	3,151	65	0	2,472	2,891	132
Val Verde	3,439	2,333	19	4	1	3,022	2,663	63	0	3,856	2,682	126
Van Zandt	5,780	3,145	17	2	0	3,999	5,776	87	0	4,750	5,406	363
Victoria	6,382	9,330	128	28	0	5,982	11,002	192	2	7,600	10,373	537
Walker	4,807	2,929	33	67	0	4,251	4,674	84	4	5,160	4,924	237
Waller	2,726	2,000	12	3	0	2,626	2,729	55	2	3,541	2,790	119
Ward	1,611	1,546	15	9	0	909	2,402	68	1	1,229	2,527	101
Washington	3,438	3,221	12	8	0	2,933	4,225	55	4	3,128	5,324	188
Webb	9,523	3,913	55	53	0	11,594	3,954	243	1	10,947	3,521	170
Wharton	5,950	3,876	21	12	0	4,136	4,962	101	0	3,939	4,794	221
Wheeler	1,172	973	1	0	0	727	1,585	24	0	884	1,191	87
Wichita	15,324	11,607	532	62	0	12,392	13,337	364	2	16,397	12,926	1,360
Wilbarger	2,820	1,631	9	2	0	1,460	1,900	28	0	1,769	1,586	102
Willacy	2,485	1,304	12	5	0	1,846	1,522	27	0	2,410	1,385	72
Williamson	10,216	8,619	138	65	0	12,437	15,516	463	0	19,737	18,148	1,034
Wilson	2,691	2,092	10	2	0	2,251	2,969	65	0	3,109	3,624	191
Winkler	1,167	1,010	3	4	0	643	1,435	37	0	644	1,419	28
Wise	4,223	2,426	18	4	0	3,086	4,584	92	1	4,458	4,255	403
Wood	3,917	2,886	13	1	0	2,912	4,729	55	1	3,479	4,678	296
Yoakum	876	1,038	9	3	0	652	1,521	44	0	676	1,204	85
Young	2,712	2,482	12	2	0	1,674	3,485	44	4	2,414	3,142	251
Zapata	1,263	611	8	1	0	1,336	790	13	0	1,111	587	13
Zavala	2,092	497	7	0	0	2,288	648	11	4	1,989	483	27
Official	1,697,870		19,143		76	1,813,779			670	1,826,431		
Totals		1,465,937		8,065		1,584,515		42,496		1,925,670		129,128
Unofficial	1,697,868		19,142		76	1,813,779			670	1,826,482		
Totals		1,465,937		8,065		1,584,515		42,496		1,925,624		129,128

Gubernatorial Candidates

In 66 gubernatorial elections since Texas joined the Union in 1845, 322 people — 310 men and 12 women — have sought the top office in state government. Miriam A. Ferguson was on the ballot six times, being elected twice, and Preston Smith was successful three times in five tries. Here is the list:

Candidate; Years; Party

Abbey, Wellington; 1950; dem.
Adams, Stanley; 1990; dem.
Adams, Tod R.; 1954; rep.
Alexander, Steve S.; 1974; dem.
Allred, James V.; 1934,1936; dem.
Andrews, Redding; 1910,1912; soc.
Armstrong, Bob; 1982; dem.
Armstrong, George W.; 1932; dem.
Atcheson, A.W.; 1906; reorep.
Atwell, W.H.; 1922; rep.
Bailey, Joseph W.; 1920; dem.
Bailey, R.P.; 1898; proh.
Ball, Thomas H.; 1914; dem.
Banks, M.T.; 1964; dem.
Barnes, Ben; 1972; dem.
Barton, Thomas D.; 1924; dem.
Beagle, Donald R.; 1978,1982; dem.
Bell, Charles K.; 1906; dem.
Bell, P.H.; 1849,1851; none.
Bilyeu, Sheila; 1986; dem.
Boynton, Alexander; 1938; rep.
Boynton, Charles A.; 1918; rep.
Brannin, Carl; 1936; soc.
Brinkley, Floyd; 1946; dem.
Briscoe, Dolph; 1968,1972,1974,1978; dem.
Briscoe III, Andrew C.; 1986; dem.
Brogdon, S.T.; 1938; dem.
Brooks, Homer; 1936,1938; comm.
Brooks, M.M.; 1906; dem.
Brooks, P.Pierce; 1936; dem.
Brown, William V.; 1946; dem.
Bryant, William R.; 1956; rep.
Bullington, Orville; 1932; rep.
Burkett, George W.; 1902; rep.
Burkett, Joe; 1924; dem.
Burks, A.J.; 1946; dem.
Butte, George C.; 1924,1930; rep.
Campbell, T.M.; 1906,1908; dem.
Capers, H.; 1920; btrep.
Carey, Edward L.; 1944; dem.
Carr, Waggoner; 1968; dem.
Carroll, G.W.; 1902; proh.
Carswell, Jack; 1962; conser.
Chambers, T.J.; 1851,1853,1861,1863; none.
Chambers, William; 1876; rep.
Choate, K.E.; 1912; soclab.
Clark, Edward; 1861; none.
Clark, George; 1892; dem.
Clark, Pat B.; 1904; peo.
Clark, Randolph; 1896; proh.
Clements, Bill; 1978,1982,1986; rep.

Cochran, A.M.; 1886; rep.
Coke, Richard; 1873,1876; dem.
Collins, Hall H.; 1942; dem.
Collins, V.A.; 1924; dem.
Colquitt, O.B.; 1906,1910,1912; dem.
Compeah, Mario C.; 1978; laraza.
Condron, R.P.; 1940; dem.
Connally, John; 1962,1964,1966; dem.
Cook, W.B.; 1908; soclab.
Cox, Jack; 1960,1962; dem., rep.
Creager, R.B.; 1916; rep.
Crichton, Jack; 1964; rep.
Crowder, A. Don; 1986; dem.
Crowley, Karl A.; 1938; dem.
Cude, Ed; 1990; rep.
Culberson, C.A.; 1894,1896; dem.
Culberson, J.G.; 1920; rep.
Cunningham, Minnie F.; 1944; dem.
Currie, Ralph W.; 1950; rep.
Dancy, John; 1853; none.
Daniel, Price; 1956,1958,1960,1962; dem.
Darnell, N.H.; 1847; none.
Davidson, Lynch; 1924,1926; dem.
Davidson, R.V.; 1910; dem.
Davidson, T.W.; 1924; dem.
Davis, A.B.Cyclon; 1954; dem.
Davis, E.J.; 1869,1873,1880; none.
Davis Jr., Cyclone; 1940; dem.
Dickson, D.C.; 1855; none.
Dixon, George W.; 1924; dem.
Dohoney, E.L.; 1886; proh.
Dowler, A.S.; 1906; soclab.
Doyle, Theresa; 1986; libetar.
Dunn, J.M.; 1894; proh.
Edwards, G.C.; 1906; soc.
Edwards, George C.; 1932,1934; soc.
Eggers, Paul; 1968,1970; rep.
Embs, Duke; 1982; rep.
Epperson, B.H.; 1851; none.
Etheridge, F.M.; 1914; prog.
Evans, L.D.; 1853; none.
Evans, Roger Q.; 1932,1940; dem.
Exum, H.E.; 1930; rep.
Farenthold, Frances; 1972,1974; dem.
Farmer, Clarence E; 1938; dem.
Fay, Albert; 1972; rep.
Ferguson, Alex M.; 1942,1944; dem.
Ferguson, James A.; 1938; dem.
Ferguson, James E.; 1914,1916,1918; dem.
Ferguson, Miriam A.;1924,1926,1930,1932, 1938,1940;dem.
Fischer, F.W.; 1936; dem.
Flanagan, W.; 1890; rep.

Formby, Marshall; 1962; dem.
Frakes, C.A.; 1932; dem.
Gaines, John P.; 1930; rep.
Gibbs, Barnett; 1898; peo.
Gillespie, Tommye; 1966; con.
Glenn, J. Ed; 1932; dem.
Gonzalez, Henry B.; 1958; dem.
Granberry, Jim; 1974; rep.
Grant, John F.; 1930; rep.
Gray, C.A.; 1906; rep.
Greer, John A.; 1851; none.
Grimes, William F.; 1944; dem.
Grover, Henry C.; 1972; rep.
Hackworthe, Johnnie M.; 1964,1966,1968; dem.
Haines, H.H.; 1926; rep.
Haley, J.Evetts; 1956; dem.
Hall Sr., John A.; 1972; rep.
Hamilton, A.J.; 1869; none.
Hamman, W.H.; 1878; grbk.
Hance, Kent; 1986,1990; rep.
Hanney, R.E.; 1900; rep
Hardaway, Enoch; 1934; comm.
Harris, C.O.; 1936; rep.
Hawkins, William E.; 1928; dem.
Hearn-Haynes, Theresa; 1990; dem.
Heath, E.C.; 1890,1908; proh.
Heitt, Otho L.; 1932; liberty.
Henderson, J.P.; 1845; none.
Hill, John; 1968,1978; dem.
Hines, Harry; 1940; dem.
Hobby, William P.; 1918; dem.
Hogg, Jim S.; 1890,1892; dem.
Holmes, Earl; 1990; dem.
Holmes, J.J.; 1954,1956; dem.
Holmes, W.H.; 1928; rep.
Hopkins, George C.; 1940; rep.
Houston, A.J.; 1892,1910,1912; refrep,proh.
Houston, Sam; 1857,1859; none.
Howe, Philip L.; 1932; comm.
Hughes, Maury; 1934; dem.
Hunter, Tom F.; 1932,1934,1936,1938; dem.
Hutchison, Charles B.; 1946,1948,1950; dem.
Hutchison, Ray; 1978; rep.
Hutzelman, David; 1982; ind.
Ireland, John; 1882,1884; dem.I
Irwin, Joe A.; 1958; dem.
Jackson, W.D.; 1904; proh.
Jenkins, J.A.; 1972; rep.
Jester, Beauford; 1946,1948; dem.
Johnson, C.W.; 1912; rep.
Johnson, Cone; 1910; dem.J
Johnson, M.T; 1851,1855; none.
Johnston, Kate M.; 1926; dem.
Johnston, Sara Jean; 1978; soc.
Jones, G.W.; 1882,1884; grbk.
Jones, J. Marion; 1910; dem.J
Jones, Martin; 1944; dem.
Kearby, J.C.; 1896; peo.
Kennerly, T.E.; 1966; rep.
King, Joseph; 1938; dem.
King, W.W.; 1922; dem.
Lane, Alvin H.; 1948; rep.

Lanham, S.W.T; 1902,1904; dem.
Lasater, Ed; 1912; prog.
Lauderdale, Ben H.; 1940; comm.
Lawrence, Benita L.M; 1950; dem.
Leitner, Frank; 1904; soclab.
Leonard, Deborah; 1972; soc.
Lewis, H.W.; 1916; proh.
Locke, Bobby; 1986; dem.
Locke, Eugene; 1968; dem.
Loeffler, Tom; 1986; rep.L
Logan, Bard; 1966; conser.
Looney, Ben F.; 1920; dem.
Looney, Robert E.; 1972; dem.
Love, Thomas B.; 1930; dem.
Loven, Paul; 1930; dem.
Lowden, J.G.; 1904; rep.
Lubbock, F.R.; 1861; none.
Luce, Tom; 1990; rep.
Makemson, W.K.; 1894; rep.
Mallett, J.M.; 1902; peo.
March, Caso; 1946,1948,1950; dem.
Marshall, H.C.; 1916; dem.
Martin, Marion; 1888; indfus.
Martin, Roger; 1970; rep.
Mattox, Jim; 1990; dem.
May, Holmes A.; 1948; dem.
Mayer, Edwin S.; 1958; rep.
Mayfield, Earle B.; 1930; dem.
Mayo, Ray Allen; 1978,1982; dem.
McBrayer, Odell; 1974; rep.
McCoy, Marvin P.; 1938; dem.
McCraw, William; 1938; dem.
McDonald, C.C.; 1934; dem.
McDonnell, S.W.; 1974; amer.
McDowell, C.K.; 1942; rep.
McElroy, Tom; 1972; rep.
McGregor, T.H.; 1920; amer.
McMinn, T.J.; 1900; peo.
McNutt, Walter S.; 1946; dem.
Meltzen, E.O.; 1914,1916; soc.
Miller, Barry; 1930; dem.
Miller, Clarence R; 1938; dem.
Miller, Earl E.; 1938; soc.
Miller, J.B.; 1845,1847; none.
Mills, Herbert E.; 1944; dem.
Mills, John T.; 1849; none.
Mills, W.H.; 1904; socdem.
Minton, W.J.; 1944,1946,1948; dem.
Moody, C.C.; 1930; dem.
Moody, Dan; 1926,1928; dem.
Morris, Charles H.; 1916; dem.
Muniz, Ramsey; 1972,1974; laraza.
Murrah, Pendleton; 1863; none.
Neff, Pat M.; 1920,1922; dem.
Nolte Jr., Eugene; 1946; dem.
Norton, A.B.; 1878,1880,1884; rep.
Nugent, T.L.; 1892,1894; peo.
O'Daniel, Pat; 1968; dem.
O'Daniel, W.Lee; 1938,1940,1956,1958; dem.
Ochiltree, W.B.; 1853; none.
Otwell, W.N.; 1990; rep.
Overholt, Gerald; 1948; proh.

Owens, Royce X.; 1990; rep.
Pearson, J.W.; 1906; proh.
Pease, Elisha M.; 1853,1855,1866; none.
Peasley, B.J.; 1944; rep.
Philp, John W.; 1914; rep.
Poindexter, William; 1910; dem.
Pope, W.E.; 1924; dem.
Porter, Gene S.; 1942,1944,1950; dem.
Posey, William H.; 1972,1974; dem.
Poteet, Bob; 1982; con.
Prendergast, D.M.; 1892; proh.
Putnam, Frank; 1930,1932; dem.
Rachal, Ray; 1990; dem.
Rainey, Homer P.; 1946; dem.
Rains, Jack; 1990; rep.
Ramsey, William F.; 1912; dem.
Reagan, David; 1972; rep.
Renfro, P.D.; 1938; dem.
Rhodes, J.C.; 1908; soc.
Rhodes, L.L.; 1920,1928; soc.
Richards, Ann W.; 1990; dem.
Roberts, O.M.; 1878,1880; none.
Robertson, Felix D.; 1924; dem.
Robertson, J.B.; 1882; inddem.
Robinson, J.J.; 1847; none.
Rogers, Fred S.; 1922; dem.
Ross, L.S. "Sul"; 1886,1888; dem.
Royall, G.H.; 1898,1900; soclab.
Runnels, Hardin; 1857,1859; none.
Russell, Edward K.; 1934; dem.
Sadler, Jerry; 1940,1946; dem.
Sanderford, Roy; 1936; dem.
Sayers, J.D.; 1898,1900; dem.
Schmidt, J.B.; 1894; lwrep.
Schmitz, Carl; 1910; soc lab.
Scott, E.P.; 1926; rep.
Self, Thomas; 1938; dem.
Sellers, Grover; 1946; dem.
Senterfitt, Reuben; 1956; dem.
Shaw, C.R.; 1946; dem.
Shivers, Allan; 1950,1952,1954; dem,rep.
Simpson, J.N.; 1908; rep.
Simpson, William D.; 1918; soc.
Sisk, Wallace; 1968; rep.
Slover, Ron; 1986; dem.
Small, Clint C.; 1930,1934; dem.
Smith, John Lee; 1946; dem.
Smith, M.A.; 1926; soc.
Smith, Preston; 1968,1970,1972,1974,1978; dem.
Smith, Sherry; 1974; soc.
Sommerville, Charles L.; 1942; dem.
Stedman, T.; 1928; commun.
Steger, William M.; 1960; rep.
Sterling, Ross S.; 1930,1932; dem.
Stevenson, Coke R.; 1942,1944; dem.
Stockton, Sumpter W.; 1948; dem.
Stuart, Hamilton; 1869; none.
Talbot, William E.; 1930; rep.
Temple, Buddy; 1982; dem.
Terrell, J.O.; 1910; rep.
Thomason, Robert E.; 1920; dem.
Thompson, Clarence; 1978; rep.

Thompson, Ernest O.; 1938,1940; dem.
Throckmorton, J.W.; 1866; none.
Trayler, Allene M.; 1952; dem.
Trice, John; 1968; rep.
Turner, Reese; 1946; dem.
Veloz, Alfonso; 1968; dem.
Waggoner, D.E.; 1934; rep.
Walker, C.E.; 1930; dem.
Walker, Edwin A.; 1962; dem.
Wardlaw, Louis J.; 1928; dem.
Warner, Harry T.; 1922; dem.
Wheeler, Hope; 1942; dem.
White, Mark; 1982,1986,1990; dem.
Whiteley, Denver S.; 1948; dem.
Whittenburg, Edward L.; 1968; dem.
Whittenburg, Roy; 1962; rep.
Williams, Clayton; 1990; rep.
Williams, John C.; 1964; conser.
Williams, R.R.; 1908; dem.
Wills, Gordon R.; 1972; dem.
Wilmans, Edith E.; 1926,1928; dem.
Wilson, Will; 1962; dem.
Witt, Edgar; 1934; dem.
Wolfe, M.H.; 1932; dem.
Wood, George T.; 1847,1849,1853,1855; none.
Woods, Stanley C.; 1966; dem.
Wren, J.M.; 1950; dem.
Wright, Herman; 1948; prog.
Yarborough, Don; 1962,1964,1968; dem.
Yarborough, Ralph W.; 1952,1954,1956; dem.
Young, David L.; 1982; dem.
Young, James; 1930; dem.
Zimmerman, O.F.; 1926; dem.
Party designations: dem., Democrat; rep., Republican; btrep., Black-and-Tan Republican; amer., American; comm., Communist; con., Constitution; conser., Conservative; grbk., Greenback; inddem., Independent Democrat; indfus., Independent-Fusion; laraza, La Raza; liberty, Liberty; libetar., Libertarian; peo., Populist; prog., Progressive; proh., Prohibition; refrep., Reform Republican; reorep., Reorganized Republican; soc., Socialist; socdem., Social Democrat; soclab., Socialist-Labor.

Counties' Political Batting Averages

This article appeared in the 1992-93 Texas Almanac

By the slimmest of margins Texas remains a state where Democratic candidates running statewide can expect to win. Qualifications to the rule are needed. Democratic gubernatorial candidates have a better than even chance at elections. U.S. Senatorial candidates need to pick the right seat. But presidential candidates are another matter, since only Jimmy Carter in 1976 carried Texas for the Democrats in the past six races for the White House. He was subsequently trounced by Republican Ronald Reagan in 1980.

The Texas Almanac reviewed the results of 22 statewide elections for governor, U.S. Senate and president beginning in 1968. This year was selected because it was a watershed year between Democrat Lyndon Johnson's landslide victory in 1964 in the wake of the assassination of John F. Kennedy and Republican Richard Nixon's romp over George McGovern in 1972, when many Texas counties voted Republican for the first time since Reconstruction.

Indeed, in 1968, American Party presidential nominee George Wallace carried 21 counties, the only third-party presidential candidate to carry counties in Texas. (For rating purposes, Wallace's victories in Angelina, Bowie, Cass, Chambers, Cherokee, Crane, Glasscock, Hardin, Harrison, Jasper, Loving, Martin, Montgomery, Newton, Orange, Panola, Rusk, San Augustine, Shelby, Tyler and Upshur counties are discounted, and the county is given to the Democrats or Republicans.

Senatorial candidates fall into two distinct camps: the Houston succession and the Rusk succession (named for Sam Houston and Thomas J. Rusk, the first U.S. Senators from Texas). Republicans have held the Houston succession since 1961 when John Tower emerged from a field of 72 candidates to win the special election to fill the seat vacated by Lyndon B. Johnson's election as vice president in 1960. Tower was re-elected in 1966, 1972 and 1978, and Republican Phil Gramm won the seat in 1984, upon Towers' retirement. Republicans have won all four races for the seat since 1968. Democrats have held the Rusk succession seat since 1875, when the radical Republican James Flanigan left office.

Incumbent Lloyd Bentsen Jr. won the office in 1970 and was re-elected in 1976, 1982 and 1988, giving the Democats a split in the eight senatorial elections since 1968.

Of eight gubernatorial elections begining in 1968, Democrats have won six, including the 1990 match between Ann Richards and Republican Clayton Williams. Only William P. Clements Jr., in 1978 and 1986, has broken the Democrats' stranglehold on the governor's mansion in Texas. And both his victories — over John Hill in 1978 and incumbent Mark White in 1986 — were considered major upsets. (Clements himself was upset by White in 1982.)

Breaking each of these 22 selected statewide elections since 1968 down by county, Democrats hold a statistical lead in victories, mostly run up in the 1960s and 1970s in gubernatorial races. In 5,588 chances to win counties (22 elections times 254 counties), Democrats have won 3,265 counties for a "batting average" of .584; Republicans have hit .416 in the same period.

There are 34 counties ranked "Heavy Democratic" by virtue of supporting the Democratic candidate 19 or more times in the 22 elections. Another 130 counties are "Leaning Democratic" with Democratic victories in 13 to 18 elections. Republicans have 11 counties considered "Heavily Republican" and 55 counties "Leaning Republican." Twenty-four small counties are considered "Swing" by virtue of giving each party 10 to 12 victories.

Seven counties — Brooks, Cottle, Duval, Maverick, Starr, Zapata and Webb — voted straight Democratic in all 22 of the statewide elections surveyed. Five counties, Hutchinson, Randall, Smith, Ochiltree and Midland, voted for Republican candidates in 21 of the 22 races.

The coin is still in the air for future projections. In 1990, voter registration in the 164 counties rated either "Heavy" or "Leaning" Democratic totaled 3,720,735, while in the 66 counties with high Republican preferences registration stood at 3,863,497. In the 24 small "Swing" counties, 117,267 persons were qualified to vote.

The face of Texas politics has changed in the past 22 statewide elections for governor, U.S. Senate and president, but it is uncertain whether the swings to Republicans are permanent. Democrats still hold most county offices and control the Legislature and most state offices. The following is a breakdown of the by-county votes in each of the selected statewide elections since 1968:

Table 56:

Votes by County
Presidential, Senatorial, Gubernatorial Elections, 1968-1990

D=Democrat; R=Republican; T=Tie; NR= No Returns
'Heavy' means 19 or more victories; 'Lean' means 13-18 victories; 'Swing' indicates 10-12 Wins.

County	P68	G68	S70	G70	P72	S72	G72	G74	P76	S76	S78	G78	P80	S82	G82	P84	S84	G86	P88	S88	S90	G90	DW/RW	Rating
Anderson	D	D	D	D	R	R	D	D	D	D	D	D	R	D	D	R	R	R	R	D	R	R	13/9	Lean Dem
Andrews	R	D	D	D	R	R	D	D	R	R	R	R	R	R	R	R	R	R	R	R	R	R	5/17	Lean GOP
Angelina	D	D	D	R	D	D	D	D	D	D	D	D	D	D	R	R	R	R	R	D	R	D	16/6	Lean Dem
Aransas	D	D	D	D	R	R	D	D	D	D	R	R	R	D	R	R	R	R	R	D	R	R	10/12	Swing
Archer	D	D	D	D	R	R	D	D	D	D	D	D	R	D	D	R	R	R	R	D	R	R	15/7	Lean Dem
Armstrong	R	R	D	D	R	R	D	D	D	D	D	D	R	D	R	R	R	R	R	R	R	R	7/15	Lean GOP
Atascosa	D	D	D	D	R	R	D	D	D	D	R	D	R	D	D	R	R	R	R	D	R	R	12/10	Swing
Austin	R	D	R	D	R	R	D	D	R	D	R	R	D	D	R	R	R	R	D	R	R	R	8/14	Lean GOP
Bailey	R	D	D	D	R	R	D	D	D	D	R	R	R	R	D	R	R	R	R	D	R	R	9/13	Lean GOP
Bandera	R	D	D	D	R	R	D	D	D	D	R	R	R	R	R	R	R	R	R	R	R	R	6/16	Lean GOP
Bastrop	D	D	D	D	R	D	D	D	D	D	D	D	D	D	D	R	R	D	D	D	D	D	18/4	Lean Dem
Baylor	D	D	D	D	R	D	D	D	D	D	D	D	D	D	D	R	R	R	D	D	D	D	18/4	Lean Dem
Bee	D	D	D	D	R	R	D	D	D	D	R	D	R	D	D	R	R	D	R	D	R	D	13/9	Lean Dem
Bell	D	D	D	D	R	R	D	D	D	D	D	D	R	D	D	R	R	R	R	D	R	D	13/9	Lean Dem
Bexar	D	D	D	D	R	R	D	D	D	D	D	D	R	D	D	R	R	D	R	D	R	D	15/7	Lean Dem
Blanco	D	D	D	D	R	R	D	D	R	D	R	R	D	R	D	R	R	R	R	D	R	R	9/13	Lean GOP
Borden	D	D	D	D	R	R	D	D	D	D	D	D	R	D	D	R	R	R	R	D	R	R	10/12	Swing
Bosque	D	D	D	D	R	R	D	D	D	D	D	D	R	D	D	R	D	R	R	D	R	R	13/9	Lean Dem
Bowie	D	D	D	D	R	R	D	D	D	D	D	D	D	D	D	R	R	D	R	D	R	D	15/7	Lean Dem
Brazoria	D	D	D	D	R	D	D	D	D	D	D	D	R	D	D	R	R	R	R	D	R	R	14/8	Lean Dem
Brazos	R	D	R	R	R	R	D	D	R	R	R	D	D	D	D	R	R	R	R	D	R	R	7/15	Lean GOP
Brewster	D	D	D	D	R	R	D	D	D	D	R	D	R	D	D	R	R	R	D	R	R	R	11/11	Swing
Briscoe	D	D	D	D	R	D	D	D	D	D	D	D	D	D	R	D	R	D	D	R	D	R	17/5	Lean Dem
Brooks	D	D	D	D	D	D	D	D	D	D	D	D	D	D	D	D	D	D	D	D	D	D	22/0	Heavy Dem
Brown	D	D	D	D	R	R	D	D	D	D	D	D	D	D	D	R	R	R	R	D	R	R	13/9	Lean Dem
Burleson	D	D	D	D	R	D	D	D	D	D	D	D	D	D	D	R	D	D	D	D	R	R	19/3	Heavy Dem
Burnet	D	D	D	D	R	R	D	D	D	D	D	D	R	D	D	R	R	R	R	D	R	R	13/9	Lean Dem
Caldwell	D	D	D	D	R	D	D	D	D	D	D	D	D	D	D	R	D	D	D	D	D	D	20/2	Heavy Dem
Calhoun	D	D	D	D	R	R	D	D	D	D	D	D	R	D	D	R	R	R	D	R	D	R	16/6	Lean Dem
Callahan	D	D	D	D	R	R	D	D	D	D	D	D	D	D	D	R	R	R	R	D	R	R	13/9	Lean Dem
Cameron	D	D	D	D	R	R	D	D	D	D	D	D	D	D	D	R	D	D	D	D	R	D	18/4	Lean Dem
Camp	D	D	D	D	R	D	D	D	D	D	D	D	D	D	D	R	D	D	D	D	R	D	19/3	Heavy Dem
Carson	R	R	D	D	R	R	D	D	D	D	D	D	R	D	D	R	R	R	R	D	R	R	11/11	Swing
Cass	D	D	D	D	R	D	D	D	D	D	D	D	D	D	D	R	R	D	D	D	R	D	17/5	Lean Dem
Castro	D	D	D	D	R	D	D	D	D	D	D	D	R	D	D	R	D	R	R	D	R	R	14/8	Lean Dem
Chambers	D	D	D	D	R	D	D	D	D	D	D	D	D	D	D	R	D	R	R	D	R	R	15/7	Lean Dem
Cherokee	D	D	D	D	R	R	D	D	D	D	D	D	D	D	D	R	R	R	R	D	R	R	14/8	Lean Dem
Childress	D	D	D	D	R	R	D	D	D	D	D	D	R	D	D	R	R	R	R	D	R	D	14/8	Lean Dem
Clay	D	D	D	D	R	D	D	D	D	D	D	D	D	D	D	R	R	R	D	D	D	R	17/5	Lean Dem
Cochran	D	D	D	D	R	R	D	D	D	D	D	D	R	D	D	R	R	R	R	D	R	D	13/9	Lean Dem
Coke	D	D	D	D	R	R	D	D	D	D	D	D	D	D	D	R	R	R	R	D	R	R	14/8	Lean Dem
Coleman	R	D	D	D	R	R	D	D	D	D	R	D	R	D	D	R	R	R	R	D	R	R	11/11	Swing
Collin	R	D	D	D	R	R	R	D	R	D	R	R	R	R	R	R	R	R	R	R	R	R	4/18	Lean GOP
Collingsworth	D	D	D	D	R	R	D	D	D	D	D	D	D	D	R	D	R	R	R	D	R	D	14/8	Lean Dem
Colorado	R	D	D	D	R	R	D	D	D	D	D	D	R	D	D	R	R	R	R	D	R	R	12/10	Swing
Comal	R	D	R	R	R	R	R	D	R	D	R	R	R	R	R	R	R	R	R	R	R	R	3/19	Heavy GOP
Comanche	D	D	D	D	R	D	D	D	D	D	D	D	D	D	D	R	R	D	T	D	R	D	16/5	Lean Dem
Concho	D	D	D	D	R	R	D	D	D	D	D	D	D	D	D	R	R	D	R	D	R	R	15/7	Lean Dem
Cooke	R	D	D	D	R	R	D	D	R	R	R	R	R	D	D	R	R	R	D	R	D	R	7/15	Lean GOP
Coryell	D	D	D	D	R	R	D	D	R	D	R	R	D	R	D	R	R	D	R	D	R	R	12/10	Swing
Cottle	D	D	D	D	D	D	D	D	D	D	D	D	D	D	D	D	D	D	D	D	D	D	22/0	Heavy Dem
Crane	D	D	D	D	R	R	D	D	R	D	T	R	R	D	R	R	R	R	D	R	D	R	9/12	Swing
Crockett	D	D	D	D	R	R	D	D	D	D	R	D	R	D	D	R	R	R	R	D	R	R	11/11	Swing
Crosby	D	D	D	D	R	D	D	D	D	D	D	D	D	D	D	R	D	D	D	D	R	D	19/3	Heavy Dem
Culberson	D	D	D	D	R	D	D	D	D	D	R	R	D	D	D	R	D	D	D	D	R	R	15/7	Lean Dem
Dallam	R	R	D	D	R	R	D	D	D	D	R	R	R	D	R	R	R	R	R	R	R	R	7/15	Lean GOP
Dallas	R	R	R	R	R	R	R	D	R	R	R	R	R	R	R	R	R	R	R	R	R	R	4/18	Lean GOP
Dawson	R	D	D	D	R	R	D	D	R	D	R	R	R	D	D	R	R	R	D	R	R	R	9/13	Lean GOP
DeWitt	R	D	D	D	R	R	D	D	R	D	R	R	R	D	R	R	R	R	R	D	R	R	8/14	Lean GOP
Deaf Smith	R	R	D	D	R	R	D	D	R	R	R	R	R	R	R	R	R	R	R	D	R	R	5/17	Lean GOP
Delta	D	D	D	D	R	R	D	D	D	D	D	D	D	D	D	D	R	D	D	D	R	R	19/3	Heavy Dem
Denton	R	D	D	R	R	R	D	D	R	R	R	R	D	D	D	D	D	D	D	D	D	D	3/19	Heavy GOP
Dickens	D	D	D	D	D	R	D	D	D	D	D	D	D	D	D	D	D	D	D	D	D	D	21/1	Heavy Dem
Dimmit	D	D	D	R	D	D	D	D	D	D	D	D	D	D	D	D	D	D	D	D	D	D	21/1	Heavy Dem
Donley	R	D	D	D	R	R	D	D	D	D	D	D	D	D	D	R	R	R	R	D	R	R	12/10	Swing
Duval	D	D	D	D	D	D	D	D	D	D	D	D	D	D	D	D	D	D	D	D	D	D	22/0	Heavy Dem
Eastland	D	D	D	D	R	R	D	D	D	D	D	D	R	D	D	R	R	R	R	D	R	R	13/9	Lean Dem
Ector	R	R	R	D	R	R	R	D	R	R	R	R	R	R	R	R	R	R	R	D	R	R	2/20	Heavy GOP
Edwards	R	D	D	D	R	R	D	D	R	D	R	R	R	R	R	R	R	R	R	D	R	R	7/15	Lean GOP
El Paso	D	D	D	D	R	R	D	D	D	D	R	D	R	D	D	R	R	D	D	D	R	D	16/6	Lean Dem
Ellis	D	D	D	D	R	R	D	D	D	D	D	D	D	D	D	R	R	R	R	D	R	R	13/9	Lean Dem
Erath	D	D	D	D	R	R	D	D	D	D	D	D	D	D	D	R	R	R	R	D	R	R	14/8	Lean Dem

Table 56:

Votes by County

County	P68	G68	S70	G70	P72	S72	G72	G74	P76	S76	S78	G78	P80	S82	G82	P84	S84	G86	P88	S88	S90	G90	DW/RW	Rating
Falls	D	D	D	D	R	D	D	D	D	D	D	D	D	D	D	R	D	R	D	D	D	D	19/3	Heavy Dem
Fannin	D	D	D	D	R	D	D	D	D	D	D	D	D	D	D	R	D	R	D	D	D	D	19/3	Heavy Dem
Fayette	R	D	D	D	R	R	D	D	D	D	D	D	R	D	D	R	R	R	R	D	R	R	12/10	Swing
Fisher	D	D	D	D	R	D	D	D	D	D	D	D	D	D	D	D	D	D	D	D	D	D	21/1	Heavy Dem
Floyd	R	D	D	D	R	R	D	D	D	D	D	D	R	D	D	R	R	R	R	D	R	R	12/10	Swing
Foard	D	D	D	D	R	D	D	D	D	D	D	D	D	D	D	D	D	D	D	D	D	D	20/2	Heavy Dem
Fort Bend	R	D	D	D	R	R	R	D	R	D	R	R	D	R	D	R	R	R	R	D	R	R	7/15	Lean GOP
Franklin	D	D	D	D	R	D	D	D	D	D	D	D	D	D	D	R	R	R	D	D	R	R	16/6	Lean Dem
Freestone	D	D	D	D	R	D	D	D	D	D	D	D	D	D	D	R	R	R	D	D	R	R	14/8	Lean Dem
Frio	D	D	D	D	R	D	D	D	D	D	D	D	D	D	D	D	D	D	D	D	D	D	21/1	Heavy Dem
Gaines	R	D	D	D	R	R	D	D	D	D	D	R	R	D	R	R	R	R	D	R	R	R	11/11	Swing
Galveston	D	D	D	D	R	D	D	D	D	D	D	D	D	D	D	R	D	D	D	D	R	R	19/3	Heavy Dem
Garza	D	D	D	D	R	R	D	D	D	D	D	D	R	D	D	R	R	R	R	D	R	R	13/9	Lean Dem
Gillespie	R	R	R	R	R	R	D	R	D	R	R	R	R	R	R	R	R	R	R	D	R	R	2/20	Heavy GOP
Glasscock	R	D	D	D	R	D	D	D	R	D	R	R	R	R	R	R	R	R	D	R	R	R	7/15	Lean GOP
Goliad	R	D	D	D	R	D	D	D	D	R	R	D	R	D	R	R	R	R	D	R	R	R	10/12	Swing
Gonzales	D	D	D	D	R	R	D	D	D	D	D	D	R	D	R	R	R	R	D	R	R	R	13/9	Lean Dem
Gray	R	R	R	R	R	R	R	D	R	D	R	R	R	R	R	R	R	R	R	R	R	R	2/20	Heavy GOP
Grayson	D	D	D	D	R	D	D	D	D	D	D	D	R	D	D	R	D	R	D	R	R	D	15/7	Lean Dem
Gregg	R	D	R	R	R	R	D	D	R	R	R	R	R	R	R	R	R	R	D	R	R	R	4/18	Lean GOP
Grimes	D	D	D	D	R	D	D	D	D	D	D	D	D	D	D	R	D	R	D	R	R	R	15/7	Lean Dem
Guadalupe	R	D	D	D	R	R	D	D	R	D	R	R	R	D	R	R	R	R	D	R	R	R	8/14	Lean GOP
Hale	R	D	D	D	R	R	D	D	D	D	R	R	R	D	R	R	R	R	D	R	R	R	9/13	Lean GOP
Hall	D	D	D	D	R	D	D	D	D	D	D	D	R	D	D	R	D	D	D	D	D	D	18/4	Lean Dem
Hamilton	R	D	D	D	R	R	D	D	D	D	D	D	R	D	D	R	D	R	D	R	R	R	12/10	Swing
Hansford	R	R	R	R	R	R	R	D	R	D	R	R	R	R	R	R	R	R	R	R	R	R	2/20	Heavy GOP
Hardeman	D	D	D	D	R	R	R	D	D	D	D	D	D	D	R	D	R	D	D	D	D	D	16/6	Lean Dem
Hardin	D	D	D	D	R	D	D	D	D	D	D	D	D	D	D	R	R	R	D	D	R	R	18/4	Lean Dem
Harris	R	R	R	R	R	R	R	D	R	D	R	R	R	D	R	R	R	D	R	D	R	D	7/15	Lean GOP
Harrison	D	D	D	D	R	R	D	D	D	D	R	D	R	D	R	R	D	R	D	R	R	D	14/8	Lean Dem
Hartley	R	R	D	D	R	R	D	D	R	D	R	R	R	R	R	R	R	R	R	R	R	R	4/18	Lean GOP
Haskell	D	D	D	D	R	D	D	D	D	D	D	D	D	D	D	R	R	R	D	R	R	D	17/5	Lean Dem
Hays	D	D	D	D	R	D	D	D	D	D	D	D	R	D	D	R	R	R	D	R	R	D	15/7	Lean Dem
Hemphill	R	R	D	D	R	R	D	D	R	D	R	R	R	D	R	R	R	R	R	R	R	R	4/18	Lean GOP
Henderson	D	D	D	D	R	R	D	D	D	D	D	D	D	D	D	R	D	R	D	R	R	D	15/7	Lean Dem
Hidalgo	D	D	D	D	R	R	D	D	D	D	D	D	D	D	D	D	D	D	D	D	R	D	19/3	Heavy Dem
Hill	D	D	D	D	R	D	D	D	D	D	D	D	D	D	D	R	R	R	D	D	R	R	15/7	Lean Dem
Hockley	D	D	D	D	R	R	D	D	D	D	D	D	R	D	D	R	R	R	D	R	R	R	13/9	Lean Dem
Hood	D	D	D	D	R	D	D	D	D	D	D	D	R	D	D	R	R	R	D	R	R	R	14/8	Lean Dem
Hopkins	D	D	D	D	R	D	D	D	D	D	D	D	D	D	D	R	R	R	D	R	R	D	16/6	Lean Dem
Houston	D	D	D	D	R	D	D	D	D	D	D	D	D	D	D	R	R	R	D	R	R	D	16/6	Lean Dem
Howard	D	D	D	D	R	D	D	D	D	D	R	R	R	D	R	R	R	R	D	R	R	R	11/11	Swing
Hudspeth	D	D	D	D	R	R	D	D	D	D	D	D	R	D	D	R	R	R	D	R	R	R	12/10	Swing
Hunt	D	D	D	D	R	R	D	D	D	D	D	D	R	D	D	R	R	R	D	R	R	R	13/9	Lean Dem
Hutchinson	R	R	R	R	R	R	R	D	R	R	R	R	R	R	R	R	R	R	R	R	R	R	1/21	Heavy GOP
Irion	R	R	D	D	R	R	D	D	D	D	R	D	R	R	D	R	R	R	R	D	R	R	9/13	Lean GOP
Jack	D	D	D	D	R	D	D	D	D	D	D	D	R	D	D	R	R	R	D	R	R	R	13/9	Lean Dem
Jackson	D	D	D	D	R	R	D	D	D	D	D	D	R	D	D	R	R	R	D	R	R	R	13/9	Lean Dem
Jasper	D	D	D	D	R	D	D	D	D	D	D	D	D	D	D	R	D	R	D	R	R	D	18/4	Lean Dem
Jeff Davis	D	D	D	D	R	D	D	D	D	R	R	D	R	D	R	R	R	R	D	R	R	R	10/12	Swing
Jefferson	D	R	D	D	R	D	D	D	D	D	D	D	D	D	D	D	D	D	D	R	R	D	18/4	Lean Dem
Jim Hogg	D	D	D	D	D	R	D	D	D	D	D	D	D	D	D	D	D	D	D	D	D	D	21/1	Heavy Dem
Jim Wells	D	D	D	D	R	D	D	D	D	D	D	D	D	D	D	D	D	D	D	D	D	D	21/1	Heavy Dem
Johnson	D	D	D	D	R	R	D	D	D	D	D	D	R	D	D	R	R	R	D	R	R	D	13/9	Lean Dem
Jones	D	D	D	D	R	D	D	D	D	D	D	D	D	D	D	R	R	R	D	R	R	R	14/8	Lean Dem
Karnes	D	D	D	D	R	D	D	D	D	D	D	R	D	D	R	R	R	R	D	R	R	D	14/8	Lean Dem
Kaufman	D	D	D	D	R	D	D	D	D	D	D	D	D	D	D	R	R	R	D	R	D	D	16/6	Lean Dem
Kendall	R	R	R	R	R	R	D	D	R	D	R	R	R	R	R	R	R	R	R	R	R	R	2/20	Heavy GOP
Kenedy	D	D	D	D	R	D	D	D	D	D	D	R	D	D	D	D	D	D	D	R	R	D	19/3	Heavy Dem
Kent	D	D	D	D	R	D	D	D	D	D	D	D	D	D	D	R	R	D	R	D	R	R	16/6	Lean Dem
Kerr	R	D	R	R	R	R	D	D	R	R	R	R	R	R	R	R	R	R	R	R	R	R	3/19	Heavy GOP
Kimble	R	D	D	D	R	R	D	D	R	D	R	R	R	R	R	R	R	R	D	R	R	R	8/14	Lean GOP
King	D	D	D	D	R	D	D	D	D	D	R	R	R	D	R	R	R	R	D	R	R	R	11/11	Swing
Kinney	D	D	D	D	R	D	NR	D	D	D	R	R	R	D	D	R	R	R	R	D	R	R	11/10	Swing
Kleberg	D	D	D	D	R	D	D	D	D	D	D	D	D	D	D	R	R	D	D	D	R	D	18/4	Lean Dem
Knox	D	D	D	D	R	D	D	D	D	D	D	D	D	D	D	R	D	R	D	D	D	D	19/3	Heavy Dem
La Salle	D	D	D	D	R	D	D	D	D	D	D	D	D	R	D	D	D	D	D	R	R	D	20/2	Heavy Dem
Lamar	D	D	D	D	R	D	D	D	D	D	D	D	D	D	D	R	R	R	D	R	R	D	15/7	Lean Dem
Lamb	R	D	D	D	R	R	D	D	D	D	R	D	R	D	D	R	R	R	D	R	D	R	11/11	Swing
Lampasas	D	D	D	D	R	D	D	D	R	R	R	R	D	R	D	R	R	R	D	R	D	R	10/12	Swing
Lavaca	D	D	D	D	R	D	D	D	D	D	D	R	D	D	R	R	R	D	R	D	R	R	14/8	Lean Dem
Lee	D	D	D	D	R	D	D	D	D	D	D	D	R	D	D	R	R	R	D	R	R	R	14/8	Lean Dem
Leon	D	D	D	D	R	D	D	D	D	D	D	D	D	D	D	R	R	R	D	R	R	R	15/7	Lean Dem
Liberty	D	D	D	D	R	D	D	D	D	D	D	D	D	D	D	R	R	R	D	R	R	R	15/7	Lean Dem
Limestone	D	D	D	D	R	D	D	D	D	D	D	D	D	D	D	R	R	D	D	R	D		17/5	Lean Dem
Lipscomb	R	R	R	R	R	R	R	D	R	D	R	R	R	R	R	R	R	R	R	R	R	R	2/20	Heavy GOP

Table 56:

County	P68	G68	S70	G70	P72	S72	G72	G74	P76	S76	S78	G78	G80	P80	S82	G82	P84	S84	G86	P88	S88	S90	G90	DW/RW	Rating
Live Oak	R	D	D	D	R	R	D	D	D	D	R	R	R	D	R	R	R	R	R	D	R	R	R	9/13	Lean GOP
Llano	D	D	D	D	R	R	D	D	D	D	D	R	R	D	D	R	R	R	R	D	R	R	R	12/10	Swing
Loving	R	D	D	D	R	R	D	D	R	D	R	R	R	R	R	R	R	R	R	R	D	R	R	7/15	Lean GOP
Lubbock	R	D	D	R	R	R	R	R	R	D	R	D	R	R	R	R	R	R	R	R	D	R	R	3/19	Heavy GOP
Lynn	D	D	D	D	R	R	D	D	D	D	D	D	R	D	D	R	R	R	R	D	R	R	R	13/9	Lean Dem
Madison	D	D	D	D	R	R	D	D	D	D	D	D	D	D	D	R	D	D	R	D	R	R	R	15/7	Lean Dem
Marion	D	D	D	D	R	R	D	D	D	D	D	D	D	D	D	R	D	D	D	D	R	D	D	18/4	Lean Dem
Martin	D	D	D	D	R	R	D	D	D	D	R	R	R	D	D	R	R	R	R	D	R	R	R	11/11	Swing
Mason	R	D	D	D	R	R	D	D	D	D	R	R	R	R	R	R	R	R	R	D	R	R	R	8/14	Lean GOP
Matagorda	D	D	D	D	R	D	D	D	D	D	D	D	R	D	D	R	R	R	R	D	R	R	R	14/8	Lean Dem
Maverick	D	D	D	D	D	D	D	D	D	D	D	D	D	D	D	D	D	D	D	D	D	D	D	22/0	Heavy Dem
McCulloch	D	D	D	D	R	R	D	D	D	D	D	D	D	D	D	R	R	R	R	D	R	R	R	14/8	Lean Dem
McLennan	D	D	D	D	R	R	D	D	D	D	D	D	R	D	D	R	R	R	R	D	R	D	R	14/8	Lean Dem
McMullen	R	D	D	D	R	R	D	D	R	D	R	R	R	R	R	R	R	R	R	R	R	R	R	6/16	Lean GOP
Medina	D	D	D	D	R	R	D	D	D	D	R	R	R	D	D	R	R	R	R	D	R	R	R	11/11	Swing
Menard	R	D	D	D	R	R	D	D	D	D	D	R	R	D	D	R	R	R	R	D	R	R	R	12/10	Swing
Midland	R	R	R	R	R	R	R	R	R	R	R	R	R	R	R	R	R	R	R	R	R	R	R	1/21	Heavy GOP
Milam	D	D	D	D	R	D	D	D	D	D	D	D	D	D	D	D	R	D	D	D	D	D	D	20/2	Heavy Dem
Mills	D	D	D	D	R	R	D	D	D	D	D	D	D	D	D	R	R	R	R	D	R	R	R	14/8	Lean Dem
Mitchell	D	D	D	D	R	R	D	D	D	D	D	D	R	D	D	R	R	R	R	D	D	R	D	15/7	Lean Dem
Montague	D	D	D	D	R	R	D	D	D	D	D	D	D	D	D	R	R	R	R	D	D	R	D	16/6	Lean Dem
Montgomery	R	D	D	R	D	R	R	D	R	D	R	R	R	R	R	R	R	R	R	R	R	R	R	5/17	Lean GOP
Moore	R	R	D	D	R	R	R	R	D	D	R	R	R	R	R	R	R	R	R	R	R	R	R	5/17	Lean GOP
Morris	D	D	D	D	R	R	D	D	D	D	D	D	D	D	D	D	D	D	D	D	D	D	D	20/2	Heavy Dem
Motley	R	D	D	D	R	R	D	D	D	D	R	R	R	D	D	R	R	R	R	D	R	R	R	9/13	Lean GOP
Nacogdoches	D	D	D	D	R	R	D	D	R	D	D	D	R	D	D	R	R	R	R	D	R	R	R	12/10	Swing
Navarro	D	D	D	D	R	R	D	D	D	D	D	D	D	D	D	R	D	D	R	D	D	R	D	18/4	Lean Dem
Newton	D	D	D	D	R	D	D	D	D	D	D	D	D	D	D	D	D	D	D	D	D	D	D	21/1	Heavy Dem
Nolan	D	D	D	D	R	R	D	D	D	D	R	D	D	D	D	R	R	R	R	D	R	R	D	15/7	Lean Dem
Nueces	D	D	D	D	R	R	D	D	D	D	D	D	D	D	R	D	R	D	D	R	D	R	D	17/5	Lean Dem
Ochiltree	R	R	R	R	R	R	R	R	R	D	R	R	R	R	R	R	R	R	R	R	R	R	R	1/21	Heavy GOP
Oldham	R	R	D	D	D	D	D	D	D	D	D	R	R	D	D	R	R	R	D	D	R	R	D	11/11	Swing
Orange	D	D	D	D	R	D	D	D	D	D	D	D	D	D	D	D	D	D	D	D	D	R	D	20/2	Heavy Dem
Palo Pinto	D	D	D	D	R	R	D	D	D	D	D	D	D	D	D	R	R	R	R	D	R	R	D	15/7	Lean Dem
Panola	D	D	D	D	R	R	D	D	D	D	D	D	D	D	D	R	R	R	D	R	D	R	R	14/8	Lean Dem
Parker	D	D	D	D	R	R	D	D	D	D	D	D	R	D	D	R	R	R	R	D	R	R	D	13/9	Lean Dem
Parmer	R	D	D	D	R	R	D	D	D	D	R	R	R	R	R	R	R	R	R	R	R	R	R	7/15	Lean GOP
Pecos	D	D	D	D	R	R	D	D	R	D	D	D	R	D	D	R	R	R	R	D	R	D	D	11/11	Swing
Polk	D	D	D	D	R	D	D	D	D	D	D	D	D	D	D	R	R	R	D	D	R	D	R	17/5	Lean Dem
Potter	R	R	R	R	R	R	R	R	D	R	D	R	R	R	R	R	R	R	R	R	R	R	R	3/19	Heavy GOP
Presidio	D	D	D	D	R	D	D	D	D	D	D	D	D	D	D	D	D	D	D	D	R	D	R	21/1	Heavy Dem
Rains	D	D	D	D	R	D	D	D	D	D	D	D	D	D	D	R	R	R	R	D	D	R	D	17/5	Lean Dem
Randall	R	R	R	R	R	R	R	R	R	D	R	R	R	R	R	R	R	R	R	R	R	R	R	1/21	Heavy GOP
Reagan	R	D	D	D	R	R	D	D	D	D	R	R	R	D	D	R	R	R	R	D	R	R	R	10/12	Swing
Real	R	D	D	D	R	R	D	D	D	D	R	R	R	D	D	R	R	R	R	D	R	R	R	11/11	Swing
Red River	D	D	D	D	R	D	D	D	D	D	D	D	D	D	D	D	R	D	D	D	D	R	D	19/3	Heavy Dem
Reeves	R	D	D	D	R	R	D	D	D	D	R	R	D	D	D	R	D	D	D	D	R	R	R	15/7	Lean Dem
Refugio	D	D	D	D	R	D	D	D	D	D	D	D	D	D	D	R	R	R	R	D	D	R	D	16/6	Lean Dem
Roberts	R	R	R	R	R	R	D	D	R	R	R	R	R	R	R	R	R	R	R	R	R	R	R	3/19	Heavy GOP
Robertson	D	D	D	D	R	D	D	D	D	D	D	D	D	D	D	D	D	D	R	R	R	D	D	21/1	Heavy Dem
Rockwall	D	D	D	D	R	R	D	D	R	R	R	R	D	D	D	R	R	R	D	D	R	R	R	6/16	Lean GOP
Runnels	R	D	D	D	R	R	D	D	D	D	R	D	D	D	R	R	R	R	R	D	R	R	R	10/12	Swing
Rusk	D	D	D	D	R	R	D	D	R	D	R	D	D	D	D	R	R	R	D	R	R	R	D	9/13	Lean GOP
Sabine	D	D	D	D	R	D	D	D	D	D	D	D	D	D	D	R	D	R	D	D	R	D	D	18/4	Lean Dem
San Augustine	D	D	D	D	R	R	D	D	D	D	D	D	D	D	D	R	D	D	D	D	R	D	R	18/4	Lean Dem
San Jacinto	D	D	D	D	R	D	D	D	D	D	D	D	D	D	D	R	R	R	D	D	R	D	R	16/6	Lean Dem
San Patricio	D	D	D	D	R	D	D	D	D	D	R	D	D	D	D	R	D	D	R	D	R	D	R	16/6	Lean Dem
San Saba	D	D	D	D	R	R	D	D	D	D	D	D	D	D	D	R	R	R	D	D	R	R	R	15/7	Lean Dem
Schleicher	R	D	D	D	R	R	D	D	D	R	D	R	R	R	D	R	R	R	R	D	R	R	R	10/12	Swing
Scurry	D	D	D	D	R	R	D	D	R	D	R	R	R	D	R	R	R	R	R	D	R	R	R	9/13	Lean GOP
Shackelford	D	D	D	D	R	R	D	D	D	D	D	R	R	D	R	R	R	R	R	D	R	R	R	13/9	Lean Dem
Shelby	D	D	D	D	R	R	D	D	D	D	D	D	D	D	D	R	R	R	D	D	R	D	R	17/5	Lean Dem
Sherman	R	R	R	R	R	R	D	D	D	D	R	R	R	R	R	R	R	R	R	R	R	R	R	4/18	Lean GOP
Smith	R	R	R	R	R	R	R	R	R	R	R	R	R	R	R	R	R	R	R	D	R	R	R	1/21	Heavy GOP
Somervell	D	D	D	D	R	D	D	D	D	D	D	D	D	D	D	R	R	R	R	D	R	R	R	15/7	Lean Dem
Starr	D	D	D	D	D	D	D	D	D	D	D	D	D	D	D	D	D	D	D	D	D	D	D	22/0	Heavy Dem
Stephens	R	D	D	D	R	R	D	D	D	D	R	R	R	D	D	R	R	R	R	D	R	R	R	10/12	Swing
Sterling	R	D	D	D	R	R	D	D	R	D	D	R	R	D	R	R	R	R	R	D	R	R	R	9/13	Lean GOP
Stonewall	D	D	D	D	R	D	D	D	D	D	D	D	D	D	D	D	R	R	D	D	D	D	D	20/2	Heavy Dem
Sutton	R	D	D	D	R	R	D	D	R	D	R	R	D	R	R	R	R	R	R	D	D	D	D	8/14	Lean GOP
Swisher	D	D	D	D	R	D	D	D	D	D	D	D	D	D	D	D	R	D	D	D	D	D	D	21/1	Heavy Dem
Tarrant	R	D	D	D	R	R	D	R	D	R	D	R	R	D	R	R	R	R	R	D	R	R	R	8/14	Lean GOP
Taylor	R	D	D	D	R	R	R	D	R	R	D	R	R	D	R	R	R	R	R	D	R	R	R	7/15	Lean GOP
Terrell	R	D	D	R	D	R	R	D	D	D	R	D	D	D	R	R	R	R	R	D	R	R	D	12/10	Swing
Terry	R	D	D	D	R	R	D	D	D	D	D	R	D	D	R	R	R	R	R	D	R	R	D	12/10	Swing
Throckmorton	D	D	D	D	R	D	D	D	D	D	D	D	D	D	D	D	R	R	R	D	R	D	D	17/5	Lean Dem

Table 56:

County	P68	G68	S70	G70	P72	S72	G72	G74	P76	S76	S78	G78	P80	S82	G82	P84	S84	G86	P88	S88	S90	G90	DW/RW	Rating
Titus	D	D	D	D	R	D	D	D	D	D	D	D	D	D	D	R	R	D	D	D	R	D	18/4	Lean Dem
Tom Green	R	D	D	D	R	R	D	D	R	D	D	R	R	D	R	R	R	R	R	D	R	R	9/13	Lean GOP
Travis	D	D	R	D	R	R	D	D	D	D	D	D	D	D	D	R	D	R	D	D	R	D	18/4	Lean Dem
Trinity	D	D	D	D	R	D	D	D	D	D	D	D	D	D	D	R	D	R	D	D	R	D	18/4	Lean Dem
Tyler	D	D	D	D	R	D	D	D	D	D	D	D	D	D	D	R	D	R	D	D	R	D	18/4	Lean Dem
Upshur	D	D	D	D	R	D	D	D	D	D	D	D	D	D	D	R	R	R	R	D	R	D	15/7	Lean Dem
Upton	R	D	D	D	R	R	R	D	R	D	R	R	R	D	D	R	R	R	R	D	R	R	8/14	Lean GOP
Uvalde	R	D	D	D	R	R	D	D	R	D	R	R	R	D	D	R	R	R	R	D	R	D	9/13	Lean GOP
Val Verde	D	D	D	D	R	R	D	D	D	D	D	D	D	D	D	R	R	R	R	D	R	D	15/7	Lean Dem
Van Zandt	D	D	D	D	R	R	D	D	D	D	D	D	D	D	D	R	R	R	R	D	R	R	14/8	Lean Dem
Victoria	R	D	D	D	R	R	D	D	R	R	R	R	R	R	R	R	R	R	R	D	R	R	6/16	Lean GOP
Walker	D	D	D	D	R	D	D	D	D	D	D	D	R	D	D	R	R	R	R	D	R	D	15/7	Lean Dem
Waller	D	D	D	D	R	D	D	D	D	D	D	D	D	D	D	R	D	R	D	D	R	D	18/4	Lean Dem
Ward	R	D	D	D	R	D	D	D	R	D	R	R	R	D	D	R	R	R	R	D	R	R	9/13	Lean GOP
Washington	R	D	R	D	R	R	R	D	R	D	R	R	R	D	D	R	R	R	R	D	R	R	7/15	Lean GOP
Webb	D	D	D	D	D	D	D	D	D	D	D	D	D	D	D	D	D	D	D	D	D	D	22/0	Heavy Dem
Whaton	D	D	D	D	R	D	D	D	D	D	D	D	R	D	D	R	R	R	R	D	R	D	14/8	Lean Dem
Wheeler	R	R	D	D	R	R	D	D	D	D	D	D	R	D	D	R	R	R	R	D	R	R	11/11	Swing
Wichita	D	R	D	D	R	R	D	D	D	D	R	D	R	D	D	R	R	R	R	D	R	D	12/10	Swing
Wilbarger	D	D	D	D	R	R	D	D	D	D	D	D	R	D	D	R	R	R	R	D	R	D	14/8	Lean Dem
Willacy	D	D	D	D	R	R	D	D	D	D	D	D	D	D	D	D	D	D	D	D	D	D	20/2	Heavy Dem
Williamson	D	D	D	D	R	R	D	D	D	D	R	D	R	D	D	R	R	R	R	D	R	D	13/9	Lean Dem
Wilson	D	D	D	D	R	D	D	D	D	D	D	D	R	D	D	R	R	R	R	D	R	R	14/8	Lean Dem
Winkler	R	D	D	D	R	R	R	D	R	D	D	R	R	D	D	R	R	R	R	D	R	R	9/13	Lean GOP
Wise	D	D	D	D	R	R	D	D	D	D	D	D	D	D	D	R	R	R	R	D	R	D	15/7	Lean Dem
Wood	D	D	D	D	R	R	D	D	D	D	D	D	R	D	D	R	R	R	R	D	R	R	13/9	Lean Dem
Yoakum	R	D	D	D	R	R	D	D	R	D	R	D	R	D	D	R	R	R	R	D	R	R	7/15	Lean GOP
Young	D	D	D	D	R	R	D	D	D	D	D	D	R	D	D	R	R	R	R	D	R	R	13/9	Lean Dem
Zapata	D	D	D	D	D	D	D	D	D	D	D	D	D	D	D	D	D	D	D	D	D	D	22/0	Heavy Dem
Zavala	D	D	D	D	D	D	D	D	D	D	D	D	D	D	D	D	D	D	D	D	D	D	21/1	Heavy Dem

Summary: Heavy Dem: 34; Lean Dem: 130; Swing: 24; Heavy GOP: 11; Lean GOP: 55

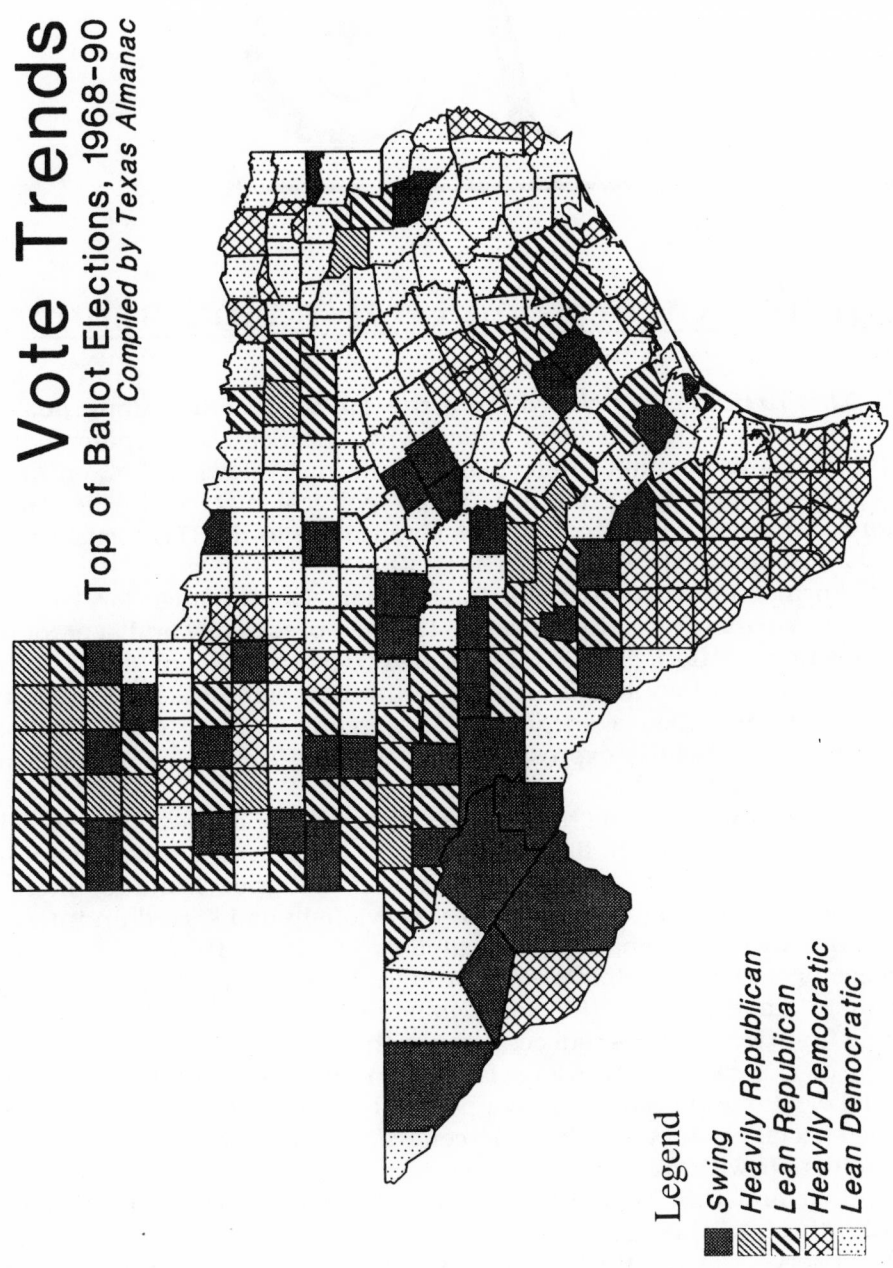

Vote Trends

Top of Ballot Elections, 1968–90
Compiled by Texas Almanac

Legend

- Swing
- Heavily Republican
- Lean Republican
- Heavily Democratic
- Lean Democratic

John Tower: The GOP's Godfather

This article is reprinted from the 1992-93 Texas Almanac.

A Texas political legend ended when former U.S. Senator John Goodwin Tower died in a tragic plane crash in Brunswick, Ga., on April 5, 1991. For practical purposes, Texas' political history can be dated before and after the diminutive Texan's election to the U.S. Senate in a special election in the spring of 1961.

Former President Lyndon B. Johnson set the stage for Tower's election by running for two offices — the vice-presidency and senator — in the same election. A political unknown, Tower was considered nothing more than a Republican irritant to the Democratic Senate majority leader. But he polled a surprising 41 percent of the general election vote, as many Texans expressed their displeasure at Johnson's dual appearance on the ballot.

The following spring, more than 70 candidates crowded the ballot for the special election to fill Johnson's seat. The favorite was William A. Blakley, a millionaire businessman and Gov. Price Daniel's interim appointee to the senate seat. (Blakley previously had served an interim appointment to the senate seat vacated by Daniel in 1957 before losing a special election to Ralph W. Yarborough. However, Blakley is the only Texan to serve in both the Sam Houston and Thomas J. Rusk, the state's first two senators, successions in the Senate.)

Tower's race the previous fall gave him name recognition in the special election and put in place a political organization. He led the field in the special election with 30.9 percent of the vote and defeated Blakley in the runoff with 50.6 percent of the vote. The election gave Republicans their first U.S. Senate seat from Texas since 1875, and sent after shocks through the ranks of the firmly entrenched Democratic party. Most observers at the time thought Tower's election was an aberration and that he would never be re-elected.

The election invigorated Texas Republicans. For most of the 20th century, Republicans were more a party of patronage than a legitimate political force in Texas. The action was within the ranks of Democratic party where conservatives battled liberals, and the Democratic nomination was tantamount to election.

Dissatisfaction with Democratic President John F. Kennedy allowed the state Republican to score victories in special elections for legislative seats in 1963, and the party appeared to be on a roll. After President Kennedy's assassination in Dallas, however, the party's fortunes tumbled. Usually conservative Texas gave Lyndon Johnson a resounding landslide in the 1964 presidential election over conservative Republican U. S. Sen. Barry Goldwater of Arizona and in the process wiped out the GOP's hard-earned gains across the state.

Only John Tower remained as the highly visible patron saint of the party, a lone rallying point. He spoke at fund-raisers across the state and in Washington developed a reputation as a solid, articulate conservative voice in the liberal atmosphere of that day in Washington. At five feet five inches tall, Tower was hardly a stereotypical rangy Texan, but he used his size to his advantage. "I'm John Tower, but I don't," he opened many after-dinner talks to the laughter of diners — and contributors. Tower, a powerful speaker whose voice would have done justice to any pulpit, was a popular orator.

Waggoner Carr, a popular conservative Democrat and former speaker of the Texas House of Representatives, challenged Tower in the 1966 general election and lost when internal strife racked the Democratic party. Barefoot Sanders, a moderate and now a federal judge in Dallas, did little better in 1970, and current Railroad Commissioner and former U.S. representative Robert Krueger ran a close campaign in 1976, only to be nipped at the wire by the now-seasoned Sen. Tower.

Though a political unknown in 1960, Tower was well prepared for office. The son and grandson of Methodist ministers, he was born in Houston on Sept. 29, 1925, and graduated from high school in Beaumont in 1942. After serving on a U.S. Navy gunboat in the Pacific in World War II, Tower took a B.A. in political science at Southwestern University in Georgetown in 1948. He worked as a radio announcer in Taylor and Beaumont and as an insurance agent in Dallas before joining the faculty as an associate professor of political science at Midwestern University in Wichita Falls in 1951.

One irony of Tower's career was his attendance at the prestigious London School of Economic and Political Science, an anathema to conservatives at the time. Tower later earned a master's degree in political science at Southern Methodist University in Dallas before returning to teach at Midwestern.

In 1956, Tower attended his first national political convention, traveling to San Francisco for the renomination of President Dwight D. Eisenhower. At home, he was a member of the 23rd Senatorial District executive committee and served as chairman of the state education and research committee.

Tower did his homework in the Senate, becoming an authority in national defense and the military. Under his guidance, defense spending rose to $211 billion a year. He was credited with bringing many lucrative defense contracts to Texas. When Republicans gained the majority in the Senate in 1981, Tower became chairman of the powerful Armed Services Committee. As important, he put together a highly competent staff to deal with his constituents' relations with the federal government, which earned him many friends among the grass-roots of the state's voters.

He also was an active fund-raiser for the party and chaired the Republican Senate Campaign Committee to elect more GOP faithful to the upper house.

As surprising as his election 23 years earlier was Tower's decision not to seek re-election in 1984, after holding some fund-raisers for his anticipated campaign. In his retirement, the former senator became a high-paid defense consultant.

The following year, President Ronald Reagan named Tower to the post of strategic arms negotiator with the Soviet Union. In 1986, Reagan appointed Tower to chair a three-member bipartisan committee to investigate the infamous Iran-contra scandal.

Ironically, it was his experience in defense that opponents used against him when President George Bush tried to appoint Tower Secretary of Defense in 1989. Critics claimed the former senator was too close to defense contractors to perform the duties of the office properly. In one of the few personal setbacks of his political career, Tower's appointment was rejected by the same Senate in which he served for more than two decades. It was the first rejection of a cabinet nominee in more than 30 years.

In a book published just before his death, *Consequences: A Personal and Political Memoir*, Tower lashed out at many who contributed to defeat of his nomination.

Tower's personal life was turbulent, including two publicized divorces. He had three daughters by his first wife, Lou, including Marian, who died with her father in the plane crash that ended his life.

At the time of Tower's death, Republicans held 10 of 27 Texas seats in the U.S. House and more than 60 seats in the Texas Legislature. Republicans also hold many local government positions, an unheard-of circumstance before Tower opened the door and led the way for development of the two-party system in the state. Despite his quips about his height, in Texas political history, John Tower indeed did — tower.

Bibliography

Barr, Alwyn, **Black Texans: A History of Negroes in Texas, 1528-1971;** Jenkins Publishing Company, Austin, 1973.

Barr, Alwyn, **Reconstruction to Reform: Texas Politics, 1876-1906;** University of Texas Press, 1971.

Brown, Norman D., **Hood, Bonnet, and Little Brown Jug: Texas Politics, 1921-1928;** Texas A&M University Press, College Station, 1984.

Crawford, Ann Fears, and Crystal Sasse Ragsdale, **Women in Texas: Their Lives, Their Experiences, Their Accomplishments;** Eakin Press, Burnet, 1982.

Davidson, Chandler, **Race and Class in Texas Politics**; Princeton University Press, Princeton, N.J., 1990.

Driskill, Frank, **Free the North Wind**; Eakin Press, Burnet, 1980.

Encyclopedia Americana, International Edition, Vol. 17; Grolier, Inc., Danbury Conn., 1990.

Final Report, Texas 1986 Sesquicentennial Commission, March 31, 1987.

Gould, Lewis L., **Progressives and Prohibitionists: Texas Democrats in the Wilson Era;** University of Texas Press, Austin, 1973.

Handbook of Texas, Vols. II & III, Walter Prescott Webb, ed.-in-chief; The Texas State Historical Association, Austin, 1952.

Hare, Maud Cuney, **Norris Wright Cuney, A Tribune of the Black People**; Originally published by The Crisis Publishing Company, New York City, 1913; Facsimile Reproduction by Steck-Vaughn Company, Austin, 1968.

Heard, Robert, **The Miracle of the Killer Bees**; Honey Hill Publishing Company, Austin, 1981.

Hine, Darlene Clark, **Black Victory, The Rise and Fall of the White Primary in Texas;** KTO Press, Millwood, NY, 1979.

Knaggs, John R., **Two-Party Texas: The John Tower Era, 1961-1984;** Eakin Press, Austin, 1986.

Laws of Texas, The, 1822-1897, Vols. I & II, compiled by H. P. N. Gammel; The Gammel Book Company, Austin, 1898.

McCallum, Jane Y., **"Activities of Women in Texas Politics," Texas Democracy,** Frank Carter Adams, ed.; Democratic Historical Association, Austin, 1937.

Olien, Roger M., **From Token to Triumph: The Texas Republicans Since 1920;** SMU Press, Dallas, 1982.

Rogers, Mary Beth, Sherry A. Smith and Janelle D. Scott, **We Can Fly: Stories of Katherine Stinson and Other Gutsy Texas Women;** Ellen C. Temple, Publisher, with the Texas Foundation for Women's Resources, Austin, 1983.

"Shall Women Vote: Expressions by Texas Statesmen on the Long Mooted Question Lately Revived"; *The Dallas Morning News,* March 20, 1894.

Taylor, A. Elizabeth, **Citizens at Last: The Woman Suffrage Movement in Texas;** Ellen C. Temple, Austin, 1987.

Texas Democracy, Frank Carter Adams, ed.;Democratic Historical Association, Austin, 1937.

Texas Through Time: Evolving Interpretations, Walter L. Buenger and Robert A. Calvert, eds.; Texas A&M University Press, College Station, 1991.

Texas Women: Finder's Guide to the Texas Women, A Celebration of History Exhibit Archives, Ruthe Winegarten, ed.; Texas Woman's University Library, Denton, 1984.

The World of Texas Politics, George Christian, ed.; Lyndon B. Johnson Library, The University of Texas, Austin, 1989.

Tower, John, **Consequences;** Little, Brown and Company, Limited, Boston, 1991.

Notes to Election Tables

The county-by-county vote counts in this book are drawn from several sources. Many are from the official returns in the Archives Section of the Texas State Library in Austin. Others are from the Texas Secretary of State's annual reports or from various editions of the Texas Almanac.

The "Official Totals" listed at the bottom of each table are the totals taken from the source of the vote counts, as mentioned above. The "Unofficial Totals" are those calculated by computer by the Almanac staff from the same county-by-county numbers. There are many possible reasons for the differences in the two figures. Among these: Some of the 19th-century returns are incomplete because of missing county returns. We may have been able to obtain the official statewide total vote count, but the individual county returns may not be available or may be only partial counts. Some of the early, hand-written returns are faint or smeared, making some of the numbers impossible to read. In other cases, there may be typographical errors in the returns, either in some county figures or in the totals. We have published here the most accurate numbers we can obtain.

Because of space limitations, names of some candidates have been abbreviated. A list of the names of all candidates for U.S. Senate is on pages 170-171. The list includes name of candidate; year(s) and type of election — whether the election was Democratic Primary (dp), Republican Primary (rp), General Election (gen), or Special Election (spl); party affiliation (an explanation of the codes is on page 318); and whether the candidate was male (m) or female (f). The list of candidates for Governor, on pages 316-318, includes name, year(s) of elections and party affiliation(s).

In the Presidential Races tables for 1848-1880 and 1884-1896 and in the Gubernatorial Races general election tables for 1863-1880, 1882-1890 and 1892-1898, there is a row below Zavala County labeled "Other." The vote count in this row is from counties that were organized at the time of the election, but no longer exist, principally Greer and Davis.

Some Democratic primaries for U.S. Senator and Governor were omitted from our tables because the county-by-county vote counts could not be obtained from any of our sources or from the political parties themselves. For Governor, these years include 1906, 1914, 1916, 1918, 1920 and 1922. In 1970, Preston Smith was unopposed, so that primary was also omitted. For Senator, the missing years include 1906 (J.W. Bailey was unopposed), 1910 (C.A. Culberson was unopposed), 1916, 1918 and 1922. After 1966, primary returns are not published here, since, with the development of a viable two-party system in Texas, the Democratic primary no longer held its place as the final decision-making process in the selection of the state's officials.

These are the political party abbreviations used with candidates' names in the election table:

A-American
A1-America First
BT-Black and Tan Republican
C-Conservative
CI-Citizens Party
CM-Communist
CO-Constitution
CU-Constitutional Union
D-Democrat
GB-Greenback
I-Independent
ID-Independent Democrat
IF-Independent Fusion
J-Jacksonian
L-Liberty
LA-Labor-Reform
LR-Lily-white Republican
LT-Libertarian
ND-National Democrat

P-Prohibition
PE-People's Party (Populists)
PR-Progressive
PUP-People's Unity Party
R-Republican
RE-Reorganized Republican
RR-Reformed Republican
RZ-La Raza Unida
S-Socialist
SD-Straight-out Democrat
SL-Socialist-Labor
SR-States' Rights
SW-Socialist Workers
TR-Texas Regulars
U-Union
UL-Union Labor
W-Whig
WI-Write-In

Additional notes on election tables:
Presidential:

Since the names of some presidential candidates have been abbreviated in the election tables, the full names are given below, along with the years they ran and their party affiliation:

Anderson, John; 1980; I.
Andrews, T. Coleman; 1956; CO.
Babson, Roger; 1940; P.
Barker, Wharton; 1900; PE.
Bell, John C.; 1860; CU.
Benson, Allan L.; 1916; S.
Bidwell, John; 1892; P.
Blaine, James G.; 1884; R.
Breckinridge, John C.; 1860; D.
Browder, Earl R.; 1936, 1940; CM.
Bryan, William J.; 1896, 1900, 1908; D.
Buchanan, James C.; 1856; D.
Bush, George; 1988; R.
Butler, Benjamin F.; 1884; GB.
Carter, Jimmy; 1976, 1980; D.
Cass, Lewis; 1848; D.
Chafin, Eugene W.; 1908, 1912; P.
Cleveland, Grover, 1884, 1888, 1892; D.
Colvin, D. Leigh; 1936; P.
Coolidge, Calvin; 1924; R.

Corregan, Charles H.; 1904; SL.
Cox, James M.; 1920; D.
Davis, John W.; 1924; D.
Debs, Eugene V.; 1900, 1904, 1908, 1912, 1920; S.
Decker, Rutherford, L.; 1960; P.
Dewey, Thomas E.; 1944, 1948; R.
Dukakis, Michael; 1988; D.
Eisenhower, Dwight D.; 1952, 1956; R.

Ferguson, James E.; 1920; A.
Fillmore, Millard; 1856; W.
Fisk, Clinton B.; 1888; P.
Ford, Gerald; 1976; R.
Foster, William Z.; 1928, 1932; CM.
Garfield, James A.; 1880; R.
Gilhaus, August; 1908; SL.
Goldwater, Barry; 1964; R.
Grant, Ulysses S.; 1872; R.
Greeley, Horace; 1872; D.
Hallinan, Vincent; 1952; PR.
Hamblen, Stuart; 1952; P.

Hancock, Winfield S.; 1880; D.
Hanly, J. Frank; 1916; P.
Harding, Warren G.; 1920; R.
Harrison, Benjamin; 1888, 1892; R.
Harvey, W.H.; 1932; L.
Hayes, Rutherford B.; 1876; R.
Hoover, Herbert C.; 1928, 1932; R.
Hughes, Charles E.; 1916, R.
Humphrey, Hubert H.; 1968; D.
Johnson, Lyndon B.; 1964; D.
Kennedy, John F.; 1960; D.
LaFollette; Robert M.; 1924; PR.
Landon, Alfred M.; 1936; R.
Lemke, William; 1936; U.
Levering, Joshua; 1896; P.
Lightburn, Joseph B.; 1964; CO.
MacArthur, Douglas; 1952; CO.
Malloney, Joseph F.; 1900; SL.
McCarthy, Eugene J.; 1976; I.
McGovern, George; 1972; D.
McKinley, William; 1896, 1900; R.
Mondale, Walter; 1984; D.
Nixon, Richard M.; 1960, 1968, 1972; R.
O'Conor, Charles; 1872; LA & SD.
Palmer, John McA.; 1896; ND.
Parker, Alton B.; 1904; D.
Pierce, Franklin; 1852; D.
Reagan, Ronald; 1980, 1984; R.

Reimer, Arthur E.; 1912; SL.
Roosevelt, Franklin D.; 1932, 1936, 1940, 1944; D.
Roosevelt, Theodore; 1904, R; 1912, PR.
St. John, John P.; 1884; P.
Scott, Winfield; 1852; W.
Smith, Alfred E.; 1928, D
Smith, Gerald L.K.; 1944; A-1.
Stevenson, Adlai E.; 1952, 1956; D.
Streeter, Alson J.; 1888; UL.
Sullivan, Charles L.; 1960; CO.
Swallow, Silas C.; 1904; P.
Taft, William H.; 1908, 1912; R.
Taylor, Zachary; 1848; W.
Thomas, Norman M.; 1928, 1932, 1936, 1940, 1944, 1948; S.
Thurmond, J. Strom; 1948, SR.
Tilden, Samuel; 1876; D.
Truman, Harry S.; 1948; D.
Wallace, George C.; 1968; A.
Wallace, Henry A.; 1948; PR.
Watson, Claude A.; 1944, 1948; P.
Watson, Thomas E.; 1904, 1908; PE.
Weaver, James B.; 1880, GB; 1892, PE.
Wilkie, Wendell L.; 1940; R.
Wilson, Woodrow; 1912, 1916; D.
Wooley, John C.; 1900; P.

Additional notes for the presidential election tables:

In 1860, Lincoln and Douglas, the winners of the nationwide election, were not on the ballot in Texas.

In 1876, the vote published here for Comanche County is for only two precincts, so the vote is incomplete.

1940: The official totals are from the State Canvassing Board with 33 counties missing. The Texas Election Bureau totals, including the 33 counties are 905,156 and 211,707. The unofficial totals include the 33 counties. There was nothing in our sources to indicate which counties are missing from the Canvassing Board count.

Senatorial Special Elections:

1941: The total number of candidates in the special election were 25 Democrats, 2 Republicans, 1 independent and 1 Communist.

In the 1957 special election, there were 23 candidates, of which 3 had withdrawn before election day, but their names had already been printed on the ballot.

The 1961 special election attracted 71 candidates, and a runoff was necessary. The vote count published here is for the runoff election.

Gubernatorial Primaries:

1982, Although Buddy Temple qualified for a runoff with Mark White, he declined, and Mark White was declared winner of the primary

Gubernatorial General Elections:

1914: K.E. Choate, the Socialist-Labor candidate, was omitted from the table for space reasons. His statewide total vote was 400. He also ran in 1912 and is included in the table for that election.

1928: J. Steadman (Communist), garnering 109 votes, and L.L. Rhodes (Socialist), with 738 votes, have been omitted from our tables because of space limitations.

1930: Although George Butte had won the Republican primary, he refused to run, and William Talbot was the Republican candidate in the general election.

1936: Carl Brannin (Socialist) and Homer Brooks (Communist) were omitted for space reasons. Brannin's statewide total vote was 962 and Brooks' was 283.

1940: Candidate Derden withdrew before the election, but his name was still on the ballot. Although a thorough search was made of available materials, we could not find this candidate's first name.

1960: Bard Logan (Constitution Party) was also a candidate, receiving 20,506 votes statewide.

1986: Column labeled "Other" contains the total vote for two write-in candidates, Charles Lee and J. Muriel.

1990: In addition to the candidates in the published tables, 19 registered write-in candidates received a total of 11,517 votes. Also, the official canvassed total vote for Jeff Daiell was 129,157.

Dates of General Elections:

Since 1878, the general election has been held on the first Tuesday after the first Monday in November. Before that time, however, the date of the general election varied. Below are listed the dates of general elections prior to 1878:

1845: Dec. 15	1859: Aug. 1
1847: Nov. 1	1861: Nov. 6
1849: Aug. 6	1863: Aug. 3
1851: Aug. 4	1866: June 25
1853: Aug. 1	1869: Nov. 30
1855: Aug. 6	1873: Dec. 2
1857: Aug. 3	1876: Feb. 15

Index